Praise for *Achieving Excellence in Fundraising*, Fifth Edition

"This Fifth Edition of *Achieving Excellence in Fundraising* offers a primer for all those engaged in the important work of securing philanthropic support for their respective organization. By combining academic insight with practitioner experience, the new edition addresses the foundations of the profession with an eye on the future. It's an important contribution to the canon for the profession."

—Sue Cunningham, President & CEO,
Council for Advancement and Support of Education

"The landscape of fundraising today is rapidly changing, so keeping up with donors' priorities and wishes is more critical than ever. *Achieving Excellence in Fundraising* is the most comprehensive and knowledgeable guide to understanding fundraising principles in a global and diverse world. Adopting the most effective fundraising strategy will not only set you up for success, but also lead to a positive impact to improve the world. This guide is what all fundraiser and nonprofit leaders need in their toolbox."

—Ann Putnam Marks, Regional Partnerships Manager,
UNICEF Private Fundraising & Partnerships

"Only a handful of books are so good to start with that the late author's colleagues gather periodically to refresh the content for new generations. *Achieving Excellence in Fundraising* is both a classic and a contemporary exploration of the topics fundraisers, nonprofit CEOs, volunteers, and students need to be confident, professional, and current in this unique role that is needed more and more around the world. The original deep experience, journalistic flair, and sheer heart of fundraising pioneer and teacher Hank Rosso is intact, with core and principles conveyed for ready application. Add in the new channels, techniques, evidence, and innovation in fundraising and you have the kind of book all will want both as brain food, and in the background of their Zoom meetings as a hallmark that they are serious professionals. The world needs more really skilled and authentic fundraisers. This book is a great contribution to that goal."

—Wendy Scaife, Director,
Australian Centre for Philanthropy and Nonprofit Studies, QUT

"Building on the previous iterations, the Fifth Edition authors provide modern and insightful perspectives on the evolution of the fundraising profession. The compilation of lived experiences and current research will energize long-tenured fundraising practitioners and inspire the next generation of fundraising professionals. I would recommend sharing this book with your teams, close colleagues, and others who desire to better understand and appreciate the breadth and depth of this noble profession."

—James H. Moore, Jr., President & CEO,
University of Illinois Foundation

"More than 50 authors affiliated with The Lilly School of Philanthropy share today's best practices guaranteed to enhance your fundraising performance. It's all in this Fifth Edition of *Achieving Excellence in Fundraising*."

—Don Campbell, Founder and Chairman Emeritus (Retired),
Campbell & Company

"Kudos to the authors of the Fifth Edition of this must-read classic. New chapters and comprehensive revisions elevate the substantial value of this book for fundraising professionals and anyone interested in the potential of philanthropy."

—Mary Tschirhart, Professor & Director,
Trachtenberg School of Public Administration and Public Policy,
The George Washington University

"Donors are now activating their philanthropy in innovative ways that are meeting the moment. In this Fifth Edition, *Achieving Excellence in Fundraising* provides a comprehensive framework for all nonprofit organizations to design and implement a fundraising strategy that engages today's donors and transforms institutions and the communities they serve."

—Helene D. Gayle, President & CEO,
The Chicago Community Trust

ACHIEVING EXCELLENCE IN
FUNDRAISING

The Instructor's Guide for the fifth edition of *Achieving Excellence in Fundraising* includes supporting materials for fundraising courses using this text. The Instructor's Guide is available free online. To download and print a copy, please visit:
www.wiley.com/college/aefr

IUPUI
INDIANA UNIVERSITY
Lilly Family School of Philanthropy

The Indiana University Lilly Family School of Philanthropy is the world's first school dedicated solely to education and research about philanthropy. Established in 2012, the school was inaugurated in 2013 and named for one of America's great philanthropic families in honor of its generations of generosity and leadership.

Indiana University (IU) has been at the vanguard of philanthropy education since the Center on Philanthropy at Indiana University was founded at Indiana University Purdue University Indianapolis (IUPUI) in 1987. Led by the center, IU established the field of philanthropic studies; established the nation's first bachelor's, master's, and Ph.D. degrees in the field; and created the nation's first endowed chair in philanthropy.

The Lilly Family School of Philanthropy prepares students, philanthropy professionals, donors, and volunteers to be thoughtful innovators and leaders who create positive and lasting change. Alumni of its programs lead national nonprofits and foundations, serve international relief organizations, and lead hands-on neighborhood human services centers.

As the pioneer of the unique, liberal arts-based field of philanthropic studies, the school and its world-class faculty offer unparalleled academic degree programs and rigorous, objective research that sets the standard for the field and provides a crucial resource for philanthropy and nonprofits. Through global partnerships, teaching and learning experiences on six continents, and an international student body, the school increases understanding of philanthropy within and across cultures.

The Lilly Family School of Philanthropy integrates innovative academic, research, international and training programs with groundbreaking resources such as The Fund Raising School, the Women's Philanthropy Institute, the Mays Family Institute on Diverse Philanthropy, and Lake Institute on Faith & Giving.

The Fund Raising School, which Hank Rosso moved to Indiana University in 1987 to form the centerpiece for the founding of the Center on Philanthropy, continues today as the premier international, university, and curriculum-based fundraising education program. For the nearly 50 years since its founding in 1974, The Fund Raising School has taught successful, ethical, systematic, mission-focused fundraising, volunteer board leadership, and nonprofit management practices to more than 50,000 people in more than 40 countries. Experienced fundraising professionals comprise The Fund Raising School's faculty, offering multiple online and in-person sessions of 22 different regularly scheduled courses in Indianapolis and in cities around the nation as well as sponsored, customized courses in locations around the globe.

As a hub for philanthropic thought and research, the Lilly Family School of Philanthropy regularly convenes innovators, scholars, philanthropists, fundraisers, nonprofit and foundation professionals, and researchers to share their diverse perspectives, exchange ideas, and develop insights that anticipate trends, address pressing issues, and shape the future of philanthropy.

For more information, please visit philanthropy.iupui.edu.

ACHIEVING EXCELLENCE IN FUNDRAISING

FIFTH EDITION

EDITORS
GENEVIEVE G. SHAKER
EUGENE R. TEMPEL
SARAH K. NATHAN
BILL STANCZYKIEWICZ

WILEY

Library of Congress Cataloging-in-Publication Data is Available:

ISBN: 9781119763758 (cloth)
ISBN: 9781119763765 (ePub)
ISBN: 9781119763772 (ePDF)

Cover Design: Wiley
Cover Image: © Patrizia Savarese/Getty Images

SKY10045615_041223

CONTENTS

LIST OF TABLES, FIGURES, AND EXHIBITS

Tables

Figures

Exhibits

FOREWORD

This book is a critical resource in a time when many institutions are struggling to demonstrate their relevance to rapidly changing social and economic conditions. This fifth edition of *Achieving Excellence in Fundraising* meets the challenge of responding to such concerns by combining rigorous research with the insights of exceptional practitioners. As lead editor of the prior three editions and intellectual successor to Hank Rosso, Dr. Gene Tempel is also welcoming a generational change with three new editors who bring fresh topics and perspectives to the endeavor. Tempel provides a valuable bridge from the founding vision of the publication to current and future practice. He has ensured that the book's enduring values continue to guide an engaging journey of discovery into what it means to excel in fundraising.

Professor Genevieve Shaker, the lead co-editor, represents the next generation of leadership on the faculty of the Indiana University Lilly Family School of Philanthropy at IUPUI. Her research focuses on fundraising and fundraisers, philanthropy in higher education, philanthropy education, and the ways people give in the workplace, drawing also on two decades of experience as a practitioner in the field. Dr. Sarah Nathan leads a community foundation while continuing her passions for teaching and scholarship, following her curiosity about those who choose fundraising as their calling. She also draws on her experiences developing cutting-edge academic curricula on fundraising as well as professional development programs for The Fund Raising School. For over six years, Professor Bill Stanczykiewicz has been leading The Fund Raising School to new levels of innovation and prominence while taking on additional responsibility for the Lilly Family School's fundraising and communications programs. As a faculty member he has strengthened the leadership and fundraising aspects of the academic curriculum, drawing on his research into board dynamics as well as many years of experience serving as chief executive of a youth-focused nonprofit.

What our new editors share with Gene Tempel is an intimate immersion in the intellectual life of the Lilly Family School, as well as a deep commitment to engaging those who fundraise as a way to improve our world. Their collaboration reveals that running deep and strong across generations is a desire to show how the joy of discovery leads to success in the field, and that the worlds of research and doing continue to build on each other in pursuit of excellence. As the founding dean of the Lilly Family School and president emeritus of the Indiana University Foundation – as a scholar and fundraiser – Tempel sets a high standard for the new generation of editors in integrating theory with practice.

This book was produced during a global pandemic, the likes of which we have not faced in living memory. The pandemic also became the stage for social justice movements based on dramatic incidents calling attention to racial and gender inequity and injustice, vivid signs of systemic discrimination, and increased political polarization. All have intensely affected the institutions most dependent on philanthropy. In normal times, keeping abreast of research and evolving practice is taxing enough. Doing so during the pandemic required additional efforts – not only because of the very human challenges our editors and authors faced, but also because the nonprofit sector and those who seek to engage it experienced novel stresses and strains that shifted the ground we seek to understand.

This volume speaks to the latest innovations in the field while addressing the perennial challenges involved in building meaningful relationships to support worthy causes. It also provides readers an opportunity to revisit the foundations of fundraising. What is the purpose of this activity? Who are its protagonists? And how does the work and those who enable it fit into conceptions of a good society and how we belong together – ideas that seem much more unsettled now than they were when the first edition of this book appeared thirty years ago.

In light of the political divisiveness of our times, as well as the global challenges exacerbated by the pandemic, it is perhaps all the more remarkable that we have a profession and a field of inquiry devoted to the relationships we build to advance the common good. As a formal profession, fundraising can be seen as a collective realization that we need to build community among the systems that modern society has created to enable us to interact at vast and impersonal scale.

Communities based on fundraising relationships are built as correctives to fix social problems. Or, they seek to ameliorate by enhancing the lives of others. Whether fixing or building, communities are valuable means to achieve important public goals, hopefully ones we can all appreciate.

To appreciate fundraising is to appreciate the scale of community, where people know each other personally and can make meaningful connections to those they aim to help. Yes, there is a universal human connection that moves us to donate to far-off strangers, but that usually relies on the salience of our common mortality to grab our attention – something like a disaster.

So, as we consider the role of fundraising in our rapidly changing world, I am impressed by its role in fostering meaningful relationships that help us define who we are. No matter how technology, the economy, and political movements upend daily life, there is lasting value in building authentic relationships that seek to improve our world.

Communities are means to other ends, but they are also valuable in their own right. This is also the case with fundraising. As you excel in the craft, you too are likely to find pleasure and satisfaction in the process of fundraising. Relationships built on the road to elsewhere are often valuable milestones that give truth to the saying that the journey is more important than the destination. The relationships you build, aided by the discoveries you will experience in this book, will add to the satisfaction you derive from advancing the causes you serve.

I suspect this is also the case with my colleagues who put together this compendium of insights, provocations, guidelines, and prompts for discussion. Seeing this book roll off the printing press (and its digital counterpart) is a moment of achievement deserving celebration. But it pales in comparison to the multitude of moments of learning and debate it will facilitate, and the countless professional and volunteer fundraisers whose talents will blossom by engaging the thoughts and experiences that have been compiled as signposts for their journey.

Achieving Excellence is a vital institution because it enables journeys of fundraising that will shape our times. *Bon voyage!*

Amir Pasic
Eugene R. Tempel Dean
Indiana University Lilly Family
School of Philanthropy
September 2021

PREFACE

As we began work on this edition in spring 2020, nonprofits and fundraisers around the world faced challenges and uncertainties like never before. The novel coronavirus was in its first months and economies were staggering with the related pressures. In the United States, a social justice movement was spotlighting historical and structural issues related to racial equity. Similar social movements were occurring around the globe. Nonprofits were reflecting deeply on their commitments to equity and inclusion. Some faced exponential rises in needs for services, and others experienced declining opportunities to deliver their missions and garner needed income.

Because of COVID-19, we could not gather in person for editorial meetings at the Indiana University (IU) Lilly Family School of Philanthropy at IUPUI. Rather, we met online as our university leaders explored the best ways to keep our community healthy and safe and maintain financial stability. Indiana University fundraisers paused to make sense of campus and community needs and expectations, rather than completing previously planned efforts. Like their peers at other colleges and universities, they called and wrote donors to check on their well-being and to provide updates. They resumed fundraising, prioritizing emergency support for students, whose need for special assistance was quickly evident.

Just as university fundraisers were navigating unknown territory, fundraisers across the wide and diverse nonprofit sector found themselves scrambling to keep up with pressing demands for more resources. Their responsibility for funding organizational missions weighed heavily and they wondered how to build relationships without seeing donors in person. Like clients, donors, and everyone else, fundraisers struggled with their own personal difficulties and uncertainties.

As it turned out, we all soon witnessed the generosity of people helping their neighbors and communities in extraordinary ways. College students creating direct aid programs, providing funds, food, and even temporary housing for one another. Monetary gifts from individuals flooded into food pantries, community health organizations, schools, and social service agencies of all kinds. Small business owners shifted from profit-making activities to providing free meals for frontline workers and making masks, isolation gowns, and hand sanitizer. Foundations responded by loosening grant restrictions, corporations made public pledges to aid in relief efforts, and both broadened commitments to social justice funding. State and local governments shifted priorities to address the pandemic, and the whole of society adjusted.

Now, two years later, we know that 2020 was the most generous year on record. Giving USA (2021) recorded $471.44 billion dollars in charitable giving driven by increased contributions from foundations and individuals. Although more difficult to track, direct giving, mutual aid, and other forms of informal giving and helping also appeared to increase in popularity (Stiffman 2021c). Online giving grew exponentially. Almost half of all households reported paying for services not used during pandemic closures such as childcare and gym memberships, while frequenting local businesses for take-out meals and other needs (Mesch et al. 2020). Most nonprofits survived, battered and exhausted by the crisis, and some with smaller teams than before, but with a sense of relief as operations resumed more normally (Parks 2021). Through it all, fundraisers' work proceeded, bringing new perspectives and practices, and overcoming challenges. As this book goes to press, the learning and adapting continues.

A Strong Tradition

In 1991, when Henry "Hank" Rosso wrote the preface for the first edition of *Achieving Excellence in Fund Raising* he noted how fundraising changed following World War II, a defining event for his generation. Like Hank's experience, our editorial perspective is shaped by a defining time period. Given the events in 2020 and 2021, this book includes a new section dedicated to contextual factors and evolving conditions. Without certainty of how the past two years will ultimately shape fundraising, we became acutely aware that conditions can change quickly. In years to come, fundraisers must be prepared to adapt more quickly and more intentionally than at any time in the recent past. Thus, throughout the book, we tried to balance innovations and changes in raising money with time-tested best practices – research that is still emerging as the book is in production – and professional habits honed over years of pre-pandemic experience. It was also important to us that this edition include many voices and that chapters draw attention to equity and justice in fundraising, including beneficiary representation and rights and ideas from community-centric fundraising.

In that first edition, Hank also noted his mission to expand knowledge about fundraising and to serve as a resource to others. He was a pioneer fundraiser and a leading consultant of an era when the fundraising occupation professionalized and the IRS codified nonprofits' tax-deductible status. He introduced much of what he taught in The Fund Raising School (TFRS) to a larger audience through *Achieving Excellence in Fund Raising*. Today, that symbiotic relationship continues with TFRS curriculum and materials, inspiring chapter authors and concepts from the book chapters and also providing source material for TFRS courses.

After Hank's passing, Gene Tempel took on the editorship with a second edition published in 2003. The third edition followed in 2011 with Tim Seiler and Eva Aldrich joining Tempel as editors. Five years later, Tempel and Seiler edited the fourth edition with Dwight Burlingame. Eva now leads CFRE International, the body that oversees the Certified Fund Raising Executive (CFRE) credential. Both Tim and Dwight recently retired after decades of leadership. They all leave an indelible mark on generations of students and professionals, including this volume's editors.

A New Era

The fifth edition, published in 2022, has been released in tandem with the Lilly Family School's tenth anniversary and nearly 50 years after the founding of TFRS. Gene Tempel has passed the baton of editorial leadership to Genevieve Shaker, associate professor of philanthropic studies and TFRS faculty member, while himself playing a guiding transitional role in the most recent edition – his fourth. Bill Stanczykiewicz, director of TFRS since 2016, has joined the editorial team, as did his TFRS predecessor Tim Seiler (1996–2015) for the prior two editions. Sarah Nathan, who assisted with the third and fourth editions, is a former associate director of TFRS, and serves currently as the executive director of the Middletown Community Foundation.

Collectively, we have experience as fundraisers and leaders in nonprofits large and small; as board members and volunteer fundraisers; as educators of undergraduates, graduate students, and professionals; and as researchers and writers. We consider ourselves "pracademics" with strong interests in using research to inform the field. We are also perpetual students of philanthropy and fundraising who are humble in our desire to learn and grow.

This volume also features a new generation of chapter authors, all of whom are Lilly Family School of Philanthropy faculty, staff, alumni, students, and friends, with a number also being affiliated with TFRS.

Of the 54 authors in the volume, 33 are writing chapters for the book for the first time. We are pleased to welcome back authors from previous editions. Several authors' involvement stretches back decades, including Gene Tempel, who has written for every edition since the first, as well as Tim Seiler, Jim Hodge, Marnie Maxwell, and Lilya Wagner – contributors since the second edition. All told, the fifth edition cohort is the most diverse thus far. It is more representative of the fundraising community of today and tomorrow, but we recognize that there is more to be done.

While preparing this book, we discovered that the previous edition has been used in some 450 colleges and universities. This is indicative of growth in formalized fundraising education and of the book's expansion from handbook to teaching tool for students of fundraising, philanthropy, and the nonprofit sector. It also continues to serve as a guide for board members, nonprofit professionals, volunteer fundraisers, those who want to "spread their wings" to other fundraising domains, and those who wish to hone their craft by applying research to their work.

Like the field itself, the editions of this book evolve as fundraising practice changes and adapts – while retaining the original purpose of achieving excellence. The gingko leaves on this cover were chosen to symbolize the book's longevity and the collective wisdom it contains. Gingko trees are among the oldest plant species on earth, displaying incredible resiliency, with many trees living for centuries. Gingkoes persist, even in the face of great adversity, including several that survived the 1945 bombing of Hiroshima, Japan. Every autumn, a group of volunteers collects the fallen seeds of these special trees. Under the banner of the Green Legacy Hiroshima Project, seeds are then sent around the world to promote peace and understanding. Recently, a sapling from one of these seeds was planted on the Indiana University–Purdue University Indianapolis (IUPUI) campus, adding additional meaning for the editorial team.

Like the gingko tree, fundraisers are resilient professionals; we hope this volume plants many seeds of knowledge for new and experienced fundraisers alike.

The New Edition

In our quest to make a new edition for a new era, we strengthened the text for academic and professional education, and for more informal use. A set of learning objectives guides each chapter, articulating reading goals and creating the organizational structure. Chapters are uniform in length and format. All chapters received repeated, rigorous content reviews by multiple editors. Each chapter was carefully read for clarity in language, recognizing that many readers are experiencing fundraising terminology for the first time and that academic approaches to presenting research are not always reader friendly. Along these lines, we asked academic faculty who wrote chapters to make sure to translate the research into practical, actionable terms for use. Likewise, we asked practitioners to draw on research, when available and applicable, to enhance their chapters. Discussion questions invite readers to review each chapter's research and best practices. For the first time, the volume includes application exercises to provide hands-on activities for readers to try out their learnings.

The book sections and their contents have been reorganized and reconceptualized. The book is organized chronologically, laying the ethical, legal, theoretical, and philosophical groundwork in the first section; next moving through contextual, organizational, and logistical considerations; and then into the landscape of fundraising programs, donor populations, and strategies. However, there is no one "right" way to navigate through the book. The 39 chapters are organized into seven sections, each of which might be the starting or focal point, depending on the reader's intended purposes.

Part One provides timeless knowledge for all fundraisers. "Developing a Personal Philosophy of Fundraising" sets the book's tone with the core values that underlie fundraising as the gentle art of teaching the joy of giving (Rosso 1991), with an added approach of empowering fundraisers to develop and acknowledge their own philosophies based on values, beliefs, and lived experience. A chapter on the joy of giving returns in this volume, bringing new research that proves Rosso's maxim. This section also includes consideration of ethical and legal implications for fundraising as well as a new chapter connecting practice to interdisciplinary theory.

The next part, "Contemporary Dynamics of Fundraising," examines the ever-changing external landscape for this work. Two of the chapters return from previous editions with significant revision (Chapters 6 and 9). Chapters 7, 8, and 10 are new to *Achieving Excellence* and contribute insights into the nuances of fundraising in challenging times and the various subsectors, and with a lens of equity and justice.

Part Three presents organizational fundamentals for executing a comprehensive fundraising program. The seven chapters in this section illuminate steps in the fundraising cycle, from examining the case for support to donor identification through donor relations and stewardship. This section also looks at how fundraising programs intersect and collaborate with marketing efforts as well as how to budget for fundraising.

The next part addresses the various roles, responsibilities, and functions of the fundraising team, broadly defined. This volume's editors lean into their research strengths, presenting data-driven understandings of the fundraising profession generally and leadership for fundraising specifically. Also in this section are newly updated chapters on engaging board members and volunteers in this work, which is especially important in smaller organizations where fundraisers wear many hats.

Part Five focuses on building and growing the base of supporters. Inviting an organization's broadest constituency to become first-time and then repeat donors is the basis of a healthy annual giving program, from which all other fundraising flows. The section presents annual fund planning tools as well as strategies meant to welcome gifts of all sizes. The chapters examine tactical aspects of inviting and retaining donors: crafting effective appeals, integrating digital strategies, and holding events with purpose.

Research – much of it completed by the Lilly Family School team – is at the core of Part Six, which examines individual donors and their many complexities. The chapters present insights into donors' motivations and behaviors, and recommendations for applying the information to practice. The section is grounded with a new chapter on donor motivation research. Chapters focus on giving by women, within communities of color, among LGBTQ households and high net worth people, as associated with faith traditions, and in reference to generational differences, collectively exploring multiple dimensions of how individuals make giving decisions and express their values through philanthropy.

Similar to Parts Three and Five, the book's seventh and concluding part provides tactical analysis of fundraising, in this case through the lens of raising funds from major donors, donor-advised funds, grantmaking foundations, and corporations. From co-creating major gifts and gift planning to organizing fundraising campaigns and understanding corporate and foundation philanthropy, the seven chapters prepare fundraisers to confidently ask for transformative gifts.

A Contribution to Philanthropy

Many of Hank Rosso's (1991) ideas continue to be foundational to how we think about fundraising, even as the field changes and develops in the United States and beyond. These include taking pride in our work and remembering that fundraising's purpose is to facilitate philanthropy. Philanthropy, in turn, is in service to the greater good and needs and interests beyond one's own. All fundraising rests on the case for support, driven by the mission, and rooted in community needs. All fundraising must be built on a foundation of respect: respect for beneficiaries, organizations, communities, fundraisers, and donors. Respect is conveyed through inclusive practices, including listening and learning; speaking in ways that uplift and do not demean beneficiaries, donors, or fundraisers; and upholding ethical standards and moral values.

Fundraising is a noble career that is meaningful, creative, and fulfilling. It is not easy work; it includes a great range of tasks and activities, and there is opportunity for many to excel and contribute. It is also a black box about which most people, at best, understand little, and at worst, misunderstand much. This book is meant to demystify fundraising by providing information and research on ethics and theory; donor motivations and behaviors; programs and tools; and guiding principles and philosophies. By improving fundraising and supporting fundraisers, we can improve philanthropy to improve the world.

ACKNOWLEDGMENTS

This edition of *Achieving Excellence in Fundraising* is a culmination of nearly 50 years of practicing, teaching, and thinking about fundraising. At the same time, it is a new beginning shaped by contemporary research on philanthropy and fundraising; evolving approaches to teaching; and distinctive social, economic, and political environments.

Accordingly, it is important to recognize those who have shaped and supported this fifth edition, as well as to acknowledge our predecessors, whose footsteps guide us. The book originated with Hank and Dottie Rosso, who founded The Fund Raising School (TFRS) in 1974 and transferred it to Indiana University and the Center on Philanthropy in 1987. Their ideas, honed through decades of consulting and educating others, appeared in *Achieving Excellence*'s first edition in 1991, which gathered fundraising luminaries to create a shared repository of experiential wisdom. Hank and Dottie continued to be advisors, mentors, and friends until their deaths in 1999 and 2020, respectively. Their legacy continues through the Dottie Rosso Scholarship, which supports fundraisers from small nonprofits to attend TFRS classes. Likewise, the Hank Rosso Scholarship supports teams of two employees to attend TFRS classes, making it easier to implement learnings at their nonprofits.

We owe a debt of gratitude to the Rossos, to TFRS, and to the Lilly Family School of Philanthropy. Not only is the Lilly Family School the academic home of the editors, it connects the authors and is a key source for much of the research and knowledge used in this book. School staff, graduate and undergraduate students, alumni, academic and practitioner faculty, leadership, and supporters together have created a culture of learning and sharing "to improve philanthropy."

Dozens of authors have written for the now five editions of *Achieving Excellence* over the past 30 years, five editors shaped the previous volumes, and several graduate assistants and staff members have worked behind the scenes to assemble hundreds of thousands of words into cohesive wholes. All have contributed to the ongoing development of knowledge for this book and for the field.

Assembling this edition during the COVID-19 pandemic and a context of social introspection and change meant asking the current authors to write their chapters in a time of great uncertainty, for nonprofits and fundraising to be sure, but also for them personally as work and life routines shifted. We are profoundly grateful that they chose to say "yes" to the request to participate.

Moreover, the authors welcomed our comments and suggestions during a time of rapid changes in perspective shaped by evolving current events. Their varied experiences and steady clarity of vision have allowed us to produce a book that will better prepare fundraisers for the future. Earlier editions have reflected changing conditions, but the fifth edition takes an even greater step forward in anticipating fundraising and philanthropic challenges for uncertain times to come.

We are grateful to have put this volume together when the academic community in nonprofit and philanthropic studies is more robust than ever. There are a number of strong media outlets specializing in reporting on the nonprofit sector. Because the field's profile is growing, as are educational opportunities, more fundraisers are choosing the profession earlier instead of "falling into it" later. And, the public discourse around philanthropy invites us to think critically about our work in new ways.

Some of these developments can be tracked back to when the Lilly Endowment gave seed money to create the center and, subsequently, its unrestricted endowment, with the goals of building the capacity of the nonprofit sector and the field of philanthropic studies. We recognize those who had a vision for an academic program dedicated to the study of and education about philanthropy, including leaders at Indiana University–Purdue University Indianapolis (IUPUI), Indiana University (IU), and in Indianapolis as well as many generous donors and funders like the Lilly Endowment, Kellogg, and the Atlantic Philanthropies.

We are humbled that so many educators chose previous editions of this book for their students and – since 1991 – that generations of practitioners have read the chapters to build and refine their fundraising skills and to support their organizations. We are grateful to our publisher, Wiley, and our editors Brian Neill and Deborah Schindlar, for continuing to provide a good home for books on nonprofits, fundraising, and philanthropy.

Our partner on this project since its inception was Pat Danahey Janin, editorial assistant and a doctoral candidate in the Lilly Family School. Putting together an edited volume with 39 chapters and more than 50 authors is a significant administrative task. Pat communicated with every author, read every chapter, and worked side-by-side with the editors on the details large and small. The authors, editors, and readers are fortunate that Pat brought her expertise, talent, and dedication to the project.

This edition pays special attention to fundraisers as central contributors to philanthropic giving and as *whole* people, driven by their own personal values and experiences. Just as fundraisers complete their work in the context of life as a whole, we created this book under unusual circumstances with children home from school, campus buildings closed, and many personal and professional transitions. We especially thank our families, friends, colleagues, and school leaders who encouraged us, informed our ideas, and supported us during the many months of preparation. We learn a great deal from each of you and from the fundraisers whose work inspires us every day.

THE EDITORS

Genevieve G. Shaker, Ph.D., is Associate Professor of Philanthropic Studies at the Indiana University Lilly Family School of Philanthropy at Indiana University–Purdue University Indianapolis (IUPUI). Previously, she was an active fundraiser for 20 years. She served as Associate Dean for Development and External Affairs for the Indiana University School of Liberal Arts, where she led communications, alumni programming, public events, and fundraising, including overseeing the school's $20 million-dollar contribution to an overall $3.9 billion university-wide campaign. She is one of a few academics whose career in fundraising forms the foundation for her work as a scholar. She teaches regularly for The Fund Raising School, where she presents research-informed insights for practicing professionals, is featured in podcasts and webinars, and comments on philanthropy for the general public. Professor Shaker is an award-winning teacher, writer, and researcher, recognized for excellence in teaching by the trustees of Indiana University and in applied scholarship by the Association of Fundraising Professionals. She is the co-author of *Fundraising Principles for Faculty and Academic Leaders* (Palgrave 2021) and publishes in peer-review journals, nonprofit publications, and popular media. She is a fellow of the Teachers Insurance and Annuity Association of America (TIAA) Institute and associate editor of the journal *Philanthropy & Education*. Professor Shaker's research focuses on fundraising and fundraisers, higher education advancement, workplace philanthropy, philanthropy and the global common good, and philanthropy education.

Eugene R. Tempel, Ed.D., is Professor Emeritus of Philanthropic Studies, Founding Dean Emeritus of the Indiana University Lilly Family School of Philanthropy, and President Emeritus of the Indiana University Foundation. Professor Tempel has three decades of philanthropy leadership, administration, and fundraising experience. He played an integral role in establishing the Lilly Family School of Philanthropy's precursor, the Center on Philanthropy at Indiana University, and served as the center's executive director from 1997 through 2008, transforming it into a leading national resource and the world's first school devoted to the study and teaching of philanthropy. Committed to strengthening the philanthropic sector, Professor Tempel chaired the national Association of Fundraising Professionals' Ethics Committee and served as a member of Independent Sector's Expert Advisory Panel, which created national guidelines for nonprofit governance and ethical behavior. He is a past chair of the Indiana Commission on Community Service and Volunteerism. He has mentored many of the nation's most successful executives in philanthropic fundraising. Professor Tempel served as the Indiana University Foundation president between 2008 and 2012 before being named founding dean of the Lilly Family School of Philanthropy. Under his guidance, the foundation completed Indiana University (IU) Bloomington's $1.1 billion Matching the Promise campaign, exceeding the goal by more than $40 million, and launched and completed the $1.25 billion IMPACT campaign at Indiana University–Purdue University Indianapolis (IUPUI). Despite a difficult economy, IU recorded the second and third highest total voluntary support numbers during his tenure. Tempel currently serves on the Board of Governors for the Riley Children's Foundation and for Antioch University. He provides pro bono consulting to the Sisters of St. Benedict of Ferdinand Indiana, where he is Chair of the Executive Advisory Committee, and to the Indiana Repertory Theatre, where he chaired a recently completed capital campaign. He earned a B.A. in English and philosophy from St. Benedict College, an M.A. in English, and a doctorate in higher education administration from IU.

Sarah K. Nathan, Ph.D., is a self-described "pracademic" who has spent her entire career in the nonprofit sector as a fundraiser, educator, volunteer, and leader. Most recently she has been focused on community philanthropy and currently serves as the Executive Director of Middletown Community Foundation in Ohio. Dr. Nathan spent five years prior as the Associate Director of The Fund Raising School (TFRS), where she managed all aspects of the curriculum designed for fundraising practitioners. As part of the innovative and collaborative TFRS team, she designed several new specialty courses and virtual learning experiences. As a course designer, she was attuned to the most recent scholarly research and industry best practices to ensure that courses included active and applied learning. In short, her creative design work translated research for a practitioner audience.

Previously, she was Assistant Professor of Nonprofit Management and Philanthropy at Bay Path University where she taught and advised online graduate students in the master's degree programs in nonprofit management and in strategic fundraising. Dr. Nathan began her philanthropy career as a 19-year-old student, calling alumni at her undergraduate alma mater, Concordia College in Moorhead, Minnesota, where she later became Associate Director of the Annual Fund. She continues to serve the college as an enthusiastic alumni ambassador. When living in Indiana, she supported her local community as a volunteer and board member of the Johnson County Community Foundation, where she helped establish the county's first giving day. Dr. Nathan is an avid Girl Scout and spends countless hours joyfully guiding young leaders. She is a proud graduate of the Lilly Family School of Philanthropy and holds an M.A. and Ph.D. in philanthropic studies.

Bill Stanczykiewicz, Ed.D., serves as Director and Rosso Fellow of The Fund Raising School (TFRS), where he designs and teaches in-person and online fundraising courses delivered in the United States and around the world. Bill also serves as Senior Assistant Dean for External Relations within the Indiana University Lilly Family School of Philanthropy, where he oversees fundraising as well as marketing and communications. As a clinical associate professor of philanthropic studies, Bill has academic teaching responsibilities that include undergraduate and graduate courses in fundraising, philanthropy, and leadership. His 25-year leadership and fundraising career includes serving as CEO of a statewide nonprofit promoting youth development and academic attainment. He also has volunteered and fundraised on boards of directors for nonprofits associated with hunger relief, community development, youth and family ministry, education, and workforce development. His civic engagement resulted in Bill being named a "Sagamore of the Wabash" by the Governor's Office of Indiana. His bachelor's degree in journalism from Northwestern University led to his 10-year career as a radio sportscaster, which included being honored as the "Indiana Sportscaster of the Year." Bill then earned a master's degree in public administration – with a concentration in nonprofit management – from George Mason University while he served on legislative staff in the United States Senate. Bill's doctoral degree in interdisciplinary leadership from Creighton University included his dissertation discovering research-based methods for increasing board engagement with fundraising. He also holds a post-graduate certificate in leadership from Vanderbilt University. Bill's professional passions include helping more nonprofits raise more money to make the world a better place through their public service missions.

AUTHOR BIOS

Katherine Badertscher, Ph.D., is Director of Graduate Programs at the Indiana University Lilly Family School of Philanthropy. She teaches a variety of B.A., M.A., and doctoral courses and The Fund Raising School's Fundraising Ethics course. She received the Women's Leadership Award (2019) from the Indiana University–Purdue University Indianapolis (IUPUI) Office for Women, the Graduate Teaching Award (2019 and 2020) from the Lilly Family School of Philanthropy as well as the Indiana University Trustees' Teaching Award (2021). Dr. Badertscher is a Coburn Place Safe Haven Board Member.

Anne Bergeron is a specialist in nonprofit cultural enterprise. She has served in senior management at the University of California, Irvine (UCI) Institute and Museum of California Art, Brown University's Arts Initiative, Dallas Museum of Art, and Solomon R. Guggenheim Museum, in addition to running her own consulting firm. In 2010–2012, she was visiting practitioner at Georgetown University's Center for Public and Nonprofit Leadership researching *Magnetic: The Art and Science of Engagement* (AAM Press 2013), her co-authored book on high-performance museums. Anne is an advisory board member of Performa, a member of The Museum Group, and currently studying philanthropy at Indiana University.

Sarah King Bhetaria is a project manager residing in Bloomington, Indiana. Committed to family-centered care, she serves as the president for national nonprofit organization Project Sweet Peas, which empowers and supports families of medically fragile babies. Sarah earned an M.A. in Philanthropic Studies from the Indiana University Lilly Family School of Philanthropy, and a B.S. in Neurobiology and Physiology from Purdue University.

Maarten Bout, CFRE, a native Dutchman, is the Director of Development, International Advancement at the Indiana University Office of the Vice President for International Affairs. He earned an M.A. from the Indiana University Lilly Family School of Philanthropy. His interest in philanthropy lies in the individual's agency to give and the nature and influence of the relationship between the donor and the fundraiser. He has written for *The Fundraiser* (NL), Association of Fundraising Professionals' *Advancing Philanthropy*, and *Giving USA*.

Beth Breeze, Ph.D., worked as a fundraiser and charity manager for a decade before founding the Centre for Philanthropy at the University of Kent, UK, in 2008, where she now leads a team conducting research and teaching courses on philanthropy and fundraising, including an innovative M.A. Philanthropic Studies taught by distance learning. Her books include: *Richer Lives: Why Rich People Give* (2013), *The New Fundraisers: Who Organises Generosity in Contemporary Society?* (2017), and *In Defence of Philanthropy* (2021).

Catherine (Cathy) Brown designs and teaches courses for The Fund Raising School. She has 20+ years' experience in nonprofit management and fundraising, plus expertise in curriculum design and instruction. Cathy received a B.A. from Hanover College, M.S. in Education from Indiana University, and Graduate Certificate in Philanthropic Studies from the Indiana University Lilly Family School of Philanthropy at Indiana University–Purdue University Indianapolis (IUPUI). She is a nationally certified Associate Professional in Talent Development.

M. Gasby Brown has an unparalleled passion for the nonprofit industry. Her work and impact are testaments to her strong belief in the necessity of outstanding boards and good philanthropic practices. She is the CEO & Executive Consultant of The Gasby Group, Inc. (TGG), a full-service strategic fundraising and organizational effectiveness powerhouse with an impressive list of clients. She has shared her strategic thinking and expertise with board members nationally and internationally.

Dwight F. Burlingame, Ph.D., is Professor Emeritus of Philanthropic Studies at Indiana University, where he taught Philanthropic and Nonprofit Studies for

31 years. He is a member of Association for Research on Nonprofit Organizations and Voluntary Action (ARNOVA), where he served a six-year term as editor of *Nonprofit and Voluntary Sector Quarterly (NVSQ)* and as treasurer. He has received numerous awards and is active in the nonprofit community. He earned a B.A. from Moorhead State University, an M.S. from the University of Illinois, and a Ph.D. from Florida State University.

Jane Chu, Ph.D., combines her academic research and professional practice in the arts, philanthropy, and business administration. In 2014, she was appointed to serve as the eleventh chairperson of the National Endowment for the Arts, completing her term in June 2018. Dr. Chu is also a practicing visual artist, and a Distinguished Visiting Scholar at the Indiana University Lilly Family School of Philanthropy.

Aaron Conley, Ed.D., is a faculty member for The Fund Raising School and founder of the consultancy Academic Advancement Partners. He consulted previously with Grenzebach Glier and Associates, where he led the teaching and coaching practice. He also held senior fundraising roles over two decades at a number of research universities. Dr. Conley has authored educational fundraising research articles, book chapters, and a book. He earned a doctorate in higher education from Indiana University.

Elizabeth J. Dale, Ph.D., is Associate Professor in Nonprofit Leadership at Seattle University and received her doctorate from the Indiana University Lilly Family School of Philanthropy. She is a former development director and CFRE, and her research interests include women's philanthropy and giving to women's and girls' causes, giving among LGBTQ donors, and the intersection of gender and philanthropy. She holds a bachelor's degree in journalism and women's and gender studies from Ohio Wesleyan University and a master's degree in women's studies from The Ohio State University.

Erik J. Daubert holds the lifetime credential of Advanced Certified Fund Raising Executive (ACFRE) from the Association of Fundraising Professionals (AFP). He is Immediate Past Chair of the AFP Research Council and Past Chair of the Growth in Giving Initiative, the Fundraising Effectiveness Project, and the ACFRE Certification Board. A faculty member with The Fund Raising School, Erik has also served as an Affiliated Scholar with the Center on Nonprofits and Philanthropy at the Urban Institute in Washington, D.C., and taught at several universities.

Roberta L. Donahue, M.B.A., CFRE, CFRM, has over 25 years in fundraising and has accumulated a wide variety of experiences in institutional advancement. In addition to serving as a faculty member of The Fund Raising School, she is currently a fundraising and management consultant. Ms. Donahue received her B.A. from Marian University in Indianapolis and her M.B.A. from the State University of New York at Binghamton.

Patrick C. Dwyer, Ph.D., is Assistant Professor of Philanthropic Studies at the Indiana University Lilly Family School of Philanthropy. He teaches courses on donor motivations, behaviors, and engagement; institutional fundraising and grant writing; and experimental research methods. His research focuses broadly on human motivation, emotion, and prosocial action. He received his Ph.D. in Social Psychology from the University of Minnesota.

Tyrone McKinley Freeman, Ph.D., is Associate Professor of Philanthropic Studies at the Indiana University Lilly Family School of Philanthropy. Formerly a professional fundraiser in community development, social services, and higher education organizations, he also served as Associate Director of The Fund Raising School. He is author of *Madam C.J. Walker's Gospel of Giving: Black Women's Philanthropy during Jim Crow,* which won the Association of Fundraising Professionals' Global Skystone Partners Research Prize in Fundraising and Philanthropy.

Jeri Patricia Gabbert serves as the Vice Chancellor for University Advancement and External Affairs at Indiana University Northwest. She is a faculty member at The Fund Raising School, serves on the Board of Directors for Council for Advancement and Support of Education (CASE) V, and holds the CFRE designation. Jeri Pat holds a B.A. degree from Hanover College and an M.A. degree from Ball State University.

LaKoya S. Gardner is the Director of Programs and Associate Director of Development for the Mays Family Institute on Diverse Philanthropy in the Indiana University Lilly Family School of Philanthropy. She has over 10 years of experience in fundraising within higher education and other nonprofits. LaKoya received her B.A. from Indiana University–Purdue University Indianapolis (IUPUI) and M.A. in Organizational Leadership from Indiana Wesleyan.

Nathan Hand serves as Chief Advancement Officer at The Oaks Academy in Indianapolis and Faculty at The Fund Raising School. He has served in leadership fundraising roles in the education sector, founded a community center, and began his career in Washington, D.C. Nathan earned his M.A. from the Indiana University Lilly Family School of Philanthropy, an Executive Certificate in Nonprofit Management from Georgetown University, and undergraduate degree from DePauw University.

Ruth K. Hansen, Ph.D., is an Assistant Professor of Management at the University of Wisconsin-Whitewater, where she teaches about the nonprofit sector, fundraising, and organizational behavior. Her research primarily focuses on the theory and practice of fundraising. Ruth has more than 20 years' professional experience as a fundraiser, during which she was recognized as a Certified Fund Raising Executive (CFRE). She earned her Ph.D. in 2018 from the Indiana University Lilly Family School of Philanthropy.

Lijun He, Ph.D., is currently a financial advisor at Merrill Lynch Wealth Management at Seattle Market. In her current role, she primarily works with high net worth individuals and families. Lijun also serves as Vice Chair of P.E.A.R.L. Institute of New York, a nonprofit dedicated to mental health well-being of Asian American and Asian Pacific Islanders. Previously, she worked as Assistant Professor in Nonprofit Management at Pace University. She earned a doctoral degree in philanthropic studies with a minor in nonprofit management at the Indiana University Lilly Family School of Philanthropy in 2015.

H. Daniel Heist, Ph.D., is an Assistant Professor of Public Administration and Nonprofit Management in the Romney Institute of Public Service and Ethics at Brigham Young University. His research focuses on charitable giving, philanthropy, and volunteering. His nine years of professional fundraising experience inform his research and teaching. Dr. Heist is a leading expert on donor-advised funds and co-founder of the Donor-Advised Fund Research Collaborative.

Patricia Snell Herzog, Ph.D., is Melvin Simon Chair and Associate Professor of Philanthropic Studies in the Indiana University Lilly Family School of Philanthropy at Indiana University–Purdue University Indianapolis (IUPUI). Prior, Herzog was an Assistant and Associate Professor of Sociology and Co-Director of the Center for Social Research at the University of Arkansas. She has published numerous articles, reports, and books, including *The Science of Generosity: Manifestations, Causes, and Consequences* (Palgrave 2020) and *American Generosity: Who Gives and Why* (OUP 2016).

James M. Hodge has spent 44 years in philanthropy working in leadership positions for universities and academic medical centers. Aligned with the Indiana University Lilly Family School of Philanthropy's philosophy, he has been a guest lecturer, teacher in The Fund Raising School, and author of several major gift chapters in *Achieving Excellence in Fundraising*. Jim is a frequent speaker, workshop presenter, and nationally recognized practitioner of benefactor-centered, relationship-based, and inquiry-driven philanthropy.

Pat Danahey Janin is a consultant, instructor, and Ph.D. candidate at the Indiana University Lilly Family School of Philanthropy. Her research is on international philanthropy and the ocean, which led her to work for the United Nations Decade of Ocean Science. She has taught at the Lilly Family School and SciencesPo Paris. Pat worked internationally for 18 years in the business, nonprofit, and government sectors, and holds an M.B.A. from ESCP Paris, a graduate degree from the Sorbonne Paris IV, and a B.A. from Colorado State University.

Russell N. James III, J.D., Ph.D., CFP®, is a chaired professor in the Department of Personal Financial Planning at Texas Tech University, where he directs the on-campus and online graduate program in Charitable Financial Planning (planned giving). He graduated, *cum laude*, from the University of Missouri School of Law and also completed a Ph.D. in consumer economics from the University of Missouri, where his dissertation was on charitable giving.

Paula J. Jenkins serves as the Vice President of Development for the Bloomington campus with the Indiana University Foundation. Paula is a faculty member at The Fund Raising School, serves on the Board of Directors for the Association of Fundraising Professionals (AFP) Indiana chapter, and has earned the CFRE designation. She has a B.S. degree from the University of Arizona Eller College of Management.

Rafia Khader is a Program Manager at the Lake Institute on Faith and Giving and the Muslim Philanthropy Initiative at the Indiana University Lilly Family School of Philanthropy. She is also the Managing Editor of the *Journal of Muslim Philanthropy & Civil Society* (Indiana University Press). She has over a decade of experience working with the American Muslim community as a nonprofit administrator, researcher, and volunteer.

David P. King, Ph.D., is the Karen Lake Buttrey Director of Lake Institute on Faith & Giving and Associate Professor of Philanthropic Studies at the Indiana University Lilly Family School of Philanthropy. His research interests include exploring the practices of twentieth and twenty-first century American and global faith communities and how the religious identity of faith-based nonprofits shapes their motivations, rhetoric, and practice. He is the author of *God's Internationalists: World Vision and the Age of Evangelical Humanitarianism* (UPenn Press 2019).

Sara Konrath, Ph.D., is a social psychologist and directs the Interdisciplinary Program on Empathy and Altruism Research at the Indiana University Lilly Family School of Philanthropy. Her research explores the science of empathy and giving. She is the former Science of Giving editor at *Nonprofit and Voluntary Sector Quarterly,* and a co-organizer of the Science of Philanthropy annual conferences. The Notre Dame Institute for Advanced Study (2020–2021) supported her while writing this chapter.

Yannan "Lukia" Li, Ph.D., is an Evaluation Associate at The Mark USA. She is also a freelancing consultant affiliated with S. Sutton & Associates. Dr. Li holds a Ph.D. degree in Philanthropic Studies and an M.A. degree in Applied Communications, both from Indiana University. Her research interests include the nonprofit use of social media, nonprofit accountability, and philanthropy ethics.

Angela Logan, Ph.D., is an Associate Teaching Professor and the St. Andre Bessette Academic Director of the Master of Nonprofit Administration in the Mendoza College of Business at the University of Notre Dame. Her research focuses on the intersection of gender, race, and nonprofit and philanthropic leadership. She is the first African American woman to earn a Ph.D. in Philanthropic Studies from the Indiana University Lilly Family School of Philanthropy.

Margaret M. Maxwell of Maxwell Associates helps nonprofits with strategic planning, governance, marketing, and business plan development. She also is a faculty member of The Fund Raising School and a BoardSource Certified Governance Consultant. Prior to consulting, she was Vice President for The Children's Museum of Indianapolis, one of the nation's premier cultural institutions, where she led the fundraising, marketing, strategic planning, and earned income programs. She received both a B.A. in journalism and an M.B.A. from Indiana University.

Debra J. Mesch, Ph.D., is Professor Emerita of Philanthropic Studies at the Indiana University Lilly Family School of Philanthropy and was the first holder of the Eileen Lamb O'Gara Chair in Women's Philanthropy. Dr. Mesch was the Director of the Women's Philanthropy Institute (WPI) from 2008 to 2018. Her primary responsibility was to guide the research agenda on the role of gender in philanthropy. Professor Mesch received both her M.B.A. and Ph.D. in organizational behavior/human resource management from Indiana University Kelley School of Business.

Heather A. O'Connor, Ph.D., CFRM, CAP®, is Managing Director, Research at Kordant Philanthropy Advisors. She is a former fundraiser with 20 years of experience serving health, education, and social service organizations. Her research interests include women's charitable giving, nonprofit messaging, and the professions of fundraising and philanthropic advising. She holds a Ph.D. in Philanthropic Studies from the Indiana University Lilly Family School of Philanthropy and an M.A. in Social Service Administration from the University of Chicago.

Una Osili, Ph.D., is the Efrymson Chair in Philanthropy at the Indiana University Lilly Family School of Philanthropy. Dr. Osili is also the Associate Dean of Research and International Programs at the Lilly Family School and the Dean's Fellow for the Mays Institute on Diverse Philanthropy. Her research is focused on household charitable behavior across low-income and high-income environments.

Amir Pasic, Ph.D., is the Eugene R. Tempel Dean of the Indiana University Lilly Family School of Philanthropy. Previously he held positions at the Council for Advancement and Support of Education (CASE), Johns Hopkins University, the Rockefeller Brothers Fund, The George Washington University, and the Library of Congress. Dr. Pasic earned his doctorate in political science at the University of Pennsylvania, a master's degree in international relations from Johns Hopkins University, and a bachelor's degree in economics and political science from Yale University.

Susan B. Perry, Associate Director of Development at the Lilly Family School of Philanthropy, is a successful fundraiser with 25+ years of experience. She has developed and implemented individual donor giving programs as well as a multi-level sponsor program. In addition to managing staff to implement an annual fund, donor appeals, and grant execution, Susan has a wide range of experience working with both large and small companies on comprehensive marketing, communication, and development skills.

Aja May Pirtle is an experienced marketing, branding, and fundraising consultant with nearly two decades of experience in government, tourism, education, and nonprofit marketing. She currently serves as Managing Director of Marketing & Communications for the Indiana University Lilly Family School of Philanthropy, a first-of-its-kind world leader in philanthropic studies, research, and training.

Anna Pruitt, Ph.D., is the Managing Editor of *Giving USA: The Annual Report on Philanthropy,* the longest-running annual report on charitable giving in the United States. She researches individual giving, donor-advised funds, regional giving, and other important topics in the field of philanthropy as a member of the research program at the Indiana University Lilly Family School of Philanthropy. Her work brings cutting edge research to donors, fundraisers, and nonprofit leaders.

Phillip M. Purcell, CFRE, has enjoyed a 30-year career in planned giving and currently serves as the Director of Planned Giving for the Central Territory of the Salvation Army. Phil is Senior Consultant and the lead gift planning attorney for the Heaton Smith Group, and serves as Editor for *Planned Giving Today,* a monthly national publication. Phil teaches courses on law and philanthropy, nonprofit organization law, and planned giving for the Indiana University Maurer School of Law, Indiana University Lilly School of Philanthropy, and The Fund Raising School. He received his B.A. degree from Wabash College, and J.D. and M.P.A. degrees from Indiana University.

Patrick Rooney, Ph.D., is the Glenn Family Chair in Philanthropy, Professor of Economics and Philanthropic Studies, and the Executive Associate Dean for Academic Programs at the Indiana University Lilly Family School of Philanthropy. A nationally recognized expert on philanthropy and charitable giving, Dr. Rooney has published many academic and practitioner-focused papers, speaks frequently across the country, and has served on nonprofit boards and advisory committees. He earned his B.A., M.A., and Ph.D. in Economics at Notre Dame.

Jeannie Infante Sager is Director of the Women's Philanthropy Institute in the Indiana University Lilly Family School of Philanthropy. In this role, Jeannie leads efforts to translate research to practice; guides strategic programming; and manages fundraising, communications, and operations. She is a nonprofit executive with over 25 years of experience in healthcare, higher education, and independent school fundraising and leadership. She received her B.A. in International Relations from Rollins College and an M.A. in Philanthropic Studies from Indiana University.

Timothy "Tim" L. Seiler, Ph.D., has served in roles such as unit development officer, capital campaign manager, vice president, program director, clinical professor, and Rosso Fellow in Philanthropic Fundraising. Author and editor in the workbook series *Excellence in Fundraising,* he also co-edited editions three and four of *Achieving Excellence in Fundraising.* In 2014, he received the Association of Fundraising Professionals' (AFP) Indiana Chapter Fundraising Executive Award and the Rosso Medal for Lifetime Achievement in Ethical Fundraising.

Charles Sellen, Ph.D., served as the inaugural Global Philanthropy Fellow at the Indiana University Lilly Family School of Philanthropy (2019–2021) and a Fulbright "NGO Leader" visiting from France. He has conducted research on philanthropy since 2004, at the intersection with international relations and global cooperation toward development. He previously worked in government (with the French Agency for Development) and the private sector and served as chairman of a French nonprofit think tank on happiness and well-being.

Shariq Siddiqui, Ph.D., is Assistant Professor of Philanthropic Studies and Director of the Muslim Philanthropy Initiative at the Indiana University Lilly Family School of Philanthropy. He has served as a nonprofit practitioner for over 20 years and is the author of research on Muslim philanthropy and nonprofit sector. Dr. Siddiqui served as the Executive Director of Association for Research on Nonprofit Organizations and Voluntary Action (ARNOVA). He has a Ph.D. and M.A. from the Lilly Family School, a J.D. from the McKinney School of Law at Indiana University, and a B.A. in History from the University of Indianapolis.

Caitlin Deranek Stewart, M.A., M.P.A., CFRE, is a Major Gift Officer at Indiana University School of Medicine focused on scholarships, women's health, and fighting blindness, among other priorities. Caitie is passionate about health equity and access to high-quality healthcare and believes that philanthropy creates innovation to improve the world. When not fundraising, Caitie is a professional musician across the Midwest, a private voice and piano teacher, and proud mom to two children.

Danielle Vance-McMullen, Ph.D., is an Assistant Professor of Public Policy and Nonprofit Management at DePaul University. She uses Big Data and behavioral experiments to research donor behavior and nonprofit competition in new charitable giving contexts. She is active in donor-advised fund research and is a co-founder of the Donor-Advised Fund Research Collaborative.

Lilya Wagner, Ph.D., was Director of the consulting firm Philanthropic Service for Institutions until early in 2020, and on the faculty of The Fund Raising School and the Indiana University Lilly Family School of Philanthropy. She was Vice President for Philanthropy at Counterpart International in Washington, D.C., an international development organization. She is a frequent international speaker and workshop presenter, and an award-winning author. Her book *Diversity and Philanthropy: Expanding the Circles of Giving* is a comprehensive volume about cultural influences on generosity.

Pamala Wiepking, Ph.D., is the Visiting Stead Family Chair in International Philanthropy and Visiting Associate Professor of Philanthropic Studies at the Indiana University Lilly Family School of Philanthropy and Professor of Societal Significance of Charity Lotteries at the Vrije Universiteit Amsterdam. She studies international and interdisciplinary explanations for philanthropy with the aim to help create more generous societies.

Kidist Yasin is a doctoral student in Philanthropic Studies at the Indiana University (IU) Lilly Family School of Philanthropy. Kidist received her B.A. and M.S.C. degrees in Economics from Dire Dawa University and Addis Ababa University, respectively, both located in Ethiopia. She also obtained an advanced Master's degree in Development and Globalization from the University of Antwerp in Belgium. She has experience lecturing university students on various economics topics and supervises undergraduate students working on research projects.

PART ONE

PHILANTHROPIC CONCEPTS FOR FUNDRAISING

CHAPTER ONE

DEVELOPING A PERSONAL PHILOSOPHY OF FUNDRAISING

By Eugene R. Tempel and Sarah K. Nathan

This chapter introduces the concept of a personal philosophy of fundraising, established by each fundraiser and made personal to one's own engagement in fundraising. The personal philosophy includes a set of guiding principles that are foundational to successfully engaging in fundraising. The chapter argues that the development of a personal philosophy of fundraising begins with reflection about one's own experience with, and understanding of, philanthropy. It evolves throughout careers in the field, based on job position, shifting organizational dynamics, evolution of fundraising structures and forms, and the complexities of the external environment, including cultures, in which individual and institutional donors exist.

As a result of this chapter, readers will:

- Understand the importance of developing a personal philosophy of fundraising.
- Examine personal and professional experiences in relation to who they are as fundraisers.
- Consider societal factors relevant to their philosophy, including the roles of philanthropy.
- Reflect on organizational conditions influencing their philosophy, including foundational principles of fundraising as professional work.
- Reflect on examples from the authors' philosophies.

Why a Philosophy of Fundraising?

Fundraising professionals are what is known as "boundary spanners," functioning in the space where the organization interacts with its external environment (Kelly 1998). They are like marketing and sales personnel in business and foreign ambassadorial staff in governments. Those who live in these roles must have the strength of character and confidence to represent the organization to its constituents, to negotiate on behalf of the organization, and to represent the views and values of constituents and donors to organizational leadership. They must become trusted agents to both internal and external parties. Thus, it becomes important for fundraisers to articulate: "I know who I am; I know what I do; and, I know why I do it."

Early leaders in the field of philanthropic studies challenged scholars and practitioners alike to work toward and advance a philosophy of fundraising (Burlingame and Hulse 1991). Thirty years ago, Hank Rosso (1991) offered his perspective on essential elements of ethical philanthropic fundraising based on a lifetime of teaching and reflection, the status of fundraising as an emerging profession, and society at the time of first edition of this book. His essay "A Philosophy of Fundraising" was printed in the subsequent editions and shared widely.

Today, we acknowledge the ever-changing dynamics of fundraising in the twenty-first century and suggest each fundraiser should have their own philosophy of fundraising based on the contexts of time and culture, study and understanding of fundraising and philanthropy, and experiences over the course of a career. This chapter will help readers develop a personal philosophy of fundraising through multiple lenses – the personal, the societal, and the organizational – and distill lived experiences, beliefs, and values. A personal philosophy of fundraising is a guiding force for a meaningful career. Throughout this chapter, the authors demonstrate the formation of a philosophy of fundraising by sharing examples from their own lives and careers.

Personal Experiences and Philanthropy

Reflection begins by looking internally. A lifetime of experiences shapes each person at any given moment in time. Formally, an individual's identity is considered "what an individual will stand for and be recognized as" (Josselson 1987, 8). Informally, identity may be considered the key attributes, preferences, and experiences that define who we are. While each person may emphasize certain attributes in different settings, one's professional identity is inseparable from personal experiences, roles, and expectations. People do not stop being parents, for example, when they walk into the office. Likewise, they do not stop being leaders or organizational representatives when in the grocery store. (This is especially true for those living in small towns like Sarah!)

Indeed, personal and professional identities are layered on top of lived experiences. Individuals see the world from their vantage point(s), for example, of gender identification, racial and ethnic background, and with a history of many or limited financial resources. Physical abilities, orientation, nationality, faith tradition, geography, parental status, and more shape each person and how they approach philanthropy.

The Philanthropic Autobiography

As educators, we use the philanthropic autobiography to help learners develop individual perspectives on philanthropy. The philanthropic autobiography is the place to begin developing a personal philosophy; it reveals the "roots" of our philanthropic self.

The autobiography identifies people's first memorable experiences of philanthropy as both givers and receivers, and from role models to experiences over time that help them modify, amplify, and develop how they help others. In teaching the philanthropic autobiography, we ask such questions as: "What are some of your earliest memories of philanthropy? What are some of your defining philanthropic moments? Who are your philanthropic role models? Describe the most meaningful gift you've received." A philosophy of fundraising begins with these principal experiences.

Gene's philanthropic autobiography begins as a six-year-old in January 1954, when his family lost its home and belongings to a house fire. The volunteer fire department (an active philanthropy in St. Meinrad, Indiana) made a valiant attempt to save the house, but the fire had a head start, and the department failed. More acts of philanthropy followed. Members of the local parish, neighbors, and the community at large organized on all-out effort to collect clothing and toys, to provide food, and to search for shelter. They did not think of themselves as fundraisers, of course. None had developed a philosophy of fundraising. But they achieved their goal of providing for Gene's family by engaging a large portion of the community in the collective effort. The experience opened his eyes to the role of *philanthropy* (a word he only learned later) in making people's lives whole. Perhaps Gene has been repaying that effort his entire life. Certainly, it is the foundation of his understanding of philanthropy as an activity focused on others.

Sarah's earliest memories of philanthropy are from the 1980s gymnasium of her parochial school and the day when volunteer parents formed an assembly line to make frozen pizzas. Students then sold and distributed the pizzas to friends and neighbors as part of an annual fundraising effort. The parents had found a unique fundraising niche that suited the times before local stores had dozens of frozen pizza options. Sarah's dad must have believed he was coaching her to "pitch" piz-zas (he was a small business owner, after all), but he was really teaching her to make the philanthropic case for support. Articulating why and how pizza sales supported her education was the case for support. Like the community members in Gene's story, the parents and children would not have called themselves fund-raisers or used a term like "case for support," but that is what was happening. Sarah learned to use her voice to advocate for a cause from which she also benefited. Money raised went toward a new school playground, which volunteer parents later installed.

Individuals' experiences as givers and receivers bring to life philanthropy focused on others, which is at the core of a philosophy of fundraising.

Philanthropy in Society

Philanthropy is about certain kinds of action (giving, volunteering, advocating), the actions' outcomes and rationales. It affirms a value, a concern for the well-being of people beyond oneself, and attention to the public good. In this context, Tempel (2003) presented the roles of philanthropy in society as:

- Through healthcare, human services, and international relief, nonprofit organizations seek to *reduce human suffering* for those who are injured or ill, to aid victims, and to assist those not able to sustain themselves. This is perhaps the oldest role of philanthropy, a role that has existed throughout recorded history.
- Nonprofit organizations *enhance human potential* through religion, education, the arts, culture and humanities, the environment, and international efforts.
- Philanthropy *promotes equity and justice* through inclusive structures and programs within the public, private, and nonprofit sectors that ensure opportunity for vulnerable, marginalized, or underrepresented people. Awareness and advocacy can advance the common good wherein every-one's human rights are assured.
- Through organizations and voluntary associations, people come together; they belong, and contribute to their neighborhood, city, state, country, or world through *community building*.
- Philanthropy *provides human fulfillment* by giving all people the opportunity to become that best image of ourselves. Through giving and sharing, humans express their ideas and values.
- Philanthropy *supports experimentation and stimulates change* by taking risks, exploring areas that the larger community or the market sector may be unwilling to enter, and often funds alternative or new solutions.

- Nonprofit organizations *foster pluralism* by allowing for multiple responses to an issue, and at its best, include a wide variety of voices. In a society in which philanthropy flourishes, parallel power structures are allowed to carry out what the government will not or cannot do.

Reflecting on these roles of philanthropy will help shape a philosophy of fundraising. Often, the first impulse in philanthropy is to make people's lives whole, by alleviating suffering and then providing enriching opportunities. For example, hospitals not only heal bodies, they also may enhance the healing process through beautiful spaces, music, and even visits from animals. Philanthropy can aid in curing disease and improving treatment through research and also in healing the spirit through artistic expression.

It is also likely that multiple roles relate to a person's philanthropic autobiography. These roles may relate to personal value systems or be the impetus of a career. Considering which roles one gravitates toward gives fundraising meaning and can influence where a fundraiser chooses to work.

Reflecting on one's philanthropic autobiography can be a reminder of teachers, mentors, religious leaders, coaches, and camp counselors who nurtured younger selves. These trusted adults were expressing philanthropy's role to enhance others' human potential. At the same time, these adults found personal fulfillment and contributed to community building through engagement with young people and causes they cared about.

Turning toward our own stories, Sarah finds satisfaction in serving as a Girl Scout troop volunteer, not only because of the activities themselves, but also because of her commitment to the organization and the special community it creates of girls and their caregivers. Gene enjoys pro bono consulting for the Sisters of St Benedict in Ferdinand, Indiana, helping them raise money for their mission because it enables him to repay them for the education they made possible for him. Professionally, Gene and Sarah both see themselves as educators whose central goal is to enhance others' potential and opportunity.

Thinking Globally and Culturally

In developing a philosophy, fundraisers must also consider philanthropic traditions and practices beyond their direct experiences. Philanthropy is not only an American phenomenon and celebrating its international and cultural forms is a key philanthropic role: fostering pluralism. It is a part of every culture across time and place, often in unique ways that must be considered for a full understanding of philanthropy (Illchman et al. 1998) (see Chapter 9).

Indigenous people, for example, practiced philanthropy before Europeans arrived in North America. Traditions of giving and receiving vary among tribal groups but share principles, including the idea that gifts are constantly in motion.

A philosophy of fundraising might be informed by another important aspect of Native American philanthropy, the gift exchange relationship: "Giving by one individual to another honors the recipient, and by receiving the gift with grace and gratitude, the recipient in turn honors the giver since the act of receiving the gift helps restore balance in the life of the giver" (Burlingame 2004, 336–337).

Advancing Social Justice and Racial Equity

Among philanthropy's roles is promoting social justice and racial equity. Today, more philanthropic dollars are flowing from individuals, corporations, and foundations toward improving opportunities for people of color and other marginalized communities and changing structures that facilitate inequity. At the heart of these efforts is advocacy (a form of philanthropy) within the racial justice movement and an enhanced awareness of need stemming from the COVID-19 pandemic that has likely changed philanthropy permanently (Classy 2020). A fundraising philosophy must take into account how one's actions, fundraising efforts, and the case for support relate to philanthropy's role in advancing equity and justice.

Again, we look to our activities to demonstrate how fundraisers might incorporate equity and justice into their personal philosophy. Gene is a long-standing volunteer with the Indiana Repertory Theatre (IRT). For him, one of the most satisfying aspects is the organization's effort to provide theater at nominal or no cost to students from across the state. By removing a significant barrier, many children from low-income rural, suburban, and urban families see live, professional theater for the first time. The development of the theater's Inclusion Series, which focuses on issues of social justice and racial equity, has further helped Gene reflect on his responsibility for helping foster educational opportunities for underrepresented communities.

Likewise for Sarah, being a part of the Girl Scout movement, among the first national youth-serving organization to publicly declare a commitment to being an antiracist organization, challenges her to create a better future for all girls in her daughter's generation. Simultaneously, as a community leader committed to advancing equity through philanthropy, she is mindful of her own ongoing process of self-reflection, learning, and discovery for what it means to lead with an equity lens.

Core Fundraising Tenants within Organizations

Another component of a philosophy of fundraising is developing an awareness of the relationship of fundraising to the organization and field of fundraising.

The following tenants are core components of professionalized fundraising that can be incorporated into a person's philosophy.

The Case for Support

Fundraising rests on the case for support (Rosso 1991; see Chapter 13). Fundraising is never an end in itself: It must be based on the case for support. The privilege to ask is made legitimate by the mission, the goals of a nonprofit organization, and by the contribution the organization makes to the public good. Put another way, the organization has a right to ask because it fulfills a community need, not because the organization has a budget shortfall or "to keep the lights on." The highest importance in fundraising is the ultimate beneficiary, that is, the client, student, family, or group whose life is changed for the better because of the organization's programs.

Philanthropy is stimulated by a vision for the future that improves on the present. Organizations exist to fulfill that vision. A philosophy of fundraising must take into account that fundraising is based on this rationale; it is not an end in itself.

Culture of Philanthropy

A strong organizational "culture of philanthropy" exists when fostering philanthropy is everyone's responsibility from the board of directors to the CEO to program staff, and not the sole duty of fundraising staff (Gibson 2016; Joyaux 2015). Recognizing fundraising as a total organizational effort, planned and led by fundraising staff, can generate higher job satisfaction for fundraisers and improves fundraising outcomes (Axelrad 2015; Crumpton 2016; Whitchurch and Comer 2016).

A culture of philanthropy also depends on a deeper tenet. Philanthropy (and fundraising) must be seen as a legitimate source of revenue for an organization as it fulfills societal roles of philanthropy. People within the organization may require coaching and resources to demystify fundraising and understand philanthropic giving before embracing a shared philanthropic responsibility. Acceptance of philanthropy as a legitimate source of support is the beginning of acceptance of one's role in fundraising, of engaging potential donors with the organization's case for support, its mission, goals, and objectives.

In a culture of philanthropy, fundraisers develop plans that orchestrate involvement of board members, volunteers, the CEO, and other staff in the fundraising process. Most agree that involvement of the board is essential to fundraising success (see Chapter 20). As with fundraising success in general, assuring board acceptance of philanthropy and participation in fundraising is essential for the culture of philanthropy and subsequent engagement of other volunteers and staff members in fundraising.

A philosophy of fundraising incorporates examination of the culture of philanthropy and how to articulate that to others. At the most elemental level, fundraisers and their allies are called to embrace philanthropy as a legitimate source of support for a worthy cause. As a leader, Sarah finds this philosophy gives her strength to reiterate to the board: "We deserve to ask!"

Integration

Fundraising is an organizational process designed to engage donors and potential donors with the organization's case, mission, goals and objectives, and its vision for the future. Fundraisers design and orchestrate this process involving themselves and others in carrying out the work. A personal philosophy of fundraising informs approaches toward structuring fundraising itself, integrating it into organizational leadership and management decision-making, and involving others in the process. Fundraising must be institutionalized; it must be integrated into the management structure of the organization. Otherwise, fundraising risks becoming disconnected from the mission and case for support. Otherwise, a culture of philanthropy cannot develop; otherwise fundraising becomes an end in itself.

Gene has always insisted that as a fundraiser he be taken seriously. He has insisted that fundraisers be involved in decisions that impact the ability of the organization to attract philanthropy. And he has insisted that fundraisers be well informed professionals who take a professional stance on matters pertaining to fundraising in the management of the organization. These commitments began with principles of fundraising and philanthropy, but also with individual reflection about actions required of fundraisers themselves.

Confidence in the Work

Among most important components of a philosophy of fundraising is one's attitude toward fundraising. Rosso's (1991) call for fundraisers to "substitute pride for apology" remains as relevant today as 30 years ago. In other words, there is no need to be sorry about asking for money and inviting gifts. Instead, fundraising is proud and honorable work enabling positive change and opportunity in society. Those who do not believe in the values being promoted by the case for support, those who see fundraising as an end in itself risk seeing fundraising as begging. Those who do not believe that the beneficiaries are worthy of support risk mistaking fundraising for being about the money rather than the cause. Those who do not understand that giving and volunteering bring joy to donors and volunteers may see fundraising as diminishing others, as taking something away, as getting people to act against their better judgement.

There are many attributions for the phrase "It's better to give than to receive." Here is how Maya Angelou (1993) put it: ". . . I have found that among its other benefits, giving liberates the soul of the giver. . . . The giver is as enriched as is the recipient, and more important, that intangible but very real psychic force of good in the world is increased" (15). In short, a philosophy of fundraising must be based on confidence that fundraisers help donors and volunteers find fulfillment through generosity to others.

Ethical Grounding

No philosophy of fundraising can be complete without attention to the ethics of fundraising and philanthropy (see Chapter 2). The "Code of Ethical Standards" of the Association of Fundraising Professionals is a good beginning. Specialized fields such as healthcare and education provide ethical perspectives as well. Commitment to a code of ethics, understanding of more general philosophical approaches to ethics, and tools for handling ethical dilemmas must undergird the individual philosophy of fundraising.

Voluntary Action

Payton (1988) defined *philanthropy* as "voluntary action for the public good." The case for support is about community benefit. But the philosophy of fundraising must also consider that philanthropy is a voluntary activity. This was one of the key pillars of Rosso's (1991) philosophy as the gentle art of teaching others the joy of giving. Fundraisers cannot pressure potential donors and must educate board members, staff, and volunteers not to push potential donors based on relationships, reciprocity, financial situations, or other factors that make it difficult for them to act freely.

Professional Responsibility

Finally, as the fundraising profession grows and matures, members have a responsibility to each other. Fundraisers serve as role models for generous behavior within their families, organizations, and communities. Indeed, they give and volunteer at a much higher rate than the general population (Shaker et al. 2020). Fundraisers' generous actions, then, become an expression of their commitment to philanthropy on and off the job.

Likewise, a component of a philosophy may also include a sense of professional responsibility to support fellow fundraisers, especially newcomers to the field and those who have historically been excluded. Sharing knowledge and encouragement, formally or informally, with colleagues reflects a larger commitment to fundraising. Gene has intentionally mentored countless fundraisers throughout his career. Sarah has created a semi-formal network of peers who she can call on for support and guidance.

Conclusion

Philanthropy is stimulated by a vision for the future that improves on the present. Fundraising is the difficult work of engaging potential donors with an organization's vision for the future, its case for support, and its mission, goals, and objectives. The first statement is idealistic; the second, the view of a realist. Articulating a philosophy of fundraising will help each fundraiser soar, inspired by their own life experiences and philanthropic journey and uplifted by a compelling case for support. And, a philosophy, undergirded by guiding principles from the field, will provide grounding for carrying out the work, institutionalizing it, developing a culture of philanthropy, and deciding on the activities, approaches, and individuals to pursue to support the cause.

Fundraisers are called to become reflective practitioners prepared to critique their own work. To do so they must develop their philosophy of fundraising, one that evolves over time to remain relevant and to guide them through complexities of a changing world and field. Individual experiences, cultural traditions, a quest for justice, and consideration of organizational and social influences all contribute to a robust philosophy of fundraising.

Discussion Questions

1. What is a personal philosophy of fundraising and why should fundraisers develop one?
2. What is a culture of philanthropy and how does it relate to one's philosophy of fundraising?
3. Consider at least three tenets covered in this chapter and describe how you will incorporate them into your philosophy of fundraising.

Application Exercises

1. Develop the beginning of your philanthropic autobiography by writing down in free form the answers to the following questions: "What are some of your earliest memories of philanthropy? What are some of your defining philanthropic moments? Who are your philanthropic role models? Describe the most meaningful gift you've received." How is fundraising present and how might you see it differently after reading this chapter?
2. Outline the initial approach you will take in your own philosophy of fundraising by considering the roles of philanthropy in society, the position of fundraising in your organizational context, and your core beliefs about fundraising as a foundation for philanthropy.

CHAPTER TWO

A COMMITMENT TO ETHICAL FUNDRAISING

By Anne Bergeron and Eugene R. Tempel

Fundraising is a noble profession, supporting organizations in the voluntary sector – arts, humanities, education, health and human services, religion, social justice, international aid, animal welfare, and the environment. Individuals, including fundraisers, are often drawn to these fields over other public-facing occupations out of service and commitment to enhancing civil society. Fundraisers wield influence in their facilitative role developing relationships among organizations, donors, and beneficiaries. They are responsible to their organizations for helping to realize institutional missions, to donors for fulfilling their gift intentions as agreed, and to beneficiaries for representing their best interests. With these responsibilities come the obligation to act ethically with care and good judgment, and create trust, the foundation of philanthropy.

Ethics is not commonly discussed for fear of sounding preachy or old-fashioned. But understanding and applying ethics is as important for fundraisers as technical skill. This chapter explicates ethical practice in fundraising.

In this chapter, readers will explore:

- The principle of trust that buttresses the nonprofit sector.
- Ethical values and philosophies that undergird moral conscience.
- Professional ethics and ethical behavior.
- Common ethical issues and dilemmas.
- Ethics and social justice.

A Foundation of Trust

The nonprofit and philanthropic sectors are built on a covenant of trust that serves the public good (Pribbenow 1994). Trust anchors nonprofit organizations, the constituencies they serve, and the patrons who support them. Although there is a correlation between trust and donor generosity (Sargeant and Lee 2001), recent studies express some contradictions. One report finds that trust in nonprofits is high among educated, upper income, urban residents, but low among those from underserved, impoverished, rural communities (Independent Sector 2020). Another finds there is little trust in institutions worldwide due to systemic injustice and bias (Edelman 2020), while a third indicates that nonprofits are viewed as more trustworthy than for-profits and government, but overall trust has declined among donors (Give.org 2020).

Trust is the foundation on which philanthropy is developed and sustained. Donors must be assured that their contributions will be used as promised and applied in ways to generate the impact intended. Benefactors and beneficiaries expect transparency and accountability from public benefit organizations. The nonprofit sector has not been immune from scandals or stories of abuse and mismanagement, and the inevitable result is an erosion of the public's confidence. Faith in the sector is restored through "stewardship of the public good" (Pribbenow 1994, 40) when nonprofit leaders and fundraisers practice ethical behavior and maintain organizational cultures that honor ". . . a set of core values that are in keeping with the historical, philosophical, moral, and religious roots of the voluntary sector" (Jeavons 2016, 207).

Philosophy of Ethics

If public trust is so critical to the nonprofit sector (Independent Sector 2002), then how does one engender trust? Trust is gained by consistently practicing the highest ethics and values (Pribbenow 1994). *Ethics* is defined as "how a moral person should behave" and values as "the inner judgments that determine how a person actually behaves" (Josephson 2002, 3). The Josephson Institute of Ethics offers the following set of values that inform professional, ethical practice:

1. Honesty,
2. Integrity,
3. Promise keeping,
4. Fidelity and loyalty,
5. Fairness,
6. Caring for others,

  7. Respect for others,
  8. Responsible citizenship,
  9. Pursuit of excellence, and
10. Accountability. (Josephson 2020)

Embracing these values and choosing to do the right thing "takes principled action as well as character worthy of human capacity" (Anderson 1996, 71). A brief primer on moral philosophy – the principles of right and wrong that govern human behavior and guide moral action – offers three traditional approaches to moral thinking. These are the ethics of care, consequentialism, and deontology, also referred to as "care-based," "end-based," and "rule-based" philosophies (Kidder 1995, 23–25).

- **Care-based ethics** advances the "well-being of care-givers and care-receivers in a network of social relations" (Sander-Staudt 2011, 1). It is often associated with the principle of the Golden Rule found in many of the world's religions, treating others as one wishes to be treated (Kidder 1995), with respect, compassion, and fairness. Its tenets are guided by self-love and love of humankind (Anderson 1996).
- **End-based consequentialism** focuses on acting morally to produce the right results (Haines 2006). For Greek philosopher and teleologist Aristotle (384–322 BC), whose virtue ethics underscores the importance of character as fundamental to a moral life, practicing beneficence and justice is paramount (Anderson 1996). For English philosophers Jeremy Benthan (1748–1832) and John Stuart Mill (1806–1873), who promoted a form of consequentialism called *utilitarianism*, the best overall outcome is one that "maximizes utility" and produces the greatest amount of good for the greatest number (Nathanson 2014, 3).
- **Rule-based deontology** addresses the concept of duty and acting morally in accordance with universal and impartial "rules that everyone could and should obey" (Jankowiak 2019, 25). German philosopher Immanuel Kant (1724–1804) expresses this theory as the *categorical imperative*.

These three principles can be applied to the situation faced by medical professionals in 2020 and 2021 when COVID-19 treatments were hampered by shortages of personnel, equipment, and medication. Doctors guided by care-based ethics would administer first to the sickest patients while offering compassion to the others. Doctors guided by consequentialism and reasoning that younger patients would have a better chance of surviving would treat them before older patients. Doctors driven by rules might apply a first-come, first-served approach to care. In the case of actual guidelines issued during the pandemic, medical ethicists favored the utilitarian principle of maximum benefit (Emanuel et al. 2020).

Professional Ethics

The Association of Fundraising Professionals (AFP) fosters ethical and best practices for fundraisers through education, training, advocacy, and research. Its "Code of Ethical Standards" guides the profession today in ways that engender trust (https://afpglobal.org/ethicsmain/code-ethical-standards). The "Donor Bill of Rights" respects those whose philanthropy makes the voluntary sector viable (https://afpglobal.org/donor-bill-rights).

Fundraisers must embrace these professional principles and think critically and carefully about ethical issues. As the "consciences of the philanthropic community," fundraisers must bring ethical courage to their work and "create communities of moral deliberation" in the organizations they serve (Pribbenow 2013, 8 and 13). While codes are guides to professional behavior (Rosen 2005), ethical fundraising is more about a right way to act than do's and don'ts. According to a 2011 AFP survey, those who routinely practice ethical fundraising share similar traits. They build trusted relationships by being honest and transparent in their dealings and communications. They are accountable for their behavior, as well as the behavior of their organizations. They embrace AFP's codes and model ethical practice, even when it is uncomfortable or unpopular. They take seriously their roles as stewards of the public trust (Pribbenow 2013).

Ethical Behavior

In *Obedience to the Unenforceable*, a report on ethical practice for nonprofit and philanthropic organizations, Independent Sector (IS) (2002) clarifies three types of ethical behavior that guide nonprofits: complying with applicable laws; doing the right thing, even in the face of hardship or discomfort; and choosing the ethical path between competing goods or conflicting values. The last, called ethical dilemmas, are the most difficult situations to address, often pitting core values against one another, so there is no easy right answer. There are commonly four types of "right versus right" ethical paradigms: truth versus loyalty, individual versus community, short-term versus long-term, and justice versus mercy (Kidder 1995, 17–18).

IS offers guidance to nonprofits in maintaining an ethical culture by adopting these shared values:

- **Commitment beyond self**, service to the public at the core of civil society.
- **Obedience of the laws**, a fundamental responsibility of stewardship, including those governing tax-exempt philanthropic and voluntary organizations.

- **Commitment beyond the law**, or "obedience to the unenforceable," the higher calling of personal responsibility to society accepted by nonprofit professionals. This phrase is taken from a speech given by British barrister and judge Lord John Fletcher Moulton (1844–1921).
- **Commitment to the public good**, requiring "those who presume to serve the public good . . . [to] assume a public trust" (Independent Sector 2002, 7).
- **Respect for the worth and dignity of individuals**, a promise that all voluntary sector staff and volunteers must fulfill.
- **Tolerance, diversity, and social justice**, reflecting civil society's rich heritage and the fundamental protections afforded to individuals in a democracy.
- **Accountability to the public**, a central responsibility of public benefit organizations.
- **Openness and honesty**, essential qualities of organizations that seek and utilize public or private funds to serve public purposes.
- **Responsible stewardship of resources**, a duty of care governance requirement that nonprofit organizations vow to uphold (Independent Sector 2002).

IS encourages nonprofit leaders, especially fundraisers, to integrate these commitments into their work. To strengthen transparency, governance, and ethical standards, IS (2015) developed *Principles for Good Governance and Ethical Practice*, a resource for organizations to establish or improve policies and procedures.

Attitude and language matter. Fundraisers are not salespeople and donors are not targets. The dignified process of inviting someone to give is not hitting them up. Philanthropy is a voluntary act, so guilt and undue pressure have no place in communications between fundraisers and donors (MacQuillan 2016). And organizations and beneficiaries are not beggars, but active agents in addressing community needs.

Conducting oneself with integrity, demonstrating moral character, and exercising good judgment can help to avoid ethical issues common in nonprofits (Burchill 2006; Rhode and Packel 2009; Rosen 2019). These include:

1. **Conflicts of interest**, when trustees, executives, or fundraisers benefit materially from insider relationships to their organizations, such as contracting services from a board member's business, or when fundraisers compromise professional relationships by accepting personal gifts from donors. Because engendering trust is crucial, nonprofits and fundraisers should avoid even the *appearance* of conflicts of interest.
2. **Accountability and reporting**, when solicitation materials or reports are inaccurate in describing the purpose of fundraising efforts and the use of funds. Transparency and candor are expected traits of nonprofits, without which trust declines.

3. **Tainted money**, when conflicts arise between an organization's mission and values, or social mores in general, and the source of donated monies. For example, a number of universities and museums were forced to reckon with gifts from the Sackler family, owner of pharmaceutical company Purdue Pharma, which helped to fuel the opioid addiction crisis (Cascone 2020a).

4. **Donor privacy**, when the confidentiality of donor information is violated, shared with those who have no need to know, or when fundraisers or consultants take donor information with them from one job to the next. Donor privacy is sacrosanct, protected by the AFP code of ethics, and donor relationships belong to the nonprofit, not the fundraiser.

5. **Compensation**, when excessive salaries and benefits awarded to senior staff or perks to trustees and high-level volunteers fall outside of what is acceptable to the IRS or breach a nonprofit's duty of care responsibility for prudent management of assets; or when fundraisers are paid a commission on monies raised, which contravenes AFP standards.

6. **Financial integrity**, when restricted funds are not applied as directed by patrons or are accepted with compromising strings attached; or when holdings in investment portfolios are at odds with institutional missions or values.

Applying Ethics

While it is vital to understand moral philosophy and to have good moral character and judgment, that is often not enough to ensure ethical behavior. Ethical issues can be complex and cause even the most principled person to falter. A disciplined approach to ethical decision-making can help prevent missteps while determining the best outcome for the circumstances.

The Markkula Center for Applied Ethics at Santa Clara University offers a useful framework for ethical decision-making in fundraising (Harrington and Varma 2020). First, objectively state the ethical issue at hand. Is there a conflict of interest or the appearance of one? Is there an ethics code violation or a legal compliance concern? Has there been a misappropriation of funds or lack of transparency in reporting? Does the situation present a controversial donor offering tainted funds?

Second, summarize all the relevant information and consider everyone with a stake in the issue – trustees, staff, donors, volunteers, beneficiaries, and the public. Confer with stakeholders, determine if the concerns of some carry more weight than others, and discuss why this might matter. "Good decisions take into account the possible consequences of words and actions on all those potentially affected by a decision" (Josephson 2002, 18).

Third, articulate various alternatives for action and their probable outcomes, assessing each relative to organizational mission and values, plus institutional relationships and one's own personal integrity (Fisher 2000).

Fourth, decide how to act and apply intuition to the decision. If it becomes front page news, can the decision be defended to one's peers or children (Levy 2013)?

Finally, take action, monitor the result, and then reflect on the outcome. Doing this in a consistent manner helps to build ethical muscle, which can be relied upon when the next ethical dilemma arises.

Just because something is legal does not make it ethical. Billionaire Leon Black, former chair and CEO of the private equity firm Apollo Global Management, was forced to step down from his corporate role, as well as his chairmanship of the Museum of Modern Art in New York, when it was reported he had paid convicted sex offender Jeffrey Epstein $158 million, which saved Black $2 billion via tax avoidance schemes (Pogrebin and Goldstein 2021). While his actions were not illegal, some view them as unethical.

Ethics and Social Justice

Contemporary society perceives deep disparities and bias in the world's economic, political, and social systems (Edelman 2020), with calls for those in power to combat structural inequities, including within the voluntary sector. Ford Foundation President Darren Walker (2019) urges philanthropists to use their capital to address systemic imbalances that create the need for charity over giving to institutions that support their privilege. Grantmaker Edgar Villanueva (2018) favors dismantling colonialist structures inherent in the foundation world by utilizing Indigenous customs that share power and foster participatory decision-making around wealth redistribution. Poet, scholar, and institutional philanthropist Elizabeth Alexander has refocused the Andrew W. Mellon Foundation from conventional arts and humanities funding to social justice initiatives that support community libraries, reading and literacy programs, and educational opportunities for the incarcerated (Florsheim 2020).

Applying social justice perspectives to nonprofit leadership and fundraising means generating new resources that offer the potential to succeed to those lacking opportunity. It means building inclusive workplaces with diverse boards and staff that reflect regional demographics and communities served. It means pursuing equity-based prospect research and cultivation programs that prioritize women and people of color alongside traditional white male corporate donors. It means retooling the annual fund as a catalyst for community building. When fundraising and philanthropy is shared by many, ". . . collective action enables people to achieve results through building equal and mutually-supportive relationships" that advance organizations and causes (Klein 2016, 3).

The field of fundraising has long taught that philanthropy is a donor-directed choice, motivated by the interests and intentions of the giver. The astute fundraiser finds the fit between organizational need and donor passion. How might fundraising change to enable justice-focused philanthropy? What if fundraisers are also taught to be beneficiary-directed, helping donors use their privilege to focus philanthropy on the root causes of inequity and its symptoms? Here, the lessons are about humility, empathy, listening, learning, deep community engagement, and trusted partnership.

Community-Centric Fundraising, guided by leaders of color and their allies, offers these core principles of socially-just fundraising practice:

1. Fundraising must be grounded in race, equity, and social justice.
2. The collective community is more important than individual organizational missions.
3. Nonprofits are generous with and mutually supportive of one another.
4. All who engage in strengthening the community are equally valued, whether staff, donor, board member, or volunteer.
5. Time is valued equally as money.
6. Donors are treated as partners, and this means being transparent, assuming the best intentions, and occasionally having difficult conversations.
7. Collaborative voluntary actions foster a sense of belonging, not othering.
8. Everyone personally benefits from engaging in the work of social justice – it is not just charity and compassion.
9. Social justice work is holistic and transformative, not transactional.
10. Healing and liberation require a commitment to economic justice (Community-Centric Fundraising 2021).

Reorienting fundraising from donor-centered to community-centered encourages power sharing in philanthropic relationships in ways that foster racial and economic justice. The authors propose the following "Beneficiary Bill of Rights" (see Exhibit 2.1) to ensure that the recipients of benevolence have agency and are active participants in collective community enrichment.

EXHIBIT 2.1. PROPOSED BENEFICIARY BILL OF RIGHTS

Beneficiary Bill of Rights

Philanthropy is based on longstanding global traditions of offering assistance and support to people and causes beyond oneself. It is a human activity that brings individuals together around common concerns that seek to enhance the quality of life for all. To ensure that philanthropy best serves those intended to benefit from charitable giving, we declare that all beneficiaries of philanthropy have these rights:

1. To be assured that donors and philanthropic and nonprofit organizations are acting in good faith to serve the best interests of the community.
2. To inform leaders of philanthropic organizations, plus donors and fundraisers, of community needs, concerns, and customs by engaging with, listening to, and being responsive to beneficiaries.
3. To be informed of and have access to the leadership of philanthropic and nonprofit organizations engaged in work designed to benefit the community.
4. To expect organizations to embrace an inclusionary practice of community development through collaborative governance that gives agency to all stakeholders.
5. To be at the center of community conversations and involved in framing issues, making plans, taking action, and evaluating outcomes through collaborative decision-making.
6. To have access to philanthropic and nonprofit organizations' most recent financial statements.
7. To be treated with dignity and respect, with opportunities for direct engagement and a voice in the decision-making process, which may include board or committee service.
8. To be free to ask questions and offer commentary without reprisal and to receive timely, honest responses.
9. To have the opportunity to participate anonymously, with personal information protected to the extent provided by law.
10. To be appropriately acknowledged for one's community advocacy, if desired.

Beneficiaries are defined as individuals or a group of people who receive direct benefit from philanthropic or nonprofit organizations working on their behalf to serve the public trust.
Source: Anne Bergeron and Eugene R. Tempel 2021. All Rights Reserved.

Conclusion

Fundraisers play a pivotal role in the nonprofit organizations they represent. Beyond securing the philanthropic resources needed to further institutional missions, fundraisers also serve as moral compasses for their organizations. By embodying moral character, observing the AFP Code of Ethical Standards, being transparent, and embracing accountability (Pribbenow 2013), fundraisers build the very trust that is needed to ensure the public good. Doing so takes discipline, courage, and principled action, but the rewards of living and working ethically justify the commitment.

Discussion Questions

1. Explain three philosophical approaches to ethics.
2. Describe the differences between an illegal act, an unethical one, and an ethical dilemma.
3. What are some differences between the Donor Bill of Rights and the Beneficiary Bill of Rights?
4. Identify and discuss at least three overlapping ideas between Josephson's values framework and Independent Sector's *Obedience to the Unenforceable*.

Application Exercises

1. Find an ethical issue concerning fundraising or nonprofits in the news and summarize how it might be resolved by applying the Markkula Center approach.
2. Describe a difficult conversation with a donor based on the Beneficiary Bill of Rights. Identify which ethical principles guide your response. Role play the conversation with a colleague.

CHAPTER THREE

LEGAL ASPECTS OF FUNDRAISING

By Philip M. Purcell

Fundraising excellence requires adherence to the letter and spirit of legal and ethical standards. The importance of the law in fundraising is evident by the attention given to charitable organizations and their fundraising practices by the U.S. Congress, Internal Revenue Service (IRS), state attorneys general, nonprofit boards of directors, and donors. The IRS lists abuses in fundraising and management by nonprofits or donors in its annual list of tax scams.

This chapter highlights the most significant legal issues. After reviewing it, readers will be able to:

- Explain the legal duties of prudent care, obedience, and loyalty relative to fundraising responsibilities and understand how to fulfill these duties.
- Identify legal issues and be aware of practices that emanate from state law such as the oversight role of the attorney general, enforcement of gift restrictions, and others.
- Identify ramifications for fundraising that emanate from federal law such as completion of the IRS 990 form, distinctions between public benefit charities, member benefit organizations and private foundations, and others.
- Describe legal considerations relative to international philanthropy, donor privacy, and confidentiality.

Background

The law that governs fundraising is a complex partnership of federal and state statutes, administrative regulations, and judicial decisions. It is dynamic and subject to change. Sources of current and accurate legal information include qualified legal counsel, independent auditors, updated reference works, consultants, and state or federal government offices.

Many legal issues are not "black and white." Resolution of a legal dilemma, similar to an ethical challenge, requires considerable discernment. First, all facts and circumstances must be accurately clarified and understood in detail. Next, applicable laws must be identified and examined. Discussion must take place with all appropriate parties as circumstances warrant: fundraisers, staff leadership, board of directors, legal counsel, and auditors, as well as volunteers, donors, and their professional advisors (e.g., legal counsel, accountant, financial advisor). Finally, a decision must be made, implemented, and monitored or modified for similar circumstances in the future.

Governance

Pursuant to state law, charitable organizations may be unincorporated associations, nonprofit corporations, charitable trusts, or other forms such as limited liability corporations. Governance structure is determined under state law by articles of association, constitution, or bylaws; trust instruments and governing statutes; or articles of incorporation and bylaws for nonprofit corporations (Fishman, Schwarz, and Mayer 2015). Nonprofit corporations are the most popular governance structure since they offer a valuable balance of liability limitation for directors and effective governance.

Once organized under state law, a charitable organization usually seeks qualification for tax exemption by the IRS as a public charity (for public or mutual benefit) or as a private foundation. For more detailed information, see IRS Form 1023 or 1023 EZ (*Application for Recognition of Exemption under 501(c)(3)*) or IRS Form 1024 (*Application for Recognition of Exemption under 501(a)*) and accompanying instructions. Also see IRS Publication 557, *Tax Exempt Status for Your Organization*.

The board of directors or trustees is responsible for the oversight of a nonprofit corporation, including the assurance of fundraising excellence. State law imposes three primary legal duties on nonprofit corporation boards of directors: prudent care, obedience, and loyalty.

Duty of Prudent Care

The duty of prudent care requires directors to exercise their responsibilities in good faith and with the diligence and skill that a prudent person would under the same circumstances. This prudent care requires carefully made decisions relative to both expenses and revenues, including generation of revenue by fundraising.

Use of development, fundraising, campaign, and other committees to oversee fundraising is an excellent means to satisfy the duty of care responsibility (see Fishman et al. 2015). State law supports prudent delegation of work to committees and independent counsel who are qualified and fulfill their assignments. A helpful resource for planning and evaluating governance and legal best practices is Independent Sector's *The Principles for Good Governance and Ethical Practices: A Guide for Charities and Foundations*.

Duty of Obedience

The duty of obedience requires a nonprofit corporation to carry out its legally stated charitable mission. The duty of obedience can be violated when fundraising is completed for programs and services that do not fulfill the organization's mission. This duty can also be violated if the nonprofit's founder prevents the board of directors from prudently fulfilling the mission by diverting attention to other projects. When directors are recruited to the board, they should be provided an orientation and manual that includes key documents such as articles of incorporation, bylaws, IRS determination letter, strategic plan, current budget, independent audit, and meeting minutes.

Duty of Loyalty

The duty of loyalty requires directors to avoid acting in any manner that may harm the nonprofit corporation or that may result in the directors' personal financial gain. The duty of loyalty is imposed by state law and involves federal oversight prohibiting excess benefits or private inurement by directors, officers, and staff. In the case of excess benefits, the IRS may impose excise tax penalties as an intermediate sanction pursuant to Internal Revenue Code Section 4958. More egregious cases of private inurement will result in loss of tax-exempt status.

Conflicts of interest can arise in the context of fundraising if directors use charitable gifts to leverage personal financial contracts. Also, directors must agree to treat the names and information about donors and gifts as confidential, respecting all requests for anonymity. The board of directors should adopt a conflict-of-interest policy requiring that conflicts of directors be disclosed and appropriately managed.

IRS Form 990 and Governance

The IRS annual Form 990 information return for larger organizations asks substantive questions relative to charitable organization governance. Information concerning the board of directors, conflict-of-interest policies, charitable gifts and other data is now collected and subject to IRS review.

Board review of the Form 990 and the annual financial audit is a best practice. Smaller organizations may submit a simple postcard or other form requiring less information. The current versions of the Form 990 and instructions are available at www.irs.gov. Completed 990 forms are available for public inspection.

State Law Considerations

Oversight of charitable organizations often rests with the state attorney general. Other state offices with oversight may include the secretary of state (e.g., nonprofit incorporation and annual certification) and Department of Revenue (e.g., application for property, sales and other tax exemptions, charity gaming such as bingo).

The attorney general typically has the legal standing on behalf of the public to bring a lawsuit in court or to impose other relief (e.g., injunctions, asset receiverships, replacement of directors or trustees) in cases where claims have been made by donors, whistleblowers, or the public that the organization is acting imprudently, ignoring donor intent, or otherwise violating the law.

State Fundraising Registration

Fundraising registration requirements differ by state. The National Association of State Charity Officials (NASCO) has oversight of solicitation by charitable organizations. NASCO offers a model charitable solicitation law, including a unified registration form that has been used or modified by some states. Some states exempt from registration those charitable organizations domiciled in the state and that use their own staff or volunteers to fundraise. However, charitable organizations located in other states may be required to register at least once or must provide an annual registration.

NASCO provides recommendations for internet fundraising called the Charleston Principles that some states may adopt. See the NASCO website for extensive information and a state-by-state list of charity offices at www.nasconet.org.

Fundraising Consultants and Solicitors

Some charities hire consultants and/or solicitors to assist in fundraising activities. The regulations for consultants and solicitors vary by state. In many states, a fundraising consultant is defined as an independently contracted person or organization hired to advise and train the charitable organization on fundraising strategies – but not to directly solicit gifts. A fundraising solicitor is an independently contracted person or organization hired to directly solicit gifts.

Many states require annual registration with the attorney general or other state office by fundraising consultants and solicitors before conducting business. The registration may require provision of a copy of the contracts, disclosure of the fees paid, and verification whether the consultant or solicitor will have custody of donations.

Definition of a Gift and Donor Restrictions

State and federal courts have required both a subjective and objective test to determine the existence of a charitable gift, especially for qualification of a tax benefit. The subjective test requires that the donor's intent must be "disinterested generosity" to support a charitable mission. The objective test requires that the gift be received by a qualified charitable organization and does not include any financial benefit or quid pro quo returned to the donor in exchange for the gift. In addition, a donor cannot impose conditions on a gift that inappropriately restrict the duty of care owed by the board of directors over the use of the gift (e.g., sale or investment of donated assets).

Donors may include specific restrictions on the use of a gift by an organization such as a designation for endowment and/or for a particular program or purpose. Charities are expected to honor donor intent as a legal and ethical best practice unless the purpose becomes impossible, impractical, or illegal. A helpful resource for honoring donor intent and restrictions is *Protecting Your Legacy: A Wise Giver's Guide to Honoring and Preserving Donor Intent*, provided by The Philanthropy Roundtable. Court cases as well as statutory law known as the Uniform Prudent Management of Institutional Funds Act (UPMIFA) includes procedures for modifying the purpose or management aspects of a gift if impossible, impractical, and so on.

Charitable Pledges

Lawsuits to enforce charitable pledges are rare, but they may be deemed enforceable contracts pursuant to state law, particularly in cases where the charitable organization has acted in reliance on the pledge (e.g., building construction begins in reliance on a major gift pledge). The Financial Accounting Standards Board (FASB) requires charitable pledges to be booked as a receivable on the audited financial statement. Donors with active pledges may be requested to confirm their commitment by the independent auditor. Private foundations cannot fulfill the personal pledges of a director, officer, founder, or staff. A donor advised fund can fulfill pledges of the donor or advisor following special rules as explained in IRS Notice 2017-73.

Charitable Endowments

All states except Pennsylvania have adopted a version of the Uniform Prudent Management of Institutional Funds Act (UPMIFA) as the law governing endowments and other types of funds. Pursuant to UPMIFA and FASB an endowment is a gift designated as restricted by a donor, either in formal communication from the donor or in response to the marketing materials of the charitable organization. A gift that is not restricted as endowment by the donor but is treated as endowment by action of the board is deemed to be quasi-endowment pursuant to FASB. Quasi-endowments may be spent at any time by action of the board of directors.

A board of directors must approve policies for the prudent investment, spending, and fees applicable to its endowments. While private foundations are legally required to spend at least five percent of their assets each year (with some exceptions), a public charity endowment does not have a required spending rate. Pursuant to UPMIFA, it is the duty of the board of directors to spend or accumulate assets as it deems prudent, balancing the short-term support from the endowment with a goal of generational equity.

Percentage Requirements

Percentage limitations imposed by state law on fundraising costs have been subject to federal and state scrutiny with courts holding that solicitors are not required to affirmatively disclose fundraising costs while making the solicitation. However, states may prosecute fraudulent practices in cases where donors and prospects are not accurately informed of how much of their gifts will be paid to the fundraising solicitors (Fishman et al. 2015).

Telemarketing

Many states through the attorney general or other office maintain "do not call" lists to prevent unwanted solicitation telephone calls. Some states exempt charitable organizations from the do not call list if the nonprofit uses its own full- or part-time staff or volunteers to make the solicitation calls.

Federal Law Considerations

The Internal Revenue Code (IRC) permits two types of charitable organizations pursuant to IRC Section 501(c)(3): public benefit charities and private foundations. A charitable organization is presumed to be a private foundation unless it proves on its annual IRS 990 information return that it is a public benefit charity.

The distinction is especially important since gifts to public charities provide greater tax benefits to donors. In addition, private foundations must comply with several very restrictive rules (see IRC Section 4940). These restrictions exist because a single donor (an individual, family, or corporation) can have significant control over the investments, grant-making, and operating programs of the private foundation.

Types of Public Benefit Charities

The IRC allows for two types of public charities. One type must pass the "public support test," which requires that one-third of the total support of the organization be derived from a broad number of donors. Community foundations are an example of this type of public benefit charity. The second type qualifies as a public benefit charity without the public support test and includes churches, schools, hospitals, medical research organizations, state university foundations, and governmental units (see IRC Section 509(a)(1)).

Supporting Organizations

Supporting organizations are not required to satisfy the public support test. Supporting organizations are created to support the charitable mission of another public benefit charity. From a fundraising perspective, supporting organizations can be helpful in several special circumstances such as accepting specific assets that may carry potential liability (e.g., real estate), accepting large gifts to avoid violation of the public support test by the supported organization, or as an "incubator" for a charitable program that may ultimately evolve into a public benefit charity.

Member Benefit Organizations

Qualified member benefit organizations include civic leagues, business leagues, chambers of commerce, real estate boards, social and recreational clubs, fraternal benefit societies or associations, and credit unions. A member benefit organization is not taxed, but gifts to these organizations generally do not qualify the donor for an income tax charitable deduction. Receipts for gifts to these organizations must disclose that the donor will not qualify for an income tax charitable deduction. However, there are a few exceptions for certain member benefit organizations. The income tax deduction is available for gifts to veterans' organizations, volunteer fire departments, fraternal societies for charitable purposes, and cemetery companies (see IRC Section 170(c)(3)-(5)).

Some member benefit organizations partner with separately incorporated public benefit charities that serve as a charitable "foundation" to accept tax deductible gifts for qualified charitable purposes, for example, a fraternal organization using a foundation to accept gifts for scholarships. (See IRS Publication 4221, *Compliance Guide for Tax-Exempt Organizations Other than 501(c)(3) Public Charities and Private Foundations.*)

Unrelated Business Taxable Income and Fundraising

Tax-exempt organizations do not normally pay income tax on fundraising or other revenue. However, revenue generated by the organization from a trade or business that is regularly carried on and not substantially related to the charitable mission will be taxed as unrelated business income (UBTI).

Exceptions to UBTI include revenue generated from qualified sponsorship payments so long as the donor recognition provided to sponsors does not become advertising. Many charitable organizations utilize sponsorships to meet resource development goals. Advertising that does not qualify as sponsor recognition includes endorsements, an inducement to purchase, and/or messages containing qualitative or comparative language, price information or other indications of savings or value. Other exceptions to UBTI include passive investment income on a charitable endowment, rental on real estate, and bingo game revenue. Other charity gaming activity may be taxed. (See IRS Publication 598, *Tax on Unrelated Business Income of Exempt Organizations.*)

Donor Privacy and Confidentiality

Federal and state privacy laws require the protection of donor privacy and confidentiality. State laws that allow access to public records may apply to donor records of organizations that receive tax revenue. While the IRS 990 form is available to the public, donor names in Schedule B or elsewhere in the 990 are not public information and may be redacted before sharing with the public.

Some public university foundation records have been deemed accessible by the public pursuant to state law (see the website of the Council for Advancement and Support of Education). Other laws that may impact donor records include the Family Educational Rights and Privacy Act (FERPA) and the Health Insurance Portability and Accountability Act (HIPAA).

Tax Benefits for Charitable Giving

The income tax charitable deduction was introduced in 1917 and the estate tax charitable deduction in 1921. The charitable deduction depends on the asset(s) donated and the type of recipient (Toce, Abbin, Pace, and Vorsatz 2020). Donors claim the greater of the standard deduction and the sum of itemized deductions, including the charitable deduction. As a result, most taxpayers do not itemize in order to claim a charitable deduction. However, gifts of appreciated assets that are worth more at the time of the gift than when purchased (cost basis) escape capital gains tax if donated in-kind to and sold by a charity.

The following summarizes the income tax benefits and annual limits of charitable gifts. The deduction is available for the year of the gift and up to five more years to carry-over excess deduction each year.

Gifts to public charities by individuals:

- Cash gifts: Limited to 60 percent of Adjusted Gross Income (AGI)/100 percent in 2020 and 2021.
- Cash gifts in 2020 and 2021 also qualified for a universal above-the-line deduction of $300 single or $600 married (2021 only).
- Long-term noncash gifts: Limited to 30 percent of AGI for fair market value (FMV) or 50 percent for cost basis.
- Short-term noncash gifts: Limited to 50 percent of AGI for cost basis of the gift.
- Ordinary income/Tangible property for unrelated use: Limited to 50 percent of AGI for cost basis of the gift.

Gifts to public charities by corporations:

- Cash gifts: Limited to 10 percent of Taxable Income/25 percent in 2020 and 2021.
- Gifts of food inventory for the needy: Limited to 15 percent of Taxable Income/25 percent in 2020 and 2021.

Gifts to private foundations by individuals:

- Cash gifts: Limited to 30 percent of AGI.
- Long-term noncash gifts: 20 percent of AGI for fair market value (FMV) for public stock only/cost basis for other assets.
- Short-term noncash gifts: Limited to 30 percent of AGI for cost basis of the gift.
- Ordinary income: Limited to 30 percent for cost basis of the gift.
- Tangible property for unrelated use: Limited to 20 percent of AGI for cost basis of the gift.

Gift and Estate Tax Benefits for Charitable Giving

There are differences among the income, gift, and estate tax benefits for charitable giving. First, the gift and estate tax charitable deductions do not have percentage limits. Second, the income tax charitable deduction is only available for gifts to domestic organizations while the estate tax deduction is available to domestic and foreign organizations. (See IRC Section 2522(a).)

Noncash Gifts

To claim an income tax charitable deduction for a noncash gift (e.g., stock, real estate, artwork, equipment, software) the donor must complete IRS form 8283 (with an exception for gifts of small value), and file it with the tax return. A deduction over $5,000 requires a qualified and independent appraisal.

A resource for noncash gift valuation is IRS Publication 561, *Determining the Value of Donated Property*. If the charity sells or disposes of the noncash gift within three years, it must complete IRS Form 8282, reporting the sale except for gifts such as publicly traded stock. The IRS compares the sale price with the deduction value. An excellent resource that reviews the tax rules for various types of gifts is IRS Publication 526, *Charitable Contributions*.

Gifts to International Organizations

The legal aspects of international fundraising and the tax benefits for donors are complex. Since 9/11, several regulations, including lists of organizations linked to terrorism, were promulgated to assure that philanthropy was not assisting terrorist activities. In general, only gifts to charitable organizations created under the laws of the United States – or gifts subject to tax treaties between the United States and select countries (e.g., Canada, Mexico, Israel) – qualify for an income tax deduction. This rule does not apply to the estate tax charitable deduction.

To support international charities, various prudent procedures may be followed, including expenditure responsibility and equivalency determination. See www.guidestar.org and the U.S. Department of the Treasury website at www.treas.gov/offices/enforcement/key-issues/protecting/index.shtml.

Gift Substantiation and Disclosure

A donor cannot claim a tax deduction for any single contribution of $250 or more unless the donor obtains a contemporaneous, written acknowledgment of the contribution. An organization can assist a donor by providing a timely, written statement containing the following information:

- Name of organization.
- Date of contribution.
- Amount of cash contribution.
- Description (but not the value) of noncash contribution.
- Statement that no goods or services were provided by the organization in return for the contribution, if that was the case.

- Description and good faith estimate of the value of goods or services, if any, that an organization provided in return for the contribution.
- Statement that goods or services, if any, that an organization provided in return for the contribution consisted entirely of intangible religious benefits, if that was the case.

For the written acknowledgment to be considered contemporaneous with the contribution, a donor must receive the acknowledgment by the earlier of the date on which the donor files their individual federal income tax return for the year of the contribution or the due date (including extensions) of the return. The acknowledgment must describe goods or services an organization provides in exchange for a contribution of $75 or more. For a summary of the gift receipt rules, see IRS Publication 1771, *Charitable Contributions – Substantiation and Disclosure Requirements.*

Conclusion

Fundraising excellence requires adherence to both the letter and spirit of the law. Prudent management of charitable organizations requires careful attention to the "black and white" legal and ethical requirements for fundraising. It also requires making good – and sometimes difficult – decisions in cases where a dilemma is presented. Good decision-making requires one to clarify the facts, understand the applicable legal and ethical standards, and make a reasonable decision. Evaluating and modifying one's decisions helps to continually improve fundraising practices. Achieving excellence in fundraising demands nothing less.

Discussion Questions

1. Explain the duties of prudent care, obedience, and loyalty relative to fundraising responsibilities.
2. What are the tax benefits for the various types of gifts?
3. What must organizations do to comply with laws of international philanthropy, donor privacy, and confidentiality?

Application Exercises

1. Visit the NASCO website (www.nasconet.org.) to learn about applicable laws in your state relative to fundraising. Is your organization in compliance?

2. Review the federal laws that govern fundraising. Does your board review the IRS 990 form with its questions and schedules that disclose fundraising-related information? Identify your organization's type: public benefit charity, supporting organization, member benefit organization, or private foundation. If your organization is a public benefit charity, does it pass the public support test? Does your organization comply with the rules for gift substantiation and disclosure?

3. Review a written acknowledgment that you received for a gift. Does it include all the required elements?

CHAPTER FOUR

THEORY IN FUNDRAISING

By Ruth K. Hansen

Philanthropic giving has attracted many theorists, but research on fundraising has been less tied to theory. This chapter first discusses the role of theory in fundraising practice, and then examines several theories that have been used to explain aspects of fundraising.

After completing this chapter, readers will:

- Understand how theory contributes to fundraising practice.
- Be able to explain how fundraisers function as boundary spanners in open systems, and the dynamics of resource dependence.
- Understand the implications of gift theory, reciprocity, and social exchange in the relationships among the donor and the organization, the organization's clients, and the fundraiser.
- Appreciate the role of self-identities, moral identities, and social identities in giving and the implications for fundraising.
- Consider how fundraisers can use symbolism and principles of dramaturgy to help the organizations, clients, and causes resonate persuasively with donors.

Theory's Role in Fundraising Practice

Until recently, fundraising has primarily been learned through practice (Duronio and Tempel 1997). How can theory clarify and improve the practice of fundraising? And what is the role of theory more generally? Maxwell (2013) offered two metaphors for understanding how theory is more than abstraction. Theory can operate as a spotlight, isolating and highlighting facets of an idea (or a practice) or enhance understanding of that idea or practice. Theory can also provide a framework to organize thinking about complex ideas, processes, or systems. Collecting evidence without some idea of how it fits together results in a jumble. Theories can be the hooks on a wall that let us place each item in relationship to others and see patterns, which may similarly help people understand what is happening and apply those insights. Maxwell (2013, 49) called this second metaphor a coat closet.

Let's add a third metaphor. A collection of theories unattached to situations is like a closet full of clothes on hangers – each may be individually well crafted, but while they hang there, they are disconnected, not fulfilling their purpose. If piled on all at once, their purposes are muddled, the potential splendid function of each obscured by the indiscriminate invocation of all. The thoughtfully styled individual selects an item (or items) appropriate for the purpose. Similarly, a collection of theories is not enough, but the perceptive selection and application of a theory activates its functional value.

This chapter provides a "closet full of spotlights." Rather than a single unified theory of fundraising, it draws on several theoretical approaches that offer diverse ways of thinking of fundraising, each of which may prompt examination of specific aspects and new insights about what we're doing.

Theoretical Approaches

The rest of the chapter introduces theoretical approaches that have been used to explain aspects of fundraising practice – what is happening, how it happens, and why. It begins by addressing macro systems theory, boundary spanning, and resource dependence. Next, it shows how gift theory and reciprocity apply to fundraising. Then, it describes the identification theory of care and how social identity theory contributes to philanthropic choices. Finally, it shows how a dramaturgical approach and symbolic interactionism can be helpful in understanding fundraising.

The Big Picture: Systems Theory, Boundary Spanning, and Resource Dependence

Systems theory provides a fundamental theoretical base for understanding fundraising (Kelly 1998; Tempel 1991). An organization that isolates itself from its environment can be considered a "closed system." One that is influenced by social and economic trends and needs, and exchanges resources within its community is an "open system." Simply put, charities do not exist in isolation. They exist within an environment and interact with that environment (Scott and Davis 2006). Typically, strong fundraising programs thrive in relatively open systems (see Chapter 11).

Individuals who raise funds for an organization function as *boundary spanners*, linking the organization with important resources in the external environment (Kelly 1998). Boundary spanners are essentially diplomatic liaisons who work to align the interests of those within and those outside the organization. Fundraisers seek to develop financial resources for an organization through cultivation, solicitation, and stewardship activities. They also listen to the interests and concerns of potential donors and look to find good linkages with the organization's mission. By interacting with potential donors on behalf of their organizations, fundraisers perform an important boundary-spanning role.

Resource dependence theory explains why fundraising occurs and suggests some common organizational dynamics. The theory states that for organizations to survive, they must acquire necessary resources, and maintain their supply (Pfeffer and Salancik 1978). This means that organizations are not wholly autonomous in their financial decision-making but rely on their environment for various resources. The greater an organization's dependence on voluntary contributions, the more volatile its revenue environment is (Carroll and Stater 2009), and the more likely it is to devote its time and personnel resources to developing financial resources (Heimovics, Herman, and Jurkiewicz Coughlin 1993; Hodge and Piccolo 2005; Nonprofit Research Collaborative 2015). This illustrates the importance of skilled fundraising.

Dependence on others leads to power considerations. When funding is scarce, the charity is more vulnerable to the demands of prospective funders, which may affect the organization's decision-making autonomy. For instance, nonprofits that receive relatively high levels of government funding are less likely to have nonprofit boards that strongly represent their client constituents (Guo 2007). This dependence dynamic is also seen in an increasing focus on donor-centered philanthropy, particularly for major donors (James III 2016c). If a donor (or grantor) is providing significant financial support, they may be keenly interested in affecting the design and administration of that program or the organization as a whole, and less attentive to the needs of the community or the organization's beneficiaries. Discerning the point at which a donor's engagement crosses the line into unwelcome or inappropriate territory can be difficult (see Chapter 2). Organizations may choose to diversify their revenue sources, including fees, dues, or commercial activities in order to lessen their dependence on any one funding source, and in so doing potentially diminish threats to control over financial and programmatic decision-making (Carroll and Stater 2009).

Social Exchanges: Gift Theory and Reciprocity

Gift theory recognizes that giving gifts is a universal aspect of social human behavior, and, further, that receiving a gift generally prompts a social obligation to reciprocate in some manner (Adloff 2016). The gifts may vary greatly – they may include money or physical items; favors such as use of resources like a boat or equipment, helping with yard work or childcare, or preferential treatment; or appreciation expressed through a thoughtful note, loyalty, or even prayers. Thus, giving is rarely one-way, but is instead a *social exchange* of some type. Many factors affect what is considered an appropriate gift: cultural traditions, the relationship and relative social status of each party, and time and place. These social considerations apply whether one is considering an initial gift, or a reciprocal expression (Adloff 2016; Mauss 1990). Breaking the social norm of *reciprocity* is viewed as a lack of appreciation and makes future giving less likely (Lindahl 2010). Gift theory tells us that giving results in reciprocal obligations, and that these create and maintain webs of both mutual interest and mutual responsibility (Gouldner 1960; Mauss 1990).

One implication of this theory is stewardship. Demonstrating to donors that their generosity is appreciated and impactful fulfills the expectations of reciprocity. When fundraisers acknowledge gifts and demonstrate stewardship, they are speaking to the social exchange aspect of giving, fulfilling the social norm of reciprocity, and maintaining a relationship of mutual interest (Alborough 2017). Gift theory explicitly recognizes the importance of relationship building in fundraising.

A second implication of gift theory concerns donor status. As noted by Lindahl (2010), ". . . making generous donations confers high status on the donor and benefits the recipient organization and the community at the same time" (93–94). The norms of reciprocity between peers suggest that the gift or favor eventually reciprocated should be of similar value. However, those of high status are often perceived as having higher social obligations to their communities (*noblesse oblige*), while those of lower status are required to reciprocate with their appreciation, which might take the form of loyalty. Thus, gift theory explains instances of conspicuous generosity, in which a person might give significantly to a cause to be recognized publicly as a member of a socially elite group.

Positive Identification: The Identification Theory of Care and Social Identity Theory

The **identification theory of care** focuses on relationships and meaning to explain why people give (Schervish and Havens 1997; 2002). Its attention to encouraging the process of engagement makes it highly applicable to the work of fundraising. The essential idea is that "voluntary assistance derives from identification, identification derives from encounter, encounter derives from relationship, and relationship derives from participation" (Schervish and Havens 2002, 50). This process is illustrated in Figure 4.1.

FIGURE 4.1. MODEL OF IDENTIFICATION THEORY

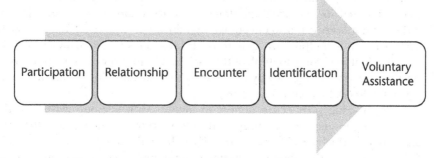

Source: Adapted from Schervish and Havens 1997; 2002.

The core of this model is the idea of *communities of participation* – that people care most about family members, friends, and those they know well from the communities in which they participate. This may include those joined in attendance at religious services, or shared membership in formal and informal groups. The social relationships formed in these communities prompt shared frameworks, or ways of thinking about the world. These frameworks influence preferences and commitment to causes. When a person identifies with others – that is, they view others as being similar to them, part of "us," or similar to those they care for – they are likely to help the others by volunteering money, time, or resources (Schervish and Havens 1997; 2002). The first important implication of this idea is that generosity is born not of selflessness, but instead of acting in accordance with values and priorities that are essential to self-identity. The second implication, and one of direct significance to fundraisers, is that encouraging an expansion of generosity means recognizing and encouraging people's current expressions of care, broadly construed (Schervish and Havens 2002). Another major implication for fundraisers is the importance of engaging potential donors with a cause and with others who support the cause.

Related to this idea, **social identity theory** helps explain how people identify as members of groups (Turner and Oakes 1986). The tendency to categorize people into groups is a *heuristic* – a mental shortcut that helps in navigating a complex world. If people see themselves as belonging to a group, that group is an "in-group"; other groups are "outgroups." People tend to favor others whom they see as sharing a *social identity* – belonging to the same "in-group" (Tajfel and Turner 1979). Applying this idea to fundraising, fundraisers may activate prospective donors' social identities that overlap with others affiliated with the organization. These might include mentioning other donors with similar identities, such as gender (Shang, Reed, and Croson 2008); mentioning a tie to an organization, such as alumni status (Drezner 2009); reminding the donor of their past giving history, and therefore, their status as a donor to the organization (Kessler and Milkman 2018); or encouraging the individual to identify with the group or cause that will directly benefit from the donation (Garvey and Drezner 2013; James III 2017). Fundraisers can also encourage identification with *moral identities*, such as someone who is "helpful" or "generous." If these adjectives already describe how an individual would like to think of themselves, a fundraiser can encourage behavior that reflects that identity by recognizing that attribute in the donor (Aquino, Freeman, Reed, Lim, and Felps 2009).

Encouraging prospective donors to identify with a group can make them more willing to help that in-group, and to support what others within that group also support (Duclos and Barasch 2014; Hysenbelli, Rubaltelli, and Rumiati 2013). On the downside, this identity activation can also make people more aware of who is not a member of that group and depress their willingness to help outsiders. However, as donors and volunteers become more involved with an organization, their affiliation with the group will become a greater part of how they view their own personal identity (Oyakawa 2015).

People who spend time together and value their relationship tend to find points of agreement and to share many priorities. **Co-orientation theory** explains how people who are within a community of participation will tend to either come to share views and priorities, or step back and spend less time and energy on their mutual relationship (Newcomb 1953, cited in Lindahl 2010). As applied to fundraising, this suggests that peer solicitation – that is, asking an existing donor to help solicit their friends and acquaintances for a cause – is likely to encourage serious consideration on the part of the prospective donor. However, this should not be done lightly. If the gift opportunity is not a good match for the prospective donor, then involving the peer solicitor can potentially damage the friendship.

Setting the Scene: Symbolic Interactionism and Dramaturgy

Symbolic interactionism, a framework derived from American pragmatism, has ties to both social psychology and microsociology. It focuses on how people interpret meaning from the objects, people, and situations of life, which then influences their decisions and actions. These meanings develop through social interaction and communication with others (Mead 1934; Schwandt 2007). Language, gestures, and physical objects can all influence the meaning one person takes from a situation, which will affect how they respond.

Dramaturgy uses theater as a metaphor to examine and understand the meaning in social interactions. Using workplaces to observe human behavior, Goffman (1959) explored how situations prompt expected roles, behavior, and expressions. Using a dramaturgical framework, a "front region" is an area or situation that interacts with customers, and a "back region" or "backstage" is a setting that is out of view from customers. Working in a backstage role requires technical expertise, while working in a front region requires expressive skill. Goffman notes that, ". . . in those interactions where the individual presents a product to others, he will tend to show them only the end product, and they will be led into judging him on the basis of something that has been finished, polished, and packaged" (44). Co-workers will work as teams to help project this polished impression – putting our best foot forward – which grants the team and its organization legitimacy in the eyes of those observing.

Applying the precepts of dramaturgy to fundraising yields four key assertions (Hansen 2018).

- First, that fundraisers incorporate an understanding of the importance of first impressions into their work.
- Second, that fundraisers actively frame situations to suggest a plan for cooperative action. This may include describing a situation, a frame for interpreting it, and an opportunity to act on that interpretation. For example, a fundraiser might describe a problem, how the organization can help address it, and ask the donor for monetary support.
- Third, that the fundraiser, the organization, and the clients who will benefit from cooperative action must all be seen as having character that aligns with being worthy of support. For instance, when fundraisers, organizations, and clients are seen as trustworthy, and the cause is easy to sympathize with, the situation is beneficial to fundraising activities.
- And fourth, that fundraisers must be sensitive to prospective donors' likely reactions, seeing themselves as prospective donors to evaluate how a letter, a call, an event, or any other situation will be seen, and if it will support a meaning that aligns with asking for cooperative action, a gift of time or money.

Taking these together makes clear the importance of taking the donor's perspective to try to understand how they will interpret communication – the words, the timing, the "costumes," the "setting," even the background music. Do all of these align to resonate with the donor's understanding of an important cause, and support their choice to act? It's probably not surprising that one of the metaphors fundraisers commonly use to describe their work is that of the choreographer (Breeze 2017).

A dramaturgical analysis also highlights that a discordant note can ring false with the donor. Something unexpected or out of place can be jarring, disrupting a potential donor's support for a worthwhile cause. For those organizations addressing change and social justice, there is an inherent tension, since the welcoming tone and controversy avoidance that may help attract and cultivate new donors can also perpetuate injustices (Hansen 2018). Dramaturgy suggests the importance of expressive competence – of finding the way to take donors' perspectives and understand likely impressions while also being honest and true to mission that is community centered. This skillful balance on the part of fundraisers paves the road to cooperative action.

Conclusion

Many theories address why people engage in philanthropy as donors, and these also inform fundraising. For example, empirical evidence shows that being asked is key to the act of making gifts (Adloff 2016). Less attention has focused on theories of how fundraising functions, and its social implications. As Russell James III (2017) noted, theoretical guidance is perhaps less important for quick, transactional models of fundraising, but can contribute greatly to aspects of fundraising that rely on developing longer term, nuanced relationships.

The process of developing and testing theoretical frameworks to help understand fundraising is ongoing (Mack, Kelly, and Wilson 2016). Many of these theories are extensions or refinements of theories originally used in other situations. Systems theory is a reminder that organizations are part of a greater environment requiring boundary spanning to ensure adequate financial resources. Resource dependence theory highlights potential power implications of revenue portfolios. Gift theory examines the social exchange aspects of philanthropy, indicating that fundraisers and donors live in a relational society. Identification theory looks to the importance of affirming a donor's sense of self and the role of communities of participation in expanding how a donor identifies with others. Dramaturgy emphasizes the importance of symbolic meaning, and how fundraisers can encourage an atmosphere and framing that aligns the importance of the cause with the donor's interests.

Taken together, these theories undergird the importance of relationships in fundraising. They imply a duty of care to donors, to treat them as whole people with personal values and preferences. They also imply a duty of care to the organizations and those they serve.

Discussion Questions

1. What are some ways in which reciprocity plays a role in how fundraisers and donors interact? Provide specific examples from your experience.
2. How can fundraisers activate a donor's identity with regard to other donors? To an organization's clients? To the organization itself? What theories apply?

3. We tend to find it easy to support others who share a social identity. What implications might this have for fundraising practice? Are any of those implications in tension with an organization's mission or other social concerns? If so, how might fundraisers and administrators mitigate those tensions?

Application Exercises

1. Make a table of different fundraising functions and/or solicitation vehicles, such as annual fund mailings, major gift solicitation, and so on. Place the theories from this chapter under the headings for the situations in which they might be most useful. List at least one new tactic based on the theories in this chapter.

2. Assume you work for a university. You are planning to meet with a donor who is an alumna of the English department and has established a scholarship fund for nontraditional students in honor of her mother. Her graduating class is nearing its 35th reunion. What topics or ideas do you want to include in your planned discussion? Use at least two theories from this chapter to analyze your choices for the meeting plan.

CHAPTER FIVE

THE JOY OF GIVING

By Sara Konrath

"It is more blessed to give than to receive."

~Acts 20:35

"Most people would rather give than get affection."

~Aristotle

The belief that it is better to give than to receive has a long history, with examples from ancient religious texts and philosophers. The earliest known scientific evidence, from the early 1970s, discovered that people learned faster when doing so helped someone avoid suffering – such altruism was motivating and rewarding. This chapter reviews scientific research on how giving time and money affects givers.

The chapter will help readers to:

- Understand how giving time and money affects psychological, social, and physical health outcomes.
- Learn about research on the joy of giving across cultures and across the lifespan.

- Be aware of benefits of giving even during challenging times.
- Know some potential limits of giving, and how to maximize the joy of giving in oneself and others.

Fundraising professionals facilitate a significant portion of donations to nonprofits. Fundraisers match people's values with opportunities to give, and in doing so, help to feed the hungry, take care of the sick, share musical and cultural experiences, and educate generations of students. When fundraisers help givers give, they may not realize that they are bringing these givers more happiness and better health. By being mindful of these benefits of giving, fundraisers can see themselves as givers too, and can personally experience the joy of giving.

Psychological Outcomes

Many of us believe that if we only had more time and money, we would be happier. In fact, there is much research finding that *giving away* our time and money makes us happier, even though after giving we have less for ourselves (for reviews, see Hui et al. 2020; Konrath 2014).

Research finds that *volunteers* have higher happiness, life satisfaction, and psychological well-being than those who do not volunteer. Of course, volunteers are different than nonvolunteers in a number of ways that could explain why they are happier. For example, they tend to have higher incomes and more social and psychological resources than nonvolunteers. But most research finds that these differences do not fully explain the happiness effects of giving time. Even when scientists statistically control for these variables, the results remain similar.

Similarly, lots of research finds that giving away *money* also promotes more well-being in givers. There are also similar benefits for *everyday kind acts* like helping strangers, sharing with neighbors, and supporting loved ones. For example, a meta-analysis that examined 201 studies with 198,213 participants found that various types of giving and helping were associated with higher well-being (Hui et al. 2020).

The best evidence for the causal effects of giving uses a *randomized control trial* (RCT), a method that is also used to test if a new drug or vaccine works. Scientists start with a group of people who are pretty similar at the beginning, and then ask half of these people to give time or money. The other half are in the control group (e.g., spend money or do kind acts for themselves). For example, one study asked participants to spend a small amount of money (either $5 or $20) on themselves versus another person, and then the researchers measured participants' mood at the end of the day. People who spent their money on someone else were happier than those who spent it on themselves, regardless of the amount of money spent.

Randomized control trials consistently find that giving money, volunteering time, and doing kind acts all lead to more psychological benefits for givers, compared to control groups.

Does the Joy of Giving Last?

Research finds that giving to oneself quickly loses its luster, whereas giving to others has lasting happiness-boosting power. Many enjoyable activities lose some of their pleasure when repeated. But when researchers compared the experience of giving money away repeatedly (up to 10 times) versus the experience of receiving it, they found that the joy people experienced from getting was quick to fade with repetition. However, the joy of giving had staying power and was less likely to fade over time.

Several studies confirm that giving is associated with long-lasting good feelings. For example, people who were asked to regularly and frequently do small kind acts for others felt happier up to two months later. There are similar effects of giving money: one study found that people who spent more of their employment bonus on others felt happier up to two months later, while another found that participants who donated more to charity at one time were happier up to nine years later.

The Joy of Giving Runs Deep

Giving time and money not only affects givers' happiness, it runs more deeply into fulfilling feelings of meaning and purpose in life. In fact, giving increases people's perceptions of a life well lived with meaning and purpose (i.e., *eudaimonic* well-being) more than their simple feelings of happiness (i.e., *hedonic* well-being).

The psychological benefits of giving extend into mental health symptoms; givers experience fewer symptoms of depression and anxiety, which, if untreated, could become full blown psychological disorders.

Fundraisers need not worry that they might erase these benefits of giving by sharing the news with potential donors. Even when people are aware of the potential happiness effects of giving, this does not diminish the psychological rewards. Indeed, one study found that people gave *more* when they learned of the potential happiness-building effects of giving.

Simply recalling, observing, or counting one's own kind acts also increases happiness as much as actually doing them. Even more incredible is that these happiness boosts seem to be noticeable by outside observers. The joy of giving is written on our faces.

The Paradox of Generosity

There is strong scientific support for these findings. And yet, when people are asked to guess which one will make them happier, spending money on themselves versus spending it on others, they think they will be happier when spending on themselves. This may help to explain the increasing prevalence of materialistic goals.

Giving money can also make people feel richer, despite having less money because they just gave some away. Giving time to others can lead to feelings of "time affluence," the subjective feeling of having a lot of free time available. Amazingly, people feel like their schedules are less rushed, even though objectively they have less time because they just gave some away. The *paradox of generosity* is that people feel happier, richer, and healthier after giving their money and time to others (Smith and Davidson 2014). Having money in itself does not make people happier, but the way people spend it can affect their happiness (Dunn and Norton 2014).

Social Outcomes

Giving is contagious: People's giving behavior spreads into their closest relationships, and into their broader social networks.

Not only is giving socially learned and replicated, it can also enrich people's reputations and social relationships. One study found that participants who gave more money to charity were more likely to be selected to represent their group as leaders, and also received more money from group members. This demonstrates how giving to charity can promote a positive reputation for givers. Kind people are likeable, and others want to be around them. Studies have found that preteens who behave more kindly are more popular with their peers. For example, in one study, preteens who performed three kind acts (versus visited three new places) each week became more popular over time.

Similar results have been found in older adults. In one study, older adults who volunteered increased in their social connections after several months, while control group participants experienced a decline. Volunteers also increased 17 percent in feelings of being socially supported, while control group participants declined 25 percent in perceived social support. Givers also report less loneliness and more feelings of social connection.

People with higher giving-related traits like empathy both provide *and* receive more social support, which suggests a balanced give-and-take in their relationships. They also try harder to maintain their relationships and report more love and affection for those they interact with. Overall, people with higher giving-related traits and behaviors have more positive and satisfying relationships.

Is generosity good for romance? Research finds that being generous can help to encourage new romances. For example, kindness is the top trait that both men and women are looking for in a romantic relationship, and generous people are seen as more desirable romantic partners. Our research has found that generous people are rated as more physically attractive: the *good-looking giver* effect. And, a large national study found that more generous single people were more likely to be in a relationship the following year.

Physical Outcomes

There are many physical health implications of giving time and money, ranging from immediate physiological processes to healthy lifestyle behaviors to health-care usage to longevity (see Bekkers, Konrath, and Smith 2016, for a review).

Brain Responses

When donating money, the pleasure and reward centers of the brain are activated as much as when receiving money. Giving support to loved ones also activates neural reward centers, while simultaneously lowering neural fear and stress areas. And when directly compared, research finds that giving to loved ones has more neural benefits than donating to charity.

Stress Hormones

Daily stressors like arguments or work deadlines can increase cortisol, a stress hormone that is toxic for health and predicts early mortality, especially cardiovascular-related. Volunteering buffers people from cortisol response to stressors – on days that people volunteer, their cortisol remains low, even in the presence of stressors. People with giving-related traits like empathy also have lower stress hormones during stressful tasks, and small actions (e.g., shifting one's focus to others, writing an affectionate letter) have similar effects.

Gene Regulation and Cellular Aging

Scientists have examined changes in people's genetic expressions after doing kind acts (versus control activities) for one month. Such kind behaviors cause inflammation-related genes to be down-regulated. Similar results are found in volunteers, in addition to the up-regulation of antiviral genes.

Strength and Energy

Giving can also make people physically stronger, at least temporarily. Researchers asked people to hold a 5-pound weight with their arms stretched horizontally for as long as they could. They were then given a $1 payment and half of them were asked to donate it to UNICEF (100 percent agreed), while the other half just kept it. People who donated the money held the 5-pound weight longer than those who didn't. Other research confirms that giving time may also have similar effects. Older adults who volunteered for 4–8 months (compared to controls) reported increased strength and energy, better grip strength, and faster walking and stair climbing speeds.

Pain Responses

Giving can also reduce physiological responses to pain. One study found that people who gave to charity tolerated higher levels of pain compared to those who kept money for themselves. Givers also show less activation in pain-related areas of their brain compared to nongivers. Volunteering and other forms of helping can even help to reduce pain among chronic pain patients.

Cardiovascular Risk

Much research examines giving and cardiovascular risk factors. It finds that volunteering, giving money, and giving support to loved ones are associated with lower blood pressure, lower blood glucose, and fewer inflammatory markers.

Most research is on older adults, who are at higher risk. However, an experiment that assigned some teens to volunteer, compared to a control group, found that volunteering for four months decreased several cardiovascular risk factors (inflammation, cholesterol, body mass index) even in this young population.

Health Behaviors and Healthcare Usage

Volunteering increases physical activity since it gets people out of the house. Volunteering is especially beneficial for older adults who were previously inactive, with one study finding that their physical activity increased 110 percent after being assigned 4–8 months of volunteering. Older adults who help others more informally also have increased physical activity.

As for healthcare usage, our research finds that older adult volunteers are more likely to use preventative healthcare services: they are 30 percent more likely to get a flu shot, 47 percent more likely to get cholesterol tests, women are 53 percent more likely to receive mammograms and 21 percent more likely to receive Pap smears, and men are 59 percent more likely to receive prostate exams. These can help to identify or prevent more serious health conditions. We also found that volunteers spent 38 percent less time in the hospital compared to nonvolunteers.

Longevity

A meta-analysis that included 14 studies with over 74,000 older adults found that volunteering was associated with a 47 percent decreased risk of dying overall, and a smaller (24 percent) decreased risk when adjusting for background factors like age, sex, socioeconomic status, physical health, health behaviors, and social connections. Since then, a high-quality national study of older adults found that volunteers were 44 percent less likely to die than nonvolunteers.

To put this in perspective, eating six or more fruit and vegetables per day lowers mortality risk by 26 percent, and regular exercise lowers mortality risk by between 23 and 33 percent. So, volunteering lowers the risk of early death at least as much as traditional health behaviors. When comparing *types* of giving, we have found that people who give *time* (volunteering, giving support, or caregiving), but not *money*, are less likely to die. Although lots of research finds that charitable giving feels good, this doesn't necessarily translate to a longer life.

The Joy of Giving around the World

Most research on the effects of giving has focused on people from Western cultures. However, there is an emerging cross-cultural literature that suggests people from all over the world experience the joy of giving and volunteering. Studies have examined between 136 to 142 countries worldwide, and confirmed that in most cultures, volunteering is associated with higher well-being (86 percent of cultures studied) and better physical health (88 percent of cultures studied) and donating to charity is associated with higher well-being (90 percent). These results are found even in poor countries where resources are scarcer, and even in an isolated rural village with limited Western influence on a South Pacific Ocean island. They are also not explained by demographic differences in givers compared to nongivers.

The Joy of Giving across the Lifespan

Most research on the effects of giving has been conducted on older adults. Yet, giving time and money also predicts better psychological well-being and health in middle-aged adults, young adults, adolescents, children, and even toddlers.

Still the benefits of giving tend to get stronger as people age. This was recently confirmed in a study of over 1.7 million people from 166 nations. Although the study found joy of giving effects at all ages, it also found that 50-year-olds experienced *double* the joy of giving compared to 20-year-olds, and 80-year-olds experienced even more – 2.74 times that of 20-year-olds. Similar patterns were found worldwide. This might be because of different types of volunteer jobs across different age groups, or different motives and emotional responses to giving as people age.

The Joy of Giving during Difficult Times

Giving time and money can promote increased happiness and health even during difficult times. For example, aging adults often face increased difficulty completing tasks like lifting heavy objects or climbing stairs. Research finds that people who have more altruistic attitudes are better able to cope emotionally with such losses of independence. Indeed, those who choose to volunteer despite these limitations live longer than those who do not.

The joy of giving has been found in other groups facing challenges, including those receiving welfare benefits, individuals with disabilities, those with traumatic brain injuries, individuals with lumbar spine disorders, spinal cord injuries, multiple sclerosis, HIV/AIDS, and older adults with dementia, other forms of cognitive impairment, or living in long-term care facilities.

Among those with ongoing psychological problems, like post-traumatic stress disorder or social anxiety, giving can help to manage their symptoms. In fact, research finds that more depressed young people experience more joy of giving than less depressed ones. And among teens who experience adverse childhood experiences, volunteering can help to buffer them from poor mental health. Even individuals who have had trouble with the law experience the joy of giving, which is a hopeful finding suggesting potential motivations and pathways for rehabilitation.

People often increase charitable giving in response to disasters and pandemics, and research finds that such increases in charitable donation are associated with increases in happiness – despite the stress and trauma of the situation itself. In the face of tragedy, giving time and money is not only good for the recipients, but for the givers themselves.

The COVID-19 pandemic created a uniquely challenging situation in that many givers found it more difficult to give, whether because of financial constraints or being homebound. Even in this time, givers experienced more positive emotions overall. However, givers who also perceived high risk to themselves or their loved ones actually experienced *more* negative emotions than less generous people. More research will help to uncover the complex implications of giving during the pandemic.

The Limits of Giving

This chapter covers *voluntary* giving behaviors like volunteering for nonprofits, giving money, and giving support to loved ones. Involuntary giving such as that required by schools, parents, or courts is unlikely to have the same benefits. In addition, caregiving is a more extreme form of giving that is often less voluntary, more intensive, and can include seeing loved ones in pain or distress. Some research finds that caregiving is associated with poorer well-being and health outcomes. Yet, other research finds that the helping itself can be beneficial, especially with enough support, even though seeing loved ones in distress can be harmful. However, this complex type of giving goes beyond the scope of this review.

When it comes to other types of giving, it is possible for people to give beyond their means. For example, studies have found that volunteering between 1 and 15 hours per week is associated with optimal health and well-being. However, joyful givers may well know their limits.

As for charitable giving, one recent study found that Americans who donated 10 percent of their incomes were happier than those who donated less. The authors used 10 percent as a cutoff point since some religions encourage tithing, however, they did not explore whether there was a point at which giving was no longer beneficial. This could be because it was highly unusual for people to give 10 percent away – only 2.7 percent of participants did so. Another study found that the more money people gave, the higher their psychological well-being, and the authors did not find any cutoff point after which there were fewer benefits of giving. In fact, spending money on others is associated with increased well-being even in lower-income countries. However, it is reasonable to assume that at a certain point, donating to charity might be bad for well-being, especially if people give to the point that they cannot take care of their own needs. Still, such over-giving is rare, and the more common problem is *under*-giving.

In general, it seems wise to give from one's surplus resources. For example, it might be better for lower income people to give their time than their money, since volunteering predicts more happiness in lower income people compared to higher income people.

Finally, when it comes to everyday kindness, the more people give, and the more they make giving part of the practice of their everyday life, the more joy they experience from giving. For example, performing nine acts of kindness per week leads to more happiness than performing three acts per week. Future research should try to better understand potential limits of giving for well-being and health.

More Joyful Giving

There are a number of practices that can help to increase the joy of giving.

Variety

Research finds that giving in a variety of ways and to different types of people makes people happier than giving the same way and to the same people over and over again. Just like a healthy diet of food, a healthy giving diet ideally involves variety to avoid the acts becoming routine.

Altruism

Altruistic attitudes also matter for happiness, like saying that you enjoy helping others or that you try to help even if others can't return the favor. In fact, research finds that altruistic attitudes can be more important for happiness than giving behaviors themselves. And my research has found seeing oneself as caring predicts a lower risk of dying in older adults than actual giving behaviors. The thought counts – being ready to serve and help matters, even if actual opportunities for helping do not present themselves.

Choice

When giving is mandatory, it does not feel as good; givers experience the most psychological benefits of giving when they can freely choose to do so. This is supported by research finding that voluntary giving activates reward centers in the brain, but required giving does not.

Concrete

Thinking about giving as more concrete (e.g., make someone smile) instead of more abstract (e.g., make someone happy) increases the joy of giving. So, fundraisers should consider designing their donation appeals to encourage simple concrete behaviors, rather than higher-level conceptual ones.

Social

The social aspects of giving also matter. For example, volunteering is associated with *double* the happiness when it involves directly interacting with others versus more indirect types of helping. There are no known studies that examine similar questions regarding charitable giving, but one might expect that giving in person (e.g., to nonprofit staff, at charity events) would increase happiness more than giving in other ways (e.g., mail, online, automatic payroll deduction).

Summary: Giving Joyfully

Many are aware of the power of vaccines, and we can increase our joy of giving by giving ourselves a V.A.C.C.S. Giving behaviors that have **V**ariety, **A**ltruism, **C**hoice, are **C**oncrete, and **S**ocial can increase the joy of giving.

Conclusion

Fundraisers are givers (see Chapter 18) and also encourage giving in others. This chapter reviews research finding that giving time and money can promote psychological well-being, the quantity and quality of social relationships, and better physical health – even a longer life. Although the majority of research has been done in Western countries and among older adults, these benefits have been found for people of all ages, and all over the world. It is even possible to experience the joy of giving during difficult times. Giving feels good because it satisfies people's core psychological needs and helps them to shift their perspectives and manage stress. Giving is more beneficial when it is voluntary and not a burden, and there are a number of practices that can help to increase the joy of giving. Some people say that we should give until it hurts, but research suggests that giving until it *feels good* may be more accurate.

Discussion Questions

1. Discuss at least three ways that volunteering is beneficial to the volunteer and the donor.
2. Describe different effects of giving time versus giving money.
3. How can fundraisers use the knowledge in this chapter to enhance donors' experiences and engagement?

Application Exercises

1. Apply this information in your professional context. How can you use the research to build your confidence as a fundraiser?
2. Talk with a donor about how they have experienced the joys of giving, including during difficult times and in consideration of potential limits to its positive outcomes. Compare what the donor says to your experience and the information in this chapter.
3. Apply the V.A.C.C.S. formula to the fundraising approach of your or another organization, identifying areas of strength and opportunity.

PART TWO

CONTEMPORARY DYNAMICS OF FUNDRAISING

CHAPTER SIX

THE PHILANTHROPIC CONTEXT FOR FUNDRAISING

By Pat Danahey Janin and Dwight F. Burlingame

The context for philanthropy and fundraisers is continually changing. Economic upswings and crises, political stability and changes, increased or decreased physical well-being, including from a pandemic, and finally, social peace or unrest all impact the focus and flow of resources destined to address societal needs. Philanthropy, too, is undergoing changes. This chapter helps readers reflect on the contemporary environment in which fundraisers work.

After completing this chapter, readers will understand:

- Philanthropy's definition and roles.
- Contemporary challenges to philanthropy.
- The nonprofit sector's size and scope.
- Digital and educational changes in philanthropy infrastructure.
- Fundraising and the changing economic, social, and political climate for philanthropy.
- Opportunities for philanthropy today.

Defining Philanthropy

Philanthropy comes from the Greek meaning love of humankind. It is a multifaceted term, with many layers of meaning in both its historical and its contemporary usages

(Sulek 2010). Indeed, there are many motivations for philanthropic activities, including the love of other persons, the beautiful, the good, the divine, and wisdom; personal excellence, civic virtue or morality, rational understanding, moral sentiment, and goodwill; and the pleasures of social interaction. The Indiana University Lilly Family School of Philanthropy uses Robert Payton's broad definition of philanthropy – voluntary action for the public good – as a foundation for its work. This voluntary action encompasses many forms of giving, volunteering, and association. In this conception, philanthropy is purposeful in both action and intention, seeking to improve the human condition and contribute to democracy through pluralism, community, and championing people's rights (Payton and Moody 2008).

Philanthropy is social action that addresses human and civic needs. Philanthropy improves the welfare of others and in doing so improves one's own life, providing multiple pathways for change and improvement. From this standpoint, the roles of philanthropy, as defined in Chapter 1 and illustrated in Figure 6.1, are generally considered to be: reducing human suffering; enhancing

FIGURE 6.1. SEVEN ROLES OF PHILANTHROPY

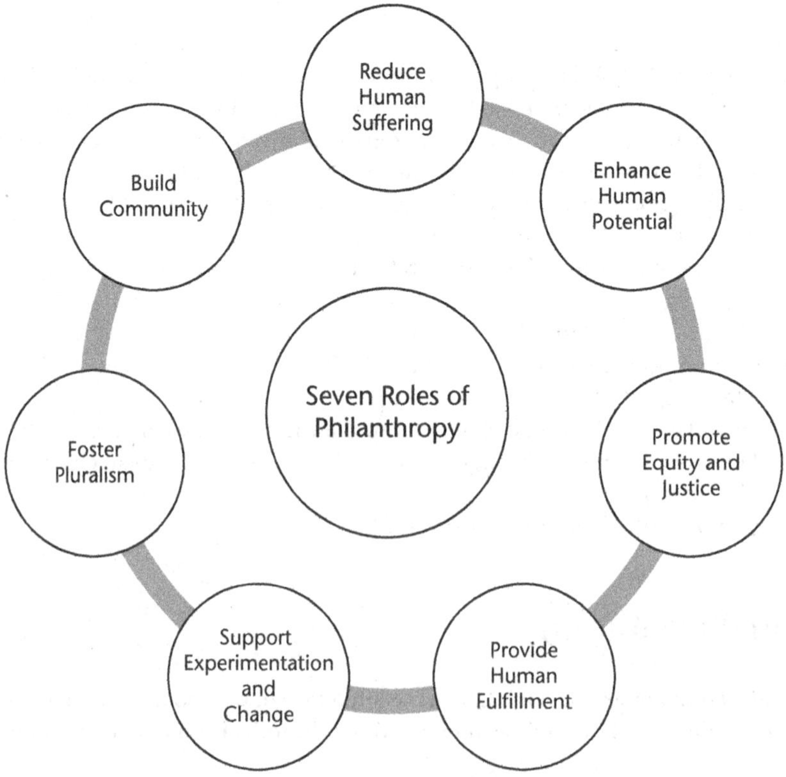

Source: Tempel 2003.

human potential; promoting equity and justice; building community; providing human fulfillment; supporting experimentation and change; and fostering pluralism (Tempel 2003). These seven roles of philanthropy can be seen as interconnected pieces, at the heart of which is community.

The Contemporary Challenges Philanthropy Faces

Philanthropy is not without challenges, critiques, and failures. The scale of philanthropy continues to increase in overall donations, in the number of registered nonprofit organizations, and in volunteer hours served (AmeriCorps 2018a, 2018b; Giving USA 2021; Urban Institute 2020). However, the percentage of Americans giving and volunteering is declining. Just over 50 percent of Americans give to charities, and rural and suburban areas are experiencing noticeable declines in volunteering (Grimm, Jr. and Dietz 2018; Zarins and Osili 2018). Fundraisers can keep abreast of these trends and new developments by consulting valuable references and contemporary reviews (see Powell and Bromley 2020, *The Chronicle of Philanthropy*, the HistPhil Blog).

American understanding of the sector as "nonprofit," "voluntary," "independent," "third," or "philanthropic" is relatively new. The sector was studied by the Commission on Private Philanthropy and Public Needs, which produced the Filer Commission report in 1975. The nonprofit sector was recognized as a powerful economic and social force with a close, yet sometimes adversarial, relationship to government.

Research reveals a long record of societal improvements through voluntary action, the numerous advances in health, education, civil rights, and the like (e.g., see reporting from *Inside Philanthropy*, *The Conversation*, *Nonprofit Quarterly*, and Philanthropy Roundtable's blog). It also has brought to light the reoccurring challenges philanthropy faces in the political choices of public and private approaches to addressing persistent social issues and inequalities. Challenges also occur when outcomes fall short of promises. Some critiques of philanthropy derive from the continued debate of the proper role of philanthropy in addressing the public good. Tensions are evident in the relation between wealth and power; in the balance between philanthropy's personal and public benefits; and in the power difference between donor and recipient. In addition, philanthropic action is challenged by desires for organizational and individual freedom and the public demand for transparency and accountability. Finally, perspectives vary as to whether philanthropic activity enhances or undermines democracy (Franks 2020).

These tensions are a reminder that philanthropic organizations themselves encounter difficulties. Although most organizations are genuinely focused on the social well-being of many, some organizations experience teleopathy or the disease of purpose or mission (Payton and Moody 2008, 120). They may lose sight of their mission and focus on maintaining their existence, rationalizing and practicing in a corrupt manner, and finally, involving themselves in morally corrupt activities such as those of the Ku Klux Klan and contemporary hate groups.

The current context of increasing disparity in wealth, racial justice, devastating environmental disasters, and political division intensifies these longstanding questions around philanthropy and highlights hazards and failures. Fundraisers benefit from understanding the possibilities and the limitations of philanthropy in order to help their organizations navigate important philosophical and practical dilemmas. Before addressing the big questions facing philanthropy, it is important to understand the size and scope of philanthropy and the available data that will inform fundraisers' daily activity.

Size and Scope

Philanthropy and nonprofit organizations play a significant role in American society. The nonprofit sector grew in both numbers and finances from 2006–2016. According to the National Center for Charitable Statistics at the Urban Institute (NCCS Project Team 2020), approximately 1.54 million nonprofits were registered with the Internal Revenue Service in 2016, an increase of 4.5 percent since 2006. This number, however, understates the sector's size by not including nonregistered groups – namely, religious organizations and churches, which are not required to register, as well as small, mostly informal groups. Between 2006 and 2016, the number of registered public charities (501(c)(3) organizations) grew by approximately 20 percent to 1.08 million of the total. Among them, human services comprise the largest subsector (35 percent), followed by education (17 percent), and health (12 percent). Among the smaller subsectors, international/foreign affairs and environment/animals saw the largest growth rates in the number of organizations, increasing by 16 and 10 percent, respectively, during the same period.

Formal and informal volunteering helps nonprofits operate while furthering community building. In 2017, 30.3 percent of adults volunteered through an organization (AmeriCorps 2018b). Volunteers donate to charity double the rate of nonvolunteers, engage in their communities, talk more frequently to neighbors, and vote more often in local elections among other civic activities.

Volunteerism acts at the intersection of instrumental and expressive values of nonprofits. Volunteers provide program delivery and help with fundraising (instrumental); and they embody values like care, hope, and equity (expressive). These values represent a shared articulation of the community values of which the nonprofit organization is a part. Fundraisers have a particular responsibility to ensure that both the instrumental and expressive contributions of volunteers are recognized and remain central to the mission of the organization (Lu Knustsen and Bower 2010).

Turning from volunteerism to donating, Giving USA (2021) estimates 2020 total giving to be $471.44 billion, or 2.3 percent of GDP, a 5.1 percent increase in current dollars (3.8 percent increase in inflation adjusted dollars) over 2019 giving. Since the end of the Great Recession in 2009, the total growth in inflation-adjusted giving is 37 percent for the 2011–2020 decade. In 2020, three of four sources of giving (individual, foundation, bequest) were at an all-time high in inflation-adjusted terms. These data reveal that giving by individuals is the largest share, nearly 70 percent. In 2020, individuals gave $324.10 billion. Individual giving and bequests when combined totaled 78 percent in 2020. Chapter 8 provides additional information about giving trends by subsector.

Finally, it is important to pay attention to donor-advised fund giving (see Chapter 37) and online giving, including crowdfunding (see Chapter 24). Despite the global crisis, #GivingTuesday (2020) reported a 29 percent increase in participants (34.8 million people) and a 25 percent total giving increase ($2.47 billion compared with $1.97 billion in 2019). Multiple charitable crowdfunding platforms attract both individual and institutional donors including foundations and corporations (Bernholz, Reich, and Saunders-Hastings 2015; Weinger 2016).

Giving USA and other specialized data sources on volunteerism, nonprofits, donor-advised funds, online giving, and crowdfunding can empower fundraisers' work. Understanding national data can help fundraisers engage in meaningful conversations with staff and board members about key trends and assist in tracking, comparing, and contextualizing the organization's progress.

Technological and Educational Advances in Philanthropy Infrastructure

The nonprofit sector has grown significantly since the Filer Commission's report, in the United States and globally. Growth of the sector has occurred alongside the adoption of an increasingly complex use of media and technology for communication and an expansion of educational programs.

The growth of community foundations globally provides an interesting example for the increasingly multifaceted communications required of nonprofits. Community foundations raise money in their communities, support nonprofit organizations, and integrate local citizens on their boards. Strategic communication and engagement with all forms of media widen their networks of relationships, engage stakeholders, and increase public awareness of their multiple roles and activities (Esposito and Besana 2018). In 2014, there were an estimated 1,800 community foundations worldwide with over 1,000 in the United States and

Canada, and 670 in Europe (Community Foundation Atlas 2014). Often connected to thematic or local community foundations are giving circles – groups of individuals who come together to support their community through funding, volunteering, and networking. Leveraging the power of the digital age, giving circles and related initiatives like Philanthropy Together (2020), are increasing not only donations but the numbers of individuals engaged in collective giving. The Philanthropy Together collective, which promotes the democratization and increase in diversity in giving circles across the United States and globally, is enhancing the ability of these groups to gather, discuss, decide, give, and engage. By the year 2020, the network had brought together 2,000 giving circles that donated $1.29 billion.

Media channels, both traditional (newspapers and radio) and digital (websites, social media platforms, podcasts, and digital downloads) are enmeshed in the daily practices and routines of nonprofit professionals, including fundraising and volunteer recruitment (Burger 2019). These practices, linked to the professionalization of the sector, require specific communication and digital literacy skill sets that are needed in all nonprofit organizations (see Chapters 16 and 24). The term *digital literacy* refers to "the ability to use information and communication technologies to find, evaluate, create, and communicate information, requiring both cognitive and technical skills" (American Library Association 2020). It is considered the next core function of any nonprofit organization alongside financial and program management (Bernholz 2017).

The size and scope of philanthropy education and research has grown significantly in the last two decades. The number of institutions offering programs has nearly doubled in just the past 15 years (Seton Hall University 2020). In 2020, there were 342 colleges and universities offering nonprofit management courses, which included 86 programs with noncredit courses, 78 continuing education programs, 252 graduate degree programs, and 82 programs with online courses. Scholarly activity about the nonprofit field has existed for nearly a century and has accelerated since 1990. Top research themes include theories of volunteering, social capital, and civic engagement. The frequent disconnect between academic research and practice calls for more collaboration between academics and practitioners and a search for new explanations of the functioning of the sector (Ma and Konrath 2018). Fundraising theory is one method to bridge this gap (see Chapter 4).

The COVID-19 pandemic accelerated the widespread use of digital platforms across the nonprofit sector for fundraising purposes. Fundraisers need to understand the difference between commercial and nonprofit entities that provide these digital platforms (Bernholz 2020b). The abrupt change to a virtual format highlighted issues of data privacy for donors and beneficiaries as well as the importance of digital access. Fundraisers increasingly must have essential – if not advanced – skills in digital fundraising perhaps acquired through academic programs in the field.

Fundraising and the Economic, Social, and Political Climate

Charitable giving is affected by economic growth and recession, social well-being and unrest, and the overall dynamic of political processes and institutions. Nonprofit organizations experience these changes daily and may be challenged due to their particular context.

Economic Climate

Analysis shows changes in giving are closely tied to economic changes, especially in household wealth, household income, and for foundations, stock market performance. When adjusting for inflation, giving usually increases in nonrecessionary years and slightly contracts in recession years (Rooney and Bergdoll 2020).

The COVID-19 pandemic unevenly impacted business, employment, health, and the nonprofit sector. People of color suffered disproportionately in the United States revealing numerous systemic barriers to economic opportunities and the precariousness of entire communities.

The coming transfer of wealth and new wealth will render Gen X and Millennial generations the most significant philanthropists who will contribute to reshaping norms in giving and engagement (see Chapter 31) (Johnson Center 2017).

Social venture philanthropy and social enterprises have grown considerably and often serve as alternative revenue streams to traditional fundraising for nonprofits. Social enterprise, LLCs, BCorps, and social cooperatives can be attractive opportunities to operate in the marketplace as businesses using revenues to advance social goals. These hybrid organizational forms are developing across the globe and present a new way to mobilize innovative ideas and resources to contribute to long-term societal challenges. However, to enter this "Frontier of Philanthropy" – described by Salamon (2014) – requires significant knowledge and recognition that traditional philanthropy and government support are needed for success. Further, "market-based" solutions need to be viewed as appropriate for the social purpose mission of the organization. Fundraisers continually need to be aware of the potential pitfalls associated with these vehicles.

Social Climate

The recent social climate has been characterized by widespread dissatisfaction. The persistent and unresolved issues of healthcare, education, poverty, greater inequalities, and racism have refocused the attention of American society. Philanthropy has been both challenged by and responsive to these issues.

Philanthropy has historically been associated with wealth of key individuals like Carnegie and Rockefeller from the Industrial Revolution or Gates and Bezos of the tech revolution. However, philanthropic action has been carried out in a multitude of ways by diverse members of society from the earliest days. Individuals crossing color or ethnic lines to save others from drowning or fire. Women raising funds for mining families, for illnesses such as tuberculosis, or for basic school supplies for classrooms. Minority veterans, doctors, and community members raising money for basic healthcare for their communities. These examples demonstrate that philanthropy has engaged individuals at all levels of society who have given "time, money and moral concern to benefit others" (Moniz 2020, para 5).

Individuals across the country and around the world are envisioning new ways of expressing generosity and care for others. Fundraisers can look at this as an opportunity to include these diverse communities and philanthropic practices in their own approaches for support.

Political Climate

Democracy is being scrutinized through questions about institutions, processes, and division among people. Philanthropy's unique role in prompting and developing civic engagement, advocating for change, and amplifying unheard voices is part of this discussion. Philanthropy and nonprofits increasingly are being asked to provide basic services in healthcare, education, environmental action, and more (Bernholz 2020c). What is the role of philanthropy and where are the limits? Bernholz asks whether it is time to "re-imagine philanthropy."

There are changing demographics of who is giving with more reliance on the super wealthy. Recent examples such as Purdue Pharma and Jeffery Epstein point to a continuing concern with tainted money and tainted donors within the practices of philanthropy (Johnson Center 2020). Critiques of "big philanthropy" from mega donors and the ultra-rich have raised concerns of decreased participation by donors with less wealth. Yet, research shows that even in the unique environment of both a global pandemic and an economic downturn, most households initially maintained both direct and indirect giving (Mesch et al. 2020). Regular people gave in various ways, including locally focused efforts and initiatives by younger generations and communities of color gathering people together to help one another, practicing unconventional generosity such as buying locally and spreading the message about safety measures on social media.

Fundraisers must remain faithful to the organization's mission, be creative, and engage board members. Connecting the nonprofit's work with the broader social issues and systems will help fundraisers identify a larger pool of donors in the future. Most of all, fundraisers must remain positive. Philanthropy is about hope for the future and fundraising is an optimistic profession that serves society well, especially in times of distress.

Opportunities for Philanthropy

Conditions including climate events (fires, floods), the pandemic, social movements, and economic crises require fundraisers to respond with agility steeped in solid understanding of their organization's context. This section describes three changes in the relationships among donors, nonprofit organizations, communities, and beneficiaries.

One change is a new appreciation for the assets of communities and their unique qualities. For example, recent studies on rural philanthropy highlight the importance of trust and common values in uncovering hidden needs in rural Iowa. Or, in New Mexico, research found that place and people who are rooted in local history and culture play a key role in devising partnerships. The local participants honored the process of sharing and equalizing power and cultivated a sense of mutual respect among all participants – donors and recipients alike (Campbell University 2020).

A second change relates to how the pandemic caused rapid adaptation in ways of giving. Giving online increased; other giving was directed through direct transfer platforms. Donor-advised funds gave more in a record amount of time. Foundations also changed funding restrictions and reporting requirements to reach vulnerable populations and to assure that nonprofits survived the pandemic and economic disruption. This demonstrates that quick pivots are possible.

A third change is some funders' embrace of trust-based philanthropy, which includes explicit attention to community voices, funding for community-driven projects, and self-determination for community members, to decide what is best. This approach acknowledges the imbalance in funder-grantee relations and seeks to address mistrust in institutions and those in power. It involves new processes, sharing, humility, and deep learning to help communities mobilize efforts from the bottom up (Wong and McGrath 2020).

The turbulent times have created a context in which philanthropic values are being reexamined. In the face of these disruptions and social reckoning, philanthropy has become a critical building block in the figurative and literal healing of many (Grant 2020).

Conclusion

Questions about philanthropy's purpose and position in society are age-old and will continue as a source of robust discussion. It is certain that fundraisers will always have to adapt to a changing context of economic, social, and political issues. New skills in technology and digital communications will be part of their daily practice, but more educational opportunities will also be available to develop these and other capacities. Engaging donors, volunteers, and staff in new ways will be important as organizations deliver their missions in a more diverse world and growing nonprofit/philanthropic sector. The power of data, a changing philanthropic narrative, and the implementation of equitable and inclusive practices are all key elements of the sector's future. As the institutional stewards of philanthropy, fundraisers should bear these changes in mind as they fulfill their role in building a just and civil society.

Discussion Questions

1. Discuss the opportunities, critiques, challenges, and failures of philanthropy reviewed in this chapter. How can fundraisers prepare to have conversations with donors and community members in relation to these concerns and possibilities?
2. Discuss how the changing economic, social, and political climate could affect distinct types of nonprofits (i.e., human service organizations versus arts organizations).

Application Exercises

1. What is an example in your community where philanthropy has made a significant, positive impact? Conversely, what is an example in your community where philanthropy has overlooked a specific need or group of people? Finally, can you find local examples of innovative efforts to better incorporate community voices into funding decision-making and philanthropic strategizing?
2. Evaluate your organization's digital literacy. Look at the following areas: Internally, do all employees understand the importance of data use, management, and privacy? Are online fundraising financial transactions secure? How do you acquire the data you use in fundraising activities? What is the approach to donor privacy? Do you address the question of data privacy with your clients? How is organizational beneficiaries' privacy protected? Externally, is your organization at risk of data breaches?

CHAPTER SEVEN

FUNDRAISING IN CHALLENGING TIMES: CRISIS, SURVIVAL, AND TRANSFORMATION

By Amir Pasic

Fundraising is no stranger to crisis or challenging times. Some crises are familiar and periodic, while others can represent fundamental discontinuities for society and the roles of fundraising and philanthropy. Fundraising can be energized by crisis and challenge, especially when the philanthropic organization is prepared to ask good questions about its purpose.

This chapter offers leadership habits and coping mechanisms for fundraisers during the stress and ambiguity of challenging times. It addresses the importance of synthesizing knowledge and reaffirming the ethical foundations of fundraising to understand the ongoing impact of challenging times.

After completing this chapter, readers will:

- Appreciate the continuum of crises that engage fundraising.
- Learn about leadership habits that can inform responses to crisis.
- Understand the roles of purpose, power, and perspective when fundraising in crisis.
- Appreciate the argument that ethical engagement is even more necessary during crisis.

Fundraising Is Never Far from a Crisis

If society did not face challenges, there would be little demand for fundraising. Fundraising arose as a response to challenging times. So, in times of crisis, fundraisers are confronted with the foundations of their craft, why they do what they do. Crises also divert attention from where fundraisers focus in normal times, from their chosen missions and approaches.

Challenges can be local, like an earthquake, or global, like a pandemic. Some fundraisers have jobs that focus on emergencies and disasters, raising funds for those experiencing grave, often mortal, challenges. After reprieve from immediate emergencies, colleagues in these jobs prepare for the next crisis.

Those who fundraise in anticipation of a disaster whose contours are not yet known rely on past knowledge. When faced with a crisis, knowledge becomes even more urgent. For example, in recessions there are often predictable patterns of behavior. However, the global recession that followed the lockdown in the wake of COVID-19 tested the limits of routine recession responses given that it was the deepest economic retrenchment since the Great Depression of the 1930s (Gopinath 2020). Even the Great Recession of 2008–2009 had unique characteristics with roots in the financial system that significantly reduced the value of real estate and other assets, not to mention its human toll (Hanke 2017).

The challenge of a crisis for fundraising clearly impacts the availability of resources and donors' ability and inclination to give. Determining the availability of resources becomes of immediate concern as does the impact of the crisis on the generosity of donors. This is the immediate challenge at hand for fundraisers during a crisis.

When crises have routine elements, fundraisers can anticipate likely responses from donors. The knowledge involved in making such an assessment is relatively stable. The fundraiser must evaluate the nature of the crisis to decide how to adjust techniques to keep donors engaged and to support them in their giving.

Crises also develop at different speeds. Sometimes they are slow-moving, like the crisis in access to health and education, or in exposure to the arts. Sometimes they are immediate, when people lose homes and jobs because of a natural disaster or economic recession. When the crisis does not possess familiar contours, how to fundraise is difficult to assess.

Fundraising in challenging times presents itself as a continuum. Certainly not every flood, earthquake, or recession will be exactly like the past. Fundraisers need to identify what is novel about any particular crisis. On the other end of the spectrum is a rare event like the COVID-19 pandemic for which the last similar case of global scope occurred 100 years ago.

The fundraiser's case for support in response to the crisis will shape how donors respond. The fundraiser's knowledge and diversity of experience, synthesized into a perspective to identify and describe the challenge or crisis, will be important in shaping the nature of the relationship with the donor during the course of a crisis. Describing what the crisis is about can help the fundraiser craft the tactical response to the case at hand. Certain tactics or habits of good fundraising may be very useful in any crisis. Indeed, fundraisers may have to rely on these while they determine the contours of a complex case that continues to evolve.

The nature of the challenge also informs the strategic resources needed to address it. Complex crises may affect strategy at its core, bringing into question not only the purpose of the cause, but also the principles of the profession itself. A crisis that has deep and broad impact on social arrangements and attitudes can bring into question how fundraisers orient themselves toward donors and the social role of the fundraising profession. As fundraisers wrestle with a strategic conundrum that may affect the foundations of the fundraising profession, they can come to appreciate and better describe the nature of the crisis.

As fundraisers confront the kind of profound social change that questions the roles of fundraisers, they look to the ethical foundations of the profession (see Chapter 2) for guidance across different contexts and crises. These bring to light the role of the fundraiser in articulating how different kinds of knowledge connect supporters and causes.

Leadership Habits in Crisis Fundraising: Purpose, Power, and Perspective

COVID-19 and the racial and other social crises it laid bare have generated a profusion of commentary on how to manage through it. Current research suggests that fundraisers should focus on purpose, power, and perspective.

Purpose

Specific guidelines are preferable to general abstractions when one is confronted with a crisis. Kerrissey and Edmondson (2020) concluded from their analysis of effective leadership during the pandemic:

> When the situation is uncertain, human instinct and basic management training can cause leaders – out of fear of taking the wrong steps and unnecessarily making people anxious – to delay action and to downplay the threat until the situation becomes clearer. But behaving in this manner means failing the coronavirus leadership test, because by the time the dimensions of the threat are clear, you're badly behind in trying to control the crisis. Passing that test requires leaders to act in an urgent,

honest, and iterative fashion, recognizing that mistakes are inevitable and correcting course – not assigning blame – is the way to deal with them when they occur.

Instead of vision, Petriglieri (2020) argued for the importance of "holding": "Because when there's a fire in a factory, a sudden drop in revenues, a natural disaster, we don't need a call to action. We are already motivated to move, but we often flail. What we need is a type of holding, so that we can move purposefully" (2). He argued that crises test visions and that they rarely survive.

Fundraisers build relationships in support of the cause they have adopted. Reaffirming these relationships by holding others through the crisis is echoed in the advice that McKinsey and Co. offered leaders during the pandemic (Dhingra et al. 2020). They recommended that organizational leaders engage with each employee's personal sense of purpose to ignite their motivation and move the organization through the crisis.

For example, The Fund Raising School demonstrated "holding" by working closely as a team to develop new strategies in response to the pandemic. Stanczykiewicz (2020a) described how intense and open communication combined with humility among team members built trust while leading to new solutions. Meanwhile, Seiler (2020) reaffirmed the fundamental principles of fundraising and the need to focus on who is served while confirming the validity of the mission. He emphasizes the steady and ethical work of engagement, and the responsiveness of communities in a crisis, including the arts organizations that normally have a hard time when the economy contracts but are nonetheless important in giving us hope and meaning. He also focuses on the staying power of storytelling, again an expression of intimate human purpose as fundraising leaders seek to "hold" others close in troubled times.

Purpose is a touchstone in crisis and is a good reminder to first be generous in engaging potential donors and colleagues. But it is not only to others that one should be generous. Self-care is important for all as they pursue their purpose in a crisis. Self-care is not a self-indulgence, but a necessity to be effective in helping others (Reese 2020).

Power

Crises expose how power is distributed. The fact that COVID-19 disproportionately affected minority and poor populations, while the wealthy segments of society increased their affluence, precipitated widespread calls for social justice across the world, often in the wake of killings of unarmed Black Americans. Beyond social attention to inequality, an important movement in the fundraising profession became more salient with its call for reconsidering the donor-based model of fundraising (Le 2017a).

Vu Le (2017b) and the community-centric fundraising movement provided a strong critique of the relative powerlessness of the fundraiser and the nonprofits they represent to the wealthy and powerful donors they cultivate. They propose a new model that recasts the role of the donor and how nonprofits approach donors as patrons. They argue that submitting to donor wishes perpetuates and worsens injustices, as meaningless measures of impact surrender too much power to donors to make decisions and to enjoy perks of status that they do not deserve. According to the community-centric movement, the community itself should be more engaged and make more decisions about the philanthropy from which it is supposed to benefit. In focusing on cultivating the wealthy, according to Vu Le (2017a), fundraisers surrender too much power to donors in return for their money. Given the turn of many donors to support communities of color and other neglected communities, the time may be ripe for the community-centric fundraising movement to gain more adherents.

Challenging times not only create rough seas, they can lay bare power relations that can recast how the work of fundraising is approached. But in addition to larger questions about power dynamics implicit in donor-centrism, there are also power dynamics that affect the everyday work of fundraisers.

Pfeffer (2019) has developed a skeptical view of many leadership nostrums. Pfeffer argues that a lot of leadership advice assumes away power relations and makes leadership sound like it is mostly about developing self-awareness, communicating well, and following some well-worn how-tos. But leadership usually means acquiring and exerting power and it comes with consequences both professional and personal.

On the leadership literature, Pfeffer (2019) wrote "although leader modesty is valued and praised in much leadership teaching, an extensive, even vast, research literature demonstrates that narcissism and unwarranted self-confidence predict being hired, obtaining promotions, and other indicators of career success, including, in some instance, aspects of job performance" (9).

On the practical uses of power, he concluded that "one of the most important outcomes from teaching people about power is to increase their sense of personal agency and also the frequency with which they take strategic actions to achieve their goals and build their influence" (Pfeffer 2019, 15). Consequently, power is not only about having or seeking the upper hand over others. It is also about taking the initiative and realizing that you have the power to move events. Power differentials do not always speak to larger injustices in society. Understanding them can help leaders identify the power they have to affect change.

The context of power in which fundraisers operate and the power they have to exercise their own agency acquire even more salience during challenging times. The power imbalance that fundraisers can experience with both major gift donors and bosses still leaves them with the power to affect how the crisis impacts them and those around them. One important way of having power to make positive change is to focus on perspective.

Perspective

High-performing gift officers tend to have the qualities of a "curious chameleon," someone who is deeply engaged both socially and intellectually, and generally open to both people and ideas (EAB 2014). Fundraisers need knowledge and social skills to be successful. It becomes even more important during the kind of crisis that upends established ways of working and understanding the world. Generating a perspective on the crisis that can engage and persuade others is a powerful skill.

Jeffrey Sonnenfeld, the senior associate dean of leadership programs for the Yale School of Management, spoke about the increasing need for leaders in all sectors to integrate complex areas of knowledge, ranging from climate change to racial and social justice to the psychology of groups and individuals (Galloway 2020). In their work to translate the missions of the causes for which they raise funds and make them compelling to donors, fundraisers need to understand the community basis for the cause and translate needs to align with the interests of donors.

In crisis, this sense-making work takes on more urgency as there is no time for tentative experiments to see if something works before it is implemented. Searching for perspective on the crisis and its impact on their responsibilities are what fundraisers do every moment no matter how difficult it is to be certain about what needs to be done. Perspective will be imperfect, but when it is based on skillful synthesis of quickly moving expertise, it can break through doubt, confusion, and paralysis. Fundraisers can be vital creators of perspective by engaging colleagues, experts, and donors, synthesizing their various viewpoints into a perspective that shows a way forward. In building relationships, fundraisers are not only preparing to ask for a gift, they are educating themselves and their interlocutors, not unlike the way that Hank Rosso (1991) conceived of the core of fundraising as the gentle art of teaching generosity.

By generating perspective, fundraisers perform a valuable service. Intensive learning for and with others is part of the important knowledge work of a fundraiser, just much intensified during a crisis. See Chapter 19 for additional insights into fundraising leadership.

The Demand for Perspective: The Mindful Work of Fundraising

Crises as far-reaching and profound as the COVID-19 pandemic bring to the fore a series of additional challenges. Bernholz (2020a), for example, referred to a "syndemic" (the pandemic coupled with endemic racism) in her quest to "reimagine philanthropy" that she argues should become more equitable and democratic after the crisis. This paradigm points to the need to understand complexity, connection, and community.

Complexity, Connection, and Community

Contemplating complexity as turmoil continues is difficult. Kruglanski (2020) described how the novelty and life-changing nature of the pandemic changed who people are. Dependence on others heightened and people came to value connections to others more. Coping with crisis, understanding it, and giving it meaning require the joining of efforts and minds.

As fundraisers meaningfully connect donors to advancing a cause, they are often at the center of the storm. They have to improvise and perform while accepted norms give way. Useful leadership habits can be helpful in times of crisis; reassurances and the reaffirmation of values can be helpful in getting through the turmoil. Engagement with others can provide perspective as fundraisers figure out what they need to know now and to prepare for the changes the crisis will bring.

Fundraisers participate in maintaining and revising key habits of social interaction that make civil society. However, they need to be wary of playing a role in perpetuating structures and processes of injustice and inequity in the nonprofit sector.

Breaking the Status Quo

During my graduate course, Philanthropy in Times of Crisis, students became interested in considering minimum giving levels for nonprofit board members. These minimums can sometimes serve as barriers to recruiting members from communities of color or from communities that the nonprofit actually serves. They also favor the wealthy and powerful who may preserve the status quo. The students were eager to embrace the responsibility of formulating and vetting the missions of boards, how to best compose them, and to consider who is responsible for articulating the purpose of a nonprofit.

Even before the pandemic, boards, especially those of museums and cultural institutions, were already under intense scrutiny (Sheonberger 2020). Criticized for hierarchical notions and granting cultural prominence to the wealthy, the movement to "decolonize," or at least seriously scrutinize established practices, seems to have become more prevalent during the crisis. "Normal" cultivation practices were seen by many as working against the noble purposes many professional fundraisers espouse.

Reconsideration of Ethical Fundamentals of the Profession

This deeper questioning of the mores and ethics of fundraising makes it like many other professions that are taking a hard look at how inequities and discriminatory practices need to be better understood and countered (*The Economist* 2020). Fundraising is a relatively new profession, with the Association of Fundraising Professionals (AFP) becoming the first national organization through its predecessor organization in 1960. In its history, it has not yet had to respond to a social upheaval that questions some of its basic orientations. And as the largest representative body of the profession, AFP is responding through its Ethics Committee. It has started a process of considering how the inequities that surfaced so starkly during the pandemic and associated crises need to inform a discussion and reformulation of the current Code of Ethical Standards.

It would seem that when challenging times call for a reconsideration of ethical fundamentals, asking us for an examination of the ends and means of the fundraiser's calling, that there is little solid ground left to stand on. As fundraisers improvise by "holding" donors and colleagues all the while striving to synthesize a vast diversity of knowledge while so much is unclear and provisional, how can they also open up the once well-settled ethical foundations that define their profession?

And yet posing fundamental questions about ethics in this environment can be useful. It acknowledges that we are in a liminal moment, a period of fluidity. Fundraisers must be open to questioning and clearly reaffirming why they do what they do and the proper tools to use.

Clearly, issues of race, equity, and inclusion are challenging the profession as they are in the broader society. Related scrutiny is focused on the concentration of wealth and power in a small number of hands. On top of this, the ways in which information is shared and consumed has created deep polarization, not seen in the United States since the Civil War. And these challenges developed amid surging needs during the pandemic while fundraisers worked to affirm the relationships that give them and those they serve a sense of purpose.

Ethically Inspired Adaptation during Crisis

With a deep and lasting crisis like the COVID pandemic, the ethical foundations of the profession become more intense and immediate. Ethics become less like permanent rules for confronting difficult cases. Instead, every day brings difficult dilemmas. In a crisis that challenges as profoundly as the pandemic and its complications, there are daily questions about the right thing to do, about values in conflict.

In such challenging moments, a simple recitation or application of a code is not enough. Fundraisers need to understand the justifications and rationales behind the codes in order to find direction and perspective.

But this should not be seen as a burden. All it means is that ethics come alive. They become a tool to use to make sense of the right things to do even when everything else seems radically unsettled. For example, several universities suspended solicitations during the early phase of the pandemic, asking only for emergency support for students who were facing hardship as a result of the pandemic. Donors to performing arts organizations made gifts to continue paying artists who could not perform and generate revenue. Fundraisers had to make countless decisions about the right thing to do as normalcy was upended. Ethically informed adaptations to the crisis provided inspirational relief and real benefits to people and organizations in distress.

Fundraisers create and maintain authentic relationships rooted in purpose. This approach is lauded by many who study successful leadership during crisis. Fundraisers also need to integrate the knowledge that connects their cause and its supporters with relevant knowledge that comes from researchers and informed commentators about the state of the world for which their cause seeks to be relevant. This is the familiar dual role of fundraisers as curious chameleons who are eager for a diversity of authentic connections while pursuing knowledge to better illuminate proposed solutions.

In a crisis, the social and the cognitive aspects of fundraising become more demanding. And if the crisis is deep and unprecedented it may bring into question the very basis of the profession. In this case, the fundraiser is called to be an applied ethicist, going beyond knowledge about what is, to options for what should be.

It is not easy, but it is reassuring first to ask the question of what should be done, even when it is not clear what the realistic options are for what can be done. Wondering about the right thing to do is never the wrong question to ask when seeking perspective, even when challenges seem too big to grasp. Ethics become even more part of the everyday, helping to clarify mission and purpose. Ironically, opening up the ethical dimension for discussion can help bring more clarity to challenging times.

Conclusion

Fundraising is not a stranger to crisis since fundraisers often seek support for causes that aim to improve or fix issues that are a crisis or on their way to becoming one. Purpose, power, and perspective can help fundraisers manage through times of crisis. Examining and re-examining the ethics of fundraising in the midst of crisis is not an added burden but a necessity for developing perspective on what is important.

Discussion Questions

1. What are some unhelpful responses to crisis that you have witnessed? What are some more positive examples?

2. How do successful fundraisers handle a crisis? What can be learned from fundraisers who regularly raise money for natural disasters and humanitarian crises?

3. What are some of the challenges for the profession of fundraising brought to the forefront by recent crises? Discuss how they could affect fundraising systems and structures in the long term.

Application Exercises

1. Consider a fundraising challenge or campaign during the pandemic. What elements of purpose, power, and perspective did it display?

2. Describe a crisis and the response. How did the fundraisers involved respond? How might they have responded differently?

3. Consider the same or a different crisis as in exercise #2. What were its ethical dimensions related to fundraising? How could it have been handled differently?

4. How will your fundraising behavior adapt to meet the next recession, the next pandemic?

Thank you to the faculty and students who participated in the Lilly Family School of Philanthropy fall 2020 course, Philanthropy in Times of Crisis. Much of this chapter is drawn from the lectures, readings, and class conversations that constituted that collective journey.

CHAPTER EIGHT

FUNDRAISING ACROSS NONPROFIT SUBSECTORS

By Anna Pruitt

The nonprofit sector is home to over 1.4 million organizations (Giving USA 2021) with diverse purposes, goals, and constituents. While charitable giving trends are instructive, nonprofit organizations deserve to be considered individually.

This chapter categorizes nonprofits into the following nine subsectors used in Giving USA:

- Religion,
- Education,
- Human Services,
- Foundations,
- Public-Society Benefit,
- Health,
- International Affairs,
- Arts, Culture, and Humanities, and
- Environment and Animals.

Fundraisers can access data for each subsector from Giving USA and other sources, analyze upcoming trends and changes in donor behavior, and identify the most useful approaches for their work. Although this chapter includes data from the 2021 edition of Giving USA, the patterns identified are part of longer-term trends that are likely to continue for the next several years.

In this chapter, readers will learn the types of organizations within each sub-sector as well as the following information:

- *Supporters and constituents:*
  - Internal strengths.
  - Major groups of constituents and donors.
  - Known patterns of giving.
- *Issues that fundraisers should consider:*
  - Current issues within the field.
  - Changing landscape for giving in recent years.
  - New landscapes and challenges for fundraisers.

Religion

Supporters and Constituents

Giving to religion includes giving to congregations, missions, and religious media. The important role of religion in many donors' lives is reflected in the size of the sector: 28 percent of all giving, by far the largest subsector (Giving USA 2021). Twenty-nine percent of households give to religion, by far the largest share of giving, with 60 percent of total dollars for the average household (GenerosityForLife n.d.). In addition, nearly half of surveyed high net worth households give to religious causes, giving an average of almost one in three charitable dollars to this cause (Indiana University Lilly Family School of Philanthropy 2016; 2021a).

Individual contributions comprise 81 percent of funding for congregations (King et al. 2019). Members of the congregation form the base of the constituents, volunteers, and donors, and 78 percent of funds are received during services (King et al. 2019). There is evidence linking higher rates of attendance at services and higher levels of giving to congregations (Austin 2017) (see Chapter 27).

Issues That Fundraisers Should Consider

When many congregations moved services online during the pandemic, online giving increased. Online giving may change religious giving patterns: One report of 2,000 churches found that online donors gave steadily throughout the year and throughout the week, with 67 percent of digital giving happening on days other than Sunday (Barry 2019).

The decline in religious affiliation and the associated decline in attendance has been an area of concern. In 2014, 22.8 percent of Americans had no religious affiliation, an all-time high (Pew Research Center 2015). However, a recent study of congregational giving found that similar percentages of congregations reported growing compared to those that reported that membership was shrinking over the three years of the study (King et al. 2019). Additionally, nearly half the congregations reported an increase in revenue.

Congregations that frame charitable giving as a key aspect of religious identity and an important way to contribute to the overall mission of the church tend to have greater and more consistent levels of support than organizations that discuss charitable giving as a necessity to keep the religious institution running (Mundey et al. 2019).

Education

Supporters and Constituents

Education includes independent and public schools, libraries, higher education, and professional schools. Only 11 percent of U.S. households donated to education, but education donors gave roughly 15 percent of their total giving dollars to this cause (GenerosityForLife n.d.). A larger percentage of high net worth donors give to education, 23 percent to K–12 organizations, and 25 percent to higher education (Indiana University Lilly Family School of Philanthropy 2021a). Education was the top cause among grants made from donor-advised funds (DAFs) from 2012 to 2015, comprising 28 percent of total grant dollars (Giving USA 2018).

The Voluntary Support of Education (VSE) Survey issued by the Council for Advancement and Support of Education (CASE) showed that foundations are the largest source of support to higher education, followed by alumni, non-alumni, grants from DAFs and other sources, and corporations (Kaplan 2020).

The robust fundraising infrastructure of educational institutions provides a wide range of tools, events, and approaches. Development teams may include different professionals working on alumni giving and the annual fund, major gifts, planned giving, and corporate and foundation giving.

Issues that Fundraisers Should Consider

Experiences within the education subsector vary widely. Many colleges with smaller alumni populations and endowments have struggled in recent years. Some schools have launched crowdfunding campaigns or appeals to donors in the region where the school is located. Meanwhile schools of all sizes can receive criticism for their endowments from critics concerned about the immediate financial needs of students, even in cases where donors have earmarked gifts to the endowment (Kim 2017).

Fundraising is growing at community colleges and independent schools. According to CASE, the average endowment for community colleges grew 76 percent between 1998 and 2018 (St. Amour 2020). Independent and K–12 public schools are also expanding their private support, with capital gifts coming from major donors.

Schools have increased engagement with donors who sometimes are overlooked such as alumni of color, members of the LGBTQ+ community, and others. Research demonstrates that a sense of belonging is associated with greater alumni giving, and that a diverse and culturally sensitive fundraising team can help grow and encourage fundraising from these groups (Drezner 2013; Drezner and Pizmony-Levy 2020).

Human Services

Supporters and Constituents

Human services organizations include food banks, homeless shelters, disaster relief, and youth-focused programs such as scouting and 4-H clubs. Human services organizations receive the third-largest share of total giving (Giving USA 2021). Giving to basic needs is one of the most popular causes for households of all types, with nearly one-fourth of all households giving to basic needs (GenerosityForLife n.d.) and over half of high net worth donors giving to this cause (Indiana University Lilly Family School of Philanthropy 2021a).

Human services organizations have often formed partnerships with corporations that can provide in-kind donations, volunteer opportunities for employees, and gifts of cash. Many large foundations support human services organizations.

Issues that Fundraisers Should Consider

For some organizations, government grants may represent a large share of their total revenue (McKeever 2015), however, the fluctuating nature of government budgets makes it difficult to plan around these funds, increasing the need for philanthropic fundraising. In addition, 50 percent of human services nonprofits in a recent study were operating at net loss (Alliance for Strong Families and Communities and the American Public Human Services Association 2018). Fundraisers can start small and gradually build up the donor base to support the financial health of the organization.

Giving to human services has changed: The percentage of households donating to basic needs, youth, and neighborhood organizations declined from 2000 to 2018 (Indiana University Lilly Family School of Philanthropy 2021c). However, total giving to these causes has grown or remained steady; fewer donors are contributing larger amounts. Demonstrating stewardship and diversifying funding streams are good strategies for fundraisers.

Many human services organizations reported a surge in giving in response to the COVID-19 pandemic. DAF grants increased nearly 80 percent in support of human services organizations in the first six months of 2020 over 2019 (National Philanthropic Trust 2021b). This is similar to the Great Recession of 2008–2009 when giving to human services increased while total giving declined (Giving USA 2021). Donors respond to perceived need. Therefore, human services organizations experiencing an uptick in donations must communicate with new donors about the ongoing importance of their work.

Foundations

Supporters and Constituents

The number of foundations is growing over time (Behrens 2016), and giving to foundations, including private, corporate, and community foundations, comprises the fourth-largest category of giving (Giving USA 2021). Most private and corporate foundations are established with a large sum that serves as the endowment through which grants are then made (Council on Foundations n.d.). Many private foundations are established due to devotion to a particular cause or geographic area (see Chapter 38). For the vast majority of private family foundations in a recent survey, the founding donor's intent and the family's connection to an issue were the primary reasons that foundations focused on a particular issue or region (Born 2020). Many businesses have established corporate foundations as a way to give back, and the primary source of funds for these foundations is generally the parent company (Petit 2010). Giving to corporate foundations can be a good way for corporations to take advantage of a surplus in a particularly strong business year and to contribute to the company's communities.

Community foundations are supported primarily by local donors who are committed to giving locally and rely on the expertise of community foundations to direct funds to impactful organizations. Community foundation giving days, usually 24-hour online fundraising events, are also a popular way to engage local donors and nonprofits, and are often accompanied by an in-person event. These events serve to energize the donor base, increase the visibility of the foundation in the community, and encourage a culture of philanthropy (Livingston 2012). There are many resources available for fundraisers planning a giving day (Bingle 2017; Knight Foundation n.d.).

Issues that Fundraisers Should Consider

A report from the Center for Effective Philanthropy found that community foundation donors' perceptions of how receptive the foundation is when they need help and how effectively the foundation is impacting the community were important predictors of a donor's giving likelihood in the next five to ten years (Buteau et al. 2014). Donors with a positive view of the community foundation had a higher likelihood of planning to give in the next five to ten years, and the reverse was also true: Donors with less favorable views of the foundation were also less likely to report plans to give to the community foundation in the future.

Fundraisers might consider the benefits of offering some flexibility in the DAFs held at community foundations. This strategy paid dividends for the Greater Kansas City Community Foundation, which created an option for no minimum to set up a DAF (most organizations have a minimum requirement of $5,000 or above) and saw strong year-over-year growth (Stiffman 2019).

Public-Society Benefit

Supporters and Constituents

Public-society benefit includes giving to pass-through organizations like United Ways, Jewish Federations, and national donor-advised funds. The subsector also includes civil rights, legal aid, public policy, and advocacy organizations such as the ACLU and the NCAAP Legal Defense Fund. It includes organizations that encourage civic engagement. Recently there has been an uptick in interest and visibility of these organizations thanks to movements for social and racial justice.

Giving to this area has experienced strong growth over the last five years, outpacing growth of total giving to make it the fifth-largest subsector (Giving USA 2021). Sixteen percent of all households give to combined purpose organizations such as United Ways and federated giving campaigns (GenerosityForLife n.d.), and rates of giving are even higher for high net worth households, at 27 percent (Indiana University Lilly Family School of Philanthropy 2021a).

Issues that Fundraisers Should Consider

This subsector's diversity requires distinct analysis of different types of organizations.

In the Philanthropy Panel Study (PPS), giving to the United Way, Jewish Federations, and other "combined purposes" organizations declined by 16.6 percent of households from 2000 to 2018 – a decline sharper than any other area of secular giving (Indiana University Lilly Family School of Philanthropy 2021c).

Giving to United Ways has declined for many years, indicating broader trends (Stiffman and Haynes 2019). Leadership from the United Way has identified the decline of workplace giving campaigns, and the decline in giving from middle and upper-middle class donors. Knowing the larger trends shaping this area of giving, fundraisers in this area may want to prioritize maintaining existing donors.

While some areas of this subsector have declined, others have increased dramatically. Legal defense funds have become a way for donors to express support for marginalized communities. In these cases, fundraisers might focus on converting these new donors into long-term donors by continuing to build relationships and demonstrating the impact of initial gifts.

Health

Supporters and Constituents

Health organizations include large hospital foundations and nonprofit hospitals as well as medical research organizations dedicated to specific diseases, addiction treatment and prevention, and mental health services. Donors often have a personal connection to the health cause that they support.

Health is one of the six largest subsectors according to Giving USA (2021). The PPS finds that 16 percent of households give to health, with health donors directing 13 percent of their total giving to these organizations (Indiana University Lilly Family School of Philanthropy 2021c). By comparison, 32 percent of high net worth donors give to health, a far larger share of households than the average (Indiana University Lilly Family School of Philanthropy 2021a).

Issues that Fundraisers Should Consider

The percentage of households giving to health declined by 6.0 percent from 2000 to 2018 – the second sharpest decline of any type of secular giving (Indiana University Lilly Family School of Philanthropy 2021c). However, giving to health over that same time period increased, which means that a smaller number of households are giving more, and perhaps that fundraisers are diversifying funding streams by reaching out to foundations and corporations as well.

As a result of a change to legislation in 2013, nonprofit hospitals have access to demographic and treatment data for patients – information that can be used to identify and engage potential donors, a practice often known as grateful patient programs (Galewitz 2019). Physicians are also sometimes part of the fundraising process, sparking some ethicists to raise concerns about patient confidentiality and conflicts of interest. However, fundraisers have outlined clear best practices to ensure that these programs are ethical and part of a comprehensive fundraising approach (Thayer 2020). Grateful patient programs are increasingly widespread – 68 out of 108 nonprofit hospitals reported having these programs according to a recent survey (Galewitz 2019).

International Affairs

Supporters and Constituents

International affairs includes U.S.-based nonprofits that work in international aid, development, or relief; those that promote international understanding; and organizations working on international peace and security issues. Since its establishment as a category of giving in 1987, the international affairs subsector has grown rapidly over time, eclipsing the arts subsector to become the seventh-largest category of giving (Giving USA 2021).

International affairs draws on high net worth donors, with 10 percent giving to this area (Indiana University Lilly Family School of Philanthropy 2021a), compared to 6 percent of households overall (GenerosityForLife n.d.). Giving to international affairs is also associated with higher levels of education – 65 percent of donors to international affairs have a college degree, compared with 49 percent of donors overall (GenerosityForLife n.d.).

The international affairs subsector receives strong support from corporations and foundations. Many corporations give in-kind or cash donations to support philanthropic efforts in the countries where they operate.

Issues that Fundraisers Should Consider

Currently, much of the foundation grantmaking is focused on supporting the United Nations' Sustainable Development Goals (SDGs). Prominent funders include the Bill & Melinda Gates Foundation, which represented 10.4 percent of total granting dollars given to advance SDGs from 2010 to 2015 (Candid n.d.).

In years with a major international disaster, giving to international affairs organizations spikes. Fundraisers should note that media coverage helps drive disaster giving – more coverage can be beneficial for raising awareness (Indiana University Lilly Family School of Philanthropy 2019).

The international affairs subsector includes innovations such as program-related investments, a type of financial investment that a foundation can make to support a social enterprise or other project as part of the foundation's larger commitment to economic development abroad. Innovations also include microloans, impact investments, and a hybrid of private investment and philanthropic dollars.

Arts, Culture, and Humanities

Supporters and Constituents

Giving to arts, culture, and humanities organizations is one of the smaller categories of overall giving, but draws on a deeply passionate donor base. Giving to this subsector is often associated with high net worth giving, with one in four giving to this subsector (Indiana University Lilly Family School of Philanthropy 2021a). By comparison, only 7 percent of U.S. households overall gave to the arts (GenerosityForLife n.d.).

Since many arts organizations are focused on producing events or exhibitions, fundraising in this subsector makes the most of these events, which may include receptions, meeting the artists, or "behind the scenes" events such as attending a performance rehearsal.

Corporate sponsors fund the arts through sponsorships, in-kind donations, and cash support.

Issues that Fundraisers Should Consider

Giving to arts, culture, and humanities organizations is negatively impacted by recessions. Organizations that successfully rebounded from the Great Recession diversified funding streams and sources of revenue to increase financial stability. Arts, culture, and humanities fundraisers need to be flexible and optimize opportunities to ask for donations. Software can help arts organizations streamline fundraising efforts by keeping ticket sales, customer relationship management, marketing, and fundraising in the same platform.

Growth is possible: a poll found the vast majority of Americans had favorable opinions about the arts, believing that arts can be a way to understand other cultures, unify communities, and serve as a source of pleasure and enjoyment (Americans for the Arts 2018). An issue in expanding giving to the arts may be access – higher rates of attendance at arts and culture events are connected to higher income. Fundraisers might enlist boards to fund accessibility efforts that are most likely to be supported by local foundations and corporations. Finally, fundraisers can work with program managers to increase awareness through small "pop-up" events at a donor's home, or in public venues like parks, parking lots, or shopping malls.

Environment and Animals

Supporters and Constituents

Environment and animals is a newer category of giving and remains the smallest, only becoming large enough to be counted in 1987 (Giving USA 2021). Giving to these types of organizations has grown rapidly since that time, outpacing the growth in total giving.

Only 9 percent of U.S. households gave to environment organizations (GenerosityForLife n.d.), but high net worth donors gave at more than twice that rate (Indiana University Lilly Family School of Philanthropy 2021a). Giving is associated with higher levels of education, with 64 percent of these donors having a college degree (GenerosityForLife n.d.) as compared with 49 percent of all donors.

Giving in this area is growing for all types of donors, including major funders, foundations, and corporations. Funding approaches include everything from conservation efforts to prize-based philanthropy for developing new "green" technologies to policymaking efforts.

Issues that Fundraisers Should Consider

Like other areas that draw largely on high net worth households, fundraisers should consider strengthening planned giving programs. Pet owners are 70 percent more likely to give a bequest than nonpet owners (Freewill 2019).

Most young people are worried about climate change and believe that environmental issues are deeply important (Cohen 2019). Fundraisers in environment organizations should connect with this younger demographic through a variety of engagement opportunities such as giving, volunteering, and advocacy, with a goal of engaging these donors long-term.

Fundraisers might also consider connecting to funders of poverty alleviation, equity, and justice. Climate change will disproportionately impact people of color and households in low-income areas (Frosch et al. 2009), and individual donors and foundations have made that connection. Mega-donors and large-scale foundations have expanded their giving to climate change, especially relating to marginalized populations.

Conclusion

This brief introduction into fundraising in the different subsectors should serve as a reminder of the importance of ongoing education for all fundraisers, since external economic factors, demographic changes, and innovative technologies can all help to shape giving to the subsectors.

Discussion Questions

1. In what subsector is your nonprofit (or another that is of special interest) categorized? How is its fundraising similar or different from the data and analysis described in the analogous segment of this chapter?

2. Pick two or three subsectors. What differences and similarities are described in the sections? How might fundraising be modified for each subsector as a result?

Application Exercises

1. Visit generosityforlife.org and explore the generosity data section. Pick a subsector, look at the fact sheets, and experiment with generosity maps. What are some additional insights to complement the information in this chapter? Write up a few recommendations for nonprofit fundraisers in that subsector.
2. Develop a list of fundraising ideas, based on the information in this chapter, to expand fundraising beyond high net worth donors, with greater incorporation of different economic, racial, and generational groups.

CHAPTER NINE

GLOBAL PHILANTHROPY AND CROSS-CULTURAL FUNDRAISING

By Charles Sellen and Lilya Wagner

Philanthropy varies across countries; however, time-tested principles of fundraising provide a basis for widespread practices. This chapter addresses how philanthropy and fundraising have proliferated globally while building on distinctive cultural, religious, and societal traditions.

After completing this chapter, readers will:

- Understand the global growth and practices of fundraising.
- Identify differences and commonalities in the roots and traditions of generosity and philanthropy among countries and cultures.
- Integrate cultural differences in giving in North America with practices in cross-border and cross-cultural fundraising.
- Cultivate an appreciation for cultural differences in philanthropy and integrate acquired knowledge into practice.
- Identify, utilize, and share dynamic, emerging, and nontraditional practices within the profession.

The U.S. model for fundraising has been adapted by cultures globally, which in turn, have influenced fundraising in the United States. Fundraisers with knowledge about these diverse methods of philanthropy and fundraising benefit themselves, their nonprofits, their communities, and their donors.

Global Perspectives on Philanthropy

Philanthropy is as ancient as human existence. All nations and cultures have traditions of giving. Philanthropy was not a free-floating activity separated from the complex elements of the societies in which it resided, but was influenced, indeed structured, by the specificity of particular cultures (Illchman, Katz, and Queen 1998). Philanthropy research, however, has focused primarily on **W**estern, higher **E**ducated, **I**ndustrialized, **R**ich, and **D**emocratic (WEIRD) countries. Recognizing the universality of altruistic behaviors is crucial to discussing definitions and connotations of philanthropy across cultures (Wiepking 2021).

Understanding philanthropy as a global practice is essential for two reasons. First, civil society organizations (CSOs) or nongovernmental organizations (NGOs) have played a critical role in shaping local civil society because shifting social and political developments are frequently supported by philanthropy. Citizens have advocated for self-expression, freedom of speech, voluntarily gathering for common vision and goals, and to aid the poorer segments of society. Beginning in the 1990s the role of government in various countries was reduced because of the emergence of new democratic cultures, technological advances in communications, and the inability of many governments to keep up with even basic services. NGOs rose as service providers and advocates.

Second, with the emergence of CSOs came attention to philanthropy, as a renewed concept or as a new endeavor based on traditions. Fundraising grew dramatically globally and has continued to proliferate. This has influenced fundraising in the United States as the influx of refugees gradually changed the faces and preferences of today's donors, and knowledgeable fundraising professionals responded. In turn, U.S.-based people from other countries are increasingly contacted by foreign fundraisers to support, for instance, higher education institutions in their countries of origin (Indiana University Lilly Family School of Philanthropy 2020b).

Giving has also benefitted from charitable trusts or public benefit foundations (institutionalized philanthropy). Many practice grantmaking internationally (Schuyt et al. 2017; Johnson 2018; OECD 2018). They often seek alignment with the United Nations Sustainable Development Goals known as the 2030 Agenda.

Two reports measure the international diversity of philanthropy. The *Global Philanthropy Environment Index* examines 79 economies and five key dimensions: Ease of operating philanthropic organizations, tax incentives, cross-border flows, political environment, and sociocultural environment (Indiana University Lilly Family School of Philanthropy 2022). The *CAF World Giving Index*, updated yearly by the Charities Aid Foundation, illustrates the impact on philanthropy of war, famine, and other external factors revealing – without judgment – that some cultures are more amenable to philanthropy than others.

Global philanthropy increasingly became organized, with experience and advice crossing borders. This also increased the need for designing a "global philanthropic infrastructure" (WINGS 2018).

Global Development of Fundraising

According to Anheier and Daly (2004), "Transnational philanthropy has been and can remain a major force for improving the lives of millions of people worldwide, particularly in regions that are underdeveloped economically and are socially and politically fragile" (174). The *Global Philanthropy Tracker* (Indiana University Lilly Family School of Philanthropy 2020a), which measures cross-border flows of charitable giving from 47 economies, reported $68 billion of charitable gifts in 2018 – a dollar amount smaller than remittances, private investment, or official development assistance (ODA). The report also tracks global generosity in response to the coronavirus and climate change.

Some regions or countries experience fundraising as something managed from the Global North (such as UNICEF or CARE), but designed to assist locally. Some have relocated their international headquarters in the Global South. Other projects instituted by U.S. or European organizations establish programs to aid in carrying out management and fundraising. Alongside these efforts philanthropic traditions continue locally. Long-term success of international approaches in country requires involvement and support of local people and beneficiaries.

As immigrants come to the United States, they bring practices and perceptions about generosity that challenge fundraisers. U.S. fundraisers can grow when they realize philanthropy is present in every culture, and they are enriched by awareness of cultural issues, sensitivity toward differences, and genuine appreciation for international fundraisers' efforts and achievements.

Another complexity within international philanthropy, even in established democracies, is how charitable organizations are often different from those in the United States. This is even more true in fragile, emerging civil societies. Therefore, cultural differences as well as foreign legal and political environments must be considered when the U.S. model of fundraising is applied, or when people from those environments and circumstances migrate to the United States' nonprofit scene.

Some fundraising methods are widespread across nations (Breeze and Scaife 2015): special events, one-to-one approaches, direct marketing appeals, and community circles. Planned giving and bequests vary by culture and law. Some cultures are uncomfortable with charitable lotteries. New technologies involving digital money and social media are growing (Nonprofit Tech for Good 2020).

It is useful for fundraisers to know which principles of fundraising are universally adaptable as well as culturally and situationally appropriate. Some of these are:

- Making a strong, compelling case for funding, and expressing this case in differing ways to different markets (i.e., corporations, foundations, individual donors).
- Understanding donor motivations.
- The need to research and know the potential markets, to practice the exchange relationship in determining why a donor might give, and to diversify funding sources whenever possible.
- The impact of national and world economies on asking for and giving funds.

Some concepts are not universally adaptable. Prospect research is difficult in some places because of lack of research resources as well as prevailing attitudes toward privacy. Consider as examples the still-lingering hostility among Germans for those who build dossiers on prospective donors and the impact of nearly fifty years of KGB activity in the former Soviet Union. Since 2018, the General Data Protection Regulation (GDPR) protects the privacy and security of people in the European Union. It restricts the collection and storage of data by third parties, as well as access to personal information that American fundraisers are accustomed to relying on. Also, tax deductibility and the concept of planned gifts are foreign to many nations, with some shifts among advanced economies (OECD 2020).

International philanthropic concepts that must be considered when working with diverse donors in U.S. communities include (Wagner 2016):

- Differences in board responsibility and board members' involvement, expectations, and actions, with training on cultural differences and philanthropic expectations.
- Proximity is significant, how close the problem is to the donor and their family or community, and how well the nonprofit serves that community.
- Planned giving often requires more education in terms of mutual benefits and rationale.
- Tax incentives are less important than other motivations.
- Recognition must be done in culturally acceptable ways.
- Fundraising strategies vary by cultures, including face-to-face interactions and relationships.
- Leadership is more vital in some cultures than others.

In established democracies, charitable organizations differ from one country to another, even more so in fragile, emerging countries. The distinction between philanthropy, remittances, private investment, and foreign aid or official development assistance (Indiana University Lilly Family School of Philanthropy 2020a) is important to recognize when considering how money flows. Also, types of organizational forms for deploying philanthropy include:

- NGOs that establish foundations in other countries in order to access local funds (e.g., a university in Nigeria opening up a foundation for fundraising in the United States).
- U.S. organizations that raise funds overseas to enhance or supplement their fundraising in the United States (e.g., as described in Koenig's (2004) *Going Global for the Greater Good*).
- International development and relief organizations based in the United States, but with offices and fundraising programs in many parts of the world (e.g., World Vision).
- Affiliations and collaboration between local grassroots organizations and U.S. nonprofits (e.g., Counterpart International and a project with Zambian Orphans of Aids).
- U.S. institutions with branches in other countries (e.g., Webster University).
- Corporate giving by American companies (e.g., companies that are channeling a growing share of donations abroad).

People within the same country and in similar situations can approach philanthropy very differently. Nevertheless, there are often still similarities across cultures and religious traditions. Core values within families, or central to people's upbringing, have an initial and powerful influence. Faith, community, perceived gaps in structures of support, concern for injustice, and passion for arts are all examples of concerns people may also share during their lifetimes (Lloyd 2012).

Understanding international NGOs and fundraising aids comprehension of what is happening in the culturally diverse world inside the borders of the United States, including in local communities.

Cultural Influences and Fundraising in the United States

An article in *Harvard Business Review* stated, "The culture in which a person is born – the home culture – plays a key role in shaping his or her identity. No matter where people end up living, they retain a sense of themselves. . . . Even if they wish to forget their ancestry, the society to which they have moved – the host culture – tends to make that difficult because it views them as different and as newcomers, even pretenders" (Kumar and Steenkamp 2013).

Immigrants have two challenges that diminish over time. The first is to maintain their cultural distinctiveness while living in a foreign society. The second is affiliating themselves with the host culture and assimilating. However, assimilation can be challenging since "... it's all too common to rely on clichés, stereotyping people from different cultures on just one or two dimensions. ... This can lead to oversimplified and erroneous assumptions" (Meyer 2014b).

Advising corporations, *The Economist* (2013) stated, "Coping with cultural differences is becoming a valued skill. The advance of globalization ... means that companies have to deal with business and consumers from a wider range of backgrounds." Some companies embrace these complex differences to their advantage and the benefit of consumers.

Given these perspectives and cautions from the corporate sector, a conclusion presented in "Contextual Intelligence" (Khanna 2014) is that management practices – extrapolated also for fundraising – do not always travel well across borders because economic development, education, language, and culture vary widely from place to place. Tarun Khanna (2014) suggested that professionals have to develop contextual intelligence, to recognize what they need to know versus what they do not know and adapt to different situations, environments, and peoples.

Wagner (2016, 2) summarized:

Increasingly, our consciousness of cultural diversity has grown as population shifts occurred, repressive governments failed and in some cases disappeared, and minorities found a voice through civil society, nonprofit organizations, or NGOs (nongovernmental groups) in many places around the globe. As these organizations proliferated, so did the awareness that culture influences generosity and that fundraising practices need to adapt to those influences. Therefore the nonprofit sector everywhere but especially in the Western Hemisphere has grown increasingly aware that services to diverse population groups must be adapted culturally, and therefore fundraising must also take place with cultural consciousness in mind.

Fundraisers should diversify their donor outreach to various cultures in the United States to enrich their organizations and help reach across transnational borders as well.

Implementing Fundraising Principles across Cultures

Fundraisers must understand international NGOs and CSOs. Understanding diversity on a global scale helps them grasp what is happening in their communities, with their prospective donors, volunteers, and colleagues. It is imperative for non-profit leaders and fundraisers to learn and act on the impact of culture on philanthropy.

The United States may have the most advanced fundraising model (see world-wide typology of fundraising regimes compiled by Breeze and Scaife 2015, 588) developed over considerable time. It may have perfected fundraising techniques for contemporary times and have much to offer in terms of sharing expertise. But professionals also have a great deal to learn from other cultures. At times, fundraisers are either overwhelmed or intimidated by the complexity of cultures and the implications for fundraising as they survey the potential donors in their community or among their constituents.

Developing Cross-Cultural Fundraising Proficiency

Considering cultural traditions, behaviors, or religious implications of a particular population group may seem daunting. Moving from awareness to proficiency in fundraising from various cultural groups can be adapted from a corporate perspective. Global leaders, whom the authors of the *Harvard Business Review* article call the global elite, are those who have the ability to create value by helping their organizations adopt a global perspective. They suggest the following steps for acquiring a global outlook (Unruh and Cabrera 2013):

- Learn by thinking. Develop a broad outlook by thinking globally, moving beyond your frame of mind to unfamiliar territory.
- Observe, ask questions, and do not assume you know the answers.
- Study, both through formal education and via all the other means available today, such as literature, websites, webinars, foreign films, and many other means.
- Keep an open mind and heart. Understand that differences are not value statements but just that – differences. Welcome new experiences. Develop empathy.
- Learn by doing, by forging relationships, and by attending events.
- Begin locally and work with others. Seek opportunities to mingle, join, and collaborate with people from other cultures.
- Go international, even if it is venturing to a club event or a church service held by a culture other than your own.

A first step in culturally sensitive fundraising is to become aware of a particular culture. Talk with community leaders, develop an advisory group or council, show a genuine interest, read background material such as information on the country of origin, and be a listening learner.

Second, involve key people from the selected cultural group in the activities of the organization. Invite people to events or give special tours. Study giving amounts and habits, preferences, and practices of the culture. Much information is now available about giving by diverse populations and is quite easily accessible. (See Wagner 2016, based both on research and best practices.)

Third, test fundraising outreach strategies on the key people invited to be involved in some way. Do not assume without checking on their preferences and behaviors. Evaluate the outcomes of this testing step and modify campaigns accordingly.

Fourth, as the knowledge base and expertise grow, branch out even more and learn about the diversity within multicultural population groups. For example, while Hispanics may have some philanthropic traits in common, begin to identify the differences among philanthropic cultures within Central and South American nations. Continue to be involved with diverse communities and encourage volunteers to work across cultures.

Fifth, integrate diverse strategies into the fundraising program gradually, ensuring that all population groups are appropriately approached. For example, in relation to women's giving, efforts could consider how women in various cultures might give, giving among different generations of women, how long a donor has been in the United States, and differences by country or geographic area.

Applying Generalizations Judiciously

While the complete list of philanthropic cultural traits among the many cultural groups residing in the United States is lengthy, some generalizations are possible. Generalizations differ from stereotypes in that they are usually more widely applicable, more reliable, and less subjective or prejudiced. Usually, generalizations are the result of observing a large number of people and coming to conclusions, acknowledging that there are exceptions to every rule. Generalizations are often based on research and insights of knowledgeable professionals, and in the case of cultural aspects of philanthropy, generalizations allow some inferences (while acknowledging the exceptions) on how people of a certain country or culture operate when it comes to philanthropy (Peterson 2018).

There are three stages of giving in most population groups. The first is *survival*, sharing among social and economic peers, within an ethnic group, and building a new home and community. The second is *helping*, when financial stability is reached, giving to the less fortunate. The third is *investing*, going beyond responding and moving to a long-term vision of helping the community. Other generalizations include:

- Philanthropy often begins with the nuclear family. Then it reaches the extended family and fictive kin. Finally, giving may extend to the broader community.

- Religion often plays a significant role in developing the habit of giving, expectations of generosity, and promising blessings of giving. Virtually all religions promote and teach philanthropic values, although with differing emphases.
- Special occasions are often a platform for giving and volunteering.
- The concept of not giving to strangers is prevalent in many cases.
- Traditional, mainstream nonprofits are often shunned and there is at times some distrust due to previous experiences.
- Philanthropy may be practiced extensively but not always in ways recognized by nonprofits and the Internal Revenue Service (IRS).
- For many cultures, philanthropy is viewed in the broadest sense – gifts of time, talent, and treasure combined or given individually – and revolves around family, church, and education.
- Level of immediate need is important. Long-term support, such as planned giving, is not often a priority.
- Most cultural groups are influenced by leaders – community, religious, professional, social, and family.
- Much giving outside of the United States is without regard to tax benefits.
- Reciprocity is an accepted concept. As has often been advised, "serve before you ask." Also, helping those in ways they themselves were helped often motivates cultural groups.

These are generalizations, providing a basic foundation for acquiring more information about specific cultural groups. Some caveats are recommended. Remember, analyzing an overarching culture, such as Asian Americans, is a starting point but ultimately will be incomplete because of the diversity of the subcultures. Knowing how various cultures wish to be identified (e.g., Hispanic versus Latinx) is important. And, there is no substitute for learning from members of the cultural group and individual donors themselves.

Achieving Cultural Competence

Acquiring cultural proficiency is a privilege, a responsibility, and a pleasure. It need not be a chore but can be considered through a stepwise progression (Winkelman 2005):

1. Ethnocentric – ignorance of and dislike of other groups.
2. Contact – initial learning leading to development or withdrawal.
3. Awareness – recognition of the importance of cultural differences.
4. Acceptance – appreciation of differences.
5. Sensitivity – capable of culturally appropriate behaviors.

6. Competence – works effectively with other cultures.
7. Proficiency – capable of teaching cultural competence to others.

Winkelman (2005) further defined the four sectors of achieving cultural competence:

- Personal – including cultural self-awareness, personal management, and cross-cultural adaptation skills.
- Cognitive – including knowledge of cultural systems and beliefs and their impacts on behavior.
- Interpersonal – particularly knowledge of intercultural process dynamics and cross-cultural skills.
- Professional – including skills in intercultural relations, relevant to specific work activities.

Demographics continue to change. The savvy professional will realize the need to broaden the definition of philanthropy to include traditions, preferences, and ways of giving by diverse populations and not attempt to use a "one size fits all" mentality. To ignore or remain unaware of the rich and varied giving traditions of the world's populations is unwise, incomplete, and unbalanced.

Conclusion

Cultures shape how people relate to philanthropy. Culturally specific groups and populations are more likely to engage in philanthropy when their preferences are respected and understood. These are important lessons for fundraisers. There are significant and numerous changes in how philanthropy is done globally and in North America.

True, resistance to cultural understanding crops up periodically and is a two-way street in the global community, but the challenge is to be savvy and embrace changes for ultimate benefit to ourselves as professionals as well as our organizations and those we serve. Failing to acquire cultural proficiency would jeopardize our work and organizations in an ever more interdependent world.

Discussion Questions

1. Considering that asking and giving are universal practices in the world, what attributes does the U.S. model provide to help fundraise in other cultural environments?

2. What difficulties may fundraisers encounter while adapting the U.S. approach elsewhere? What can be learned from foreign countries' experiences and traditions?

3. Fundraisers sometimes adopt a "one size fits all" mentality in their strategies. Why might this attitude be detrimental to a culturally inclusive fundraising plan and what can a fundraiser do to overcome this mindset?

4. Describe how a fundraiser could evolve from developing recognition of another culture and its altruistic traditions and behaviors to proficiency in interacting with the culture and its donors.

Application Exercises

1. Examine the roots of your family and culture (whether recent or several generations back) and ask yourself the following questions: What traditions, behaviors, and communication styles are appropriate in your culture that are still current for you? What forms of philanthropy have been present?

2. With a critical eye, watch a movie (or TV program) addressing cultural differences that you may have not been aware of. How would you rewrite the script to make it more appropriate, now that your cultural sensitivity has been awakened?

3. Speak to a donor (or find a video of one online), who is from a different culture, about their philanthropy. Ask them about their influences and priorities and consider what they share in light of the generalizations and other information in this chapter.

4. Using a web search, explore the fundraising communications of an international nonprofit (i.e., World Vision, UNICEF), including reading their websites for different countries. Make a list of 3 to 5 differences in how the organization makes philanthropic requests, represents beneficiaries, and communicates its case for support across the countries.

CHAPTER TEN

FUNDRAISING FOR ADVOCACY AND SOCIAL CHANGE

By Shariq Siddiqui and Katherine Badertscher

Civil society has long centered around advocating for social change. Inequality, injustice, and marginalization have created conditions that galvanize dissenting voices. Social movements fight poverty, racism, violence, misogyny, climate security, discrimination based on sexual orientation, and other issues. Social movements require time, talent, and money to further their positive vision. There is a strong correlation between volunteering and fundraising (see Chapter 21). Those who put their time and talent into a cause are more likely to contribute financially.

After completing this chapter, readers will:

- Understand and explain how social justice nonprofit organizations develop and how their fundraising evolves.
- Explain why both service provisions and social change are fundraising goals for social justice organizations.
- Recognize social justice nonprofits' distinguishing characteristics and how they shape the organizations' fundraising approaches.
- Learn about the importance of advocacy to social justice fundraising.
- Understand how social movements establish institutional identity through fundraising.

Amplifying Social Movements

Sometimes external crises challenge social movements. In 2020 and 2021, the world faced a global pandemic with the COVID-19 virus outbreak, devastating the nonprofit sector. Demand for services increased while human and financial resources were depleted. Furthermore, the pandemic disproportionately impacted minority and vulnerable communities in the United States. Nonprofits led by people of color and women were less likely to receive government grants (Dorsey, Bradach, and Kim 2020). The American Civil Liberties Union observed that the CARES Act deprived many immigrants of benefits due to them, including testing and care, cash rebates, and unemployment insurance (Waheer and Moussavian 2020). Another report identified banks managing CARES Act loans giving White customers preferential treatment over Black customers (NCRC 2019).

COVID-19 forced most family members to remain at home, increasing isolation and exacerbating domestic violence. Stay-at-home orders, intended to protect the public and prevent widespread infection, left many women and children trapped with their abusers. Those most vulnerable were the least able to reach hotlines, shelters, or other resources (Evans, Lindauer, and Farrell 2020; Taub 2020). The murder of George Floyd by police officers in Minneapolis amplified long structural racism within the United States against African Americans and minorities. This event brought together people across the world to speak out against the treatment of Black people.

Fundraising Trends during COVID-19 and the Racial Justice Movement

The COVID-19 pandemic emerged and quickly spread worldwide. Recent reports suggest that nonprofits were able to use this crisis to strengthen their relationships with their donors through innovative practices. Engaging volunteers remotely, connecting with donors virtually, and reminding donors of organizations' cases for support were important ways in which nonprofits furthered their relationships and fundraising.

Donors, moreover, rose to meet the challenges of COVID-19 and the decline in individual income. These donations included an explosion of grant making from donor-advised funds (Theis 2020). Similarly, private and community foundations showed flexibility in their existing grant programs while giving out needed funds to their supported organizations, as many created emergency relief funds or shifted to providing general operating support.

Research from the Mays Family Institute on Diverse Philanthropy in the Indiana University Lilly Family School of Philanthropy (2021b) reported that the murder of George Floyd and similar incidents inspired a significant increase in racial justice charitable giving. Four trends in donor activity were identified:

- Crowdfunding to support the victims and their families.
- Direct support to Black-led grassroots organizations.
- Historically Black Colleges and Universities (HBCU) received more donations.
- With Black philanthropists leading the way, philanthropists of all backgrounds turned their attention to racial equity.

Muslim Americans provide an example of the unique ways particular groups and causes' fundraising was challenged by the pandemic. The pandemic was declared a month prior to the Muslim holy month of Ramadan. Ramadan is a time when most Muslim-American organizations raise a majority of their funds through event-based fundraisers. A marginalized racialized minority, Muslim Americans sought to reinvent their fundraising programs to meet the challenge of the pandemic.

Fundraising Resulting from Advocacy for Social Change

Two case studies – resisting Islamophobia and combating domestic violence – depict social justice movements that have followed a common trajectory. Both represent social movements of collective action that challenge systems of oppression, power, and control (Domestic Violence Network 2020; Pence 1987). Social movements originate with visionary leaders who identify a social issue and create local, grassroots networks. Networks then coalesce into formal nonprofit organizations that signal legitimacy and provide structures that outlive founders. Nonprofit organizations then deliver services, mobilize advocacy, and attract and retain human and financial resources for the long term. While local nonprofits originate to address community needs and raise funds, they often reflect and adapt to national and international movements.

A Racialized Religious Minority's Quest for Equality

Muslim Americans have been the subject of prejudice and negative attacks since the birth of the United States. Thomas Jefferson was attacked as being a secret Muslim for his argument that the U.S. president should not have to meet a religious test (Spellberg 2014). Spellberg argued that "by 1776 most American

Protestants . . . had generally been primed not only from the pulpit but by books and theater to think the worst about Islam and Muslims."

Muslim Americans have sought to give and raise resources for social good. Enslaved Muslim women in Georgia are reported to collect small quantities of rice every day from the rice paddies. They would also save small quantities of sugar from their rations. These Muslim Georgian women would then make a saraka cake given to children. It is argued that the word *saraka* comes from the Arabic word *sadaqah*, a form of Islamic charity. A famous enslaved Muslim-American, Prince Abdul Rahman, went to the North to raise funds to purchase the freedom of his children who remained in slavery. He was presented as a convert to Christianity (GhaneaBassiri 2012).

At the end of the nineteenth century, there were initial efforts to further Islam in America by Alexander Russell Webb, the former American consul to the Philippines, who established the American Mission (Abd-Allah 2006). In 1910, a leader of the Sufi order came to the United States and established the Sufi Order of America under the leadership of his earliest convert in San Francisco, Ada Martin (Curtis 2009; 2010).

No serious institutional building by Muslims occurred until the twentieth century through the efforts of African Americans, Indian missionaries, and Arabs. These include Moorish Science Temple in 1913, the Nation of Islam in 1930, the Federation of Islamic Associations in 1953 in the wake of Pan-Arabism, and the Muslim Student Association in 1963. All of these institutions were developed to protect and preserve Muslim religious identity in America during sustained anti-Muslim bigotry in America.

Muslim American veterans of World War II established the Federation of Islamic Associations (FIA) in 1954 to fight for the right of Muslim American soldiers to have an "I" (designating Islamic faith) rather than "x" (designating unknown or nothing) on their military dog tags. The FIA is significant for a number of reasons. First, it indicates a larger community of Islamic organizations in the country that sought to "federate" or organize together. Second, this organization was established by second and third generation Muslim American veterans. Finally, it predates the wave of Muslim immigrants to the United States that are a significant proportion of that community today.

Since 1990, several national public advocacy organizations have also been established, including the Council of American–Islamic Relations, Muslim Public Affairs Council, EmGage, and Muslim Advocates. Muslim Americans also have established many smaller regional or local public advocacy organizations.

Muslim nonprofits play an increasingly vibrant role in Muslim civic life in the United States today. However, Muslim nonprofits are smaller than average nonprofits, and many of them manage within severely meagre resources (www.guidestar.org). They often have inadequate cash reserves to maintain their standing amid financial recession, leaving them vulnerable to the pandemic-related economic downturn. Furthermore, many Muslims save the bulk of their charitable contributions for the most spiritual month of the year, Ramadan (Bakar 2008). Muslim Americans rely heavily upon fundraising events during Ramadan for their annual funding. Because COVID-19 measures were put in place a month before Ramadan, Muslim-American organizations had to quickly adapt to ensure continuity of their missions. This included leveraging technology to host virtual fundraisers. In addition, the organizations called on peer-to-peer networks to help meet their fundraising goals. They also invested heavily in digital marketing and fundraising. Finally, these organizations focused on personalized (yet virtual) relationship building to secure major gift fundraising. Many of these nonprofits were able to succeed despite challenges that were unique to them during the Covid pandemic. For example, Islamic Relief (USA), Helping Hand for Relief and Development, and other major charities report having their strongest fundraising years in history.

Recent academic studies about Muslim Americans provide further understanding of philanthropy among Muslim Americans. Despite the heightened levels of Islamophobia, Muslim Americans have consistently prioritized their religious institutions, domestic poverty relief, and education over civil rights, legal advocacy, and international causes.

Women Stand Up to Domestic and Gender-Based Violence

The social movement to combat domestic violence exemplifies an international call to action for broad social change and to meet desperately unmet needs (Carson 2001; Wilson 1977). The movement ushered in social change and public policy modifications at the local, state, and federal levels that created new fundraising opportunities and challenges. Advocates built on the momentum of the second-wave women's rights movement of the 1960s and 1970s to make domestic violence a public issue, initiate the shelter movement, and hold abusers accountable for violent behavior.

The movement to combat domestic violence and serve those who fled violent homes began with survivors (Pence 1987). Until the 1970s, survivors of wife beating had few resources: individual strategies for survival, help from willing friends or family, and child-welfare agencies, which might choose to remove their children from their homes (Gordon 2002). Successful advocacy on behalf of survivors resonated by the 1980s as the public gradually accepted that "battered" women were truly trapped in abusive relationships and that public intervention was justified (Rothenberg 2002; 2003). By 1990, "domestic violence" was the legally and commonly recognized description for the issue (Pleck 2004, 194).

The domestic violence movement's history addresses fundraising only tangentially. Erin Pizzey's *Scream Quietly or the Neighbors Will Hear* (1974) broke the silence about the hidden tragedy of battered wives. After opening a women's community center in 1971 in Chiswick, England, Pizzey realized that sheltering abused wives would be the center's mission. She operated on a shoestring budget, relying on individual giving and volunteering, yet virtually overnight became a model for the world.

By 1976, twenty safe houses existed; by 1982 more than 300, and by 1986 over 1,000 shelters operated across the United States (Pence 1987; Pleck 2004). In the seminal *Battered Wives* (1976), National Organization for Women (NOW) board member Del Martin outlined the operations and fundraising tactics of the first eight U.S. shelters, complete with the primer, "How to Set Up a Refuge and Prepare a Funding Proposal" (Martin 1976). The embryonic shelter system relied on founding coalitions as volunteer fundraisers, scraping together $1 and $2 gifts and in-kind donations to furnish safe houses. Volunteers staffed hotlines, ran shelters, and offered peer counseling. Occasionally county or state health departments made small grants, but community foundations and United Way branches eschewed most shelter startups. Martin (1976) recognized that most grassroots groups were "weak on fundraising" and warned, "Your whole project rests on your ability to raise funds, so you must fly in the teeth of the dragon" (247). Her funding proposal design has stood the test of time as well as her recognition that only with a national network of fundraising, public education, and lobbying could individual women's safety and public policy profoundly improve.

The change in public discourse about violence against women exploded longstanding myths about family unity and marital bliss. Once the silence shattered, fundraising for formerly taboo causes became increasingly acceptable. NOW's National Task Force on Battered Women/Household Violence (1975) further raised public consciousness and promoted shelters. Because the social movement arose simultaneously with the urgent plea for safe places, fundraising for the service provision of shelters became intertwined with public policy and social change (Dobash and Dobash 2000, 199).

Fundraising appeals that promised a values exchange with donors evolved in tandem with the social movement's success. Public sentiment, and therefore, donations, did not favor survivors until the domestic violence movement gained traction in the 1980s. Constant fundraising was required to keep shelters open, operate crisis services, provide security, and pay salaries (Tierney 1982). Early shelters followed either of two ideological orientations: feminist coalitions aligned with NOW or traditional social service organizations such as the YWCA. Shelters that conveyed goals, ideologies, and operations compatible with a broad range of donors, comparable to other social service agencies, were able to raise funds. Those that projected a militant, radical image were less successful. A shelter operator captured the fundraising climate: "traditional social service groups will be more likely to [raise] money than feminist organizations operating with a grassroots orientation" (Tierney 1982, 217). Leaders of the pathbreaking Duluth, Minnesota, Domestic Abuse Intervention Project (DAIP) recalled the early atmosphere of distrust as existing institutions, including funders, saw shelter advocates as "pushy, single issue, and inherently biased outsiders" (Pence and McDonnell 2000, 252). The more radical organizations, therefore, tamed their messaging toward safety and protection in exchange for state legislation and funding (Pleck 2004).

The movement influenced public policy in lockstep with shelter formation. Between 1976 and 1980, 44 states passed laws concerning wife abuse and eliminated the marital exemption from rape statutes. Advocates educated and enlisted local law enforcement to gradually erode institutional assumptions about domestic violence (Van Eck 2017). By the late 1980s, shelters had developed diversified funding sources that included private donations and a patchwork of local, state, and federal funds.

Two decades of advocacy culminated with the federal Violence Against Women Act (VAWA), part of the Violent Crime Control and Law Enforcement Act of 1994. VAWA included $1.6 billion in federal funding for a national hotline for survivors, shelters, and police departments (The Women's Legal Defense and Education Fund n.d.). VAWA represented crucial broad recognition of domestic violence as a public issue, signaling wide acceptance and social change in tandem with the service provision for basic needs: a true social justice achievement (Van Eck 2017).

The Julian Center in Indianapolis illustrates fundraising for the domestic violence movement. Founded in 1975 as the Julian Mission, it formed with equal missions of advocacy and guidance for women seeking to improve their quality of life through a "ministry of listening." Within two years, domestic violence formed the core of its mission; trauma-informed counseling and programming guided its work. In 1982, the Julian Center opened the state's first shelter at a confidential location with this fundraising appeal, "Now the words 'battered wife' are almost universally known and . . . there are shelters where battered women can stay when life at home becomes too violent" ("Backers" 1981, 10). Fundraising evolved from small, individual donations to include the United Way, Lilly Endowment, and Indianapolis Foundation. Local events brought concerns over rape, stalking, and domestic violence into public discourse and further raised the Julian Center's profile.

The Julian Center undertook a multi-year, multi-pronged approach to "change the public perception about domestic violence as a first step to reducing the incidence of domestic violence in homes." The organization ran concurrent public relations, public education, annual fundraising, and phased capital campaigns. The innovative campaign drew donated property and capital contributions from individuals, United Way, Lilly Endowment, and Central Indiana Community Foundation – rejecting named gifts because of the nature of the mission. The Julian Center headquarters, counseling center, and newly established Indianapolis Police Department domestic violence unit resulted ("To Combat" 2000, B1).

The ten-person police unit was a model nonprofit/government partnership. The shelter opened in 2001 and was filled to capacity almost immediately. By the early 2000s, the Julian Center had diversified its revenue sources to include private donations, special events, earned income from its thrift shop, earned income from county stipends, federated giving, and public and private grants (Julian Center private collection n.d.).

The Julian Center in 2010 stated its mission as twofold: (1) To provide counseling, safe shelter, and education for survivors, and (2) To educate the community about domestic violence and its impact on *all* lives (emphasis by author; Julian Center private collection n.d.). Yet domestic violence remains tragically high, and the unmet need overwhelming, despite the social justice advances of the past two generations (Domestic Violence Network 2020; "Domestic" 2021, A2; NNEDV 2020). VAWA federal legislation has been sustained and provides a predictable revenue source. Philanthropic and government support for family and gender-based violence organizations has grown steadily since 2012 (Mesch et al. 2020). Fundraisers and advocates continue to work hard and succeed, but the next generation has more work to do on behalf of survivors.

Conclusion

The case studies illustrate how fundraising for advocacy and social change develops and sustains nonprofit organizations that further social movements. The COVID-19 pandemic created unique challenges for social movements for survivors of domestic violence and Muslim Americans fighting islamophobia. Engaging these communities through their unique histories is crucial to continued fundraising for social change and advocacy. Centering fundraising approaches on experiences of those at the heart of the issues empowers the volunteers who drive these movements. Constantly engaging with the diverse narratives that come from these movements is critical to fundraising success.

Discussion Questions

1. How does a nonprofit organization's history influence its fundraising strategy?
2. How can a nonprofit organization balance social change and service delivery in its fundraising appeals?
3. Describe how your organization or another is connected to a national or international movement. Why is the connection relevant to the fundraising strategy?

Application Exercises

1. Research an advocacy or social justice nonprofit that interests you.
   a. What are its major sources of funds?
   b. How do you explain its fundraising model?
   c. How has it changed over time?
2. Your organization wants to expand its fundraising to Muslim-American donors. How will you increase fundraising through various vehicles? What do you think holds most promise for your organization?
3. Review a fundraising letter or other fundraising communication from a social justice nonprofit. Or watch a video of a staff member describing the organization's work and seeking support. What can you discover about how it seeks to connect with donors and express its mission? How does it describe beneficiaries of the cause with respect and inclusivity? What can be learned from its approach by other nonprofits?

PART THREE

AN ORGANIZATIONAL FOUNDATION FOR FUNDRAISING

CHAPTER ELEVEN

PREPARING THE ORGANIZATION FOR FUNDRAISING

By Jane Chu

Donors are gratified when their charitable support positively impacts the public good. Whether the work connects to education, health, human services, arts and culture, the environment, or serves those underrepresented, a competent non-profit attends to key operational components that build a strong organization and demonstrate legitimacy, paving the way for donors to consider making phil-anthropic contributions. This chapter addresses the organizational components of human resources and planning, and how the nonprofit relates to its external environment.

After completing this chapter, readers will be able to:

- Identify the fundamental components in a nonprofit organizational structure.
- Explain why each component is integral to successful fundraising.
- Understand how to align the parts within each component with fundraising.
- Differentiate between open and closed systems of interacting with the community.

Capable Human Resources

A prerequisite for fundraising in any organization is the human capacity to run the organization and its programs, and to design and implement a strategy for raising money.

Engaged Board of Directors

Nonprofit boards oversee the organization through governance and policy, and the directors are selected for their interest in and support of the organization (see Chapter 20). Board members have skills related to different aspects of the operations, and they participate in fundraising through personal donations and identifying prospective donors.

In addition to its legal duties, an engaged board should be representative of the community through racial and ethnic diversity as well as gender and age. However, nonprofit boards often lack diversity (Indiana University Lilly Family School of Philanthropy 2018b). An analysis of 1,456 nonprofit CEOs and their boards found more effective governance within organizations with diversity policies and inclusive behaviors in place (Buse et al. 2016). These organizations created a culture of inquiry to expand information, knowledge, and perspectives to ensure that their programs and services better reflected the needs and interests of the community.

Adequate Staffing and Volunteers

Hiring fundraising staff is a top priority, and the lead development director must serve on the nonprofit's senior leadership team. Nonprofits cannot solely depend on the development director to singularly produce the funds needed without investing in and providing training for a development team to support the fundraising process and systems (Bell and Cornelius 2013). Hiring and training a fundraising team can increase funding available to support the rest of the organization, including for other staff positions.

The CEO also can engage donors and prospective donors. Gone are the days when the CEO only led administrative operations, leaving the fundraising to the development team. All employees – including those in nonfundraising occupations – are valuable to the fundraising process. For example, if a prospective donor is interested in how the nonprofit's financials are structured, an employee on the accounting team might accompany the executive leadership to meet with the donor to help answer questions.

Operational volunteers also send out a meaningful message to the community when they get involved with the organization. These folks have stepped forward to help while receiving no financial remuneration.

Comprehensive Planning

Written plans convey stability, signaling to potential donors that the nonprofit is confident of its future and empowered by its vision for a thriving society. An attainable and inspiring strategic plan together with an operational plan that articulates how the strategic plan will be achieved and holds the organization accountable for results provide evidence of an effective organization.

A Sound Strategic Plan

A compelling strategic plan of an effective nonprofit has five components: (1) setting goals and objectives, (2) analyzing the situation, (3) considering and selecting alternatives, (4) implementing the plan, and (5) evaluating the plan. The strategic plan is cultivated through learning gained from previous plans and operational experiences. The tools nonprofits use and the myriad organizational characteristics (e.g., organizational age, budget size, revenue streams, number of participants or clients) may lead to differences in how nonprofits execute their plans (Crittenden and Crittenden 2000). At the same time, the benefits from creating a strategic plan include making decisions that are tied to the organization's purpose, improving coordinated responses, collaborating with external partners to address broader public issues, and improving the morale and competency of the organization (Bryson 2010). An operations plan aligned with strategy directs finite resources for greatest impact.

A Comprehensive Operations Plan

An effective operational plan involves every aspect of the organization, not just programs and services. What are the nonprofit's financial goals? How are volunteers utilized? What do the annual income and expenses look like for each program, in the current year and future forecasts, and how does this inform fundraising?

Employees in every department and team know the organization's direction. They associate their specific jobs with achieving goals while having ownership of the big picture strategy. Documenting an operational plan not only identifies the best resources to use, it also helps employees make better decisions on how best to utilize those resources. The fundraising plan ultimately is crafted to facilitate the operations and achieve the mission articulated in the strategic plan.

Other Forces

In crafting their plans, nonprofits must be aware of the forces that may influence their desired trajectory and activities. Are there potential roadblocks? If so, how might they be addressed? Is the nonprofit entering a capital campaign? If so, are there other capital campaigns in the community that may share similar prospective donors, ending in a competition for the same dollars?

Effective nonprofits also incorporate crisis planning – a process revealed by the COVID-19 pandemic as essential. Will current strategies be able to adjust to unforeseen changes? Are there multiple scenarios of the plan waiting in the wings, if needed? An examination of 43 nonprofit leaders identified potential crises ranging from disasters and inability to carry out their mission to internal stakeholder challenges and unanticipated occurrences (Gilstrap et al. 2016). When organizations created a systematic plan that simulated a crisis and how they might respond, they were able to be better prepared for the unexpected. They analyzed their strengths and vulnerabilities, identified the needed components of a responsive contingency plan, and designed a crisis communication process to give internal and external stakeholders a sense that a plan of action was in place, generating enough calm to better address abnormal situations.

A Commitment to Evaluation

A tangible way for nonprofits to show credibility and worthiness of donor contributions is by building an evaluation component into the organizational plan. Evaluation signals that the nonprofit holds itself accountable for its own performance. Fundraisers can utilize the evaluation findings to help donors see the organization's progress when the results of the work are measured against initial goals, objectives, and strategies. That same evidence also can identify needed improvements. Donors can deduce that the effective nonprofit is a responsible steward of their contributions.

The demand for evaluating results has increased over the past two decades, augmented by a surge in the number of nonprofits. Between 2005 and 2015, the number of nonprofits registered with the Internal Revenue Service (IRS) increased 10 percent from 1.41 million to 1.54 million (McKeever 2018). Simultaneously, waves of economic decline have increased the need for additional nonprofit services in the community. Donors feel the pinch of shrinking revenues, and must discern where their scarce dollars should go, so they look to evaluation findings as verifiable evidence of which nonprofits are higher performers (Vaughan 2010).

Different types of nonprofits serve the public in distinctive and sometimes contrasting ways, and their evaluation measures will reflect this. Despite the variety of evaluation approaches, three precautionary pitfalls can inform the creation of relevant measurement guidelines for any nonprofit.

It's More than Just Financial

There has been a propensity for donors to consider a nonprofit's financial profit margin or administrative percentage to determine a return on their investment. The tendency to apply a lone financial metric to determine the nonprofit's overall effectiveness can bypass the nonprofit's mission and overemphasize efficiency (Vaughan 2010). To be sure, nonprofits must follow good business practices and be cost-effective while simultaneously delivering quality programs for mission impact.

Outputs versus Outcomes

Sometimes, when nonprofits assemble their data for evaluation reports, there is a tendency to confuse outputs with outcomes, even though the two measurement categories are distinct. Externally, donors are looking for outcomes to evaluate the nonprofit's impact, while internally, nonprofits identify specific output measures as part of their program activities.

Outputs are valuable for nonprofits to insert into their strategic plan. How many people will the organization train? What types of workshops will be produced? Did the education team visit three schools or ten? These outputs represent the nonprofit's productivity level. Outcomes, on the other hand, provide longer-term results of the nonprofit's work. How were constituents affected by the services provided? Did they increase their skills? Did unemployed clients get a job? Did the participants gain insights as a result of the nonprofit's work? Strickhouser and Wright (2015) note that outcomes shift the nonprofit's reporting requirements from counting outputs to conceptualizing, measuring, and reporting results.

Quantitative versus Qualitative

Is it better to utilize quantitative indicators and statistics or case studies and stories to show a nonprofit's effectiveness? Quantitative measures, it is argued, are more objective, while case studies and stories are subjective. But Hall (2014) cautioned that one particular approach to evaluation is not fundamentally superior to another; rather, there are inherent strengths and weaknesses to all evaluation techniques. Instead of identifying the single best evaluation approach to apply to the entire nonprofit sector, it is more effective to understand the advantages and disadvantages of an array of evaluation tools, depending on what results need to be measured, coupled with the type of service each nonprofit provides (Willems, Boenigk, and Jegers 2014).

While donors and nonprofits both agree on the importance of evaluation, each tends to utilize evaluation feedback for different purposes, with donors wanting to validate where to give their dollars and nonprofits wanting to apply the findings to improve their services and client responsiveness. These discordant purposes may lead to selecting measurement indicators that are less relevant to one side than the other. Campbell, Lambright, and Bronstein (2012) suggested that donors and nonprofits collaborate in advance to develop optimal evaluation processes and measures, also incorporating ways to learn from those clients who benefit from the nonprofit's work.

Two case studies demonstrate how organizations can align strategy, planning, and evaluation, laying the groundwork for both successful programs and fundraising.

Case Study 1: Carnegie Hall Lullaby Project – New York

Many people recognize Carnegie Hall in New York as a legendary venue, presenting the world's greatest artist to its stages for more than a century. But Carnegie Hall also believes in the power of the arts to reach out and instill well-being into the community, so through its Weill Music Institute education program, it launched the Lullaby Project in several national and international locations, where pregnant women and new mothers worked with professional musicians to compose personal lullabies for their babies. In New York City, the Lullaby Project served mothers at ten sites, from clinics, hospitals, and homeless shelters to programs for adolescent and young mothers, correctional facilities, and other community programs, representing a diverse group of racial and ethnic participants: Black American (50 percent), Hispanic/Latina (33 percent), mixed heritage (9 percent), and other/unspecified (8 percent).

From the beginning, Carnegie Hall wanted to know how and why the Lullaby Project mattered, and its evaluation process grew as the project evolved. The organization chose to utilize qualitative data to assess the impact of its work. Internally, it created outputs to determine whom it wanted to reach and evaluated 66 participating mothers from select New York City sites. The data were collected through naturally occurring evidence from the project itself: attendance sheets with demographics from participating mothers, audio-recorded and transcribed songwriting work sessions between the mothers and professional musicians, mothers' lullaby journals in which they wrote letters to their babies and sketched ideas for their songs, and the lullaby lyrics.

Carnegie Hall Lullaby Project outcomes included mothers noting that out of the process of writing and composing a lullaby, they experienced sharing and support from their social and family networks. The Lullaby Project lyrics, written in multiple languages, helped their young children to hear new vocabulary and language. Mothers also discovered insights, positive emotions, and a sense of personal meaning and hope for the future, in comparison with their earlier, less positive, more matter-of-fact comments reflecting a level of uncertainty (Wolf 2020).

Case Study 2: KC Scholars – Kansas City

The KC Scholars organization was created to increase the opportunities for low- and modest-income students and adults to attend college. The organization provides scholarships, financial incentives to promote college savings, and support services for those who likely would not have otherwise attended or completed a post-secondary credential or degree. From its inception, KC Scholars built an evaluation component into the program. As it understood more about how and where the program made an impact, it updated its evaluation measures accordingly in order to be relevant.

KC Scholars keeps track of its outputs, making approximately 500 scholarship awards and jumpstarting 500 college savings accounts each year. To date, it has supported more than 10,000 ethnically and racially diverse participants. The KC Scholars program noted a vulnerable time when such students might want to drop out of college, so as part of its evaluation process, the KC Scholars program tracked longer-term outcomes to reveal that 92 percent of adult learners persisted in college from the first semester to the second semester of year one (Tankersley-Bankhead personal communication 2020 and 2021).

Fundraising Operational Requirements

What are the fundamental elements needed on a daily basis to maintain a smooth operational fundraising process for a nonprofit organization?

Personnel

Fundraising management positions vary by the needs of the organization, depending on the amount of time and capacity required for the task. These personnel range from volunteers and part-time employees to full-time development teams. Long-term successful fundraising necessitates having the attention of someone who is competent to plan, organize, and manage the fundraising process. Professional staff on a development team understand the value of involving board members, volunteers, and other appropriate staff to assist in the fundraising process. Fundraisers also understand the importance of diversifying their funding sources instead of depending on one or two major gifts to carry out the annual operations. They coordinate when and how to best approach each of their sources of support, including individual donors, corporations, foundations, and government, and continuously identify and cultivate new and prospective donors while also soliciting current donors.

Case for Support

A compelling case for support inspires potential donors to give to the organization. It should align with the organizational plan, emphasize the strategies, and serve as a communication tool for the organizational leaders, not just with the fundraising team (see Chapter 13). Include stories and illustrations of the nonprofit's work and the subsequent results, gleaned through evaluation. Ask the question: "What would be at stake, if not for the work of this nonprofit?"

Donor Database

The donor database allows a nonprofit to create a centralized, comprehensive list of current and prospective donors. Each donor record in the database provides information on previous giving alongside other personal characteristics that are helpful for long-term relationship cultivation. An array of donor database software programs is available, ranging from basic spreadsheets with donor information to complex systems with deluxe fundraising metrics and elaborate donor search functions. Regardless of which donor database the nonprofit employs, fundraising staff should keep the database current with each donor's giving records as well as the occasions and events where each donor was engaged and ensure that the donors' giving amounts align with the organization's finance and accounting records.

Gift Range Chart

The gift range chart estimates how many donors are needed at different giving levels to achieve the nonprofit's overall fundraising goal. Typically, only a handful of donors are able to make contributions of significant amounts, and as the gift range levels descend, the number of donors giving more modest amounts will increase. Although gift range charts have often been associated with capital campaigns, they are also valuable for annual fundraising and other purposes (see Chapters 22 and 35).

Gift Acceptance Policy

A gift acceptance policy informs the kinds of gifts a nonprofit can accept. In addition to cash, can the nonprofit accept other assets (i.e., stocks, property, automobiles), and if so, under what conditions? Are there gift sources that run counter to the organizational mission (i.e., an alcohol company and addiction recovery nonprofit) and cannot be accepted? Occasionally, a nonprofit is also offered a significant contribution from a donor who has a tainted reputation that contradicts the mission and integrity of the organization. Should the nonprofit accept the contribution? A gift policy created in advance and approved by the non-profit's board of directors can provide guidance on such dilemmas.

A Fundraising Culture

Effective nonprofits understand that fundraising is not just relegated to their development staff. Creating a culture of philanthropy requires establishing a shared vision and priorities that involve their board members, executive leadership, and staff across the organization who believe in philanthropy as a legitimate source of support (see Chapter 1). All can participate in raising funds as ambassadors of the organization, and in cultivating relationships in the community (Bell and Cornelius 2013). Having a philanthropic culture elevates fundraising from being an appendage that brings in money to developing a set of values and behaviors that are fundamental to the nonprofit's mission.

Connecting with the External Environment

Fundraising readiness also depends on being relevant and transparent to the external environment. Over the past 25 years, nonprofits have increasingly moved away from a closed-system mindset of sequestering themselves from the community, and toward an open-system approach of cooperating and adapting to their surroundings (Lu Knutsen and Brock 2014), which, in turn, can open the door to a broader base of support. These nonprofits understand the strong relationship between how well they function and communicate internally – from individual employees across departments, part-time workers, contractors, and volunteers to executive leadership and board members – as well as externally, including donors, civic and business leaders, and community partners. They create lists of constituents, asking themselves, who needs to know about the work we are doing? What do they want to know? How often should we communicate with them? What approaches should we take to inform them? Astute nonprofits communicate the results and reasons for their work, and how their performance will be measured, setting context for their constituents as to how the operations align with the organizational mission. Accountability is essential to the good stewardship of constituents. Consistent updates, internally and externally, inspire board members, employees, volunteers, donors, and other external stakeholders to stay connected through their time, expertise, and donations.

In an open system, nonprofits demonstrate agility when their external environment changes. During the COVID-19 pandemic, nonprofits had to quickly adjust the ways they carried out their services. For example, in San Diego, California, 428 nonprofit leaders noted that their services were dramatically disrupted, even while community needs, such as food and supplies for vulnerable populations, increased (Dietrick et al. 2020). Nonprofit financials revealed a decline in program revenues and fees for services that made paying their employees difficult. In addition to needing emergency supplemental funding, the nonprofits noted that advanced scenario planning, especially in finance and dealing with ambiguity, and staying in touch with donors and constituents would be their top recommendations for dealing with future crises.

Those in the philanthropic sector attuned to social inequities work to even the playing field for people who are marginalized and underrepresented. For example, the Ford Foundation committed all its grantmaking to take a stand against inequality, and the Andrew W. Mellon Foundation prioritized programs that reinforce equity and social justice (Cascone 2020b). Warner Music Group and the Blavatnik Family Foundation set up a $100 million fund to strengthen the music industry and combat racism following the 2020 violence incurred on Black people and the global health emergency that inordinately affected people of color (Klinge and James 2020). By supporting leadership, programs, structures, and systems that demonstrate the principles of diversity, equity, inclusion, and access, these organizations connected to their external environment to initiate necessary societal changes.

Conclusion

Nonprofits, no matter their size, can pave the way for philanthropic contributions when they are simultaneously working in the community and strengthening their internal operations. They build strong organizations through capable boards, employees, and volunteers. Their strategic and operational plans address work throughout the organization and are tied to tactics and evaluation measures. They dedicate the necessary time and resources toward integrating their fundraising program, including people and systems, as a core function necessary for mission attainment. They create a culture of philanthropy within and outside of their organization. They proactively stay engaged with constituents and ensure that their services are relevant in the community. They hold themselves accountable for their performance. Donors are attracted to supporting nonprofits that deliver effective work in the community and operate with productive and sustainable results.

Discussion Questions

1. Why is it important to make the fundraising staff and systems a priority in the organization?
2. Review the two case studies in the chapter and assess what makes their evaluation efforts successful. What are some potential pitfalls in how nonprofits evaluate their performance?
3. Describe the differences in nonprofit behavior within closed systems versus open systems.

Application Exercise

Select a nonprofit organization. Examine its website and create a general analysis of the organization's structural components:

1. How many board members and staff does it have?
2. In what ways do the board and staff represent the diversity of the community?
3. Does it publish an organizational plan? Does it meet the criteria in this chapter?
4. What kind of evaluation information is provided?
5. Is the leader of the development staff included in the executive leadership team?
6. What else can you discover about the fundraising personnel?
7. Can you discern whether the nonprofit operates as an open or closed system?

CHAPTER TWELVE

BUILDING A COMPREHENSIVE FUNDRAISING PROGRAM

By Jeri Patricia Gabbert and Paula J. Jenkins

A comprehensive fundraising program focused on the growth of the organizational mission requires approaching fundraising with a development perspective and structuring fundraising through careful planning and attentive communications. It also requires attention to donors at all levels who give through the multitude of fundraising channels available to organizations.

After completing this chapter, readers will be able to:

- Identify and explain the primary purposes of each component of an integrated and comprehensive development program.
- Recognize the multistep process of the fundraising cycle.
- Identify and distinguish among fundraising programs and purposes.
- Assess strengths and weaknesses in fundraising planning and execution.

The main ideas, concepts, and language in this chapter are largely drawn from foundational works by Hank Rosso (1991) and Tim Seiler (2016a, 2016b), which appeared in previous editions of this book and remain central to successful fundraising.

Development Planning and Communications

Ethical fundraising is more than just asking for money. Instead, fundraising is a complex process and a function of development. Development involves fostering an understanding of another person's philanthropic interests and values; exploring how those values may be aligned with the values of an organization; and connecting those values through an invitation to participate in the three central behaviors of philanthropy – donating time, financial resources, and voice through advocacy. The development process creates and enhances relationships with (potential) donors to ensure current and future funding, and requires thoughtful planning and communication. The knowledge gained through the development process then can be utilized by the fundraiser to invite prospective donors to become donors.

Organizations with fundraising plans are likely to raise more money than organizations without a plan (Nonprofit Research Collaborative 2019). Planning calls for vision and leadership and sets the direction for the future by answering the following questions (Seiler 2016b):

- Who are we?
- What distinguishes us from other nonprofits?
- What do we want to accomplish?
- How will we reach our goals?
- How do we hold ourselves accountable?
- Why is our organization best poised to address this human/societal need?

The answers inform all aspects of organizational life, including mission, goals, objectives, programs, and evaluation, which are then the basis of fundraising. Chapters 11 and 19 provide structural tools for organizational and fundraising planning.

Planning provides the direction and script for communications. The best communications strategies in the most effective development programs help to cultivate and nurture in-depth relationships with prospective and current donors. Effective communication provides opportunities for constituencies to understand the organization's case for support, to endorse the case, and to become involved in the active articulation of the case.

A solid development program will serve the organization well regardless of unforeseen circumstances that may arise such as a natural disaster or health crisis. A comprehensive, strategic, timely, and thoughtful development program implemented before a crisis or other unexpected events will help the nonprofit navigate and endure obstacles and challenges. History has shown that even in times of crisis donors still contribute, and oftentimes give even more (Giving USA 2021).

A comprehensive development program also addresses the moral imperative of inclusive communications and fundraising. Prioritizing inclusivity in communications and fundraising strategies and practices advances diversity, equity, and inclusion (DEI) while grounding fundraising practices in equality, antiracism, and justice.

The Fundraising Cycle

Fundraising is straightforward and common-sense: the right person or persons asking the right prospective donor(s) for the right gift for the right program at the right time in the right way (Rosso 1991). It is not, however, easy. Fundraising is a multifaceted process requiring extensive involvement of staff and volunteers in a series of interrelated steps described in the fundraising cycle, a tool developed by Hank Rosso (1991). When effectively managed, this complex process leads to the successful alignment of all the six "rights": right donor, right solicitor(s), right amount, right time, right reason, and right way. The professional fundraising executive oversees the process, serving as catalyst and coach for all involved in its planning and execution.

Fundraising is cyclical (Seiler 2016a). The fundraising cycle is based on the awareness of marketing principles and how they are applied to the fundraising process (see Figure 12.1). The continuous cycle is a disciplined planning and management tool, continuously addressing the internal work that is required (and sometimes overlooked) prior to donor solicitation. The fundraising cycle ensures that the nonprofit has appropriate systems and processes in place to address shortcomings and support meaningful donor engagement.

The cycle includes many discrete steps constituting the whole (Seiler 2016a). Step 1 is labeled "Planning Checkpoint: Examine the Case" and 13 additional steps follow, proceeding clockwise. Soliciting a gift comes at step 13, demonstrating the cycle's emphasis on comprehensive planning before asking for charitable donations. The cycle includes many planning checkpoints – for preparatory tasks to be completed "behind the scenes." It includes action checkpoints to involve volunteers and generate the gifts, as well as one strategic checkpoint following contributions, before beginning anew. Skipping or shortchanging steps could lead to gaps in the fundraising plan or generate oversights, leading to less-than-desirable fundraising results. The cycle describes all the elements necessary for establishing a fundraising program. Once the program is established, it is not necessary to repeat all the steps of the cycle on an annual basis. That does not mean the cycle should be "retired," but rather returned to periodically as a tool for evaluation in changing circumstances.

FIGURE 12.1. THE FUNDRAISING CYCLE

The Fundraising Cycle
Awareness of Marketing Principles

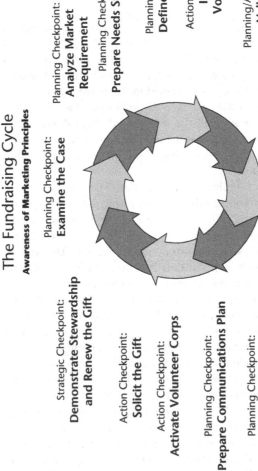

Planning Checkpoint:
Examine the Case

Planning Checkpoint:
Analyze Market Requirement

Planning Checkpoint:
Prepare Needs Statement

Planning Checkpoint:
Define Objectives

Action Checkpoint:
Involve Volunteers

Planning/Action Checkpoint:
Validate Needs Statement

Planning Checkpoint:
Evaluate Gift Markets

Planning Checkpoint:
Select Fundraising Vehicle

Planning Checkpoint:
Identify Potential Giving Sources

Planning Checkpoint:
Prepare Fundraising Plan

Planning Checkpoint:
Prepare Communications Plan

Action Checkpoint:
Activate Volunteer Corps

Action Checkpoint:
Solicit the Gift

Strategic Checkpoint:
Demonstrate Stewardship and Renew the Gift

Source: Tempel, Seiler, and Aldrich, eds., *Achieving Excellence in Fund Raising, 3rd ed.,* p. 11. Copyright © 2010 Jossey-Bass Inc., Publishers. Reprinted by permission of Jossey-Bass Inc., a subsidiary of John Wiley & Sons, Inc.

Step 1: Planning Checkpoint: Examine the Case

The first step is the examination of the case for support. The organization's case for support justifies its existence and articulates all the reasons it deserves philanthropic funding. Each nonprofit organization must develop a distinctive case based on clearly defined and understood community needs. The case for support describes how the nonprofit is distinct and different than others in the community while being managed effectively and efficiently. Importantly, the case explains how the donor's gift will make a difference. It must provide persuasive and intelligent responses to questions potential donors and others may ask (see Chapter 13).

The case for support provides the backdrop for developing fundraising materials, and creates the basis for institutional priority-setting, decision-making, and evaluation. It should be a living document, reviewed regularly by internal stakeholders such as board members, executive leadership and staff, volunteers and donors, keeping it relevant and fresh rather than stagnant and dated.

Step 2: Planning Checkpoint: Analyze Market Requirements

In analyzing market requirements, the nonprofit must validate its case for support against the wants and needs of populations of potential gift sources. For example, if an organization serving the homeless wants to build a new shelter to house more clients, does that idea resonate with individuals in the community? The corporate sector? Foundations? Do the potential donors in each of these markets believe the organization's capabilities to address the issue in a way that warrants philanthropic support?

Coupled with significant attention and response to feedback from organizational beneficiaries and information derived from research and best practice, the marketplace of prospective donors and funders provides validation for the nonprofit's proposed solution. Market validation is critical to successful fundraising. If the organization seeks funding from individual, corporate, and foundation markets, it must test its case for support in each group.

If the respective markets do not understand or accept the importance of the needs being addressed by the nonprofit or the nonprofit's strategy, fundraising faces a serious obstacle. Donors give to those organizations that address the needs they are aware of and care about and approach the issues in ways that are effective.

Step 3: Planning Checkpoint: Prepare Needs Statement

The needs statement results from the organization's plan for carrying out its work toward mission fulfillment. After annual and long-term program plans are designed, financial planning defines the resources required to implement the programs and produce results. The revenue needed to support the program plan is a justification for fundraising.

Needs statement preparation involves the board members, some major donors, and other key volunteers who can affect the organization and its fundraising potential. The needs statement shapes future fundraising goals and objectives and must include ongoing programmatic needs as well as longer-term needs for capital improvements and financial stability such as an endowment.

Step 4: Planning Checkpoint: Define Objectives

Organizational objectives, as determined through strategic planning, must be translated into specific and measurable solutions for identified problems. If the mission statement explains "Why," and goal statements answer "What," objectives become the "How." Earning credibility among market sources (individuals, corporations, and foundations) requires objectives that are realistic and achievable. Seiler (2016a) provided the acronym **SMART** to help clarify what effective objectives must be:

- **S**pecific,
- **M**easurable,
- **A**chievable,
- **R**esults-oriented, and
- **T**ime-determined.

Fundraising objectives would follow the same principles. For example, a fundraising objective would be: "The organization needs a reliable stream of operating support to invest in new technology infrastructure. By developing a monthly giving program, we will enhance the stability of the annual fund by converting 10 percent of annual donors to this program in the next year." This objective gives a specific illustration of how the organization will achieve an organizational purpose and execute the activities through the fundraising plan.

Step 5: Action Checkpoint: Involve Volunteers

While board members have been involved in the planning and management process thus far, they continue to play a critical volunteer role in the next steps of the fundraising cycle. Fundraising responsibility and authority rests with the entire governing board, and the development committee will likely take an active role in identification, cultivation, solicitation, and stewardship of potential and current donors. An effective gift solicitor is one who believes in and is committed to the cause, and early involvement prepares volunteers to be solicitors of their peers. Since people give to people and peers give to peers, mindful attention must be given to diversity, equity, and inclusion. The most effective gift solicitation is that of a peer volunteer asking for gifts in a face-to-face solicitation (Schervish and Havens 1997).

Step 6: Planning/Action Checkpoint: Validate Needs Statement

Volunteers should be involved in the study and validation of the organization's needs. Are they defensible and credible? Staff cannot assume that past acceptance of needs during planning is sufficient for volunteers to continue donating and raising philanthropic support. It is also important that those staff other than fundraisers and leadership are informed and invited to contribute to planning in this stage or before. Ongoing review and corroboration are required.

Step 7: Planning Checkpoint: Evaluate Gift Markets

Gift markets should be identified and evaluated to determine ability and perceived ability to support the nonprofit's programs through charitable gifts. Each market should be analyzed according to the potential and complexity of the source of funding and the resources needed to raise that funding. Encouraging a diversity of gift market sources is essential for achieving a resilient donor base in the dynamic and ever-changing fundraising environment.

As noted previously, the most likely sources of gifts are individuals and foundations. Including bequests, giving from individuals constitutes 78 percent of all charitable giving (Giving USA 2021). Meanwhile, foundations account for 19 percent of donated dollars, with growth in the foundation sector resulting from increased giving to community foundations and family foundations. Another reason is the phenomenal growth in donor-advised funds (DAFs), which have increased by 80 percent since 2015 (National Philanthropic Trust 2021a). Meanwhile, 4 percent of charitable support is provided by corporations (Giving USA 2021). (The combined percentage for individuals, foundations, and corporations exceeds 100 percent due to rounding.)

Step 8: Planning Checkpoint: Select Fundraising Vehicle

Next, fundraising staff must now select the appropriate fundraising vehicles and strategies for each market based on organizational needs. Fundraising vehicles include annual fund, capital campaigns, major/special gifts, and planned giving. Strategies include direct mail, special events, grant proposals, personal solicitation, telephone calling, and digital fundraising. Each of these activities is a piece of a larger plan to achieve fundraising goals.

Just as market evaluation calls for diversity of funding, selection of fundraising vehicles should explore every opportunity for raising gift funds to carry out the organization's mission. The management process of analysis, planning, execution, control, and evaluation is key to the successful use of vehicles and determining fundraising effectiveness.

Step 9: Planning Checkpoint: Identify Potential Giving Sources

This step refines the gift market evaluation process and identifies prospective donors in each market. Prospective donor development is based on identification of data, which provides baseline information on each prospective donor's linkage, ability, and interest (see Chapter 14). Instinctually, for many the exercise of finding prospective donors begins with identifying individuals, corporations, and foundations with the most money (ability). However, such exercises are futile unless immediately followed with efforts to determine linkage to the nonprofit and interest in the cause. When lacking the latter two characteristics, there is no real reason for a funder to choose a particular nonprofit to support.

Volunteer leaders can play a helpful role in this step by assisting in the development of priority lists of specific giving sources. This type of involvement builds ownership of the fundraising plan and process among volunteers (see Chapters 20 and 21).

Step 10: Planning Checkpoint: Prepare Fundraising Plan

The previous steps focused on analysis, information gathering, and preliminary planning. The results now can be translated into a proposed fundraising action plan. Professional fundraising staff draft the fundraising plan and involve volunteer leaders in refining and validating the plan.

The plan should:

- allocate the resources necessary for implementation.
- quantify how much money will be raised for what purposes.
- include a calendar and timeframe.
- define the methods for each fundraising program.
- include roles and responsibilities of fundraising staff, other team members, and volunteers.
- include methods for monitoring and evaluating to facilitate modification as needed.

Step 11: Planning Checkpoint: Prepare Communications Plan

The next planning step is the preparation of a communications plan. Donors' awareness of the organization's mission, goals, and objectives is fundamental to successful fundraising. Assuring this knowledge requires a strategy and diligent attention from fundraisers and communications professionals (see Chapter 16).

Fundraising communications must go beyond the casual dissemination of information and instead facilitate an external understanding of the nonprofit and its purposes, resulting in a desire to contribute to mission fulfillment. Effective fundraising communications create a "values exchange" whereby interpersonal relationships are built through two-way interaction providing a means for sharing mutual interests and concerns.

Step 12: Action Checkpoint: Activate Volunteer Corps

The effective nonprofit organization must continually attend to and expand its volunteer corps to strengthen fundraising results. It must also build structures to support volunteer involvement in fundraising, such as training, confidentiality agreements, and job descriptions (see Chapter 21).

One in three adults (30.3%) volunteers at a philanthropic organization and fundraising is a common activity (AmeriCorps 2018a). Although nonprofits rely on volunteers to fundraise in varying degrees, peer-to-peer efforts remain a powerful source of philanthropic inspiration for donors to all sorts of organizations. While some larger nonprofit organizations such as colleges, universities, and hospitals may not use volunteers in active gift solicitation, there is still a critical role for the volunteer leader in other parts of the fundraising cycle. And, volunteer engagement is in itself a form of donor development since the giving rate for volunteers is higher than nonvolunteers (AmeriCorps 2018a).

Step 13: Action Checkpoint: Solicit the Gift

Twelve phases of the cycle have been completed. Some gifts – from the board, the staff, and key volunteers – may have been discussed or documented already. But, generally speaking the process now culminates in asking for charitable donations.

Solicitations are made in person, through direct mail, on the telephone, in a grant proposal, via digital media, or at a special event. The solicitations are driven by the case for support, align with the fundraising plan, and are shaped with information about the prospective donors. Solicitations may take the form of thoughtfully constructed letters with compelling requests and email follow-ups echoing the core message (see Chapters 23 and 24). For larger gifts, fundraisers, organizational leadership, and volunteers personally visit potential donors, typically following a longer relationship (see Chapters 33 and 34). No solicitation is more compelling than one conducted by volunteers who personally request gifts for "their" nonprofit. For example, a bank president and nonprofit board member who accompany a gift officer on a solicitation to another local banker are showing their commitment while also legitimizing the organization and request.

A missed step or inadequate completion of any previous step will now become evident when a request, in any form, does not resonate with donors and fundraising goals cannot be met.

Ultimately, this step is a dignified process of asking with pride for help with the nonprofit's important work and sharing of the joy of giving (Rosso 1991).

Step 14: Strategic Checkpoint: Demonstrate Stewardship and Renew the Gift

Successfully soliciting gifts is not the end of the cycle. In fact, it is only the beginning of a deepening relationship between the nonprofit and a donor who is invited to become more involved as a volunteer, advocate, event attendee, and/or renewed donor. Appropriate acknowledgment, stewardship, accountability, and disclosure are key components to renewed and increased gift support from donors (see Chapter 17).

The fundraising cycle then is occasionally refreshed and revisited to demonstrate continued need, worth, and effectiveness.

The Four-Legged Stool of Fundraising

Funding acquired through the fundraising cycle serves the organizations' financial needs, which fall into several categories: ongoing operating and general program support, special purposes, capital (building and equipment), and endowment (Seiler 2016b). A comprehensive fundraising program generally includes annual giving (the annual fund), major gifts, capital campaign, and planned giving, as illustrated by the Four-Legged Stool, shown in Figure 12.2, and briefly described in the subsequent paragraphs.

The annual fund is the first building block for all fundraising programs. Donors' contributions support current, ongoing programs that fulfill the organization's mission (see Chapter 22). Often, the annual fundraising goal is determined by the organization's budget: philanthropic contributions fill the "gap" that other sources of revenue do not cover to meet the organization's programmatic and operating needs. The annual fundraising program builds donor loyalty to the organization through recurring gifts, and donors with the habit of giving grow more interested in and involved with the organization. Over time, these regular givers become the base group for the other fundraising programs: major and planned gifts and capital campaigns (Rosso 1991; Seiler 2016b).

FIGURE 12.2. THE FOUR-LEGGED STOOL OF FUNDRAISING

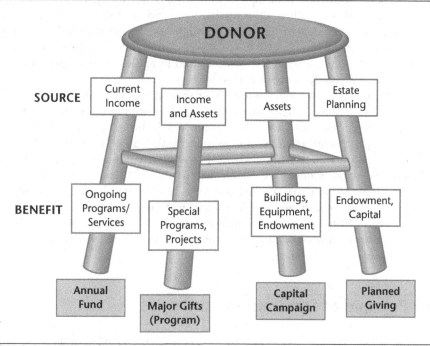

Source: The Fund Raising School 2021, 34.

Major gifts are larger than the typical gift to the annual fund, raising the donor's commitment level and bonding them to the organization (see Chapter 33). Major gifts are not only defined by the amount, but by the importance to the organization and by their relative complexity, compared to an annual gift, in both fundraising strategy and donor effort. These gifts are often restricted for particular and special purposes within the organization and can be made through asset transfers (like stocks) and other means in addition to cash contributions. Major gifts themselves can be counted within an annual fund and are an essential part of fundraising campaigns with larger goals.

Campaign fundraising is defined through an established timeline and clear goal amount (see Chapter 35). The term *capital campaign* originally indicated a focus on expanding an organization's physical assets (i.e., the building, facilities, land); it also has come to be understood as a structure for increasing assets of all kinds. Capital campaigns also support program development and expansion, and increasingly, they support the creation and expansion of endowments. Comprehensive capital campaigns are also common in universities and other large nonprofits whereby all fundraising (annual fund, endowment, capital) is positioned under a campaign umbrella. Although campaigns will include gifts of many sizes, large gifts are imperative to reach goals, often requiring donors to give from resources beyond their regular income (and to exceed their regular gift levels). Gifts are often pledged over a period of years.

Planned gifts are contributions other than immediate cash gifts. They require "planning" as a result. They are commitments made in the present – sometimes without organizational knowledge – from which the organization benefits later, usually at the death of the donor or a surviving beneficiary (Seiler 2016b) (see Chapter 36). Planned giving has been a growth area in fundraising in recent years (National Association of Charitable Gift Planners 2020). Charitable bequests, within donors' wills, are the simplest form of planned gift, but there are many other options of varying complexity and with a range of different donor and organizational benefits. Every nonprofit seeking to build an integrated development program should be involved in planned giving at least through wills, retirement plans, and insurance policies.

Donor Pyramid of Fundraising Strategies

A model for visualizing fundraising is the Donor Pyramid of Fundraising Strategies, showing how organizations distinguish fundraising programs and orient donor giving and engagement with a positive trajectory. Donors move from making annual gifts to major gifts, to the capital gift, and ultimately to the planned gift (Seiler 2016b) (see Figure 12.3).

The pyramid illustrates the common nonprofit approach for organizing fundraising programs functionally and philosophically to make decisions about staffing, resource delineation, and planning. The goal is to create avenues for engaging prospective donors and strengthening relationships with those with the greatest capacity and interest, thereby moving them up the pyramid. The fundraising strategies become increasingly personalized in each tier of the pyramid. Impersonal, annual giving strategies are used to build a broad base of donors. Long-term, relationship-based strategies are deployed as donors grow their involvement and larger gifts are made. The number of donors who advance up the pyramid grows smaller at each tier. While there are some exceptions to the trajectory – a surprise planned gift or a major gift early in a fundraising relationship – this model is the baseline for structuring most fundraising programs.

FIGURE 12.3. DONOR PYRAMID OF FUNDRAISING STRATEGIES

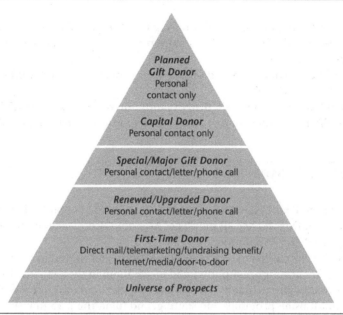

Source: The Fund Raising School 2021, 73.

The donor pyramid demonstrates how the components of the integrated development program are interwoven (Seiler 2016b). Effective fundraising recognizes the interdependencies of each program with the others and manages the programs as mutually reinforcing.

Conclusion

Sustainable fundraising that stands the test of time requires strategy, communications, and a comprehensive approach. The Fundraising Cycle provides a step-by-step process to begin and maintain a fundraising program. The Four-Legged Stool and the Donor Pyramid are additional planning tools for structuring programs and allocating human and financial resources. This chapter is a framework to orient subsequent chapters in this book. It organizes efforts such as annual fundraising, major giving, and planned giving as part of a larger whole, whereby success in annual giving begets positive outcomes further up the pyramid in major and planned giving. All manner of organizations can create, explain, review, and renew their comprehensive fundraising program using principles from this chapter.

Discussion Questions

1. What are the steps in the Fundraising Cycle? How might the difficulty of completing the steps vary for organizations of different ages, sizes, and cause-orientations?
2. How should volunteers and other constituents be engaged within the Fundraising Cycle?
3. What kinds of resources will an organization need to be successful in each of the different fundraising programs and approaches described in this chapter?

Application Exercises

1. Using the Four-Legged Stool model, illustrate your organization's fundraising program. Does it have all four legs? Are some stronger than others? Which legs need greater attention?
2. Use the Donor Pyramid of Fundraising Strategies to track current fundraising strategies at your organization and locate them in the pyramid. Identify areas of strength and weakness. (Or find an organization of interest online, explore its fundraising programs and staffing, and fill in the pyramid with what you discover.)

CHAPTER THIRTEEN

ARTICULATING A CASE FOR SUPPORT

By Timothy L. Seiler

Hank Rosso sometimes began teaching a case for support with the tongue-in-cheek statement: "We need money. You've got it. Give it to us." He was then quick to stifle the ensuing laughter by insisting that this is NOT how to articulate a case for support.

Nonprofit organizations seem to assume intuitively that their work merits philanthropic gift support. If they assume potential donors and funders share this intuitive knowledge, they are mistaken. Nonprofit organizations require a case for support, one more compelling than Rosso's make-believe expression of a case.

This chapter proceeds from the development of the general case for support to the case statement. The chapter also describes the roles of staff and volunteers in doing the work of case preparation.

After completing this chapter, readers will be able to:

- Explain the case for support as the justification for philanthropic fundraising.
- Identify the components that help build a case for support.
- Enumerate the key elements in fundraising case statements.

Defining Case for Support and Case Statement

A case for support is a *sine qua non* for nonprofits. It is the rationale underlying fundraising, the reason nonprofit organizations deserve philanthropic support, not why they need money. Without a case for support, a nonprofit does not have a right to seek philanthropic support, to raise money.

It is important to understand that *case for support* as a phrase might be daunting to some, even a cause for panic. Andy Brommel, Director of Communications Consulting at Campbell & Company, fears that the term is fundraising jargon that confuses more than clarifies. Brommel believes that when fundraisers hear case for support, they think, "Oh, no. I have to write some long document." However, the case for support is "not a long document; it's a set of messages that prepare prospective donors and funders for solicitation" (Brommel 2020).

A case for support is an argument or set of arguments explaining why a nonprofit deserves gift support. The case for support is bigger than the organization and relates to a cause being served. The case for support is an encyclopedic accumulation of information, parts of which are used in different iterations to argue that the organization deserves gift support for working in service to the cause.

A *case statement* is a particular articulation of the case for support. A specific case statement is not as large or universal as the case for support; that is, a case statement is a specific illustration of some of the elements making up the case for support. A case statement selects and articulates specific points from the overall case for support (Seiler 2001).

Preparing the Case for Support

The case for support is central to an organization's work, and examining the case is the first step in the fundraising cycle, a step-by-step planning and implementation model addressed in Chapter 12.

The preparation of the case begins with understanding that nonprofit organizations raise money to meet community needs. Unmet social needs leads to the creation of nonprofit organizations, and the case for support is built on how well the organization meets those needs. The effectiveness of the case depends on how well the organization serves the cause.

The case for support is the bedrock on which philanthropic fundraising is built. It is the urgent call for a solution to a problem, the meeting of a need. The persuasiveness of the case relates directly to the nonprofit's ability to solve problems and to adjust to changing market or societal needs. The case for support is the expression of the cause, addressing why anyone should contribute to the advancement of the cause. The case is larger than the organization's financial needs; it is larger than the organization.

Preparation, development, and validation of the case begins with staff. Organizations with communications or marketing staff often draw on their writing expertise for case development. For smaller organizations, development staff, or whoever has responsibility for managing development and fundraising, need to take the lead. Development professionals typically serve as interpreters of the concerns, interests, and needs of the external constituencies. The staff must be able and willing to report on constituencies' perceptions of the organization, especially perceptions of prospective and current donors and organizational clients and beneficiaries.

It is not uncommon for fundraisers to discover that not everything is perfect among the constituencies. Occasionally, constituencies are misinformed or uninformed. Sometimes there are perceptions that the organization is not effective. Perhaps constituencies lack confidence that gifts are needed or that they make a difference. Finding out how to address these concerns will strengthen the case for support. Fundraising staff must know the organization inside and out and must represent the constituencies as well.

Getting others involved, though, in case development is important. Seeking the ideas of key constituencies – board members, volunteers, donors, and potential donors – is particularly effective in enlisting leadership for articulation of the case in fundraising. Having a role in developing and validating the case increases the enthusiasm of those who will articulate the case. They will question what puzzles them or challenge what disturbs them. If they are representative of others from whom gifts will be sought, their questions and challenges will strengthen the case for support. "Involve those you want to own and use the case. Facilitate structured discussions of key questions and clarify core messages before writing any long document. Test your case via surveys, focus groups, maybe even a feasibility study" (Brommel 2020).

Key Information Components of a Case for Support

The development of the overall case for support begins with compiling and collating information components that provide the background for everything a potential donor might want to know about the nonprofit organization. These components probably already exist in the organization. They become an information bank, from which case statements are developed. The information database is a starting point for the development of specific case statements.

The following 10 key components, adapted from Rosso (1991), must be in ready form inside the organization and must be available, accessible, and retrievable when needed for developing a case for support:

1. *Mission statement* articulates awareness of the cause and provides insight into the problem the organization addresses.
2. *Planning and evaluation* illustrate strategic, operational, fundraising, and program plans that demonstrate commitments and provide evidence of strengths and impact.
3. *Goals* articulate what the organization aspires to achieve in solving the problem.
4. *Objectives* state what will be accomplished by reaching the goals.
5. *Governance* illustrates the character and quality of the organization as shown in its volunteer leadership and governance structure.
6. *Staffing* illustrates the competence and qualifications of the staff.
7. *Finances* describe expenses associated with providing programs and services as validation for philanthropic gift support beyond earned income and fees for service.
8. *Programs and services* explain how the nonprofit serves its constituencies and the community.
9. *Service delivery* points out advantages, strengths, and effectiveness of how people access the programs and services.
10. *History* tells of the organization's successes over time and demonstrates legitimacy.

Mission Statement

A mission statement is a philosophical statement of the human or societal needs the nonprofit organization meets; it explains why the nonprofit exists. A mission statement is an expression of the values in which the organization believes and around which it does its work.

It is often believed that mission statements express what an organization does, as exemplified by a statement such as "It is the mission of the agency to provide after-school care." This is more a goal or purpose statement rather than a mission statement.

A statement containing an infinitive phrase – to deliver, to provide, to serve – is a goal or purpose statement, telling what the organization does. A mission statement, on the other hand, explains *why* the organization does what it does. An effective mission statement provides a base for identifying beliefs and values. A good mission statement often begins with words such as "We believe" or "We value." For example, a shelter for animals might use the following as its mission statement: *Concern for Animals* believes that all animals deserve humane treatment. Because we care about all animals, *Concern for Animals* provides shelter and food for abandoned and unwanted animals.

Here is another example of a statement that is more of a goal or purpose statement than a mission statement and a suggested revision to reveal more clearly the values/beliefs of the organization.

Original text:

• "The mission of Global Hope is to combine the resources of individuals and organizations around the world to provide emergency relief and economic and social development."

Suggested revision:

• "Global Hope believes that wherever people are suffering, compassion and hope can help them endure and thrive. Global Hope exists to mobilize people and resources to meet the needs of suffering people in a hurting world. This is achieved through a variety of programs, including disaster relief and agricultural, education, medical, and economic assistance." (Seiler 2001, 22–23)

The mission statement gives donors and potential donors an opportunity to find the shared values between them and the nonprofit organization. Because people give to organizations with values they share, it is important for organizations to express their values clearly. Because the first step in the fundraising cycle is to examine the case for support, and the first element in the case is the mission statement, it is critical that the mission statement be one of values. Mission is "why," and even in the corporate world, good business starts with "why." Simon Sinek (2011) popularized this idea in his book about how great organizations and great leaders do things differently. Sinek argues that people become deeply involved with a product, service, movement, or idea only when they understand the why behind it. It all starts with why.

Planning and Evaluation

This component should describe the process used for planning and the measures taken for evaluation. Program plans precede fundraising plans and validate the need for service. Therefore, the first step in beginning to develop a case for support originates in the organization's strategic plan. The organizational plan articulates where the organization is going and what it takes to get there. Fundraising plans demonstrate the need for philanthropic support for the organization to carry out its strategic plan.

Evaluation provides a means for demonstrating effectiveness and efficiency in programs and accountability and stewardship of philanthropic resources. Evaluation processes must be determined as early as possible and be constantly updated. They need to show responsiveness to those who are served.

Planning and evaluation documents show that the organization takes its work seriously and holds itself accountable. This inspires confidence in donors and potential donors.

Goals

If the mission statement answers "why"; goals answers "what." What does the organization do? Goal statements are general expressions explaining what the organization wants to accomplish as it seeks to meet the needs or resolve the problem described in the mission statement. Goals are usually stated in ambitious terms and often come out of strategic planning processes. Goal statements guide the organization toward fulfilling the beliefs expressed in the mission statement. Because organizations frequently have multiple programs, goals will be multiple; that is, the organization will have several program-related goals, some of which require funding, and funding the program goals leads to the formulation of fund-raising goals.

Objectives

Objectives differ from goals in degree of specificity. Objectives are more precise and more measurable than goals and explains "how" the organization expects to reach its goals. These, too, should be defined as part of strategic or annual planning efforts.

A fundraising goal might be "To increase annual fund income." Objectives for how to reach that goal might be "To increase annual giving from individuals by 5 percent in the next fiscal year" and "To increase corporate giving and corporate sponsorship by 15 percent in the next fiscal year."

Governance

The issue of governance of nonprofits is critical in attracting charitable gifts. The governance structure indicates the character and quality of the institution. This component should contain relevant information about how the board is composed and how it functions. Complete dossiers of board members and organizational material such as by-laws and conflict-of-interest statements should be part of the governance component.

Staffing

As governance is a matter of integrity and quality, staffing is an indicator of competence and professionalism. Descriptions of staff should illustrate the credentials and qualifications of staff, paid and volunteer, and include resumés as appropriate. Staffing patterns reveal how the organization delivers programs and services effectively.

Competent, skilled staff, together with dedicated, energetic board members, offer a persuasive case for potential contributors to make charitable gifts. It is essential to keep this component current. Staff members should review their resumés at least annually, updating continuing education and professional development activities.

Finances

Financial information about the organization links budgeting with objectives and program descriptions. Information about finances gives a clear picture of how the organization acquires and spends financial resources. This financial overview establishes and validates the need for philanthropic gift support, justifying fundraising. The overview also offers the opportunity to demonstrate fiscal responsibility and accountability for prudent use of funds.

In short, the fundraising plan needs to be based on the organization's full financial plan. Making a case for philanthropic support requires the ability to show a clear picture of all income and expenses for the organization.

Programs and Services

The programs and services component should include descriptions of how the organization provides services to its clients and meets community needs.

One of the best ways to show the importance and impact of the programs and services is to collect testimonials from clients and beneficiaries telling their personal stories of how the organization helped them. If confidentiality issues constrain the use of personal testimonials or stories, third-party endorsements provide a helpful substitute, as can anonymous statements and data about the types of people served and the outcomes.

Potential donors and funders are more likely to respond to fundraising appeals when they recognize that people are truly benefiting from the nonprofit's work.

Service Delivery

The next component is explaining the delivery of programs and services. This should explain how people access programs and services – in person, online, or through other means. Occasionally, an organization's facility is a distinguishing factor: visibility, accessibility, and convenience are advantages for both physical and virtual service provision.

This component might include plans for renovation, expansion, or new construction, and will help make the case for capital fundraising.

History

In talking about its history, a nonprofit should focus on its accomplishments in terms of how it has served its constituencies and its communities. The history should capture the spirit of the people, both service providers and beneficiaries. The focus should be on the organization's heroes as exemplified by the stories people tell about the organization and its impact. History is the heroic saga of the organization and proves its legitimacy and trustworthiness.

With these components in place, an organization is ready to develop case statements, for fundraising and for informing other types of constituent communications.

Case Statements

Case statements order and present information for communications, public relations, and fundraising, and take the form of brochures, foundation and corporation grant proposals, direct mail letters, email messages, website information, campaign prospectuses, news releases, newsletters, speeches, even face-to-face gift solicitations. It is helpful to think of a case statement as the "case at work" (Rosso 1991).

In developing case statements, the focus is on answering these questions:

1. What is the problem or social need central to our concern?
2. What services or programs do we deliver to respond to this need?
3. Why are the problem and the services important?
4. What constitutes the markets (funding sources) for our services?
5. What distinguishes us from others who are seeking support from the same markets?
6. Do we have a written plan with a statement of philosophy (i.e., mission, vision, values), goals and objectives, and programs and evaluation?
7. What are the specific financial needs for which we seek gift support?
8. How do we demonstrate our competence to carry out our defined programs?
9. Who is associated with our organization: staff, key volunteers, trustees, or directors?
10. Who is likely to support us?

FIGURE 13.1. AD FROM DANA-FARBER CANCER INSTITUTE

At Dana-Farber, defeating cancer is more than our purpose. It's our passion.

THE

Our team of Harvard Medical School physicians and researchers works relentlessly...turning our discoveries into life-saving

THRILL

breakthroughs for patients everywhere. Here, we've created personalized vaccines that can shut down melanoma.

OF

And we helped develop a blood test for lung cancer patients that eliminates the need for invasive biopsies.

DEFEAT

This is the art of defeating cancer and, here, we have it down to a science.

DANA-FARBER
CANCER INSTITUTE

Let's defeat cancer...once and for all. Visit **dana-farber.org/defeatcancer** 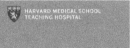 HARVARD MEDICAL SCHOOL
TEACHING HOSPITAL

Source: Used with the permission of Jan Lawlor, Vice President, Philanthropy Marketing, Dana-Farber Cancer Institute and The Jimmy Fund Division of Philanthropy, Brookline, MA.

In writing such case statements, it is helpful to remember that the purpose is to stimulate potential donors and funders to take a series of steps, ultimately ending in the decision to make a gift or grant. Certain qualities of writing must exist to stimulate this sequence:

- Relevance of the issue – to capture attention.
- Proximity to donors – to engage their interest.
- A sense of the future – to build confidence
- Immediacy – to instill conviction.
- Excitement – to create a desire to act.
- Importance – to take action.

Successful case statements move potential donors/funders to take action; that is, to motivate them to participate in the nonprofit's work by making a gift or grant.

One writing strategy to capture attention is to take something normal, or expected, and reverse it or "turn it on its head." The following example from the Dana-Farber Cancer Institute (see Figure 13.1) is an outstanding example of how to do this. While this is not an advertisement designed to fundraise, it grabs attention and compels the reader to read what is between the lines.

Capitalizing on the television sports show *Wide World of Sports*, which was known for the familiar opening voice-over, "The thrill of victory, and the agony of defeat," this ad's bold inversion of the wording captures attention and demands a reading of the full text. This is a compelling device for capturing attention and likely leads to the next steps in the sequence designed to prompt the reader to take action.

The process of developing and articulating a case for support takes a series of steps, from creating and/or collating key components to developing "long documents" (see the beginning of this chapter) for information, education, and fundraising.

Tailored to the Audience and Supporting the Mission

Case statements must fit the interests and needs of donors and funders, including individuals, corporations, foundations, and others. Case statements, then, are tailored to the audience – recipients of direct mail like new donors, donors renewing gifts, and donors upgrading their gifts; recipients of email messages and readers of social media posts; corporations and foundations receiving formal grant proposals; and donors being asked for gifts in personal, face-to-face (or virtual) meetings.

While the iteration of the case is specific in each instance, what all case statements have in common is adherence to the mission of the organization. It is the thread that holds everything together.

Effective fundraising case statements must do the following:

1. State a need: a community need, the cause being served.
2. Document the need: external evidence that confirms the problem.
3. Propose strategies to meet the need: organizational goals, objectives, programs.
4. Identify who benefits: recipients, beneficiaries, community at large.
5. Demonstrate organizational competence: governance, staffing, mechanics of service delivery.
6. Specify resources required: philanthropic support being sought.
7. Tell how to make gifts: checks, credit/debit cards, stocks, donor advised funds, online, mobile devices.
8. Explain benefits of giving: answer the question "What's in it for me?" as a donor/funder; show what the organization will do with gifts.

The answers to the questions should all be found in the 10 components that help build the case for support.

Conclusion

In articulating the case for support, it is critical to keep the donor/funder uppermost in mind. Case statements must be understandable to the audience; it is unwise to assume the audience knows the organization at all, let alone as well as the creators of the case know the organization. Case statements should avoid "insider language," what Brommel (2020) referred to as jargon, and must be written in the clear, precise language of the vernacular.

Developing and articulating a case for support is the first step in the fundraising process. Reviewing the case occasionally is a way to ensure that it is current and relevant. The following questions can be a starting point for a review:

1. Who are we and why do we exist?
2. What do we want to accomplish?
3. How will we accomplish it?
4. How do we hold ourselves accountable?
5. What distinguishes us from others doing similar work?

Answering these questions regularly validates the organization's case for support, and prepares the organization to develop messages that articulate boldly and compellingly why it deserves gift support.

Discussion Questions

1. What is the difference between "case for support" and "case statement"? Which group of people inside and outside an organization need to be included in the development of each one?
2. What challenges could an organization face in developing a case for philanthropic support and articulating through your various messages? What are the potential ramifications for fundraising and what are some ideas for overcoming these difficulties?

Application Exercises

1. Review the mission statements for several organizations. What types of words are used to express the "why"? Decide which one is the most effective illustration of why the organization does what it does and why the organization matters. (Note: You may also want to consider your organization's mission and vision statements for this exercise.)
2. Using "The Thrill of Defeat" ad in this chapter as an example, consider how to take the ordinary and "turn it on its head" in developing a short case for your organization or one you are interested in.
3. Find an example of a case statement online. Review it to see how it responds to the questions in the "Case Statements" section of this chapter and whether it demonstrates the qualities of writing that are recommended in the same section.
4. Because stories help move people emotionally, engage your board (or development committee) in a storytelling exercise in which all participants tell their own stories of why they are engaged with your organization. (Or find some videos of donors and volunteers talking about their nonprofit involvement.) Compare what you hear to the eight components of effective case studies in the last section of this chapter.

CHAPTER FOURTEEN

IDENTIFYING AND QUALIFYING POTENTIAL DONORS

By Catherine Brown and LaKoya S. Gardner

While stewarding current donor relationships, fundraisers also continually search for new donors to strengthen and grow the nonprofit organization. Well-established tools and processes can be utilized to identify which potential donors represent fundraisers' best opportunities to cultivate new charitable gifts.

After completing this chapter, readers will be able to:

- Understand and use the Rosso Constituency Circle Model.
- Identify, qualify, and develop donors using the Linkage Ability Interest (LAI) and Linkage Involvement Advocacy (LIA) principles.
- Follow a three-part framework for donor research, including the roles and responsibilities tool.
- Understand the importance of ethical research and management of donor information.

Introduction

Identifying and qualifying donors can be like standing in a crowded venue. People attending a sporting event or concert have at least some interest in the activity or they would not be there. How much interest can be discerned by observing various clues? Some may be wearing the team jersey or the singer's concert T-shirt. Some are sitting in the upper deck while family members, friends, longtime fans, or celebrities are in those seats closest to the stage or field. The level of the seat they have chosen can be a signal to their connection or linkage to the team or performer and ability or capacity to afford those seats.

The Rosso Constituency Model

The arena or stadium in the context of fundraising is illustrated by the Rosso Constituency Model (see Figure 14.1), named after Henry Rosso, the founder of The Fund Raising School. The nonprofit and those it serves are at the center of the model just as actors are on the stage or athletes are on the field. The model is not intended to value the donor as lesser or more important, but to provide a strategy to organize fundraising planning time and resources.

FIGURE 14.1. ROSSO CONSTITUENCY MODEL

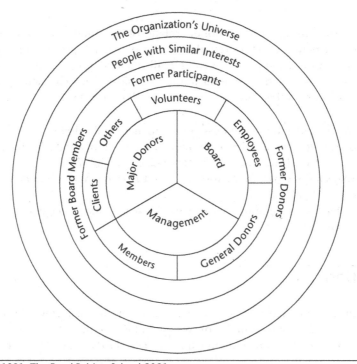

Source: Rosso 1991; The Fund Raising School 2021.

Similar to the people sitting in the front row of the arena, donors who are most closely connected and committed to the nonprofit and the organization's mission are at the center of the model's concentric circles. Board members, well-established major donors with long giving histories, and management staff are typically the most committed constituents. The first two complete circles from the center include those who are somewhat connected or involved, but not as deeply as those in the center. This might include volunteers, employees, general donors, staff, former donors, or previous board members. The outer rings of the constituency model, or the seats in the top sections of the arena, contain those who are aware of the nonprofit's mission and work, but less so than the other levels. These people have similar interests (i.e., soccer fans in the baseball stadium or opera buffs in the symphony theater) or have a similar but general interest (i.e., sports fans or music lovers).

To be effective in these conversations, fundraisers must learn about donor motivations and variations in philanthropy among groups of people. Part Six of this book provides a place to begin.

Expanding the Circle

Several methods are available for adding new names to the donor database. A nonprofit can purchase or rent lists of names of people whose interests are the same or similar to its mission. Smaller and newer organizations without a budget for this type of investment can gather new names more informally through asking board members, friends, and volunteers.

This first draft of a filled-in Rosso Constituency Model should be analyzed for diversity. Complete a donor grid showing age, race, gender, ethnicity, and demographics of an organization's current donors. Is there a good mix of ages, races, genders, and ethnicities? If not, the fundraiser now has an opportunity to work with the board of directors, other staff members, donors, and volunteers to identify diverse communities of donors.

Expanding the number of prospective new donors should occur while remaining mindful of reaching diverse audiences that are reflective of the nonprofit's mission and values. For example, researching the history and current concerns of minority and marginalized populations can help identify specific LAI characteristics unique to these groups. In addition, volunteer committees that are diverse, equitable, and inclusive can help identify people in the constituencies the nonprofit seeks to reach. The committee can develop relationships with gender or ethnic based organizations such as a minority focused chamber of commerce or women's giving circle. The committee can also connect with young professionals' groups, community foundations that manage a range of racial and ethnic funds, or education initiatives that focus on diverse audiences (e.g., students of color or women in STEM).

Instead of focusing solely on who is included in the donor database and on the prospective donor list, the fundraiser also can continue asking: Who is missing? One way to work to alleviate the gap is through a social media campaign inviting the nonprofit's followers to share information with their networks (see Chapter 24). Written content and photos should enable diverse audiences to see themselves in the organization's social media postings, the social media shared by followers, and in all marketing materials.

The "easiest" place to begin donor identification is at the center, in those "seats" closest to the stage or playing field, and then work outward, up into the next level of seating in the arena, all the way to the upper deck. At each level, fundraisers need to understand who is in each seating area, where they spend their time, and how they prefer to receive information in order to offer inclusive opportunities to participate.

Navigating the Circle

Traditionally, donors and organizations follow a basic path: potential donor (heard about the concert or game), first-time donor (sat in the top row of the arena), established donor (returned to the next show or game), upgraded or mid-level donor (moved down to seats closer to the stage), major donor (in the front row). There are always exceptions, of course, but analyzing and categorizing donors in this way can help build strategy and effectively engage each donor or donor group.

Examples can be found in the ways different donors responded to the unique events of 2020. Pandemic treatment and vaccinations, social justice issues, and economic decline prompted some donors to jump right into the mid-level seats or even the front rows without testing out the upper deck first. For example, institutional funders and large donors contributed over $5.9 billion to organizations primarily engaged in racial equity work in 2020 (Williams-Pulfer and Osili 2020). These donors were known to the organizations they supported, which were then charged with providing good stewardship, including being accountable and reporting on outcomes and working toward repeat gifts (i.e., closer arena seats).

At the same time, crowdfunding related to victims of racial injustice skyrocketed. GoFundMe crowdfunding pages for George Floyd, Ahmaud Arbery, Breonna Taylor, and Jacob Blake have each raised over $1 million. GoFundMe memorial campaigns inspired by social justice issues saw more donations than any other campaign in the online platform's history, raising over $14 million from 500,000 donors in 140 countries. Many of the gifts received were $5 gifts or less (Williams-Pulfer and Osili 2020). Many of these donors' gifts showed a connection to the cause – they were "people with similar interests" but provided direct aid to victims' families rather than to nonprofit organizations. Nonprofits and fundraisers for social justice causes now have the challenge of building on this societal momentum to expand their constituency circles through outreach, awareness building, and marketing. The LAI Principle can help.

The LAI Principle

Analysis of donors and prospective donors can be conducted through the lens of LAI (Rosso 1991). The following terms help identify potential donors as well as where they "sit" in the Constituency Model. This analysis allows fundraisers to then utilize their time, energy, and other resources most effectively.

Linkage describes how someone is connected to the nonprofit. *Ability* reveals the prospective donor's financial capacity to donate. *Interest* explains the individual's demonstrated knowledge about the mission and involvement in the mission work. Indicators of each can take many forms; a few possibilities follow:

- Linkage Indicators
  - Has received services.
  - Knows a board member, volunteer, staff person.
  - Refers others to services.
- Ability Indicators
  - Has given to other nonprofit organizations.
  - Shows evidence of discretionary income.
  - Time of life changes – empty nest, retirement, sale of business.
- Interest Indicators
  - Attends an event or activity.
  - Participates regularly on social media.
  - Has a history of giving to this organization and/or similar organizations.

Using the LAI Principles and the Rosso Constituency Model allow fundraisers to become more specific when identifying potential donors. The categories will vary among organizations. For example, a university may break down "former participants" into groups like "Alumni" who are "1–3 years out from graduation," "4–6 years out from graduation," "7–10 years out from graduation," and so on. Often, larger universities will take that further by school (i.e., engineering) or department (i.e., mechanical engineering).

A small- or medium-sized nonprofit, such as an animal shelter, could categorize prospective donors into one of two lists: people who have adopted an animal and people who have not. The first list then can be analyzed further by creating subcategories of people who adopted cats or dogs or other animals.

When prioritizing how best to use time for fund development, the fundraiser starts at the center of the Rosso Constituency Model, with those most closely connected to the nonprofit. These are the people sitting in the "front seats" of the nonprofit's donor data management system, which is generally referred to as the donor database.

Qualifying Donors

Once potential donors have been identified (i.e., linkages discovered), each individual (or entity) can be analyzed for qualification, which explores ability and interest in making a gift. In this stage of analysis, fundraisers look for indicators to support initial cues that the prospective donor might be willing to make a gift. Qualifying donors today includes capturing verbatims, that is, what donors reveal directly or indirectly through surveys, and monitoring digital body language, or, what they do online (Warner 2020). Seeking and capturing this information helps fundraisers better understand their donors' interests, passions, and concerns, as well as their demographics and psychographics, to prioritize those most interested in building or deepening a relationship and making a gift.

The analysis should be as deep and precise as the fundraiser and the nonprofit have capacity for doing. For individuals near the center of the constituency model, gathering this additional information is often done through in-person or virtual meetings or calls. For those farther away from the center, donor surveys, email, social media outreach, and special event activities are often more strategic and effective approaches.

Fundraisers must be conscious of their donor communication patterns and regularly review and analyze their materials. Do marketing materials speak to donors of color? Can they see individuals who look like them? How does the cause relate to their concerns and circumstances? Furthermore, if there is a lack of response from constituents of color or others, learn why. Test current and new marketing materials with a diverse range of people and make revisions based on their feedback.

Draw on available research to inform the messaging. For instance, donors of color respond best and have greater respect for community, racial, and ethnic organizations with a strong business model and effective service delivery strategy (W.K. Kellogg Foundation 2012). Many donors of color see education as a direct connection to health, housing, and overall quality of life issues. Education is the key to realizing personal dreams and hope for a better society. This is passed on through generations. Their verbatims and digital body language likely support these beliefs, which can, in turn, be considered in fundraiser conversations and nonprofit messaging around educational causes.

LIA, the Other Principle

The outer rings of the Rosso Constituency Model can be filled by using the indicators of linkage (Whom do they know?), ability (Are they willing and able to give?), and interest (How do we know they care?). Bringing new donors into the organization, as described in the previous sections, is called *donor acquisition.*

When growing the mid-level and inner circles of the constituency model, termed *donor development*, the indicators shift slightly as guided by the acronym LIA (Linkage Involvement Advocacy).

Linkage continues to be important. Whom does the donor know, and what is the connection? Those closer to the center have already indicated their interest through previous attendance, participation, and giving.

The analysis continues by looking for more indicators of *Involvement.* Have they served on a committee or the board? Have they volunteered at several activities? Have they served as a mentor or been involved with service recipients? Have they not only donated to a crowdfunding campaign, but hosted one or shared one on their social media? These are indicators of deeper involvement, stronger values exchange, and the potential for larger or more frequent gifts.

Donors at this level have also indicated their ability through previous gifts, typically, so the analysis then continues by examining indicators of *Advocacy.* How are they advocating for the mission within their circles of influence? Are they bringing others to the nonprofit organization? Are they sending their neighbors emails or sharing the nonprofit's posts on social media? These types of indicators reveal that the prospective donor has internalized the mission and the message, and wants to provide that information to others.

Prospective Donor Research

In large organizations, there are often entire teams or departments dedicated to researching potential donors for the organization. They may have access to sophisticated software, wealth screening companies and wealth indicator reports, and a multitude of other resources to help qualify donors for future gifts. The research provided by these teams is driven by facts and indicators of readiness to make a gift at a particular level. They are not stalkers seeking to invade the privacy of donors, but instead use public information to create reports to help fundraisers better understand the LAI or LIA indicators.

However, most organizations are smaller and do not have advanced research teams. Over 66 percent of all nonprofits have less than a $1 million budget and are considered grassroots organizations (Frailey 2017). These nonprofits typically have fewer staff members, smaller reach and focus, and fewer resources. Staff who fill multiple roles can conduct initial and yet highly useful research by using search engines, asking board members and friends, and drawing on other local resources.

Three Levels of Research

There are three levels of prospective donor research that identify the LAI/LIA indicators for constituency groups and individual constituents or donors.

Level 1 is the *basic* level, and includes name, address, phone number, email, profession, and other relevant demographic information helpful to qualify a donor. This information can be utilized to determine if donors are even aware of the nonprofit or can easily access the nonprofit's programs and services. The information also can help determine how the nonprofit can best send information to them.

Level 2 focuses on *affiliations and interests*, which may include religious affiliation, board and volunteer roles, hobbies, memberships, or political interests. For example, people who attend religious services monthly are 11 times more likely to give to religious congregations, and they give an average of $1,737 more than people who attend less than once a month (Austin 2017). Those who donate at least $2,500 to political campaigns are 15 times more likely to give a charitable donation than those who do not (DonorSearch n.d.). Knowledge of these types of interests and behaviors can help fundraisers qualify the donor's particular interests in the nonprofit as well as the donor's potential range of future contributions.

Level 3 research is information relevant for *giving decisions*. This level includes more detailed financial information, including wealth markers such as real estate holdings, stock ownership, and Federal Election Commission (FEC) filings. This information can be utilized to prioritize which donors to work with and how best to cultivate those relationships. For example, donors who own over $2 million in real estate are 17 times more likely to make a charitable contribution than those with less wealth in real estate (DonorSearch n.d.). Yet, net worth alone does not guarantee giving, and perceptions of one's own wealth can vary greatly. Individual values and circumstances will always affect how wealth is used (see Chapter 26). "African American High Net Worth donors are actively building their wealth, their social and political capital, and are less likely to inherit money from family" (Vaid and Maxton 2017, 20).

Wheel of Roles and Responsibilities

Another visual framework for qualifying donors and useful for analyzing donor research is the Wheel of Roles and Responsibilities (see Figure 14.2) (Rosso 1991).

FIGURE 14.2. WHEEL OF ROLES AND RESPONSIBILITIES

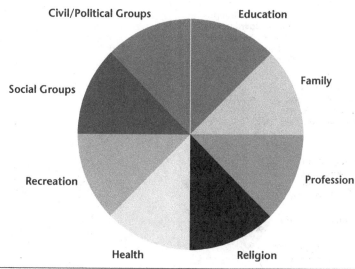

Source: Rosso 1991.

The donor or donor group sits at the center of the wheel, and spokes represent roles and responsibilities common to life today. These roles and responsibilities each influence the amount of time, energy, resources, and interest they might be willing to invest in engaging with the nonprofit organization. Any of these roles can influence this relationship positively or negatively, and the amount of influence each has may differ for different constituencies.

Consider the following scenarios.

Family 1 (see Figure 14.3):

- Level 1: Early 40s, lives in suburbs, African American, blended family with five children ranging from 7 to 21 years old.
- Level 2: Educated and pursuing advanced degrees, male/female soon to be married, one adult child, one teenager, and three younger children, one grandchild; active religious affiliation; no health concerns; interest in travelling frequently, shopping, sports and recreation; evidence of community social groups, community boards and volunteering within sports and recreational organizations; participation in service clubs and giving circles.
- Level 3: Wealth indicators: one real estate holding; little political giving.

FIGURE 14.3. WHEEL EXAMPLE FAMILY 1

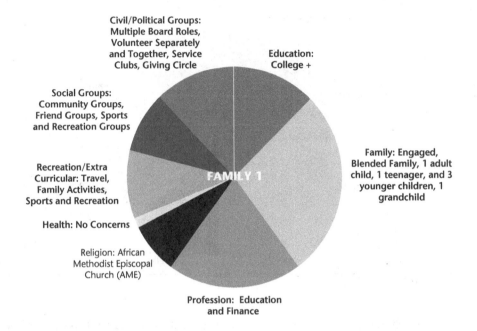

Family 2 (see Figure 14.4):

- Level 1: Early 80s, lives in suburbs – snowbirds in winter, white, adult children and grandchildren, pet owners.
- Level 2: Educated, male/female marriage; two adult children, three adult grandchildren; retired – previously sales and business ownership; somewhat active religious affiliation; some health concerns; interest in golf, community recreation; evidence of various community social groups; current and previous board service; volunteer together; previously active in service clubs.
- Level 3: Wealth indicators: two real estate holdings; evidence of political giving; multiple investments.

Data points such as these can help define the LAI of each family. If, for example, the nonprofit in question has an education mission, the linkage could apply to both families. The interest may be higher in Family 1 because there are children still in school and the parents are considering additional degree programs. Might that influence ability for Family 1? Maybe, but more information would be needed. If the mission of the organization is animal care, Family 2 may have stronger linkage as pet owners. Analyzed in this manner, the three levels of research help

FIGURE 14.4. WHEEL EXAMPLE FAMILY 2

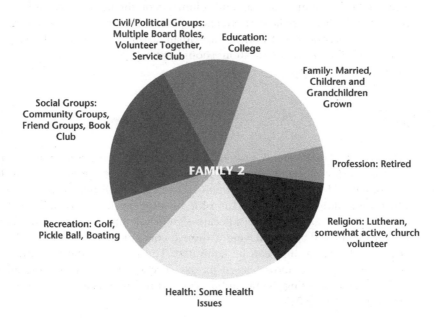

fundraisers better understand donors and groups of donors and determine where the LAI is strongest.

Ethical Considerations

The intent in gathering the information described in this chapter is to identify and qualify, or disqualify, the constituents or constituency groups who have been identified for further attention and engagement. Both the *Donor Bill of Rights* and the Association of Prospect Researchers for Advancement (APRA) provide ethical guidance for gathering and managing this information. As Prine and Lesem (2016, 82) wrote in the prior version of this chapter:

> These fundamental principles . . . include a commitment to confidentiality, accuracy, and relevance of information gathered on prospective donors; a responsibility to lead by example in creating and following policies that support ethical prospective donor research; honesty and truthfulness regarding their role as prospective donor of researchers and the role of research at the organization; and avoidance of conflicts of interest.

These principles insist on protecting donor data, including sensitive information, through a secure database, restricting access to information to only those who need it, and educating staff and volunteers on the importance and aspects of confidentiality. Clear policies should be in place to maintain sensitive information, and with consequences if policies are violated. Donors can, and do, request to review their files, thus organizations should assure the data within is only relevant to the gift relationship.

Conclusion

Identifying and qualifying donors effectively means understanding the nonprofit's current constituency and who may be missing or underrepresented. The Rosso Constituency Model, analyzed through LAI and LIA indicators, can be utilized as a basis for building a positive relationship focusing on the compatibility of shared values. Effective organizations allocate significant time, energy, and resources toward identifying and qualifying a diverse constituent community with whom meaningful relationships can be cultivated. The ultimate goal is to invite each donor over time to move closer to the core of the nonprofit organization (Seiler 2016b) or, using the metaphor within this chapter, closer to the action on the stage or playing field.

Discussion Questions

1. What are additional indicators for LAI beyond the examples listed?
2. What biases should fundraisers be aware of when building constituency models?
3. Considering the Wheel of Roles and Responsibilities and examples in this chapter, what additional information would you seek for Family 1 to determine its LAI for a particular mission or organization? What about Family 2?

Application Exercises

1. Create a Rosso Constituency Model for your organization. If you are not involved with an organization yet, pick a cause that is important to you, and build a model of your extended family and friend group illustrating their LAI. Who would be in each circle?

2. Do some research on yourself or someone you are close to. Find proof of the following and share where you found it:
   a. Level 1 Basic – name, address, phone number, email, education, profession, race, gender preference, spouse or significant other, children, pets.
   b. Level 2 Interests and Affiliations – religious affiliation, volunteer roles, hobbies, memberships, political interests, service clubs or social groups.
   c. Level 3 Giving Decisions – real estate holdings, stock ownership, previous giving.

   Once the research is complete, discuss how and where you found proof, and any inaccuracies or misinformation you found.

CHAPTER FIFTEEN

BUDGETING AND EVALUATION IN FUNDRAISING

By Erik J. Daubert

An excellent fundraising budgeter will advocate for the fundraising department before, during, and after the budgeting process. Doing so greatly improves the chances of the organization providing sufficient financial resources for fundraising to succeed. Budgeting for the expected (such as annual, capital, endowment, major gifts, and grants) and planning for the unexpected (such as new ideas, opportunities, and building organizational reserves) represent just some of the many responsible strategies and tactics fundraising executives and nonprofits can use when planning for the future.

After reading this chapter, fundraisers will:

- Understand the significance of leadership in the fundraising budget and evaluation process.
- See and value the importance of including fundraising within the larger nonprofit budget process.
- Understand basic fundraising budget terms, including indirect, direct, and general administration cost elements and formulas.
- Be able to create a fundraising budget using time study analysis and sound budgeting principles.
- Be able to develop fundraising reports using various free and available resources.

Constructing the Fundraising Budget

Fundraising is a management function and includes developing the fundraising budget. Fundraisers should discuss the nonprofit's budget and the fundraising departmental budget with leadership. Connecting with those who make budget decisions will position fundraising to have the best chance for success when funding decisions are made.

One of the first things a good fundraising executive can do is understand the budget.

- How was it formulated?
- What period of time does it cover?
- Who put it together?
- What do "line items" represent and what is contained in each?
- What level of detail does it cover?

All of these questions – and more that will arise on reviewing the budget – seek essential information about the fundraising plan for the upcoming or existing time period.

Rarely has fundraising budgeting been as challenging as it is today. With nonprofit business models seeming less sure than ever due to environmental conditions ranging from pandemics to the economy and more, the budgeting and evaluation processes must include "what if" scenarios that involve a Plan A, a Plan B, and even a Plan C, D, or E.

Budgeting for Success in Fundraising

Understanding current budget and fundraising performance is a great first step in building a future budget.

- How is the current fundraising program doing?
- How much money did the organization raise this year?
- Is the board and CEO/Executive Director mostly happy with how fundraising is going at the organization?

Some questions regarding the future budget process might include:

- Will incremental budgeting (raise all the expense and income lines by X percent) or zero-based budgeting (start from scratch and build the budget from the ground up) be used?

- How will other departmental and organizational needs affect budget needs in the coming year(s)?

Understanding the current fundraising budget – and current fundraising environment – can empower fundraisers to budget more effectively for the coming year.

Leadership and the Fundraising Budget

Nonprofits need to spend money to raise money, explaining why the fundraiser needs to be involved in the nonprofit's budget creation meetings. For example, rather than deciding the nonprofit is going to build a new building next year and then deciding that it needs to raise $X to make it happen, fundraising should be represented in discussions about the new building before and while these decisions are being made.

Another example of providing leadership in the fundraising budget is in looking ahead on important issues that empower the nonprofit to move forward effectively – issues such as diversity, equity, and inclusion (DEI). Diversifying the nonprofit's donor population likely will incur direct expenses such as hiring a more diverse staff and providing training on diversity and cultural differences. These expenses must be accounted for in the budget process. By budgeting for expenses – and appropriate revenues – through DEI efforts, the nonprofit is taking a necessary step toward mission fulfillment in ways that expand the nonprofit's constituencies and fundraising.

Fundraising staff need to not only be proactive in leading fundraising discussion topics but also contributing to decision-making as part of a high functioning nonprofit leadership team.

Fundraising Expenses Are an Investment in Fundraising

Fundraising represents one of the highest returns on investment activities that a nonprofit organization can make. The return on investment (ROI) of fundraising is often the very highest ROI activity a nonprofit can activate. Therefore, strategic higher investment in fundraising can generate a higher return on impact to the nonprofit mission. Consider the following:

- Nonprofit invests $50,000 into starting major gifts fundraising.
- In year one, the nonprofit raises $50,000 in new gifts.
- Some of the new donors donate again in subsequent years.
- In year five, one of these donors makes a $100,000 gift, five other major donors contribute $10,000 each, and two become board members.

Overall charitable giving now significantly exceeds the first-year investment of $50,000.

This hypothetical example reveals how donors who are retained over time create lasting value to the nonprofit not only from the dollars raised, but also from the value of relationships built. Unlike most other departments within the nonprofit, fundraising generates returns in the first year and in future years as well.

Program Budgeting

Responsible fundraising budgeting involves understanding a few key terms.

- *Indirect costs* are general nonprofit expenses, regardless of whether fundraising is happening or not. Examples of this are things like building rent, accounting expenses, and utilities.
- *Direct costs* are expenses that happen specifically because the program exists. Some examples of this in the fundraising budget might be fundraiser salary, fundraiser conference and training expense, cost of a fundraising consultant, mileage expense related to fundraising, and so on.

Understanding these two distinct types of expenses can help staff, volunteers, and donors see the full cost of the fundraising program and any other programs a nonprofit operates. While some donors prefer only to fund direct program costs, it is important to understand that without indirect costs, many programs do not happen. An example of this in a hospital is custodial and electrical expenses in a surgical center. While a donor may only want to fund the surgical center direct costs, no one wants to have surgery in a dark and dirty operating room!

Fundraising Revenue

Fundraising revenue (sometimes called "contributions" or "income") is generally categorized in two distinct ways:

- *Restricted contributions* are gifts that have been designated for specific purposes. An example of this is a "$500 gift for children's books for the after-school program." Using this money for anything else is inappropriate and unethical (see Chapter 2).
- *Unrestricted contributions* are gifts that the nonprofit can use as it determines to further the mission of the organization. Examples of this might be "a $500 gift to XYZ Nonprofit Organization." Because the gift has no specific determination as to how it must be used, it may be used as the nonprofit sees fit.

While nonprofits can raise more money for their mission by allowing donors to make restricted gifts to current funding priorities (Eckel, Herberish, and Meer 2014), raising both restricted and unrestricted contributions strengthens the nonprofit's capabilities toward mission fulfillment.

Creating the Fundraising Budget

A typical nonprofit budget has a separate column for each program, including a column for fundraising. Next year's budget is often constructed by using the current year's budget as its basis. A departmental budget worksheet like that pictured in Exhibit 15.1 is a common way to begin. This budget shows how direct and indirect expenses combine to build the fundraising budget for the coming year.

Fundraising Performance and Evaluation

Creating the departmental budget also includes planning for fundraising outputs.

- What fundraising goals and objectives will be accomplished and how will they be the same or different from last year?
- How much money is being sought from how many donors?
- If trying to raise more funds, will more investment be needed for the fundraising department?
- Are different results expected from the same fundraising approaches?
- How will next year be better or different from this year?

Key terms and equations for fundraising performance include:

- *Cost to Raise a Dollar* (CRD): How much it really costs to raise one contributed dollar. Remember, when converting a word problem into a fraction, the first word is the numerator, and the second word is the denominator. Therefore, the formula for "cost" to "raise a dollar" is fundraising expense (cost) divided by revenue (raise a dollar). For example, if $10,000 is spent on direct mail that raises $30,000, then $10,000/$30,000 = $.33 to raise a dollar.

EXHIBIT 15.1. THE DEPARTMENTAL BUDGET WORKSHEET

THE DEPARTMENTAL BUDGET WORKSHEET

The combination of direct costs (program expense) with office operations (indirect costs) represents the true and complete budget required for fundraising. Preparation of the budget for the year should be based on an analysis of both prior years' expenses and individual program results.

Current Fiscal Year			Next Fiscal Year
	Budget	Actual	Budget Estimate
A. Administration/Salaries			
Director of Development	$ _____	$ _____	$ _____
Professional Staff Office	$ _____	$ _____	$ _____
Support Staff/Part-Time	$ _____	$ _____	$ _____
Workers/Temporary Workers	$ _____	$ _____	$ _____
Subtotal	$ _____	$ _____	$ _____
Fringe Benefits (%)	$ _____	$ _____	$ _____
Pay Increases (%)	$ _____	$ _____	$ _____
TOTAL	$ _____	$ _____	$ _____
B. Office Operations/Office Supplies			
Telephone Charges	$ _____	$ _____	$ _____
Telephone Equipment	$ _____	$ _____	$ _____
Rental Equipment	$ _____	$ _____	$ _____
List Fees	$ _____	$ _____	$ _____
Postage Fees	$ _____	$ _____	$ _____
Printing Costs	$ _____	$ _____	$ _____
Books/Periodicals	$ _____	$ _____	$ _____
Travel (trips)/	$ _____	$ _____	$ _____
Travel (local)	$ _____	$ _____	$ _____
Entertainment Awards/Plaques	$ _____	$ _____	$ _____
Dues/Memberships	$ _____	$ _____	$ _____
Professional Development	$ _____	$ _____	$ _____
Insurance	$ _____	$ _____	$ _____
Office Rental	$ _____	$ _____	$ _____
New Equipment	$ _____	$ _____	$ _____
Equipment Maintenance	$ _____	$ _____	$ _____
Consultant Fees	$ _____	$ _____	$ _____
Services Purchased	$ _____	$ _____	$ _____
Other	$ _____	$ _____	$ _____
Subtotal	$ _____	$ _____	$ _____
C. Budget Summary			
(A + B)	$ _____	$ _____	$ _____

Excerpted: AFP Fundamentals of Fundraising Course © Association of Fundraising Professionals 2017.

- *Net Fundraising Return* (often called *fundraising return on investment* or ROI): The amount of money raised based on the amount of money spent on fundraising. This figure is obtained by dividing "net fundraising revenue" by "total fundraising expenses." For example, a nonprofit spends $10 to raise $100. The net revenue is $100 − $10 = $90. Therefore, the net fundraising return is $90/$10 = $9. This result describes how every $1 spent on fundraising generates a net return of $9.

Analyzing needed resources and anticipated fundraising results positions departments to achieve fundraising goals and objectives. The more effort put into determining needed resources before and during the budget process, the more likely these resources will be available for fundraising and the nonprofit when they are needed.

Evaluating Fundraising Programs with Measurement and Evaluation Tools

There are a number of tools and resources available to measure and evaluate fundraising performance. Many fundraising software programs include built-in tools; learn to leverage those tools as effectively as possible. This section describes freely available tools that can augment fundraising software as needed.

Fundraising Fitness Test

The Fundraising Fitness Test (available for free from the Fundraising Effectiveness Project at https://afpglobal.org/feptools) enables a nonprofit organization to evaluate several fundraising metrics. The test requires three fields of information: donor id number, gift date, and gift amount. The spreadsheet program then generates key metrics such as:

- New donor retention,
- New donor acquisition,
- Repeat donor retention,
- Donor gains, and
- Dollar gains.

By running this analysis, fundraisers can begin to understand how the nonprofit performed in the past and also make plans for how to improve fundraising in the future. Exhibit 15.2 demonstrates some of the many outputs available from the Fundraising Fitness Test.

EXHIBIT 15.2. FUNDRAISING FITNESS TEST TOP INDICATORS TAB

No.	Fundraising Performance Indicator	All Donors	Under $100	$100-$249	$250-$999	$1,000- $4,999	$5,000 & Up
	Donor retention rate						
1	New donor retention rate	37%	23%	49%	48%	66%	73%
2	Repeat donor retention rate	72%	52%	66%	76%	81%	88%
3	Overall donor retention rate	64%	36%	61%	72%	80%	87%
	Donor acquisition rate						
6a	New donor acquisition rate	31%	78%	33%	13%	6%	3%
6b	Repeat donor re-acquisition rate	13%	12%	17%	15%	10%	9%
6	Overall donor acquisition rate	45%	90%	50%	28%	16%	13%
	Donor gains, losses & net						

Source: Fundraising Effectiveness Project (FEP). 2020a. "Fundraising Fitness Test (FFT)."

Understanding Employee Time and the Fundraising Budget

In 2016, the Federal Accounting Standards Board (FASB) created Accounting Standard Update (ASU) Number 2016-14, which impacts nonprofit accounting (Financial Accounting Foundation 2016). This update changed nonprofit financial reporting by stating that a Statement of Functional Expenses must be provided at the major program level. ASU 2016-14 also explains that nonprofit organizations must disclose in their footnotes how they allocate costs and be able to defend their methodology as appropriate. These changes have created new challenges in nonprofit accounting – including for fundraising costs. ASU 2016-14 requires nonprofits to provide time-based reporting for employees at the program level, including the fundraising department.

Allotting employee time to fundraising costs is a process that begins with some simple questions:

- How much time does the executive director spend on fundraising?
- How does the nonprofit account for time with program staff who interact with donors?

- How much time does the professional fundraiser spend on fundraising – rather than program or administrative work?

Questions like these can be answered by understanding the investments of time made by each of these employees in the course of their workday, week, month, and year.

An excellent way to understand where an organization's time and fundraising efforts are spent is to do a time study, which is explained in this section.

The first step in performing a time study is to estimate how much time each staff member spends on general administration and programming. Use a spreadsheet like the one shown in Exhibit 15.3 to break out staff time by category. A full-time employee (FTE) is budgeted at 2,080 hours per year, so a half-time person would be 1,040 hours.

In Exhibit 15.3, time has been allocated for each employee, and each employee has some time budgeted for fundraising. Program personnel spend most of their time on programming, while other staff may play smaller or larger roles in making fundraising happen at the nonprofit. Note how each employee's time is spent for each program area. In the example, in the Total row of the spreadsheet, the nonprofit is spending $11,300 in salaries on general administration, $60,150 on fundraising, $101,650 on Program #1, and $99,900 on Program #2.

Next, calculate the time study factor. To do this, take the total number of hours for each of the four activities and divide each of these hours by the total employee hours for the organization. This allows for showing a portion of what were indirect costs as direct costs to programming. In the preceding example, 624 hours divided by the total nonprofit hours equals a general administration time factor of 0.0333 (624/18720 = 0.0333).

We next put the time study factor into Exhibit 15.4 along with the salaries and benefits used in Exhibit 15.3. For this example, benefits are estimated as 30 percent of salaries (30 percent of $273,000 is $81,900).

By using the time study factor along with earlier budgeted totals for salaries, benefits, rent/utilities, postage, printing/design, and so on, respective totals can be filled in for each department's expenses. Note in the previous exhibit how all departments have expense allocations utilizing the time study factor for each expense category. Some examples of this are the General Administration salaries line, which takes 0.0333 × $273,000 = $11,300. Another is Fundraising, which is 0.1833 × $273,000 = $60,150. By doing this for each area, the entire spreadsheet can be completed for expenses. For some expense lines, actual figures may be

EXHIBIT 15.3. TIME STUDY FACTOR WORKSHEET, PART 1

POSITION	SALARY	Hours	Gen. Admin. TIME	Gen. Admin. $$	Gen. Admin. Hrs.	Fundraising TIME	Fundraising $$	Fundraising HRs.	PRO. (#1)	P.(#1) $$	P.(#1) HRs.	PRO. (#2)	P.(#2) $$	P.(#2) HRs.
Executive Director	$40,000	2080	0.1	$4,000	208	0.5	$20,000	1040	0.2	$8,000	416	0.2	$8,000	416
Director of Fund. Dev.	$38,000	2080	0.1	$3,800	208	0.8	$30,400	1664	0.05	$1,900	104	0.05	$1,900	104
Program Director	$35,000	2080	0.1	$3,500	208	0.05	$1,750	104	0.45	$15,750	936	0.4	$14,000	832
Program Manager	$30,000	2080	0	$0	0	0.05	$1,500	104	0.95	$28,500	1976	0	$0	0
Program Manager	$30,000	2080	0	$0	0	0.05	$1,500	104	0	$0	0	0.95	$28,500	1976
Program Associate	$25,000	2080	0	$0	0	0.05	$1,250	104	0.5	$12,500	1040	0.45	$11,250	936
Program Associate	$25,000	2080	0	$0	0	0.05	$1,250	104	0.5	$12,500	1040	0.45	$11,250	936
Program Associate	$25,000	2080	0	$0	0	0.05	$1,250	104	0.45	$11,250	936	0.5	$12,500	1040
Program Associate	$25,000	2080	0	$0	0	0.05	$1,250	104	0.45	$11,250	936	0.5	$12,500	1040
TOTAL:	$273,000	18720		$11,300	624		$60,150	3432		$101,650	7384		$99,900	7280
Time Study Factor			0.0333			0.1833			0.3944			0.389		

Source: The Fund Raising School, Principles and Techniques of Fundraising Course 2021, 236.

EXHIBIT 15.4. TIME STUDY FACTOR WORKSHEET, PART 2

INCOME	GEN. ADMN.	FUNDRAISING	PRO. (#1)	PRO. (#2)	TOTAL
Individuals					
Corp. & Foundations					
Government					
Program Revenues					
In Kind					
Interest					
Reserves					
TOTAL	0	0	0	0	0
Time Study Factor	0.0333	0.1833	0.3944	0.389	1
EXPENSE	GEN. ADMN.	FUNDRAISING	PRO. (#1)	PRO. (#2)	TOTAL
Salary	11,300	60,150	101,650	99,900	273,000
Benefits	3390	18045	30495	29970	81900
Rent/Utilities	799.2	4399.2	9465.6	9336	24000
Telephone	199.8	1099.8	2366.4	2344	6000
Postage					
Printing/Design					
Supplies					
Equipment	599.4	3299.4	7099.2	7002	18000
Maintenance/Repair	166.5	916.5	1972	1945	5000
Travel/Lodging					
Mileage					
Facility/Food					
Staff Development	233.1	1283.1	2760.8	2723	7000
Program Marketing					
TOTAL	16,688	89,193	155,809	153,210	414,900

Source: The Fund Raising School, Principles and Techniques of Fundraising Course 2021, 238.

known (such as postage), while other expenses will require using time study allocations to generate the figures. Note how the entire expense portion of the table can be filled in using this process.

Exhibit 15.5 takes everything done so far and focuses on the top portion of the sheet to break out fundraising income. By planning how much is expected to be raised in each fundraising segment (individuals, corporations and foundations, government, in kind, etc.) and starting with the total for each area (e.g., $200,000 from individuals) the time study factor can be used to determine expected funding needs for each program. In this way, funding from the income section for Program #2 is now $167,275 and so on. This shows what each program really costs and how fundraising dollars can be allocated for each non-profit program.

With this information, program totals can be broken out to determine a per-person cost for each program. For example, in Program #2, the $167,275/500 people served = $334.55 per-person cost. This is powerful information for explaining the real cost of programs to donors and other interested parties.

The percentage of funds spent on general administration relative to program support can be calculated using this equation: (General Administration + Fundraising)/Total Budget = General Administration and Fundraising %. Example here is ($18,038 + $96,293)/$451,090 = 25%.

EXHIBIT 15.5. TIME STUDY FACTOR WORKSHEET, PART 3

INCOME	GEN. ADMN.	FUNDRAISING	PRO. (#1)	PRO. (#2)	TOTAL
Individuals	11,538	80,443	59,494	48,525	200,000
Corp. & Foundations	—	—	66,000	45,000	111,000
Government	—	—	—	30,000	30,000
Program Revenues	5,000	10,000	42,990	42,500	100,490
In Kind	1,000	4,850	1,000	1,000	7,850
Interest	500	1,000	—	250	1,750
Reserves	—	—	—	—	—
TOTAL	18,038	96,293	169,494	167,275	451,090
Time Study Factor	0.0333	0.1833	0.3944	0.389	1

EXPENSE	GEN. ADMN	FUNDRAISING	PRO. (#1)	PRO. (#2)	TOTAL
Salary	11,300	60,150	101,650	99,900	273,000
Benefits	3390	18045	30495	29970	81900
Rent/Utilities	799.2	4399.2	9465.6	9336	24000
Telephone	199.8	1099.8	2366.4	2344	6000
Postage	100	1,500	375	290	2265
Printing/Design	0	2,000	1,250	4,000	7,250
Supplies	150	250	5,000	3,750	9,150
Equipment	599.4	3299.4	7099.2	7002	18000
Maintenance/Repair	166.5	916.5	1972	1945	5000
Travel/Lodging	600	500	600	750	2,450
Mileage	250	250	450	500	1,450
Facility/Food	250	100	4,000	3,275	7,625
Staff Development	233.1	1283.1	2760.8	2723	7000
Program Marketing	0	2,500	2,000	1,500	6,000
TOTAL	18,038	96,293	169,484	167,275	451,090
Admin. Percentage	0.25				
Per Unit (500 people)			338.97	334.55	451.09

Source: The Fund Raising School, Principles and Techniques of Fundraising Course 2021, 239.

Fundraising Net Analyzer

Additional resources addressing ASU 2016-14 can be found through the Fundraising Effectiveness Project's Activity Based Management (FEP-ABM) project. By working with accountants on activity-based management for fundraising, FEP-ABM is bridging the gap that has traditionally existed between the allotment of time for fundraising efforts and properly accounting for fundraising costs as it relates to staff time allotment to program costs and to fundraising costs as well.

The Fundraising Net Analyzer resources and tools help nonprofits navigate and manage fundraising costs using ideas contained in ASU 2016-14. These free resources have been developed by AFP's Research Council along with the Greater Washington Society of CPAs and others.

Exhibit 15.6 shows a sample output from the Fundraising Net Analyzer such as staffing costs and costs to raise a dollar for each fundraising program.

EXHIBIT 15.6. FUNDRAISING NET ANALYZER – MFE CALCULATING FUNDRAISING MEASURES

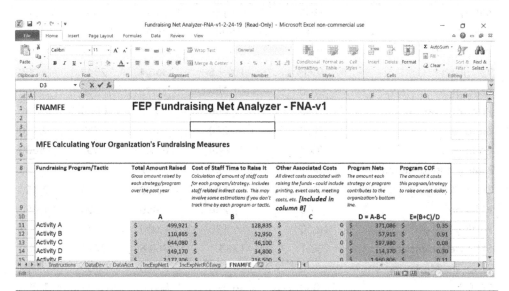

Fundraising Program/Tactic	Total Amount Raised	Cost of Staff Time to Raise It	Other Associated Costs	Program Nets	Program COF
	Gross amount raised by each strategy/program over the past year	Calculation of amount of staff costs for each program/strategy. Includes staff related indirect costs. This may involve some estimations if you don't track time by each program or tactic.	All direct costs associated with raising the funds - could include printing, event costs, meeting costs, etc. *[Included in column B]*	The amount each strategy or program contributes to the organization's bottom line.	The amount it costs this program/strategy to raise one net dollar.
	A	B	C	D = A-B-C	E=(B+C)/D
Activity A	$ 499,921	$ 128,835	$ 0	$ 371,086	$ 0.35
Activity B	$ 110,865	$ 52,950	$ 0	$ 57,915	$ 0.91
Activity C	$ 644,080	$ 46,100	$ 0	$ 597,980	$ 0.08
Activity D	$ 149,170	$ 34,800	$ 0	$ 114,370	$ 0.30
Activity E	$ 2,177,306	$ 216,500	$ 0	$ 1,960,806	$ 0.11

Source: Fundraising Effectiveness Project (FEP). 2020b. "Fundraising Net Analyzer (FNA),"

The Fundraising Net Analyzer toolkit can be utilized to understand and manage fundraising costs and is downloadable from https://afpglobal.org/feptools (Fundraising Effectiveness Project 2020b).

One question that is often asked in fundraising is: "What is an appropriate amount of money to spend to raise a dollar?" According to Charity Watch (accessed 2021), a charity watch group described by *The New York Times* as "the pit bull of watch dog groups," a good fundraising expense ratio to aim for is 25 percent or less.

While some donors might complain that this percentage is too high, fundraisers can respond with confidence by explaining how the nonprofit relies on skilled employees who deserve just wages and benefits. These employees also need training, technology, and other resources to fulfill the nonprofit's mission. For most nonprofits, fundraising is actually the highest margin program it operates. This means that when reviewing all the programs it offers, fundraising raises more money for organizational operations per dollar invested than any other program in the organization. Fundraising is generally a good investment.

It is also important to note that many experts are now moving away from hard and fast percentages for rating nonprofit performance. Smaller nonprofits and those with smaller fundraising goals may find lower fundraising costs difficult to obtain as larger fundraising programs tend to have lower fundraising expense ratios due to economies of scale.

Conclusion

By utilizing the strategies, tactics, tools, and resources outlined in this chapter, nonprofit executives can prepare and implement more effective fundraising efforts. Discussing, advocating, planning, and applying strong fundraising budget practices can lead nonprofits to better-implemented and better-resourced fundraising efforts. By using powerful evaluation tools to show how needed resources are creating desired results, fundraisers can make a solid case for investing in fundraising and, ultimately, raise more money to do more mission work. By communicating with staff, board, and government about fundraising performance through sound reporting, nonprofits can show constituencies that their nonprofit and those it serves are worthy of sound investment.

Good budgeting leads to strong fundraising planning, which leads to better fundraising. Empowered by these resources, fundraisers can create fiscally savvy departments, contribute to healthier organizations, and do more to accomplish the mission.

Discussion Questions

1. Nonprofit leadership in the budgeting process determines how an organization spends its resources on many different and important aspects of its operations. Discuss some strategies and tactics for elevating and valuing the fundraising budget in the overall nonprofit budget process.
2. The accounting and fundraising departments often struggle with fundraising reporting. What are some strategies and tactics for making sure that these departments and the entire nonprofit organization – including boards and leadership staff – report fundraising results in ways that are appreciated and understood by all?
3. Issues like "cost to raise a dollar" and "appropriate general administration and fundraising costs" have challenged nonprofit professionals for decades. What is the right amount? Is there a percentage that is best for all nonprofits? Why are the percentage costs for these areas at your nonprofit not only acceptable but worthy of celebration? If you do not currently work at a nonprofit organization, choose one that you like and use their information for this discussion.

Application Exercises

1. Perform a time study analysis on your nonprofit. If you are creating your own nonprofit or choosing one you would like to get to know better, for the purposes of this exercise, make the nonprofit have at least three programs in addition to fundraising.

2. Using data from your nonprofit organization (or one that you have selected), run a Fundraising Fitness Test to obtain key metrics on donor retention, new donor acquisition, and more. If you do not have and cannot gain access to a dataset, use created data of at least 100 gifts. What are your key metrics for the following data points?

   a. Number of gifts
   b. New donor acquisition
   c. Repeat donor retention
   d. Donor gains
   e. Donor losses

CHAPTER SIXTEEN

MARKETING FOR STRATEGIC FUNDRAISING

By Aja May Pirtle and Margaret M. Maxwell

Marketing builds strong relationships between an organization and its associated stakeholders. This chapter explores how marketers complement the work fundraisers do to build and strengthen relationships with donors. An effective partnership between marketers and fundraisers helps both parties be more effective in communicating the values exchange that is beneficial to organization and donor alike (Rosso 1991).

Understanding the marketing process helps nonprofits engage deeply with their donors, benefiting the organization's fundraising efforts and the donor's diverse needs.

After completing this chapter, the reader will be able to:

- Describe how marketers and fundraisers can work together effectively to enhance fundraising.
- Explain the elements of an organization's brand.
- Assess which key audiences and donor groups may be most important to their particular organization.
- Select market research strategies that can enhance understanding of donors and potential donors.
- Practice storytelling activities to bring the case for support to life for donors.

Marketing as the Linchpin

At one time, marketing was often seen as synonymous with advertising, invoking visions of decanter-filled offices and people creating iconic pitches, commercials, and taglines. Today, marketing is acknowledged to be a more holistic approach for building strong relationships between an organization and its constituency. The marketing exchange relationship is easily understood in the context of the for-profit sector, as widgets and whatnots are sold to an eager consuming public. In the context of the philanthropic sector, marketing becomes an integral partner in building the values exchange that attracts patrons, volunteers, and donors.

Both sectors, however, share the same definition of *marketing*, provided in 2017 by the American Marketing Association (AMA): "Marketing is the activity, set of institutions, and processes for creating, communicating, delivering, and exchanging offerings that have value for customers, clients, partners, and society at large." In other words, marketing helps make the connection between an organization and the community (local or global) that it serves. A good marketing strategy can help tell the organization's stories, communicate its needs, and organize its communications clearly and accessibly.

Marketing Is a Team Sport

In many organizations, the marketing and development teams are seated within the same department, or at the very least, adjacent departments. And that's no surprise: Marketers serve as storytellers and conduits for a relationship with a brand, and fundraisers are relationship builders and personal representatives of the organizations they serve.

By implementing a few key strategies, marketers and fundraisers can help create a meaningful, substantive, and creative partnership built on shared goals, common tactics, and a love for the organization. Indeed, this partnership often can be life-giving for an organization, for its staff, and for its mission fulfillment.

From a marketing perspective, attention to a short list of considerations lays the groundwork for a successful collaboration with fundraising.

Gather the Right Team with the Right Skills

Whether the team works remotely or in-person, fundraising and marketing staff must have the technology skills to collaborate and communicate effectively with each other and with the organization's constituents. The COVID-19 pandemic accelerated the push for nonprofits to develop robust online content and engagement strategies to ensure they remained relevant during a challenging time. Meetings, database management, solicitation efforts, cultivation activities, program delivery, and communications messaging were all delivered virtually by staff working in their homes. While in-person activities will likely never be completely displaced in the post-pandemic world, the enhanced reliance on technology applications demonstrated clearly the need to have a staff that is flexible and technology-literate.

Bring Marketers in Early

Marketers can help shape messaging, ensure a consistent brand experience, and gather and tell stories to donors and other stakeholder groups. They can also help strategize on the best ways to reach donors through a variety of channels, brainstorming the perfect campaign to reach a new or challenging audience and then helping put it into action.

One of the biggest challenges a marketing department faces is making sure there is adequate space on the schedule to push out key messages at the right time. Development staff can help the planning process by alerting its marketing colleagues to key fundraising events, goals, or deadlines.

Talk about Data

Marketing departments often have a wealth of information about the audiences the organization serves, and existing or future research can also inform development work.

Conversely, the donor database can be immensely helpful to a marketing department as it refines its own knowledge about the organization's core audiences. Marketers can mine the donor database for rich information about trends, demographics, and even psychographic information, which can help both marketing and fundraising initiatives.

Use a Multi-Channel Approach

Development is most often about personal relationships, which is where the development officers shine. They know their portfolio and their donors' needs on a personal basis. If they share that information with the marketing team, it can help shape marketing strategies and content.

The marketing department can help expand the potential donors at the base of the pyramid through a multi-channel approach. Long gone are the days in which twice-a-year appeal letters were the only option. Now there are crowdfunding, social media campaigns, giving day campaigns, appeal videos, and other similar vehicles (see Chapter 24). By working together, marketing and development staff can leverage the strengths of both departments in a meaningful way.

Share in Successes and Results

Fundraisers should communicate back to the marketing team about the results of a particular fundraising goal or campaign. This gives the marketing team a real goal to aim for and also important feedback about what is working (and what is not).

Sharing in the work can also bring about important and affirming relationships between colleagues so that when big challenges arise, there is a firm foundation of trust and context.

A Quick Guide to Branding

Over the past two decades, a marketing-related term has made its way into society's collective vocabulary: branding. Too often, a brand is equated with an organization's visual elements: the logo, colors, and font. But a brand has much more meaning and is a much more powerful tool than a logo could ever be by itself.

The AMA (2017) described a brand as a name, term, design, symbol, or any other feature that identifies one seller's goods or service as distinct from those of other sellers. Famed marketer Marty Neumeier (2007) put it this way: "A brand is a person's gut feeling about a service, organization, or product" (19). It's that feeling of elation coffee drinkers get when they see the green and white mermaid beckoning them to the drive-through. In the context of nonprofits, it's the feeling associated when the giant red cross appears in a community after a natural disaster or the sound of bell rings alongside a red kettle during the holidays. That's a brand at work.

A brand itself can have many moving parts, but these elements can be most helpful when developing a marketing strategy (Faust, personal communication 2021):

- **Brand Proposition:** A three- to five-word description of the most compelling idea to convey about the organization's mission.
- **Brand Values:** What the brand stands for, the things it holds dear, and the values that define how it behaves.
- **Brand Personality:** The human characteristics that are attributed to and personify the brand.
- **Brand Drivers:** The unique and differentiating benefits of the organization.

FIGURE 16.1. BRAND PYRAMID INDIANA UNIVERSITY LILLY FAMILY SCHOOL OF PHILANTHROPY

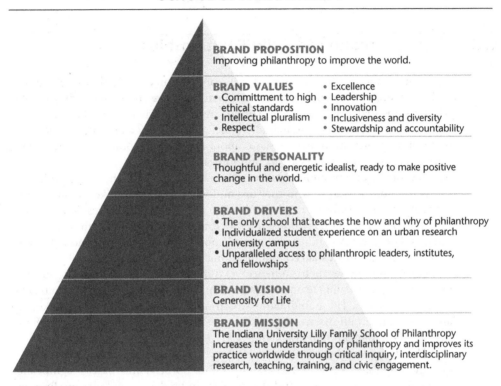

BRAND PROPOSITION
Improving philanthropy to improve the world.

BRAND VALUES
- Committment to high ethical standards
- Intellectual pluralism
- Respect
- Excellence
- Leadership
- Innovation
- Inclusiveness and diversity
- Stewardship and accountability

BRAND PERSONALITY
Thoughtful and energetic idealist, ready to make positive change in the world.

BRAND DRIVERS
- The only school that teaches the how and why of philanthropy
- Individualized student experience on an urban research university campus
- Unparalleled access to philanthropic leaders, institutes, and fellowships

BRAND VISION
Generosity for Life

BRAND MISSION
The Indiana University Lilly Family School of Philanthropy increases the understanding of philanthropy and improves its practice worldwide through critical inquiry, interdisciplinary research, teaching, training, and civic engagement.

Definition of Terms

Brand Proposition	Brand Values	Brand Personality	Brand Drivers
The most inspiring and compelling idea we can convey about the brand to our target audiences	What the brand stands for, the things it holds dear, and principles that define how it behaves	The human characteristics that are attributed to and personify the brand	The unique and differentiating benefits of the brand

Source: Indiana University Lilly Family School of Philanthropy 2021.

Together, these elements create a full picture of the brand. They can be used in a variety of ways, but a brand pyramid is one tool to help consolidate these ideas. A sample pyramid is presented in Figure 16.1. If the logo, font, and color scheme are the clothes of a brand, the pyramid is the foundational character and soul of a brand. It is also a way to make sure that the marketing department's materials are fully consistent with the case for support as well as the overall fundraising plan.

Gathering Information to Build Relationships

Just as branding is critical to building and managing an organization's reputation, gathering information about customers and donors is essential for building strong relationships that result in giving, volunteering, and advocacy on behalf of the organization. Fundraisers and marketers each play a role in gathering information that will drive organizational decisions about how best to communicate with current and prospective donors across multiple channels.

Too often, organizations (and marketers) think about what their audience needs to know instead of who they are and what they would like to know. This focus on the organization's needs rather than the audience's can result in marketing and communications that are one-sided and are often met with an uninterested and deaf ear. An audience-centered approach can break this bad habit and breathe fresh air into a stale communications strategy.

Fundraisers know their audiences extremely well and can provide critical insights to the marketing team as they develop a multi-channel approach to reaching key audiences. These foundational steps are critical to make sure marketing and development efforts are aligned to meet an organization's audiences where they are, both digitally and in-person.

The distinction between market research (typically led by marketing staff) and the fundraiser's role in researching the in-house donor base is significant, although both functions can and should work in tandem. The following foundational steps can help align information-gathering efforts.

Identify the Key Audiences

Most organizations have the ability to access a database that records a tremendous amount of helpful information for the fundraiser. In addition to the basics – Who are the donors? How much have they given? What are their addresses, phone numbers, and email addresses? – the database ideally permits the organization to segment donors into subgroups of similar types, maintain a giving history for each donor, assess giving capability, and record additional information gleaned through donor conversations.

Fundraisers can use this in-house data to make a list of constituent groups that they know (or suspect) might be important to their organization's fundraising success (see Chapter 14). Demographic factors, current or potential involvement with the organization's programs and services, and relationship connections are some of the important determinants of who makes up a key constituent group.

The marketing team can also identify who is interacting with the organization on social channels. Working together, the fundraiser and marketer should be able to identify three to five key audience groups, including a mix of current, former, and prospective donors.

Find Out More about Them

To set a research agenda, the fundraiser must decide what needs to be known to effectively ask for a gift, steward the gift, and renew the gift. For example, if one of the key audiences is donors who pledge online, it will be helpful and actionable to know how these donors want to receive pledge reminders and how frequently they want to be reminded. Do they prefer the reminders to come through email or a letter? A postcard or a brochure?

In addition to answering these basic questions, researching key audiences involves unpacking emotions, feelings, and impressions about the organization and the brand. The Indiana State Museum, for example, learned about how to grow its membership (the museum's annual fund) by talking with, following, and meeting with "mommy bloggers." These hard-working women had found a niche in providing fun opportunities for families and had a huge local following. Through their blogs and those ongoing conversations, the museum learned more about why these women came to the museum, what membership benefits were attractive to them, and for what reasons. Indy Moms became one of the museum's key audience groups, and the museum's membership numbers grew because of that focus.

Meet Them Where They Are

Seasoned fundraisers are very familiar with tailoring their work to the communications preferences of donors. Is email, social media, or print the preferred communication channel for particular donors? Usually the donor database will have a field for exactly that reason – everyone has different communications habits.

Similarly, organizations have their own (sometimes limited) communications resources. With the increasingly complex landscape of marketing channels, it is important to focus on the ones that the organization's donors and volunteers are on and that the organization can resource effectively. That focus might mean choosing a couple of social media channels rather than chasing every fad, or perhaps dedicating resources to direct mail because the organization's patrons respond best to an appeal that goes to an actual mailbox.

Measure It

More and more, marketing and communications tactics can be measured. While there are still the intangible "impressions," there are also likes, follows, comments, visits, open rates, and click-throughs. Did an email that had a high click-through rate result in similarly high-giving engagement? Does the landing page reveal any disconnects between the email and the website? All of these measurements can help paint a picture of an organization's full marketing success.

Test It

Market research is focused on gathering external information that can help facilitate effective donor communication about the case for support. It provides a perspective about the organization's donors and documents the effectiveness of different fundraising and communication strategies. It also assists fundraisers by providing the means to test and evaluate creative communication strategies long before they are refined and sent to donors.

What words and phrases best communicate the message? Do donors understand and have empathy with the organization's mission? What kinds of photo images best communicate the organization's work? What news sources do the donors trust? What obstacles does the organization face in increasing the size of an annual gift? How does an economic downturn affect how donors feel about giving to the organization?

Board members and volunteers are a great first audience to test communications with – assuming they align with the audience the organization is trying to reach and bring diverse perspectives. Sending a draft version to a close group of trusted opinion leaders is an easy way to gather feedback before implementing a communications strategy broadly.

> In 2019, the United Nations Children's Fund (UNICEF) reached historic giving levels through an online engagement campaign. By using data gained from their digital marketing insights, development officers have shaped emails and other communications to appeal to donors' interests. By doing so, they are reaching a new generation of donors and creating lasting relationships that will serve the organization and its beneficiaries for years to come (Stiffman 2020).

Incorporating Market Research

Market research can be either quantitative or qualitative, and both types are valuable to fundraisers.

Quantitative market research, which focuses on generating an appropriate number of responses in order to make generalized statements of fact, is often gathered through surveys and web analytic inquiries. A well-crafted quantitative market research study, for example, can help a fundraiser say with reasonable certainty, "80 percent of our donors are unsure of the value of unrestricted giving to our organization."

Qualitative market research is more concerned with subjective factors such as impressions, feelings, and emotions and is often gathered through focus groups or individual interviews (like those done in campaign feasibility studies). Questions posed through qualitative research are open-ended rather than yes/no, which means the results are difficult (if not impossible) to quantify with certainty. However, if an organization conducts multiple focus groups and/or individual interviews and hears the same feedback being shared, some generalizations can be drawn.

A qualitative study might, for example, produce conclusions such as, "First-time donors perceive our newer programs as more relevant to the community than our legacy programming, which is why they became involved. They'd like to know more about the impact these programs have before they consider giving again." It might also provide an organization with some of the compelling words or imagery that may end up in a case statement (see Chapter 13).

Qualitative and quantitative research can be used together to gain better insights about data. For example, themes that arise through focus group discussions can be tested more broadly with a quantitative survey to determine if these impressions can be extrapolated across a broader group of donors. Conversely, survey data can sometimes report "what" is going on, but not why. Unpacking an issue through individual interviews or focus groups can provide a richer understanding of the "why" behind the survey results.

Working together, marketing and development staff can determine the best way(s) to approach gathering the information needed. The following are several types of market research that might be helpful in an organization's fundraising planning, along with a representative question that each type might answer.

- *Brand Testing:* How is the organization perceived by donors and clients?
- *Concept Testing:* Will this idea work with our donors?
- *Copy Testing:* Does this copy communicate accurately, and is it memorable?
- *Donor Satisfaction Studies:* What do donors like and dislike about the organization's events?
- *Focus Groups:* How do first-time donors evaluate a proposed ad campaign, and how does that differ from repeat donors' perceptions?
- *In-Person or Telephone Interviews:* Is "leaving a legacy" a goal for our donors?
- *Campaign Planning Studies:* How compelling is our case for support?

- *Mall Intercept:* What does the "person on the street" think about holiday giving this year?
- *Mystery or Secret Shopping:* How easy is it to make an online gift to a competitor, and how does that compare to our web capabilities?

There is not one single "best way" to do market research with donors. In the end, the research tool(s) selected must match with the nonprofit's personality as well as the informational needs of the organization; the time available to the nonprofit to gather, analyze, and act on the data; and the organizational resources available to conduct various types of research. What is necessary, however, is that the organization recognizes that making "guesses" about donors is much less effective than basing decisions on real information.

Storytelling: Making Authentic, Long-Term Connections

"Once upon a time . . ." These magical words draw young children into myriad stories that help them develop interests in ideas and characters they have never met. These stories are often how children first appreciate the intricacies of language and human emotions and learn how to process and portray them. It's no surprise then that adults become wired to be drawn into stories.

Consider this study, conducted with analytically minded MBA students. Two groups were told positive statistics about a particular winery and its potential success. A third group was given the same statistics, along with a final statement: "And my father would be so proud to sip this wine." Overwhelmingly, the third group believed in the success of the winery (Kaufman 2003). In other words, the story matters.

What, then, does an MBA class experiment have to do with marketing and fundraising? It means that while organizations often share the various data points and numbers with donors, what the donors will most often connect with is a story. They, like all adults, want to hear about what those numbers, plans, and budgets mean in the context of the humans and communities being served.

Here are some ideas to help bring an organization's story to life:

- Ask a board member to open each meeting with their own personal story of involvement. It will not only be an insight into their own life and motivations for giving back, but will often provide fuel for a powerful example that can be shared.
- Make videos of volunteers and create short clips that tell stories of why they are involved with the organization. Use the video clips to recruit more volunteers and cheer on the existing volunteer base.
- Pictures can tell the story, too. Invest in strong photography that visually compels people to learn more about what the organization is doing in the

community. Create a social media campaign that shares the stories of the people involved with or served by the organization. Share it over a series of days with compelling photography and copy that entices the reader to follow the organization regularly and learn more.

- Be mindful to use images that are representative of the community along with words and messages that are culturally relevant to the intended audience.

> Giving toward racial justice has taken center stage after many years, fueled by the fundamentals of storytelling: direct video footage, first-hand testimonies, and emotionally compelling messaging from the Movement for Black Lives, National Association for the Advancement of Colored People (NAACP), and others. The GoFundMe pages crowdfunding to seek justice for George Floyd, Ahmaud Arbery, Breonna Taylor, and Jacob Blake all attracted at least $1 million. By early 2021, Floyd's GoFundMe memorial campaign garnered more donations than any other campaign in the online platform's history, raising over $14 million from 500,000 individual donors in 140 countries worldwide. Many of these gifts to the families impacted by police violence were for $5, and few were for $50,000 or more (Williams-Pulfer and Osili 2020).

Conclusion

Understanding the brand, identifying key audiences, conducting appropriate market research to select appropriate communications messages and channels, and developing compelling stories to bring the organization's case to life are the building blocks to successful nonprofit marketing efforts. The next steps – implementing appropriate marketing and communications strategies – usually fall to the marketing professionals. Though fundraisers also play a role, especially in one-to-one communication efforts with donors. In small organizations or integrated advancement teams, fundraisers may also find themselves with designated marketing duties as well as fundraising tasks.

Keeping the website and social media channels fresh and sharing information through newsletters and blogs enables the organization to focus on delivering content directly to stakeholders and donors. Other reputation-building initiatives, including writing and placing op-eds and speaking at service clubs or civic organizations, are activities that can reinforce for current donors the importance of being involved in the organization. These same activities can also help educate prospective donors about an organization.

People who are unschooled about the diverse elements that factor into an effective marketing program may tend to jump to these end products and assume they are what "marketing" is. In fact, newsletters, social media posts, and other communications activities are the end result of a carefully thought through process that leads to better understanding between organizations and their audiences. The end product is only successful if the key audiences are actively engaged in the process.

Discussion Questions

1. What are ways to build a strong sense of partnership between the marketers and fundraisers in an organization?
2. Discuss how to assess the communications resources and capabilities of an organization along with the communications preferences of its donors to determine the "best" way to effectively reach donors.
3. How can an organization evaluate the success of its marketing and communications efforts?

Application Exercises

1. Select a nonprofit organization that you are familiar with and put together an assessment of its brand proposition, brand values, brand personality, and brand drivers. Discuss your findings and recommendations with someone at the organization to see how your assessment matches with how the organization sees itself.
2. Develop three open-ended questions to elicit stories from volunteers about why they choose to be involved with an organization. Practice the questions with an active volunteer you know and record a short video. Or, if you have access to a nonprofit's volunteers: pose these questions to them and create short video interviews that can be used on the website or through social media volunteer recruitment efforts. Measure audience engagement with the videos.

CHAPTER SEVENTEEN

INTEGRATING PRINCIPLES OF DONOR RELATIONS

By Patrick C. Dwyer and Susan B. Perry

The key to developing a consistent stream of philanthropic support rests in building relationships. Once donors give to an organization, they are much more likely to donate again if they feel a sense of connection to the organization and its mission. Retaining current donors is highly valuable, especially when considering potential lifetime contributions (Sargeant 2001). Donor engagement, allowing donors to feel connected year after year, is vital to retention and requires significant time and effort.

This chapter integrates principles of donor relations and considers their importance to operating a successful fundraising program.

This chapter will help readers:

- Identify key features of donor relations.
- Recognize the role of expressing gratitude in donor relations.
- Understand the concept of stewardship and how it applies to different kinds of gifts.
- Appreciate transparency and accountability and the organization's responsibility for building trust.
- Apply chapter principles during times of crisis.
- Consider donor relations and diversity, equity, and inclusion.

What Is Donor Relations?

According to the Association of Donor Relations Professionals (ADRP), *donor relations* is "the comprehensive effort of any nonprofit that seeks philanthropic support to ensure that donors experience high-quality interactions with the organization to foster long-term engagement and investment" (ADRP.net). This effort can take place at many points in The Fundraising Cycle. When thinking about engaging donors and prospective donors to give generously in support of an organization's work, the focus may be primarily on presenting the programs, initiatives, and projects that best support the mission. Experience and research have shown that implementing intentional strategies that also carefully take the donor into consideration can help create a rich culture of donor engagement and is essential to increasing gifts over time. The way fundraisers and organizations acknowledge, manage, recognize, and report gifts can go a long way in building a robust culture of giving.

Gift Acknowledgment

The first aspect of donor relations is gift acknowledgment. How an organization responds to a gift affects the donor's sense of whether the gift is truly valued. From a donor's perspective, components of an efficient gift acknowledgment include timeliness, the inclusion of tax receipt language, and meaningful expressions of gratitude.

Generally, a gift should be acknowledged and receipted within 48 hours of acceptance. Traditionally, this is done through signed, hard-copy letters sent via postal mail. However, for gifts made online, many giving platforms ask donors to opt-in to receive a gift acknowledgment and receipt via email. It is important to remember that the donor who gives online may sometimes want a hard-copy receipt for tax purposes. Therefore, asking how donors would like to receive their gift receipt can be useful.

It is also important to affirm the amount of the gift with language that addresses Internal Revenue Service (IRS) requirements, such as: "(Nonprofit name) is a 501(c)(3) nonprofit organization. Your contribution is tax-deductible to the extent allowed by law. No goods or services were provided in exchange for your financial donation." In addition to these standard practices, organizations that acknowledge gifts with high levels of effectiveness will engage other personalized gift acknowledgment strategies, such as visiting with donors to express gratitude on behalf of the organization, engaging volunteers in the acknowledgment process (e.g., through thankathon calling sessions and handwritten notes) and sending special acknowledgments for gifts that show a personalized level of stewardship. Taking the time to handwrite a thank you note or make a quick phone call to the donor shows a culture of care and that an organization is efficient.

In addition to letters, notes, calls, and emails, gifts can be acknowledged with brief, personalized videos. There are software platforms available for this, or fundraisers could also record a brief, personalized video using a webcam or smartphone, and then email the video to the donor. A survey by Google found that more than half of donors who saw a video about a nonprofit went on to donate (Gross 2013).

Moreover, gifts can be acknowledged, and gratitude expressed, by anyone who knows the donor or who has benefited from the donor's gift. This can include board members, staff members, volunteers, other donors, and when appropriate, program participants (such as students thanking donors for funding scholarships). This also means that a gift can be acknowledged, and gratitude expressed, more than once. If multiple people reach out to the donor during the year, this can keep the organization at the forefront in the donor's mind.

Expressing Gratitude

Expressing gratitude is an essential aspect of donor relations. However, as obvious as this may sound, fundraisers often fall short of thanking donors effectively, if at all (Craver 2017). Researchers have found that people underestimate the positive impacts their expressions of gratitude have on other people, and this can prevent them from expressing gratitude (Kumar and Epley 2018). This is unfortunate, as expressing gratitude can have important downstream consequences on a donor's future relationship and involvement with the nonprofit organization.

Research reveals the importance of expressing gratitude for charitable gifts. For example, several studies have found that thanking a person for performing a desirable behavior in the past makes them more likely to do so in the future (e.g., Clark, Northrop, and Barkshire 1988; Grant and Gino 2010; Panagopoulos 2011). A handwritten "Thanks!" from a restaurant server on customers' checks leads to higher tips (Rind and Bordia 1995). In addition, a research study examining university fundraisers who solicited alumni donations over the phone found that those fundraisers who were thanked by their supervisor ended up making more calls over the next month compared with those who were not (Grant and Gino 2010).

However, it is important to note that not all studies have revealed benefits from expressing gratitude (e.g., Samek and Longfield 2019), suggesting there may be characteristics of gratitude expressions or the contexts in which they are delivered that make them more (or less) effective. For example, whether a "thank you" seems sincere can influence how it affects a recipient, and gratitude expressions can even backfire if they appear to be driven by ulterior motives (Dwyer 2015). Therefore, when thanking donors, fundraisers should try to avoid immediately asking for another gift and avoid using expressions like "thank you in advance for your gift." Expressions of thanks that stand on their own, apart from further requests, will likely be seen as more sincere expressions of gratefulness.

In addition, expressions of thanks can involve a "self-oriented" aspect (getting something that the nonprofit wanted) as well as an "other-oriented" aspect (because of the donor's actions). Research suggests that other-oriented gratitude, praising the benefactor, more effectively fosters donor relationships than emphasizing the gift's benefit to the recipient (Algoe, Kurtz, and Hilaire 2016). This also appears to hold for a donor's future giving behavior (Dwyer and Vaz 2020). Other-oriented gratitude expressions appear to be more effective because they are seen as more responsive to the donor's needs and have been referred to as a way of "putting you in thank you." Examples include statements such as, "You went out of your way to support us," "This shows what a generous person you are," and "We think you're great!"

Interestingly, recent work also finds that a single expression of gratitude can influence not only the person toward whom it was directed, it can also have ripple effects throughout social networks, organizations, and communities. Simply witnessing an expression of thanks from one person to another also promotes helping and relationship-building actions from the person who witnesses the expression of gratitude (Algoe, Dwyer, Younge, and Oveis 2020). Here, the effect of expressed gratitude again appears to be driven by its other-praising elements, which bolster perceptions of the expresser's responsiveness.

Consequently, there may be added benefits of expressing one's gratitude to donors in public, as opposed to (or in addition to) private settings. Public donor recognition activities may help draw new donors toward the organization. Examples of these activities include social gatherings to recognize donors, which could take place either in person or online, and using traditional and social media platforms to thank donors.

Stewardship and Donor Relations

Beyond expressing gratitude to donors, organizations have a responsibility to be good stewards of their gifts by using them as they intended and updating donors on the impact. Stewardship involves ". . . . being responsible for something valuable on behalf of someone who has entered it into our care" (Conway 2003, 432). As the team behind the Qgiv (2021) fundraising platform stated, "ultimately, stewardship is about meeting a donor's gift intentions and expectations within the parameters of your organization to create a long-term, mutually beneficial relationship."

Nevertheless, when it comes to fundraising, the word *stewardship* is not perfect. After all, we do not really steward people – we steward resources. However, many today apply the concept of stewardship to donors. Donor relations activities that fall within this broader definition of stewardship include the following:

- Calling donors to create personal connections through conversation.
- Providing opportunities for supporters to get involved in other ways besides their charitable giving.
- Finding creative ways to remain engaged with donors without always asking for the next gift.

Reporting to donors how their gift was used to further the organization's mission is a key aspect of stewardship. This is true of both unrestricted and restricted gifts. Those who make unrestricted gifts deserve stewardship of their gifts, just as do those whose gifts have more parameters. Both types of donors have a right to hear from the organization how their gifts were used or how they made a difference per the Association of Fundraising Professionals' (AFP) "Donor Bill of Rights." Organizations today receive a lower percentage of gifts unrestricted than they did a decade ago, perhaps because these gifts were not stewarded as well.

All donors and all gifts are important. Therefore, donors who make smaller gifts should be viewed as being special to the nonprofit, like the donors who make larger gifts. This applies to donors whose small unrestricted gifts help pay for everyday operational expenses and to donors whose larger gifts are restricted to a specific purpose.

It is always critically important to carefully construct the language of fundraising appeals and gift forms to be clear to donors about how their funds could be used. When donors make restricted gifts, organizations agree to act as trustees to carry out the purposes for which the gifts were solicited or for which the gifts were intended. There is no minimum financial amount for following donor intent. Fundraisers have a shared ethical obligation with other leaders within the nonprofit to make sure that the donor's intentions are honored. But this is more than an ethical obligation; it is a legal one and one with important ramifications for the public trust.

Transparency, Accountability, and Trust

Serious regard for the public trust is the soul of stewardship (Conway 2003). Nonprofit organizations build and maintain trust in their role as servants to the public good by remaining true to their philanthropic missions and their donors' intentions. As Tempel and Seiler (2016b) wrote, "trust is the stock and trade of philanthropy" (431), explaining the adage that fundraising happens at the speed of trust.

Psychologists have even suggested that trust "may be the single most important ingredient for the development and maintenance of happy, well-functioning relationships" (Simpson 2007, 264). Research has found that trust is a central feature of thriving relationships (e.g., Kim et al. 2015; Rempel, Holmes, and Zanna 1985) and is related to whether and how much people give (Light 2008).

Unfortunately, trust in nonprofits, as in many other social institutions, is lower than it used to be (Edelman Trust Barometer 2020). However, there are mechanisms through which fundraisers and nonprofits can combat this negativity. Transparency and accountability are two key ways of fostering trust among donors.

Transparency and accountability are two distinct but related principles that are essential to the fundraising process. The principle of transparency involves being open and clear about one's actions. Fundraisers should demonstrate to donors and potential donors that they have nothing to hide.

The principle of accountability emphasizes the importance of taking responsibility for one's actions. Whereas transparency involves being open about what you are doing, accountability involves doing what you are supposed to and behaving in accordance with expectations.

Accountability and transparency are intimately connected. While transparency promotes openness and honesty, accountability involves justifying why specific decisions were made and actions were taken, or not taken (Brown 2015). The organization needs to explain how it operates and how the money is used.

In the past, donors were more likely to trust that an organization would use a gift wisely, efficiently, and following the mission of the nonprofit. Today, financial transparency is very important to donors. "There are more nonprofits than ever, which means there is more competition for donations. To complicate matters further, donors are more informed and savvier than ever. They know good fundraising, and they are cautious givers. Donors have access to more information, thanks to the internet, and are becoming more sophisticated givers" (Forbes 2020).

Additionally, high net worth donors report they would give more if they were confident that their donations were having the desired impact (Indiana University Lilly Family School of Philanthropy 2014; Tempel and Seiler 2016b). Thus, greater transparency and accountability can help unlock future giving.

Donor Relations in Times of Crisis

Lessons learned about stewardship during a crisis can inform donor relations for future challenges such as natural disasters, power grid failures, economic downturns, and other forms of social upheaval. During the COVID-19 pandemic, for example, an updated plan for donor relations became essential for fundraisers to engage donors and prospective supporters virtually.

Fundraisers typically view face-to-face interactions as an ideal way to connect with donors, but the pandemic rendered these meetings impossible and then problematic. As a result, fundraisers and donors alike embraced virtual visits, video calls, and live-streaming events as ways to meaningfully connect across the country and the world. The "Zoom call" has since become a popular way to conduct personal visits and is expected to remain a useful tool for fundraisers.

How might fundraisers shape a donor engagement strategy in such a rapidly changing environment? Lessons learned from prior situations can be used to be more responsive in any crisis. Here are four ways to get started (Hilsner-Wiles 2020):

- *Show care.* Check in with donors to see how they are doing. Proactively communicating with donors, without asking for a gift, can help maintain or even enhance connections with them in what may be challenging times in their lives.
- *Enlist leaders to communicate with donors.* What is the president's or executive director's perspective on the crisis, and how does this person plan to move forward? Donors will appreciate hearing directly from an organization's leaders. Options can include small sessions with donors and friends, tailored messages for major donors, and invitations for supporters to share their feedback and insights with leaders. Updates on the organization's short-term response and information about adaptations to long-term plans are two ways of supplying reassurance.
- *Emphasize the nonprofit's expertise.* Provide data and stories illustrating how donors' gifts support programs, services, and research, particularly those that are relevant to the crisis. Highlight organizational expertise and staff knowledge, and how it enables informed decision-making and responsiveness to beneficiaries' needs.
- *Use virtual tools to keep donors engaged.* Keeping true to the culture of the organization, use technology to communicate with donors in ways that are feasible for them. Host a webinar to spotlight those working on the organization's mission; present organizational circumstances, accomplishments, and requests for support. Share photos and videos, as appropriate for the organizational mission and clients, so that donors can see the organization's efforts for themselves, even if from a distance.

Diversity, Equity, and Inclusion (DEI)

Considerations of DEI are imperative, especially during a crisis. Listening to diverse voices and perspectives is essential in providing insights into problems and considering a wide range of possible solutions. Crises and other widespread societal events can also have differing consequences for different communities, which presents challenges and opportunities for donor relations. It becomes all the more important for fundraisers to understand how members of various communities might be affected by social circumstances, which in turn, may impact how they give, or why they might not, how these dynamics might change in response to different events, and how to interact with supporters appropriately.

In addition, practical solutions to ease the burden of stressful times on vulnerable groups include fostering a culture of inclusion that avoids marginalizing or stigmatizing group members, communicating in ways that are reassuring to donors, and encouraging donors and potential donors to ask questions of the organization. It is also important to maintain a clear and consistent message in the face of these challenges. Inclusive leadership requires proactive communication as well as flexibility and transparency (YW Boston 2020).

Fundraisers need to be intentional about stewarding donors with different backgrounds and be aware of cultural differences associated with communication and relationship building. Other chapters in this book provide insights (see Chapter 9 and the chapters in Part Six) into various groups of donors, with the caveat that it is best to understand donors' preferences individually, as feasible. Communicating to donors about intentional steps taken to ensure DEI can be significant within an overall approach to donor relations. Transparency on these complex topics can help fundraisers build and deepen trust with donors while increasing the level of credibility and stability that donors perceive in the nonprofit.

Conclusion

Donors are becoming more sophisticated and more informed every day. The activities and processes that form a high-functioning donor relations program enable appropriate responses to donor expectations and rights. Beyond thanking and recognizing donors, managing gifts, and reporting back, the ultimate goal of a donor relations program is to strengthen the role and perceived value of giving and deepen the relationship between the donor and organization. To achieve this, donor relations must be viewed as an organizational priority, and stewardship of donor funds must be recognized as an ethical and legal mandate.

As Kay Sprinkle Grace (2020), one of the first faculty members at The Fund Raising School and recipient of the Association of Fundraising Professionals' 2020 Global Fundraising Professional of the Year Award, noted, "Our durability is based on our responses to the ever-changing needs and interests of our communities and the growing aspirations of our donors." Doing this work well highlights the importance of donors and of giving to beneficiaries while serving as the first step toward unlocking future gifts. In the end, making the effort to engage donors meaningfully and with dignity is the most promising cultivation exercise fundraisers can perform.

Discussion Questions

1. Discuss the role of expressing gratitude in donor relations.
2. What is the difference between donor relations and stewardship?
3. How can fundraisers cultivate trust?
4. What is the role of donor relations in time of crisis? How can donors be engaged during difficult times?

Application Exercises

1. Use a smartphone to record a thank you video to a hypothetical donor, and practice sending that brief video via email.
2. Write a personalized thank you note that is other-focused (focused on the donor) as opposed to self-focused (focused on the nonprofit).
3. Describe in detail three donor stewardship activities that can be implemented or expanded by a nonprofit organization you are familiar with.

PART FOUR

THE FUNDRAISING TEAM

CHAPTER EIGHTEEN

FUNDRAISERS: STEWARDS OF PHILANTHROPY

By Genevieve G. Shaker and Sarah K. Nathan

Fundraisers facilitate charitable giving, but are understudied and often underappreciated for their contributions to philanthropy. Understanding fundraisers' role in philanthropy will help practitioners do their best work, build awareness for reflection and improvement, combat uncertainties and isolation, and develop the professional community.

Readers of this chapter will:

- Review the history of formalized fundraising.
- Examine fundraisers' demographics and responsibilities.
- Consider research about the nature of fundraising.
- Assess opportunities and challenges for the field.

The Formalization of Fundraising

In the United States, the first documented secular efforts to raise money are associated with early colleges, including Harvard and the University of Pennsylvania (Cutlip 1990). Fundraising, however, was typically a secondary task of institutional leaders, depended on occasional contributions from the wealthy few, and relied on a small number of personal appeals.

TABLE 18.1. THE EVOLUTION OF FUNDRAISING AS AN ORGANIZATIONAL FUNCTION IN THE UNITED STATES, 1900–2000

Era and approximate timeframe	Aspects of era
Era of nonspecialists 1900s to 1910s	• fundraising as a part-time activity • some external paid solicitors • Federal income tax provisions for charitable deductions enacted • YMCA is the most recognizable fundraising organization
Era of fundraising consultants 1910s to 1940s	• first nationwide fund drive, successfully completed by the Red Cross • popularization of the "Ward Method" for campaigns with set goals and timeframes • fundraising consultancies founded to advise organizations on how to fundraise instead of serving as paid, external solicitors • in-house fundraising still conducted by nonspecialists • first recorded use of the term *development* to indicate raising money in higher education
Era of transition 1940s to 1960s	• wider adoption of fundraising as organizational revenue source • charitable organizations and private colleges hire dedicated fundraising staff • division of work between in-house staff (annual giving) and external consultants (campaigns) • first recorded use of the term *fundraiser*
Era of staff fundraisers 1960s to 1990s	• fundraising solidified as an internal function • rise of fundraising at hospitals, public universities • fundraising education programs created (e.g., The Fund Raising School, founded in 1974) • additional government oversight for nonprofits • expansion of fundraising methods

Source: Modified from Kelly 1998.

More systematic fundraising emerged around 1900 with larger scale philanthropy and broader solicitation of the general public (Cutlip 1990). Kelly (1998) described fundraising within organizations as having a four-phase evolution during the twentieth century (see Table 18.1).

Although women and people of color are usually overlooked in fundraising histories, evidence shows their early and ongoing contributions. Jane Adams regularly raised money for Hull-House (founded in 1889) to provide social and educational opportunities for Chicago's working class (Kelly 1998). Black school and college leaders, including Booker T. Washington at Tuskegee Institute (founded in 1881), raised money for scholarships and operating purposes (Washington 1900). Archives reveal that women were active in mid-twentieth-century fundraising consulting firms (Kelly 1998).

In the twenty-first century, fundraising is entrenched within most U.S. nonprofits and is mission-critical. Designated staff fundraisers are the norm in large- and medium-sized nonprofits, though executives, external consultants, and volunteers remain important partners in raising money.

Breeze and Scaife (2015) identified the United States as the only nation with an "advanced" fundraising structure, including the presence of highly developed professional practices and strong professional associations. Other nations are categorized as having fundraising structures that are established (Australia, Canada, United Kingdom), evident (Austria, Japan, Israel), emerging (Bulgaria, Caribbean, China), and embryonic (Indonesia, Lebanon). Breeze and Scaife predict that global demand for trustworthy, professional fundraisers will increase.

An ongoing debate centers on whether fundraising has achieved the status of a "profession." A profession has an established theoretical knowledge base, the ability to certify expertise and self-regulate, an ethical code, and a duty to the common good (MacQuillin 2017). Traditionally, professional status signaled expertise, accountability, legitimacy, and recognition in the public sphere. There is agreement that the field is progressing significantly, even giving rise to alternate conceptions (e.g., fundraisers as creative professionals) (Breeze 2017). The quest to develop recognized standards of practice, systems of accountability, and public understandings of fundraising work continues even as the term *professional* is more widely applied to fundraisers.

Fundraisers and Their Work

According to the Bureau of Labor Statistics (2019a, 2019b), 108,000 U.S. individuals are classified as paid fundraisers, and another 88,000 are public relations and fundraising managers. These numbers seem low in consideration of the country's 1.56 million nonprofit organizations (Urban Institute 2018), suggesting that fundraising remains interwoven with other responsibilities in some settings. Other countries report fewer fundraisers. The United Kingdom (U.K.) estimates range from 10,000 to 31,000; Association of Fundraising Professionals (AFP) has 3,600 Canadian members as compared to 30,000 U.S. members (AFP 2019; Breeze 2017).

The AFP conducts an annual survey of its U.S. and Canadian membership. Of 3,600 participants in 2020, 80 percent were female, 19 percent were male, and 1 percent indicated other (in the overall AFP membership 75 percent are female). The average salary was approximately $85,000; 51 percent had a bachelor's degree and 38 percent had a master's degree.

Fundraising does not require a particular academic credential, professional certification, or formal licensure. According to the AFP (2020) the largest cluster of fundraisers previously worked in business, sales, marketing, PR, financial planning, or banking (35 percent total). Fundraising knowledge is often acquired informally. Only 11 percent of U.K. fundraisers reported primarily learning fundraising through courses; 81 percent learned on the job (Breeze 2017). Fifty-two percent reported accidentally becoming fundraisers. This also occurs in the United States; however, more are entering fundraising earlier and with intentionality (Nathan and Tempel 2017).

Fundraisers in large organizations often are specialists (annual giving, major giving, planned giving, corporate and foundation giving, stewardship, donor relations) with distinctive responsibilities. In smaller organizations, fundraisers may be generalists doing all manner of fundraising (and other) tasks. The international Certified Fund Raising Executive (CFRE) Job Analysis survey (2015) structured the dimensions of fundraising as: (1) donor research; (2) securing the gift; (3) relationship building; (4) volunteer involvement; (5) leadership and management; (6) ethics, accountability, and professionalism (Aldrich 2016). Breeze (2017) proposed a three-part model explaining fundraising conceptually as fostering a philanthropic culture, framing needs, and facilitating donations.

Fundraising as Art, Science, or Both?

Some portray fundraising as an "art," entirely reliant on inherent personal traits, perhaps because the relational aspects of raising money are difficult to document (Breeze 2017). Unfortunately, this furthers the misconception that fundraising success simply requires a certain personality type. Some studies of fundraisers also examine additional factors, such as personal experiences, and the "science" of fundraising knowledge and fundraising education (i.e., Breeze 2017; Shaker and Nathan 2017). Table 18.2 categorizes effective fundraisers' key traits, skills, and knowledge from several studies. Notably, few studies reflect donors' impressions, and most studies examine only the fundraisers who work directly with donors.

The science of fundraising is found in academic fundraising education (Mirabella 2007), professional training programs, and certification programs (e.g., CFRE). The chapters in this book also demonstrate the development of fundraising's research base, common language, ethical standards, and evidence-based best practices.

Ultimately, effective fundraisers must be artful and scientific in varying degree and depending on their particular job functions. Breeze (2017) writes, "There is therefore no such thing as a 'typical' or 'perfect' fundraiser, any more than there is an 'ideal' type of teacher, doctor, or lawyer" (65).

TABLE 18.2. CHARACTERISTICS OF SUCCESSFUL FUNDRAISERS FROM RESEARCH

Date, Authorship, Country, Participants	Key Traits	Key Skills	Key Knowledge
1997, Duronio and Tempel U.S., Fundraisers	• Commitment to the cause/organization • Authenticity and warmth • Honesty and integrity • Hard working	• Communication • Management and organization • Fundraising (i.e., solicitation)	• Fundraising domains (e.g., planned giving, tax/legal, gift administration) • Organizational capacity • Leadership • Academic training
2011, Scaife, McDonald, and Smyllie Australia, Major gift fundraisers and major donors	• Cause knowledge and passion • Integrity	• Communication • Marketing • Management	
2014, Nagaraj U.S. and Canada, Higher education major gift fundraisers and chief development officers	• Linguistic and behavioral dexterity • Intellectual and social curiosity	• Information distillation • Strategic solicitation	
2017, Breeze U.K., Fundraisers and "million pound asker" fundraisers	• As compared to the public, fundraisers are more: • Trusting • Extraverted, open, conscientious, agreeable, and neurotic • Emotionally intelligent • Sociable and likely to organize social gatherings		
2017, Shaker and Nathan U.S., Higher education fundraisers	• Emotionally intelligent (including interpersonal communication skills) • Achievement oriented • Ethically grounded • Other centered • Mission focused • Intellectually adept	• Oral/written communication • Interpersonal communication • Listening • Donor engagement	• Managing the fundraising process • Fundraising programs and strategies • Maintaining professional outlook • Organizational functions for fundraising • Communicating effectively

Note: Studies include industry reports and academic research, with significant range in sample size and methodologies.

The Field's Challenges and Opportunities

From natural disasters and health crises to adaptive technologies and shifting ideas about philanthropy in society, fundraising takes place in an ever-changing environment. Current conversations are calling into question some foundational principles of raising money as being too centered on donors rather than beneficiaries and social justice (see Chapters 2 and 7). Fundraisers must keep their practices adaptable, dynamic, and in tune with social dynamics. These demands may be especially difficult for fundraisers in smaller organizations with few fundraising colleagues, limited resources for professional development, and multifaceted expectations.

Fundraisers must and do rise to many challenges. Compared to the public, fundraisers in Breeze's (2017) U.K.-based study tended to be more open to new ideas and experiences and more be extraverted; display more agreeable behaviors such as helping others; and less likely to feel depressed, tense, or worried. These characteristics match research showing that resilient people demonstrate optimism, a moral compass, cognitive and emotional flexibility, and social connectedness (Zimmerman 2020). Traits that make fundraisers' resilient enable them to navigate professional difficulties while seizing opportunities.

Overcoming Misperceptions about Fundraising

Fundraisers globally experience stigma, often based on negative perceptions about discussing or asking for money (Breeze and Scaife 2015). In the United States, these views hark back at least as far as the early twentieth century when independent, paid solicitors displayed poor stewardship of donations (Kelly 1998). Even today, people often perceive that asking for money is not proper, honest, or acceptable (Meisenbach et al. 2019). Although 91 percent of fundraisers feel positive about the field, only 41 percent believe that the public views fundraising positively (Nathan and Tempel 2017).

To counter these perceptions, fundraisers must create a "culture of philanthropy" within organizations (Gibson 2016). This approach includes the belief that fundraising spans job functions and activities – from the board table to the all-staff meeting (see Chapter 11). Organizations that nurture this mindset transform donor relations into a collective undertaking while breaking down internal silos by revealing what fundraisers do each day.

Fundraisers should also reflect on why they fundraise, be able describe what their work achieves, and be prepared to articulate this information to others (see Chapter 1). This may also require explaining philanthropy, why people give, and what giving and volunteering returns to the donor (see Chapters 5 and 26). Fundraising also requires a personal commitment to improving society and the well-being of others as part of values-based, ethical practice (Duronio and Tempel 1997). In one research study, nearly 100 percent of the fundraisers were donors and more than 80 percent volunteered in their communities, demonstrating their commitment to the public good (Shaker et al. 2020). Being open about one's own philanthropy counters negative stereotypes.

Supporting Fundraisers' Retention and Success

There is concern about fundraiser turnover. Some say average tenure is 18–24 months and fundraisers are perpetually looking for new opportunities, but the evidence is nuanced. An industry report found 51 percent of fundraisers anticipated leaving their positions (Joslyn 2019). Academic research, however, found that only 20 percent intended to leave their organization and current job tenure was 3.6 years (the median job tenure was 2 years) (Shaker et al. under review). The same study found as fundraisers become more experienced (10+ years) their job tenure increases. A 2020 AFP report also showed an upward trend in job tenure with averages of over five years. This suggests that a good proportion of fundraisers stay longer than commonly thought and fewer may end up leaving their jobs than some surveys suggest.

Regardless, good fundraisers cannot stay long enough. The relational nature of fundraising means time and trust are lost when fundraisers depart. Yet, few nonprofits have formal employee retention plans (Nonprofit HR 2019). When asked why they are considering leaving, fundraisers report the overwhelming pressure to succeed, feeling unappreciated, and a lack of advancement opportunities (Joslyn 2019). More research is needed to understand why fundraisers leave (or stay), and which "interventions" generate meaningful results.

To help with retention, organizations can invest in their fundraisers through professional development, value philanthropy as a legitimate source of revenue, and include the chief fundraiser at the decision-making table (Bell and Cornelius 2013).

Participation in professional associations, such as the AFP, provides fundraisers with training, networking, and mentoring. When nonprofits lack the funds for staff to join associations, attend conferences, or take part in trainings, fundraisers can connect with local peers and other low-cost professional development opportunities (Nathan et al. 2021). Informal peer networks require time, but not budget, and can help overcome isolation felt by some fundraisers. Video conferencing technologies have also expanded global networking opportunities.

Making the Profession More Diverse, Equitable, and Inclusive

Institutionalized philanthropy is associated with large transfers of wealth, most often by white men to organizations governed by white men. Philanthropy in communities of color, meanwhile, does not receive the same level of attention and often takes place informally and outside formal volunteering or fundraising structures (see Chapter 29). Not surprisingly, therefore, the majority of U.S. fundraisers are white (AFP 2020). Today, improving equity and inclusion within nonprofits and fundraising (and adapting fundraising practice) is a moral imperative and important for continued success in serving social needs and raising money.

Fundraisers of color face multiple barriers, including microaggressions, implicit bias, difficulty navigating predominantly white spaces, and a sector that largely upholds structures of institutional racism (CauseEffective 2019). This environment can be especially difficult as most fundraisers of color develop careers without persons of color as mentors, leaving them feeling particularly isolated. There are examples of people of color in major leadership roles in foundations and nonprofits, but broad diversification of leadership positions remains a key imperative (Rendon 2019).

With the social justice movement, associations and nonprofits redoubled diversity, equity, and inclusion commitments. As organizations create new ways to attract, sustain, and retain people of color, fundraising associations (AFP, Council for Advancement and Support of Education) have programs (i.e., internships, conference scholarships) to welcome people with diverse backgrounds into the field. Nonprofits need to actively recruit people of color for fundraising positions, strive to ensure that, when feasible, there are multiple candidates of color for job openings, and build structures to ensure inclusivity, not just diversity.

Individual fundraisers can also be influential. The sector has avenues for learning about and engaging in equity and inclusion efforts. Being an informed, intentional ally for colleagues of color may ease some daily struggles and contribute to a culture of inclusion. New research specifically suggests that a CEO who supports fundraising staff of color "in external situations and create[s] a culture of equity internally" (CauseEffective 2019, 14) is singularly important.

Addressing Gender Disparities

Over the last 75 years, the fundraising profession moved from predominately male to predominately female (Dale 2017; Duronio and Tempel 1997). Gender disparities persist, hampering women's ability to reach the highest fundraising (and organizational) positions and receive equitable remuneration. According to the AFP (2020), female fundraisers were paid 22 percent less then male fundraisers. Similarly, in the United Kingdom, men are more likely to be fundraisers in the largest, most-resourced organizations, women are more likely to work part-time, and male fundraisers ultimately make 14.5 percent more than female fundraisers despite comparable starting salaries (Breeze and Dale 2020). AFP-sponsored research shows an alarming percentage of fundraisers who have experienced some form of sexual harassment in their careers (females: 73%, males 59%) (LePere-Schloop and Beaton 2021).

Structural barriers hampering gender equality across the global economy also affect fundraisers. Examples include childcare and pregnancy leaves, secrecy around salaries, and disparities in family responsibilities (Rendon 2021). These barriers keep women from leadership positions and are even more challenging for women of color.

Progress requires significant changes in government and organizational policies and practices. A ban on employers asking job candidates about previous salaries reduces pay gaps (Rendon 2021). Transparency in posting salary ranges is now widely considered a best practice across the sector. The presence of women on nonprofit boards, and as chairs, increases the likelihood that women will be promoted or hired into leadership positions (Lee 2019). As women assume leadership roles, they can help transform the culture by serving as mentors, guides, and public voices for equity.

Studying the Profession

There is a growing body of research about and increasing attention to fundraisers, helping to fill a knowledge gap. Researchers are exploring fundraisers' roles in philanthropy and what facilitates positive fundraising outcomes – including overcoming barriers created by biases around race, ethnicity, gender, and accessibility. Research brings added legitimacy to the profession and provides insights into how to strengthen the field, better prepare fundraisers, create effective fundraising programs, and build sound organizational practices to help fundraisers succeed.

Research is establishing fundraisers as an additional component in the organization and donor dynamic. Chapman (2019) documented how the relationship among donor, fundraiser, and beneficiary influences giving decisions. Taking a sociological approach, Alborough (2017) found that fundraiser-facilitated relationships fit into several models based on frequency of contact and depth of interaction, and that fundraisers provide a central avenue for donors to express reciprocity toward the organization and its beneficiaries. Fundraising was more than the sum of an internal, managerial process. Additionally, Breeze's (2017) U.K. study uncovered useful metaphors – such as the chameleon, swan, and honest broker – describing the work of fundraisers.

Recognizing, understanding, applying, and participating in research about fundraising practices and the role of fundraisers can provide practitioners with effective tools for professional development and operational effectiveness.

Conclusion

Driven by mission, equipped with industry knowledge and research, and guided by a duty to social responsibility, the fundraising field is ever evolving to meet nonprofit and community needs. As fundraising takes its place as a recognized profession, defined ethical practices, transparency, and accountability will elevate its status through the actions of individual fundraisers. It is important that fundraisers thus reflect on their own personal experiences within the larger professional context. By being active within the field, fundraisers help grow the profession, build its authority and respect, and enhance justice and equity within fundraising.

Collectively, fundraisers' personal and professional optimism; respect for donors and recipients alike; and willingness to learn, innovate, and serve will put the field on a path to win professional respect and continue to make a meaningful and positive difference to society. As the stewards of philanthropy, fundraisers are envoys of trust, agents of transformation, caretakers of dreams.

Discussion Questions

1. How has fundraising developed within organizations with which you are familiar? Discuss in relation to the information in Table 18.1 and its chapter section.
2. How do organizational and national differences affect fundraisers' work and experiences?
3. How would you prioritize the challenges faced by fundraisers and why? Considering other information in the book and resources, what other critical issues do you find?

Application Exercises

1. Compare your experiences as a fundraiser, or understandings of the fundraising profession, to the content of this chapter.
2. Consider Table 18.2 and the related discussion about successful fundraising. What study themes and differences stand out? How can this information be useful to fundraisers and organizations?
3. Choose one of the challenges or opportunities presented in the chapter and brainstorm ways that you can learn more about it and make a contribution.

CHAPTER NINETEEN

FUNDRAISING PLANNING, MANAGEMENT, AND LEADERSHIP

By Bill Stanczykiewicz

Fundraising is a management function. The fundraising plan is a management document with specific goals aimed at achieving strategy, paying for programs, and satisfying the budget. Fundraisers use the plan to determine which fundraising activities happen and when, holding the nonprofit accountable for fundraising results while helping donors enjoy the joy of giving.

Fundraisers also are leaders even though they rarely serve in the nonprofit's top staff position. The chief development officer leads the nonprofit's fundraising team, leads peers across the organization, and "leads up" to the CEO as well as the board of directors.

Management and leadership can be interwoven but essentially are distinct. Fundraisers need to know the difference between these two important functions and become adept at both.

Consequently, readers of this chapter will learn:

- The tasks and tools of fundraising management.
- The traits and skills of fundraising leadership.
- How transformational leadership can accomplish fundraising strategy.
- How to navigate the complexities of power dynamics when leading.
- The unique aspects of fundraising leadership during a crisis.

Management

Management focuses on today and keeps track of details, all while ensuring things get done. Leadership examines the future and explores possibilities, all while providing big picture inspiration. Table 19.1 displays how Bennis (2009) summarized the distinction between management and leadership.

As Bennis (2009) explained, leaders passionately describe a guiding vision with an integrity that builds trust, while managers ensure that the right steps are being taken to achieve that vision. In the context of fundraising, leaders "develop" an "innovative" vision aimed at accomplishing the "what and why" (the mission) of the nonprofit organization. Managers, meanwhile, "administer" the "systems and structures" of the fundraising plan, which describes the "how and when" of each fundraising vehicle and market, all while "measuring for results."

Fundraising Planning

Fundraising is a complex endeavor that requires specific goals and measurable outcomes that are systematized through a formal fundraising plan (Elkas 2016). This plan allows fundraising managers to plan and prioritize as well as implement and execute, while celebrating successes, identifying gaps, and holding themselves and the rest of the nonprofit accountable for fundraising results.

The exact format of the fundraising plan is not as important as ensuring that there is a written plan and that everyone associated with the nonprofit knows what is expected for successful implementation. The fundraising plan can be written text describing:

- The fundraising case for support.
- The financial need of the nonprofit overall and by program or activity.
- A gift range chart for achieving the fundraising goal.
- A description of gift markets (i.e., individual donors, foundations, corporations) and fundraising goals within each market.
- The philanthropic interest and financial range of major gift donors.
- A list of foundations and corporations and the grant, gift, and sponsorship amounts that will be requested from those funders.
- The vehicles utilized to pursue charitable support (i.e., one-on-one meetings with donors, special events, annual fund letters, digital fundraising, grant proposals, sponsorship requests).
- A specific timeline for implementing each vehicle.
- A description of board and staff responsibilities for implementing the plan.
- A detailed fundraising budget to pay for this comprehensive work.

Exhibit 19.2 lists projected donations by source, and the remaining columns can be filled in with the monetary amount – either a precise number or a range – that

TABLE 19.1. MANAGEMENT VERSUS LEADERSHIP ACTIVITIES

Manager	Leader
Administers	Innovates
Maintains	Develops
Systems and Structures	People
Control (measure for results)	Trust
Short-Range View	Long-Range View
How and When	What and Why

Source: Based on Bennis 2009.

EXHIBIT 19.2. FUNDRAISING PLAN TEMPLATE

SOURCE	UNRESTRICTED Amount	PROGRAM #1 Amount	PROGRAM #2 Amount	TOTAL GOAL
INDIVIDUAL DONORS				
Board of Directors	$ _____	$ _____	$ _____	$ _____
Board Member	$ _____	$ _____	$ _____	$ _____
Board Member	$ _____	$ _____	$ _____	$ _____
Board Member	$ _____	$ _____	$ _____	$ _____
Staff	$ _____	$ _____	$ _____	$ _____
Volunteers	$ _____	$ _____	$ _____	$ _____
In-Person Meetings	$ _____	$ _____	$ _____	$ _____
Donor	$ _____	$ _____	$ _____	$ _____
Donor	$ _____	$ _____	$ _____	$ _____
Donor	$ _____	$ _____	$ _____	$ _____
Direct Mail	$ _____	$ _____	$ _____	$ _____
Digital	$ _____	$ _____	$ _____	$ _____
Special Events	$ _____	$ _____	$ _____	$ _____
Euchre Tournament	$ _____	$ _____	$ _____	$ _____
FOUNDATIONS				
Big Town Foundation	$ _____	$ _____	$ _____	$ _____
Fam Lee Foundation	$ _____	$ _____	$ _____	$ _____
CORPORATIONS				
Bill's Produce & Supermarket	$ _____	$ _____	$ _____	$ _____
Pat's Peugeot Dealership	$ _____	$ _____	$ _____	$ _____
Gene's Gym	$ _____	$ _____	$ _____	$ _____
Gen & Sarah's Bookstore	$ _____	$ _____	$ _____	$ _____

the fundraiser plans on receiving from the source (individual, foundation, or corporation) or vehicle (special event, direct mail, or digital) during that year. Exhibit 19.3, meanwhile, provides a timeline for these fundraising activities.

EXHIBIT 19.3. SAMPLE FUNDRAISING TIMELINE

ACTIVITY	MONTH OF THE YEAR											
	J	F	M	A	M	J	J	A	S	O	N	D
INDIVIDUALS												
Board of Directors												
Annual appeal	X											
Board prospective donor list development				X								
"Work the list"					X	X	X	X	X	X	X	X
Staff – Annual Appeal									X			
Volunteers – Annual Appeal							X					
Individual Donors – Major Gifts												
One-on-one meetings	X	X	X	X	X	X	X	X	X	X	X	X
Ongoing cultivation and stewardship	X	X	X	X	X	X	X	X	X	X	X	X
Individual Donors – Direct Mail												
Prepare the letter									X			
Mail the letter										X		
Receive, record, steward gifts											X	X
Digital												
Review social for likes, shares, comments	X			X			X			X		
Fundraising appeals		X			X			X			X	
Special Event – Euchre Tournament												
Plan and invite			X	X	X	X	X					
Host the event								X				
Debrief and follow-up									X	X	X	
FOUNDATIONS												
Big Town Foundation												
Meet with program officer			X									
Grant proposal deadline								X				
Fam Lee Foundation												
Grant application deadline							X					
CORPORATIONS												
Meet with businesses during budgeting	X	X	X	X	X	X	X					
Invite business sponsors to special event						X	X					
Submit requests for business donations							X	X	X	X	X	X

The fundraiser, in the role of manager, then can follow the fundraising plan to prioritize fundraising activities, schedule tasks and activities, ensure quality completion of each activity, and measure results.

Staying organized in this manner is an example of the fundraiser's professional stance, demonstrating the seriousness of their profession, the credibility of the nonprofit, and the stewardship of donor relationships.

The fundraising plan also guides the fundraising activities of other people in the nonprofit organization. The fundraising team, the CEO, staff colleagues, and the board of directors all can see themselves in the plan and throughout the timeline.

Fundraisers can function as managers while concurrently serving as leaders. However, an important distinction needs to be made. Fundraisers should not use the fundraising plan to manage people, not even people on the fundraising team. Instead, fundraisers should lead people and manage agreements. In this context, the fundraising plan is that agreement.

Leadership

If fundraisers had as many donors as there are explanations of the word *leadership*, this textbook would not be needed. A recent online search discovered nearly 300 million results in response to a search for that definition, but some leadership principles stand the test of time.

Roles of the Nonprofit Leader

The Fund Raising School relies on the description provided by James MacGregor Burns whose book, *Leadership*, sparked considerable research into effective leadership practice. Burns (1978) wrote, "Leadership is relational, collective, and purposeful. Leadership shares with power the central function of achieving purpose" (18).

Notice that leadership is "relational," indicating people working together, not situating the leader above everyone else. The team's work is "collective," as the leader encourages team members to share their recommendations, skills, abilities, and concerns to achieve overall organizational success. While each individual should be celebrated for their contributions, the team's collective efforts are aimed at "achieving purpose" – fulfilling the nonprofit's mission while donors experience the joy of giving.

In the context of fundraising leadership, *purposeful* does not mean meeting metrics. Those measurements matter to the fundraiser as manager. The fundraiser as leader is, instead, focused on achieving the purpose of the nonprofit's vision and mission; on behalf of the people (or animals or environment) being served; for the cause being championed. The fundraiser as leader focuses on "why" the

FIGURE 19.4. FOUR ROLES OF THE NONPROFIT – INCLUDING FUNDRAISING – LEADER

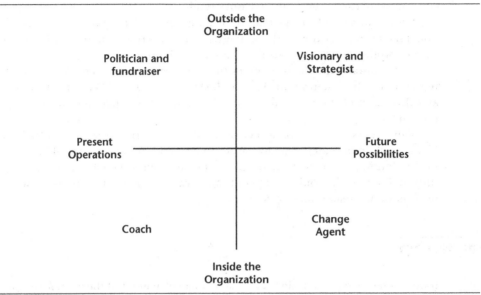

Source: Based on Nanus and Dobbs 1999.

resources are being raised, not on "how," and the "why" galvanizes the fundraising team – and the entire nonprofit – into vibrant action (Bennis 2009).

The four roles of the nonprofit leader articulated by Nanus and Dobbs (1999) can serve as a road map for the fundraising leader. Figure 19.4 reveals how the first responsibility of the leader – located in the top right quadrant – is to look outside of the organization and into the future. The fundraising leader, for example, can examine economic trends and forecasts, public policy proposals and events, as well as evolving cultural factors and conditions, when devising the new fundraising strategy.

The fundraising leader then continues to look into the future but moves inside the nonprofit – into the bottom right quadrant – providing change leadership by describing the new strategy, answering questions, and addressing concerns, thereby ensuring that the entire organization is on board with the new strategy. In the bottom left quadrant, the fundraising leader – still inside the organization but now in the present – serves as a coach, providing big-picture oversight while celebrating successes, identifying gaps, expecting the unexpected, and fostering continuous improvement.

With a vibrant vision, organizational consensus, and a thorough plan, the fundraising leader then can remain in the present but venture outside the organization – into the top left quadrant – to lead the nonprofit's fundraising.

Transformational Leadership

Leading the team toward the nonprofit's overall mission – and leading the nonprofit's fundraising to fulfill that mission – is the essence of transformational leadership (Bass and Avolio 1993). Transformational leaders promote organizational interests over self-interests (Robbins and Judge 2016). Elevating the organization's success over any one individual's success also enhances the likelihood that the team will adhere to ethical standards since behaving unethically would not only diminish the reputation of the individual, but also the persuasiveness of the cause (Johnson 2018a). Therefore, employing transformational leadership deploys ethical fundraising.

These descriptions of transformational leadership also reveal why fundraisers are well suited for leadership, and in fact, already are leaders. The successful fundraiser aligns the philanthropic values of donors and funders with the nonprofit's values and mission. The effective fundraiser articulates how that alignment strengthens the nonprofit's pursuit of the mission and how achieving the mission strengthens the community. In these capacities, the fundraiser is leading toward donor intent and organizational impact, not personal success.

As Wagner (2004) noted astutely, fundraisers already are transformational leaders – focused on donors, the nonprofit, and the community instead of on themselves.

Bass (1985) characterized transformational leadership into categories that can be translated into fundraising leadership practice.

- *Idealized influence* – Fundraisers exemplify the nonprofit's values while placing the needs of donors, colleagues, program participants, and other stakeholders above their own.
- *Inspirational motivation* – Fundraisers with an abundance (as opposed to a scarcity) of mentality demonstrate a continual sense of possibility to everyone associated with the nonprofit.
- *Intellectual stimulation* – The listening skills, empathy, and emotional intelligence utilized by fundraisers in their relationships with donors also can be utilized to encourage ideas for new approaches and recommendations for continual improvement from throughout the philanthropic organization.
- *Individualized consideration* – Just as fundraisers tailor each philanthropic request to the specific motivations of each donor, fundraisers as leaders focus on the strengths and opportunities for growth of each member of the team.

Leadership is a social influence process – leaders explicitly work socially (with others) to influence the team toward a shared purpose (McAllister 2018). This positive view of leadership is inspiring but also incomplete. There is one more word from Burns' (1978) description of leadership that fundraising leaders need to confront.

Power

Leaders in the philanthropic sector might be uneasy with the word *power*. While serving the poor and marginalized, overcoming injustice, and promoting equality, nonprofit leaders can become uncomfortable with the notion of holding power.

While leaders, including fundraisers, continually pursue tangible progress toward the timeless ideals of justice, leaders need to come to terms with their own reservoir of power. The question is not "if" leaders have power – they do. The question instead is "how" leaders utilize power – either effectively or not. After all, while Burns (1978) described leadership as relational and collective and aimed at achieving purpose, he also called attention to leadership's association with power.

Types of Power

French and Raven (1959) provided guidance for how leaders can wisely and competently utilize their power. They explained that there are two types of power that all leaders can access. *Hard power* (which many people think of when they hear the word *power*) consists of reward, coercive, and legitimate power. *Soft power* (which often is neither detected nor discussed) consists of information, expertise, and referent power.

The utilization of hard power seems obvious. Examples include fundraising managers who reward team members with raises and promotions, while using coercive power when placing a team member on a performance improvement plan. Legitimate power is based on having the title and the position on the staff chart to make decisions.

Conversely, soft power starts with the information the leader uses to inform recommendations, guidance, and decisions. For example, when recommending or deciding on a fundraising strategy, the fundraising leader can cite the latest data on charitable giving from Giving USA, current research on how economic factors influence donor behaviors, and recent trends discerned from the donor database.

Soft power continues with expertise, a close cousin of information, which helps the leader be viewed as an expert. Expertise is evident, for instance, when fundraising leaders exhibit their mastery of fundraising techniques; demonstrate how best to relate with donors; stay up to date on digital fundraising methods; or speak the language of the business sector when raising funds.

Soft power also is referent, meaning the rest of the organization can refer to the leader as a fully committed member of the team – someone who has demonstrated commitment to the cause and to the nonprofit's well-being. Having earned referent power, the fundraising leader's decisions for the team and recommendations to

TABLE 19.5. EFFECTIVENESS OF DIMENSIONS OF POWER FOR FUNDRAISING LEADERS

HARD / SOFT POWER	DIMENSION	SUPERVISORS (CEO / Board)	PEERS (Other VPs)	TEAM (Fundraising Staff)
Hard	Reward	Low	Low	Moderate
Hard	Coercive	Low	Low	High
Hard	Legitimate	Low	Low	High
Soft	Information	High	High	High
Soft	Expertise	High	High	High
Soft	Referent	Moderate	High	High

Source: Based on French and Raven 1959.

superiors (known as "leading up") are viewed not as an individual insisting on being right or winning an argument but as a team member who is completely dedicated to the success of the organization.

Interestingly, hard power at best has a neutral effect, and at worst has a negative effect on organizational culture and results (Robbins and Judge 2016). Soft power, meanwhile, has a positive influence on individual and team effectiveness.

The difference between hard and soft power especially is noteworthy for fundraisers who rarely have the top staff position in the nonprofit but who always have soft power. Table 19.5, based on French and Raven's (1959) research, reveals how a fundraiser's soft power is impactful when leading the fundraising team, influencing peers with similar positions in the nonprofit, and leading up to the CEO and the board of directors.

In-Group Leadership

The fundraising leader's use of power can be both maximized and mitigated by using "in-group" leadership. According to Haslam, Reicher, and Platow (2011), an in-group leader:

- Reflects the group by understanding the group's culture and what matters most to group members.
- Represents the group by serving as a typical member of the group and championing the group to others.
- Realizes group achievements by fostering in-group collaboration and celebrating group success.

In-group leaders emphasize what they have in common with their colleagues. This strong sense of shared identity has a positive influence on how team members view the leader and on how well the team works together toward shared results (Van Knippenberg et al. 1994).

Fundraising leaders "reflect the group" when they continually remind the fundraising team, staff colleagues, CEO, and board members of the reasons why money is being raised. Fundraising leaders "represent the group" when they advocate to the CEO and the board of directors of the necessity to plan fundraising alongside the program plan and budget – as well as the importance of providing the fundraising team with sufficient resources to fundraise effectively. "In-group" leadership also is evident when fundraising leaders realize and celebrate the team's successes.

Fundraising leaders, mindful of their hard and soft power while exemplifying the traits of "in-group" leadership, are well positioned to lead effectively (according to Burns 1978) in ways that are relational, collective, and aimed toward achieving purpose. These attributes take on added importance during seasons of crisis.

Fundraising Leadership during Times of Crisis

A once-in-a-century pandemic beginning early in 2020 ignited deadly health concerns while slamming the brakes on the world economy. Soon afterward, tragic murders of unarmed Black citizens reignited political, economic, and social movements toward racial justice and reconciliation.

Many nonprofits were directly involved with COVID-19 relief or racial justice advocacy, and all nonprofits needed to continue fundraising in a perfect storm of crisis. Fundraising therefore required responsive skills in crisis leadership – a need that remains perpetual (see Chapter 7).

Crisis leadership is defined as "the set of preparatory and response activities aimed at the containment of the threat and its consequences" (Ansell and Boin 2019, 1082). Notice how crisis leadership starts with being prepared and planning ahead. This allows the crisis leader to respond promptly, not to end the threat, but to contain the threat and any resulting consequences.

Fundraisers, who already are guided by a sense of possibility, need to realize that a crisis always is possible and that action steps responding to crises also are possible (Boin 2004). Therefore, whether the crisis is a world health calamity, the failure of a state's electric grid, an economic recession, a local tornado or flood, or the unexpected closing of a community's major employer, fundraising leaders should realize that crises are normal and not unusual, allowing them to approach the crisis with calm and confidence (Ansell and Boin 2019).

Crisis Planning

One preparatory step is for the fundraising leader to budget and raise funds in a manner that builds an operating surplus that can be utilized during economic recessions, including financial downturns caused by crisis (see Chapter 15). This can be challenging, requires ongoing attention, and can require an organizational shift. Unsurprisingly, nonprofits with endowments and operating reserves were most likely to endure during the COVID-19 pandemic (Kim and Mason 2020).

When a crisis hits, leaders need – in this order – to save lives and save infrastructure (Boin et al. 2013). Ensuring the safety of any and all people associated with the nonprofit is the leader's first priority before then turning to the building, the vehicles, the technology, the bank account, and other aspects of the nonprofit's infrastructure.

The leader's next response involves guarding the nonprofit's reputation (Boin et al. 2013). For example, the fundraising leader can describe the nonprofit's prompt actions in the first two steps – saving lives and saving infrastructure – when communicating with donors, reassuring donors of the nonprofit's legitimacy and competence.

After urgent and immediate needs have been addressed to save lives, protect infrastructure, and guard reputation, the fundraising leader then turns to scenario planning – identifying several different possibilities for the near- and long-term future (Uitdewilligen and Waller 2018). The fundraiser who is accustomed to leading toward a well-defined vision now needs to adapt to complex, incomplete, and conflicting information (Ansell and Boin 2019). The fundraising leader also needs to be comfortable with making provisional decisions that can be revised or reversed as new information becomes available (Ansell and Boin 2019; Crichton and Flin 2004).

Despite the crisis, fundraising needs to continue. The nonprofit's financial needs are at least the same and likely are greater due to the crisis, and fundraising during a crisis provides donors with an enhanced opportunity to experience the joy of giving. As Tim Seiler noted at the start of the COVID-19 pandemic, philanthropy – with a message of making the world a better place – ultimately delivers a message of hope (Stanczykiewicz 2020b).

Conclusion

Fundraising responsibilities include management and leadership. Fundraisers are managers when they implement the fundraising plan and measure progress. Fundraisers are leaders when they continually point toward why funds are being raised (the nonprofit's mission), and fundraisers lead when they reflect the nonprofit's values and exemplify an inspiring sense of possibility and abundance.

All leaders have power, and fundraising leaders need to use their power well when leading their teams, leading across the organization with peers, and when leading up to the CEO and the board of directors. Exhibiting in-group leadership increases the fundraising leader's abilities to properly utilize power.

Fundraising leaders also need to adapt their leadership skills to times of crisis. How the nonprofit navigates the crisis actually can help fundraising leaders maintain and build trust with donors, especially since fundraising needs to continue during the crisis.

Discussion Questions

1. Explain the dimensions of fundraising management in comparison with leadership.
2. What are some central concepts of leadership described in this chapter and how do they apply in the fundraising context?
3. How can fundraisers best "lead up" to the CEO and to the board of directors?
4. What messages should the fundraising leader communicate to donors during times of crisis?

Application Exercises

1. Review Figure 19.4. In the top right quadrant, look outside of your organization (or an organization you want to research) and into the future. What economic, political, cultural, or other trends could affect the organization's future fundraising strategies?
2. How comfortable (or not) are you with the word *power*? How would you utilize your power as a leader to lead up, lead across, and lead the team that reports to you?
3. What are some specific ways to be an "in-group" leader? Have a conversation with a person who you believe leads in this way to add to the ideas in this chapter.

CHAPTER TWENTY

ENGAGING THE BOARD FOR FUNDRAISING

By M. Gasby Brown

"Many nonprofits don't get the board they need; they get the board they deserve." This admonition reveals the due diligence required to intentionally develop a highly engaged board of directors of a nonprofit organization.

Members of the nonprofit's board of directors should be the organization's first donors and first fundraisers (Tempel and Seiler 2016a). However, fewer than half of nonprofits have boards that are fully engaged with fundraising (Board-Source 2017).

There are four types of board members. Those who make things happen. Those who watch things happen. Those to whom things happen. And those who don't even know what's happening. Nonprofits should be interested in the first type of board engagement at all costs. Building the right board development structure and procedures will exponentially enhance the likelihood of creating a highly involved, generous board.

In this chapter, readers will learn:

- How to recruit board members.
- How to retain engaged board members.
- How to request board member charitable gifts and fundraising support.

Recruiting Board Members

The board of directors holds the ultimate legal responsibility over the nonprofit organization (Herman et al. 1996), which is a key reason why all board members should be donors (Brown and Guo 2010). Miller-Millesen (2003) organized board member responsibilities into three categories:

- Monitoring:
  - Determining the nonprofit's mission.
  - Creating and overseeing the nonprofit's strategic plan.
  - Monitoring program results.
  - Keeping fiscal control.
  - Evaluating the CEO.
- Boundary-Spanning:
  - Fostering external relationships.
  - Reducing risk.
  - Overseeing charitable donations and fundraising.
- Conforming:
  - Ensuring legal compliance.

Helping all board members see donating and fundraising as part of their responsibilities – and helping them understand how donating and fundraising financially support all other board member duties – can increase the board's engagement with fundraising. However, board members often need ongoing information and encouragement from the nonprofit's staff, including fundraisers, to fulfill their fund development duties (Cumberland et al. 2015).

Just as paid staff are hired with great intentionality, board members also should be carefully identified, recruited, and selected. In fact, intentional recruitment and retention of board members is a consistent best practice among nonprofits with 100% board giving (Stanczykiewicz 2020c). Remaining mindful of racial, gender, and age diversity is crucial, especially since many nonprofit boards remain predominantly White, male, and older (Indiana University Lilly Family School of Philanthropy et al. 2018). Boards with higher percentages of female board members or people younger than 40 tend to be more engaged with governance and fund development. Meanwhile, diversity also increases the number and variety of people that a nonprofit can meet, thereby increasing the prospective donor possibilities (Wagner 2016).

Nonprofits need to follow a systematic approach for board recruitment, as illustrated in Figure 20.1, with distinct activities and goals.

FIGURE 20.1. EIGHT-STEP BOARD RECRUITMENT PROCESS

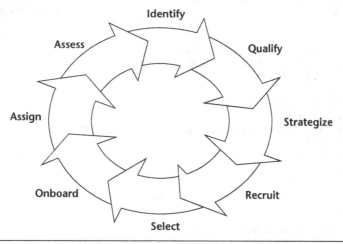

Source: Developed by M. Gasby Brown, The Gasby Group, Inc.

1. *Identify* – Do not wait until there is a vacancy. The nominating/governance committee should create and maintain an ongoing roster of prospective board members recommended by existing board members, staff, donors, and other stakeholders. Media stories and civic leaders also can be sources of information about potential volunteers for board service.

2. *Qualify* – Review the organization's list of board needs and requirements in relation to current board members and potential board candidates' qualifications and profiles. Candidates' passion for the cause and mission must be a core consideration as should be their ability to contribute to fundraising goals. Candidates' demographics, professional skills, personal attributes, giving capacity, and community connectivity also should be considered. Develop a matrix, like the sample in Exhibit 20.2, to explore current board capacities and ascertain needs.

3. *Strategize* – Similar to planning how to cultivate a relationship with a prospective major donor, nonprofits need to determine the best approach for "cultivating" each prospective board member and design individual plans. This includes being prepared with a specific answer when the prospective board member asks, "Why me?"

EXHIBIT 20.2. BOARD NEEDS MATRIX

Category	Board Member Names

Skill Set
Human resource capacity and policies
Fundraising/Resource development
Administration/Management
Entrepreneurship
Communications/Marketing/PR
Strategic planning
Nonprofit governance, program design, and evaluation
IT/Technology
Government/Policy
Legal
Mission-related
Analytics

Qualities
Passionate about mission
Leadership skills/motivator
Team-oriented
Willingness to work/availability
Understanding of community needs

Personal Style
Good communicator
Visionary
Strategist
Bridge/Consensus builder

Resources
Money to give
Willingness to give
Access to other resources
Availability/Willingness for active participation

Community Connections/Capital
Religious organizations
Community organizations/Social services
Media
Political

Demographics
Age
Gender
Race/Ethnicity
Religion
Location

Other
Other board commitments
Conflicts of interest

Terms
Year joined
Number of terms

4. *Recruit* – Execute the strategy. Provide ample time for the prospective board member to talk with staff and board leadership; to tour the nonprofit's programs; and to meet with other stakeholders such as beneficiaries and volunteers. Be transparent about board responsibilities, time commitment, and support provided by staff. Board members are eleven times more likely to donate and fundraise when clear expectations are communicated during new board member recruitment (Stanczykiewicz 2020c).

5. *Select* – If there is a fit between the parties and a clear mutual understanding of expectations, the nominating/governance committee then presents a board candidate for a vote by the entire board. If a nomination is ratified, a formal invitation is extended, and hopefully, accepted.

6. *Onboard* – Conduct a comprehensive orientation by reviewing a board manual that includes materials such as by-laws, organizational chart, strategic plan, gift acceptance policy, audited financials, and annual report. Onboarding should also include signing a conflict of interest form and board expectations agreement.

7. *Assign* – Pair new board members with existing board members who can provide additional information and support. Peer-to-peer relationships among board members increase the likelihood of 100 percent board participation in fundraising (Stanczykiewicz 2020c).

8. *Assess* – Annually assess the board recruitment process. Identify the board's strengths, weaknesses, and gaps. This information can inform the nonprofit's ongoing identification and recruitment of board members who are passionate about the nonprofit while reflecting all necessary aspects of diversity.

Retaining Board Members

Effectively identifying and recruiting board members is just the first step. The same intentionality is necessary to retain board members. Providing opportunities for meaningful engagement – during and between board meetings – while the nonprofit's CEO and fundraising staff maintain consistent communication are best practices associated with nonprofits with 100 percent board engagement with donating and fundraising (Stanczykiewicz 2020c).

In considering the retention of diverse board members, it is important to take an "equity" approach that creates a sense of equal ownership of the board role (Brown and Solomon 2020). This is different from a "diversity" approach that entails simply checking off boxes for membership or an "inclusion" view, which invites people to the table as guests. Some reflection questions to examine board diversity, equity, and inclusion include:

- In what ways is the organization removing the barriers that limit outreach opportunities for board members of color or other underrepresented communities?
- Does the organization seek "excellent" and "super qualified" underrepresented board members while accepting less than excellent white board members?
- Conversely, does the organization seek less than excellent people of color to check off a box while seeking "the best" white board members?
- What is the retention plan for board members of color? Trainings and resources are available to aid in self-assessment and development of equitable systems.

Nonprofits can retain engaged board members in a systematic way using the "Eight Stages in Board Retention" process shown in Figure 20.3 and described in the subsequent sections.

1. *Thank* – Thank board members in meaningful ways. Opportunities are available at board meetings, during one-on-one conversations, in the annual report, through social media, and on the nonprofit's website.
2. *Assess* – Annually assess individual board members and the board as a whole in relation to member responsibilities. This process celebrates successes, identifies gaps, and reinforces expectations. The assessment of each board member's fundraising activities, and the overall fundraising effectiveness of the board, can be performed by the board's fundraising committee.
3. *Involve* – Involving board members starts with interesting and productive board meetings. Start meetings with a "mission moment" highlighting the nonprofit's reach and influence. These brief stories can: describe a recent success; show impact; feature a testimonial from a beneficiary; introduce donors explaining why they give; and highlight a civic leader describing the difference the nonprofit makes in the community. Including a mission moment reminds board members why they agreed to volunteer for this important responsibility, and this practice is consistent among nonprofits with high levels of board member participation in fundraising (Stanczykiewicz 2020c).

FIGURE 20.3. EIGHT STAGES OF BOARD RETENTION

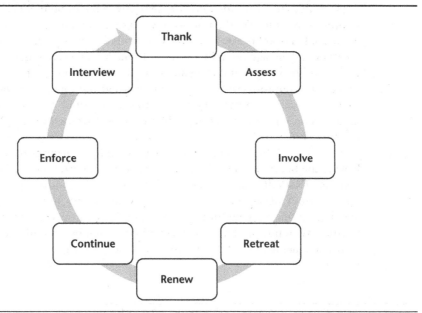

Source: Developed by M. Gasby Brown, The Gasby Group, Inc.

Also, ensure that board meetings go beyond document reviews and committee reports to explore a big question, examine a significant opportunity, or solve a key problem. Asking board members what they think and inviting insights from their respective areas of expertise strengthens board engagement.

Nonprofit boards that organize their work through committees tend to be more effective (Bradshaw et al. 1992; Brudney and Murray 1998). Each board member should serve on at least one committee.

4. *Retreat* – Ensure that the board retreat is a treat to attend. Important strategy discussions should be joined with opportunities to bond, share experiences, meet donors and recipients, and become empowered to take action at a higher level.

5. *Renew* – Invite eligible board members to renew their board service. Meanwhile, board members who are not fulfilling the nonprofit's list of board expectations should be asked to volunteer in other ways. Removing underperforming board members is consistent among nonprofits with high levels of board engagement with fundraising (Stanczykiewicz 2020c).

6. *Continue Involvement* – Match each board member's interests with specific opportunities for continued involvement. Invite board members to tour the nonprofit, volunteer in the nonprofit's programs, and attend its events and activities. Fundraisers also can pursue individual meetings with each board member and engage them in a variety of fundraising tasks. Ongoing engagement with the nonprofit during and outside of board meetings is a consistent practice of nonprofits with 100 percent board giving (Stanczykiewicz 2020c).

7. *Enforce Term Limits* – Serving on the board should not be a lifetime appointment. Enforcing term limits allows boards to be refreshed while avoiding the creation of inertia within the organization.

8. *Exit Interview* – Obtain valuable information and perspectives from members leaving the board. Find opportunities for former board members to stay involved. Examples can include task forces created to address problems or opportunities; occasional meetings to provide updates and stay connected; and a program of asking former board members for introductions to prospective donors and others. Former board members should be invited to continue making annual donations and are also strong candidates for planned gifts.

Requesting Support from Board Members

The nonprofit's financial stability is a primary responsibility of the board of directors. This responsibility is fulfilled through fiscal oversight and also through donating and fundraising.

Donating

All board members should be donors, ideally from their personal wealth. The board member's invaluable volunteer time and connections to other funding sources are not a replacement for their personal financial engagement. If those who are closest to the nonprofit do not donate, why expect others to give?

Each board member should be invited to contribute at a level of generosity commensurate to their respective income and wealth. While nonprofits can establish a minimum donation level for board members (a so-called "board minimum"), nonprofits with 100 percent board giving tend not to impose a board minimum for charitable gifts (Stanczykiewicz 2020c).

Importantly, establishing a board minimum can be discriminatory, preventing otherwise capable people from serving on the board. A volunteer with unique wisdom, expertise, knowledge, and connections could be excluded from board service simply because the board minimum is beyond the reach of their relative income and wealth.

Nonprofits also should be hesitant when considering the implementation of a "give or get" policy that allows board members to raise and/or donate a minimum dollar amount. Such a policy could encourage board members only to fundraise from others instead of fulfilling their responsibility of providing a charitable donation from their personal wealth.

When board members donate, they are leading by example. This includes making pledges and donations to comprehensive campaigns above and beyond their annual charitable gift. Board members also are responsible for external relations, promoting the nonprofit through their circles of influence. This duty of "boundary-spanning" takes on added importance during times of crisis, such as the Great Recession and the COVID-19 pandemic (Alexander 2000).

Fundraising

Board members need to be involved in fundraising beyond their own charitable giving (Tempel and Seiler 2016a). Emphasizing all nine board member responsibilities (Miller-Millesen 2003) encourages board members to be fully engaged in all of their duties while avoiding the misperception that the nonprofit only is interested in the board member's charitable giving and fundraising. This approach also helps board members understand how fundraising strengthens their other areas of responsibility. For example, programs are more likely to fulfill the nonprofit's board-approved strategic plan when they are adequately funded.

A fundraising committee within the board of directors – also known as a development committee or an advancement committee – is foundational for maximizing board engagement with fund development. This committee reviews the staff's proposed fundraising plan and – if satisfied – recommends that plan to the full board for approval. The committee then monitors progress toward achieving the fundraising plan while continually encouraging board members to donate and fundraise.

Imagine the impact when board members observe and continually hear from their peers on the development committee. In fact, the odds of board member engagement with fundraising nearly double when the board has a fundraising committee (Stanczykiewicz 2020c). Inviting board members to approve the fundraising plan and providing the full board with updates on plan implementation provide natural opportunities to remind board members of their opportunities to provide a charitable gift and fundraise.

Board members should assist the organization with donor identification and qualification. Through social and business networks, members likely know people with potential interest and the financial capacity to be generous. Access to potential donors is critical to an organization's fundraising success. Fundraisers should ask the board to participate in donor-rating sessions or peer screening to identify which prospective donors might be interested in giving and appropriate gift ranges.

Provide options and ideas for members to think about the importance of their involvement. Fundraisers must be specific in asking the board for help with individuals: "We need to meet with X. Do you know them? Can you help with this potential donor?" The direct approach versus casting a broad net of names may yield better results. Board members also can host events, from receptions in their home to luncheons at a club, their place of employment, a local restaurant, or at the nonprofit organization.

Board members additionally can assist in fundraising by helping develop and implement cultivation strategies to engage individuals, typically with major gift potential, as well as corporations and foundations. Cultivation of prospective donors takes board members closer to engagement in solicitations by recognizing the importance of relationships, on which successful fundraising depends.

With proper training and preparation, board members should be invited to join staff at meetings with donors. Fundraising staff can help board members understand how the fundraising process is mutually transformational and not "selling" or transactional by teaching board members a solicitation approach that has integrity, avoids surprising the potential donor, and creates an atmosphere in which gift discussions honor mutual respect. While some board members might be comfortable asking for the charitable gift, other board members can add value to these solicitation meetings by explaining why they serve on the board or by telling a compelling story about the nonprofit's impact. Most importantly, effective solicitation is a partnership between board members and fundraising staff.

Board members also are uniquely influential in donor stewardship. Thanking donors in person, writing notes, sending personalized letters, and making phone calls allow board members to convey gratitude to donors for their charitable gifts. Donors are positively affected when hearing from unpaid board members. At the same time, donor stewardship can help board members become more comfortable with their other fundraising responsibilities.

Organizations can encourage and assist board members in completing their giving and fundraising responsibilities with a board development commitment form. An example is provided in Exhibit 20.4.

The next section features a case study that demonstrates how one organization worked to better integrate fundraising into their board's activities.

EXHIBIT 20.4. BOARD RESOURCE DEVELOPMENT COMMITMENT AND TRACKING FORM

Board Resource Development Commitment and Tracking Form

Board member:
Date completed:
Year of Commitment:
During this program year, I pledge to participate in the fundraising efforts of the organization in the following ways:

I.   **Board Giving**

My personal gift will be $ Paid $

Additionally, I will   I completed

☐   Become a campaign matching donor   ☐
Include (name of organization) in my will

II.   **Individual Giving**

I will   I completed

☐   Introduce (X) prospects to the development team   ☐

☐   Invite at least two new prospective donors to join my table at the dinner   ☐

☐   Provide at least five new names for the mailing list   ☐

☐   Personally sign 20 thank you letters to donors   ☐

☐   Make (X) donor calls for stewardship (non-ask calls)   ☐

☐   Join the executive director or other staff at up to five major donor meetings   ☐

☐   Participate in fundraising campaign calls to donors   ☐

☐   Share (X) campaigns with (X) people from my network   ☐

III.   **Events**

I will   I completed

☐   Host a dinner/reception for prospective donors   ☐

☐   Identify another host and facilitate introduction   ☐

☐   Attend two events (cultivation and/or fundraising)   ☐

☐   Do one presentation to a donor or potential donor group   ☐

☐   Buy a table at the annual dinner Help/volunteer at an event   ☐

(Continued)

EXHIBIT 20.4. (CONTINUED)

Board Resource Development Commitment and Tracking Form

IV.   **Foundations and Corporations**
I will   I completed
☐   Connect X to at least one new foundation   ☐
☐   Connect X to at least one   ☐
              corporation/business

V.   **Other**
I will   I completed
☐   Serve on the development committee   ☐
☐   Attend a workshop on fundraising to   ☐
              upgrade my skill set

Other offers of engagement in resource development:

Thank you for lending your voice and leveraging your networks in support of the mission!

Source: Adapted from the Institute for Social Policy and Understanding (ISPU) 2021.

Case Study: How a Crisis Transformed One Board's Fundraising Engagement for the Better

The Institute for Social Policy and Understanding (ISPU) is a nearly 20-year-old, Washington, DC, and Dearborn, MI, research and education nonprofit. The organization received the Center for Nonprofit Advancement's annual Board Leadership Award in 2020. The award recognizes outstanding leadership of highly successful boards and provides an opportunity for others to learn from their journey.

A consideration in the process was the board's engagement in fundraising (Neggaz 2020). ISPU shared a tale of two crises. In 2017, due entirely to external factors, ISPU lost its largest multiyear institutional funder. Overnight, one quarter of ISPU's committed funding, much of it unrestricted, disappeared. ISPU's board members gave regularly to the organization and had been involved in fundraising in a somewhat ad hoc way. Organizational leadership realized quickly that getting through the crisis and achieving long-term sustainability would require further and systematic empowerment of board members to deliberately build up unrestricted reserves.

Over the next three years, the organization developed a major gifts program, with the board leading the way. The organization implemented an agreement for members detailing expectations for participation and fundraising. The board also implemented a formal assessment process, including a self-reflection questionnaire and involvement conversations with the governance committee. The board strengthened the development committee, enlisting a highly engaged chair and committed members with fundraising experience. The development committee asked to be invited to other subcommittee meetings to share information and learn more about their activities. ISPU developed a stewardship strategy that more strategically included board members. As a result, the organization consistently maintained 8–10 months of unrestricted cash on hand to shore up against future shocks.

Consequently, ISPU was better prepared for COVID-19 and the shocks of 2020. The board was well equipped and excited to help. Despite the pandemic, which required deep reflection about retaining staff and the fate of important research projects as well as extensive scenario planning, the board led the charge in surpassing the fundraising goal for spring 2020. The board members made larger gift commitments and broadened their solicitations to more people in their spheres of influence. Each board member treated the fundraising as a personal campaign. A few members even gave to each other's campaigns as well as their own. Imagine that! A vigorous recognition campaign also followed with board members writing personal notes and making thank you calls.

ISPU was announced as the Board Leadership Awardee in the summer of 2020. Winning has been a game changer for ISPU; it reinforced the importance of good governance, good leadership, and a genuine collective commitment to mission. ISPU shared the win with its constituents through social media, traditional media, and email. The win communicated that ISPU was an impactful organization, well run, well respected, and well recognized for board engagement in fundraising. This built the legitimacy of the organization for new and potential donors, who now have additional evidence that ISPU holds itself to the highest standards and operates with integrity.

Conclusion

Fundraising by the board of directors strengthens the nonprofit's effectiveness (Green and Griesinger 1996). Following the three R's – Recruit, Retain, and Request – can help nonprofits create and maintain an engaged board, increasing the likelihood that members will be fully involved as donors and fundraisers.

Great governing boards of charitable organizations do not just happen; they must be designed for greatness, constantly tuned and honed (Frantzreb 1997). Organizations that intentionally follow successful board strategies while customizing tactics that best suit their organizational environment are more likely to successfully create a culture of philanthropy with their board and, consequently, throughout the entire organization

Discussion Questions

1. What are the steps in the board recruitment process and how might they be implemented in different organizational contexts?
2. What is your greatest confidence – and greatest concern – when thinking about communicating fundraising expectations to incoming and current board members?
3. List as many ideas as possible for involving board members in fundraising. What would a nonprofit need to do or have in place in order to implement each idea?

Application Exercises

1. Create a list of expectations, including donating and fundraising, for a nonprofit's board of directors. Use the list to create a board agreement for members.
2. Review the current roster of your board of directors. Create a matrix describing board members' demographics, professional skills, and other personal attributes. What gaps exist? What steps can be taken to increase (or continually ensure) the board's racial, gender, age, and other forms of diversity?
3. Develop a plan for board retention using the eight steps described in this chapter. Then, expand the plan by developing an engagement program for an individual board member.

CHAPTER TWENTY-ONE

WORKING WITH VOLUNTEER FUNDRAISERS

By Tyrone McKinley Freeman and Beth Breeze

When properly engaged and well managed, volunteer fundraisers can be vital sources of moral support and concentrated labor to maximize the success of fundraising programs. Their participation can help small fundraising shops extend the reach of limited staffing and budgets. They can imbue larger fundraising operations with energy and excitement. Volunteers can work directly with staff-driven fundraising programs or conduct their own supporter-driven fundraising outside of organizations. In either case, volunteer fundraisers provide notable resources to advance resource development in support of organizational visions and missions.

As a result of reading this chapter, readers will:

- Understand the strategic role and value of volunteer fundraisers.
- Distinguish two main types of volunteer fundraisers.
- Learn about volunteer trends.
- Gain insight about volunteer motivations.
- Understand the six steps for successful volunteer integration.

Research from AmeriCorps (2018a) has repeatedly confirmed the connection between volunteering and other acts of civic engagement related to fundraising in the United States. According to the agency, volunteers donate to charity at two times the rate of nonvolunteers. Their example of giving is essential for cultivating the interests of other potential givers. These volunteers do favors for their neighbors and good things for their neighborhoods at two times and three times the rates of nonvolunteers, respectively. They are also five times more likely to belong to a civic group or community association than their nonvolunteering peers. Further, fundraising is the No. 1 activity that volunteers report doing when they serve (AmeriCorps 2018).

While these facts may be surprising to some, they demonstrate the investment volunteers have in their communities as well as the social networks they can bring into fundraising programs. These qualities are in keeping with the volunteers' strategic role and value to fundraising.

Strategic Role and Value of Volunteer Fundraisers

Volunteers represent an internalization of an organization's values that is vital for successful fundraising. They embody the mission and can serve as powerful advocates of its validity and impact because they are not financially compensated for their service and have no vested financial interest. Volunteers have their own lives, jobs, and many other responsibilities related to family, work, and community. The fact that they choose to serve an organization speaks highly of its work and should be utilized to support fundraising.

Volunteer fundraisers can play useful roles at any stage of The Fundraising Cycle (see Chapter 12), which is a powerful tool for engaging supporters. When examining the case for support, analyzing market requirements, and defining and validating needs statements and objectives, volunteers can serve as bellwethers for assessing the local community's needs and responsiveness to particular cases for support. Through their local involvement as citizens, they can provide insights to keep fundraising activities fresh and relevant.

When evaluating gift markets, selecting fundraising vehicles, identifying potential giving sources, and creating fundraising and communications plans, volunteers can provide recommendations, contacts, and other valuable inputs for decision-making processes. Here, their belief in philanthropic support and example as organizational donors is paramount. Given the connection between volunteerism and philanthropic giving, fundraisers would be remiss in their responsibilities if volunteers were not provided opportunities to add financial support to their contributions of time and talent. This is particularly true of volunteers involved with solicitation. Before asking others to give financially, they should be givers themselves.

With training and encouragement, volunteers can help solicit gifts, demonstrate stewardship, and renew gifts through strategic engagement with donors.

Here, their linkages to donors and prospective donors are essential. The principle of Linkage Ability Interest (LAI) (see Chapter 14) states that the greatest potential for a gift exists when a prospective donor has a linkage or connection to an organization, the ability to give at the desired level, and an interest in the cause. Volunteers can help make these connections and discern donor interests and giving capacities through their social networks. In support of prospective donor research, volunteers can help assess donor lists for likelihood of giving and help organizational staff build meaningful relationships with donors.

Volunteers can be powerful witnesses and organizational advocates when put before an individual donor, foundation officer, or corporate giving committee. They can passionately convey the importance of the mission, especially those who have personally benefited from it. Creating appropriate opportunities for sharing their enthusiasm can help solidify donor relationships and illustrate an organization's impact in personal ways.

The experience of nonprofits affected by external shocks, such as economic recessions and global pandemics, highlights the profound value of being able to draw on nonsalaried help when faced with periods of financial insecurity or surges in demand for services. Being prepared for these moments, however, requires fundraisers to regularly think about meaningful volunteer engagement so that programs and teams can be built in this manner.

There are two broad categories of fundraising volunteers:

- *Staff-driven*: Volunteers who have been recruited to help with fundraising efforts including administrative support, events, campaigns, and committee service. They fundraise on behalf of the organization and are authorized representatives.
- *Supporter-driven*: Volunteers operating independently to fundraise in aid of a nonprofit organization. Nonprofits may not be aware that these volunteers are holding events or crowdfunding campaigns until the final sum is passed on to the organization.

Whatever combination of "staff-driven" and "supporter-driven" volunteer fundraising is suitable for an organization, responsibility for all fundraising begins and ends with an organization's board of directors (see Chapter 20). Integrating board members into the fundraising program is a central task for fundraisers to address.

This chapter focuses primarily on staff-driven volunteers, but fundraisers should also be prepared to engage with supporter-driven volunteers when made aware of their efforts. An awareness of volunteer trends is important for developing formal programs for volunteer fundraisers.

Volunteer Trends

Volunteering is universal. The United Nations (2018) estimated that the annual hours of service produced by volunteers globally represents the equivalent of a labor force comprised of over 109 million full-time workers. Every day, these volunteers provide vital services and acts of care important to community life around the world. Only 30 percent of this volunteer work force participated through formal nonprofit organizations. The majority of this service to others was rendered person-to-person with individuals living outside the volunteer's household. Together, volunteers in Asia and the Pacific, Europe and Central Asia, and North America comprised 72 percent of the voluntary labor force. Across the globe, women dominate the volunteer ranks.

In the United States, 2018 AmeriCorps data shows 77.4 million Americans (or 30.3 percent of the adult population) formally volunteer for nonprofit organizations, contributing nearly 7 billion hours of service worth more than $167 billion in labor. This represents a significant increase in rates of volunteering over the past decade. In response to the 9/11 national emergency in 2001, American volunteerism grew. The deep recession later in that decade reversed that trend. Steady decline following the Great Recession continued into 2015 with a low of 24.9 percent of the population volunteering. The 2018 nearly six-point boost in volunteerism was a positive sign, but it occurred prior to the COVID-19 global pandemic of the early 2020s, which wreaked havoc on the global economy and nonprofit organizations reliant on volunteers.

In the early weeks of the pandemic, Gallup reported a decline in American volunteerism to 58 percent from 64 percent three years prior (Jones 2020). However, VolunteerMatch (2021), the popular recruiting website, surveyed users during the pandemic and found that just as the rest of the economy went virtual due to shutdowns and quarantines, so did volunteerism as supporters connected online with nonprofits. People also assisted others in their communities. Numerous media reports about volunteers' grocery shopping for struggling neighbors and making masks for first responders captured ways in which citizens responded to the crises as governments were overwhelmed (U.S. Bureau of Labor Statistics 2020b). However, the long-term effects of the pandemic on volunteerism remain to be seen.

Most American volunteers give their time to religious organizations (AmeriCorps 2018a). Sport, hobby, arts, and culture organizations are the second-largest sites for volunteer service followed by educational and youth-serving organizations; civic, political, professional, and international organizations; hospital and other health organizations; public safety organizations; and environmental and animal care organizations. In keeping with global trends, American women gave 3.9 billion hours of volunteer service, while men gave 3 billion hours. Demographically,

Generation X leads American volunteer rates (36.4 percent) followed by Baby Boomers (30.75 percent), Millennials (28.2 percent), Generation Y (26.1 percent), and the Silent Generation (24.8 percent).

Volunteer Motivations

Before attempting to manage volunteer fundraisers, staff needs to understand them. People volunteer for many reasons, including those related to valuing particular organizational missions, wanting to learn, interacting with others, developing employable skills, and coping with difficult life experiences (Musick and Wilson 2008). Many volunteers have altruistic desires to make a difference through service and be part of programs positively impacting community life. Some volunteer by utilizing special knowledge or skills in order to develop themselves personally or professionally (Fashant and Evan 2020). Volunteerism is also an avenue for acquiring new skills, gaining meaningful work-related experiences, and developing networking opportunities that may lead to employment or promotion (Faletehan, van Burg, Thompson, and Wempe 2020). Many professionals also volunteer as they transition from work to retirement, and retirees often increase their volunteer commitments to fill portions of their newly available time (AmeriCorps 2018). Volunteerism can fulfill a need for camaraderie, belonging, and greater life satisfaction from being helpful to others. These motivations are not mutually exclusive. Indeed, volunteers often have both self- and other-oriented motives animating their service.

Volunteer service can be integral to the success of an organization's fundraising efforts. Major donors and employers are two sources of highly motivated volunteer labor for fundraising. Major donors can be effective peer ambassadors because of their preexisting relationships with organizations and other potential donors. Those who become involved as volunteer fundraisers are motivated to make a practical difference for a nonprofit they are passionate about by using their access to networks of wealthy people and their personal credibility to ask for sizeable gifts (Breeze and Lloyd 2013).

Employee fundraising is a common feature of fundraising around the world (Breeze and Scaife 2015) and is comprised of numerous programs, often including corporate matching gifts. Programs typically include workplace giving, donations to nonprofits where employees volunteer, and disaster relief (CECP 2020). Money donated in the name of a corporation is often raised by staff that solicited colleagues and customers. "Shop floor" employees are increasingly involved in selecting which nonprofits will benefit from these efforts, leading to choices based more on personal experiences and philanthropic preferences rather than corporate goals (Breeze and Wiepking 2020). Employers facilitate these efforts in order to support the communities in which their staff and customers live, and also to secure additional benefits relating to marketing, personnel recruitment and retention, and enhanced corporate reputation (Gautier and Pache 2015).

Whether volunteer fundraisers originate from employer or major donor relationships, or from elsewhere, professional fundraisers must be prepared to manage varying motivations, conflicts, needs, and expectations in order to maximize the volunteers' experience and impact.

Six Steps for Successful Volunteer Fundraiser Involvement

Effectively utilizing staff-driven volunteers in fundraising requires planning and ongoing attention. Recalling The Fundraising Cycle, the six steps in this section (see Figure 21.1) offer a process for maximizing the engagement of staff-driven

FIGURE 21.1. SIX STEPS FOR SUCCESSFUL VOLUNTEER FUNDRAISER INVOLVEMENT

6 Step Six:
Recognize and Retain Fundraising Volunteers

5 Step Five:
Manage Fundraising Volunteers' Performance

4 Step Four:
Ensure Meaningful Engagement

3 Step Three:
Welcome and Develop Fundraising Volunteers

2 Step Two:
Identify and Recruit Volunteers

1 Step One:
Determine the Organization's Needs

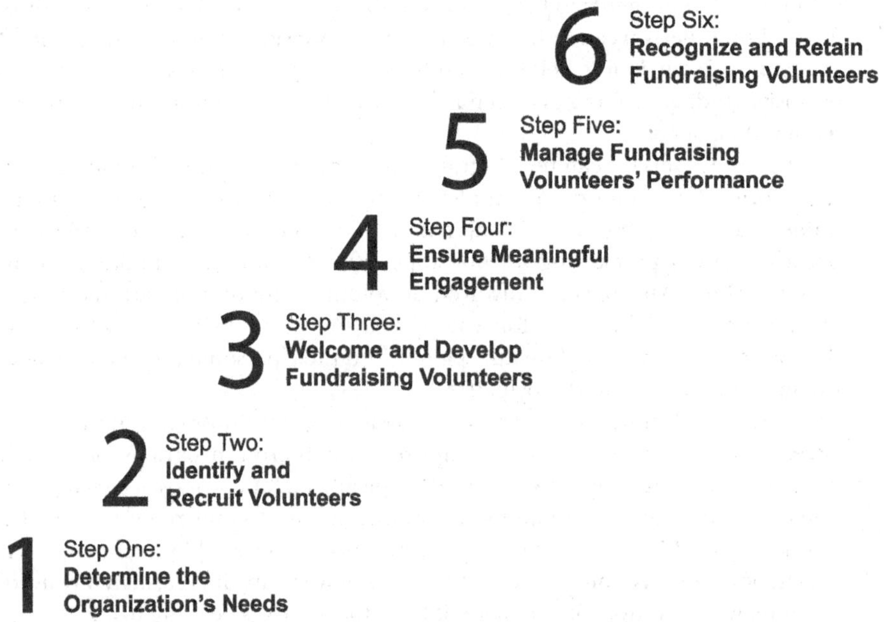

volunteers. Supporter-driven fundraising volunteers are, by definition, outside organizations' direct control, but the following advice can still be relevant for supporting, acknowledging, and retaining them.

Step One: Determine the Organization's Needs

It is essential to clarify what kind of voluntary fundraising help is needed. Volunteers do not take a salary but they do incur costs, notably staff management time, which must be accounted for to ensure a net benefit. To avoid volunteer-driven drift, fundraising strategy must remain central. Consult the Fundraising Cycle to identify the specific areas where volunteer fundraisers may add value to program planning and implementation. Consider donor development and review the specific donor identification, cultivation, solicitation, and stewardship activities where assistance from volunteers is needed to advance a campaign. With key needs identified, fundraisers will be better able to properly channel volunteer energy into the optimal fundraising activities.

This step also includes legal considerations and researching best practices to help guide volunteer engagement. This information can then be operationalized through development of policies and procedures. For instance, organizations working with children and vulnerable groups commonly require background security checks for volunteers who might interact with beneficiaries. Privacy, confidentiality of donor records, and basic ethical practice are some areas to address early in the volunteer fundraiser planning process.

Step Two: Identify and Recruit Volunteers

After establishing the parameters of volunteer service, it is time to seek interested individuals. Some use informal methods – such as word of mouth and social media, or advertising through organizations that promote volunteerism such as local United Ways, community foundations, service clubs, and corporations – to seek one-time volunteers for simple tasks. Volunteers may also come from within existing organizational networks. They can rise in their levels of engagement from other areas of the organization. For instance, letting donors know that volunteers are needed can enhance efforts to attract interested participants. Becoming involved as volunteers should strengthen donors' overall commitment to the nonprofit if it is a fulfilling experience and may generate benefits in positive psychological well-being (Konrath 2014). Volunteers on advisory councils or in program and service-related roles may be interested in participating in some fundraising capacity as extensions of their commitments.

For significant volunteer roles, such as chairing a capital campaign committee or running a major fundraising event, it is important to develop detailed job descriptions. For more transient and less risky tasks, such as seeking helpers for a fundraising event who may greet guests or set up decorations, activity descriptions can be simple. Whatever the scale and nature of the role, pay attention to achieving a good fit between potential volunteers' skills and preferences, and the tasks that need doing. A gregarious volunteer will be frustrated if asked to process event registrations alone in a room, a task which could be well suited to a volunteer who prefers – or needs – to do volunteering from home.

Step Three: Welcome and Develop Fundraising Volunteers

After volunteers are recruited, providing orientation and training helps them feel welcome and gain the necessary skills and knowledge to become effective team members. Volunteers will have different training needs based on their roles and history with the organization, but all should receive sufficient organizational information to help them thrive. A firm grounding in the mission, operations, programmatic needs, case for support, and cultivation and solicitation techniques is necessary for interacting with donors. To ensure that staff act ethically and fairly toward all volunteers, it is important to have formal policies covering topics such as recruitment (including diversity, equity, and inclusion considerations), training, expenses, supervision, health and safety, confidentiality, and complaint procedures (Galloway 2019).

Offer continual opportunities for volunteers to gain deeper knowledge. Use volunteer job descriptions and work backward to create training opportunities aligned with the tasks to be completed. Also, more experienced volunteer fundraisers can help induct newer ones, which reinforces knowledge and builds relationships for both groups.

For volunteers interested in direct solicitation, plan to gradually increase their activities. It is best to begin by involving these volunteers in nonsolicitation tasks such as making thank you phone calls, inviting friends to events, and accompanying staff on donor visits before conducting face-to-face solicitations. Further, fundraising volunteers should be oriented to gift acceptance policies.

Step Four: Ensure Meaningful Engagement

Assign volunteer tasks and communicate expectations in ways that are mindful of individual interests, talents, and temperaments. For volunteers to find meaning in their service, they must feel connected to their work, capable of successfully completing it, and find it personally enriching. If a younger volunteer is seeking suitable experience to build their resumé, or an older volunteer is seeking a companionable environment, determine if the organization can realistically meet those needs. If not, it is important to be clear up front to avoid disappointment and possibly ineffective volunteer service. Similarly, never miss an opportunity to connect volunteers' contributions to the mission.

Do not forget to provide ongoing training, validation, and support as necessary throughout the course of volunteer assignments. The goal is not busywork, but to meaningfully engage volunteers in advancing the mission.

Step Five: Manage Fundraising Volunteers' Performance

Volunteers, like salaried employees, must be managed, but the process is different, and lacks financial remuneration and other considerations. Volunteers likely want to feel ownership of their tasks and also need the backing of the organization to be successful. Be aware of generational differences. For example, Millennials may well prefer and perform better with more flexibility and more empowerment to be self-directed in what they do (Saxton et al. 2015).

Keep in close touch with volunteers, especially at the planning and evaluation stages of fundraising activities. Regular reviews, which can include informal chats, can help ensure that the role is meeting their hopes and expectations. These conversations can also help reveal other skills and connections held by the volunteer that could enhance their contribution and the organization's volunteer efforts (Galloway 2019). If areas of concern arise in relation to their work, provide constructive feedback, specific recommendations, and support to facilitate the desired changes. For those who continue to struggle, it may be necessary to provide further training, to identify a different mode of service, or to terminate the volunteer relationship altogether. These can be difficult conversations but sometimes can come as a relief to volunteers who are already aware of an issue. Expressing deep appreciation for a volunteer's contributions and explaining changes as related to organizational needs may assuage the volunteer's feelings in other cases.

Step Six: Recognize and Retain Fundraising Volunteers

The final step in successful fundraising volunteer involvement is to provide ongoing personalized recognition. Express thanks regularly so that volunteers feel known and appreciated. Marking milestones, such as after their first fundraising event or following their participation in soliciting a significant donation and celebrating anniversaries of service are important. If they make behind-the-scenes contributions, such as maintaining the donor database or training other volunteers, explain the results of that work – for example, new income, a stronger organization, and positive impact for beneficiaries.

As much as feasible, recognition should be tailored to suit each volunteer. Some will enjoy public recognition, such as thanks at staff meetings, being featured on the website, or honored at an event. Others may prefer private recognition, such as a handwritten note from the organization leader or from beneficiaries (if appropriate). Research shows that people who regularly volunteer are less concerned about enhancing their public image, so private incentives may be preferable to public ones

(Exley 2018). Regardless of its form, recognition is essential to supporting volunteers, ensuring their satisfaction, and showing appreciation for their service.

While there are many external factors beyond fundraisers' control that influence volunteer attrition, research shows that volunteers tend to end their involvement due to poor matches between their skills and available volunteer activities; inadequate acknowledgment and recognition practices; poor training and support; and inadequate leadership and supervision (Eisner et al. 2009). Unlike other external factors such as volunteer time constraints, these factors can be avoided if fundraising professionals demonstrate care for their volunteers by providing orientation, training, support, and recognition.

Conclusion

Helping nonprofit organizations to raise funds is one of the most common types of volunteering across the world, and volunteers are also likely to be donors themselves. Through their freely chosen and uncompensated involvement, volunteers embody passion and commitment to the cause, which is inspirational to potential donors, and therefore adds special value to fundraising efforts.

All types and sizes of nonprofits can successfully recruit and retain volunteer fundraisers, as John Ramsey, co-founder of the UK Association of Volunteer Managers, explains, "Brilliant volunteer involvement isn't the preserve of money-rich organisations, it's the preserve of people-rich organisations" (cited in Saxton et al. 2015, 2). Professional fundraisers should make every effort to create meaningful opportunities to involve volunteers across The Fundraising Cycle, using the six steps in this chapter. Not only will volunteers help secure resources to fulfill nonprofit missions, they can become trusted advisors and allies for fundraising within the organization and beyond.

Discussion Questions

1. What distinctive value can volunteer fundraisers provide to organizations? List three ways in which volunteer fundraisers are best placed to assist with securing resources.
2. What is noteworthy about the motivations of volunteer fundraisers? How can this information aid organizations in identifying, recruiting, and retaining volunteers?
3. Which of the Six Steps for Successful Volunteer Fundraiser Involvement seems most challenging and why? What are some ideas for addressing the challenges?

Application Exercises

1. Find an online volunteer handbook for an organization and compare it to the Six Steps of Volunteer Fundraiser Involvement. Write a one-page analysis of the manual and how well it is or is not in alignment with the six steps. Consider what the manual reveals about how the organization thinks about volunteer motivation, training, and recognition.

2. Use the six steps to interview a volunteer who has fundraised in an official capacity with an organization. Develop one question per step in order to ask about the person's experience with organizational needs, being recruited, being oriented and trained, having meaningful engagement, receiving feedback on contributions, and feeling recognized. Consider the volunteer's responses and reflect on how the interviewee's comments could help you best support volunteers.

3. Brainstorm some imaginative ways of recognizing contributions of volunteer fundraisers. Develop a list of three ways each to meaningfully recognize: (1) the corporate executive who volunteered as chair of a fundraising campaign committee; (2) the celebrity guest who served as an event MC; and (3) the college student who made phone calls to donors during a thank-a-thon.

PART FIVE

BUILDING AND SUPPORTING THE DONOR BASE

CHAPTER TWENTY-TWO

THE ANNUAL GIVING PROGRAM

By Sarah K. Nathan

Big gifts and the wealthiest donors get the lion's share of attention. Major donors' names appear on sports fields, concert halls, classroom doors, and all variety of physical spaces. Their stories are shared in press releases, videos, and online. No doubt, large gifts are important for nonprofit organizations.

Still, the accolades make it easy for the public to overlook organizations' many other donors. Fundraisers know, however, that the significance of large gifts does *not* mean smaller gifts are unimportant. Rather, many small gifts, gathered under the banner of the annual fund, are the core of a comprehensive fundraising program and future fundraising success.

In this chapter, readers will:

- Recognize the importance of gifts of all sizes.
- Understand the role of an organization's annual giving program.
- Apply annual fund tools, including the annual fund profile and gift range chart.
- Examine key concerns about the donor base and donor retention.

All Gifts Matter

Human generosity comes in all forms and in actions big and small. Indeed, philanthropy as an expression of one's love of others has existed across time and place. For fundraisers, tasked with developing financial resources, it is easy to measure philanthropy by the dollars requested and received. Yet, an expansive definition of *philanthropy* captures the many ways that individuals engage with each other in community (Faculty of the Lilly Family School 2020). For example, acts of informal giving and mutual aid are difficult to quantify, but are no less important to a community's quality of life. Especially in times of crisis, giving directly to individuals through mutual aid channels, rather than through organizations, can be a powerful and quick way to deploy help (Gamboa and Hadero 2021; Stiffman 2021b).

Recognizing the abundance of generous behaviors, philanthropy is not reserved for the ultra-wealthy. There is potential in every prospective constituent to contribute something meaningful to an organization's mission. Embracing the philosophy that "all gifts matter" elevates fundraising from simply counting financial transactions to helping others express their hopes and dreams. Indeed, organizations that adopt, embrace, and celebrate all gifts, regardless of type and size, generally have a stronger "culture of philanthropy" (Gibson 2016), which begets greater fundraising success.

Organizations that subscribe to this philosophy recognize the most important thing is that people make gifts regardless of size (Gibson 2016). A $3 donation from a person who is on a limited income is just as valuable as the $10,000 major gift. When organizations affirm that "it's not always about the money" the opportunity to engage people in their mission thrives. Small gifts often lead to larger gifts (Faculty of the Lilly Family School 2019). For some donors, small gifts are one way to know the organization over time, deepening the relationship that can lead to bigger gifts. The story of World Vision United States donors Dave and Dana Dornseif exemplifies this phenomenon: In the 1980s, they first became donors to the organization giving less than $20 a month, by 2015 they had given $35 million (Faculty of the Lilly Family School 2019). Of course, most people do not have this level of financial ability, but many do have the ability to give significantly more than their first gift amount.

Monthly giving programs harness the power of small gifts. A "major" gift may be out of reach for some donors, but through 12 smaller gifts, their ability to give is amplified and the impact is greater than any single contribution. Not only is this strategy useful for organizations, allowing them to plan based on a more reliable source of income, but it establishes an individual's habit of giving. In an increasingly subscription-based culture, monthly giving is a growing trend (Waasdorp 2021). Strategies like these keep an organization close to constituents through consistent engagement. Every month the organization has a reason to reach out and thank the donor while sharing stories of mission and outcomes, further solidifying the philanthropic relationship.

Crowdfunding has further demonstrated the power of collecting many small gifts. From #GivingTuesday to Facebook birthday campaigns, crowdfunding is ubiquitous and positively recognized by most individuals, although only about one-third of individuals typically contribute to crowdfunding projects (Osili et al. 2021b). These donors tend to be younger, which is good news for organizations seeking to attract new donors and establish a habit of giving early on. Likewise, crowdfunding gifts tend to be smaller, an average of $189 in 2019 (Osili et al. 2021b). In its easy and peer-to-peer nature, crowdfunding celebrates the "every day" philanthropist whose impact is found in the collective.

Annual Giving

The *annual giving program* or *annual fund* is the foundation of all successful fundraising. Donors contribute to yearly fundraising efforts to support current, ongoing programs and operations that fulfill the organization's mission (AFP 2003). The annual fundraising effort may follow a calendar or fiscal year that aligns with the organization's budgeting cycle.

The annual giving effort is a core component of an organization's comprehensive fundraising program and the lifeblood of the organization's gift income. Its direct purpose is to seek gifts on a recurring basis – at least once a year but many organizations solicit more frequently – to fund the ongoing programs and needs of the organization. Usually, annual dollars raised are budget relieving, but in some larger organizations, the annual fund provides additional discretionary resources for special initiatives. It also serves many other goals for the organization, as delineated by Hank Rosso (1991) in the first edition of this book.

Annual fundraising often focuses on seeking unrestricted gifts, necessary for meeting organizations' general needs as determined by organizational leadership, such as operations, facility maintenance, and programs. While some estimates suggest that as little as 20 percent of all giving is unrestricted, recent attention has renewed interest in this type of giving. These annual, unrestricted gifts provide flexibility, and therefore a type of stability, serving a different purpose from most restricted gifts (Shaker and Wiepking 2021).

The annual fundraising program bonds a large constituency to the organization and is the tool for encouraging recurring and upgraded gifts. Gifts to the annual fund can come from all sources (individuals, corporations, foundations, associations, and donor-advised funds), but the focus is on individuals who comprise the largest source of all charitable giving and who have been most inclined toward unrestricted giving (Giving USA 2021). Some individuals, including those enrolled in a monthly donation program, may make multiple gifts in any given 12-month period. For these donors, an "annual gift" is the culmination of multiple gifts.

As donors develop a history of giving, they grow more interested in and involved with the success of the organization. They "test" the organization and develop trust based on experiences of strong stewardship. They become accustomed to giving, and it becomes a habit. They demonstrate their ongoing interest over time. This base of regular givers is the most likely core group for larger major, capital, and planned gifts. The best place to begin looking for these donors is within the organization's existing constituency of annual fund donors.

Annual giving programs maintain community awareness and appreciation of the organization's value and the quality of its programs and services. This effort requires ongoing validation of the organization's mission, goals, and objectives, and tests its accountability and stewardship. It fosters regular attention to community and beneficiary needs, to the development of new programs as appropriate and to refreshing fundraising approaches and messages. A strong partnership with the organization's marketing team is essential in this work as it requires engaging multiple constituencies in the potential donor landscape across all communication channels (see Chapter 16).

The annual giving program is a multifaceted fundraising activity, but goes beyond serving a fundraising purpose. It achieves many crucial organizational needs and functions. It is a systematic review of the relevance of the organization's case for support, a validation of the program and special needs of the organization, and an outreach effort to identify, inform, and involve multiple constituencies in the work of the organization.

Tools for Annual Fund Planning

Annual fundraising tactics usually include direct mail fundraising, digital efforts (email, social media, crowdfunding), special events, and telephone solicitation, most of which are explored in subsequent chapters. Major donors, a focus in the last section of this book, are also a consideration in annual fundraising. These "leadership" annual gifts are often garnered through face-to-face methods. Organizations are also increasingly focused on mid-level donors with ongoing giving using increasingly personalized strategies, including face-to-face meetings and calls.

Annual fundraising requires careful planning, in alignment with organizations' overall financial needs, and integration among annual fund approaches and between these approaches and efforts with major donors, corporations, and foundations. This section focuses on the profile of the annual fund and gift range chart, core tools for organizing annual giving to be used in conjunction with a comprehensive fundraising plan (see Chapters 12 and 19).

Profile of the Annual Fund

A healthy annual fund is based on the Pareto Principle – also known as the 80/20 rule – in which 80 percent of results come from 20 percent of actors/effort (Worth 2016). The principle has been used to explain all kinds of human activity from healthcare usage to product purchases. It has even been applied to one's wardrobe – most people wear about 20 percent of the clothes in their closet 80 percent of the time!

For fundraising, the 80/20 rule is applied to the number of donors and amount of money raised and visualized in the profile of the annual fund (Figure 22.1). At the bottom of the triangle is the base of supporters, or 70 percent of the total number of donors who give about 20 percent of all money raised. At the top, 10 percent of donors give 60 percent of the total amount raised. And, in the middle, another 20 percent of upgraded, or mid-level, donors give another 20 percent of funds raised.

The 80/20 rule and the annual fund profile represent an ideal or model of a healthy annual fund. It can help organize internal operations and fundraising strategies, but it does not always perfectly predict a particular donor's behavior. While it is common that many donors will increase their giving over time, sometimes a donor's first gift may be near the top of the triangle rather than the bottom.

FIGURE 22.1. PROFILE OF THE ANNUAL FUND

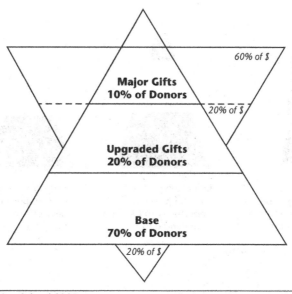

Source: The Fund Raising School 2021.

Likewise, not all organizations have a perfectly formed triangle. An organization with fewer general donors will have a smaller base and a very steep peak (Worth 2016). Another may have a bifurcated triangle with few mid-level donors. An organization without a fully developed major gifts program will have a plateau rather than an equilateral triangle. The shape of the annual fund profile can be used as a tool to identify opportunity areas (see Figure 22.2).

Gift Range Chart

Gift range charts are mathematical representations of patterns of giving in a fundraising program (Rosso 1991). They visualize *how* the team will reach its annual fund goal and are often included as a component of the organization's overall fundraising plan. The quickest way to the annual goal, of course, is a single gift of that total goal amount; however, such a fundraising effort is wishful thinking and unsustainable for most nonprofits. As a planning instrument, the gift range chart determines the pattern of giving that will result in a successful campaign while measuring the availability of prospective donors at specific gift levels. Likewise, at the conclusion of the annual campaign, a return to the gift range chart to evaluate the fundraising effort provides an answer to how the outcome related back to the original plans.

FIGURE 22.2. ANNUAL FUND PROFILE SHAPES

Steep pyramid = limited donor base, may be over-reliant on a few major gifts

Bifurcated pyramid = few mid-level donors, opportunity to focus on upgrading gifts

Plateau = many small gifts, opportunity to develop a major gift program

Source: Adapted from Worth 2016.

The gift range chart should be created with input from the team and shared with the board. Doing so builds consensus around the goal and accompanying strategies. Occasionally, it is useful to share the chart with prospective or upgrade donors as a way to raise their giving sights.

Calculating the Gift Range Chart

To prepare an annual fund gift range chart for planning, as well as for prospective donor identification and evaluation, The Fund Raising School (2021) recommends the following mathematical steps:

1. The first two gifts should equal 10 percent of the goal, or 5 percent each.
2. The next four gifts equal an additional 10 percent of the goal.
3. The chart is flexibly developed beyond this point, depending on available prospective donors, gift history, and common gift levels.
4. The prospective donors to donor ratio begins at the top level at 5:1 and gradually reduces to 2:1, assuming that some donors will give at lower levels than the original solicitation amount.

In addition to the total number of gifts needed and at what levels, another key revelation of a completed gift range chart is the total number of constituents solicited. In the following example the total number of prospective donors is 1,406, which would result in 580 gifts (see Table 22.3). If an organization did not already have 1,406 known constituents with verifiable contact information, reaching the goal would be difficult. A limited constituency requires more large gifts – or an expanded effort to reach new audiences – to make the goal, and the gift range chart needs to be created with this knowledge in mind.

Notice that the three tiers of the gift range chart mirror the annual fund triangle (Figure 22.1). The largest gifts come from fewer individuals at the top, while the base consists of hundreds of gifts of a smaller size. Likewise, gifts in the middle of the chart most likely came from donors who previously gave less than $100.

Remember that a gift range chart begins in a mechanical fashion, as a tool to chart the number of gifts and prospective donors needed to reach the dollar goal. With consistent use, organizations can begin to list the names of prospective donors at higher gift levels, further bringing the chart to life. While immersed in the actual fundraising, keep flexibility in mind: Gift ranges and numbers of gifts may need to be adjusted as the year goes on to align with emerging giving patterns.

Two final notes about the gift range chart. First, the mathematics supporting the annual fund gift range chart are dramatically different than a capital campaign gift range chart as presented in Chapter 35. The biggest difference is that in the campaign chart the largest gifts are even larger and usually from fewer donors (upward of 60 percent of the goal may come from a handful of donors).

TABLE 22.3. EXAMPLE ANNUAL FUND GIFT RANGE CHART, $60,000 GOAL

Gift Range $	# of Gifts	Cumulative # of Gifts	Prospective Donors #	Cumulative # of Prospective Donors	$ per Range	Cumulative $
$3,000	2	2	10 (5:1)	10	$6,000	$6,000
$1,500	4	6	20 (5:1)	30	$6,000	$12,000
$750	12	18	48 (4:1)	78	$9,000	$21,000
$500	18	36	72 (4:1)	150	$9,000	$30,000
$250	24	60	96 (4:1)	246	$6,000	$36,000
	10% of donors				**60% of goal**	
$100	120	180	360 (3:1)	606	$12,000	$48,000
	20% of donors				**20% of goal**	
Under $100 Average $30	400	580	800 (2:1)	1,406	$12,000	$60,000
	70% of donors				**20% of goal**	

Source: The Fund Raising School 2021.

In addition, the ratios are reversed, with fewer potential donors at the top of the chart and more at the bottom. The campaign chart is also usually constructed to span multiple years rather than one. Second, the annual fund gift range chart works best for goals of more than $25,000. With smaller goals, the gift levels become too compressed.

Annual Fund Concerns

The models and tools presented in this chapter reflect an ideal. Organizations are encouraged to adapt the models to fit their circumstances. For example, a young organization may have a small existing constituency, requiring more large gifts at the top of the gift range chart. While a well-known organization may have a much broader base to draw from. The key here is to use data to understand an organization's own giving trends in the context of larger philanthropic phenomena.

A Shrinking Donor Base?

While the 80/20 rule has been an industry standard, many organizations report a shift in their contributions that follows more of a 90/10 trend in which 90 percent of the money is coming from 10 percent of the donors. Recent research provides some insights.

The Philanthropy Panel Study (PPS) is the longest running, nationally representative survey of charitable giving by Americans. In 2000, when the PPS began tracking, 66 percent of American households donated. In 2018, 50 percent of American households donated to charity, the lowest percentage recorded (Osili et al. 2021a). Declines in household giving occurred among almost all sociodemographic groups, including by race, age, income, and education level. The percentage began to decline around the Great Recession and has not recovered. Although total charitable giving has increased in the last several years, the number of overall donors declined – a trend experienced by many organizations. While changes in income and wealth have impacted these phenomena to some degree, they do not fully account for other social and cultural shifts that may influence giving. For example, signs point to an increase in direct aid, from one individual to another and not through a nonprofit, with the advent of platforms like GoFundMe, but there is yet to be evidence that there is a correlation between a rise in this form of giving and the decline in participation in giving through formal charitable channels (Stiffman 2021b).

The Fundraising Effectiveness Project (FEP) has been collecting data since 2012, amounting to 241 million giving transactions from approximately 9,500 organizations. While not as robust and representative as the PPS data, the FEP provides quarterly reports that may signal emerging trends in giving. In the first half of 2020, it measured a promising increase in gifts under $250 (FEP 2021). These gifts, likely in response to immediate pandemic-related needs, fueled organizations' work in those early days. It became clear again that many small gifts made a significant difference in times of crisis and that changes to the donor base are ongoing.

It is important to remember that not all organizations experience these trends in the same way, and growth in giving has been uneven (Haynes 2021b). Nationally aggregated data provides just one benchmark for an organization's effectiveness. Chapter 15 provides additional information to help organizations use this kind of data analysis for fundraising evaluation.

Donor Retention

Donor retention remains a persistent challenge for many organizations (Stiffman 2021a). The FEP (2021) found that the percentage of donors who gave to a charity in both 2019 and 2020 declined. The overall 2020 donor retention rate was 44 percent, the lowest rate charted by the FEP. That decline was driven by new donors who gave to a charity for the first time in 2019, but did not give to the same organization in the following year. On the other hand, the FEP reports that giving in 2021 may counter this long-standing trend as new donors in 2020 repeated their gifts in early 2021. For organizations that experienced growth in 2020, efforts to continually engage donors will be key in retaining those donors in the future.

FIGURE 22.4. DONOR RETENTION CALCULATION AND EXAMPLE

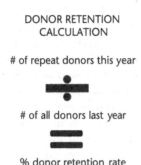

DONOR RETENTION CALCULATION	EXAMPLE CALCULATION
# of repeat donors this year	# of repeat donors in 2021 = 361
÷	÷
# of all donors last year	# of all donors in 2020 = 604
=	=
% donor retention rate	57.9% donor retention rate

The donor retention rate is calculated by dividing the number of repeat donors in the current year by the total number that donated last year (see Figure 22.4). For example, if an organization has 361 donors who gave again this year, but had 604 who gave last year, the donor retention rate would be approximately 58 percent.

Tracking the retention rate over time and comparing it to the national average provides an indication of an annual fund's overall health. The lower the retention rate, the more new donors an organization must attract each year. Developing strategies to improve retention through meaningful donor engagement is especially important given the higher cost to acquire new donors.

Conclusion

A robust annual giving program that welcomes and celebrates gifts of all sizes is essential for every nonprofit organization. First-time, repeated, and upgraded gifts that come through the mail, online, or in person at a special event comprise elements of the annual fund, with leadership level annual giving also a consideration. Each interaction with these donors provides an opportunity to deepen their relationships with the organization. Because the annual giving program relies on volume – the large number of donors – several tools are helpful to match strategies and tactics to the annual fundraising goal. The annual fund profile, the gift range chart, and calculating donor retention are quantitative and visual ways to set strategies, track progress, and assess effectiveness over time. Yet, at the heart of the annual giving effort is a fundamental belief that "everyday" donors can make a significant impact through their collective efforts. Everyone can be a philanthropist because each person has something to contribute.

Discussion Questions

1. Why are gifts of all sizes important for every organization?
2. What is the annual fund and how is it defined at your organization or others?
3. How should the annual fund profile and gift range chart be used as planning tools?

Application Exercises

1. Calculate and visualize your organization's annual fund profile. What shape does it take? What does it indicate about the annual fund's health? Identify areas for growth, and discuss the pros and cons of a triangle with your current shape.
2. Create a gift range chart for an organization's annual program goal. Share it with colleagues and compare it with the organization's current fundraising plan (do the strategies align with the gift levels?) or use it to inform a new fundraising plan. Alternatively, create a gift range chart for a $100,000 goal.

CHAPTER TWENTY-THREE

CRAFTING COMPELLING APPEALS

By Heather A. O'Connor

Think about the last time you received an appeal for a charitable organization. What led you to open the envelope, email, or social media link? How did you feel when you read the message or watched the video?

The decision to respond to a charitable appeal is often influenced by a mixture of motivations that is shaped by the characteristics of the donor, beneficiaries, organization, and solicitation as well as the relationships between them.

The term *appeal* refers to any communication – whether delivered in person, through phone, mail, or online – that asks the recipient(s) to take a specific action such as supporting the organization through volunteering (time), lending expertise (talent), or making a financial gift (treasure).

After completing this chapter, readers will be able to:

- Plan appeals for different audiences.
- Apply research to develop appeal contents.
- Develop calls to action.
- Review aspects of appeal creation and deployment.
- Navigate ethical concerns in sharing stories.

What Is a Compelling Appeal?

A compelling appeal is the central tool "to invite, involve, and bond the constituency to the organization, making it a cornerstone of organizational sustainability" (Rosso 2010, 63). When crafted as part of an integrated marketing and development program (see Chapter 16), appeals serve as more than solicitations – they educate constituencies about programs and services, report on outcomes, share stories that emotionally engage donors with their charitable impact, and help build a positive public image of the organization.

Compelling appeals emerge from the organization's case for support (see Chapter 13), carefully articulate the case for specific audiences, and strategically deliver returns across multiple formats. Achieving this requires internal and external awareness, and creative ideas that can be tailored to address various audiences from potential donors to long-term donors. When done correctly, appeals can be revised and reimagined to be applicable across formats, such as scripts for telephone solicitations, direct mail letters, face-to-face requests, and crowdfunding messages, among others.

Differentiating Appeals for Distinct Audiences

All giving is personal, and motivations to give are often as varied as the person giving (see Chapter 26). The most compelling appeals always keep donors' motivations and their relationship with the organization in mind.

First, consider the organization's network in terms of its differing relationships with groups of donors, also known as "donor segmenting." Each segment has a unique perspective of, experience with, and level of relationship with the organization. Segmenting helps organizations conceive more personal and impactful messages by orienting them to each audience. For example, a message that is appropriate for someone unfamiliar with the organization (an acquisition appeal) would likely cause offense if sent to a loyal, long-term donor or volunteer. A message highlighting a particular program or aspect of the case for support may do little to entice a donor who has a history of supporting a different program within the organization.

Donor segments may capture donors' organizational ties, or further categorize donors by giving frequency or amount. The number of segments may differ by the size of the list or the aims of the particular appeal. For example, one appeal may aim to invite annual donors to upgrade their regular gift amounts. Another may ask donors to switch from giving once a year to giving through automatic monthly payments. The categories below are suggestions to begin the process of segmenting an organization's list of current and potential supporters.

- Relationship or potential tie with the organization:
  - Current and past board or staff members.
  - Donors who have established a planned gift.
  - Prospective donors who attended the last event.

- Giving frequency:
  - Regular donors who did not give in the previous year.
  - Donors who have given consistently for a set number of years.
  - Potential donors who have not yet made a gift.

- Gift level:
  - Donors whose last gift was above a specific level.
  - Donors with the capacity to make a major gift.
  - Donors whose cumulative giving is at a set level.

Careful segmenting can help maximize return on the cost of producing and sending appeals (Fundraising Effectiveness Project 2019). Roughly half of current donors will repeat their last gift amount, and 15 percent will increase their amount if explicitly asked. Loyal donors, giving annually for five or more years, tend to make gifts that average five to eight times larger than a typical first gift. Thus, organizations need to address returning donors in a specialized way, systematically increase the request amounts, and be consistent in working to renew the gifts.

How does an organization discover tomorrow's loyal annual donors today? Commonly, an acquisition appeal is sent to members of the community who have no or weak ties to the organization, for example, event attendees who have not previously donated. Some organizations may purchase lists based on demographics, location, or other characteristics. In the absence of information about appeal recipients, the contents must be carefully crafted to speak to an audience that may not be familiar with the organization.

While considering list segmentation and appeal goals, explore which media might be most effective for the chosen audience. For clues, look to donors' giving behavior. Were recent gifts mailed? Alternatively, did they give online? Did they share the organization's enewsletter on their social media? While some generalities about communication preferences among donor populations may be useful, look to organizational data about donors' giving behaviors whenever possible. In addition, consider asking donors their contact preferences on giving forms or in acknowledgment communications, or ask within a donor survey.

Each appeal, including its medium and audience, should be conceived as part of a larger fundraising plan that includes all fundraising programs and aligns their strategies in ways that meet organizational goals while respecting beneficiaries and donors.

Research-Informed Strategies for Developing the Message

This section briefly summarizes the growing body of philanthropic research that provides insight into how various appeal framings can elicit responses. An appeal may incorporate multiple strategies.

Positive or Negative Framing

An appeal can highlight the positive outcomes of making a donation (i.e., "your gift will provide a meal for a child in need") or the negative consequences of not contributing (i.e., "without your support, more children will be hungry"). Research has found that positive framing of opportunities to "save lives" tends to generate less support than the negative framing to "prevent death" (Cao 2016; Chou and Murnighan 2013). The use of a negative frame is usually more effective when combined with a rational appeal that highlights statistics or other empirical facts. However, using a positive frame tends to be more effective when combined with an emotional appeal, such as a client story (Das, Kerkhof, and Kuiper 2008; Shen and Bigsby 2013).

When writing the call to action, consider the message's overall aim and context, and choose a frame that complements the approach.

Trustworthiness

Donors donate to organizations they trust. Fundraisers can show an organization's trustworthiness by highlighting how recipients need support, explaining how the organization makes wise use of donor funds, and acknowledging donors (Bekkers and Wiepking 2011a; James III 2017). Campaigns that appeal to the charity's credibility produce the highest donations (Goering et al. 2011).

To encourage greater trust, highlight the organization's charitable impact, longevity, and 501(c)3 status. This can be done through an endorsement from a well-known and well-regarded member of the community, or by including web links to a third-party rating system. Perhaps most important, consider using a peer-to-peer approach when calling for action. People donate more when asked by those they know (Meer 2011).

Organizations should help supporters share their enthusiasm by providing example letters and talking points to use in communicating with peers.

Identifiable Victim Effect

Sometimes thinking about the extent of a social problem can be overwhelming. Donors are more likely to respond to the needs of an individual than to respond to the needs of a large group (Kogut and Ritov 2007).

Consider starting an appeal with a narrative about a client, rather than overwhelming the reader with information about the full scale of the social problem.

Social Norms/Social Information

Research has found that behavior is influenced by social norms. Social norms are the behaviors that are common, valued, and accepted by others. For example, people are more likely to give when other people are present to witness the generosity (Alpízar and Martinsson 2013). Information about what other donors give can also influence the giving decision (Martin and Randal 2008) and amount (Shang and Croson 2009). One way this takes place is through peer-to-peer solicitation. For example, a board member might invite a group of friends to dinner, and then discuss their gift and why the organization is worthy of support. In crowdfunding, potential donors can often see names and amounts given by others they know.

Some organizations post donor "honor rolls" – acknowledgment lists – on their website or annual report to recognize all donors or groups such as long-term donors, major donors, or planned gift donors.

Since donors are motivated, in part, by how philanthropy can increase their reputation, promising public recognition for generosity can also increase charitable giving (Bekkers and Wiepking 2011; Mason 2016). There are many ways to recognize donors, including interviews in newsletters and signage with donor names. Donors should be asked about their recognition preferences.

Emotion

Emotional engagement in a cause has been found to increase donors' intentions to give (Dickert, Sagara, and Slovic 2011). Prompting a sense of hope and optimism has also been shown to increase giving (Hudson et al. 2016). Appeals that prompt negative emotions, such as fear, guilt, and sadness, can also lead to increased donations (Albouy 2017; van Rijn, Barham, and Sundaram-Stukel 2017). However, this approach can backfire if the negative emotion triggers personal distress in the reader (Kim and Kou 2014). Furthermore, repeatedly activating guilt may cause donors to conclude that their giving does not help, leading them to reduce support over time (Hudson et al. 2016).

Use negative emotion sparingly in initial communications to potential new donors and highlight the impact of gifts to generate positive emotion in regular donors.

Visuals

Photos attract donor attention and help them to identify and process information about those in need (Bae 2019). Photos that feature direct eye contact with the viewer can positively affect viewers' attitudes toward giving (Ekström 2012). Emotional expressions in recipients' faces also influence giving. Generally, sad expressions stimulate sympathy, increasing intention to donate (Albouy 2017; Small and Verrochi 2009). However, this influence may depend on the viewer's relationship to the organization. Sad images tend to result in stronger intentions to donate among viewers who are not already involved, and happy images encourage donations in viewers with existing relationships (Cao and Jia 2017).

Choose visuals to inspire new donors and show committed donors that their giving is making a difference.

Social Identities, Identification, and Perspective-Taking

People are more likely to help others who are like themselves in some way (Ben-Ner et al. 2009). Likewise, some donors are more likely to give when they share similarities with organizational beneficiaries, fundraisers, or other donors (Drezner 2018; Schervish 2005). Relatedly, philanthropic action increases when donors imagine themselves in comparable circumstances as being in need (Cao 2016; Hung and Wyer 2009).

Consider highlighting similarities between the prospective donor and those served by the organization by including details such as religious faith, gender, age, race or ethnicity, or a lived experience. When telling a client story or describing the population served by the organization, highlight common features that may resonate with donors.

Planning the Call to Action

The call to action is a crucial part of the appeal. Recipients need to know what the request is and how they should proceed. The following characteristics ensure a strong call to action.

1. *Be specific.* While the organization might have an inspiriting vision to improve the world, communicating only large or long-term goals may leave the audience feeling like they cannot do enough to make a difference. Instead, ask donors to take on a specific, tangible action and illustrate how that contribution will make a real impact. ("Donate $20 to feed a family in our community for a week," not "End hunger!")

2. *Be feasible.* Ask for an action that is realistic for donors. This is where donor segmentation comes in. Do not ask nondonors for unlikely amounts or alienate potential long-term donors by requesting actions that do not match known information about ability or level of interest. Most major gifts come from donors who have given small amounts to an organization in the past. Not everyone is ready to make a large gift right away.

3. *Present a clear priority.* There may be several ways to help the organization, but presenting them all at once may be overwhelming. Most likely, the first priority is to encourage someone to make a gift that enables the organization to carry out its work. Make a stand-alone request for that. Some formats (like a letter) may allow a brief mention of other options, such as volunteering or advocacy actions, but others, like a single social media post, may not.

4. *Make it easy.* Honor donors' time by making the giving process as quick and simple as possible. Is the organization's website and donation page easy to find? Are giving steps explained? Is contact information available for the fundraising team?

Deploying Effective Appeals

The appeal format influences its contents. For example, a tweet is not long enough to simultaneously demonstrate impact, trust, need, and potential donor benefits. A video appeal intended for general distribution should not request gifts of a specific amount. This list includes considerations for longer appeals but is informative for other types as well.

Preparation

- Plan the appeal as part of an integrated campaign so the organization's communications complement and reinforce each other.
- Segment the list and craft personalized messages for maximum impact.
- Select the medium/media for the appeal.
- Develop a system to track and evaluate appeal results.
- Plan to acknowledge gifts quickly and with language associated with the appeal.

First Impression

- Attract attention with a well-crafted email subject line or design on the outer envelope.
- Write a compelling opening appropriate for the recipient's relationship with the organization.
- Acknowledge the donor's past support and involvement, when appropriate.

Body

- Use stories or data to illustrate the extent of the problem and organizational solution.
- Pay attention to visuals and format. Use color and images, clear and accessible language, concise sentences, short paragraphs, and formatting features such as bullet points or bold font on select text.
- Strike a conversational style and professional tone.
- Create a sense of urgency when presenting the need and goals. Why should the donor respond now to this appeal?
- Include a clear call to action. What should the donor do? How?
- Ask for a specific amount, if applicable, and illustrate the impact of a gift at that level.

Closing

- Describe the recognition or other psychological or tangible benefits the donor might receive or experience.
- Choose the best person to sign. That may be the executive director, a board member, or a volunteer known to the recipient.
- Include a P.S. that reinforces the call to action.

Writing Ethical Appeals

One way to educate and motivate donors is to include the voices, perspectives, and stories of beneficiaries in fundraising materials – particularly those who are marginalized and rarely have opportunity to share their experiences (Bhati and Eikenberry 2016). Yet fundraisers, especially those who serve marginalized communities, must be mindful of potentially causing harm to those they are trying to help. Many appeals may include graphic images or describe shocking situations to stimulate giving out of sympathy or guilt (van Rijn, Barham, and Sundaram-Stukel 2017), and such images and language may perpetuate negative stereotypes and diminished expectations of the client group (Bhati and Eikenberry 2016). Individuals experiencing homelessness and those with disabilities have responded negatively to their portrayals in charitable appeals, even as they recognize the good intentions (Barnett and Hammond 1999; Breeze and Dean 2012).

These guidelines can help fundraisers share clients' stories while preserving their safety and authenticity:

- Always ask for clients' consent before using their story or image. Ensure they understand how the materials will be used and who might see them. Be aware of the power differential inherent in any organization asking a favor of a client. Make clear that sharing their story is optional and discuss the rationale for including it.

- Give clients a role in telling their story. Ask them to share how they see themselves. Gain insight into who they were before and after engaging with the organization to build knowledge of the whole person – including values, preferences, interests, and goals. Develop a respectful appeal with this knowledge in mind.
- Review the appeal content with a critical eye and ask others to as well. Does it use language in an inclusive and appropriate manner? Does it convey the person's story with authenticity and respect? Ask the client to review the draft.

Just as fundraisers have ethical obligations to those they serve, they also have obligations to donors (see Chapter 2). Donors trust organizations to use their gifts prudently and to maintain their personal identification information properly. Practice good data hygiene by ensuring names are correct, individuals are addressed appropriately, and that all private donor information is kept confidential and secure. Confirm that data systems are accessible only to the appropriate individuals within the organization and are properly maintained with security software.

Conclusion

Crafting a compelling appeal begins with the mission and case for support and then relies on understanding donors' perspectives, their personal motivations, and their relationship with the organization. This chapter discusses these considerations through the processes of segmenting lists, applying behavioral research to plan the message, and drafting components of the appeal strategically and with awareness of ethical obligations to both beneficiaries and donors. Fundraising is a process that requires careful planning, thoughtful attention, and constant follow through – whether communicating with a single donor or thousands.

Discussion Questions

1. What are some approaches to segmenting, and how can it increase the effectiveness of appeals?
2. Discuss the research findings about appeal framing and explore which approaches could work together within an appeal or series of appeals.
3. What ethical concerns should be considered when drafting an appeal, and how might they present different challenges at different kinds of organizations?

Application Exercises

1. Analyze pieces of direct mail or email appeals. What made you open the envelope or email? Was the message compelling? What kinds of motivations were evoked? What was the call to action?

2. Create your own checklist for writing fundraising appeals. What information will you need to set the goal and audience? Who at your organization will be responsible for which task?

CHAPTER TWENTY-FOUR

DEVELOPING DIGITAL FUNDRAISING STRATEGIES

By Nathan Hand and Yannan Li

Today, tweets can start movements and rally supporters. Individuals can build enormous followings and rival billion-dollar companies. Likewise, digital fundraising presents an extraordinary opportunity to leverage technology to advance organizational missions and serve social purposes. Building authentic relationships in the online space requires mindfulness.

After completing this chapter, readers will gain confidence for online fundraising by:

- Understanding management of digital fundraising programs.
- Recognizing strategies for content development and engaging people online.
- Examining crowdfunding methods and other vehicles for conducting digital fundraising.
- Studying social media metrics and considerations.

Each passing year brings developments to the wide-ranging digital fundraising space, which is why this chapter simultaneously covers the book's fastest growing topic and is the most quickly outdated. Consequently, it focuses on principles and strategies that span digital tools and stand the test of time.

Managing Digital

Relationship fundraising – or attending to the needs and interests of supporters within the fundraising process – should be the basis for implementing digital fundraising strategies. Digital fundraising and its efficiencies are not counter to relationship building and can enhance it. An email list of 50,000 is not a group to solicit only when and every time an organization is in need. Behind every email address, Twitter handle, and digital footprint is a person. Online relationships are an extension of the organization and its fundraising (and communications) staff, and form a community to achieve the mission.

As digital tools transform how nonprofit professionals raise and manage funds, best fundraising practice and research provide important underlying principles. Online fundraising efforts can be structured within an organization's overall planning to maximize contributions and participation.

Planning and Strategy Development

How an organization chooses to manage its online presence contributes greatly to the success of its strategies. Often these efforts combine the expertise, personnel, and goals of the marketing and fundraising departments and are an extraordinary opportunity for collaboration between teams. The marketing approach keeps the messages, delivery mechanisms, tools, and strategies consistent with the organization's branding and audience interests, while the fundraising approach focuses on fundraising strategy, activation, and the subsequent topics.

Multi-Channel Campaigns

Better outcomes result from using a combination of tools and media to convey a common message. For example, direct mail recipients might be encouraged to go online to see the "rest of the story" from a mailed appeal. Alternatively, emails can be sent prior to a mailed appeal so recipients can "watch their mailbox" in anticipation. Also, emails can be sent after the receipt of a mailed piece, encouraging the recipient to "save a stamp and donate online instead." Crowdfunding campaigns can include email as well as social media requests. Cross-channel campaigns should utilize shared messages, branding, images, and calls to action across all communications.

Personnel and Policies

For years, many nonprofit organizations assigned digital fundraising strategies to interns or volunteers, or to their youngest employees, assuming they were digital natives and most likely to understand the tools. Unfortunately, personal social media use rarely translates into strong organizational strategizing. Organizations have begun to understand that investing in professionally trained and skilled digital marketers is necessary. Social media managers and online fundraising specialists – often full-time, paid employees or teams of employees – interact with fans and followers and support the digital donor journey, through acquisition, engagement, giving, and stewardship.

To make incremental progress in digital marketing, small organizations should dedicate at least a portion of a full-time employee to develop digital performance indicators and content, build comprehensive communication calendars, and design policies and approval processes. Social media management tools and software are available to ease implementation, scheduling, and review.

Privacy policies, data security, and ethical practices are also important to consider when managing digital responsibilities. Most online transactions are hosted by a third party; but if keeping credit card information, for example, there are required compliance measures to ensure data privacy, notably from the payment card industry.

Content Strategy

Organizations take different approaches toward social media, as illustrated in Table 24.1. Similar to other fundraising efforts, success is proportional to the time and resources invested in cultivating community and relationship building.

Fundraisers should utilize content strategies to foster dialogue between the organization and supporters. The internet, particularly social media, enables individuals to engage with information in a way that traditional mediums do not. Comments and "shares" and "likes" are how people express their opinions in the digital era. Such dialogue helps build relationships with trust and mutual understanding and is essential as nonprofit organizations seek permission for further communication (Stanger 2016). Strong, two-way communication will inspire donors to upgrade from allowing organizational social media updates to giving permission to send them emails, receive snail mail, accept event invitations, consider larger gifts, and so on.

How can organizations encourage interactive dialogue? On social media, followers are more likely to respond to prompting questions. Questions that are related to the mission and followers' own interests are effective rapport builders (i.e., When was the last time you took care of a sick family member? How do you want your kids to be educated?). One study shows the risk of exposure to offensive comments is the major factor that prevents people from engaging on social media (Li 2018). Organizations can lead and guide dialogue in a constructive way and have policies and systems in place for negative interactions.

TABLE 24.1. LEVELS OF ORGANIZATIONAL ENGAGEMENT IN CONTENT CREATION

	No engagement	Basic engagement	Content creator
Full-time employee(s) assigned	None	.25–.75 FTE	1+
Platforms	Varied	Selected	Optimized
Posting	Random	Occasional	Often
Metrics	None	"More"	Defined
Follower engagement	None	Limited	Regular
Common activity	One-direction statements	Posting others' content	Posting organization's own, created content, facilitating two-way communications
Likelihood of digital fundraising success	Zero	Low	Possible

Source: Authors 2021.

Social Proof

People are more likely to take action that follows others and provides "social proof" (Cialdini 2001). Strategies that normalize people's beliefs about a behavior (e.g., putting money in a tip jar, giving to a friend's birthday fundraiser) are more likely to motivate people to complete the behavior (Shearman and Yoo 2007). In traditional capital campaigns, the idea of a "lead gift" leverages social proof. The gift is valuable not just for its financial impact. It also builds momentum by conveying the campaign and organization's credibility.

Social proof is important in crowdfunding and online fundraising campaigns. Consider the common "fundraising thermometer," a concept also derived from the capital campaign model, which visualizes dollars raised toward a goal. Social media feeds are often full of requests to donate, incorporating the thermometer illustration. If a thermometer is empty or includes only a gift or two (often from the organizer themselves), people often continue to scroll. In a fraction of a second, people see the goal as either unimportant or unachievable (or both) because others have not invested. Conversely, if a fundraising thermometer is 90 percent full, then a different reaction is likely. The goal becomes feasible, others are supporting it, and it may be donation worthy. Fewer individuals contribute to a cause with an empty thermometer than one close to the goal.

Communicating Impact

When an organization understands its costs and impact, and can clarify its fundraising messages with statistical evidence, engagement and giving often increase (Chang and Lee 2010). Many successful online fundraising efforts for operational needs, for example, are marketed in a way that reflect ideas of sponsorship. In addition, research finds that details that help donors to picture the impact of their contributions can increase their confidence in giving (Cryder et al. 2013). Messages like "For $2.37, you can provide a Thanksgiving meal to someone in need" or "$40 a month covers the food, supplies, vaccinations, and lodging for a pet at our shelter while they await their forever home" clearly articulate the cost and impact of a particular gift amount. These concepts are easily transferable to an online donation form, monthly giving program, or donor upgrade or acquisition campaign.

Crowdfunding Basics

Crowdfunding is the act of raising funds for a project from a larger number of smaller donations, and can allow good ideas and groups to come together to make an incredible difference. A highly successful crowdfunding effort is born from a phenomenal idea and a large number of people who contribute to and share the effort with their networks. Success can come from a single individual organizer or an organization leveraging its tools and networks. If the organization has either a strong idea or a good-sized crowd but not both, it may be successful but it will take significant effort. Importantly, many nonprofits think their case or project is inherently important enough to "go viral." They are appropriately passionate, but often incorrectly assess the project's popularity. Slowly testing ideas and projects in the support community will give the best sense of what is truly possible.

Peer-to-Peer Methods

Highly successful, organizationally driven crowdfunding efforts are often built around a peer-to-peer strategy. Rather than hoping a campaign goes viral, nonprofits intentionally engage team captains responsible for raising certain amounts from their networks. In Figure 24.2, each team captain works to raise funds and engage their own network. This strategy distributes the responsibility for fundraising success among many. Then, when captains combine resources raised, ideally, the goal is met and project completed.

This approach requires that organizations secure volunteers and develop tools and resources for captains. This is a worthwhile investment; research finds that team captains play a pivotal role in peer-to-peer fundraising because donors

FIGURE 24.2. PEER-TO-PEER FUNDRAISING

give more out of care for their friend/family member/coworker/acquaintance than interest in the cause (Scharf and Smith 2016). The approach widens the universe of possible donors while decentralizing and loosening control over the solicitations. Captains who hold a strong belief in the cause or the charity are also more motivated to perform best fundraising practice (Chapman, Masser, and Louis 2019). Nonprofits will benefit most from captains who are strongly identified with their cause.

Giving Days

Organizations often experiment with crowdfunding using a "giving day" approach, such as #GivingTuesday, founded in 2012 as a day for people to join together to do good. Always the first Tuesday after Thanksgiving, it follows Black Friday and Cyber Monday – traditional holiday shopping days in the United States. According to #GivingTuesday Data Commons, approximately 34.8 million people gave $2.47 billion in 2020. Empirical evidence shows that #GivingTuesday-types of solicitations do not significantly decrease giving to year-end appeals; instead, they may lift overall giving and benefit organizations that are perceived as "impressive, impactful, and familiar" by donors (Vance-McMullen 2018).

As more organizations have adopted a #GivingTuesday strategy, competition for donor attention has increased within social media feeds and email inboxes. Some organizations (i.e., colleges and universities, community foundations) now choose a date on the calendar and design a specialized marketing campaign for their own giving day. Many organizations offer matches, challenge programs, countdowns, and contests to unify the supporter community.

Again using traditional campaign models and social proof approaches, many giving days include lead gifts, large donation announcements, affinity group competitions, all-day social media updates, and email marketing. All efforts leverage the collective excitement of the supporter community to create positive energy and raise as much as possible in association with that day.

Crowdfunding Complexities

Crowdfunding campaigns often engage many individual contributors and build awareness among broad audiences. Some individuals are new to the organization and can be developed into longtime supporters. Acquiring these contributors increases the value of crowdfunding beyond attaining short-term fundraising goals. Donors have a "lifetime value," the monetary value of their gifts throughout their association with the organization (Sargeant 2001). Over time, donors who keep giving ultimately contribute much more than their first gift and more than the organization's initial investment in acquiring their first gift.

However, donors' long-term engagement and loyalty is often proportional to the motivation for the original gift. If contributors gave to support a strong team captain or a viral phenomenon rather than from cause affinity, future renewal is more difficult and less likely. The Ice Bucket Challenge was an incredible success, raising $115 million from 2.5 million new donors for the ALS (amyotrophic lateral sclerosis) Association. But this kind of momentum is near impossible to maintain, and in the second year of the campaign, only $500,000 was raised (Haid 2015). It is important to retain team captains as supporters and crowdfunders, and to also work to build independent connections with their supporters over time. Ultimately, those donors who already had an association with the mission or who develop one through experiencing a compelling story or manifestation of the mission will have higher rates of post-campaign engagement. It is unrealistic to expect to retain all crowdfunding supporters.

Digital Tools and Considerations

Organizations' use of online tools should be comprehensively designed and engineered to assist in conversions from, for example, stranger to subscriber, subscriber to first-time contributor, and first-time contributor to loyal monthly supporter. Technology and human interaction together create donors' journeys, which combine each individual's organizational experiences and touchpoints.

Website

Websites are an organization's front door for a multitude of future supporters, clients, volunteers, staff, and community members. Today, it is easier than ever to design and create a website using freely available web-building platforms. Website visitors should instantly understand what the organization does, the mission, and how to subscribe, give, or find relevant content. The website should be updated regularly with the latest news, blogs, and other content to maximize engagement and searchability. The website navigation should enhance conversions by providing avenues for visitors to become subscribers, supporters, volunteers, advocates, employees, or clients. A basic checklist for nonprofit websites, with fundraising in mind, includes:

- Strong visual design.
- Clear and friendly text.
- Accessible design and coding.
- Connections to social media platforms.
- Optimization for all devices (mobile, tablet, etc.).
- Information about mission, impact, board, staff.
- Donation button (at the top, right-hand side of the homepage) and ways to give.
- Opportunity to subscribe, opt-in to emails, volunteer, be involved.
- Information on services and programs.
- Sharable, fresh content.

Even as platforms such as Facebook become increasingly important information sources, organizational websites remain a crucial pillar of their online presence and legitimacy and merit regular attention.

Email

Email is still one of the most used communication tools. The total number of email users was projected to reach 4.04 billion in 2020, with a total of 306.4 billion emails sent and received per day (The Radicati Group 2019). The average office worker receives 121 emails every day. That means an organization's email is competing for attention with scores of other email messages.

Email has several advantages, and understanding the roles it can play aids organizations in designing the appropriate usage strategies. Done correctly, emails can inform, inspire, and appeal to readers, motivating them to take various actions to support the cause.

As noted previously, nonprofits need to acquire a higher level of permission before sending email appeals (Stranger 2016). Essentially, the organization should desire subscribers who truly are interested in the mission. It is better to have 10,000 email subscribers who opted in, open the email, and click on content than 100,000 subscribers who did not opt in and rarely open the messages. Further, CAN-SPAM Act of 2003 in the United States and more stringent regulations in other countries prohibit perpetual emailing to addressees who have not given permission. Organizations that send email to nonsubscribers risk being marked as spam and losing the ability to communicate using email marketing tools.

All organizations should seek to improve their use of email. Most often, basic email metrics for organizations to track and improve include:

- Number of subscribers.
- Open rate.
- Click-through rates.
- Conversion rates.
- Unsubscribes.
- Spam reports.

Social Media

About seven in ten Americans with internet access use some type of social media, and the number is still climbing. Although Millennials were the first generation to adopt social media for communication and social networking, other generations are quickly catching up.

With so many social media platforms to choose from, fundraisers need to consider how to align the key features of platforms with their objectives. The interactive features of Facebook, for instance, have demonstrated advantages in generating and maintaining conversations, whereas Twitter, with its character limitation and capacity to redistribute content, is more supportive in directing traffic to homepages and raising brand awareness (Phethean et al. 2013). Meanwhile, photo and short video sharing apps such as Instagram and TikTok have further broadened the social media space with an emergence of visual cultures, which nonprofit organizations might consider tapping into to engage their followers more effectively (Leaver et al. 2020).

Reach. Reach refers to the number of different people who experience a piece of content on a social platform. As of November 2020, Facebook ranked the third most visited website in the United States with a total of 3.67 billion visits. It had more traffic than any other social media platform, and its user base was most representative of the general population (see Figure 24.3). Statistics indicate 69 percent of U.S. adults are using Facebook, spread comparatively evenly across generations. Nearly half (46 percent) of people age 65+ are on Facebook, whereas only 8 percent of this group are using Instagram (Pew Research Center 2019). All told, these data indicate that Facebook has a wide reach that will appeal to many organizations.

FIGURE 24.3. PERCENTAGE OF SOCIAL MEDIA USERS IN GENERAL POPULATION, BY AGE

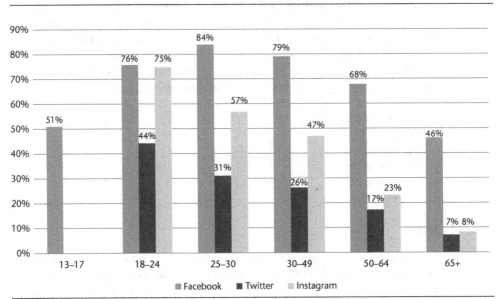

Source: "Social Media Fact Sheet." Pew Research Center, June 12, 2019.

In choosing social media platforms, fundraisers should consider whom they want to reach and whether Facebook and/or other platforms provide the most likely audience for their cause.

Engagement. Engagement measures how people are interacting with social media content, including the number of comments, likes, and shares. Studies find organizations and brands make more posts on Twitter (195 posts per month) compared with Facebook (60 posts per month) or Instagram (25 posts per month) (Socialinsider 2019). Yet, users are found to engage more on Instagram; they spend an average of 192 seconds on the platform, 45 percent longer than Facebook visitors and 40 percent longer than Twitter visitors (Alter 2020).

Social media users are more captivated by content that makes them feel "human" (Li 2018). Adding a personal tone to a post can help people relate, and thus become more receptive to the message. Another effective way to inform donors is through data visualization. Desktop users have an attention span of 2.5 seconds on Facebook, whereas for mobile users, it is even less at 1.7 seconds (Stefanski 2020). This means readers are less likely to scroll through long text than to internalize an infographic or photo representing the message. Indeed, social media professionals have found that easy-to-share content such as themed pictures are more likely to draw the attention of followers and foster conversations (Li 2018).

Locality. Another consideration is the popularity of platforms in geographic areas, particularly if raising funds outside the United States. Facebook and YouTube, for instance, are blocked in countries like Mainland China and Iran. Sina Weibo, a Chinese microblogging website that incorporates features of Facebook and Twitter, is an alternative platform used by many Chinese. Statistics show that active Weibo users reached 523 million in the second quarter of 2020 (Tomala 2021) – that is more than one-third of the entire Chinese population. Weibo has become a major vehicle for China's grassroots nongovernmental organizations (NGOs) to carry out fundraising campaigns.

Artificial Intelligence

Imagine for a moment . . .

- A preferred smart home device that enables people to send money to a favorite cause using a short, verbal instruction.
- An app where a subscriber can choose to be connected to a volunteer opportunity a block away to sort food, or to a neighbor who needs a ride to a doctor's appointment.
- A software program that automatically screens an online donor's wealth rating, and on a high rating, sends a welcoming email from the development professional, inviting them to lunch at a nearby restaurant (that is well reviewed online) and providing available dates based on the development officer's calendar.
- Geo-locating software that pushes out pop-up donation requests based on people having most recently driven by an organization.

As of publishing, these scenarios are rare, but all already exist to a certain extent. Gains in efficiency are important, but relationship building is inherently inefficient. Those that advocate for these (inevitable) developments argue, "The most exciting opportunity AI [artificial intelligence] presents is freeing staff to focus on strengthening relationships with doers and donors" (Fine and Kanter 2020). It remains to be seen whether this prediction will manifest.

When leveraging technology, it is always important to consider both what can be gained and what may be lost. Technology should foster deeper relationship building and not replace it.

Acceleration of Digital Adoption in a Pandemic

The COVID-19 pandemic amplified the adoption of digital methods of fundraising, including all of the tools in this section, and people gave more online than ever before. Also, virtual video fundraising from individuals and virtual events became a necessity. The authors predict that these strategies will continue to flourish even as in-person fundraising returns to normal. This adoption will allow broader and more efficient engagement across geographies, but may also reduce the depth of relationships. Maintaining loyalty, authenticity, and commitment to the cause may prove more difficult with donors who do not regularly witness the mission in person.

Conclusion

As digital platforms continue to evolve, so will nonprofits' use of them. Consider the resources available and audience preferences to choose the most effective combination of digital tools for the organization and situation. Importantly, hold firm to foundational principles of fundraising while keeping abreast of the changing landscape. Focus first on the comprehensive fundraising strategy rather than the digital platform itself. Then harness these powerful social tools to cultivate and empower a collective community to support important causes.

Discussion Questions

1. What investments and efforts are needed for an organization to leverage and manage the use of social media and content creation?
2. How might an organization frame its needs and outcomes and strategize tactics for a crowdfunding campaign?
3. What are benefits and challenges of peer-to-peer fundraising and crowdfunding?
4. How should an organization conceptualize an email fundraising program and measure its effectiveness?

Application Exercises

1. You work for a small nonprofit organization with 3.5 full-time employees dedicated to development and marketing. How will you divide responsibilities and manage your social media and digital presence?

2. An organization is seeking to launch its first crowdfunding campaign. Select a compelling project and feasible monetary goal. Identify sources for team captains and reasonable goals for funds raised and donors engaged. Describe how supporters could be engaged after the fact.

3. Your mid-sized nonprofit is planning to participate in #GivingTuesday for the first time. How will you decide which mediums and tools to use? What are some strategies – both in terms of content and peer-to-peer approaches – to try and what other key considerations need to be articulated within the organization?

CHAPTER TWENTY-FIVE

PLANNING EVENTS WITH PURPOSE

By Roberta L. Donahue and Caitlin Deranek Stewart

From the glitzy hotel ballroom to the interactive online experience, special events are one way that fundraisers engage supporters and prospective donors. Yet, there is a persistent misconception that events are a quick and easy method to raise lots of money (Wade 2019). Experience shows that events are neither quick nor easy. In fact, when viewed as stand-alone fundraising vehicles, many events are costly, especially when considering staff and volunteer time, and may not break even. As it turns out, events are neither a panacea nor a curse. They are one fundraising tool among many through which fundraisers help donors build meaningful relationships with causes and organizations.

After completing this chapter, readers will be able to:

- Explain cultivation, solicitation, peer-to-peer, and stewardship events.
- Describe the planning requirements for successful events.
- Engage staff in creating compelling experiences for current and prospective donor attendees.

Differentiating Events by Purpose

No matter their delivery mode, special events are most successful as part of an integrated and strategic fundraising program. Events are never a quick solution to a larger fundraising shortfall. Rather, fundraisers can use special events as a strategic opportunity to strengthen relationships between donors and organizations at various points of The Fundraising Cycle (see Chapter 12). Therefore, decisions about special events should be part of annual and strategic planning. Leadership and the development team, broadly defined, should review and endorse dates, times, locations, themes, audiences, and objectives for events as part of the overall organizational and fundraising plan.

The follow sections apply regardless of events' format or size and describe how special events can achieve various strategic functions within fundraising.

Cultivation Events

The goal of a cultivation event is "to engage and maintain the interest and involvement of a donor, prospective donor or volunteer with an organization's people, programs and plans" (AFP 2017). Optimizing cultivation requires integrating strategies at all levels of the organization and customizing opportunities for different types of donors based on giving levels and interests. Events can create unique opportunities on a large scale that lead to acquisition, renewal, and upgrade of giving.

New prospective donors are on fact-finding missions when they attend an event for a charity to which they have not contributed. Any number of factors may have drawn them to the event including:

- A general interest in the mission.
- An appealing activity or format.
- A personal invitation from a friend.
- A featured guest or speaker.
- A location of interest.

Once they arrive, the ultimate goal is to engage the guest in the cause and ignite a passion to act as a volunteer or donor. If an attendee enjoys the event but quickly forgets the organization, the experience is like an artistic commercial with memorable visuals but a forgotten product. Neither is effective in inspiring action.

Organizations must carefully design each event component to ensure that the whole is engaging and people focused. Cultivation events for former and current donors focus on invigorating and energizing the bond to the mission. The format should remind guests why they got involved with the organization and show the difference they can continue to make through their involvement. Staff, volunteers, and clients (as appropriate) can share organizational mission and impact. Organizations planning cultivation events must strive to reaffirm the importance of their work through memorable experiences. Afterward, following up promptly and personally, thanking individuals for attending, and inviting support are all important.

Creatively conceived events can achieve all of these goals. For example, as part of a dinner event, an organization put a small wooden box at each place setting. Prior to dinner, the host asked each guest to open the box. Inside was a wish from one of the organization's clients. Guests then read their client's request aloud at their table. As they read, the prospective donors were introduced to eight lives that the nonprofit was working to change – even if they had come only to hear the featured speaker. This created an interactive experience that encouraged guests to think deeply about the organization's mission.

Another example is an organization that invited prospective donors to virtually attend the unveiling of a newly constructed school in West Africa. This school was created by donations from one family and the family wanted to share the excitement with their circle of influence. Attendees watched from thousands of miles away as local craftspeople put the finishing touches on the school, celebrating with the donors as the community resource was created. As part of the follow-up strategy, the organization invited attendees to financially support the construction of another school. Many chose to do so.

Solicitation Events

Solicitation events include asking the guests for contributions of time, talent, or treasure. This type of event may not fit every organization and must be carefully considered in relation to organizational constituents and culture.

High-level solicitation events can be very successful when approached with the same general principles that apply to personal, face-to-face solicitation (see Chapter 34). For example, advance and onsite messaging should indicate that gifts will be solicited, and that guests' individual circumstances will be considered.

Such events must include time for attendees to get comfortable, feel included, and focus on the organization and mission. The organization's leaders, especially volunteers, play an important role in meeting, greeting, and introducing guests to one another. This inclusion leads to the involvement phase of the event. Well-trained volunteer and staff hosts are prepared to share their own stories and invite others to do the same. Questions such as, "Have you heard about this recent success story?" or "Can I tell you about the difference the ABC program has made?" focus conversations on the organization's mission.

It is during the presentation that an event really differs from one-to-one solicitation. Visual aids, expert witnesses, and organizational beneficiaries (as appropriate) showcase accomplishments, articulate the need for financial support, and embody the results of contributions. Prospective donors should also get to engage and ask questions, with either event speakers or hosts.

When the steps are effectively completed, most attendees will be ready, and even expect, to be asked for a financial commitment. Many will be eager to hear how they can be involved, having witnessed the difference they can make. A challenge is determining the right amount to solicit. There are several ways this can be resolved.

- Customized pledge cards are given to the prospective donors with their name and a suggested amount.
- When personalized cards are not possible or feasible, a standardized card is provided and includes flexibility for a personal commitment.
- The host recommends a range of gifts that is appropriate for the group around the (virtual or physical) table.
- The featured speaker or another trusted organizational representative suggests a minimum gift.

Another approach combines the best of events and face-to-face solicitations. The donors join others for the presentation and the event excitement, but an individualized face-to-face solicitation occurs before the end of the event or follows the event in a timely fashion. For this approach, donors must be carefully matched with designated solicitors who have been pre-identified based on mutual experience or relationship.

Peer-to-Peer Events

In recent years, organizations have adapted to donor and volunteer desires to activate their networks for causes through the development and promotion of peer-to-peer events. This type of engagement can range from personal fundraising via social media on giving days to walk-a-thons undertaken individually for a cause to other in-person gatherings hosted privately with donations collected for a nonprofit.

The power of peer-to-peer events is in the personal appeal and stories from each participant (Castillo, Petrie, and Wardell 2014). They can be excellent acquisition opportunities as new donors are attracted through a personal relationship with the volunteer and direct experience of the organization's impact. Ease with which donations are made is critical, as is a prompt and thorough follow-up.

Peer-to-peer provides a new opportunity for strategically engaging supporters and for new donor acquisition, but also includes challenges around identifying and acknowledging donors, ascertaining interest beyond the volunteer who connected them, and managing representation of the organization. While volunteers are making the solicitations associated with these events, coordinating and supporting peer-to-peer fundraising is a significant task for staff. Volunteers are passionate but do not always have the means or experience to effectively craft a solicitation without support. Staff should consider creating toolkits with standardized language and setting aside significant time for training and coaching to ensure success.

Stewardship Events

Stewardship is "the process whereby an organization seeks to be worthy of continued philanthropic support, including the acknowledgment of gifts, donor recognition, honoring of donor intent, prudent investment of gifts, and the effective and efficient use of funds to further the mission of the organization" (AFP 2017). In other words, stewardship events are an opportunity to demonstrate the judicious and impactful use of donors' financial contributions (see Chapter 17).

Stewardship events are about the donor, not the organization. They can include large gatherings for numerous supporters, or personalized experiences honoring one donor's support. As in other events, the venue and logistics matter: the organization should consider location, timing, and convenience to donors. For example, if donors from across the country contributed to a building project, a livestream of a hardhat tour could reach a large audience, helping them feel like a major part of the experience no matter where they live.

It should not come as a surprise that donors want to learn more about the organization's good work. Donors may be viewed as investors or stakeholders, eager to learn how their contributions make a difference. They want to understand outcomes of the nonprofit's work and to build their sense of personal connection. Attendees may share stories, learn program news, and hear testimonials during casual conversation. Donors find it reassuring to be in the company of peers who are committed to the same cause. Furthermore, being at an event with others interested in the mission builds community.

Consider the powerful feelings created by touring a new, donor-supported facility for a nonprofit's clients or watch the emotion in a donor's eyes as they meet a scholarship recipient. Stewardship events are critical to strengthening donors' belief in the mission, trust in the organization's operations, and can lead to future support.

Critical Factors for Event Success

From beginning to end, events require careful attention to myriad considerations and details. This section includes several primary recommendations.

A Financially Sound Plan

Events can be expensive ways to raise money; funding is needed for venues or virtual platforms, entertainment, catering contracts, and event promotion. A budget is an important planning tool even if raising funds may not be the primary purpose of the event. Consider income and expenses, including in-kind support. Costs that are often overlooked include staff time and complimentary meals. For large events, the board should approve the budget.

Event planners should also consider whether introducing multiple revenue sources makes sense. Options include:

- Inviting supporters to sponsor tables or invite guests.
- Charging a fee for entry (ticket cost).
- Seeking general event sponsorships, including in-kind donations.
- Encouraging participants to raise funds in their networks beforehand.
- Selling branded merchandise.
- Offering multiple ways to support onsite, such as special appeals and auctions.

Logistic Planning for Mission Alignment

The ambience of the event should be in accordance to its purpose and the organization's mission. Even if an event itself is exciting, if the organization is not authentically represented, outcomes may be unsatisfying. Rather than hosting a formal gala with expensive tickets, a children's after-school organization might host something casual for families of supporters and clients, and raise money through sponsorships and personal solicitations. People in attendance will feel more connected to the mission when the event reflects the organization and its priorities.

In their book *Made to Stick: Why Some Ideas Survive and Others Die,* Chip and Dan Heath (2008) claim that a compelling message must be simple, unexpected, concrete, credible, and emotional. Inspiring action from event attendees requires a carefully designed message on the importance of the organization's mission and work. Balancing an emotionally compelling case with direct, actionable steps that attendees can take to help alleviate the problem will increase response and make follow-up that much easier. Planners must also consider who should deliver the message, share the organization's story effectively in a way that speaks to the emotion, and if included, complete the solicitation.

Event planners must thoroughly consider all other logistical elements. The timing of the event, both in terms of time of year and time of day, can make a large difference as well. Ensure that events are not scheduled on religious or other holidays, and avoid other major conflicts within the organization or locally.

Events depend on a thoughtfully constructed guest list. Making sure the list is accurate and inclusive helps to build goodwill while avoiding hurt feelings. The planning group should consider the constituencies to include (i.e., donors, prospective donors, clients, volunteers). If a special guest will be honored at the event, that individual should also be given the opportunity to add people to the list.

Event Planning Team

Events are often organizations' largest and most public opportunities to reach a wide audience and inspire action on behalf of the cause.

Consider the planning team carefully. To ensure that the event is well executed and inclusive, it is essential that the planning team include a diversity of backgrounds and perspectives. This helps to ensure accessibility within the event and associated materials, create respectful and inclusive event programs, and make inclusive decisions about event tone, setting, and timing. The integration of diverse voices makes events stronger and more appealing to a broader group of potential attendees.

Consider what else the staff – and, if feasible, volunteer – planning team can help with (i.e., logistical decisions, site visits, promotion, sponsorship solicitation). Which staff members work in the area highlighted during the event? Which fundraisers work with the donor population?

Staff buy-in for an event is critical and aided by planning team communication about the event goals and requirements. Keeping staff informed about the details of the attendee list, event messaging, and logistics increases the likelihood that they will find the event valuable, volunteer their time to make it better, and encourage constituents to participate.

Contingency Planning

Unplanned happenings are inevitable and range from minor issues such as a loud party in the next room to major issues like a featured speaker being snowed in and unable to make the event entirely. Weather, low participation, food problems, and a large number of no-shows are all possible concerns. A well-planned event accounts for as many factors as possible, takes multiple preventative measures, and includes contingency measures. On event day, one staff person should be designated as the decision-maker to handle unforeseen changes, allowing quick, responsive solutions to be enacted.

Natural disasters, including the COVID-19 pandemic, can make community gatherings impossible or unwise. In such cases, an online event may fill the need, but should not be considered an easy fix. Online events require the same careful planning as in-person events and may necessitate additional skills and experience such as video production. A strong social media presence, quality email connections, and engaged followers are indicators of an effective online event. Factors for success include a condensed and engaging event timeline, dependable and simple technology interfaces, and clear communication with attendees as plans shift.

Fundraisers should think through contingency plans as early as possible.

Follow-Up Planning

Nonprofits are busy places. After an event it is common to quickly move to the next task. This means that the team should develop the follow-up plan for attendees before the event takes place.

What happens post-event? After an event, development professionals and other organizational leadership should reach out to attendees to build on the momentum. Thoughtful, personal follow-up can contribute to strengthening donors' relationships with the organization and lead to increased donations. Tasks include thank you notes to volunteers, sponsors, and others involved in creating the event, but that is just the beginning. Other techniques range from sharing event photographs to sending recorded programs to interested individuals who were unable to attend to surveying participants for their evaluations. Being able to do these things may require special efforts during the event itself.

There should be a debriefing with those involved in the inner circle of the event as well as event summaries collected from hosts, board members, and other key volunteers who engaged in conversations with donors and prospective donors.

Considering Internal Event Dynamics

In organizations, depending on the approach, special events can be rallying points or unwelcome distractions that divert energy and resources away from the mission. The elements that make events meaningful experiences for donors can also be applied to developing an internal planning process that excites and engages staff. This can also help foster a culture of philanthropy in which all in the organization understand philanthropy and see their own ability to contribute to the fundraising process. Rather than taking for granted that all staff are on board, providing ways for team members to draw on or expand their expertise through event planning or implementation can enable events to be perceived in a different and positive light.

Clear Event Purpose

Well-defined events have clearly articulated goals, for both the donor experience and related to organizational outcomes. Staff should understand the desired outcomes, be part of determining the goals, and help decide if an event is the logical way to accomplish these aims.

What does the organization need from the event? Internally, there may appear to be an easy answer to this question: "money." However, that may not be the real answer. As stated earlier, events do not necessarily generate substantial money, thanks to high up-front expenses like catering, venue, and video production. The desired outcome may not be solicitation; rather, it could be cultivation or stewardship with an eye to eventual solicitation. Based on this realization, with all the members of the leadership team in agreement, special events can be woven into the entire fabric of a donor-focused fundraising plan. Fundraisers can plan their strategies for their donors around the recognized internal purpose.

Opportunities for Donor Interaction

Events provide donors with avenues to engage with various organizational representatives and with different forms of information about the programs. Fundraising staff have unique opportunities for interaction with donors and prospective donors in these moments. Carefully orchestrated introductions and guided conversations can enable fundraisers to meet and learn about individual donors. Other staff can also be asked to take part in planning or implementing these activities during the events.

Post-event follow-up activities can continue to build the community feeling within the organization as well as with donors. Staff should be invited to debrief on the event program and evaluate event outcomes for their areas.

Connection to Mission

Events can reinforce donors' mission connection in different ways than individual interactions. Personal stories of experiences, benefits, and histories with the organization draw others closer to the case for support. In a social setting with peers, the prospective donor or current donor may be more open to engaging in a way that deepens their knowledge and commitment.

To facilitate and maximize the connection, staff and volunteers often need guidance or training. They can seek pertinent and critical information that may be missing from a prospective donor's profile. Through casual conversation, a host can learn values, family history, and other involvements. A debrief can help to make sure that the information gets into the prospective donor's file.

Engaging volunteer hosts as part of an event can be one way to deepen engagement with current donors. Hosts inform, connect, and invite their peers to join them in supporting the organization. The qualities of a good host are similar to those of many volunteers: active support and advocacy; reliable and dedicated; connected and respected; and, willingness to invite their circles of influence to give.

Engaging staff and volunteers alike in the event planning team can strengthen their commitment to and understanding of the organization.

Measuring the Impact

The event must be fully evaluated afterward to "prove" its value. Events often require staff members to take time away from their other work, flex their working schedules, and use skills outside of their normal workflow. These commitments require that the value to the organization is clear.

A post-event evaluation should be based on the original event plan and on the benefits to other fundraising activities. In addition, a staff and volunteer meeting discussing everything from event logistics to attendee experience and dollars raised will allow leadership to determine if this event should be continued, modified, or canceled in the future. It also provides an opportunity for the involved parties to present their ideas and opinions.

Conclusion

Well-designed special events are valuable for organizations and can strengthen community awareness and philanthropic support for the mission. Events are flexible, creative opportunities that can serve numerous purposes including cultivation, solicitation, and stewardship. Strong events are aligned with organizational missions, responsive to the larger environment and current conditions, inclusive of constituents and stakeholders, and closely managed and reviewed for effectiveness. They can provide multiple ways for donors and volunteers to be involved through peer-to-peer events, event planning committees, and onsite (or online) on event day. Staff throughout the organization may also participate, resulting in benefits for the team and culture of philanthropy. While significant work and planning is required, if done properly, events can serve important purposes throughout the fundraising cycle and as one component of a comprehensive development program.

Discussion Questions

1. When is an event the correct vehicle for fundraising? When should the fundraiser or nonprofit leader push back on the idea of planning an event?
2. How should cultivation, solicitation, and stewardship events differ? Which factors should change, and which should remain the same? How do peer-to-peer events fit with these other event forms?
3. As a fundraiser, post-event follow-up can be just as important, if not more important, as the event itself. How would the plan differ for follow-up with an individual just learning about the organization versus a major gift prospective donor?

Application Exercises

1. You have been asked by the board to launch a new event. Describe the process you would follow to determine what type of event could meet the organization's fundraising goals.
2. Develop a to-do list for planning an event using the "Critical Factors for Event Success" section.
3. Reflect on a special event that you attended. What type of event was it? What was its purpose? What details are memorable? What was the follow-up?
4. Interview a staff member or volunteer who has helped plan an event. Explore whether this person's experience aligned with the information in the internal event dynamics section of the chapter.

PART SIX

ENGAGING THE DIVERSITY OF INDIVIDUAL DONORS

CHAPTER TWENTY-SIX

UNDERSTANDING INDIVIDUAL DONORS

By Pamala Wiepking

When MacKenzie Scott donated an astonishing $6 billion in 2020, people hurried to discuss the motivations behind her extraordinary giving. Was it because she wanted to create more equity in the world, as a substantial part of the donations were directed at historically black colleges and universities? Or did she want to give back "freely and abundantly" from the wealth she had gained disproportionally through "an infinite series of influences and lucky breaks we can never fully understand," as she writes in her letter for the Giving Pledge (Scott 2019)? Or maybe she wanted to "get even" with her ex-husband Jeff Bezos "by doing what he does not: sharing his unbelievable, unconscionable, indescribable wealth with those he makes his money off of, i.e. everyone else in the world" (Bryant 2020; Safronova 2021).

Like MacKenzie Scott, all donors have a multitude of reasons for giving. Charitable donations are a result of many factors, including the resources that people can access, their personal experiences, and their motivations. In addition, people's social interactions and the context in which they live also influence giving decisions. Exploring these factors reveals much about individual donors and their giving behavior. Understanding why donors give is of key importance for fundraisers seeking to engage donors with organizations in a meaningful way.

After completing this chapter, readers will be able to:

- Describe the relevance of resources for individual donors' giving.
- Describe how socio-demographic characteristics influence individual donors' giving.
- Discuss the key motivations, including values and mechanisms, that explain why individual donors give.
- Demonstrate the ability to implement knowledge about a donor's motivations in fundraising.

Resources for Giving

People need a variety of resources in order to make charitable donations. First among these is access to income or wealth. Research consistently finds that people with higher levels of income and wealth give more to charity (Wiepking and Bekkers 2012). However, all people deserve the opportunity to participate in philanthropy. Fundraisers should seek contributions from people across the financial resource spectrum, not just those with greater income and wealth. People across all income levels give to charity, and there is even evidence that those with lower incomes donate relatively more: They give a higher percentage of their income (Neumayr and Pennerstorfer 2020).

Absolute income and wealth are also not the only financial resources that matter. Wiepking and Breeze (2012) showed that people's *perception* of their financial resources may be an even more important factor in giving behavior. People need to feel that their and their family's financial future are secure, before considering making substantial donations. Surprisingly, even people with access to multiple millions can feel financially insecure, and hence, will not give much to charitable causes.

There are several other key resources people hold that potentially enable higher charitable giving. Table 26.1 lists three of these resources, and briefly explains why they influence individual donor giving.

How Socio-demographic Characteristics Relate to Giving

Resources enable people to give, but personal experiences lead them to give in certain ways and to specific causes. While every donor has their own unique motivations for giving, trends can be identified among similar groups of people. Lived experience is, of course, an important motivation for people to connect with a specific

TABLE 26.1. INDIVIDUAL DONOR RESOURCES THAT CAN ENABLE CHARITABLE GIVING

Resource	Why it can enable charitable giving
Education	Education typically increases people's income and wealth. Through education, people also learn about social and societal needs, not just in their own community but also across the world. They also typically develop stronger personal values that motivate caring about others. Those with higher levels of education also are typically more socially connected, which leads to more opportunities for giving and gift requests.
Social connections	Those who are connected with a greater number and a more diverse range of people are more likely to come across opportunities for giving and receive gift requests.
Family characteristics	Having a partner and children leads to more social connectedness, and thus opportunities and requests for giving, for example, through the children's school or sport clubs.

Sources: Based on Bekkers and Wiepking 2011b; Wiepking and Bekkers 2012.

cause or organization. Think, for example, about someone who experienced a serious illness themselves or within their family, or someone who experienced a traumatic event like a school shooting, or someone whose child has a disability and encounters barriers for participation in society. These experiences may motivate them to make donations to associated charities.

Subsequent chapters in this section explain unique motivations and giving patterns for people with different socio-demographic characteristics, including women, people who identify as LGBTQ, and people who are religiously affiliated. Chapters in this section also explore giving among communities of color and across different generations as well as among those with significant financial resources. And, almost all individuals logically fall into more than one of these categories or others; a reminder to use all information about giving trends judiciously when interacting with individual donors.

The Complex Dynamics of Individual Giving Behavior

Both resources and socio-demographic characteristics influence individual donor behavior. But knowing which people are more likely to give, and give more, to an organization does not always reveal *why* they give to an organization. For fundraisers, understanding *why* people give is highly relevant for building long-term relationships with donors.

As illustrated with the MacKenzie Scott example, donors may have a multitude of motivations that exist simultaneously. Motivations for giving can be either *intrinsic* or *extrinsic*. Charitable behavior based on intrinsic motivations derives from care for others and desire to contribute to human and societal well-being, including concern for the natural environment. People who give out of intrinsic motivations give because they care about the needs of others (altruism) or because their personal values align with the values of the charitable organization. Giving based on extrinsic motivations results from the personal benefits to be received, including feeling good about one's self, increasing one's social reputation, and receiving tax benefits.

Scholars have worked to develop a more comprehensive understanding of the complex dynamics of giving motivations and two articles provide structures for organizing and using that knowledge. The first is a seminal article by Konrath and Handy (2017a), in which they reviewed the academic literature, surveyed 800 Americans, and developed the "Motives to Donate"–Scale. This scale includes six key motivations for donors.

Trust. Trusting that organizations will make a difference with their gift.
Altruism. Giving to help others in need, caring about the beneficiaries.
Social. Giving because others also give or because they know that giving is important for others.
Tax. Lowering the absolute costs for giving through the use of fiscal incentives.
Egoism. Giving to receive benefits, including increasing social reputation or experiencing the joy of giving.
Constraints. Perceiving financial constraints that limit people's charitable giving.

These are easy to remember, as Konrath and Handy (2017b) devised a clever acronym: "a **TASTE** for **C**harity."

In a second academic article that sheds light on donor motivations, Bekkers and Wiepking (2011a) conducted an extensive review of the academic literature examining charitable giving behavior. They distilled eight *mechanisms* that drive people's charitable donations. Simply put, mechanisms relate to all the different processes that lead to a certain outcome, in this case, charitable giving. Mechanisms include personal motivations for giving, like the six key motivations included the "Motives to Donate"–Scale, but mechanisms also include other external influences on donor behavior, such as the influence of a gift solicitation.

Figure 26.2 shows the eight mechanisms for giving, clustered in four categories: the opportunity to give, values for giving, costs and benefits in relation to giving, and efficacy motivations for giving.

FIGURE 26.2. EIGHT MECHANISMS THAT DRIVE CHARITABLE GIVING

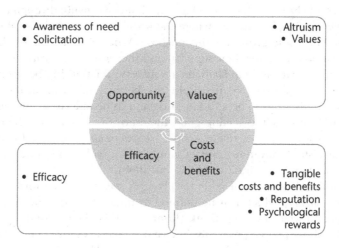

Source: Developed from Bekkers and Wiepking 2011a.

The Opportunity to Give

The first cluster relates to the opportunity to give. People need to be *aware of a need* and of a way to donate money – typically through *solicitation* – to relieve this need before they can consider making a donation. Awareness of need increases with the urgency of a need. People can become aware of needs through conventional and social media. For example, news coverage of a natural disaster often inspires people to make a donation to a nonprofit organization like the Red Cross. When friends post a message on social media about the needs of a local animal shelter, people become aware of this need and can decide to donate to support that cause.

The opportunity to give is often created by fundraisers through solicitation. An increasingly common form of solicitation is through peer-to-peer crowdfunding on behalf of nonprofit organizations. Both volunteer and professional fundraisers play a major role in individual donor behavior by asking people to donate. Research estimates that up to 85 percent of donations are made in response to a request (Bryant et al. 2003). Breeze (2017) put this markedly in her seminal work on the fundraising profession: Charitable gifts are not just given; they are asked for.

Values

The second cluster includes mechanisms that drive giving through a donor's personal *values*. People want to change the world in line with their values, and they can use charitable giving for this purpose. When donors' values align with the organization asking for their support, and they give to this cause out of *altruistic* motivations, that can help facilitate a long-term relationship between the donors and the organization. When people give because of altruism, they give out of intrinsic motivations to benefit the cause and its beneficiaries, and not for extrinsic motivations such as feeling good themselves or enhancing their reputation. Research shows that in actuality people are *impure altruists*: They do not give out of pure altruistic motivations, but in combination with other, often extrinsic and more self-serving, motivations (Andreoni 1990).

Another key personal value for giving is *empathy*. A first form of empathy is *cognitive empathy*, which can be defined as understanding how someone else is feeling, and what they may think (Konrath 2017). The second type is *emotional empathy*, where people physically feel what someone else is feeling. Both of these types of empathy can motivate charitable giving. However, one specific form of emotional empathy, empathic distress, hampers rather than helps giving behavior. When a person physically takes over the emotional distress of someone in need, this can lead to feeling "paralyzed" by the other person's emotion. And when people are focused on relieving their own distress, they will not (and cannot) help or give money. Fundraising organizations need to be careful to avoid generating empathic distress with intense negative emotional appeals, as these may be counterproductive.

Other personal values that motivate giving include religious values, biospheric values, "noblesse oblige," and social injustice. All major world religions advocate to support others in need. When people have stronger religious values, they typically also have stronger altruistic values, motivating them to give money to both religious and secular organizations (Bekkers and Schuyt 2008). Biospheric values relate to caring about nature and environmental protection, which people find increasingly important in times of climate change. "Noblesse oblige" includes motivations to give back, out of gratitude of what you have received from others and society. Addressing social injustice is also a strong motivation for giving, as shown by the influx of donations to the Black Lives Matter movement in 2020.

Costs and Benefits

The mechanisms identified in the third cluster relate to costs and benefits. First, people are more inclined to give, and give more, when the *tangible, absolute costs* of a gift are lower, and the *benefits* are higher. Tax incentives lower the absolute costs of a gift, as do matching and multiplication schemes where a third party increases a donor's gift amount. Tangible benefits of donations include small items like a pen or T-shirt, but also substantial benefits like season tickets to the opera. Social costs and benefits are also relevant: Bekkers and Wiepking (2011a) called this the *reputation mechanism,* others sometimes refer to this as *image motivation* (Ariely, Bracha, and Meier 2009). Through charitable donations, people can strengthen their social reputation. Giving is typically seen as positive behavior, and hence, socially rewarded. People like to see themselves as "prosocial persons," who care about others and contribute to their lives in positive ways. People also typically want to be perceived as being prosocial by others; this can also motivate them to make charitable donations, especially when other people will see their giving. Failing to give, in front of others and especially in settings where giving is expected (i.e., charity events, peer-to-peer crowdfunding), can also harm one's social reputation.

There are also *psychological costs and benefits* of giving. Giving makes people happy (see Chapter 5). Moreover, not giving when asked can damage a person's own self-image and belief that they are prosocial. This sometimes causes people to become "sophisticated altruists." When given the opportunity to avoid a gift request, people will do this in order to escape the dreaded anticipated guilt for not giving. Examples include taking a different exit at the supermarket to avoid the Girl Scouts selling cookies or declining a meeting where a gift request is anticipated. As Andreoni et al. (2017) put it: "Just as a sophisticated eater will avoid exposure to the chocolate cake, a sophisticated altruist can avoid being asked" (627).

Efficacy

The fourth cluster only includes a single, but important, factor: the perceived *efficacy* of giving. People who believe that their gift makes more of a difference, are more likely to give and give higher amounts. The perceived efficacy of giving can be increased by endorsements or leadership gifts from other trusted donors, including celebrities (Gneezy, Keenan, and Gneezy 2014). Interestingly, donors are less concerned about the actual effectiveness of their chosen charitable organizations, in part, because this information is so hard to come by and interpret (Bowman 2006; Coupet and Broussard 2021).

Donors do typically care about the "overhead" costs, which can relate to the percentage of an organization's income that is spent on staffing, facilities, and fundraising. Donors prefer their donations to go directly toward the programs the organization runs, and not toward sustaining the organization itself. They dislike having their gifts spent on overhead costs, under the assumption that charities with higher overhead costs are less effective than those with lower overhead costs (Gneezy, Keenan, and Gneezy 2014). Ironically, research shows that organizations with higher overhead spending can be just as effective in achieving their goals (Lecy, Schmitz, and Swedlund 2012; Qu and Daniel 2020), suggesting that this concern by donors may be misattributed. In his famous TED talk, fundraiser Dan Palotta (2013) explained why fundraising costs, in particular, can actually contribute to increased organizational effectiveness.

Implications for Practice: Assessing Donor Motivations

Ideally, a donor's motivation for giving becomes clear through his or her involvement with an organization or through personal conversations with fundraisers or board members. When lacking information about a donor's specific motivations for giving to an organization, it can be helpful to assess (and document) their motivations based on the broad mechanisms (Bekkers and Wiepking (2011a), and distinguish between intrinsic and extrinsic motivations. For example, are donors intrinsically motivated because their values align with those of the organization? Or did donors start giving to the organization because they participated in a gala event with lots of exposure, allowing them to increase their social reputation and fueling their extrinsic motivations?

When building a relationship with major donors, it is also important to take their motivations into account, which can be done using the TASTE for Charity approach (Konrath and Handy 2017b). If donors who give to an organization out of extrinsic reputational motivations are approached for a gift using a value-based proposition, without opportunities for social exposure, this limits the likelihood that they will give. The same holds true for donors who give out of altruistic motivations. They want their donation to benefit the end-beneficiaries and goals as much as possible. Providing them with tangible benefits for the donation, such as a small token of thanks, will not be appreciated as they feel that the costs of this present should have gone to the cause.

One way to assess which mechanisms from Bekkers and Wiepking (2011a) are most relevant for a specific donor, is to complete the spiderplot included in Figure 26.3 (Wiepking and Beltman 2016). Typically, donors will be motivated by a few of the mechanisms, not all. Based on the completed spiderplot, fundraisers can easily assess the most prominent mechanisms that drive a specific donor's charitable giving behavior. This information can be used to continue to develop the relationship by creating specialized opportunities to resonate with their motivations.

It is not always possible to have personal conversations with every donor, especially when fundraisers rely on annual giving campaigns to solicit donations, but knowledge about donor motivations can still be helpful. For example, a fundraiser at a large charity with thousands of small donors can still explore their motivations by talking with a limited number of donors and then can align communication to

FIGURE 26.3. SPIDERPLOT OF MECHANISMS FOR GIVING

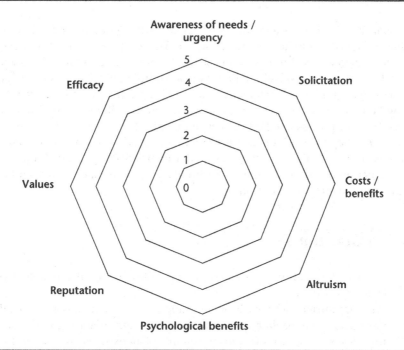

Source: Wiepking and Beltman 2016.

fit what is learned. Fundraisers can also use the spiderplot in Figure 26.3 to craft appeal letters, digital media, and programs for special events (see Chapters 23, 24, and 25). Different mechanisms for giving can be incorporated to try to attract donors. The spiderplot can be used to evaluate the extent to which a fundraising appeal is based on one or more mechanisms from Bekkers and Wiepking (2011a). Appeal responses can also be reviewed to see what was most fruitful and to try to discern the motivations of donors who responded. A good appeal typically does not include all of the mechanisms.

Surveys are another tool often used to assess donor motivations for large groups of supporters. Aim for any donor survey to be short and requiring only about five minutes to avoid annoyance and survey fatigue. A survey can assess donors' motivations for giving to specific projects within an organization as well as asking questions about why they give, including some rationales based on intrinsic and extrinsic motivations. It can be useful to work with a specialized agency that has experience in conducting donor surveys or to at least review the survey draft with a small group of close donors before launch.

Conclusion

Philanthropic giving is a deeply personal act, making donor motivations and giving influences multifaceted and complex. This chapter discusses how resources such as income, wealth, education, social connections, and family characteristics enable donors to make charitable donations. In addition, it notes how people's socio-demographic characteristics and their lived experiences influence their giving behavior. It focuses significant attention on the different motivations people can have for giving, based on the key findings in the academic literature.

The chapter concludes by illustrating how fundraisers can use the research to assess donors' different motivations. With this knowledge in hand, fundraisers will be better prepared to communicate with donors in ways that resonate and to build stronger long-term relationships.

Discussion Questions

1. Name and explain three resources that people can have that enable their charitable giving.
2. What are intrinsic and extrinsic motivations? Give examples of specific donor motivations that would classify as an intrinsic motivation for giving to a homeless shelter. And provide an example of an extrinsic motivation for giving to a university.
3. What are the four clusters of mechanisms that drive charitable donations identified by Bekkers and Wiepking (2011a)? For each cluster, name and explain one mechanism for giving.

Application Exercises

1. Indicate how the six TASTE for Charity motivations from the "Motives to Give"–Scale from Konrath and Handy (2017a) relate to the eight mechanisms for giving from Bekkers and Wiepking (2011a). Make a chart showing how TASTE for Charity motivations overlap with the mechanisms. Are there mechanisms that are not reflected in the TASTE for Charity motivations?
2. Examine one or several fundraising appeals (i.e., television commercial, direct mail, other medium). Using the spiderplot from Figure 26.3, indicate to what extent the fundraising appeal uses each of the mechanisms to motivate people to donate. Typically, campaigns will include a few of the

mechanisms, not all. After completing the spiderplot, consider how the most prominent mechanisms in the campaign may have influenced who gave and what you can now discern about donors to the organization/s.

3. Visit the Giving Pledge website (www.givingpledge.org) where each of the signatories have included a letter explaining their motivations. Select a letter to read and find evidence of at least three mechanisms, values, or motivations articulated by the donor. Then, read another letter and compare the two.

CHAPTER TWENTY-SEVEN

THE ROLE OF RELIGION IN GIVING

By David P. King and Rafia Khader

Religious faith has undergirded much of philanthropy for centuries. Indeed, most American donors find some religious or spiritual meaning in their giving (Smith and Davidson 2014). In an increasingly global society where people of different backgrounds live side by side, fundraisers need to have a breadth and depth of understanding around faith in philanthropy. This entails studying how religious identity and activity affect giving to religious nonprofits in particular as well as giving to nonprofits in general. At the same time, making sense of the consequences of rising religious disaffiliation and evolving spirituality on overall giving is also becoming increasingly important, as this chapter shows.

Engaging faith in fundraising requires embracing various ways of expressing faith, having multiple expectations among diverse constituencies, and welcoming people's personal stories of religion and spirituality.

After completing this chapter, readers will be able to:

- Describe the role of religious giving in the philanthropic sector.
- Describe the shift in religious giving and its effects on cultivating donor relationships.
- Understand the impact of increasing religious diversity and disaffiliation on fundraising.
- Explain multiple religious and spiritual motivations that inspire donors.
- Understand core principles of giving across various religious traditions.

The Landscape of Religious Giving

Religious beliefs and practices are a primary motivation for a significant amount of charitable giving. Moreover, almost all religious organizations ask for financial support to sustain their activities. Studying faith and philanthropy, therefore, requires understanding the nature of religious giving as well as the ways in which religious institutions simultaneously inspire and benefit from philanthropy.

Defining Religious Giving

Following IRS categories, Giving USA (2021) defines *religious giving* narrowly as going to congregations, denominations, missionary societies, and religious media. Under this rubric, donations to a Catholic hospital or religious college, for example, are not counted as giving to religion (but instead to health and higher education, respectively).

Yet, giving to religion, even when defined this way, dwarfs all other subsectors. According to Giving USA, religious giving made up 28 percent of all charitable giving in 2020, increasing 1 percent in current dollars from 2019, followed by education with just 15 percent of overall giving. Despite this prominence, from its height of 56 percent of total giving in the 1980s, religious giving has declined by more than 25 percent.

Religiously motivated giving has not necessarily decreased at the same pace. When asked, Americans say that 73 percent of their charitable giving goes to organizations with religious ties (McKitrick et al. 2013). Congregations make up 41 percent of that giving, but individuals categorize another 32 percent of their donations as going to religiously identified organizations (RIOs). While these organizations appear in other programmatic categories in Giving USA rather than in the religion subsector, many RIOs have faith or religious identity as a significant part of their mission (e.g., Catholic Charities, World Vision, Jewish Federations, Zakat Foundation, etc.). Donors indicate that they often give to these organizations because they value their religious identity.

Differentiating religious and secular nonprofits is not always easy, as nonprofits categorized as secular may not necessarily function as such in practice. Religion can influence nonprofits through the religious beliefs and practices of their founders, staff, and volunteers. Fifteen percent of nonprofit organizations not categorized as religious nonetheless use religious language in their names or mission statements (Fulton 2020). Furthermore, within the Giving USA categories of education, health, human services, and international affairs, at least 15 percent appear to be faith-based. Counting the 350,000+ congregations along with the 150,000 faith-based organizations that are not specifically categorized as religious, there are at least 500,000 religious nonprofit organizations in the United States.

While donors who support religious congregations allocate the majority of their charitable giving to organizations with religious ties (80 percent), they often support nonreligiously identified organizations (NRIOs), too (McKitrick et al. 2013). Even donors making gifts for secular purposes often find their charitable giving going to organizations with religious ties.

While individuals contribute most to religion, and almost 80 percent of all gifts to congregations come from individuals (King et al. 2019), some foundations also fund religion. In a study looking at philanthropy and religious diversity, Lake Institute on Faith & Giving, Aspen Institute, and Public Research Religion Institute (PRRI) found that a majority of the 33 surveyed foundations funded religious causes (Inclusive America Project 2020). While the majority of dollars support mono-faith initiatives, foundations also indicated that religious literacy (64 percent) and inter-faith or multi-faith engagement (52 percent) were also strategic priorities. What this demonstrates is that though institutional and individual donors may still have strong roots and commitments to a specific faith tradition, trends point toward funding broader forms of religious engagement as well.

Across the nonprofit and philanthropic sector, an organization's religious identity (or donors' perceptions of it) as well as the faith-based giving of individual and institutional donors is multifaceted. Whether a nonprofit considers itself religious or not, religion or spirituality is likely motivating some of its donors.

Religious Congregations

The Pew Research Center (2015) estimated that 37 percent of U.S. adults attend worship services weekly, while another 33 percent attend monthly or yearly, down from historic levels. Attendance is one of the best predictors of religious giving. Following a similar trend, individuals' membership or belonging to a religious community has fallen below 50 percent for the first time in almost 80 years of polling (Jones 2021).

Numerous studies show that people who are members of or regularly attend a house of worship (at least twice a month) are between two and four times more generous in their giving to religious causes than those who attend less frequently or not at all (Austin 2017). Perhaps it is not just attendance, but the benefits of social networks actualized in regular attendance that lead to increased giving. Other scholars point to the increased solicitations experienced by frequent attenders during religious services (Bekkers and Wiepking 2007). Indeed, the nation's largest study of congregational finances finds that most donations are made during worship services (78 percent) (King 2020). Yet, half of all congregations raise money for outside organizations such as other nonprofits, denominations, or ministries, meaning that most attendees are exposed to multiple funding requests through their faith community.

The COVID-19 pandemic brought changes to the attendance patterns and giving of congregants. While 52 percent of congregations saw an increase in participation, 41 percent saw a decline in giving (King 2020). Comparing giving month to month between the summer of 2019 and 2020, giving overall was down 4.4 percent. Small Catholic parishes and congregations (weekly attendance under 50) saw declines in participation and giving more than other groups.

Even before the pandemic, digital giving in congregations was growing, and by the spring of 2020, 84 percent of all congregations reported they were capable of receiving gifts online (King 2020). Generally speaking, religious institutions need to become habituated to conveying philanthropic requests beyond in-person services and must work to form social relationships within their community – virtually and in person. The case for support also may require updating. Leaders should not expect congregants will automatically understand congregations' needs as their organizations evolve to face new external and internal challenges.

Religious Affiliation and Spirituality

Religious affiliation has changed drastically in recent years as interest in institutional affiliation has declined across society generally. Between 2007 and 2014, the U.S. Christian population declined from 78 percent to 71 percent and the religiously unaffiliated population grew to 23 percent (second to evangelical Protestants at 25 percent) (Pew Research Center 2015). More than one in five Americans no longer affiliate with any religious tradition. Among Americans under the age of 30, only 1 in 3 are religiously affiliated. Those who were nominally associated with a religious tradition are now much more likely to report no religious affiliation; the negative public perception of religion in sociopolitical issues has pushed others to dissociate.

However, the majority of the religiously unaffiliated are not irreligious and many identify as spiritual (Fetzer Institute 2020). Researchers have found that 57 percent of Americans engage in some type of spiritually meaningful philanthropic activity, and 51 percent find their giving to be spiritually meaningful, regardless of whether the benefiting organization was secular or religious (Steensland and Wang forthcoming). Moreover, those who identify as highly spiritual, as compared to those who are less spiritual or not spiritual at all, are more likely to personally emphasize making a difference in their communities and the wider world (Fetzer Institute 2020). When it comes to giving, having a spiritual identity matters (Steensland and Wang forthcoming). Fundraisers can therefore encourage potential donors to consider giving as a method of living out their spirituality, transforming both donors and organizations.

Age, Race, and Religious Tradition

An examination of Philanthropy Panel Study data showed that age was positively correlated with participation in religious giving (Austin 2017). Only 23 percent of individuals under the age of 40 gave to religion as compared to 37 percent of those between the ages of 40 and 64. Approximately 54 percent of people over 65 gave to religion. Framed more broadly, millennials are less likely to partake in spiritually meaningful philanthropic practices compared to older Americans, with one noted exception: social activism (Steensland and Wang forthcoming).

Although race is not a significant predictor in terms of the amount of giving, it does play a role in religious giving. For example, while White people are more likely to give and at higher amounts, African Americans are more likely to give to religious causes, after controlling for income (Austin 2017).

When comparing giving, individuals across traditions have been found to give at similar rates to congregations, RIOs, and NRIOs, taking into account income and education levels (McKitrick et al. 2013). In a study breaking out five of the largest religious groups in the United States (Black Protestant, evangelical Protestant, Jewish, mainline Protestant, and Roman Catholic), the only notable difference was that fewer Jewish people gave to congregations.

Religious Giving Motivations and Perspectives

What many religious people share is the motivation to give in order to be in a right relationship with God, a religious community, or the wider world. According to Hudnut-Beumler (2007), four kinds of motivations shape religious giving.

1. *Giving to achieve reciprocity with God.* This is a way to achieve a closer relationship with God.
2. *Giving to achieve reciprocity with a particular religious group.* This reflects donors' desire to do their fair share in a community, gain recognition, or elevate into a position of leadership.
3. *Giving as an extension of the self.* This giving reflects causes people believe in and their desire to honor institutions that have been a source of blessing to them.
4. *Giving as an act of thankfulness or altruism.* This commemorates a family or life event or honors the memory of a loved one.

Giving is at the heart of most religious traditions. The teachings of these traditions remain foundational in religious followers' understandings of the "how" and "why" of giving. These traditions, however, do not characterize philanthropy in the same way. Attending to the language that various religious traditions use in framing philanthropy is important while engaging with donors.

Judaism

In the Hebrew Scriptures, the word *tzedakah* reflects the Jewish understanding of charitable giving. From the root word meaning "justice," *tzedakah* is often framed as a practice of giving in order to help the poor and to rectify social imbalance. It is considered a *mitzvah*, or commandment and obligation that Jews must follow. Many Jews also use the phrase *tikkun olam* to describe their charitable giving. Often translated as "to repair or fix the world," this phrase has been adopted by many philanthropic causes to describe the dedication of time, energy, and resources for others' benefit. It has developed resonance far beyond the Jewish community.

Jewishness is a religious and cultural identity, and the practices, motivations, and recipients of Jewish giving are diverse. With Jews making up 2 percent of the U.S. population (Pew Research Center 2020), roughly 31 percent of Jewish adults belong to a synagogue or temple (Pew Research Center 2013) where donating through a system of annual dues is often expected. While 23 percent of American Jewish giving is focused on congregations, 39 percent is tied to other Jewish nonprofits that work to sustain cultural identity and provide social services, healthcare, and education. Most Jewish communities are serviced by a Jewish federation, operating as an umbrella organization for receiving and distributing philanthropy. The remaining 39 percent of Jewish giving is concentrated on non-Jewish organizations.

Christianity

Nearly 71 percent of Americans identify as Christian (Pew Research Center 2015). In many Christian traditions, followers look to the Hebrew Bible for a precedent of the tithe (giving one-tenth of one's income to God). Some see this giving as directed first to the church, while some consider other religious or secular donations as a part of their 10 percent. Regardless, only a small percentage of Christians give a tithe (Smith et al. 2008). Within the narrower definition of *religious giving*, some Christian denominations give a higher percentage of their total income to charity than others. Mormons represented the highest percentage of per capita giving (5.6 percent) followed by Pentecostals (2.9 percent), nondenominational Protestants (2.6 percent), and Baptists (2 percent). While some see a tithe as an obligation or command from God, most Christian communities operate out of free-will offerings.

In the New Testament, Jesus talks of giving not only of a tithe but also challenged followers to give far beyond it. For instance, the Christian monastic tradition has seen men and women take vows of poverty to give themselves fully to the work of their faith. Employing one's resources to participate in God's work in the world is another consistent aspect of Christian theology. Language of responding with gratitude to God's generosity or stewarding the possessions entrusted by God by giving back to communities of faith or the needy is often central to Christian traditions of giving.

Islam

Muslims make up 1 percent of the U.S. population (Pew Research Center 2015). Muslim giving is primarily motivated by religious obligation and a belief that those with more should help those with less (Mahmood 2019). One of the five pillars of Islam, *zakat* (literally "to grow in purity"), is an annual payment of 2.5 percent of one's assets. Zakat is understood as a return of wealth and a right of the poor and needy. Often given during the holy month of Ramadan, zakat has eight categories of worthy recipients. Attesting to the appropriateness of one's gift to meet the requirements of zakat is necessary for nonprofits that engage with Muslim donors.

Islam also has a long history of giving beyond the required zakat, called *sadaqah* (akin to the Jewish root *tzedakah*, justice). One type of sadaqah, called *waqf*, is an endowment initiated to establish schools, mosques, shrines, and other institutions. While mosques are top recipients of Muslim giving, Muslims spend more than other American faith groups on civil rights protections (Mahmood 2019).

In Islam (and other faith traditions for that matter), there is debate about whether to apply charitable giving to local or global contexts and within the religious community specifically or more broadly to those in need. When it comes to giving outside their faith community, a large percentage of Muslims cite domestic poverty alleviation as their top concern (Mahmood 2019).

Dharmic Religions

Dharmic religions, originated in the Indian subcontinent, include Buddhism, Hinduism, Jainism, and Sikhism. While these traditions have long and distinct histories, their philanthropic impulses are similar to the three Abrahamic traditions discussed previously (Ilchman, Katz, and Queen 1998). In Dharmic religions, *dāna* refers to charity or giving alms. It is a central aspect of the practice of these faiths, but it does not connote the same sense of obligation as scriptural mandates within Islam or Judaism. By giving away material possessions, one accumulates spiritual merit. Donors give alms to the poor as well as more specifically to those who have chosen a life of poverty (i.e., Brahmins tied to a life of study in Hinduism, Buddhist monks who shun most possessions).

The intent of one's gift, as well as the worthiness of the recipient, is extremely important. If one gives out of the wrong motives, merits of the gift may be undermined. At the same time, the gift must be given without attachment. For many, giving the gift is freeing oneself from material possessions. Therefore, nonprofits that are keen on reporting achieved outcomes and proper accountability may find less interest from a Buddhist donor who would rather detach from the gift (Ilchman et al. 1998).

These brief summaries demonstrate the centrality of religious giving in sacred texts and practice. Yet, these are living traditions with multiple interpretations that must always be explored when working with individuals and communities.

Fundraising within a Religious Context

In relationships with donors, different forms of fundraising are appropriate and effective, based on distinct ways of inviting contributions and reasons for making them.

The Budget Appeal, Obligatory Giving

This is the most common, instinctual form of fundraising for many religious institutions and the predominant form in most congregations aimed at raising operating funds. For donors, the motivations to give may range from casually "chipping in," an obligation to "do their fair share," or resulting from regular religious practice. Inviting a donation within this dimension is simple and direct. The case for support is presented, including needs and impacts. There is an emphasis on members' duty/obligation/opportunity to support the institution to which they belong. The budget appeal should not be dismissed as unimportant. It is essential for fiscal sustainability, and this form of giving may be meaningful for brand-new givers as well as longstanding supporters who see giving as a spiritual practice for its own sake.

Programmatic Investment, Relational Giving

This dimension of fundraising emerges as individuals become more involved in the work of a religious institution and wish to identify with the organization and further its impact. Giving may be spontaneous or strategic, based on the donor's own giving patterns. Inviting a donation within this dimension will be a product of the organization's impact on potential givers. Relational giving is more personal and experiential than obligatory giving, as it is an outcome of the donor's participation in the organization's programs and the programs' impact on their lives. These gifts may be designated to specific initiatives, but they may also be received as contributions to the general fund.

Donor Care, Transformative Giving

This element of religious fundraising goes hand in hand with deep personal connection and spiritual transformation. Here, donors are discovering and deepening their life purpose through giving. Inviting a donation within this dimension will generally be part of a well-developed relationship, often with a pastoral connection or personal spiritual friendship. This form of giving may be sparked by significant transitional events in a donor's life (e.g., inheritance, retirement, end-of-life planning, spiritual awakening). Transformative giving is generous, and may often focus on a special campaign, an entrepreneurial venture, or an endowment or capital effort. Questions of legacy, spiritual breakthroughs, lasting impact, and attention to healing or changing the world are at stake in this type of religious fundraising and giving.

Faith and Fundraising

Donors are increasingly motivated by personal values in their giving. Yet, while three-quarters of high-net-worth donors point to values as a leading motivator, two-thirds of those same donors admit that they often have trouble identifying what they care about and connecting it to their giving (Indiana University Lilly Family School of Philanthropy 2018).

As society becomes increasingly diverse, fundraisers must develop a broader understanding of the variety of religious, spiritual, and moral traditions that motivate donors. At the same time, fundraisers must also develop a strong comfort level in helping donors to discover their passions and values. Discerning questions that lead donors to consider their aspirations and hopes for the future as well as reflect on their own moral and ethical frameworks will allow donors and fundraisers to build healthier relationships with one another. Such questions also will help donors to better understand their own values and motivations for giving.

Although religious or spiritual identity is not donors' only motivation, attention to these values should be central to fundraisers in faith-based and secular institutions. No matter a fundraiser's own religious sensibilities, a broad understanding of diverse religious motivations as well as a willingness to engage the donors' values and religious foundations is vital to almost all nonprofit organizations' success.

Conclusion

Though the number of Americans who affiliate with a particular religious tradition has decreased over the past few decades, religious and spiritual beliefs continue to serve as a primary motivation for charitable giving overall. Giving is at the heart of most religious traditions.

Fundraisers must understand the various ways religious traditions frame people's giving. Cultivating not only the giving capacities but also the values and faith motivations among donors is an important long-term strategy for building deep relationships with donors who share a passion for the mission. Fundraisers in long-term relationships with donors may find themselves pivoting from obligatory giving appeals to truly transformative giving – and this has the potential of transforming the organization, donor, and even the fundraiser.

While the institutions, forms of giving, and motivations are likely to change in the coming years, all signs indicate that faith will continue to be a significant factor in philanthropy in the long term.

Discussion Questions

1. What role does religion play in the philanthropic sector?
2. What motivates religious people to give? What are the distinctions among different faith traditions? Where are their similarities?
3. What are different approaches to fundraising within a religious context?

Application Exercises

1. Reflect on your own approach to giving or that of someone you know. How do religious and spiritual values impact the giving stories?
2. Interview a religious leader to understand how they frame the opportunities and challenges around faith and giving.
3. Review the website of a religiously identified organization. How is religious identity demonstrated in its mission and values, staffing, and programming? How does it frame the case for support?
4. Put yourself in the position of a donor to an organization. Given that the majority of American donors give in part from a sense of religious/spiritual values, how do (or can) the fundraising materials make space for these concerns? How would this need to vary by organizational mission and values?

CHAPTER TWENTY-EIGHT

WOMEN AND PHILANTHROPY

By Jeannie Infante Sager and Debra J. Mesch

Globally, women are more influential than ever before and using their influence to catalyze social change. Philanthropy is complex and influenced by many factors, including income, wealth, and education. Today, women have more of all three – giving them more power. Still, there remains tremendous opportunity to enhance women's charitable giving.

Research from the Lilly Family School of Philanthropy's Women's Philanthropy Institute (WPI) shows that the practice of philanthropy is not gender neutral. Gender impacts how, why, where, and when people give to charitable causes. Understanding how gender influences philanthropy can help unlock a new era of philanthropy and ultimately drive more giving. As the twenty-first century continues to unfold, nonprofit practitioners – CEOs, fundraisers, board members, and volunteers – and donors must recognize that neither philanthropy nor fundraising follow a one-size-fits-all format. This chapter explores some of the challenges and opportunities in working with women donors and encourages all to pay more attention to women.

After completing this chapter, readers will appreciate how gender influences giving by:

- Understanding women's potential as donors.
- Examining ways in which women and men differ in their giving.
- Identifying attitudes and behaviors of women as donors.
- Exploring fundraising strategies that resonate for women donors.

The Potential of Women as Donors

MacKenzie Scott made headlines in 2020 by giving $6 billion for social justice purposes to hundreds of organizations. Her philanthropy was extraordinary. Its scope, scale, transparency, and planned impact exemplify the potential of women to change society and philanthropy. Scott also joins a growing movement to increase the visibility and voice of women as donors (Safronova 2021).

In the United States, women are more than 50 percent of the population (U.S. Census 2019b). More women have better access to education, higher income, and greater wealth, all key predictors of philanthropic giving (Bekkers and Wiepking 2011b; Wiepking and Bekkers 2012). Since 1995, globally, female enrollment has tripled in tertiary education (UNESCO 2020). Women's labor force participation and median earnings continue to rise (U.S. Bureau of Labor Statistics 2020a). In around 40 percent of households with children, women are the primary breadwinners (Wang et al. 2013). Women control 32 percent of global wealth and are predicted to have total accumulated assets of up to $93 trillion by 2023 (Zakrzewski et al. 2020). Additionally, women are poised to inherit a large share of $30 trillion in wealth in the next decade (Baghai et al. 2020).

Research from the WPI shows that women's growing wealth is good news for the philanthropic sector. Women give differently, and are more likely to give more, than their male counterparts, across age, race/ethnicity, and income levels. The more women's wealth grows, the more they will give to charitable organizations (Mesch et al. 2015). How women think about wealth differs, too. According to a U.S. Trust (2013) study of high-net-worth donors, women are nearly twice as likely as men to say that giving to charity is the most satisfying aspect of having wealth. Women are happier when they give more; and for single and married women, life satisfaction increases most when they increase their giving as a percentage of income (Mesch et al. 2017).

Challenging Assumptions

Despite the overwhelming evidence of the potential and power of women in philanthropy, societal perceptions persist that suggest women are less philanthropic than men, defer to their husbands in charitable decision-making, and do not make big gifts. Consequently, women donors are underrepresented and overlooked. Recent research counters these perceptions.

Women Are More Philanthropic Than Men

The WPI *Women Give* series provides empirical data affirming that, in general, women are more likely to give to charitable organizations, compared to similarly situated men. WPI's body of research includes the foundational finding that single female households give more than comparable single male households across income and marital status (Mesch 2010). Since the initial study, WPI research has delved deeper, seeking insight into which women are most philanthropic. The findings around single female households remain true regardless of age, race, and season of life. *Women Give 2012* found that Baby Boomer and older women are more likely to give and give more across all giving levels than their male counterparts (Mesch 2012). Moreover, *Women Give 2019* confirmed this finding across racial and ethnic groups (Mesch et al. 2019). Research demonstrates that this continues in retirement. Single women and married couples give more and more consistently than single men and are more likely to volunteer (Osili et al. 2018a).

Women Drive Decision-Making

Women are deeply involved in household charitable decision-making and tend to take more responsibility for charitable decisions than men. Most U.S. couples make giving decisions jointly (Mesch et al. 2021). However, women are more likely than men to be the sole deciders. Young Generation X/Millennial married women have more of a say in charitable decisions than their Boomer/pre-Boomer counterparts did 40 years earlier (Mesch et al. 2016). Couples in the younger generation are giving higher amounts now than Boomer/pre-Boomers did in the past. Both single and married women are increasingly influential individually and within their families and have the capacity to give at ever-greater levels.

Women Make Big Gifts

Women have the potential to make sizable gifts. For example, Women Moving Millions (WMM), an initiative started by sisters Helen LaKelly Hunt and Swanee Hunt, raises million-dollar gifts from women for women's and girls' causes. According to the WMM website, since the organization's founding in 2007, WMM has committed nearly $800 million to organizations with over 340 high-net-worth women around the world, pledging to donate at least $1 million during their lifetimes. A search of the Lilly Family School of Philanthropy's Million Dollar List (milliondollarlist.org) offers more evidence that women make substantial gifts. The database includes hundreds of publicly announced gifts of $1 million or more by women to all subsectors. Moreover, women have proven they do not have to be millionaires to make big gifts. Oseola McCarty, a washerwoman for most of her life, made a $150,000 bequest, creating scholarships for African American students at Southern Mississippi University and making front-page news (Bragg 1996).

The evidence is clear: Fundraisers need to put aside misconceptions and build more relationships with women as potential donors. Practitioners should develop questions to explore philanthropic decision-making considerations for married couples. These conversations can explore giving decision processes and identify ways fundraisers can aid women in talking to their families about philanthropy. Fundraisers can also treat philanthropy as a family endeavor and encourage male donors to bring their female partners into the process. As Millennials and Gen Xers come into their own as donors, organizations should consider how they are inviting younger donors to learn about their missions and create appealing opportunities for engagement and giving for these groups. Engaging more women and supporting them as big donors requires examining the full spectrum of fundraising, including marketing, communications, special events, and stewardship practices to ensure that they appeal to both men and women. This includes knowing how and whom to thank, and capturing this information in databases. Importantly, development professionals should ask women to give. The vast majority of gifts follow a request for support and failing to invite women to give is a mistake based on false assumptions.

Identifying How and Why Women Give

Gender matters in philanthropy and the structures that support fundraising have not fully developed the tools and strategies that resonate with women. As fundraising professionalized in the 1960s, white wealthy men were the focus population. Tactics to reach them such as campaigns, recognition, giving levels, competition, and peer pressure were effective and have raised millions of dollars over the years. Generally, these approaches do not work as well for women and other populations underrepresented in the donor base. Today there is opportunity to change these structures.

Research has identified four tangible ways in which women's giving differs from men's: Women distribute their gifts more broadly, often give together, leverage technology, and look at giving holistically. This information can be used to help fundraisers with "traditional" strategies (i.e., direct mail, major giving) and newer philanthropic forms (i.e., giving circles, crowdfunding, impact investing).

Give Broadly

A consistent finding is that women tend to distribute their charitable giving among more organizations than men (Mesch et al. 2015). They also may be more constant in supporting organizations throughout their lives. If a woman gives $100 annually to each of ten organizations, however, no one fundraiser will appreciate the full sense of her generosity. Because of this, women are less likely to appear on lists of prospective major or planned gift donors. Careful review of the database for these hidden contributors, especially women who have given gifts of $100 to $500 for years, may well reveal significant gift potential.

Women are drawn to an expanded definition of *philanthropy* that encompasses both formal and informal definitions of the word rooted in the idea of "giving back." Research shows that women tend to give more than money, using their time, expertise, advocacy, and networks to apply all their resources to work for good (Mesch et al. 2020). This is especially important for communities of color, where women can be seen as "bridge builders" within philanthropy, embracing a rich and broad definition of *philanthropy*, and using their giving to celebrate and support their communities (Mesch et al. 2019). Giving during the COVID-19 pandemic and other disasters resonates with this broad definition and reflects a larger reimagining of philanthropy that considers indirect giving and mutual aid. Examples of indirect giving include supporting a local restaurant with takeout orders or gift card purchases or continuing to pay individuals and businesses for services they could not render (Mesch et al. 2020).

Fundraisers should review their fundraising portfolio to gauge whether they are engaging women and men as well as donors of all racial and ethnic groups (see Chapter 29). Recognizing and acknowledging the importance of individuals' intersecting identities within philanthropy is central to engaging them. Many women are interested in involvement with causes and building a relationship with an organization through volunteering, leadership, and educational opportunities prior to making a significant gift. Once engaged, women tend to be loyal donors and give more over time to the causes in which they are actively engaged.

Give Collectively

Many women prefer to give collectively to fully maximize their impact (Carboni and Eikenberry 2018). Giving circles appeal to women because of their collaborative and democratic process. In a giving circle or collective giving group, individuals pool their contributions and decide together how and where funding will be allocated. The number of giving circles has tripled in the last decade, and the circles have granted nearly $1.3 billion since their inception. While women represent the majority of giving circle members, the ecosystem is becoming more diverse with LGBTQ, men-only, Jewish, African American, Latinx, and Asian American groups forming.

The growth of the giving circle movement has provided countless opportunities for women in philanthropy. Women have stepped fully into leadership roles, learned about their communities, engaged deeply with nonprofits, and in some cases, influenced public policy. Because giving circles are deeply embedded in their communities and partner closely with the nonprofits, giving circles also often become frontline responders in addressing pandemic and disaster relief locally (Wright 2020).

According to one study, female giving circle members may access their social networks more strategically for philanthropic advice and have more diverse philanthropic networks than donors acting independently (Carboni and Eikenberry 2018). Furthermore, the study affirmed that women engaged in giving circles give more, give more strategically and proactively, and give to a wider array of organizations and causes. They are also more likely to engage in civic activity.

Organizations that host giving circles realize significant benefits that include building a culture of philanthropy, reaching new donors, attracting a more diverse set of donors, and increasing community visibility (Bearman and Franklin 2018). Fundraisers who develop strategies and opportunities that speak to women's interest in giving together can not only increase giving for their organization but also create a more satisfying giving experience for their female donors.

Use Technology

Research shows women use tech platforms more than men and give more than men online (Mesch et al. 2020). On digital platforms and social media, women give nearly two-thirds of total online gifts and more than 50 percent of total dollars. These online gifts tend to be smaller and go to smaller charitable organizations.

A WPI study found that women are more likely than men to give on #GivingTuesday (Osili et al. 2017). While giving goes up sharply for both men and women on that day each year and they give approximately equal amounts, women's greater participation means greater total donations from women. In this analysis, women donors gave 61 percent of the total dollars contributed on #GivingTuesday.

Nonprofits and fundraisers should be using digital platforms to foster community, build trust, and appeal to women and a diverse range of donors in general. At minimum, organizations should not only have a social media presence, but they also need to make giving online easy. Fundraisers can encourage online connectivity of their volunteers to help amplify messaging and create personal fundraising campaigns to bring in new gifts. Organizations should leverage technology at all stages of the fundraising cycle with confidence that such efforts will resonate with women.

Give Holistically

Women are more motivated than men by empathy for others. For men, giving is often about self-interest (Mesch et al. 2015). This is a matter of degree and priority; it is not that men are not empathetic. Because women are socialized from an early age into more helping, nurturing, and caring roles, these behaviors become ingrained and form the basis for many of their actions, including philanthropy. Empathy also drives women's deep engagement with nonprofits.

Research has shown that women are more likely to give to organizations where they have a personal connection or an alignment with political or philosophical beliefs. Single women are more likely than single men to cite being on a board or volunteering for an organization as motivating their giving (Mesch et al. 2015).

High-net-worth women are known to approach giving in strategic and holistic ways. A study seeking to understand high-net-worth donors' support for women and girls revealed that women donors connect wealth with responsibility, seek to educate themselves before making funding decisions, are willing to take risks with their philanthropy, value return on investment, and prefer investing in organizations and programs focused on systemic change (Dale, Small, and O'Connor 2018). In addition, when looking at high-net-worth donors who support women's funds and foundations, research found that philanthropy is a fully integrated aspect of their lives (Dale et al. 2019). The women identified as activist donors and philanthropic leaders who give during their careers and are motivated to give through board service and volunteering. Fundraisers who understand these characteristics of high-net-worth women's giving can shape conversations, engagement activities, and reporting efforts that better advance their relationships.

Gender differences in impact investing also highlight women's holistic approach to giving. This relatively new model in the philanthropy landscape involves financial investments in companies or funds to generate social as well as financial returns. Men are more likely than women to use impact investing *in place of* charitable giving (Osili et al. 2018b). Women are more likely to use it to *complement* their charitable giving. According to one survey, 59% of women are interested in sustainable investing (Morningstar 2019). Perhaps these women donors are thinking comprehensively about all the financial resources and assets they can bring to address priority issues. Fundraisers should learn about these new tools and facilitate conversations about how the tools can build on a donor's giving rather than replace it.

Conclusion: A New Era in Women's Philanthropy

MacKenzie Scott's multibillion-dollar commitments in 2020 were remarkable and may reveal a new era in women's philanthropy. Her data-driven approach, quick disbursement of unsolicited and unrestricted gifts, and invitation for others to join her exemplifies how women engage in bold, strategic, and impactful philanthropy. She is part of a growing movement among women philanthropists like Dr. Priscilla Chan and Melinda French Gates purposefully adopting platforms to leverage their philanthropy and exert influence on others. They have elevated their giving by being more vocal and transparent, even pooling resources to support innovation in addressing systemic issues such as social justice and gender equity. It is not only wealthy women who are becoming more outspoken and visible in their giving. Exponential growth of giving circles indicates that philanthropy appeals to many donors at many gift levels. Recognition of a broader definition of philanthropy also brings attention to women's giving that has been happening all along, reminding fundraisers that paying attention to female donors means also paying attention to women of color and from other marginalized communities in society.

Fundraisers should take note and acknowledge that gender matters in philanthropy. Investing in efforts that align with women's patterns of giving will lead to increased charitable giving by all. Intentional and inclusive fundraising strategies that resonate with women can transform the fundraising culture, build long-term loyal donors, and generate more resources to help fulfill organizations' missions and philanthropic purpose.

Discussion Questions

1. What are some of the assumptions and truths about women as donors? How can this information hamper or help organizations' fundraising success?
2. What are some of the differences between women and men's charitable giving behaviors?
3. What kinds of opportunities for generosity and involvement may appeal to women donors? What does the research say to support expanding these programs and efforts?
4. How might an organization communicate in ways that inspire women donors and appeal to their ways of giving?

Application Exercises

1. Identify one of your organization's women donors. What are her philanthropic motivations and how do they connect to your mission? Create a narrative that shares her story and highlights the way gender may have influenced her philanthropy. Alternatively, research a woman philanthropist using articles and information online. Compare what you learn to the information in this article.
2. Consider what structures organizations should have in place to encourage more attention to women. This can include brainstorming metrics to encourage fundraisers to engage more women, database analyses to reveal loyal women supporters, and other ideas developed from this chapter.

CHAPTER TWENTY-NINE

PHILANTHROPY AMONG COMMUNITIES OF COLOR

By Una Osili and Sarah King Bhetaria

There is a growing recognition that the philanthropic sector can learn from long traditions of philanthropy in communities of color. The COVID-19 pandemic and the Black Lives Matter movement made apparent centuries of racial injustice and awakened the nation's conscience (Osili 2020). One outcome has been an outpouring of support for causes that address racial and social justice issues (Williams-Pulfer and Osili 2020). When protests erupted after the murder of George Floyd in 2020, his family's memorial campaign raised over $14 million from 500,000 donors.

With the growth of diversity in communities across the United States, defining *philanthropy* in a rapidly changing U.S. social and economic context means expanding the lens to include the vast and complex ways that communities of color engage in sharing resources (Vaid and Maxton 2017).

To reach current and future donors from a broad array of racial, ethnic, and cultural backgrounds, the sector needs to go beyond acknowledging and accepting differences and bring diversity, equity, and inclusion to the forefront.

In this chapter, readers will:

- Examine demographic trends in U.S. ethnic and racially diverse populations.
- Explore philanthropic understandings regarding communities of color.
- Apply research about philanthropy in communities of color to fundraising.
- Develop ideas for increasing diversity, equity, and inclusion within organizations and fundraising.

The Context of U.S. Racial/Ethnic Diversity

In this chapter the term *communities of color* is used to describe minority populations and to focus on African American or Black, Hispanic or Latinx, Asian American or Asian/Pacific Islander, and American Indian or Native American peoples. Noting that terminology preferences differ vastly among people of color, this term was chosen for purposes of clarity, ease, and to align with current practices in the literature.

The U.S. racial and ethnic landscape is complex and changing. As of July 2019, approximately 36.9 percent of the population belonged to a racial or ethnic minority group (U.S. Census Bureau 2019a). By 2060, non-Hispanic whites will account for 44 percent of the population, down from 76.3 percent in 2019. From 2016 to 2060, the Hispanic and Asian American populations are projected to double, and the population of people who are two or more races is expected to triple in size from 7.5 million in 2016 to 23.8 million in 2060, making it the fastest growing ethnic group (U.S. Census Bureau 2020a). The U.S. Census Bureau's (2021a) new "Diversity Index" indicates the chance that two people chosen at random will be from different racial and ethnic groups. In 2020, that chance for the United States on the whole was just over 61 percent. Hawaii has the highest percentage variable distribution of diversity (76 percent), and Maine the lowest (18.5 percent) (U.S. Census Bureau, 2021b). Additionally, the new measures used in the 2020 Census move away from the concept of "majority" and "minority" groups for measuring diversity to better reflect complexities of race and ethnicity and the multiple identities of individuals (U.S. Census Bureau 2021a).

A significant portion of immigrants to the United States are also people of color, who bring their own philanthropic influences. The Pew Research Center tracks immigration trends and estimates that more than 1 million immigrants arrive in the United States. each year (Budiman 2020). In 2018, a record 44.8 million immigrants lived in the United States, representing 13.7 percent of the nation's population. The same year the highest number of new U.S. immigrants came from China (149,000 people), followed by India (129,000 people), Mexico (120,000 people), and the Philippines (46,000 people) (Budiman 2020). Over 47 percent of immigrants who arrived in the United States between 2010 and 2019 had a bachelor's degree or higher compared to 31.5 percent of native-born Americans with the same level of education (U.S. Census Bureau 2020b).

Education, age and median income are all important indicators for fundraisers to understand the diversity among ethnic groups within the United States. The following examples illustrate the variety of situations individuals from different ethnic groups experience. The level of educational attainment for native-born Americans varies across all ethnic groups. For example, in 2016, the postsecondary graduation rates for first-time, full-time undergraduate students were highest for Asian American students (74 percent), and lowest for American Indian/Alaska

Native students (39 percent) (U.S. Census Bureau 2020b). Overall, the median age of ethnic and racial populations was 31 years, lower than the U.S. median age of 38 years (Schaeffer 2019). Finally, with the exception of Asian Americans, the median income of people of color still lags below the national median (U.S. Census Bureau 2017).

Examining Philanthropy in Communities of Color

Philanthropy across communities of color has received limited attention even though it is a vital component of all Americans' lives, cutting across race, ethnicity, and cultural backgrounds. The pandemic and civic protest around racial injustice has brought to light the transfers of resources within and across communities. Communities of color have primarily created independent philanthropic structures and practices, with similarities and differences among ethnic groups and in relation to the White population.

Communities of color understand philanthropy broadly, and include within it giving to formal institutions as well as sharing resources within informal networks, often with people the givers know well. For many ethnically diverse populations, philanthropy is embedded in family, religious congregations, and educational groups; it includes gifts of time, talent, and treasure – and increasingly testimony, which seeks to acknowledge the lived experiences of those in need of help (Milken Institute 2020). Giving behavior may be highly influenced by faith, community, professional, and family leaders.

Philanthropy is a valued approach to addressing social issues across ethnic groups. Prioritization of informal giving practices, rather than formal structures, among communities of color may stem from mistrust of traditional nonprofits and the need for immediate support. Direct financial aid to children and the elderly is common as are activities like caretaking within extended families. Mutual aid and reciprocity are accepted concepts. Givers are often motivated to help others as others helped them. From sheltering a neighbor in need to supporting a grass-roots movement, giving generously through direct, non-institutional means is important for people of color (Indiana University Lilly Family School of Philanthropy 2021b).

Similarly, informal philanthropy to extended family and mutual aid societies is prevalent within immigrant households, many of which are headed by people of color. Motivated by social networks and sometimes reciprocity, immigrants are 10 percent more likely to send private transfers (i.e., remittances) to individuals living outside of the household, particularly to those living in their countries of origin (Osili and Du 2005). Immigrants' philanthropic activities are often influenced by the philanthropic practices of their countries of origin. Immigrants from countries with similar philanthropic institutions to the United States, may adapt their practices at faster rates than immigrants from countries with dissimilar traditions (Jackson et al. 2012). Overall, however, studies of various forms of philanthropic action have also shown no differences between immigrants and native-born people, after accounting for factors such as permanent income (Aldrich 2011; Osili and Du 2005).

The formal philanthropic sector has the opportunity to bring more diverse voices to the decision-making table. Diversity is "a value that brings unique perspective or life experience to the decision-making table" with a particular focus on racial and ethnic groups, LGBTQ populations, people with disabilities, and women (D5 2016). Nonprofits can foster equitable practices that promote fair treatment, opportunities, as they address barriers to participation. Within organizations and beyond, an inclusive philanthropic sector promotes a culture where individuals feel respected and heard, and every person is included in decision-making.

Achieving these aims requires intentional and sustained practices and tailored approaches to align with a variety of donor interests and values. Fundraising professionals need to increase their knowledge and understanding of communities of color, their contributions and preferences, the disparities they face, and their philanthropic philosophies (Anft 2002).

Research about Philanthropy in Communities of Color

Analysis of the Philanthropy Panel Study (PPS) suggests that ethnic and racial identity exert a major influence in philanthropic behavior (Indiana University Lilly Family School of Philanthropy 2017). Nonminority American households give to charity at the highest rate (59.8 percent) and with the highest average donation at $3,000, followed by Asian households that give at a rate of 58.2 percent and with an average donation of $2,402. A lower percentage of African American (32.9 percent) and Hispanic households (34.2 percent) give to charitable causes and average total donation amounts for these households were less than the average donations of nonminority and Asian American households. These statistics do not account for differences in income, education, wealth, and socio-economic conditions. When these factors are considered, African American and/or Hispanic-headed households still differ from other ethnicities but the differences in giving rates are much smaller (see Table 29.1).

Another approach for studying giving behavior is to consider the share of income and wealth allocated to charitable giving. According to the PPS data (Indiana University Lilly Family School of Philanthropy 2017), African American-headed households give the largest percentage of their wealth (2.04 percent). Asian American households closely follow, giving 1.77 percent of their wealth. Hispanic and nonminority households give similar percentages of their wealth, 1.04 percent and 0.95 percent, respectively. However, when adjusted for income,

TABLE 29.1. OVERALL GIVING BY HOUSEHOLD'S RACE

Race	Giving Rate (%)	Average Total Donation – All Households	Average Total Donation – Donor Households	Giving as Percentage of Income	Giving as Percentage of Wealth*
Nonminority	59.77%	$1,793	$3,000	2.11%	0.95%
Hispanic	34.28%	$ 429	$1,251	0.93%	1.04%
African American	32.89%	$ 605	$1,839	1.28%	2.04%
Asian American	58.22%	$1,398	$2,402	1.02%	1.77%
Other Race	52.12%	$1,145	$2,197	1.56%	1.83%

Source: Authors' analysis of data from the Indiana University Lilly Family School of Philanthropy, Philanthropy Panel Study 2017. Note: All samples included and PSID Family weights applied. Race is based on households' reference person. No controls applied.
* Excluding home value.

wealth, and demographic variables, there are few significant differences in the fraction of wealth given to charity.

Informal giving is greater among minority households as a whole compared to nonminority households (see Table 29.2). The differences tend to remain statistically significant when differences in income, wealth, and socioeconomic conditions are considered. African American households had the highest overall private giving rate of 12.3 percent while "Other" Americans follow at 11.3 percent.

TABLE 29.2. INFORMAL GIVING INCIDENCE BY HOUSEHOLD'S RACE

Race	Informal Giving Incidence (%)
Nonminority	9.97%
Hispanic	9.89%
African American	12.28%
Asian American	6.52%
Other Race	11.25%

Source: Authors' analysis of data from the Indiana University Lilly Family School of Philanthropy, Philanthropy Panel Study 2017. Note: All samples included and PSID Family weights applied. Race is based on households' reference person. No controls applied.

Hispanic and nonminority households exhibit similar giving rates of 9.9 percent and 10.0 percent, and Asian American households' rate was lowest at 6.5 percent.

High-net-worth African American households (85 percent) give at a similar rate to all other high-net-worth families (89 percent) according to data from the "Bank of America Study of Philanthropy: Charitable Giving by Affluent Households" (Indiana University Lilly Family School of Philanthropy 2021d). African American households gave the most, followed by Asian households, white households, "other" households, and Hispanic households (see Chapter 32).

The "Everyday Donors of Color" study (Indiana University Lilly Family School of Philanthropy 2021b) collected additional information about how communities of color give. For example, 53 percent of donors of color volunteer, 34 percent donate, and 70 percent donate physical items. Crowdfunding presents a good opportunity for fundraisers. About 52 percent of people in the study agreed that crowdfunding makes giving easy and 34 percent had given through a crowdfunding site. For those donors who gave to support racial and social justice causes, about 59 percent reported giving through crowdfunding. More Asian Americans and Black Americans gave to racial and social justice causes compared to White counterparts.

Identity-Based Philanthropy

Identity-based philanthropy has several definitions. In academic circles the term refers to the ways in which people's social identities – particularly those from marginalized groups – may affect their philanthropy (Drezner and Garvey 2016). In practice, it can also be "the practice of raising and leveraging resources by and from a community on its own behalf, where *community* is defined not by geography but by race, ethnicity, gender, or sexual orientation" (W.K. Kellogg Foundation 2012, 3).

Both definitions point to the importance of different forms and processes of expressing generosity as a function of personal identity. For minority donor populations, identity-based philanthropy is a movement that challenges the divides that persist within mainstream philanthropic institutions and promotes the ways ethnic groups express generosity. Examples of specific forms of identity-based giving include giving circles and inclusive crowdfunding platforms (W.K. Kellogg Foundation 2019).

Giving Circles

Giving circles are a multidimensional form of identity-based giving. They enable a group to collectively invest its time, talent, and money. Together – democratically by voting – the group members decide the future direction of the circle and the allocation of its funds (Indiana University 2020). These forums allow members to learn to give or volunteer more strategically (Carboni and Eikenberry 2018), have a safe space to discuss their perspectives, and deepen their understanding around community issues.

According to a Collective Giving Research Group study, there were 1,313 giving circles in 2017 – triple the number of circles that existed in 2007 (Bearman et al. 2017). Today, giving circle members tend to be more diverse in terms of age, income, gender, and race than previously (Carboni and Eikenberry 2018). National identity-specific networks have formed in recent years and are largely responsible for this trend, including Amplifier, Asian Americans/Pacific Islanders in Philanthropy (AAPIP), and the Community Investment Network (CIN). Out of 1,313 giving circles, Collective Giving Research Group found 106 Jewish groups, 53 Asian/Pacific Islander groups, 40 African American groups, and 19 Latinx groups in 2016 (Bearman et al. 2017). The powerful rise in giving circles in communities of color has promoted a sense of belonging and trust in the philanthropic process. Historically excluded from decision-making, ethnically diverse members use giving circles as strategic vehicles to make meaningful, responsive change in their communities.

Charitable Crowdfunding

Charitable crowdfunding is the practice of raising small gifts from a large group of people ("the crowd") to fund a cause or help others. Social media and online platforms have contributed to the exponential growth of this form of fundraising for individuals and organizations in the nonprofit sector and enhanced direct aid in diverse communities. According to the Indiana University, Lilly Family School of Philanthropy report "Charitable Crowdfunding: Who Gives, to What, and Why?" (2021e), the triple challenges of the COVID-19 pandemic, calls for social and racial justice, and a recession in 2020–2021 brought new emphasis to crowdfunding in general and for identity-based groups in particular, notably those engaged in the social justice movement. The study found that crowdfunding donors are younger, less religious, single, and noticeably more diverse. Race has an effect on social justice giving on crowdfunding platforms with more African American households giving compared to Hispanic and White households. More than half of the donors surveyed in the study contributed to individuals (close family members or close friends). Nearly one-third gave to a stranger although in lower amounts. Charitable crowdfunding corresponds to the historic practice of communities of color to react quickly and directly to fundraising appeals by those close to them and in need.

Toward Inclusive Philanthropy

Embracing diversity, equity, and inclusion (DEI) in fundraising first requires organizations to look internally. This may entail training at all levels and programs that create awareness of diversity issues. This also requires self-reflection and recognition of biases and issues faced by diverse nonprofit constituents, including employees, especially as related to identities (Danso 2016; Kennedy 2020). It is important for top-level leadership to champion initiatives as well as promote diversity in organizational ranks, including among fundraisers.

On average, 21.4 percent of nonprofit board members are people of color (Indiana University Lilly Family School of Philanthropy 2018). This is not reflective of the demographics of a diverse America; communities of color comprise nearly 36.9 percent of the population (U.S. Census Bureau 2019a). Boards that are reflective of their communities promote an inclusive and equity-focused framework for their staff, donors, and beneficiaries.

Another important component of inclusive philanthropy includes crafting a diversity, equity, and inclusion statement to serve as a guide, demonstrate an organization's willingness to embrace diversity, and reflect how diversity issues fit into its framework. Organizations' diverse donors, beneficiaries, and other constituents should be engaged in the process.

In 2021, organizations are progressing by leveraging resources, diversifying support, and empowering diverse communities to elevate social change. Donors and people of color have mobilized to provide information about equity and community needs, and to act as catalysts for change as well as intermediaries among donors, organizations, and the wider community (Indiana University Lilly Family School of Philanthropy 2021b).

Recommendations for Fundraising

Enhancing organizations' ability to reach diverse groups is a critical component of building and managing credible, comprehensive fundraising programs. Ethnically diverse groups may be associated with identifiable, distinct, and significant philanthropic characteristics and traits. Engaging with diverse communities can require reimagining fundraising and incorporating one or many of the different approaches and philosophies to inclusive practices throughout the organization. Approaches to consider and try include:

- Re-examining the relationships among donors, nonprofits, and the community served (e.g., see Community-Centric Fundraising) and valuing all forms of philanthropic engagement including volunteering.
- Seeking input from identity-based affinity groups and community leaders regarding outreach to diverse communities.
- Engaging in ongoing education to develop understandings of philanthropy in communities of color and making adaptations to fundraising practices based on research.

- Integrating volunteers who represent various ethnic groups to help shape campaigns and strategies.
- Locating new and affirming identity-based giving mechanisms such as giving circles to develop an inclusive donor base.
- Customizing appeals to the prospective donors' customs and sensibilities. Segmentation based on ethnicity, race, and other demographics provides a better understanding of the perspectives and experiences of multiracial individuals as well as other intersecting identities.

All these approaches take time, and learning will happen throughout the ongoing process. As fundraisers move forward in their work to include more ethnically and racially diverse donors, they should keep in mind that "To establish more inclusive and equitable philanthropic fundraising approaches, a variety of informal and formal giving practices needs to be considered" (Indiana University Lilly Family School of Philanthropy 2021b, 34).

Conclusion

There is a heightened recognition of implications of diversity for communities throughout the United States. It is critical that organizations understand and interact with rich differences in cultural practices, values, and philanthropic approaches. Fundraisers need to diversify strategies to meet donors' unique interests and priorities. However, embracing diversity extends beyond fundraising among diverse constituents; promoting diverse voices should be at the core of organizations. Equitable representation and inclusion among internal and external stakeholders is increasingly a priority for many nonprofit institutions. With more tools and resources, fundraisers can develop more inclusive and equitable philanthropic fundraising approaches and strategies that encompass a spectrum of values and formal and informal giving practices.

Discussion Questions

1. Why should fundraisers be concerned about philanthropy in communities of color?
2. How might the distribution of diversity across the United States impact fundraising practices in different states?
3. Which ways of giving (formal or informal) might be favored over others depending on the racial group? How might this affect the way a community of color may engage with a cause?

Application Exercises

1. Engage in a conversation with a friend, colleague, or family member who is a person of color and/or an immigrant, and explore cultural practices, values, and common philanthropic approaches. What do you discover that aligns with the information in this chapter?

2. Look through the board list, donor information, and staff within your own organization or an organization of your choosing. What kind and level of diversity do you discern? Does it reflect the community and the organizational mission? Brainstorm ideas to provide more entry points for diverse perspectives.

3. Review a fundraising strategy or appeal and consider whether diverse people are appropriately represented, while also taking into consideration the organization's mission, location, and other factors.

CHAPTER THIRTY

LGBTQ PHILANTHROPY

By Elizabeth J. Dale

Today, philanthropy scholars and fundraising practitioners are increasingly aware of the diversity of donors' experiences of and motivations for giving. Significant segments of donors do not fit the white, male, cis-gender, heterosexual "norm," as demonstrated by the diverse support generated for movements such as Black Lives Matter, #MeToo, and LGBTQ equality. These donors' philanthropic participation is often influenced by their personal identities, especially in the contexts of identities that have been marginalized and discriminated against in society (Drezner 2013). Amid calls for fundraising to become more diverse, equitable, and inclusive, organizations and fundraisers are increasingly considering how best to engage lesbian, gay, bisexual, transgender, and queer (LGBTQ) constituents and donors.

The LGBTQ community has made significant gains in the past two decades, including rapidly growing cultural acceptance, marriage equality, adoption rights, and the ability to serve openly in the U.S. military. However, federal law does not explicitly prohibit discrimination on the basis of sexual orientation and gender identity. Moreover, even in cities and states with nondiscrimination protections, many LGBTQ individuals still encounter discrimination. This chapter examines how LGBTQ individuals' experiences can create unique motivations for charitable giving and considers how fundraisers can best work with this community.

After completing this chapter, readers will:

- Understand LGBTQ donors' similarities and differences from the general donor population.
- Gain insight into the motivations that inspire LGBTQ donors.
- Understand differences in LGBTQ couples' management of household finances, which can impact giving decisions.
- Be able to apply research to improve fundraising policies and practices to build relationships with LGBTQ donors.

Expanding LGBTQ Rights: An Evolving Movement

Decades of activism and increased visibility have made LGBTQ equality one of the most prominent social movements of the twenty-first century, leading to growth in social acceptance and legal protections for LGBTQ people in the United States and around the globe. More than 13 million people ages 13 and older in the United States identify as LGBTQ, a number that has increased with growing social acceptance (Conron and Goldberg 2020). The millennial generation has embraced more expansive definitions of *gender identity* and *sexual orientation* than any previous generation, with one survey finding that 20 percent of people ages 18 to 34 identify as LGBTQ (GLAAD 2017).

Two significant legal decisions have dramatically expanded LGBTQ rights. In 2015, the U.S. Supreme Court ruled that same-sex couples have the right to marry, ending the patchwork nature of same-sex marriage and civil union laws across states. A second Supreme Court decision in 2020, *Bostock v. Clayton County*, affirmed that Title VII protects against employment discrimination based on sexual orientation and gender identity under the broader category of discrimination based on sex. Scholars believe this ruling will pave the way for other protections, including housing, public accommodations, education, and credit (Mallory, Vasquez, and Meredith 2020). Despite these significant judicial victories, legal and political backlash and ongoing claims of "religious liberty" have continued to be used to justify restricting and removing LGBTQ rights. In 2016, a record 144 anti-LGBTQ bills were introduced in state legislatures and the Trump administration reversed several significant pro-LGBTQ policies secured under the Obama administration (Evelyn and Walter Haas, Jr. Fund 2020).

While LGBTQ individuals may share common experiences with one another, it is important to understand that the LGBTQ community is richly diverse and represents a complexity of experiences. LGBTQ identities interweave with other aspects of who people are, including their race and ethnicity, social class, generational cohort, and physical ability. The significance of each identity for philanthropy varies for each individual. Noting that conventions for referring to the LGBTQ community continue to evolve, this chapter predominantly uses the acronym LGBTQ. When citing specific research, the acronym used in that particular study is used for accuracy.

Contributions of time and money from LGBTQ people have seeded the LGBTQ movement and built numerous community organizations as well as national advocacy organizations, such as Lambda Legal and the Human Rights Campaign. Today, LGBTQ organizations often serve the most vulnerable community members who experience multiple forms of oppression, including people of color, trans women, youth, and seniors. However, these organizations often struggle to raise money, even among individual donors. The LGBT Giving Project found that only 3.4 percent of LGBT Americans gave to the country's 39 largest LGBTQ advocacy organizations (Evelyn and Walter Haas, Jr. Fund 2020).

LGBTQ Patterns of Giving

Research on LGBTQ donors is increasing; yet overall, LGBTQ people remain an understudied donor population. Even with the recent progress in LGBTQ equality, there is no truly comprehensive study of LGBTQ individuals' philanthropic giving from a nationally representative sample. For example, we do not know the percentage of the 13 million LBGTQ U.S. individuals that give, and cannot make a comparison with the general population. In addition, a significant portion of existing research focuses on LGBTQ giving to LGBTQ causes, but only one subset of LGBTQ individuals' total giving (see Horizons Foundation 2008 and Evelyn and Walter Haas, Jr. Fund 2020 for examples). Finally, existing research is more likely to reflect the experiences of current donors, rather than the LGBTQ population at-large, as current donors are easier to reach. Researchers also infrequently track informal types of giving, like supporting friends and family, crowdfunding, and donations of tangible items, which may be forms of mutual aid, a type of support that is often present in social movements (Spade 2020).

For all people, giving decisions result from complex combinations of interests, personal experiences, financial ability, and charitable information. Early research found that, on average, LGBT donors contributed an equal or slightly greater amount of their personal income compared to the general population (Badgett and Cunningham 1998). A more recent study also found LGB+ donors to be more likely to give and to give higher amounts, even to non-LGBTQ causes (Chan 2020). Several studies found that, contrary to what many might assume, LGBTQ people do not direct most of their giving to LGBTQ causes. Estimates are that LGBT donors may contribute between 50 and 75 percent of their giving to non-LGBT organizations (Badgett and Cunningham 1998; Rose 1998). Similarly, a qualitative study of 19 same-sex couples found that, while many had supported an LGBTQ nonprofit in the past year, the majority of their philanthropy was to non-LGBTQ organizations (Dale 2016).

While LGBTQ donors give to a wide variety of nonprofit causes – from animal welfare and arts organizations to health groups and higher education – some unique giving patterns have emerged. First, LGBTQ donors are much more likely to support advocacy and civil rights organizations than the general population, including LGBTQ-specific organizations as well as general civil rights organizations like the American Civil Liberties Union (ACLU) (Badgett and Cunningham 1998; Horizons Foundation 2008). Second, LGBTQ donors – in general and in the high-net-worth population – are about half as likely to give to religious organizations (Badgett and Cunningham 1998; Horizons Foundation 2008; Indiana University Lilly Family School of Philanthropy 2018). LGBTQ donors are also four times more likely to support arts and culture organizations and twice as likely to give to health-related causes (Horizons Foundation 2008).

LGBTQ high-net-worth donors support more organizations on average than their straight counterparts, but depending on the study, show different patterns of giving. Beginning in 2016, the U.S. Trust Study of High Net Worth Philanthropy included an oversample of LGBT respondents, enabling comparisons between the giving practices of LGBT and straight individuals. The study found that LGBT donors gave to two more organizations on average than non-LGBT donors (9.6 vs. 7.5 organizations); were more likely to donate to arts and culture, animals, and the environment, and international issues; and were more likely to have a budget for their giving (57 percent compared to 48 percent) (Indiana University Lilly Family School of Philanthropy 2016). The 2018 U.S. Trust study found slightly different giving patterns for high-net-worth LGBTQ households: LGBTQ donors were less likely to give to health-related organizations, combined charities like the United Way, and youth or family services (Indiana University Lilly Family School of Philanthropy 2018).

The 2018 U.S. Trust study also found that 43 percent of LGBTQ households gave to LGBTQ-focused causes, and 24 percent supported women's and girls' organizations the prior year (Indiana University Lilly Family School of Philanthropy 2018). Beyond charitable giving, LGBTQ donors to LGBTQ organizations are more likely to have engaged in civic action, like contacting elected officials, attending a rally, or volunteering with a nonprofit, as compared to the general LGBTQ population (Evelyn and Walter Haas, Jr. Fund 2020). The 2016 U.S. Trust study found that high-net-worth LGBT individuals were more likely than their non-LGBT peers to have contributed to a political candidate or campaign (38 percent compared to 28 percent) (Indiana University Lilly Family School of Philanthropy 2016). In essence, researchers believe that LGBTQ donors have a heightened awareness and sophistication around using philanthropy as a tool to create social change and combine their giving with other civic and political activities.

Finally, several studies specifically examine LGBTQ donors' interest in planned giving. Older LGBTQ adults are less likely to have children, making them stronger candidates for estate gifts. The generation of LGBTQ people who witnessed the 1969 Stonewall Inn Riots in New York – a response to a police raid of the LGBTQ bar and key event in the movement for LGBTQ equal rights – is beginning to pass away and transfer wealth. Among current planned giving donors, researchers found that, on average, LGBTQ donors write wills and make a first planned gift at a slightly younger age (Dale, Krupa, Walker, and Neitzel 2019). Other research found that 16 percent of LGBTQ donors had made a planned gift commitment to support an LGBTQ organization and that 46 percent of LGBT people would consider adding a planned gift to an LGBTQ organization in their will (Evelyn and Walter Haas, Jr. Fund 2020). Finally, the 2018 U.S. Trust study found that 37 percent of high-net-worth LGBTQ donors had a planned gift intention, compared to 9 percent among others in the study (Indiana University Lilly Family School of Philanthropy 2018).

LGBTQ Motivations for Giving

Among LGBTQ people, researchers have documented many motivations for giving, some unique to LGBTQ identity and others shared with many donors. It is important to note motivations might serve as unconscious influences for donors, without being articulated to fundraisers or researchers.

Common Motivations for All Donors

Like many donors, LGBTQ donors often have personal connections to organizations or personal experiences with nonprofits as volunteers, clients, or board members. These reflect motivations that are explored in Chapter 26 as related to awareness of need and to raising the likelihood of being asked to give (Dale 2016). Many LGBTQ donors also express belief in organizations' leadership and/or effectiveness, another common motivation for giving (Dale 2016; Drezner and Garvey 2016). Some also are interested in receiving perks for their giving, such as special access to exhibits or performances, and many donors say that tax benefits are a plus, but not central to their giving (Dale 2016).

Unique Motives: Social Identity, Empathy, Justice, and Visibility

Personal identity, including sexual orientation and gender identity, can be a giving motivation. This is the "social identification" theory of giving whereby donors see themselves in "the needs and aspirations of others" (Schervish and Havens 1997, 236). Many LGBTQ donors desire to strengthen the LGBTQ community and give younger generations a smoother path to acceptance because of their own experiences of coming out and with discrimination (Garvey and Drezner 2013; Evelyn and Walter Haas, Jr. Fund 2020). In an experiment, Drezner (2018) found that donors gave more when they shared the same marginalized identity as the recipient described in a fundraising letter; this result even extended to other marginalized groups. Chan (2020) found that LGB+ individuals who reported more experiences with discrimination had greater empathy, and in turn, were more likely to make charitable gifts, even to non-LGBTQ causes like disaster relief.

Another distinct motivation reflects a "justice-oriented" approach. This motivation is often directed at fixing injustice, which might be expressed through giving to advocacy, legal, or policy organizations, and designed to influence changes to public policy or law (Dale 2016; Gallo 2001). One study found that older LGBTQ donors were more likely to be motivated by issues of policy change and ending discrimination, whereas younger donors were more likely to consider the diversity of an organization's staff and leadership when deciding whether to give (Evelyn and Walter Haas, Jr. Fund 2020). Research has also shown how "unjust" circumstances can be a barrier to giving: for example, the desire to avoid supporting organizations that actively discriminate, such as the Boy Scouts of America during the period when it banned openly gay leaders. Even after such policies change to become more inclusive, as the ban on gay scouting leaders did in 2013, the effects of these discriminatory practices may linger and prevent LGBTQ giving (Dale 2016; Drezner and Garvey 2016).

Another unique motivation is that philanthropy can be a way to assert LGBTQ presence in mainstream organizations (Dale 2016). Horizons Foundation (2008) found that many LGBT people did not consciously think about their giving in an LGBT/non-LGBT framework. One donor said, "I don't put my giving in buckets. You need to be part of the mainstream – being part of other [non-LGBT] organizations advances us" (Horizons Foundation 2008, 25). Same-sex couples used public donor recognition, like being included together on a donor honor roll, to draw attention to LGBTQ people as supporters of an organization (Dale 2018).

Household Financial Management and LGBTQ Giving

Research indicates that same-sex couples may approach financial matters very differently than straight donor couples. Straight couples overwhelmingly combine their financial resources, known as joint pooling or joint management, but same-sex couples are more likely to use financial systems that reflect power sharing and independent control over money (Burgoyne, Reibstein, Edmunds, and Dolman 2007; Burns, Burgoyne, and Clarke 2008). These management systems include partial pooling with partners having a joint account and two independent accounts

FIGURE 30.1. PARTIAL POOLING FINANCIAL MANAGEMENT

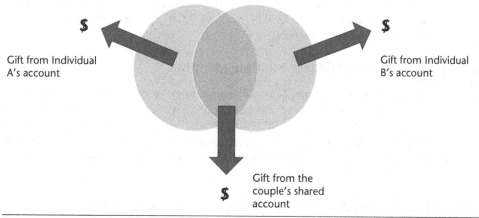

Gift from Individual
A's account

Gift from Individual
B's account

Gift from the
couple's shared
account

Source: Based on Dale 2018.

as well as completely independent control via separate accounts. Polyamorous relationships present even more potential for variation in financial management.

Regardless of the overall system of money management used by a same-sex couple, research shows that charitable giving may not follow the same pattern (Dale 2018). Multiple accounts may be used for giving, and the decision to donate may sometimes be individual and sometimes joint (see Figure 30.1). In interviews with same-sex couples, joint poolers sometimes made separate, individual gifts. Among couples with independent accounts, one person might pay for the gift, but add their partner's name for recognition purposes. Same-sex couples often saw giving as a "shared value," and few couples expressed disagreement or even bargaining about how much to give (Dale 2018). Even if the organization represented the interests of one person, their partner was generally supportive of making the gift. For example, one participant described giving to the hospital where his husband worked as a "two-minute conversation." Another supported their partner making gifts to Planned Parenthood from the joint account, even though she would not have made those gifts herself.

Recommendations for Equitable and Inclusive Fundraising

At its core, fundraising within the LGBTQ community is no different than working with any other donor group (Fender 2011). Successful fundraising is driven by reciprocal relationships and personal communication, whether from a development officer or a peer passionate about an organization. There are several steps organizations and fundraisers can take to increase the involvement and support of the LGBTQ community to LGBTQ and non-LGBTQ causes, many of which emulate fundraising best practices.

Recognize LGBTQ Individuals' Multiple Identities

Identifying as lesbian, gay, bisexual, transgender, or queer may be an important aspect of someone's identity and rarely can be ignored; however, all people hold multiple identities that are likely to impact personal philanthropic interests. LGBTQ identity is important, but it may also be important for a lesbian to support feminist causes, a Latino man to support the local Hispanic community, or a couple to support the alma mater where they met.

Make a Public Commitment to Diversity, Equity, and Inclusion

Nonprofits should publicize their efforts to further diversity, equity, and inclusion (DEI) in their organizations. Having LGBTQ staff, volunteers, board trustees, and advisory committee members, in addition to building gender and racial/ethnic diversity, builds trust among donors from different backgrounds. Organizations also should avoid having a "token" member who is expected to speak for an entire community and recruit in pairs when possible. Human resource policies should also make commitments to diversity clear: include sexual orientation and gender identity in the organization's nondiscrimination policies and ensure personnel and benefits policies apply equally to LGBTQ and non-LGBTQ employees, including extending benefits to same-sex partners. Beyond modeling inclusion, these actions signal to donors that LGBTQ people are welcomed and valued.

Avoid Common Mistakes When Recognizing or Communicating with LGBTQ Donors

Organizations show cultural competency by properly recognizing LGBTQ donors, particularly couples and transgender individuals. "If organizations want to get it right, they need to openly talk to their donors, queer or straight, about how they want to be recognized (or solicited or communicated with for that matter)" (Fender 2011, 90–91). That can mean acknowledging a gay man's spouse as his husband in a newsletter profile, addressing a lesbian couple's mail as "Ms. and Ms.," or using first names or full names without titles. Provide donors and guests the ability to specify their pronouns at events as well as in data collection and correspondence.

Begin Building the Data Foundation for the Future Today

Having data systems that are flexible and allow for capturing diverse identities and household relationships is crucial. It is particularly important to formally document donor identification preferences in database systems, as development officers may change and reliance on manual edits often leads to mistakes. If an organization lacks donor demographic data, begin collecting sexual orientation, gender identity, pronouns, and recognition preferences through online gift forms, a donor survey, or individual visits or calls.

Engage in Active, Authentic Outreach to the LGBTQ Community

Outreach can include LGBTQ-specific programming or establishing affinity groups, celebrating Pride month, or aligning the organization with movements for LGBTQ equality. It also means highlighting the efforts of LGBTQ donors and volunteers in newsletters and other publications. As one fundraiser said, "It means a lot to LGBT people to feel like somebody is speaking to them in a meaningful and authentic way, and that they're acknowledging who they are and celebrating who they are" (Flandez 2013).

Cultivate and Ask LGBTQ Donors

While it may sound fundamental, simply ensuring donors are routinely asked to give goes a long way. Many LGBTQ donors report giving because they were asked, and a significant portion of LGBT individuals say they have not given because they have not been asked (Horizons Foundation 2008). As with all donors at higher gift levels, personalized cultivation is key. Recognize that LGBTQ couples may approach financial decision-making differently than same-sex couples, tailor requests for support that align with donors' interests, and make planned giving part of donor strategies and conversations. Understanding how any couple manages money and makes giving decisions can be instructive for fundraisers, but for same-sex couples it is especially important to avoid assumptions and understand the dynamics of each donor.

Ensure Strong Stewardship That Builds Trust in the Organization

Donors want to know that an organization is well run and that gifts are used for the intended purposes. Maintaining high-quality stewardship practices will enhance donor loyalty and may be essential for securing planned gifts. This includes accuracy in data management, honoring recognition preferences, and highlighting LGBTQ donors in fundraising communication.

Conclusion

Identity matters in philanthropy, shaping the ways that potential donors feel about a cause and even how some giving decisions are made. Across the nonprofit sector, organizations and fundraisers are looking to expand their communities of support, and LGBTQ people are just one constituency receiving increased attention. With a rich history of activism and political participation, LGBTQ people may be poised to give to not just LGBTQ causes, but all types of nonprofit organizations. Research indicates they are waiting to be asked. Organizations that commit to inclusive practices and values at the leadership level and take the time to understand the unique motivations of LGBTQ donors will be best positioned to build authentic and lasting philanthropic relationships.

Discussion Questions

1. How is giving by LGBTQ individuals similar to and different from other donors?
2. An organization wants to focus on cultivating and engaging more LGBTQ people. What steps can be taken to build relationships with LGBTQ donors? How can the organization demonstrate equity and inclusivity?
3. How might the approach to building a relationship with an LGBTQ couple differ from a straight couple, if at all?

Application Exercises

1. Research a prominent LGBTQ donor (or donor couple) and identify what appears to motivate their giving and how, if at all, their LGBTQ identity may have influenced their philanthropy.
2. Craft a welcome email to a first-time donor that includes a brief set of questions to build the organization's understanding of their demographic background and recognition preferences.
3. Review several nonprofit organizations' websites from the perspective of a prospective LGBTQ supporter. Do the organizations publish or mention a nondiscrimination policy? Do they use inclusive language or feature LGBTQ people?

CHAPTER THIRTY-ONE

DIFFERENTIATING GENERATIONS AND THEIR GIVING

By Patricia Snell Herzog

It is commonly understood that contemporary society has evolved, resulting in younger generations being markedly distinct from prior generations. Consequently, generations signify changes over time. Yet, increased life expectancy means more generations live alongside one another than ever before. Attending to multiple generations is another way to segment fundraising constituents to discern what donors value and support.

After completing this chapter, readers will understand the following topics:

- Generational changes: identifying cohorts, social context, and technology.
- Life course development: emerging adulthood and transitions to adulthood.
- Organizational engagement: earning, learning, believing, serving, and giving.
- Data: statistics on giving across, within, and between generations.

Generational Changes

It is necessary to examine generational changes broadly. This includes grasping what is meant by generations, alongside grappling with social context and technology changes.

Identifying Generations

Coming of age during an increasingly digital context no doubt aided the wide-spread availability of discussions about the Millennial generation and its potential for change. Examples of public attention include assertions that the mindsets of young people are "worlds apart" from older mindsets (Bomar 2011). Evaluations of younger generations span from harsh critiques regarding the selfishness of the "me me me generation" (Stein 2013) to optimism that younger generations will change the world for the better (e.g., Raymo and Raymo 2014).

Careful research reveals a complex story. For example, in a study of 7,000 teenagers, Schneider and Stevenson (2000) found that younger generations voiced ambition within a social context that was fragmented and offered few consistent directions, resulting in many finishing college without the skills or career experiences needed to turn their dreams into reality. Based on 1,200 interviews with young people, Rainer and Rainer (2010) concluded that Millennials are characterized by a wider social net in terms of their desire for diversity and inclusion in broad matters, while also being defined by closer-knit circles than previous generations.

There is no consensus on a specific year when one generation ends and another begins, yet there are some consistent markers. Generations are shaped by significant and widespread historical events, such that those alive before and after are markedly different from those alive only after. For example, the Great Depression, World War II, and the Vietnam War marked people of those time periods, with high commonalities among people who endured those experiences and a low degree of shared experiences with those who were not yet alive. The COVID-19 pandemic will likely become such an event for demarcating generations around 2020. It is a tragedy that the events that are most successful in uniting a generation are those with significantly negative impacts. Alternatively, the greatest degree of ambiguity around generational groups exists during times of high prosperity.

In this regard, the Millennial generation is perhaps one of the most uniquely demarcated since the generation is largely defined as those who were coming of age around the millennium (circa 2000). Rather than "split hairs" over an exact year in which a new generation begins, those born in the middle of a generation's bounds (e.g., a Millennial born 1995) are more distinct from prior and subsequent generations than those born near to the age boundaries (e.g., a Millennial born 1982). In this regard, hindsight is 20/20. Retroactively, the Millennial generation is now understood to be those who were coming of age when the 9/11 terrorist attack occurred in 2001.

Identifying generations requires a historically situated understanding of important events and changes over time that bound members of a generation together and simultaneously set them apart from members of another generation (see Figure 31.1). Major changes have occurred in the social context that deserve attention in situating generations.

FIGURE 31.1. GENERATIONAL COHORTS IN HISTORICAL AND SOCIAL CONTEXT

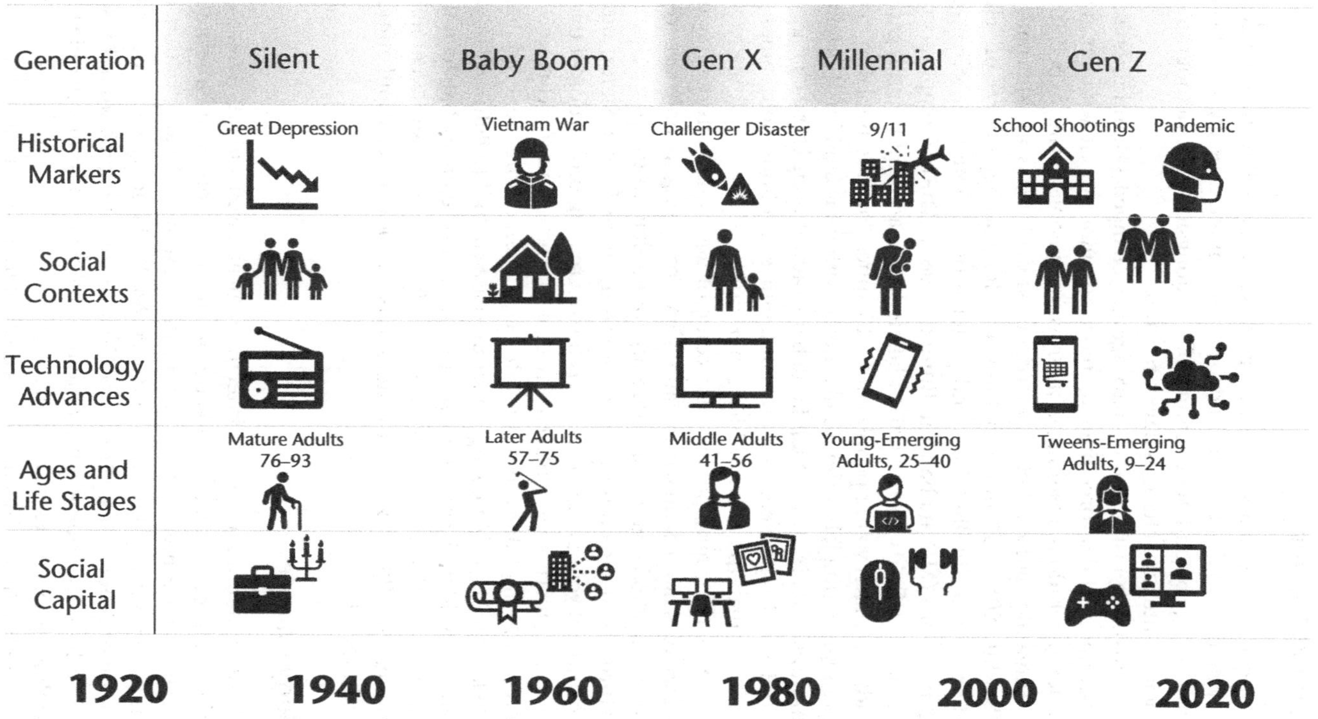

Generation	Silent	Baby Boom	Gen X	Millennial	Gen Z
Historical Markers	Great Depression	Vietnam War	Challenger Disaster	9/11	School Shootings Pandemic
Social Contexts					
Technology Advances					
Ages and Life Stages	Mature Adults 76–93	Later Adults 57–75	Middle Adults 41–56	Young–Emerging Adults, 25–40	Tweens–Emerging Adults, 9–24
Social Capital					
	1920 1940	1960	1980	2000	2020

359

Social Context Changes

Comparative scholars from a range of disciplines find that generations differ in key demographic characteristics, such as gender, race, class, and geographic location (Bengtson and Achenbaum 1993). Alongside these demographics, four major social contextual changes have occurred.

First, the institution of marriage has changed (Manning et al. 2007). Family disruptions and divorce rates are more common among younger generations than older generations, resulting in many young people having expectations to live with a romantic partner before marriage, and often as an alternative to marriage (Sawhill 2014). Family instability has long-lasting effects on child well-being (Fomby and Cherlin 2007), and patterns of disruption are often repeated across generations (McLanahan and Bumpass 1988). The contemporary reality of family life is what Goldscheider (2012) labeled, "the accordion family" and "boomerang kids," in which young people with difficulties entering the labor market and landing high-paying jobs often return home with their families of origin for periods of months or years during their launch into adulthood. These changes result in more fluid and dynamic constructions of families and households among younger generations than those from older generations.

Second, young people have come of age amid considerably more favorable views of same-sex marriage and views of young people are reshaping older Americans to be generally more accepting than in the past (Hart-Brinson 2014). Third, racial and ethnic diversity are rising in the United States, and one of the key features of younger generations is the decreasing proportion of the White population and increasing replacement of a majority-minority (Lichter 2013). Fourth, evolutions in values and attitudes can characterize generational gaps (Smith 2005). One notable change is an increase in "polite culture," in which what was once considered criticism can now be interpreted as harsh, unfeeling, or off-putting, and is supplanted by an emphasis on excessively complimentary comments (Sica 2012). Younger generations are more diverse and emphasize different cultural values.

Technology Changes

Another important change is technological advancement. Whereas older generations can recall a before-and-after to the invention of the internet, younger generations have lived entirely within the existence of Googlization, smart phones, and constant social media use (Clark 2009). While it may be common to describe younger generations as "digital natives" or the "net generation," research into digital skills finds tremendous variation in the ability of young people to navigate their online social contexts (Hargittai 2010).

Relatedly, dating culture has evolved to involve a substantial portion of online activity, including mobile dating and app-based hook-ups (Albury et al. 2017).

Indeed, the dating market has dramatically altered from one which involved romantic partners finding their mate in grade schools and neighborhoods toward strangers meeting online (Rosenfeld and Thomas 2012).

Technological advancements are also evolving the nature of work and the needs of higher education, with the advent of functional artificial intelligence and machine learning redefining the kinds of human skills that are needed for the future of learning and working (Aoun 2017). In summary, a central defining feature of younger generations is the ubiquity and depth of technology in their lives, yet tremendous variability remains in the width of skills in using it.

Life Course Development

A major complexity that deserves attention is the dynamic changes that occur throughout life as people grow and mature. Generations provide snapshots in time of people who are within a certain life stage. For example, Millennials are currently in young adulthood, and Baby Boomers are currently in later adulthood, with many now retired. Ignoring this risks conflating life stages with stable generational personality characteristics. Indeed, a common misunderstanding is that younger generations are more selfish than prior generations, rather than being in a self-focused life stage.

Emerging Adulthood

Arnett (2006) described emerging adulthood as a relatively new stage of life between adolescence and young adulthood. This life stage is characterized by a high degree of optimism about personal futures as well as an acute self-focus as young people turn inward to center on launching their own lives and distilling their personal aspirations. While this can be an exciting period of life, there are also embedded struggles that can involve high degrees of anxiety and self-doubt, even periods of depression, largely resulting from encountering disappointments in launching desired careers, unstable relationships, and underuse of talents that were concertedly developed during earlier life stages (Konstam 2015). Moreover, young people have a range of existing social networks to draw on as they enter college and pursue jobs (Nichols and Islas 2015). Intersecting generations and life stages results in understanding the Millennials and GenZers as coming of age through emerging adulthood.

Transitions to Adulthood

Transitions to adulthood have evolved markedly over recent decades (Settersten et al. 2008). Beginning in the late 1990s, young people began to understand adulthood as less characterized by having reached a set of external markers and more about achieving a sense of individual responsibility and parental independence (Arnett 1997). Adulthood has become understood as more akin to a state of mind, the perception of oneself as an adult (Shanahan et al. 2005). While this high degree of self-agency can be admirable, it also can inadvertently obscure attention to inequality in the paths young people traverse in transitioning into adulthood (Osgood et al. 2005). It is important to recognize that many vulnerable youth come up short in adulthood launches (Silva 2013). Family relations can replicate social inequality across generations (Swartz 2009), and many aspiring adults do not receive constructive help in setting directions toward their aspirations (Arum and Roksa 2014).

In this regard, aging poses a challenge to simplistic understandings of social life (Kohli 1988). Time must be understood as signifying historical changes across generations, alongside human agency in constructing a dynamic life course trajectory that is shaped by common social and psychological patterns to growing up and maturing (Elder 1994). Understanding philanthropy across generations requires attending to generational changes engagement patterns over time as well as understanding people as a work in progress amidst dynamic life course development processes. The extended period that young people spend launching into adulthood impacts how they engage in organizations, acquire social capital, and participate in society.

Organizational Engagement and Social Capital

Younger generations are generally less likely to join associations, clubs, organizations, and other community groups than prior generations (Schwadel and Stout 2012). Each generation is less involved than the one before because parents pass on their practices to their children. Together with the delays in transitioning to adulthood, this means people are settling down later and pushing back the ages at which they are anchoring in communities and becoming involved in local organizations. In fact, concern for future generations (social generativity) is a defining feature of later adulthood (Morselli and Passini 2015), and since young people are entering that stage of life later than prior generations, it makes sense that community engagement is also occurring later. Cumulatively, this results in a net loss of people engaged in communities and organizations. Since younger generations tend to think less within organizational terms than prior generations, the next sections are named by actions, followed by parentheses with organizationally based terms of older generations.

Earning (Work)

The organizational engagement changes that have received the greatest attention are in workplaces. A vibrant array of consultation businesses has sprung around how to support multi-generational workforces. Yet, whether generations truly represent distinct values has received mixed results (Lyons and Kuron 2014; Schullery 2013). It is important to understand generational categories as, in part, a representation of changing demographics, such as more female leaders and their associated diverse leadership styles, rising immigrant laborers and their diverse cultural styles, and the erosion of the middle class and its associated polarization between managerial and manual labor classes (Hershatter and Epstein 2010). It is helpful to view multiple generations as representing workforce segments that present meaningful opportunities to improve equity and inclusion.

Learning (Education)

One clear generational distinction is in parenting and the resulting approaches to learning within educational organizations. As compared to generations of the past, in which college was a new opportunity for most, many young people today arrive to campuses with a sense of academic entitlement that assumes success is deserved irrespective of effort or quality (Boswell 2012). Moreover, Millennials and younger generations expect changes to instructional delivery, most notably including digital formats (Monaco and Martin 2007). Young people are not equally exposed to updated information about what skills and knowledge work requires (Olson 2014), and it is increasingly necessary to teach students the metacognitive skills needed to navigate college toward myriad career opportunities (Herzog et al. 2020). Learning needs and expectations have evolved; young people have a range of opportunities in accessing updated information; and it would be beneficial for organizations to provide support for lifelong learning.

Believing (Religion)

The most well-documented generational change is decline in social forms of religious involvement (Crockett and Voas 2006). In the United States, personal religiosity remains relatively constant over time, but the frequency of participation in activities surrounding religiosity (religious service attendance) has declined (Wuthnow 2010). The result is what some refer to as 'spiritual but not religious' (Zhai et al. 2008). One contributing factor is family disruptions and conflicts in families over religious socialization (Uecker and Ellison 2012). An inadvertent consequence is declines in other forms of organizational engagement, including decreased academic achievement, extracurricular engagement, and service (Glanville et al. 2008). Younger generations tend to be less organized and organizational, with more fluid and episodic engagement in formal institutions.

Serving (Volunteering)

Nearly two decades ago, a group of concerned scholars called for a more expansive definition of *civic engagement* as key to involving youth in service (Youniss et al.

2002). That tradition continues, with contemporary authors advising organizations to engage younger generations on their own terms by focusing on the causes, motivations, and impacts that young people care about (Spiegel 2013). Most notably, expansive access to the internet and social media platforms have altered the variety of ways that people can join and amplify their voices to serve others and create civic changes (Banaji and Buckingham 2009). Nevertheless, some trends remain timeless, such as the importance of learning to serve and volunteer in organizations from parents (Bekkers 2007). The service of young people is also less organizationally based, channeled, and directed, with the emphasis instead being on causes and the ability to mobilize in diffuse ways online without formal organizations.

Giving (Donating)

As with other forms of organizational engagement, giving behaviors have evolved across generations, and modified strategies are needed to engage younger donors (Goldseker and Moody 2017). Of particular importance are two trends. One is the rising critique among younger generations of philanthropy as potentially anti-democratic or elite (Giridharadas 2018). The second is the social network effect, and the need for fundraisers to seek donors through online social media connections (Saxton and Wang 2013). There are marked declines across all forms of organizational engagement among younger generations, yet it is important to understand this as a function of decreased involvement with formal channels associated with the diffuse availability of digital and social media activities. In this context, it is not accurate to say that young people are disengaged, rather they are less formally channeled and more focused on activities online and within social networks.

Giving across Generations Data

How much do Americans from different generations give to charitable and religious causes? To answer this, the first step is to address giving rates overall and to acknowledge a degree of variability in the rates reported for American giving. Gallup reports that Americans reached a new low of 73 percent giving to charitable causes in 2020 (Jones 2020), which is close to the 70 percent giving rate reported by Independent Sector (Cnaan et al. 2011). However, this rate remains higher than what is reported by other sources, such as the Philanthropy Roundtable Almanac (2021) reporting about 60 percent of Americans give, which is closer to the 55 percent reported by the Science of Generosity study (Herzog and Price 2016). A similar variance exists within reporting of giving rates by generation, in part, because not all sources utilize the same definitional boundaries to demarcate generational cohorts.

TABLE 31.2. GIVING RATES AND AVERAGE GIVING AMOUNTS ACROSS FOUR GENERATIONAL COHORTS

NPS 2021	Greatest/Silent	Baby Boomers	Gen Xers	Millennials
% population	12%	24%	20%	26%
% givers	88%	72%	—	84%
$ amount given	$1,367	$1,212	—	$481
COPPS 2003	**Greatest/Silent**	**Baby Boomers**	**Gen Xers**	**Millennials**
% givers	80%	75%	53%	—
$ amount given	$1,764	$1,254	$1,100	—
Blackbaud 2016	**Greatest/Silent**	**Baby Boomers**	**Gen Xers**	**Millennials**
% givers	88%	72%	59%	60%
$ amount given	$1,367	$1,212	$732	$481
NSP 2018	**Greatest/Silent & Baby Boomers**		**Gen Xers & Millennials**	
$ amount given	$624		$443	

Sources: Based on NPS 2021, Steinberg and Wilhelm 2003, Thayer and Feldman 2016, Rooney et al. 2018.

Relying on the generational demarcations used by the Pew Research Center, the Silent Generation (or the Greatest Generation) are those born between 1928 and 1945; Baby Boomers, between 1946 and 1964; Gen Xers, between 1965 and 1980; and Millennials born after 1980 (Taylor 2014). Utilizing these age ranges, Table 31.2 presents the giving rates reported by a variety of sources. Despite some variability, a common trend is that younger generations give less, as a percent of the population and in average dollar amounts. Nevertheless, it remains important to be vigilant against mischaracterizing all younger generations as selfish (Koczanski and Rosen 2019). Keep in mind that life course development intersects with generations, and charitable giving is generally found to increase by age (Havens et al. 2006). When comparing generations at the same age (with dollar amounts adjusted for inflation), young people today give on average $180 less.

Conclusion

Understanding giving across generations requires four central elements. First, generational changes need to be contextualized within key historical events. Beyond specific events, generational groups reflect confluences of social context and technology changes. Second, generational cohorts also segment people by age, and younger generations are coming of age through an extended developmental period of emerging adulthood. Third, the deformalization enabled by digital social apps results in actions for the good of others being less organizationally based than in the past. Younger generations tend to be more fluid, episodic, and cause-based in their engagement patterns than what formal organizations provide. Engaging young people requires connecting online and advancing beyond taking philanthropy for granted as necessarily good toward explaining the targeted causes, approaches, and measured outcomes. Fourth, multiple data sources reveal a common trend: The percentage of givers and average amount of giving declines across generations, yet people also tend to give more across their lifespan as they age, settle down, and grow community roots.

Discussion Questions

1. Why is there a lack of consensus regarding exactly where one generation begins and ends? What is generally required to clearly demarcate generations, and why?
2. How are generations commonly stereotyped, and how does engaging a life course developmental approach help to understand people as dynamic and complex?
3. What are important generational and technological changes, and how have these impacted the organizational engagement levels and approaches of younger generations?
4. In considering multiple data sources, what are the overall trends in giving across generations?

Application Exercise

1. Ask a young person how they feel about philanthropy and what kinds of digital and social media platforms they have given through and why.
2. Then, have the same conversation with a person from a different generation.
3. Compare and contrast responses to consider differences and similarities relative to the information in this chapter.
4. Next, evaluate how knowing this information about generational similarities and differences could be helpful for an organization's comprehensive fundraising program.

CHAPTER THIRTY-TWO

HIGH NET WORTH HOUSEHOLD GIVING INSIGHTS

By Patrick Rooney, Kidist Yasin, and Lijun He

This chapter documents philanthropic behaviors of the wealthy, described here as High Net Worth Households (HNWHs), an important population for nonprofits and fundraisers.

Readers of this chapter will explore:

- HNWH charitable giving patterns and trends.
- Motivations and decision-making within HNWH philanthropy.
- Implications of political donations and tax policy for charitable giving.
- Implications for fundraising.

Context and Patterns of Charitable Behavior

Data from 2010 forward show nonprofits' increasing reliance on large gifts and a declining number of small and medium-sized gifts (Rooney 2019). Notably, the events of 2020, including the COVID-19 pandemic and renewed attention to racial and social inequities, may have led to some new donors. But Giving USA (2021) did not show a change in numbers of donors to cause a bump in the overall giving participation trend line.

The public dialogue of the current period includes a strong critique of the fundamental aspects of capitalism and growing concentration of income and wealth, which may be fueling a boom in mega-gifts, and concern about philanthropy as a potential tool/strategy to advance the political/social agenda of the wealthy (e.g., Collins et al. 2021; Giridharadas 2018; Reich 2018; Villanueva 2018). There are also alternate perspectives defending capitalism's systems and the right of the wealthy to earn their wealth and donate how much they think appropriate, anonymously or not; where, when, and why they elect to do so; and most importantly, honoring donor intent (Westhoff 2020) (see Chapter 6).

This chapter provides context for these phenomena by providing information on how wealthy people give. It is based on a nationally representative survey developed by the Indiana University Lilly Family School of Philanthropy's Research Department and a team from Bank of America (BOA). Over 1,600 U.S. households completed the survey in early 2021. For the purposes of the study, *HNWHs* were defined as having either $1 million in assets, excluding their primary residence, and/or earning over $200,000 annually. According to the U.S. Census Bureau (2021c), these households were in the top 10 percent of earners in 2020.

It is important to acknowledge that a survey of this kind has potential biases, limitations of sample size, and potential for exceptional behaviors to skew the results. Fundraisers can and should use these data to inform their thinking and strategies, but also should rely on their own conversations with donors and additional insights from other research sources.

Who Gives and How Much?

A supermajority (87 percent) of the HNWHs donated at least something to one or more charities (see Table 32.1). On average, they donated $12,544 (median = 1,750) with a maximum of just over $5 million. Given the high propensity to give among the HNWHs, the numbers are similar for the subsample of donors only (mean = $14,396; median = $2,500; max =$5 million). (The median amounts are the donations of the person in the middle of the distribution, so are more reflective of the "typical" donor in this sample. The mean amounts are the sum of all donations in that category divided by the total number of donors in that category. Hence, the "average" gift.)

These numbers are down from past surveys (e.g., Indiana University Lilly Family School of Philanthropy 2016, 2018a). This may simply be because different people responded to the survey or it could relate to the difficult social and economic context of 2020–2021 (or a combination of both).

HNWHs donated to almost seven different organizations on average (6.75), but there was a vast range from one to 900 (median = 4). Together, the mean and the median suggest that most of the HNWHs are targeted in their philanthropic giving.

TABLE 32.1. HIGH NET WORTH HOUSEHOLD CHARITABLE GIVING BY SECTOR (OVERALL MEAN AND MEDIAN)

Sector	Incidence	Amount (Mean)	Amount (Median)	Amount Donor only (Mean)	Amount Donor only (Median)
Total	87.1%	$12,544	$ 1,750	$14,396	$ 2,500
Religion	46.9%	$4,069	$ 0	$8,691	$ 1,800
Secular *(all the below)*	84.9%	$8,476	$ 1,000	$9,990	$ 1,300
Combination purposes	27.2%	$524	$ 0	$1,933	$ 500
Basic needs	57.0%	$2,501	$ 90	$4,388	$ 500
Youth	29.7%	$263	$ 0	$887	$ 250
Health	32.1%	$545	$ 0	$1,702	$ 250
K–12	23.1%	$780	$ 0	$3,383	$ 200
Higher ed	24.5%	$1,204	$ 0	$4,923	$ 500
Education (combined)	36.1%	$1,984	$ 0	$5,510	$ 500
Arts/Culture	26.5%	$648	$ 0	$2,454	$ 250
Social or racial justice causes	21.6%	$618	$ 0	$2,873	$ 300
Environment	20.2%	$308	$ 0	$1,531	$ 200
Animals	27.4%	$235	$ 0	$861	$ 200
Environment/Animals (combined)	36.0%	$542	$ 0	$1,510	$ 240
International aid	10.2%	$124	$ 0	$1,230	$ 250
Disaster relief	21.5%	$225	$ 0	$1,051	$ 190
COVID-19	11.7%	$119	$ 0	$1,029	$ 200
Other	23.4%	$382	$ 0	$1,637	$ 300

Note: In the subsectors in which the median is zero, at least half (or more) of the households in the sample gave exactly zero to that subsector.
Source: Authors' calculations using unpublished data from *The 2021 Bank of America Study of Philanthropy: Charitable Giving by Affluent Households,* researched and written by the Indiana University Lilly Family School of Philanthropy 2021a.

To What Purposes?

Almost half of the HNWHs (47 percent) donated to religion (church, mosque, synagogue, congregation), averaging just over $4,000 (median = 0; max = $330,000). More than four-fifths of HNWHs donated something to other charities (85 percent), and these gifts averaged almost $8,500 (median = $1,000) with a max of $5 million.

The largest share of households gifts made were to help meet basic needs (57 percent) with donors averaging $1,900 (rounded to nearest $100) (median = $500). Education (higher ed and K–12 combined) brought in the next largest share of donors (36 percent) with donors averaging $5,500 (median = $500). COVID-19 and racial/social justice captured a great deal of the news cycle in 2020, but not a large share of giving by HNWHs. COVID-19 gifts were made by only 12 percent of the sample and giving averaged $1,000 (median = $200). Social and racial justice gifts played a larger role (22 percent donating; mean = $2,900; median = $300). Note that donors' gifts to other subsectors (e.g., health, basic needs, international, youth, disaster relief) may have also been meant to help with the pandemic or support social/racial justice.

Giving by Race/Ethnicity

In this survey, respondents who were White were the most likely to give (89 percent), but did not donate the largest average amounts ($13,229 donors only; $11,750 for all households) (see Table 32.2). Black households were the third most likely to give (85 percent) and donated much larger mean amounts per household ($41,808 for donors only; $35,399 for all households) than other groups. The mean giving of Hispanic households was $7,478; the 80 percent of Hispanic households that donated gave a mean amount of $9,332. Although giving was least frequent among Asian donors, they gave large amounts ($18,544 for donors; $14,088 for all households). "Other" households were the second most likely to give at all (88 percent), but they tended to donate smaller amounts ($9,636 donors only; $8,845 for all households).

Black families were the most likely to give to religion (60 percent), but gave the second most to that purpose ($11,286) after Asians whose households donated to religion ($38,243). White households were the most likely to give to secular nonprofits at 87 percent, followed by "Other" households (86 percent). Black families donated the most dollars to secular charities for both donors only ($36,539) and all households ($28,623). Black HNWHs were also the most likely to donate to social or racial justice causes (37 percent), and donated the most dollars per household to social/racial justice causes ($8,406 for all households; $22,572 for donors only). Finally, regarding donating to COVID-19, Black HNWHs led that category both in terms of share of donors (22 percent) and the dollars given ($726 for all households; $3,355 for donor only households). For Asian donors, basic needs and education were key priorities while Hispanic donors were prone to give in the areas of education, youth, social justice, and environment. "Other" households were relatively small donors to religion and secular (combined), but gave the second highest amount (by race/ethnicity) to COVID-19 ($1,067). "Other" households also gave over $5,000 to higher education, and approximately $1,500 to both basic needs and health.

TABLE 32.2. HIGH NET WORTH HOUSEHOLD CHARITABLE GIVING BY SECTOR AND RACE/ETHNICITY

Charitable giving by sector	Race / Ethnicity				
	White	Black	Hispanic	Asian	Other
Total					
Incidence	88.8%	84.7%	80.2%	75.9%	88.2%
Amount	$11,750	$35,399	$7,478	$14,088	$8,485
Amount (donors only)	$13,229	$41,808	$9,332	$18,554	$9,636
Religion					
Incidence	47.5%	60.2%	45.4%	32.5%	42.8%
Amount	$3,693	$6,776	$1,254	$12,417	$2,995
Amount (donors only)	$7,770	$11,286	$2,771	$38,243	$7,086
Secular (all the below)					
Incidence	86.7%	78.4%	78.6%	73.8%	85.7%
Amount	$8,058	$28,623	$6,224	$1,676	$5,490
Amount (donors only)	$9,289	$36,539	$7,921	$2,270	$6,417
Combination Purposes					
Incidence	25.7%	43.3%	35.7%	18.1%	27.6%
Amount	$379	$3,343	$339	$188	$390
Amount (donors only)	$1,476	$7,749	$952	$1,041	$1,446
Basic Needs					
Incidence	58.2%	62.9%	53.4%	41.2%	57.4%
Amount	$2,833	$5,219	$702	$242	$858
Amount (donors only)	$4,870	$8,311	$1,317	$588	$1,507
Youth					
Incidence	29.7%	41.2%	32.4%	14.4%	29.0%
Amount	$249	$493	$311	$91	$304
Amount (donors only)	$839	$1,183	$966	$629	$1,072
Health					
Incidence	31.8%	41.5%	34.6%	21.6%	32.7%
Amount	$479	$1,332	$948	$137	$471
Amount (donors only)	$1,506	$3,228	$2,755	$634	$1,468
K–12					
Incidence	41.6%	32.2%	27.2%	21.4%	22.2%
Amount	$764	$2,721	$297	$504	$277
Amount (donors only)	$3,432	$8,516	$1,099	$2,352	$1,290
Higher Ed					
Incidence	24.9%	35.4%	19.9%	20.0%	21.6%
Amount	$1,308	$1726	$301	$108	$1,619
Amount (donors only)	$5,254	$4,901	$1,524	$540	$7,759

(Continued)

TABLE 32.2. (CONTINUED)

Charitable giving by sector	Race / Ethnicity				
	White	Black	Hispanic	Asian	Other
Education (combined)					
Incidence	35.9%	44.5%	32.6%	37.1%	34.9%
Amount	$2,071	$4,447	$5,97	$6,12	$1,896
Amount (donors only)	$5,769	$10,031	$1,839	$1,650	$5,531
Arts/Culture					
Incidence	27.6%	31.4%	25.9%	16.4%	20.0%
Amount	$724	$498	$866	$76	$161
Amount (donors only)	$2,623	$1,597	$3,369	$460	$836
Social or racial justice causes					
Incidence	21.4%	37.4%	22.6%	16.3%	14.6%
Amount	$179	$8,406	$297	$37	$143
Amount (donors only)	$838	$22,572	$1,326	$229	$1,035
Environment					
Incidence	20.1%	22.3%	21.1%	17.0%	20.8%
Amount	$229	$2,231	$116	$26	$122
Amount (donors only)	$1,139	$10,128	$554	$152	$608
Animals					
Incidence	27.9%	24.6%	30.5%	15.4%	29.2%
Amount	$218	$386	$366	$13	$302
Amount (donors only)	$783	$1,585	$,1208	$82	$1,059
Environment/Animals (combined)					
Incidence	37.4%	29.0%	35.5%	27.0%	34.2%
Amount	$447	$2,617	$482	$38	$424
Amount (donors only)	$1,197	$9,032	$1,364	$142	$1,264
International Aid					
Incidence	9.3%	16.0%	13.3%	5.9%	14.1%
Amount	$87	$652	$110	$143	$119
Amount (donors only)	$927	$4,148	$844	$2,433	$898
Disaster Relief					
Incidence	21.4%	29.7%	19.9%	15.6%	23.0%
Amount	$487	$185	$448	$47	$299
Amount (donors only)	$866	$1,518	$2,472	$301	$1,342
COVID-19					
Incidence	10.3%	21.9%	17.5%	11.6%	11.6%
Amount	$81	$726	$124	$36	$115
Amount (donors only)	$790	$3,355	$718	$313	$1,067
Other					
Incidence	24.5%	23.2%	21.3%	10.6%	24.2%
Amount	$344	$443	$961	$29	$309
Amount (donors only)	$1,405	$1,929	$4,545	$278	$1,312

Source: Authors' calculations using unpublished data from *The 2021 Bank of America Study of Philanthropy: Charitable Giving by Affluent Households,* researched and written by the Indiana University Lilly Family School of Philanthropy 2021a.

Giving Vehicles

While only 9 percent of the HNWHs used one or more of the specialized giving vehicles included in the survey (see Table 32.3), those who did donated an average of $23,659 (median = $1,500; max = $3.3 million), which is about double that given by the full sample of those who donated. Something that stands out is how few of the HNWH donors used specialty giving vehicles, meaning that they were much more likely to give cash, stock, or other assets. One can surmise that this result would be quite different among the ultra-wealthy (Collins et al. 2021).

Volunteering

Under one-third (30 percent) of HNWHs volunteered in 2020. However, this rate is higher than Americans generally (25 percent) (National Conference on Citizenship 2015). HNWHs who volunteered served an average of 139 hours (median = 50). It is likely that many donors' largest gifts are associated with how they spend their volunteer hours.

Giving Motivations and Decision-Making

Understanding donor motivations is a complex endeavor (see Chapter 26). This survey provided participants with a list of reasons for giving – and not giving – and

TABLE 32.3. HIGH NET WORTH HOUSEHOLD GIVING VEHICLES

Giving Vehicles			
Incidence	9.2%		
Amount (donors only)	$23,659		
Established Giving Vehicles	**Incidence**		
	Have	**Don't have**	**Plan to establish (in next 3 years)**
Private foundation	5.1%	92.8%	2.1%
Donor-advised fund	6.6%	91.6%	1.9%
Planned giving instrument	7.4%	89.8%	2.8%
A will with specific charitable provisions	16.5%	77.3%	6.2%
Endowment fund with an organization	4.5%	93.5%	2.0%
Qualified Charitable Distribution from an IRA	8.0%	90.2%	1.8%
A giving circle	4.2%	94.3%	1.5%

Source: Authors' calculations using unpublished data from *The 2021 Bank of America Study of Philanthropy: Charitable Giving by Affluent Households,* researched and written by the Indiana University Lilly Family School of Philanthropy 2021a.

TABLE 32.4. HIGH NET WORTH HOUSEHOLD MOTIVATIONS FOR GIVING

Motivations for Giving	Incidence		
	Never	Sometimes	Always
1. When you are asked	12.1%	82.3%	5.7%
2. Spontaneously in response to a need	11.2%	80.1%	8.8%
3. When you believe that your gift can make a difference	4.0%	50.9%	45.1%
4. To remedy issues that have affected you or those close to you (e.g., cancer, drug addiction)	22.5%	63.9%	13.6%
5. Because you believe in the mission of the organization	3.4%	38.4%	58.2%
6. In order to give back to your community	7.8%	63.6%	28.6%
7. In order to help address global issues	32.5%	59.5%	8.0%
8. To receive a tax benefit	40.7%	44.8%	14.5%
9. Because I want to support social justice aims	39.7%	47.5%	12.9%
10. For personal satisfaction, enjoyment, or fulfillment	12.3%	56.3%	31.4%

Source: Authors' calculations using unpublished data from *The 2021 Bank of America Study of Philanthropy: Charitable Giving by Affluent Households*, researched and written by the Indiana University Lilly Family School of Philanthropy 2021a.

asked them to select all that applied. This approach makes it difficult to parse which reasons are most important, but it does show which ones were most common (see Table 32.4).

The results give credence to the notion that "people don't give if they are not asked," but also shows that people do not always give when asked. More than half of people said that they must always believe in the mission of the organization in order to give. Believing the gift can make a difference appears to be a consistently important motivation.

On the other hand, tax motivations are never relevant to 41 percent of people and always important to only 15 percent. This result may have been (and will be in the future) affected by the Tax Cuts and Jobs Act (TCJA) passed in December 2017 and enacted in 2018. One of its key provisions was the near doubling of the standard deduction and the State and Local Tax (SALT) limits, which coalesced to reduce households' likelihood of itemizing their taxes. Even among HNWHs, many former itemizers found themselves as non-itemizers, so taxes will literally play no role in their decision-making.

The "demotivations" for giving (why not give?) are more easily interpreted (see Table 32.5). Almost 20 percent of HNWHs said they did not give because they were not asked. One-fifth of respondents (21 percent) said they just did not want to give. Another 22 percent did not give when they did not have a connection to the charity. Finally, the single largest reason donors did not give to a charity was the desire to take care of their family's needs (32 percent).

TABLE 32.5. HIGH NET WORTH HOUSEHOLDS' "DEMOTIVATIONS" FOR GIVING (WHY NOT GIVE?)

Why not give?	Incidence
1. I was not asked to give to charity.	19.8%
2. The timing of the request was not optimal.	9.9%
3. I did not have a connection to an organization.	21.9%
4. I did not know what causes to give to.	8.9%
5. The giving process was too complicated.	2.3%
6. I did not have the resources to give to charity.	14.9%
7. My gift would not have made a difference.	7.6%
8. My priority was to take care of my family's needs.	30.9%
9. I did not want to give to charity.	20.8%
10. I plan to do all my giving at the end of my life.	10.5%
11. Other.	9.1%
12. I don't know.	13.9%

Source: Authors' calculations using unpublished data from *The 2021 Bank of America Study of Philanthropy: Charitable Giving by Affluent Households,* researched and written by the Indiana University Lilly Family School of Philanthropy 2021a.

Who Decides?

In a partner/spouse relationship, the survey asked "who decides" about the couple's philanthropic decisions. Not surprisingly, there were a range of answers. In 28 percent of the HNWHs, one person was the sole decision-maker. In almost half (49 percent) of the couples, charitable decisions were made jointly. The remainder were fairly evenly split between making the decisions completely separately (11 percent) and making them separately but after conferring with each other (12 percent). One can imagine that there might be more permutations (e.g., we confer on large gifts [however defined] and decide separately on small gifts [however defined]).

Policy Issues

The survey also explored whether donations to political campaigns or tax policy issues affected philanthropic giving.

Keeping in mind that political contributions are never tax deductible, almost one-third (32 percent) of the HNWHs reported giving this way. These gifts do not appear to have displaced private philanthropic giving. Political giving was far less common, and the political giving levels were much smaller (mean political = $2,134 [median = $300] vs. philanthropic mean = $12,544 [median = 1,750]).

The maximum political gift was also just a fraction of the maximum philanthropic gift ($267,757 vs. just over $5 million).

Itemizers are households for whom their legal itemized deductions (e.g., charitable donations, mortgage interest, property taxes, medical expenses, etc.) exceed the non-itemizer, standard deduction. The standard deduction is the amount the IRS permits a household to deduct from its income without any evidence as a way of simplifying tax filing and tax enforcement. The standard deduction was recently (2018) doubled as part of TCJA. Charitable contributions are deductible without a cap for itemizers, but usually not for non-itemizers. As a part of the COVID-19 recovery efforts, charitable donations can be deducted for non-itemizers up to $300 for singles and $600 for couples filing jointly. TCJA made it more likely that all households would become non-itemizers, including HNWHs. This is important because it dramatically raises the after-tax cost of giving.

While most respondents said they were not motivated to give because of the tax deduction, this change in policy will cause many itemizers to become non-itemizers, which then represents a very large percentage increase (nearly two-thirds) in their after-tax cost of giving. Half of those who did the survey said that they were still itemizers, but one-third said they were not, with the difference being those who were unsure if they itemized or not (17 percent).

The survey asked the HNWHs what would happen to their charitable giving if they received no income tax deductions for their charitable gifts. Almost three-fourths (72 percent) said giving would remain the same, with 6 percent suggesting their gifts would increase (which seems illogical). Almost one-fourth of the respondents (22 percent) replied that their charitable giving would decrease somewhat or dramatically.

Another policy variable affected by TCJA was the estate tax. While the estate tax was not eliminated completely, it now applies to only the wealthiest households. To keep things simple, the survey asked HNWHs how the permanent elimination of the estate tax would affect their charitable bequest giving. While a few said it would decrease somewhat (2 percent) or dramatically (2 percent), nearly three-fourths (73 percent) replied that it would remain the same, and almost one-quarter (23 percent) said it would increase somewhat or dramatically.

Implications for Fundraisers

The survey found that most gifts went to help those in need, followed by religious nonprofits, then educational purposes. The year 2020 was unusual in being marked by the pandemic and demands for social and racial justice. However, with some important exceptions, HNWHs did not allocate a large number of gifts or dollars to these causes. Rather, they tended to give to the causes as they had before. This suggests that these donors tend to be relatively consistent in their philanthropic priorities. It is worth noting, however, that these donors may well have supported specific efforts addressed at these purposes within organizations with broader missions.

As the nation continues to become more diverse, it is increasingly important to attend to how communities of color give. In this study, Black HNWHs were third most likely to give at all (following White and Other). Notably, Black HNWHs donated the most overall – both for donors only and all households. They also lead the donor list in a wide range of issues compared to the other groups. Fundraisers need to actively break through false assumptions about Black donors (like they only support certain missions or they do not make large gifts), and create new organizational practices to make Black donors and other donors of color feel welcome.

Relatively few (9 percent) of the HNWHs used specialized giving vehicles, but those that did gave dramatically more than their study peers. If donors signal that they are using various giving vehicles, pay attention. Networking with legal, tax, and financial professionals could also be beneficial for fundraisers to meet new potential donors with mission interests, and these vehicles are already in place. If HNWH donors do not use these tools, there is an opportunity to provide information and resources.

In good times and bad, it is imperative that fundraisers strategically cultivate and solicit donors. While household giving overall was flat in 2020 (Giving USA 2021), almost all HNWHs still made donations that year, but usually only if they were asked. The majority of donors always must believe in the mission in order to give and it is also powerful for them to know the gift will make a difference. Being true to the mission, engaging, and educating constituents are the basis of fundraising. The fact that HNWHs are more likely to volunteer and for more hours than is typical in the United States is promising for fundraisers in their quest for engagement with this population. However, charities and fundraisers need to think about how to make both volunteering and donating experiences go well: Create synergies not disappointments.

Many households, including HNWHs, were financially affected by TCJA. However, most of the respondents reported that this did not and would not affect their charitable giving. That said, for some HNWHs, which were itemizers and then became non-itemizers, the after-tax price of giving went up by almost two-thirds. Most people would notice a price increase of two-thirds for a house, car, or even clothes, so fundraisers need be prepared to have conversations about tax changes.

Conclusion

Many were glad to see 2020 come to an end. Philanthropy was a key source of support for society's difficulties and HNWH donors were able to continue giving at high rates. Some HNWH donors gave in new ways related to the pandemic and social and racial justice concerns, but the group's overall giving priorities remained consistent. People of color are an important population of HNWH donors who present key opportunities for fundraisers and nonprofits. The fact that HNWHs are not necessarily using sophisticated giving platforms should remind fundraisers that they have expertise to bring to bear that can (even) benefit the wealthy. As always, fundraisers should be sensitive to the personal circumstances of each household, while using data like those in this chapter to inform their efforts.

Discussion Questions

1. Explore the information in this chapter about HNWH giving by subsector. Then compare what you learn with the information available in Chapter 8 from Giving USA about overall giving by subsector. What is similar? What might account for the differences?
2. Review the section on policy changes. How might fundraising (and giving) be affected? How could a nonprofit prepare for possible changes facing its HNWH donors?

Application Exercises

1. Discuss key motivations (and "demotivations") for HNWH donors and how they might affect fundraising strategies. Develop a short list of questions to ask an HNWH donor about what can hamper their giving.
2. Talk with a fundraiser about their work with HNWHs in general or regarding a particular example. What have they witnessed about decision-making processes in couples? How do they navigate these conversations and others around practical issues such as specialized giving vehicles and tax considerations?

PART SEVEN

STRATEGIES FOR MAJOR DONORS AND INSTITUTIONAL FUNDERS

CHAPTER THIRTY-THREE

CO-CREATING MAJOR GIFTS

By Maarten Bout and James M. Hodge

Major gifts, *principal gifts*, and *gifts of significance* describe gifts of magnitude with transformational value to nonprofits and benefactors. Fundraising these gifts emphasizes personal relationships, requires specific knowledge and skills, features attention to donors' passions and values, and focuses on compelling and worthy philanthropic ideas.

This chapter will enable readers to:

- Describe the major giving paradigm, including fundraisers' roles and responsibilities.
- Understand how to co-create the major giving experience with benefactors.
- Consider holistic approaches to managing the major gift program.

The Major Giving Paradigm

Major gifts play an essential role in organizations' vitality and sustainably. With the ever-widening wealth gap in the United States, many organizations are finding that 75–95 percent of contributions come from 5–10 percent of the benefactors (Rooney 2019). Gifts of $10 million dollars or more to charitable institutions have soared over the last ten years (Marts and Lundy 2017).

Major (and planned) giving fundraising is complex and sophisticated. Major gifts require thought; making such commitments takes time, often 18–24 months. They may involve multiple decision-makers: family members, financial planners, and legal advisors. Gifts of significance are more likely to support a designated project and to include restrictions. Major gifts typically support important organizational priorities and provide meaning for organizations and benefactors alike.

The Point of Philanthropic Inevitability

The major giving paradigm involves ever-deepening relationships among the fundraiser (relying on professional expertise), the benefactor (considering beliefs and passions), and organizational leaders (shaping compelling shared visions) (see Figure 33.1). Gifts happen when the benefactor's value system overlaps with the organization's mission, vision, and values. Fundraisers' consistent and excellent work at this intersection brings donors to the *point of philanthropic inevitability*, where the cause, the benefactor, and the organization transform through a shared commitment.

Hank Rosso (1991) explained that fundraising is the gentle art of teaching the joy of giving. He understood "transformational-engaged philanthropy" and knew that major gifts required relationship building. The "why of giving" is more important than the "how of giving," resulting in a shift from transactional to transformational, relationship-based, benefactor-centric, inquiry-driven fundraising (see Figure 33.2). To go from a needs-based to a vision-based approach, fundraisers must to be able to identify, develop, and articulate the organization's investment-worthy ideas. Major gift fundraisers must be change agents or "intrapreneurs" within the organization as well as valued and trusted individuals in benefactors' eyes.

FIGURE 33.1. INTERSECTION WHERE MAJOR GIFTS OCCUR

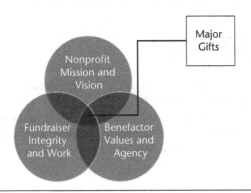

FIGURE 33.2. TRANSACTIONAL TO TRANSFORMATIONAL FUNDRAISING

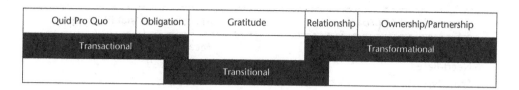

Quid Pro Quo	Obligation	Gratitude	Relationship	Ownership/Partnership
Transactional			Transformational	
	Transitional			

Morals, Meaning, and Money

In major gifts, the word *fundraiser* falls short of what the work actually entails. More time is spent tending relationships and co-creating a shared donor/organizational understanding than asking for money (Duronio and Tempel 1997). O'Neill (1993) saw development professionals as moral trainers, Nouwen and Mogabgab (2011) described major gift officers as missionaries, and Breeze (2017) portrayed fundraisers as honest brokers. Fundraisers promote compelling visions and possibilities for the betterment of humankind.

On their deathbeds, individuals measure their life's meaning based on whether they were their authentic selves, made a difference in the world, and left a lasting legacy (Kübler-Ross 1997). Through philanthropy, development officers and volunteers can help donors provide meaningful answers to lifelong questions. Table 33.3 shows some of the shifts that happen when benefactors and fundraisers move from a transactional relationship to a transformational relationship. Many prospective major benefactors know how to accumulate "means" but not add "meaning" in their lives. In the major gift paradigm described here, fundraisers help organizations and donors co-create a vision for the future, which is informed by the experiences and voices of those the organization serves.

A benefactor-centric, inquiry-driven practice is only possible through ascribing agency to the donor and building trust. Trust between the organization and the benefactor increases the emotional and financial equity of the benefactor in the organization.

Trust-building relies on fundraisers' *empathic mindset* and seeing the world through the donor's eyes. Davis (1983) described *empathy* broadly as the intellectual/cognitive and emotional reactions of one to the observation of the experiences of another. If fundraisers are to be honest brokers (Breeze 2017) between donors and organizations, they must be able to discern donors' values. Major gift fundraisers who rely strongly on cognitive empathy may have enhanced giving outcomes (Bout 2018).

The donor's empathic mindset can be nurtured as well; by telling stories of the mission and introducing them to organizational clients and participants, fundraisers can help benefactors' shift from primarily intrinsic to more extrinsic

TABLE 33.3. ESSENTIAL SHIFTS FROM TRANSACTIONAL TO TRANSFORMATIONAL RELATIONSHIPS

Transactional Approach	Transformational Philosophy
Money	Meaning
Need-Based	Vision-Based
Scarcity	Abundance
Transaction	Partnership
Telling and Selling	Compelling
Helping and Fixing	Serving
Organization-Centric	Benefactor-Centric

motivations, from self-centered to other-centered, and from independent to interdependent (Riess 2018).

Trust also requires being observant and self-aware; gestures, facial expressions, and other nonverbal cues are revealing (Ekman 2003). A donor may light up when presented with one idea, but show no emotion in response to another. Cultural sensitivities are critical as well. A gesture in one culture may be misperceived as something altogether different in another (Meyer 2014a).

Self-awareness also requires attention to one's own personal experiences and their impact on fundraisers as professionals. Everyone carries unconscious biases (Benaji and Greenwald 2016), and there are classic stories about fundraisers who fail to recognize potential donors based on preconceived ideas. Fundraisers must be open-minded in determining who has philanthropic ability and curious about philanthropic approaches that are different than their own. At the same time, fundraisers deserve fair, appropriate, and respectful treatment from donors that is inclusive of their gender identity, race/ethnicity, ability, sexual orientation, and background.

The Major Gift Cycle

Relationships with major benefactors are highly personalized and context specific. The Fund Raising School's Major Gift Cycle (see Figure 33.4) offers a roadmap with steps that may vary in degree or sequence. The fundraiser and the benefactor must explore new paths together, based on their ever-deepening relationship. New major gift officers or high-level fundraising volunteers often nervously ask the question "What do you talk about with a major benefactor?" The main driver of inquiry-driven major gift fundraising is asking "What is known about a benefactor and what is yet to be known," and structuring and planning questions accordingly.

FIGURE 33.4. THE EIGHT-STEP MAJOR GIFT MANAGEMENT CYCLE

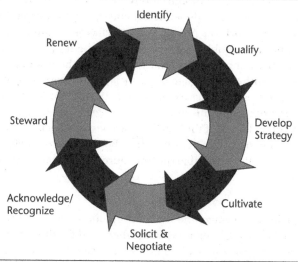

Source: The Fund Raising School 2021.

Identify

A necessary condition for a major gift is the donor's financial ability. However, wealth alone is not a sufficient condition to consider someone a potential benefactor. Staff and volunteers must place equal or greater emphasis on those individuals with a charitable nature and a passion for their cause. There is a difference between a donor who *could* support the organization and one who *would* support the organization. Selecting the right donors to engage is critical, and narrowing down the list is important for a successful major giving program. Doing so also comes with a set of ethical considerations about mission alignment (i.e., an environmental organization and a potential donor whose company is notorious for polluting waterways) (see Chapters 2 and 14).

While unanticipated gifts sometimes occur, benefactors typically emerge from the *communities of the committed*, those constituencies with established organizational relationships and mission commitment. These communities consist of existing donors, volunteers, prior recipients of organizational services, board members, involved alumni, and other close constituents. Research will reveal those individuals in the organization's orbit who might welcome a conversation with the fundraiser. Wealth screening tools are becoming more accurate, but they are imperfect, make some uncomfortable, and are not considered ethical in some contexts. The identification stage provides a preliminary evaluation of a benefactor's financial capacity and inclination to make a major gift.

Although wealthy people give to a variety of causes for many reasons, some research shows they favor organizations they find benefit from (like the arts) or on whose services they once depended themselves (like hospitals) (Schervish 2008; 2005). A classic work on prospective benefactor research prioritized "interests, concerns, passions, hobbies and eccentricities; education; family history and values, spouse partner and children; experience in the nonprofit world; residences; civic and philanthropic engagement, social and fraternal positions; and religion" of potential major benefactors (Frantzreb 1991, 120). Might an individual have a passion for a particular mission component? Do they have a philanthropic mindset? What is the degree of their social awareness and social responsibility of wealth? The key is to know as much as possible about the donor before engaging in conversations – with the caveat that the best source of information is the donor themself.

Qualify

In the qualification stage, the basic information about a donor's Linkage Ability Interest (LAI) (see Chapter 14) is weighed, and fundraiser and donor may meet for the first time or interact in a new way. Development officers explore the philanthropic nature and the financial capacity of prospective benefactors and their attraction to the mission. Volunteers may provide important insights as well as introductions and ideas for making contacts.

The fundraiser visits (or calls) the donor to begin or transform a relationship for gift making. It is imperative that the fundraiser take time to earn the trust of the donor. In *The Speed of Trust,* Covey and Merrill wrote about behaviors that engender trust, including being honest, demonstrating respect, being transparent, listening, and being accountable and realistic.

Trusted fundraisers can ask questions that respectfully probe a benefactor's value systems, interests, passion, and vision. Curating questions for various relationship stages reduces stress, and steadily deepens knowledge of the role and meaning of giving in the benefactor's life.

- Who is someone who inspired you?
- What would the world look like for your children and for others' children?
- What makes the sun come up for you in the morning?
- If you could right one wrong, what would this be?

Conversations, rather than research alone, clarify the donor's capacity and inclination to give. Discovering that a benefactor does not have the linkage, ability, or interest, and removing them from the list is also a valid and important outcome of major benefactor work.

Develop Strategy

When more is known about the donor and a decision is made to proceed, the gift officer considers which organizational priorities might most intrigue the donor and creates a strategy for engagement. The strategy has two key ingredients: the right people on the team and the right ideas.

Team. A team approach, facilitated by the fundraiser, connects the donor to the organization and avoids potential devastating consequences if a key player leaves the nonprofit. Every nonprofit needs a *visionary*, a leader(s) who brings the mission to life for benefactors, and staff members who transform vision to action. Major gift officers advance the relationship between the prospective benefactor and the organization. Board members can be instrumental in providing insights about the donor and showing their own philanthropic involvement to the donor. Other staff members, such as content experts, program personnel, and faculty members, make the mission "come to life" by providing testimony.

As much as possible, teams should be diverse in background and experience (race/ethnicity, age, gender, disability, sexual orientation, etc.) to create synergies with donors, represent communities served by the organization, facilitate learning, and achieve goals of equity and justice.

Ideation. The strategy is shaped through the development of compelling ideas to explore with the donor. Ideas align with the organization's mission, build on initial knowledge about the donor, are stronger with team input, and require fundraisers to synthesize information into new forms. Organizational leadership must create the right circumstances and environment for developing appropriate and creative ideas for gift proposals. The option of requesting unrestricted support for the organization also must not be forgotten or automatically eliminated based on the assumption that it will not be of interest to donors.

Cultivate (Engage)

Two goals of this stage are to understand the potential benefactor better and to cultivate an ownership position in the mission of the organization.

The first goal includes continuously engaging donors in conversation, being attentive to their responses, and organizing experiences to add depth to their connection to the cause. Through this process, donors' motivations and the match between the values of the donors and the organization are discerned (see Chapter 26).

The second goal, cultivating ownership, can take many different forms, which will be particular to the organization. Donors:

- Could be taken on a "field trip" to experience service delivery.
- May be invited to be a program volunteer.
- May be asked to teach a class or speak with program participants.
- Could be asked to share their expertise or opinion about a particular issue or opportunity.

Valuable clues emerge through donors' responses to carefully selected engagement opportunities. Listening for shifts in language used by donors from "me" to "we" is an important clue to increasing ownership equity. A turning point in the relationship is when, instead of saying "I think YOU should," a donor says, "I think WE should." This signals the evolution from friend to ally for the cause.

A part of the relationship-building process is inviting the potential benefactor to make first or "step" gifts to the organization. Invitations for early investments allow the development officer to determine what ideas harmonize with a donor's core values. Step gifts set the stage for the deeper involvement necessary for funding a transformational idea. Consider step gifts that can grow into important initiatives.

Solicit and Negotiate (Invite the Gift)

Gift requests usually come after exploring donor values, considering appropriate gift levels, assessing outcomes and measurable impacts, and choosing the team. Major gift officers and the team must ask themselves several questions:

- Do we know this donor sufficiently and have we earned the right to ask for a major gift?
- Is the donor meaningfully engaged in the work of our organization?
- Is this an appropriate time for this request?
- Will the project or the gift purpose resonate with the benefactor?
- Are we requesting a respectful amount and considering what gift vehicle and appropriate asset would be best for the benefactor?
- Is the team prepared to articulate the vision and make the request?

The more significant the potential gift, the longer and more complex the solicitation preparation will be. Prior to meeting with the donor and inviting the gift, solicitation team members need to be satisfied that the proper preparation is completed, the donor is well-understood, and the invitation is likely to be well received. This critical process is explored in detail in the next chapter.

Acknowledge/Recognize

Acknowledgment is the stage in which the donor is thanked. Receipts and standardized thank you letters are merely a start. Fundraisers must create benefactor-specific ways to acknowledge and recognize donor commitments. This can be as simple as a heartfelt note or call or as complex as a groundbreaking ceremony.

Through an inquiry-driven process, the fundraiser will learn how the donor prefers to be recognized. Some donors eschew attention. Some *say* recognition does not matter to them, when it eventually might. Cultural and emotional attunement is an important consideration. For example, most Dutch donors would be mortified if their name were called from the stage of an arena (Wiepking and Bekkers 2015), whereas many American donors appreciate public attention for their giving.

Steward

Stewardship is an ongoing process that further deepens relationships with donors. Demonstrating a gift's impact informs donors of how an investment is improving the lives of the intended recipients. Letters from scholarship recipients, financial reports, program tours, documentation of construction projects, personal visits, and high-level volunteer service opportunities can strengthen donor ties to the nonprofit, validate their involvement, and show a contribution's efficacy.

Stewardship, including the management of donor funds and donor intent, is ethically required and encourages future contributions. It is more than an afterthought for donors. Generation X and Millennials, for example, care more about tangible results and proof of impact than generations before (Goldseker and Moody 2017). "Effective altruists" base decision-making on utilitarian principles measuring the good of their giving by the tangible outcomes (Singer 2015). Fundraisers must attend to individual donor's stewardship preferences.

Renew

Gift renewal signals the continuous, evolving, and even overlapping nature of the eight-cycle stages. It is harder and more costly to gain new donors than to retain existing ones, and many organizations have low retention rates (Barber and Levis 2013).

Successful renewal can depend on how well the organization fulfills its mission and involves the benefactor in the implementation of the transformational gift. With attention to all the stages, there is a good chance the donor will continue the partnership. Renewal, however, requires reexamination of the donor's giving capacity, the evolution of the donor's relationship with the organization, and the donor's values and current priorities. This stage requires consistent communication, active listening, and awareness of changes in the donor's life.

Strategies for Managing the Unmeasurable

The major giving paradigm followed in this chapter prioritizes long-term relationships and requires that fundraisers' success is measured accordingly. Organizations need to take specific actions with their management systems and structures to support such programs.

Managing Donor Information

Each philanthropic relationship requires systematic documentation. Ensuring that this knowledge frames organizational interactions, even in the face of staff turnover and gaps in contact, requires prioritizing careful recordkeeping about each relationship. Because donor record systems are integrated with customer facing interfaces (e.g., ticket sales in the arts) and communication mechanisms (e.g., bulk email solutions), it is easy to record and store too much information, which may become confusing, cause analysis paralysis, and hinder visionary thinking.

Individual donor records are essential and must follow the highest standards for privacy and ethical record keeping. Contact reports should be mindful of the donor's personal circumstances, their relationship to the organization and cause, the donor and organization's shared experience, and ensure continuity of understanding within the organization. Focus needs to be on observations that give insight into the benefactor's perspective. A good guide is to only include facts, notes, or comments from benefactor visits that could be read "over your shoulder" by the benefactors themselves without discomfort.

Research suggests a connection between giving and recording fundraisers' evaluations of visits and writing next steps in contact reports (Bout 2018). It is unclear whether the connection is causal, but it may be that fundraisers who consider donors' next steps produce more effective donor communications and conversations. Training in writing contact reports and choosing the appropriate, ethical, and relevant information to include is essential.

Evaluating Fundraiser Success

Evaluation systems for major gift programs' efficacy should be based on holistic measurements, to reward long-term relationships not merely short-term results. Most models of major gift fundraising set metrics for specific numbers of personal visits with potential major benefactors, number of proposals presented, and total dollars raised each year. These metrics include aspects of a strong fundraising program. However, they do not credit all parties involved in a gift, describe the quality of engagements, or express the gratification and satisfaction of the donor.

In transformational giving, it is important to measure the fundraiser or others' impact on a donor's sense of belonging to the nonprofit, and the quality and progression of the relationship. One way to accomplish this is through periodic evaluation and discussion of contact reports, designing qualitative metrics for assessing relationships' depth and development, and conversations with the donor about their experiences.

Allocating Resources

Major gift fundraising must focus on potential benefactors with the greatest LAI. Relationship building requires a significant investment of time and energy. Major gift officers are often highly salaried professionals, and funds are usually required for travel, proposal development, and entertaining donors. Achieving a high return on investment of major gift programs requires that resources are judiciously directed and monitored.

Measuring only activity and not quality or depth of the relationship between the organization and the benefactor cannot adequately describe whether the major gift fundraising program delivers a certain return on investment. More sophistication is required in setting the major gift fundraising budget. If 95 percent of gift income comes from 5 percent of donors, this provides guidance. However, often donors balk at high expenses directed to fundraising, even though it might be the very thing that enables the organization to exist (Putnam-Walkerly 2020). Deliberate allocation of resources based on data (i.e., quantitative and qualitative) is essential to get the desired returns and justify the expenses.

Conclusion – Let's Take a Long Walk Together

In major gift work, fundraisers have the opportunity and responsibility to explore who donors are at their core, how they identify with others and their plights, what formative experiences shaped their lives, and what values are important for them to preserve. Fundraisers must be open-minded, ask important questions, inquire and explore without judgment, and find essential connections to the cause. Fundraisers must be empathic to each unique individual donor and pay attention to how they engage with the world through philanthropy.

Following the steps of the Eight-Step Major Gift Cycle using this mindset, fundraisers help donors strengthen their cause connection through carefully conceived engagement. This engagement reveals the ideas that resonate with each donor as the most investment-worthy opportunities, and the donor can be invited to partner in a shared vision. As a result, fundraisers and organizations add meaning to donors' lives, and donors bring transformational resources to organizations. In the best-case scenario, donor, organization, and fundraiser will enjoy a long-term relationship that is based on walking a path to a shared vision of the future and providing what organizational beneficiaries need.

Discussion Questions

1. What is a major gift, and what are the necessary conditions for one to emerge?
2. Who are potential major gift donors, and how do they reveal themselves?
3. What are some questions to ask donors that will reveal values that are important to them?
4. How can you make the mission of your organization come to life for donors?
5. What are the key questions to answer before approaching donors with a proposal?

Application Exercises

1. Imagine you are the chief development officer of a large medical research institution. How would you identify, approach, and develop the relationship with a potential major benefactor?
2. Create the outline of a proposal for a major gift for a hypothetical donor with financial capacity. Think through their connection to your organization, the engagement program, and the things you may learn about them.
3. Describe your most deeply held values and hopes for your life contributions to a friend, family member, or colleague. Ask them to summarize what they learned about you. Then reverse the exercise and discuss what it means for philanthropy.

CHAPTER THIRTY-FOUR

THE INVITATION TO GIVE

By Genevieve G. Shaker

The number of Americans making small and medium-sized gifts declined in recent years (Rooney 2019). While the events of 2020 and 2021 may reenergize these donors, major gift fundraising remains increasingly important. People give after being asked in the vast majority of philanthropic contributions, and individualized requests are especially vital for raising large gifts (Bryant, Jeon-Slaughter, Kang, and Tax 2003; Kelly 1998; Yörük 2012).

This chapter presents a holistic, four-part process for preparing and making in-person invitations to give (i.e., "asks" for donations, requests for contributions).

In this chapter, readers will:

- Build confidence for making invitations to give.
- Apply research insights relevant to donor engagement and gift invitations.
- Learn preparation strategies for inviting gifts.
- Examine a framework for gift conversations.

Preparing Personally to Invite Gifts

Commitment to the cause and organizational and donor knowledge are prerequisites to successful giving invitations, but so too is fundraiser self-knowledge.

A common refrain from family, friends, and strangers is: "You're a fundraiser? I don't know how you do it. I could never ask people for money." The implications are clear: Asking people for money is something to dread. Many new fundraisers and even accomplished fundraisers approach "making the ask" with trepidation. Others, however, perceive invitations to give as special opportunities resulting from careful preparation (Breeze and Jollymore 2017) that provide donors with meaning, satisfaction, and even health benefits (see Chapter 5). Embracing the excitement of inviting gifts requires developing authentic and assured approaches through reflection and practice. The subsequent paragraphs provide a guiding strategy.

Audit Asking Anxieties and Strengths

External forces and individual considerations affect feelings about asking for contributions (Fredricks 2017; McCrea, Walker, and Weber 2013). External forces can include cultural, societal, and familial views regarding money (Furnham and Argyle 2014). In many contexts, talking about money is impolite; in some, discussing personal philanthropic gift amounts or publicly recognizing large gifts is inappropriate. Individual considerations can include fears of failure, discomfort with uncertainty, concern about power dynamics, and differing communication styles (McCrea, Walker, and Weber 2013). Fundraisers' own socio-economic circumstances, personal experiences with philanthropy, religious views, and social identities are also relevant in discerning asking anxieties – and identifying strengths. Developing a written audit of one's own perspectives and experiences is an essential precursor to communicating with major donors.

Question Asking Assumptions

Once fundraisers can articulate asking anxieties and strengths, anxieties can be explored, and strengths can be reinforced. By referring to their own history, fundraisers can ask what experiences caused a fear of asking or, alternatively, empowered them to request support. They can explore who influenced their thinking about the privacy of money and their approaches to coping with uncertainties of various kinds. Fundraisers themselves can then recall their own experiences as givers and the positive results of those gifts. Defining personal feelings and potential outcomes of asking for money – most of which are positive – can break through assumptions about the "cost" of asking.

Transform Asking into Inviting

A personal philosophy of fundraising grounded in life experiences and honed through knowledge about philanthropy and professional ethics is a central tool for transforming asking anxieties into the joy of inviting (see Chapters 1 and 2). This transformation can include developing affirmative statements about gifts' purposes that reflect fundraisers' ethical mandate and professional capacity. The most effective statements are individually crafted, reflect philanthropic and personal values, and focus on what philanthropy achieves. Such statements include:

- By inviting gifts, I facilitate achieving our mission and contribute to something important to me.
- By inviting gifts, I help others respond to community needs and help make the world a better place.
- By inviting gifts, I provide donors opportunities to achieve their philanthropic purpose and bring important experiences to their lives.
- By inviting gifts, I inspire others to ask, multiply support for the cause, and do something that others cannot.

Philanthropy's legitimacy of purpose infuses these personal statements with meaning that is logical, emotional, and professional (i.e., the cause is important to humanity. My desire to help is more powerful than my fear of rejection). Writing such statements down and reading them aloud is empowering.

Build Knowledge and Seek Experience

Many fundraisers begin in annual giving, shaping written words into requests for support. Shifting the requests into oral form is daunting. Fundraisers can learn from listening and watching how others invite contributions. They can build knowledge by seeing how donors speak about their gifts and the fundraisers who asked. Fundraisers can practice asking for money, in smaller amounts, with each other and tolerant friends. By doing this, fundraisers can hear and speak the language of philanthropy, making it more familiar and reassuring each time. Fundraisers should use the many available resources and trainings to hone their approach. The commitment to improving as a facilitator of philanthropy should be career-spanning.

Reflection and intentional practice, as described in this section, enable fundraisers to become more empathetic to benefactors and beneficiaries – they too are products of their experiences and environment. These activities are avenues for resetting assumptions, being courageous, and excelling as a fundraiser. Ultimately, asking for money can become the transformational act of inviting gifts on behalf of the mission.

Advancing toward the Invitation

This chapter focuses on donors with the capacity to make large gifts and on inviting those gifts in person. Some such gifts are donor-initiated, leading to spontaneous and accelerated gift-making processes (Greer and Kostoff 2020). More often, major gifts follow a fundraiser-executed, step-by-step, engagement program, oriented toward strengthening donors' organizational association and leading to philanthropic generosity (see Chapter 33).

These engagement programs are mechanisms for developing relationships between donors and organizations (and their beneficiaries), thus differentiating philanthropy from mere financial transactions. Ethical best practice supports the formation of bonds between donors and organizations, with fundraisers as facilitators, conduits, and mediators. This section highlights research that advances relationships through engagement to the gift discussion.

Shape Strategic Conversations

Giving is motivated by an array of intersecting factors, including values, awareness of need, reputational concerns, practical costs and benefits, psychological factors, and the solicitation itself (Bekkers and Wiepking 2011a; see Chapter 26). The nature of an individual invitation to give should be intimately associated with a donor's motivations. Without talking and listening to donors, fundraisers cannot know donors' priorities, their personal circumstances, or their organizational perceptions.

Fundraisers can shape conversations – and their own behaviors – to elicit information and insights. Questions can be researched and designed to explore donors' personal values and goals, philanthropic experiences, and priorities. Questions can be used to discern who the donor should know in the organization and what organizational experience to create. Through active empathic listening (AEL), fundraisers can envision themselves in donors' experiences and work to assess the underlying meanings of donors' words and expressions. AEL behaviors include attentiveness, verbal acknowledgments, affirmative body language, responsiveness to nonverbal signals, and repeating key information (Drollinger et al. 2006). This approach is not limited to single conversations, but can become a signature feature of all interactions with a donor (Drollinger 2018).

Informed and encouraging questions with disciplined listening will generate information about the strength of the donor's linkage to the organization, their capacity to give, and alignment of donor intent with organizational need. These methods develop trust, which is all the more important in an era of increased scrutiny on philanthropy and reduced confidence in nonprofits (Theis 2019). These approaches also foster conversational rapport and provide essential insights for structuring personalized engagement strategies.

Form Meaningful Relationships

People develop, change, and evolve as donors (Jones 2018). In the strongest philanthropic relationships, donors know they are valued for more than their money; the best solicitations emerge from trusting relationships that fairly represent donors' and organizations' respective interests (Alborough 2017; Breeze and Jollymore 2017; Shaker and Nelson 2021). Fundraisers say that reciprocity in giving relationships (i.e., reports to donors on what their gifts achieve) enhances the connection between benefactors and beneficiaries, while facilitating organizational understandings of donors (Alborough 2017). According to donors, professionalism (i.e., following up, keeping commitments, acting with integrity) is also critical in deepening relationships (Shaker and Nelson 2021).

Fundraisers must question their own assumptions, biases, and practices. When unexamined, these can hamper openness to potential donors, including unexpected or atypical donors, and the ability to craft appropriate engagement programs based on actual donor information. Fundraisers and donors may analyze their relationships in similar ways, but fundraisers cannot fully understand donors' perspectives without learning about them and their experiences (Waters 2009).

Research documents that donors require individualized cultivation approaches (Shaker and Nelson 2021). As much as possible within organizational resources, each major donor experience should be intentional and imaginative, developed through sufficient analysis and preparation. All the relational dynamics can then be reviewed in determining the details of the eventual giving invitation.

Apply Interpersonal Communication Skills

Research on interpersonal communication can be used to form a competence framework for fundraisers (Ragsdale 1995). Competent communicators recognize the mutuality of balancing the need to attain a gift with the "need to preserve the prospective donor's personhood" (30). To do this, fundraisers need to communicate in ways that show affiliation and support for the donor, put the donor at ease, express empathy, demonstrate behavioral sensitivity, and reflect conversational norms, such as speaking in turn and not interrupting (Wiemann 1977). People perceive interpersonal communication to be high quality when it is frequent, interesting, and unique; has depth and breadth; and takes place with ease, flexibility, spontaneity, and open expression (Knapp, Ellis, and Williams 1980).

Fundraisers who develop self-awareness and strong interpersonal skills create positive and enjoyable experiences that donors anticipate with pleasure. When this pattern is established, moving toward the invitation to give is a natural progression.

Strategizing for the Giving Invitation

As relationships between potential donors and organizations evolve, donors and fundraisers simultaneously gain knowledge and insights. As each comes to know the other better, discovering the match between donor interest and organization mission gives relationships purpose and direction and provides clues about when and how to invite a gift. Fundraisers who cultivate versatility and responsiveness in their interactions develop diverse methods of curating, connecting, and communicating information; those who lean into their curiosity about people and their experiences have the greatest success in developing relationships and inviting gifts (Nagaraj 2013).

Initiate the Meeting Request

During the cultivation/engagement phase, fundraisers intentionally progress toward an invitation to give by attending to societal circumstances, organizational (and beneficiary) needs, and donors' concerns. Fundraisers' own professional performance expectations may also be a factor. These complex dynamics all affect timing the invitation.

At times, donors begin gift conversations without a cultivation period. A potential donor may approach an organization after following its activities in the local media or volunteering for one of its programs. In most circumstances, however, organizations and fundraisers initiate gift conversations. Regardless, happenstance can require working off-plan or ahead of schedule; rigidity in these instances can alienate donors (Greer and Kostoff 2020).

In a planned approach, progressing to the giving invitation requires strong familiarity with the donor's priorities and circumstances as well as their interface with the organization. Fundraisers need to "test" their knowledge to assess whether enough is known about the donor. Reflecting on statements like these can help.

- The donor's philanthropic priorities align with the organization, and this is evident to both donor and organization.
- The fundraiser has provided ample information about the organization's mission, opportunities, and challenges.
- The donor's personal circumstances and financial situation appear conducive to the proposed gift.
- The donor's preferences for organizational involvement are known and feasible.
- The interpersonal dynamic between the donor and organizational staff is understood.

Trial and error, experience, and instinct inform this process, but there is no substitute for using critical and careful analysis to guide decisions. If these statements show significant knowledge gaps, then more information is needed before the gift conversation.

No request for a major gift should surprise the donor. Fundraisers should provide signals that the invitation is coming. Seeking a gift conversation is strategic. A well-conceived request alerts the donor to the meeting's purpose, and with their acceptance, grants permission to proceed. Decision points shaping the request include: Who should seek the meeting? How should the gift conversation request be conveyed? Who should be involved from the organization and the donor's life? What format should the meeting follow (i.e., time of day, location/setting, length)? What organizational items (i.e., a rendering of a new building, resolution of a fiscal issue, creation of printed matter) need to be in place before meeting?

Choices need to be logical and specific to the donor, not be based on generalizations. For example, if the fundraiser typically calls to schedule meetings, receiving an email from the executive director requesting a visit may be off-putting. Alternatively, if one spouse/partner holds the relationship, inviting the other to participate without consulting them could be unwelcome (see Chapters 28 and 30).

Regardless of thoughtful preparation, donors sometimes decline and delay gift conversations because they are not ready, not in the right financial position, or more committed to other priorities – all reasons outside of the organization's control. Fundraisers can seek to understand these donors' circumstances and decisions, reassess and regroup, and diligently address and manage the factors within their influence.

Prepare for the Invitation

By agreeing to meet, donors signal interest in what the organization will say. They may arrive open-minded, ready to give, prepared with their own plan, or determined not to contribute. In every instance, the gift conversation is an opportunity to build appreciation for the mission regardless of the outcome. Preparation should be guided by this principle.

Anticipate. Imagine the gift conversation. Donors want to know: What will the gift accomplish? Why is the gift important now? How does the gift fit with my priorities (Fredericks 2017)? Review ways the donor might respond to the invitation – with technical questions and practical inquiries; with their own suggestions; with options to continue; or with a request to disengage. Prepare by anticipating all eventualities and writing a list of donor approaches and various responses.

Plan. Use a simple and flexible template to map out key information about the proposed gift, goals for each part of the conversation, and responsibilities of the asker/s. Decide whether the gift conversation should happen one-on-one or be a team effort with organizational leadership, programmatic staff, or a peer donor or volunteer. At times, the fundraiser will not even be present, making preparation even more important. Decide whether collateral materials are needed to illustrate the request. Write out the gift invitation in a few sentences including the "what" and "why."

Practice. Keep in mind that invitations must be authentic and sincere, and require practice. Repeat aloud the sentences inviting the gift, including the amount. In a team environment, a rehearsal acclimates colleagues to their conversational roles and provides coaching to address fears. Fundraisers making the invitation individually can gain self-confidence by practicing key conversations with coworkers.

Thank and Confirm. After scheduling the meeting with the donor(s), thank them for agreeing to talk, affirm the meeting, and as needed, update them on any changes in what to expect.

Figure 34.1 summarizes the process for inviting gifts described throughout this chapter, including the components of the invitation to give itself.

FIGURE 34.1. A PROCESS FOR PREPARING, FORMULATING, AND MAKING THE INVITATION TO GIVE

Making the Invitation to Give

The invitation to give is a conversation with simple and recognizable elements, not a one-way presentation, speech, or lecture. Recognizing the difference is foundational to crafting effective invitations to give. Experienced fundraisers also know that successful requests come through preparing, asking, reflecting, adapting, and asking anew. Skill and good humor will grow as fundraisers navigate a diversity of surprising, interesting, fulfilling, and even disappointing gift conversations.

Invitations to give require a structure, like the one described here. This framework, built on The Fund Raising School (2021) curriculum, provides a baseline that can – and should – be modified to suit donor, fundraiser, and organizational styles.

Open with Intentionality

Use existing relational patterns to inform how the meeting begins. Note that the presence of others may require introductions to establish rapport. Exchanging pleasantries and catching up are typical openings, but for the active empathic listener such preliminaries also reveal mood, tone, pace, and invitation appropriateness. If donors share a recent change in their circumstances, for example, the request may require a different or delayed approach. Throughout the conversation, fundraisers should evoke the traits already demonstrated in the relationship – openness, honesty, authenticity, curiosity – to create a familiar environment.

Donors' time is valuable, and this step is likely to be brief, although the conversational pace should match their preferences.

Involve the Donor

Provide context by thanking the donor for past philanthropic or volunteer support, reflecting on their future with the organization, and expressing appreciation for meeting. It is easy for the fundraising team to dominate the conversation, but important that the donor speak more. Ask the donor about organizational experiences, feedback on a recent effort, reactions to an event affecting the organization, or thoughts about a new initiative. Reference awareness of the donor's philanthropic motivations. Revisit key moments in the cultivation process, drawing on the donor's own words, all moving toward the invitation.

Reconfirm the conversation's purpose to orient the donor, seek their approval to proceed, and segue the conversation to its predetermined purpose.

Invite the Gift

Begin by reviewing the big need or opportunity that the organization's mission serves. Explain what the gift will achieve for the organization and why the timing is right, but be prepared to adapt based on reactions. Speak to how the proposed gift aligns with the donor's interests and expectations of the organization. Be concise, direct, confident, and positive. Persuade the donor with conviction about the cause and shared values.

End with a question, including the gift amount and purpose. Phrase the question in a way that warrants a response with some explanation: Will you join [us/others who care about what you do/our efforts] with a gift of [amount] for [purpose]? Will you give [amount] to respond to [need/opportunity], something I know you care about? A gift of [amount] would make a real difference for [purpose/need/people] – will you give?

Remember that this moment is not a surprise. Pause and silently await the answer. Give the donor space to think and respond. Be an engaged listener, maintaining eye contact. The temptation to fill the silence will be strong, in alignment with norms of interpersonal communication. Resist that desire and cede conversational control to the donor.

Develop the Invitation

There is always more to discuss once the invitation is made, and a prepared fundraiser has considered the donor's many potential responses. The response may be "no" or "not now" or "I need more information" or "that's not exactly what I care most about." The donor may say "yes" or "I could be interested in that" or "tell me more." The fundraiser is ready to respond with respect, restate what the donor said, and ask polite, probing questions to understand the donor's response.

Discussions take myriad forms and may:

- Revolve around questions of the gifts' purpose and specifications. Donors often desire more details or adjustments, even after everything appears settled.
- Center on how the organization will assess results and be accountable.
- Focus on mechanics of making the gift, including the gift's timing and format. Donors may wish to give less or give more, which must be considered in meeting the organizational purpose and achieving the donor's desired impact.
- Raise organizational concerns or include suggestions. Donors may have lingering issues they wish to address.
- Reflect on obstacles preventing the donor from making the gift, opportunities to leverage the gift to generate others, or forms of recognition.

The conversation is likely to carry across multiple meetings.

Close with a Plan

Work with the donor to establish a course of action. For affirmative conversations, a next step could be reviewing a draft gift agreement or exploring ways of structuring the gift. For a redirected or declined invitation, a follow-up could be a new request for a different amount or purpose, a return to the conversation at an agreed-upon date, a referral to engage differently with the organization, or even a connection to another organization better aligned with the donor's interests.

Thank the donor for engaging in the conversation. Within 24 hours, call, write, or email the donor to express gratitude and confirm the action steps. Fundraisers should also take a moment to celebrate their role in the invitation.

Conclusion

This chapter outlines a practical preparation process to guide invitations to give, originating in the cause and honed through fundraiser reflection and self-awareness. It applies research to utilize throughout the donor relationship, creating a pathway to well-conceived requests. It advocates structured and carefully prepared gift conversations. It refers to a variety of resources that provide donor, fundraiser, and scholarly perspectives.

Invitations to give are key philanthropic moments, but they are beginnings, not endings. They are components of donors' organizational journeys. They are prologues to witnessing gifts' impact on causes and needs and people. To invite gifts and facilitate philanthropy is a profession, privilege, and calling.

Discussion Questions

1. What makes gift invitations important? What makes invitations difficult?
2. How can you use research about donor motivations, active listening, interpersonal competence, and fundraiser/donor relationships to develop engagement plans and invitations to give?
3. What techniques and donor information can be used to determine appropriate timing and approaches for invitations to give?

Application Exercises

1. Revisit your feelings about asking for money. Complete the personal preparation process described in the chapter.

2. Engage in an active listening exercise by encouraging a colleague, friend, or family member to talk about an important topic. Use the information in this chapter to assess your listening skills afterward.

3. Ask a fundraiser to share stories of their invitations to give. Find out how they made decisions about when and how to ask. Also talk to a donor about their experiences. Summarize what you learned.

4. Create a simple role-playing scenario and practice the invitation to give conversation. Take turns playing the donor and the fundraiser. Debrief afterward, considering each perspective.

CHAPTER THIRTY-FIVE

CAMPAIGN ESSENTIALS

By Aaron Conley

The nonprofit sector has changed in many ways since the first edition of this book, but campaigns have remained an important fundraising tool. This chapter builds on Rosso's campaign principles (1991) and addresses contemporary questions.

This chapter will help readers to:

- Distinguish among types of campaigns.
- Understand the importance of planning (and the risks incurred by not planning).
- Learn how to structure and conduct a campaign.

Campaign Types

The campaign concept can be traced to 1905 when the YMCA in Washington, DC, retained Charles Sumner Ward of Chicago to help raise funds for a new building (Cutlip 1965). Shortly thereafter, the University of Pittsburgh hired him to apply the "Ward method" to manage a $3 million campaign. Fundamentals included careful planning and organization, committed volunteers, prestigious leadership figures, recognition and publicity, matching gifts, accurate records and reporting, and a definite time limit. These elements remain applicable across nonprofit organizations and campaign efforts, while another feature is becoming increasingly present.

Modern campaigns now take place with greater recognition of individual donors' diversity. Understandings of philanthropy are more inclusive. Women are assuming more visible and prominent roles in driving philanthropic initiatives, as are younger donors and those from diverse backgrounds and gender identities. Successful campaigns need to recognize the importance of diverse donor populations (and the concerns of a diverse society in general) and engage all interested parties in giving *and* in planning and leading campaigns (Grant and Shiller 2020).

Comprehensive Campaign

This chapter focuses specifically on comprehensive campaigns, which are especially prevalent within large organizations such as hospitals, colleges and universities, and major arts and cultural institutions. These multi-year efforts include a defined set of campaign priorities with dollar goals collectively adding up to an overall goal. Gifts and documented pledges from all sources are counted, from annual gifts to multimillion-dollar commitments and bequest intentions. The value of in-kind contributions may also be incorporated depending on the organization's counting policies. General guidance and recommendations on counting and reporting are available from the National Association of Charitable Gift Planners (2017). A similar reference for education campaigns is available from the Council for Advancement and Support of Education (2021).

Rosso (1991) identified three other campaign types, which are summarized here along with an additional contemporary form. Each can be incorporated within a comprehensive campaign or be a stand-alone effort.

Capital Campaign

This term is often incorrectly applied today to comprehensive campaigns. Its historical use referenced an organization's physical assets (Kelly 1998). These include "capital" purposes, such as building construction, renovation, large equipment investments, and real estate to facilitate expansion. Such campaigns may also focus on increasing endowment resources to help maintain capital assets. The distinguishing feature between capital and comprehensive campaigns is that dollars raised for noncapital purposes, such as unrestricted annual fund gifts or bequests, would not count toward a capital campaign goal.

Endowment Campaign

This type also applies many principles of a capital or comprehensive campaign, except with greater emphasis on bequests and other deferred gifts designated specifically for endowed purposes. Older individuals are the primary donor constituency. Corporations and foundations with policies allowing endowment gifts may also be solicited.

Major Gift/Special Project Campaign

Organizations that do not undertake comprehensive campaigns or that are between such efforts often pursue smaller and shorter campaigns with narrowly defined outcomes. Dove (2000) called these "single-purpose campaigns." He also defines *sub campaigns* as part of an organization's continuous major gift program that address smaller initiatives in concert with overall priorities. For example, colleges seeking to increase planned gifts may offer challenge funds to motivate potential donors for a limited time.

Giving Day Campaign

This relatively new campaign form features an intensely brief timeframe but shares the other characteristics of the Ward method. These may take place on #GivingTuesday (in the week after the U.S. Thanksgiving holiday), on any day designated by the organization, or on a date established by a community foundation to raise support for nonprofits in a city, county, state, or region. While most visibly associated with raising large numbers of small gifts through a dedicated website, these popular campaigns also increasingly seek commitments from major donors and include peer-to-peer solicitations (see Chapter 24).

Fundamental Structure of a Campaign

Rosso (1991) defined a campaign as an "intensive function designed to raise a specified sum of money within a defined timeframe to meet the varied asset-building needs of the organization" (80). This section provides insight into structuring campaigns to meet these objectives and requirements.

An organization's governing board must be involved in the planning process, long before any recommendation or approval is granted to undertake a campaign. This commonly takes the form of a planning committee comprised of board members who are supported by fundraising staff, and potentially, external fundraising counsel. One desired outcome is a board that is well-informed on potential campaign priorities and parameters, including the time period. All too often, campaign end dates are not formally established or officially announced. Organizations that conduct campaigns without an end date may be sparing themselves the potential of failure in their constituents' eyes. However, they are also diminishing a campaign's most vital attribute: a sense of urgency to act.

An end date first serves as an internal commitment before the campaign goes public. Then, this date allows for visualization of progress toward the goal, creating the urgency of a defined timeframe. Figure 35.1 provides a sample progress chart for a $10 million goal over five years. The straight diagonal line represents the

FIGURE 35.1. SAMPLE CAMPAIGN PROGRESS CHART FOR A $10 MILLION CAMPAIGN

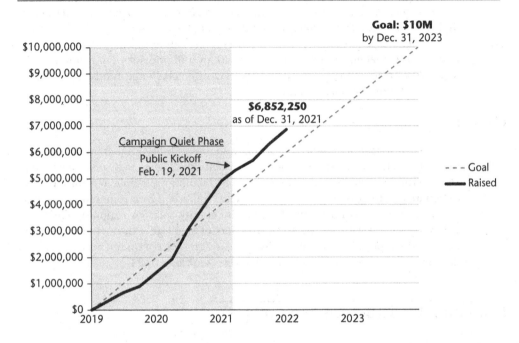

necessary projected dollars at specific time points – in this case, $2 million annually or $500,000 quarterly. This format affirms whether a campaign is ahead or behind the necessary pace when the amount raised is above or below the diagonal baseline.

Figure 35.2 uses the same concept of time and dollars to illustrate campaign phases and critical steps within each. Note that two phases fall outside the formal boundaries of the campaign's official timeframe.

Precampaign Planning

Campaign plans should align with the organization's strategic plan. Organizations without a strategic plan at a minimum should have a "statement of strategic direction" that explains the organization's identity and vision for the future (O'Brien 2005). Precampaign planning is critical to orient everyone – executives and board members, fundraising staff, and volunteer leaders – to consider the campaign from both the organization and donor perspective. Exhibit 35.3 is adapted from Rosso's (1991) campaign readiness exercise to test the internal campaign capacity (also sometimes completed through a development audit). Some of the components are more critical and weighted accordingly.

FIGURE 35.2. PHASES OF A CAMPAIGN

PRECAMPAIGN PLANNING	QUIET PHASE	CAMPAIGN KICKOFF & PUBLIC PHASE	CAMPAIGN CLOSING & CELEBRATION	STEWARDSHIP & CAMPAIGN IMPACT
Assess internal readiness	Select a start date when gifts begin counting toward goal	Set final dollar goal and campaign end date	Use end date as tool to secure new donors	Steward all campaign donors
Review past giving history	Solicit gifts from longtime donors, volunteer leaders and org. leaders	Publicly launch campaign through formal event(s), promote to wider audience with press and social media announcements	Go back to the "uncommitted" for a final ask	Create campaign impact report or summary
Conduct feasibility study	Finalize campaign case for support	Continue soliciting gifts from closest supporters	Formally end campaign with event(s), public announcement	Share campaign impact stories through website and social media
Secure and train volunteer leaders	Generate communication tools for public phase	Begin soliciting gifts from new sources		Assess processes in preparation for future campaigns
Test your campaign case		Tell impactful stories of donor support		
Develop communication plan		Communicate regularly with volunteer leadership		

DOLLARS RAISED

CAMPAIGN TIMELINE

409

EXHIBIT 35.3. CAMPAIGN READINESS TEST (ADAPTED FROM ROSSO 1991)

Score (0 to 5)

_____ 1.   Institutional plans. *Is there a strategic plan or other multi-year plan identifying specific needs prepared by senior leaders and approved by the board?*

_____ 2.   Written statement of case, needs, and goals. *Does a written case exist identifying the mission as an expression of organizational values?*

_____ 3.   Constituency. *Have constituencies been identified beyond those who are already closely involved? Is a cultivation program in place to engage them?*

_____ 4.   Market involvement. *Can staff and board members identify groups of potential gift sources, including individuals, corporations, and foundations? Are there structures to appeal to the interests of different groups?*

_____ 5.   Gift support history. *Is there a history of sustained fundraising activity for current program support, capital, endowment, and special gifts? Is historical information available to analyze the potential for campaigns?*

_____ 6.   Prospective donor development plan. *Is there an active prospective donor development plan in place? Is there a prospective donor development committee, and is time devoted regularly by staff and volunteers to discuss this population?*

_____ 7.   Efficient recordkeeping system. *Are gift-receiving, gift-recording, gift-reporting, and gift-acknowledging procedures established and functioning properly?*

_____ 8.   Communications. *Are communications a two-way system of informing and receiving feedback from constituencies, including beneficiaries?*

Score (0 to 10)

_____ 9.   Fundraising staff. *Is competent, qualified staff available to plan and direct the campaign and to provide the support that volunteer leaders will require? Will the organization's management and all staff fully support the fundraising staff throughout the campaign?*

Score (0 to 15)

_____ 10. Involved board. *Have board members asserted themselves as primary stewards of the organization? Has the board been actively involved in generating resources through fundraising? Are board members willing to give according to their abilities and ask others?*

_____ 11. Potential large gifts. *Have enough valid prospects been identified for the top levels of a draft campaign gift range chart?*

Score (0 to 20)

_____ 12. Fundraising leadership. *Does the organization have the quality of volunteer leadership that will give the energy, enthusiasm, and drive needed for success?*

_____ **TOTAL** (Maximum score = 100)

A score of 75 to 100 indicates a reasonable chance for success.

A score of 50 to 75 means there are some issues to address before any decision can be made to move forward with a campaign.

A score below 50 serves as a warning that the organization is likely not ready. The lowest-scoring components should be closely examined and resolved before proceeding with campaign plans.

Precampaign Study. Often referred to as a feasibility or planning study, this exercise allows for deeper exploration into many of the readiness test components. A consultant is commonly engaged to assist with elements beyond organizational expertise or capacity. This may include drafting the case, assessing past giving, interpreting wealth screening projections, and evaluating publications and communication strategies (Maxwell 2011). Board members and close donors sometimes help underwrite expenses related to the precampaign study.

Case Statement. This statement articulates how a campaign will enable supporters to fulfill the need(s) the organization exists to serve as established in the strategic plan. A case statement is first developed within the organization and will go through several iterations as the process forces critical thinking about the organization's mission, structure, and effectiveness in service delivery. The case will then be shared externally with a limited number of potential lead donors to determine whether it resonates with them and the larger constituencies who will be solicited later in the public phase. A consultant often conducts personal and confidential interviews on behalf of an organization to gather this critical feedback.

Revisions should continue as initial lead gifts are made. Some of these donors may not have been involved in the planning study and will be seeing the case for the first time. Acknowledging and considering feedback can help refine the case and involve all lead donors in a meaningful way prior to the public launch.

Board Preparation. Board members may have previous campaign experience from other organizations, and new board members can also be sought with fundraising experience. If needed, local community foundations or Association of Fundraising Professionals' chapters may offer campaign seminars or other expert guidance. Larger service providers, including The Fund Raising School, may also be engaged for training.

Setting a Goal. Among this stage's most critical outcomes is a projected dollar goal based on a realistic assessment of the donor base, articulated through a gift range chart. Failure to determine whether there are enough prospective donors to meet the goal is one of the most common causes of an unsuccessful campaign. An initial chart can be developed early in preplanning to educate board members and others on numbers and levels of gifts needed to meet a desired goal. Findings from the feasibility study should then be used to refine the projection. Table 35.4 is a sample gift range chart based on the same $10 million campaign represented in Figure 35.1.

Organizations must use their own data and knowledge about their current and potential donors to create a campaign gift range chart. These charts are not one size fits all. Table 35.4 assumes that candidates for the top levels of gifts are known to the organization and uses a 3-to-1 ratio before increasing the ratio of

TABLE 35.4. POTENTIAL GIFT RANGE CHART FOR A $10 MILLION CAMPAIGN

Gift Amount	Gifts Needed	Potential Donors Needed	Cumulative Total	Cumulative % Toward Goal
$2,000,000	1	3	$2,000,000	20%
$1,000,000	2	6	$4,000,000	40%
$500,000	4	12	$6,000,000	60%
$100,000	10	40	$7,000,000	70%
$50,000	15	60	$7,750,000	78%
$25,000	20	80	$8,250,000	82.5%
$10,000	50	200	$8,750,000	87.5%
< $10,000	Many	Many	**$10,000,000**	**100%**

potential donors for the next group of gifts to 4-to-1. A more complex chart could further break down gifts below $10,000 with ratios of 5-to-1 and beyond. These ratios and gift levels will vary by organization. Charts can also follow an estimate of the percentage of donors to dollars. Historically, it was common to use a baseline of about 80 percent of campaign dollars coming from 20 percent of the donors. This rule has shifted in recent decades to 90/10 and even 95/5. A long-running study of higher education campaigns conducted by the Council for Advancement and Support of Education (2017) noted that 79 percent of campaign dollars in 2015 came from the top 1 percent of donors, an increase from 64 percent in 2006.

Campaign Budget. An initial chart also helps inform projections for a campaign budget. The size and scope of potential donor populations at the various gift levels enables organizations to estimate the campaign's necessary investments. For example, upper-level donors will likely require personal contact with associated travel costs. The Fund Raising School recommends initially estimating a budget based on 5 to 15 percent of the campaign goal (2018). Again, using a $10 million goal, a 10 percent budget estimate would total $1 million overall, or $200,000, for each of the five campaign years. This amount is in addition to the existing fundraising budget.

Volunteer Leadership. Campaign volunteer structures and sizes vary widely and may include honorary chairs who add value by lending their names as public endorsements. There may be subcommittees for different gift sources and amounts, units within large organizations, and aspects of the campaign (i.e., planning campaign events). All volunteer leaders should know the expectation for a campaign gift and the utilization of their time. Volunteers may also participate in the campaign in other, one-time, or more limited capacities.

Communication Plan. A plan should be developed in this phase to articulate how various constituencies will be informed about the campaign. These plans are defined by available budget resources, as costs must be closely examined for creating websites, videos, and print and digital communication tools for solicitation and generating broader awareness.

Quiet Phase

This phase commences on the date selected to begin counting gifts toward the goal, although this can sometimes be retroactive to incorporate early and unexpected large gifts, and includes completing any remaining planning items. This date is initially known only among the leadership and governing board, key volunteers, and fundraising staff. Through the planning study, a potential dollar goal or range should be accepted among the campaign's leadership, with the understanding that a finalized figure will be established later.

Rosso's (1991) model of sequential solicitation, defined through the dual processes of "top-down" and "inside-out," guides the progression of this phase. Top-down is the process of soliciting lead gifts from prospective donors identified at the top of the gift range chart and sequentially proceeding into the next levels. As Rosso observed, campaigns do not begin effectively with a mass solicitation to all possible donors; "Small gifts are graciously received, but they do not contribute as much to the desired outcome as do the larger gifts" (92).

Inside-out drives gift participation at all levels, beginning with those inside the organization who are not in the top tiers of the gift range chart. This includes employees, volunteers, and potentially some board members. These will be relatively small gifts, but strong early participation by these groups can later be compelling to potential major donors.

Consensus is needed on the final dollar goal and the campaign end date to conclude the quiet phase. Both will be informed by the top-down process, outcomes of initial solicitations, and the feasibility study. The quiet phase should be long enough to determine if the recommended dollar goal (from the planning study) is proving realistic. If there is less support than was anticipated, the quiet phase provides the opportunity to lower the goal or lengthen the timeframe before launching publicly. This reinforces the importance of not publicizing the goal and timeframe before the public launch and ensuring both are approved by the governing board.

Campaign Kickoff and Public Phase

This phase represents the most visible and exciting time in a campaign as the growing donor base and dollars raised generate substantial momentum. It can also be time-intensive and stressful as the organization publicly commences the campaign.

Methods of formally launching a campaign vary greatly, but commonly align with an organization's culture and budget resources. Some use a large and formal ceremony catering to major donors, while others opt for an informal, grassroots approach that engages a broad constituency. Widely available technologies even allow for completely virtual launches aimed at reaching donors through social media.

Regardless of the form of kickoff vehicle to be used, the last step prior to setting the campaign launch date is an assessment of gifts raised and the remaining potential major donor pool yet to be solicited. Most organizations begin the public phase after raising approximately 50 percent of the goal. Commencing this phase with less, such as 20 to 30 percent, may give the impression that the campaign lacks momentum. Launching with more, such as 70 to 80 percent, may leave potential donors feeling success can be achieved without their support.

This phase also includes solicitations for smaller gifts from broader audiences, while continuing the focus on major gifts. Potential mid-level donors may be influenced by the larger gifts announced at the public kickoff. Multiple studies note that donations can be strongly related to social influences and pressures (Bekkers and Wiepking 2011a).

Campaign Closing and Celebration

The campaign closing brings two important solicitation opportunities. The first is to encourage new donors to be part of a successful effort. This emphasis on participation can be invaluable in expanding the donor base and thereby improve the potential for larger future campaigns. The other opportunity is to go back to the "uncommitted," prospective major gift donors who were approached earlier but deferred due to poor timing or other reasons.

The final and most visible activity of this phase is a closing event or announcement to recognize the campaign total and celebrate success. A campaign closing should demonstrate that the hospital, museum, food pantry, or other institution did not undertake the campaign simply to raise money, but rather to serve a larger purpose.

Stewardship and Campaign Impact

The campaign celebration indicates the effort's official end, but follow-through activities position future achievements. Most prominently, a successful campaign has engaged long-time donors and welcomes a vital population of first-time supporters. A notable challenge is determining how to effectively thank a base of donors across multiple gift levels, and one that has likely expanded significantly.

Wherever possible, there is no substitute for personal engagement. The executive leadership team should commit to speak with as many campaign donors as possible for the sole purpose of expressing thanks. This not only includes the largest donors, but those new donors who show promise for long-term engagement and future support.

Other stewardship strategies can provide this personal element while reaching far greater numbers of donors. Some suggestions include:

- Small group events (virtual and in-person) for volunteers or donors who gave above a specified level.
- Publications such as an impact report that summarizes campaign outcomes and recognizes donors.
- Digital messaging (text and video) disseminated via email, social media channels, and the organization's website.
- Permanent signage acknowledging the amount raised and impact. This could also highlight names of volunteer leadership, major donors, or other key figures.

Last, a comprehensive review yields helpful insights to inform future campaigns. A post-campaign assessment should address such questions as:

- Was the increase in gift volume managed effectively with timely processing and acknowledgments?
- Was timely research information provided to staff and volunteers about prospective donors?
- Could gift proposals be drafted, reviewed, and approved more quickly?
- Was the process effective for scheduling time for the leader(s) to meet with donors?
- Are there ways to improve internal processes, such as arranging travel and reimbursing expenses?
- Did staff and volunteers feel informed regarding campaign progress?

Operational matters should obviously be addressed as they arise, but the demands of a campaign can easily overshadow ongoing processes. A post-campaign assessment, internally led or with help from a consultant, gives the entire organizational team the opportunity to provide feedback.

Conclusion

The global pandemic and economic turbulence of 2020–2021 widely affected charitable giving. Many organizations proceeded with campaigns, but adjusted how they engaged with donors and volunteers (CCS 2021; 2020; Haynes 2021a). As organizations face crises and unexpected events with significant consequences for their communities or services, they must maintain a focus on the 10 to 20 individuals, foundations, or corporations representing the top potential donors within their gift range chart. The economic health of these donors and their philanthropic priorities will always help determine if a campaign is feasible, and their continued engagement will inform campaign priorities, goal setting, and messaging.

Campaigns challenge the patience and resolve of staff, senior management, and boards. They require significant resources along with confidence there will be a justifiable return on investment. And they will test every operational function of a fundraising program. However, a well-planned and carefully initiated campaign's benefits far outweigh short-term strife.

Periodic, successful campaigns as a complement to a regular fundraising program benefit organizations financially. They also substantially expand organizations' brand and visibility, engage new constituencies, and draw on various sources of philanthropic support. Campaigns may represent a new form of fundraising for many organizations, but as Rosso (1991) noted, "Diversity of funding is the secret of financial stability. Diversity of fundraising methods adds to that security" (292).

Discussion Questions

1. Identify the core features of a comprehensive campaign. Explain how one or more of the other types of campaigns could be incorporated into a larger comprehensive campaign.
2. Name and explain the phases of campaigns and their components. How could the activities in each phase be tailored for a particular organization or campaign type?
3. Why is it important to publicly announce an end date for a campaign? What if the board chair objects to listing an end date on the campaign website and other promotional materials?

Application Exercises

1. Construct a gift range chart with an initial goal of $25 million. Next, explore how you would modify the chart, while retaining the $25 million goal, if the solicitations for the top gift are all unsuccessful during the quiet phase.
2. Complete the Campaign Readiness Test for an organization you are familiar with. If you are unable to rate some of the components, what information is needed for finishing the assessment?
3. Explore the promotional materials for one organization's campaign. How does what you discover align with the information in the chapter about necessary elements of successful campaigns?

CHAPTER THIRTY-SIX

PLANNED GIVING PRINCIPLES

By Russell N. James III

For many fundraisers, planned giving just feels scary. It has so many rules about taxes, asset, and trusts. How can you know everything? Worse, it often deals with death! How do you talk to someone about their death? And yet, planned giving can be powerful. It can help donors and nonprofits do more than they ever thought possible.

Fear not! Planned giving does not have to be hyper-technical. It does not have to focus on death. There are answers.

This chapter reviews the latest research and practices so that readers will be able to:

- Recognize organizational and donor motivations for using planned giving.
- Understand the basic ideas behind various planned giving instruments.
- Describe research-based principles for communicating on planned giving topics.
- Identify key audience members for planned giving messages.

The Justification: Why Planned Giving?

In order to understand why planned giving is important, it helps to know what it is. In its broadest form, planned giving is any donation other than an immediate cash gift. It includes a wide variety of instruments, strategies, and approaches. It achieves donors' philanthropic priorities, bringing them a number of positive outcomes (see Chapter 5), and can provide extra donor benefits, including tax avoidance, income, and continued management or control of wealth. It can combine current, future, estate, and asset gifts. (Combinations with current gifts can also be called "blended" gifts.)

The justification for planned gift fundraising usually starts with bequest gifts. In the United States, over $41 billion in charitable bequests were transferred in 2020 (Giving USA 2021). With an aging population, such gifts are expected to grow. Further, compared with previous generations, the "Baby Boom" generation is not just larger, but also more likely to be childless and have higher education – both of which predict increased propensity to make charitable bequests (James III 2015).

Another justification for planned giving is that it allows donors to give much more than they otherwise could. As creative planning increases tax or income benefits, it reduces the cost of the gift. It also allows that cost to be spread out in a way that fits with the donor's other financial goals, such as retirement planning.

Another important argument for planned giving is its behavioral effects. Planned giving is special because it usually involves gifts from assets, rather than disposable income. This is a key mindset difference for donors. Gifts from disposable income tend to be compared with other daily or weekly expenditures, a relatively small reference point (Gourville 1998). Gifts from assets tend to be compared with wealth, a relatively large reference point. Thus, the same size gift might feel ridiculously large when compared with other disposable income purchases, but quite reasonable when compared with total wealth. In experiments, reminding people of their wealth changes spending behavior (Morewedge, Holtzman, and Epley 2007). People are more generous with irregular, unearned money than with regular, earned income (Reinstein and Riener 2012). Thus shifting donors toward gifts of appreciated assets, rather than gifts of disposable income, may dramatically increase giving.

Some national empirical evidence supports this idea. One analysis of over a million nonprofit tax returns found that raising funds from noncash assets predicted future fundraising success (James III 2018a). For example, nonprofits receiving gifts from securities, on average, experienced a 106 percent greater growth in total contributions five years later. This relationship was true regardless of the organization's size or cause type.

Bequest gifts are also a planned gift of assets. A "before and after" comparison from a national dataset found that annual inflation-adjusted giving increased about 77 percent after donors added charity to their estate plans (James III 2020). This dramatic increase was sustained two, four, six, and even eight years later. Thus, far from cannibalizing current giving, planning an estate gift preceded a dramatic increase in current giving. Such plans also can generate estate gifts and may increase interest in irrevocable alternatives (discussed later) that provide more tax and income benefits.

The Tools: What Can You Do with It?

Planned giving can get complicated. There are tax laws, trust laws, detailed accounting, and acronyms. However, in most cases, the planned giving tools either trade a gift for income or increase tax benefits.

Trade a Gift for Income

Several tools provide income in different ways.

- *Charitable Gift Annuity (CGA):* A donor makes a gift to a charity, and in return, receives fixed payments for life from the charity. This can be paid to and for the life of any one or two people selected by the donor. Payments may start immediately or after a period of time.
- *Charitable Remainder Uni-Trust (CRUT):* A donor makes a gift to a trust, and in return, receives payments of a set percentage (5–50 percent) of the annual value of the trust for life (or a period of up to 20 years) from the trust. Anything left at the end goes to a selected charity. (If payments are a fixed amount, rather than a fixed percentage, this is a *Charitable Remainder Annuity Trust (CRAT)*.) Payments can also be made to (and for the life of) other people selected by the donor. Variations include,
  - *Net Income CRUT or NICRUT:* Payments may not exceed annual income of the trust.
  - *Net Income Makeup CRUT or NIMCRUT:* Payments may not exceed annual income of the trust, but past deficiencies can be made up if future income is larger.
  - *Flip-CRUT:* Payments may not exceed income only at first, but then "flip" to mandatory payments after an event such as the donor reaching retirement age or the sale of a difficult-to-market asset.
- *Pooled Income Fund (PIF).* A donor makes a gift that is pooled with other donors' gifts and invested. The donor receives a share of income earned each year by the pooled funds for the donor's life.

Increase Tax Benefits

Planned giving can also create tax benefits from giving by helping avoid capital gains taxes, estate taxes, and income taxes.

Avoid Capital Gains Taxes. A donor can write a $1,000 check. The donor gets a $1,000 tax deduction, worth up to $370 ($1,000 × 37%) on a federal tax return. But suppose the donor instead gives a $1,000 asset purchased for $100 over a year ago. The donor still gets a $1,000 tax deduction, plus the donor avoids $214.20 in federal capital gains tax ($900 capital gain × 23.8%). This capital gains tax benefit does not require the donor to be itemizing their tax deductions.

This need not even require changing the donor's portfolio. In a "charitable swap," instead of giving $1,000 of cash to the charity, the donor gives $1,000 of appreciated stock and uses the cash to immediately purchase identical shares of the same stock. Afterward, the portfolio looks the same, except the newly purchased shares have no capital gain.

Avoiding capital gains tax becomes even more powerful when the donor is also getting income from the gift. Suppose a donor has a $1,000,000 nonincome-producing asset originally purchased for $100,000. The donor wants to sell it, invest it, and use the 5 percent annual earnings for retirement. But selling it means paying capital gains tax. A $900,000 capital gain × 23.8% = $214,200 in tax. Thus, after a sale, the $1,000,000 becomes just $785,800. The donor's income is only $39,290 ($785,800 × 5%). If instead, the donor gives it to their CRUT, the CRUT can sell the asset with no up-front capital gains taxes. After a sale, the full $1,000,000 is still available. The donor's income is $50,000 ($1,000,000 × 5%).

Avoid Income Taxes. With planned giving, a donor can take an income tax deduction today, even though a public charity will not receive a gift for many years. For example, a gift to a *Donor-Advised Fund* (DAF) or *Private Foundation* creates an immediate income tax deduction, but provides the donor time to disburse the funds to a public charity (see Chapters 37 and 38). If a donor puts assets inside a *Grantor Charitable Lead Trust* that will make annual payments to charity, the donor immediately gets an income tax deduction for the present value of all the years of future gifts. Plus, the donor gets anything left over in the trust at the end.

With a *CRUT*, the charity receives anything left over at the end of the donor's life (or the life of whomever the donor chooses as the lifetime beneficiary or after a set period of years). This transfer is often many decades away. Nevertheless, the donor immediately gets an income tax deduction based on the estimated value of this future transfer. Similarly, donating the inheritance rights to farmland or a personal residence by deed (called a *Retained Life Estate*) also creates an immediate income tax deduction.

Charitable instruments can also shelter investments from ongoing taxation. For example, suppose a *CRUT* invested $1 million that was later sold for $2 million. At the sale, no taxes are paid. The full $2 million is still available. At a 5 percent payout, the donor's income is now $100,000 ($2,000,000 × 5%). If the donor's retirement investments had not been in a *CRUT*, that sale would have created $1 million of income along with a large tax bill due immediately. In the same way, investment growth inside a donor advised fund is tax free and inside a private foundation pays only 1.39 percent of net investment income.

For donors age 70+, a gift directly from an IRA, called a *Qualified Charitable Distribution*, avoids income taxes. Money inside an Individual Retirement Account (IRA) has not yet been taxed. When it is taken out, either voluntarily, or starting at age 72, through a *Required Minimum Distribution*, income taxes must be paid. But a *Qualified Charitable Distribution* counts against the *Required Minimum Distribution*, thus avoiding those income taxes.

Avoid Estate Taxes. Anything left to charity in an estate plan avoids estate taxation. Any money in an IRA inherited by a charity avoids the income taxes that would otherwise have to be paid.

Assets transferred into a *Non-Grantor Charitable Lead Trust* make fixed payments to charity for a set number of years with any remaining amount going to selected heirs. Gift or estate taxes are paid only on the amount that is *projected* to be left over at the end for heirs. Nothing is paid on the amount *actually* transferred to heirs. Thus, any growth above the initial § 7520 interest rate goes to heirs completely free of estate and gift taxes. For a donor who was already planning to make such donations, using this instrument with a $0 *projected* remainder for heirs provides a no-cost chance at tax-free *actual* transfers to heirs.

Finally, these income, estate, and capital gains tax benefits can be stacked together. An estate plan can include a gift to a *Non-Grantor Charitable Lead Trust* making annual payments to the decedent's *Private Family Foundation* for 20 years with the remainder going to heirs. A complex appreciated asset can go to a *Charitable Remainder Trust* that pays income for life and then goes to a *Donor-Advised Fund*. The income and tax benefits, including state-level tax benefits, can stack together to produce extreme results (Yeoman 2014).

The Messages: How Should You Say It?

Planned giving can get complicated. But ultimately these are just methods that allow a donor to make a larger gift. Planned giving is for those moments when the donor says, "I wish I could do more, but. . . ." When that barrier is a financial concern, planned giving can sometimes help address that circumstance by delaying the gift or providing income or tax benefits. Nevertheless, a gift must still be motivated by the desire to accomplish a philanthropic goal, not just a financial one. Uncovering these philanthropic desires – and any financial barriers – often comes through personal conversations predicated on strong relationships.

And how, then, should fundraisers discuss these complicated options with donors? Experimental research suggests the power of the old rule: Keep it simple. For example, using technical, financial, "insider" terms (e.g., *Charitable Remainder Trust, Charitable Gift Annuity*) rather than simply describing what the arrangement actually *does*, reduced interest in making the gift (James III 2018b).

Despite all this potential intricacy, for most charities, the bulk of planned giving contributions come as estate gifts. How should fundraisers talk about these? The same simplicity rule still applies. For example, people were much more interested in learning about "gifts in wills" rather than "estate giving," "legacy giving," or "bequest gifts" (James III 2018c).

Simplicity helps, but this does not deal with one major issue. Most planned giving is about death. Specifically, it is about the donor's death. This can make such conversations feel scary, or at least uncomfortable. How should we talk about death?

To answer this question, it helps to understand some academic research. The psychological problem with death is that you disappear. The solutions are to ignore the problem (called "avoidance") and/or to live on after death (called pursuit of "symbolic immortality" or "lasting social impact") (James III 2016a; Kosloff, Anderson, Nottbohm, and Hoshiko 2019).

Avoidance can be expressed by ignoring, staying away from, or postponing interactions with death reminders. Thus, if we want to attract a larger audience, it is often a good idea not to lead with death. In experiments, people were significantly more willing to "Make a gift to charity in my last will & testament" than to "Make a gift to charity in my last will & testament that will take effect at my death" (James III 2016b). Stories about planned gifts in wills by other *living* donors were more influential than identical stories about *deceased* donors (James III and Routley 2016). Similarly, people were much more interested in reading about "Other ways to give smarter" (which is not focused on death), rather than reading about "Planned giving" (which is more associated with death planning), even though they expected to receive estate planning information with either description (James III 2018c).

The desire to live on ("symbolic immortality") makes *permanence* particularly attractive in death-related contexts. In one experiment, a poverty relief charity was described as either "meeting the immediate needs of people" or "creating lasting improvements that would benefit people in the future" (Wade-Benzoni, Tost, Hernandez, and Larrick 2012). Normally, the first description generated more donations. But for people who were first reminded of their mortality, the results reversed, and the permanence language generated more donations. In another experiment, the most powerful motivation to make a second gift in memory of a loved one was the chance to make their named fund permanent (James III 2019a). Thus, in planned giving, donors may be particularly attracted to endowments, scholarships, building namings, or other options that provide a sense of permanence.

For this permanence to be meaningful, it must be a lasting expression of the donor's identity (i.e., the donor's people, values, or life story). In other words, it must provide a way for the donor's story or values to "live on." Thus, it is essential that the organization's case for support matches with the donor's values and life story. The importance of connecting the donor's life story with the bequest gift has arisen in research using qualitative interviews (Routley and Sargeant 2015), neuroimaging (James III and O'Boyle 2014), and phrasing experiments.

For example, in one study testing 24 different bequest gift descriptions among nearly 10,000 participants, the phrase generating the highest intention to give was "Make a gift to charity in your will to support causes that have been important in your life" (James III 2016b). Similarly, the social norm statement, "Many people like to leave a gift to charity in their will" became more powerful when it was changed to "Many people like to leave a gift to charity in their will because they care about causes that are important in their lives."

Another way to connect with the donor's life story is to suggest a charitable bequest gift in honor of a family member with a connection to the cause. Experimental research shows that such suggestions increase intentions to leave a bequest for many people (James III 2015b).

The Audience: Where Should You Focus?

Fundraisers do not have time to talk to everyone. So, where should you spend your time? Some people are more open to making a charitable bequest than others. Both consistent donors and the childless are much more likely to plan such gifts (James III 2009). Wealth is important. A donor who does not have it cannot leave it to an organization. As wealth increases, both the likelihood of leaving a gift to charity and the average share of the estate going to charity increases (James III 2019b). Black people and Hispanic people express relatively high interest in leaving a charitable bequest (Lehman and James III 2018) and are just as likely as non-Hispanic White people to include charity when completing a will or trust document, but they are dramatically less likely to have a will or trust documents (James III 2009). This matches other research finding lower access to formal legal services among minority groups, and suggests that fundraisers and advisors can serve an important role in helping to overcome this estate planning documentation barrier (James III 2020). Age is a dominant factor for charitable bequests. For estates over $1 million, 55 percent of charitable dollars came from decedents older than 85, while only 4 percent came from those under 65 (Joulfaian 2005). Why? First, wealthy people tend to live longer (Makaroun, Brown, Diaz-Ramirez, Ahalt, Boscardin, Lang-Brown, and Lee 2017). Second, among the wealthy (top 5% of wealth holders), wealth increases with age every year – even to age 95 and beyond (Kopczuk 2007). Finally, as people age, they become more likely to include charity in their estate plans (Joulfaian 2005). With increasing longevity, the dominance of older decedents is increasing. Among estate returns filed in 1963, 1970, 1973, 1983, 1990, and for 2003 decedents, those aged 75 and older made up, respectively, 65 percent, 70 percent, 72 percent, 77 percent, 83 percent, and 83 percent of all charitable bequest donors.

Charitable dollars are transferred at the oldest ages. This explains why, despite some lofty predictions, inflation-adjusted bequest giving was essentially flat from 2000 to 2013 (Giving USA 2021). Although media attention was focused on the "Baby Boom" generation, those in the over-80 age group who generate the bulk of charitable bequest dollars were from the "Baby Bust" generation. This depression-era cohort was part of a dramatic drop in fertility.

Charitable bequest decisions that control final transfers appear to be made at the oldest ages and near the end of life. For example, a national sample of Australian wills found that 76 percent of all charitable bequest dollars were transferred by wills signed in the 80s or older (James III and Baker 2015). In the same study, most probated charitable wills were signed within five years of death. A longitudinal study in the United States found that among adults over 50, the ten-year retention rate of a charitable estate component was about 55 percent. Further, the majority of decedents making charitable estate transfers had no charity in their estate plan at some point within five years of death.

Taken together, the evidence shows a high level of older age and end-of-life fluidity in charitable bequest plans. Although such fluidity is not a concern for irrevocable planned giving instruments, these gifts are also typically made at somewhat older ages. Charitable remainder trust creation tends to peak between ages 70–74 (Franey and James III 2013) and charitable gift annuity creation peaks between ages 75–79 (American Council on Gift Annuities 2018).

The fluidity of revocable charitable bequest decisions means that organizations need to keep donors engaged after gift commitments are made. One study found that among 700 decedents who had confirmed having a planned bequest gift to the charity, 35 percent generated no estate gift (Wishart and James III in press). This loss rate averaged 24 percent when the charity had at least one communication with the decedent within two years of death, and 48 percent otherwise.

Conclusion

Understanding planned giving requires work on the part of the fundraiser. But it can help both the nonprofit and the donor. Although potentially complex, most instruments aim to increase tax benefits or trade a gift for income. Such benefits can allow the donor to give much more than would otherwise be possible. Powerful messages often focus on simple terms, stories of others like the donor, and giving opportunities that provide permanence and match the donor's values and life story. Key audiences for planned giving fundraising, especially in bequest giving, are older adults, consistent donors, the wealthy, and the childless.

Discussion Questions

1. What is an example of a real-world scenario where planned giving might allow a donor to give more than would otherwise be possible?
2. How would the communication principles discussed here affect the typical "planned giving" brochure?
3. How well do metrics for planned giving success at your nonprofit match the realities of decision-making in revocable charitable bequests?

Application Exercises

1. Find the factors available in your organization's donor database that would help to identify those most likely to include a gift to charity such as age, consistency of donations, and so on. How would you rank these potential donors?
2. Find articles and stories online that reference a planned gift or donor. What is included about the donor's motivations and the technical elements of the planned gift?
3. Find your choice for the "best" and "worst" planned giving advertisements online. What makes the good ones good? What makes the other ads not as good?

CHAPTER THIRTY-SEVEN

DONOR-ADVISED FUND (DAF) BASICS

By Danielle Vance-McMullen and H. Daniel Heist

Donor-advised funds (DAFs) are the fastest-growing form of philanthropy in the United States (National Philanthropic Trust 2021a), and they are changing the way many donors give to charity. DAFs are unusual because, although the assets are managed by institutions like community foundations, DAF giving decisions are essentially made by individual donors. This chapter describes the key characteristics of DAFs and the history and growth of DAF giving. Next, the DAF giving process and benefits to donors are explained, and fundraisers learn how to work with donors who have DAF accounts. The chapter concludes by explaining some of the limitations and criticisms of DAFs.

After reading this chapter, fundraisers will be able to:

- Explain how a DAF works.
- Describe the prevalence of DAFs as a philanthropic vehicle.
- Articulate the DAF giving process and the various strategies donors use with DAFs.
- List the benefits that DAFs offer to donors.
- Develop solicitation strategies for DAF donors.
- Consider critiques of DAFs.

Overview of Donor-Advised Funds

DAFs function like a hybrid between a checking account and an investment account for charitable giving purposes. Donors open a *fund (or account)* by making tax-deductible *contributions* to a DAF *sponsor,* a 501(c)(3) public charity that holds and manages the funds. Donors then use *advisory privileges* to recommend grants from the DAF sponsor to another public charity or private operating foundation. Legally, the sponsor controls the funds; however, the donor recommendations are nearly always followed. In many cases, sponsors also give donors discretion on how funds are invested. Each DAF account may have multiple *donor advisors* authorized to make recommendations. The DAF vehicle provides tremendous flexibility for supporting donors' philanthropic goals.

DAF sponsor organizations can be categorized into three types of varying popularity (see Table 37.1):

- *National* – National sponsor organizations serve a broad client base. These organizations include subsidiaries of commercial financial services providers as well as employer-supported workplace giving organizations.
- *Community Foundation* – Many community foundations (CFs) offer donor-advised funds to local donors. They focus on serving donors within a specific geographic area and promote community-based philanthropy.
- *Cause-related* – Some DAF sponsors were organized to serve donors who associate with a specific cause, typically a religious affiliation. Here, the term *cause-related* is being used in lieu of the term *single-issue* used by National Philanthropic Trust (2021a). Many cause-related DAF sponsors facilitate giving to a variety of issues.

Different types of sponsor organizations appear to serve donors with different giving patterns (Heist and Vance McMullen 2019). Overall, the DAF vehicle facilitates a wide variety of philanthropic activity.

TABLE 37.1. OVERVIEW OF DAF SPONSOR TYPES

Sponsor Type	Number of Sponsors	Number of Funds	% of Total Funds	2020 Assets (Billions)	% of Total Assets
National	53	731,110	84%	$87.23	61%
Community Foundation	607	83,185	10%	$40.22	28%
Cause-Related	333	58,933	7%	$14.50	10%

Source: Based on National Philanthropic Trust 2021.

Donor-Advised Fund History

Arrangements similar to modern DAFs began at CFs in the early twentieth century. During this time, the introduction of the income tax and the deduction for charitable giving incentivized private citizens to become more involved in supporting public charities. After the Tax Act of 1969, private foundations were more regulated, and DAFs began to emerge as an alternative to private foundations (Berman 2015). In the 1990s, commercial investment firms, beginning with Fidelity Investments, created subsidiary charitable organizations to offer their clients "giving accounts." The number of DAFs proliferated through the early 2000s, mostly through national commercial sponsors, and more recently, through workplace giving accounts. The increasing use of DAFs has also contributed to the growth of community foundations.

Donor-Advised Fund Growth

Over the past several decades, DAFs have grown to make a substantial impact on the sector. DAF grantmaking, donations, and assets have set records each year since 2010. The expansion of DAFs is especially striking when compared to other charitable giving vehicles during this same time. Importantly, the growth is caused primarily by the increase in the number of donors who have chosen to give using DAFs.

Assets. The assets held in DAFs have increased steadily in recent years, with total DAF assets reaching $142 billion by the end of fiscal year 2019, which represents approximately 14 percent of the funds held by all private (independent) foundations (Board of Governors of the Federal Reserve System 2020). For community foundations, DAF assets represent a substantial portion of organizations' funds. A survey of CFs found that DAFs make up 22 percent of organizational assets on average, with the largest CFs reporting that DAFs make up more than 36 percent of assets, on average (Candid 2020).

Understanding the average DAF account is more relevant than aggregate national figures for fundraising practice. While some national reports have noted that the mean DAF account size is $162,556, this number is skewed by a few ultralarge DAF accounts (National Philanthropic Trust 2021a). The assets of a typical DAF account vary somewhat based on the policies of the DAF sponsor, especially policies around minimum opening balances. Fidelity Charitable, which has no minimum contribution, reported a median account balance of $21,637 in 2020. Silicon Valley Community Foundation, which has a $5,000 minimum contribution, reported that around 55 percent of accounts had balances less than $100,000 in 2019.

Grantmaking. DAFs granted approximately $27.8 billion to nonprofits in fiscal year 2019 (National Philanthropic Trust 2021a). This figure is approximately one-half of the grantmaking by private (independent) foundations and around 9 percent of the giving by individuals in 2019, according to Giving USA (2020). While overall the pattern of grants from DAFs seems to follow individual giving, DAF grantmaking is more likely to go to education, public-society benefit, and the arts and a bit less likely to go to religion than the other forms of giving (Giving USA 2018).

Grantmaking by DAFs has increased substantially over time. Over the past five years, DAF grants rose by 93 percent (National Philanthropic Trust 2021a). All growth calculations in this section are in current dollars. In comparison, aggregate individual giving rose 17 percent over this time (Giving USA 2020). In periods of economic downturns, DAF grantmaking typically remains relatively robust, especially compared to other areas of philanthropic giving by individuals (Heist and Vance-McMullen 2019). Moreover, DAF grantmaking increased significantly in 2020 in response to the COVID-19 pandemic. During the first six months of 2020, a survey of large DAF sponsors found that the number of DAF grants increased by 37.4 percent and the total value of DAF grants increased by 29.8 percent, compared to 2019 grants for the same period (National Philanthropic Trust 2021b).

Contributions. In fiscal year 2019, $39 billion was contributed to DAFs (National Philanthropic Trust 2021a). These donations represent nearly 13 percent of individual giving in that period. This sum has increased 81 percent over the past five years, far surpassing the five-year growth in overall philanthropy, which was 20 percent (Giving USA 2020). In recent years, Fidelity Charitable and other national DAF sponsors have been among the largest recipients of philanthropic donations in the United States (Lindsay et al. 2016).

DAF Giving Process

Making donations through a DAF involves several decisions made at different points in time. When setting up a DAF, donors choose where to open their account, how (and how much) to initially fund the account, and usually select some investment options. Later, they make decisions about where, when, and how much to grant to nonprofit recipients. Over time, donors will often contribute more to their DAF, recommend more grants, and make other decisions such as family involvement and even post-mortem plans.

Opening a DAF Account

Starting a DAF is much easier than setting up a private foundation or charitable trust. Many DAF accounts can be set up online in a matter of minutes. Donors decide where to set up their accounts for various reasons. Many choose a commercial sponsor (e.g., Fidelity, Vanguard, Schwab) for ease of use in coordination with an investment account. Others choose a community foundation because of a desire to engage in community-based philanthropy. Still others pick cause-related sponsors, such as a Christian or Jewish organization, to align more closely with their values. Donors also decide how much to contribute and what resources to use. Some DAF sponsors have minimum initial contribution requirements (such as $5K or $25K). The initial contribution may be related to a recent or upcoming liquidity event, for which a donor is trying to offset tax liabilities. Once the initial contribution is complete, the donor usually has options for how the money will be invested, ranging from long-term to more short-term investment approaches. Some donors prefer socially responsible or impact-related investments.

Making Grant Recommendations

After funding the account, donors "recommend" grants by listing the name or EIN of the charity and the amount of the grant. The DAF sponsor reviews this recommendation and mails a check or transfers money directly to the charity. Donors' names are normally included with the checks so recipients know who recommended the grant. However, donors can choose to remain anonymous. In rare occasions when grant recommendations are denied, the legal status of the charity may be in question, or the charity may conflict with the sponsor's stated guidelines or IRS regulations, which are described later in this chapter.

DAF Strategies and Uses

Donors continue using DAF accounts by adding contributions into the account and making more grant recommendations from the account. The type, timing, and amounts of these transactions depend on donors' strategies and circumstances. The following are some common approaches that donors use with DAFs. These strategies are not mutually exclusive; donors may also change strategies over time.

- *Annual DAF giving* – Some donors give through their DAF with a short-term (usually annual) budget in mind. They make contributions based on the previous year's giving and have predetermined plans for upcoming grants.
- *Bunching* – Some donors create a multi-year plan for giving (i.e., 2–3 years) and make a larger contribution into their DAF to cover grantmaking over this

period. Bunching allows donors to deduct several years of donations within one tax year. This is a more prominent strategy since the 2017 Tax Cuts and Jobs Act increased the standard deduction for personal income taxes, resulting in fewer households itemizing deductions.

- *Event DAF giving* – Many donors set up and contribute to their DAFs when they experience liquidity events or the sale of a large asset. DAFs allow donors to reduce their tax liability within the same year as the event, while deferring grantmaking decisions.
- *Long-term DAF giving* – Some donors use their DAF for long-term philanthropic planning. These donors may use the DAF like a private foundation or an endowment, making grants from investment income and preserving the principal for future giving. Some donors use the DAF like a long-term savings account, building up assets for a future major gift. And some donors have postmortem plans for their DAF resources.
- *Family involvement* – Because DAFs allow multiple people to act as donor advisors, many donors involve family members, regardless of other strategies. Some family involvement includes concurrent giving, while other strategies involve family in the future.

Benefits of DAF Giving

As mentioned throughout the chapter, DAFs provide substantive benefits to donors that act as strong incentives::

- DAFs are easy to set up. Donors do not need lawyers or professional advisers to set up an account; the process can often be completed online.
- DAFs are relatively inexpensive. Minimum initial contributions range from $0 to $25,000, making DAFs accessible to even the most modest philanthropists.
- DAF contributions are immediately tax-deductible. This allows donors to maximize tax savings within a given year.
- DAFs offer grantmaking flexibility. There are no time limits on DAF grantmaking. (See DAF critiques later in this chapter.)
- DAFs simplify recordkeeping. Giving through a DAF allows donors to keep their giving records in one place.
- DAFs facilitate family involvement. DAFs make it easy for multiple people to use the same account for charitable giving.

Fundraising Approaches for DAF Donors

To this point, this chapter has covered what a DAF is, how donors may be using their DAF, and why. With this understanding, fundraisers can develop strategies for engaging and soliciting DAF donors and demonstrating stewardship of their gifts. A recent study showed that "87% of organizations that solicited DAF gifts received a DAF gift in the past 3 years" and even "42% of organizations that did not solicit DAF gifts received a DAF gift" in the same period (Osili et al. 2020). Proactive organizations will be more likely to raise money from DAF donors.

Cultivation

There are three groups of prospective DAF donors: (1) current donors who are already using a DAF, (2) current donors who would benefit from using a DAF, and (3) DAF donors who are not current donors. Identifying this last group of donors is often top-of-mind for fundraisers, but identifying the first two groups will help an organization better prepare for finding the third group. Here are some strategies related to these first two types of potential DAF donors.

1. Ask current donors whether they use a DAF. If so, ask them about their DAF:
   a. When did you open your DAF? Where? Why?
   b. What assets do you use to contribute to your DAF?
   c. How often do you grant from your DAF? What kinds of grants do you make from your DAF?
   d. Who are the "donor advisors" on your DAF?
2. Keep track of this data in the donor database to develop solicitation strategies.
3. Talk with current donors about DAFs and share knowledge about the benefits of DAFs. It may seem counterintuitive to help donors set up a DAF because that adds one more step to closing gifts, but remember that fundraising is about long-term relationships. Helping a donor discover the benefits of DAFs builds a mutually beneficial relationship that will increase the likelihood of future donations.
4. Build relationships with DAF sponsors. Community foundations and cause-related sponsors are sometimes asked to recommend organizations to donors and may also have initiatives to engage their donors with community-based or values-based causes. Sponsors will not provide donor information to a soliciting organization, but they will often provide organizational information to a donor.

Solicitation

To start, make it easy for donors to make a DAF grant to the organization. Discuss the use of DAFs on the website and other solicitation materials. List the EIN and mailing address clearly; DAF donors will need this information when making a grant recommendation. Consider using a DAF giving widget, which helps link the organization's giving page with DAF sponsor grantmaking sites.

Next, build strategies for soliciting DAF donors based on the information gleaned from the engagement questions (previously listed). Depending on what strategies donors use for their DAF giving, the following solicitation approaches may be used:

- *Annual DAF giving* – Ask the donor to consider setting up an automatic grant recommendation to the organization, if offered by the sponsor.
- *Bunching DAF giving* – Look for short-term projects that donors can support. Help them envision how they can make a difference to the organization over the next two to three years so that they can plan their bunched contributions accordingly.
- *Event DAF giving* – These donors are likely to have major gift capacity and a major-gift mindset. Follow typical major gift solicitation approaches (as described in Chapters 33 and 34).
- *Long-term DAF giving* – If the donor is using the DAF like an endowment, follow the annual DAF giving strategy. Also consider major gift and planned gift opportunities. Remember that donors can name remainder beneficiaries on DAF accounts (see Chapter 36).

Acknowledgment and Stewardship

Engage DAF donors just like any other donor. While, technically speaking, the check came from the sponsor organization, remember that the donor directed the grant to the organization. Give the donor credit for the grant in the donor database to ensure the donor is properly recognized, engaged, and cultivated for future gifts beginning with demonstration of wise use of previous contributions. Note, however, that donors do not need a receipt for tax purposes because they received their deduction when contributing to the DAF sponsor. Instead, acknowledge the amount and purpose of the grant received without mention of tax deductibility. If the grant lacks the donor's name or contact information, some sponsor organizations will transmit acknowledgment and stewardship communications for you. Completely anonymous donors may still be recognized as such in annual reports or donor recognition walls. Report to both those who recommended the grant and the organization from which it came on the use and impact of the grant.

Limitations on DAF Giving

While DAF giving is quite flexible, fundraisers should be aware that both federal regulations and sponsoring organization policies place some limits on DAF donations. IRS Code Section 4967 states that gifts made by DAFs cannot confer "a more than incidental benefit" to DAF donors or advisors (26 U.S. Code § 4967(a) (1)). In addition, the Pension Protection Act of 2006 specified that DAF grants must not be given to organizations that provide "excess benefits" to DAF donors, advisors, or their relatives or to certain types of "supporting organizations" without 501(c)(3) status.

In general, DAF sponsors have been left to interpret what constitutes "a more than incidental benefit" to DAF donors and advisors. In 2017, the IRS issued additional proposed guidance on this topic (IRS Notice 2017-73). The guidance, which has not been finalized, specified that grants should not pay for event attendance or participation. The guidance also noted that, in some cases, DAF grants that the receiving nonprofit "treats as fulfilling a pledge made by a donor, donor advisor, or related person" may be allowed if certain requirements are met. Fundraisers should check with DAF sponsors to understand pledge-related restrictions as each sponsor has different ways of handling this "gray area."

Furthermore, sponsoring organizations may place restrictions on DAF grant-making. This may include a prohibition on giving to hate groups or, in the case of certain religiously affiliated sponsoring organizations, prohibitions on giving to nonprofits that contradict religious values.

Critiques of DAFs

The controversies surrounding DAFs are centered on not only concerns about DAFs' outsized role in American philanthropy and the immediate tax benefits they provide, but also issues related to gift timing, transparency, and trust.

Speed of Grantmaking

Currently, there are no federal regulations regarding how soon or at what rate funds donated into DAF accounts must be granted to operating charities. The rate of donations is measured as a payout rate, which roughly translates to a percent of assets distributed in a year. This rate varies widely by sponsor characteristics and over time (Heist and Vance-McMullen 2019). Typical aggregate payout rates tend to hover around 14 percent to 22 percent, depending on the calculation method used (Andreoni and Madoff 2020). Another way of measuring the speed of grant-making is by looking at "shelf life," or time between contributions and grantmaking. On aggregate, DAF "shelf life" has been estimated at around 4 years (Andreoni 2018).

The time lag between contributions into DAFs (and tax benefits) and grants from DAF accounts has been routinely questioned. Critics have proposed a maximum shelf life for funds (Madoff and Colinvaux 2017). They have also proposed delaying some or all tax benefits to donors until grants are distributed to operating charities (Colinvaux and Madoff 2019). However, others have argued that an immediate tax deduction acts as an important incentive for contributions, and flexibility in payout rules allows donors to give more strategically (Kridler et al. 2017; Stanford Law School 2020).

Transparency

In addition, critics are concerned about the lack of transparency in giving from DAFs because there is little reporting required. DAF sponsors report aggregated statistics on the IRS form 990, which means that the public cannot observe which donors made grants to which charities. This anonymity is similar to the privacy afforded to individual donors; foundations' requirements mandate much more transparency. As a result, some private foundations elect to make donations to DAFs to keep their giving anonymous. This behavior has been criticized, largely because these private foundation donations can still be counted as foundation payouts (Madoff and Colinvaux 2017).

Trust

Finally, there is a degree of mistrust of DAF sponsors, particularly those with commercial affiliations. Critics are concerned that these institutions benefit from DAF investment and management fees and encourage donors to maintain high asset balances rather than maximize payouts (Colinvaux 2019). While the fees from managing DAFs do support operations at DAF sponsors, there is little empirical evidence to support the claim that sponsors purposely encourage donors to maintain high asset balances to maximize fees.

Conclusion

DAFs play an important role in the modern philanthropic landscape. Development professionals must understand why donors choose to use DAFs as philanthropic vehicles and how to work with donors and their various DAF giving strategies. In addition, development professionals should stay informed of the limitations on DAF giving and the critiques of DAFs to address any concerns that may arise. Ultimately, DAF donors have made a commitment to charitable giving, and this commitment can benefit nonprofit missions when DAF holders are solicited effectively.

Discussion Questions

1. Explain three reasons why a philanthropic individual would use a DAF.
2. In what ways is DAF giving similar to or different from non-DAF individual giving?
3. In what ways is DAF giving similar to or different from foundation/institutional giving?

Application Exercises

1. If you were a policymaker, which aspect or aspects of DAF regulation would you change? Explain your choice, emphasizing the consequences you expect the change to have on contributions to DAFs and grants from DAFs.
2. A new donor has been introduced to your organization, and you believe they may have a DAF. What questions would you ask the donor to explore their capacity and willingness to make a DAF gift to an organization like yours?
3. You are a new director of development at a nonprofit. The board's fundraising committee asks you to develop a strategy for increasing DAF grants. Committee members offer to set up a meeting with a contact at the local community foundation to solicit DAF grants. What would you include in a DAF-specific fundraising strategy? As part of this strategy, what education might you offer to the fundraising committee on DAF giving?

CHAPTER THIRTY-EIGHT

OVERVIEW OF GRANTMAKING FOUNDATIONS

By Pat Danahey Janin and Angela Logan

The number of U.S. grantmaking foundations and the amount they give have steadily increased since the late twentieth century. This is primarily due to accelerated wealth generation notably in technology and finance. In 2020, foundations gave $88.55 billion (19 percent of the total given by all donors to nonprofits) (Giving USA 2021). In 2021, there were 127,595 private foundations (i.e., independent, operating, and corporate) and community foundations in the United States holding $1.2 trillion in assets (Candid 2021). Most foundations carry out their public responsibilities by making grants to nonprofit organizations that are public charities.

Given the complexity of the foundation field and its increasing importance in the giving landscape, this chapter will enable readers to:

- Distinguish the different types of foundations.
- Understand the size and scope of foundations and their activities.
- Adopt basic steps to pursue foundation funding.
- Identify trends and tensions in foundation relationships to grantees and giving.

A Short History of Grantmaking Foundations

In the United States, philanthropic foundations can be traced back to the American Revolution (Hammack 2018). A series of court cases in the nineteenth century (*Dartmouth College v. Woodward* 1816; *Vidal v. Girard's Executors* 1844) established the distinctly private nature of voluntary organizations, including philanthropic foundations and their freedom of action. Private foundations follow the donor's intent within state and federal regulations for charitable activities (Hammack 2018; Soskis 2020). In the United States, four types of foundations came into being at separate times.

- The oldest type is the *private operating foundation* whose existence dates back to 1770 (Toepler 1999). Operating foundations operate their own services, which have the benefit of economic independence from donor provided funds or endowment (Toepler 1999).
- *Private (nonoperating and grantmaking) foundations* came into being at the beginning of the twentieth century as a scientifically based, rationalized approach to tackling social issues distinct from traditional charitable relief organizations. The Carnegie Corporation (founded in 1911) and The Rockefeller Foundation (founded in 1913) were the first philanthropic foundations to make significant contributions to the educational, institutional, and cultural landscape of the United States.
- The *community foundation (CF)*, supported by and serving a geographical community, came into being in 1914 thanks to F.M. Goff who created the Cleveland Foundation. This type of foundation allowed charitable trust funds to be managed by and for the community (Colinvaux 2018). The community foundation is considered a public charity since funds are raised from a large number of donors (individuals, families, businesses).
- *Corporate foundations* are traced back to the post–World War II period when a court case ruled that a corporation could make donations that were not related to its business (*A.P. Smith Mfg. Co. v. Barlow*). In the 1980s, corporations began directing their charitable donations toward causes more in line with their economic interests (Tremblay-Boire 2020).

Examples of ultimate outcomes of foundation grantmaking include well-known art museums, public libraries, nature preserves, the establishment of education standards and research universities, and many key developments of American science, notably in the medical field.

Foundation Practices and Types

Private foundations are divided into three principal categories: independent, operating, and corporate. Private foundations are created with funds from wealthy individuals, families, or small and large businesses. Independent foundations are the most common type (90 percent) and give most of dollars ($64 billion) (Candid 2021). Operating foundations are second in number (over 8,500 representing just over 6 percent), giving $8 billion. Corporate foundations are legally separate from their affiliated companies but giving is often linked to business interests; they give $7 billion. A fourth category is the community foundation, established by members of a community who raise funds from others to support that community. These are fewer in number (less than 1 percent), and give substantially ($10 billion, over 11 percent) to nonprofits (Candid 2021).

Most foundations invest the corpus of their assets in an endowment and all but operating foundations must distribute a percentage of their annual income or assets as grants to nonprofit organizations (COF 2021). Funding typically comes in five different forms:

- *Operations or unrestricted grants* support the ongoing activities and general expenses of the nonprofit.
- *Program grants* support a specific project or specified purpose.
- *Capital grants* support building construction, purchase of equipment, or endowment support.
- *Pilot grants* support new programs or initiatives as trial efforts.
- *Challenge or matching grants* are often used to support capital projects and made under specific conditions: a determined timeframe, the raising of a specified amount of funds from other sources, and a grant disbursement once the other funds are in hand.

Fundraisers will need to research a foundation's funding types and make sure there is alignment with the organization's needs.

In an earlier edition of this book, Davis (2011) provided fundraisers with an overview of foundation types; this work serves as the basis for the following sections. Table 38.1 also summarizes the types of foundations and several key characteristics.

Independent Foundations

The Internal Revenue Service (IRS) defines *independent foundations* as private foundations established to provide support or distributions to nonprofits through grants. Individuals or families usually establish these foundations, and they are named for the funders. These foundations do not accept or seek donations from the general public.

Large, well-established independent foundations generally have a full-time staff, often in proportion to their asset base. Examples include the Bill and Melinda Gates Foundation, the W.K. Kellogg Foundation, and Lilly Endowment Inc. Smaller foundations may have only one full-time person dedicated to daily operations.

TABLE 38.1. FOUNDATION TYPES, FINANCING, AND REQUIREMENTS

Foundation Type	Primary Activity	Financial Base	Use of funds	IRS Fund Distribution requirement
Independent Foundation	Grantmaking	Endowed	Grants to NPOs, Program-Related Investments	5% of endowment annually
Independent Family Foundation	Grantmaking, enactment and inculcation of values across generations	Endowed	Grants to NPOs	5% of endowment annually
Corporate Foundation	Grantmaking and community relations	May or may not be endowed	Grants to NPOs	5% of net investment assets
Operating Foundation	Program administration and grantmaking	May be endowed, and/or receive funding from other sources	Operation of internal programs, occasional grants	Required to spend at least 85% percent of income to support own programs
Community Foundation	Grantmaking and fundraising	Seeks to build endowment, DAFs	Grants to local or defined community of NPOs	Exempt from 5% minimum distribution requirement

Source: Based on Frumkin 2006, 219–236; IRS n.d.

Although not an official term and with no legal definition, the expression *family foundation* is often used to describe an independent foundation that has family dimensions. Those dimensions may be self-identification as a family institution, family involvement and influence in governance, strategic planning, or operations, donor intent and legacy that determine decision-making, and assets coming primarily from family sources (Moody, Knapp, and Corrado 2011). The Bloomberg Family Foundation, located in New York City, is an example.. Family foundations make up a large part of the foundation landscape and are present in communities across the United States.

Operating Foundations

Operating foundations are preferred by donors who wish to be involved in the charitable work more directly rather than acting through public charities. They are dedicated to conducting research and/or operating programs to support the goals of the original charter or governing body and often are actively fundraising themselves. Some operating foundations also make grants to nonprofit organizations (COF 2021). They are often a resource as conveners for nonprofits engaged in complementary research, work, and programs rather than cash grants. Examples of operating foundations are the Terra Foundation for American Art, which funds the Terra Museum for American Art and two Paris museums, and the Indiana University Foundation.

Corporate Foundations

Corporate foundations generally are funded by an associated for-profit company and act as a philanthropic arm and grantmaking vehicle for the company. Some corporate foundations fundraise for additional monies to support their grantmaking (i.e., Finish Line Foundation provides opportunities for store customers to make contributions toward its programs). Mission and funding interests mirror the company's interests, and the foundation typically works in concert with the company's community relations – and sometimes marketing – efforts (see Chapter 39). A corporate foundation often has a separate board of directors, usually comprised of employees and individuals related to the company. The Walmart Foundation and the KPMG Foundation are examples of corporate foundations.

Community Foundations

CFs receive gifts and also make grants through special IRS provisions. As public charities, they must receive assets from a large pool of donors and, consequently, fund a wide range of community needs. Most CFs limit their interests and grants to a particular geographical area, although some are thematic (The Ocean Foundation is a thematic example) and others now open their programs to allow donors to distribute their funds broadly. CFs also house donor-advised funds (DAFs), which allow individuals to donate funds to the CF for distribution to their priority causes (see Chapter 37). Generally, these foundations consider it a primary mission to support community-wide initiatives and develop unrestricted funds specifically for this purpose. Examples of CFs include the New York Community Trust, the Hartford Community Foundation, and the Pride Foundation.

Factors Influencing Foundation Giving

Most foundations are created to exist in perpetuity rather than for a limited time, which influences their approach to financial management and grantmaking. When the economy contracts and stock market returns decline, foundations often decrease their grantmaking to maintain their endowment existence in the long term. When the economy expands, and stock market returns are on the rise, foundations may (or may not) increase their payout rate above the 5 percent payout rate (Rooney and Bergdoll 2020). This payout dynamic is subject to fierce debate in the face of increasing immediate needs due to recurring and unpredictable economic downturns and additional crises (i.e., environmental disasters, the pandemic) (Kramer 2021). Many foundations increased their payout rates significantly in response to the pandemic with gifts increasing 15.6 percent or $11.94 billion in 2020 (Dubb 2021). Foundations seek to be responsive to social needs in the present, and yet need to keep an eye on their long-term viability for the future. Fundraisers attentive to this dynamic and the associated debate will be able to understand funding flows and how they may vary by foundation.

Put simply, the typical foundation process has been to set guidelines, receive proposals from nonprofits, make selections, disburse funds, and then evaluate the reported outcomes. Today foundations may take on much more active roles with nonprofits. For example, foundations may adopt a donor-investor role with more involvement in grantee operations, or foundations may use impact grants for specific sectors, which include providing technical support and convening peer learning communities of multiple grantees. New approaches are also emerging such as participatory grantmaking engaging communities in the whole grantmaking process (Candid n.d.). Foundations often work together on issues and form funder groups or networks. Fundraisers need to be aware of the requirements of various foundation approaches and alternate vehicles to obtain funding, carry out operations, and monitor progress (Fyffe 2016). Foundation identity and internal operating culture also play a large part in grantmaking practices. Scherer (2017) found three distinct foundation grantmaking practices.

- Foundations that identify as "agenda setters" look to be catalysts or change agents with direct action, clear outcomes, and information sharing. They employ expert program officers in their focus field(s).
- Foundations that identify as "supporters" carry out indirect actions, turn to nonprofit leaders to show the way, and work on capacity-building for the sector.
- Foundations that identify as "community builders" are open to different purposes of funding depending on the community need. They invest in community relations and spend time meeting with all stakeholders.

Fundraisers will benefit from paying attention to the financial, operational, and individual factors that affect and may modify foundation giving practices over time.

Organizing for Foundation Fundraising

Foundation fundraising should be considered as one element of a diversified fundraising program. A grant seeker will need to demonstrate that support for the organization is coming from multiple sources in the community: clients, friends, community members, other organizations.

Fundraising from foundations has some similarities to fundraising from individuals and corporations. The principles of Linkage Ability Interest (LAI) found in individual fundraising (see Chapter 14) apply as do cultivation techniques used before soliciting a gift. Presenting a case for support tailored to the foundation's interests resembles the approach needed in corporate fundraising (see Chapter 39) with the caveats that (most) foundations are focused on philanthropic interests and foundations may be less likely to seek widespread public visibility from their support.

There are a number of further caveats to consider in relation to foundation fundraising including:

- Keep in mind that the vast majority of foundations are independent private foundations; most interest areas are related to the founder's life experience, concerns, or family legacy. This shapes the foundation's mission, although in long-standing foundations the founding vision may be interpreted differently as time passes, founders' pass, leadership and staffing evolve, and social needs change.
- Foundations usually require a formal application and have an established grant cycle and internal decision-making process that includes board approval. These processes ensure internal and external accountability.
- A negative response from a foundation does not rule out future grants. Foundations receive more funding requests than they can support.
- Foundations are attentive to matching levels of operations and focus in funding requests. For example, it makes sense for a locally focused nonprofit to seek funding from a locally based foundation (Teitel 2012).

Six Elements of Approaching Grantmaking Foundations

Although fundraising from a foundation is just as tailored as individual major gift fundraising, there is general consistency regarding several essential tasks.

Research

It is important to understand what a foundation will fund, how much, when, and whom. Research should focus on local, regional, and national foundations based on the issue area, type of project, and level of funding sought. Foundations provide guidelines that indicate the particular process for grant applications, deadlines, and often state what they will not fund.

Only 10 percent of foundations have websites, and two-thirds of foundations accept grant applications by invitation only (Glasspockets 2021). The directory Candid is a key resource for researching funders and their past grantmaking as well as collecting general information about foundation fundraising (see https://fconline-foundationcenter-org and https://learning.candid.org/resources/knowledge-base/).

Mission Congruency

The mission of the grant-seeking organization needs to align with the mission and vision of the foundation. The fundraiser's ability to find those common areas of interest and objectives are key to opening a constructive and long-term relationship. When funding priorities are not in concert, it is important to focus elsewhere.

Relationships

Foundations require a long-term outlook coupled with relationship building. In most cases, program officers are available to answer questions and discuss possibilities. Think of the foundation as a partner. If the foundation does not accept unsolicited proposals and there is mission alignment, begin by assessing what type of relationship can be built. How can the organization inform the foundation about its activities, communities served, and outcomes?

Proposal Development

Foundations may require a letter of inquiry (often submitted electronically) as a preliminary screening step. These are short presentations that indicate the organization's focus, programs, development, and summarize the funding request. If there is a perceived fit, then a full proposal may be invited. Each foundation will has its own guidelines, although proposals generally include the following items:

- Cover sheet, including appropriate contact information,
- Executive summary,
- Needs statement,
- Case statement,
- Proposed solution,

- Expected outcomes,
- Evaluation plan,
- Governance and staffing,
- Budget and budget explanation, and
- Project timeline.

Follow-Up

Once a grant is awarded, the cultivation of this relationship includes consistent communication, information transmission on how the organization is serving the community, and a reiteration of interest in developing an ongoing partnership.

Evaluation

A common expectation is that nonprofits will provide information back to the funder on the use of the budgeted funds and their outcomes on the particular nonprofit's mission work. As partners, nonprofits and their foundation funders are highly invested in knowing what is successful in attaining the goals and what is not going as well. Ongoing assessment is a healthy way to keep the dialogue current and responsive to changing circumstances, particularly essential in multi-year funding. A final report and evaluation of the use of funds is also a tool to cultivate the next grant.

Trends and Tensions

After a century, the U.S. foundations may be at a change point with increasing calls for more inclusive management structures and grantmaking processes. This section briefly summarizes critiques and ways foundations are adapting (or struggling) to better accommodate community concerns and nonprofit interests.

Internal Foundation Practices

Although the foundation sector is increasingly embarking on the long-term process of changing organizational structures to incorporate diversity, equity, and inclusion (DEI) (Young, Love, Csuti, and King 2017), organizations continue to struggle to have decision-makers whose identities reflect the clients and communities they serve (BoardSource 2021). Boards that are more diverse tend to adopt DEI practices more frequently than others, creating a cycle of change. Foundations have been slow to adopt a DEI lens to their own hiring practices (Mills 2016). Villancuva's (2018) experience of working inside a foundation as a person of color attests to the gradual pace of change and has heightened the call for less talk and more action in changing foundation culture and practices.

External Foundation Grantmaking Practices

In the second decade of the twenty-first century, long-standing calls for more participatory, inclusive, and community oriented grantmaking practices became particularly acute amidst public health and social challenges in American society.

COVID-19's health, economic, and social crises renewed a call for foundations to operate in more innovative and transformative ways. Numerous foundations responded by putting in practice fewer restrictions on grants, asking less of grant applicants, and making new grants unrestricted (Orensten and Buteau 2020) as well as by questioning their own practices, policies, and processes. Some foundations, for example, adopted the practice of accepting previously submitted applications or creating a standardized grant application (Caplan 2020). Others put initiated "Trust-Based Philanthropy," based on long-term support, dialogue, and partnership-oriented relationships (Nonprofit Quarterly 2019). Furthermore, in 2020, a foundation-led "pledge of action" garnered over 800 foundations to agree to eight commitments that lighten the demands on grantees, enhance community-based responses, and engage foundations in advocacy and partnerships (COF 2020).

Widespread social protest in response to the George Floyd murder in the summer of 2020 raised the Black Lives Matter (BLM) movement to the level of the largest civil movement in U.S. history (Gyamfi and Konadu 2021). Advocating against unjustified killings of African Americans by police, the BLM Global Network Foundation raised over $90 million in 2020, from foundations, corporations, and individual donors (Morrison 2021). In this context, nonprofit organizations, particularly those with a primary focus on social justice and DEI work, reignited conversations around the inherent power imbalance in the relationships between foundations and nonprofit organizations. One prominent grantmaker proposed Artificial Intelligence (AI) as a possibility for equitably introducing and matching funders and grant seekers as a gateway to building trust and data analysis and pinpointing neglected organizations or areas in need of support (Liebling 2020). Moreover, vocal calls are demanding an interrogation of the totality of history, looking at where philanthropic dollars originated, and whether the current forms of philanthropy are truly meeting the needs of communities or merely perpetuating the status quo (Giridharadas 2018; Villanueva 2018).

Changes in grantmaking processes may be on the horizon in the years to come and merit close monitoring by fundraisers.

Conclusion

The foundation landscape is diverse and made up of independent, operating, corporate, and community foundations. It accounts for nearly a fifth of U.S. charitable giving. Foundation grants support charitable organizations with programmatic funds, unrestricted contributions, and capital contributions, among other options. Foundation fundraising requires a distinct understanding of the origins, interest areas, funding levels, and application processes specific to each organization.

Key fundraising practices for long-term foundation support include carrying out research, assuring mission alignment, building a relationship, developing a proposal according to foundation processes, following up, and systematically carrying out evaluations. Foundation practices around DEI are evolving, albeit slowly, in response to the pandemic and widespread civil protests.

Fundraisers attentive to their communities' needs, the foundation landscape, and changing practices may harness the benefits of foundation partnerships for their organization's mission.

Discussion Questions

1. Review the foundation types described in this chapter and develop a list of questions about how each form works.
2. What steps and information are needed for an organization to incorporate grant seeking and proposal writing into its fundraising operations? What are the necessary elements to build a long-term partnership with a foundation?
3. How have the tensions in society influenced foundation practices (internal and external)? Think of two ways this could change a foundation's relationship with the community at large and fundraisers in particular.

Application Exercises

1. Consult the Foundation Center database for foundations in your area (geographical or program focus). Use the principle of Linkage Ability Interest to identify one or two foundations whose funding priorities, levels, and scope match the mission of an organization you are familiar with. Identify the foundation type and implications for the grant-seeking process.
2. Review a foundation website and look for its history, program areas, grant application process, and signs of DEI.

CHAPTER THIRTY-NINE

BUSINESS SECTOR FUNDRAISING

By Dwight F. Burlingame and Bill Stanczykiewicz

Corporations approach charitable giving carefully, often establishing overall allocations as part of annual budgeting and planning. Thus, nonprofits also need to take a strategic approach to business sector fundraising. Like individual donors, each business has distinct values, motivations, and interests guiding its philanthropic activities. Most corporate charitable giving, however, shares the commonality that donations are made within companies' overall interest in profitability.

In this chapter, readers will learn:

- The history and context of business sector charitable giving.
- Different forms of corporate contributions.
- Four ways of understanding corporate charitable giving.
- How to approach businesses as part of the 14-Step Fundraising Cycle.

Background and Current Conditions of Corporate Giving

Companies have traditionally supported nonprofit organizations to improve the environment for successful business to take place. The argument that "the healthier the community, the more business one will be able to conduct" is globally espoused. In many countries, business giving accounts for a higher percentage of nonprofit philanthropic revenue than in the United States (Wiepking and Handy 2015).

In the United States, corporate support of charitable activities is a twentieth-century invention. Previously, most court rulings rendered corporate giving for charitable purposes inappropriate unless such giving was business-related. Laissez-faire arguments of the time were similar to Milton Friedman's (1970) assertion that company management could not give away stockholders' money since it was the "social responsibility of business . . . to increase its profits" (123). Many pin-point railroads' early twentieth-century support of YMCA efforts to provide "safe" housing for workers as the beginning of strategic corporate giving, perhaps based on enlightened self-interest (Smith 1997).

In 1935, the Internal Revenue Code was amended to allow companies to deduct charitable gifts supporting the promotion of business purposes, thus initiating the modern era of regularized corporate giving programs (Smith 1997).

In 1936, federal corporate income tax forms document business giving at around $30 million (Schwartz 1968). By 2020, this figure had grown to an estimated $16.88 billion (Giving USA 2021). Most of the expansion in corporate giving occurred in the last 40 years and can be explained by growth in the size and number of companies as well as the removal of additional legal obstacles. The most significant case was 1953's *A.P. Smith Mfg Co. v. Barlow*, in which the New Jersey Supreme Court refused to overturn the decision of corporate management regarding a charitable gift with no known business benefit. This case reflected the increasing recognition of the importance of businesses' broader economic and social roles.

Even with the growth in dollar amounts of corporate giving, on average, corporate profits have risen much more quickly than corporate giving. For example, from 1986 to 1996, corporate giving as a percentage of profits went down from 2 to 1 percent. During the first two decades of the twenty-first century, giving averaged around 0.9 percent before declining to 0.8 percent in 2020 (Giving USA 2021). Smaller firms generally donate a larger share of their income to nonprofits. Various estimates suggest that only a third of companies claim philanthropic contributions on their federal corporate income taxes, electing to maximize distribution of profits to shareholders. Still, company chief executives are highly positive about their corporate social responsibility and philanthropy programs. The programs help drive long-term business success through charitable gifts, community investment grants, and commercial activities that support nonprofits (Chief Executives for Corporate Purpose 2020).

Corporations are most interested in supporting causes that (1) form a link with the company and the nonprofit that will benefit the company economically and socially, and (2) are relatively proactive and narrow in scope. Of course, many companies still do a considerable amount of reactive giving to many different organizations. According to Giving USA 2021, 29 percent of corporate charitable giving supported health and social services, 19 percent went to education (9 percent to higher education and 10 percent to K–12), and 13 percent went to community and economic development.

Individual companies' changes in giving emphases and funding amounts can be driven by shifts in corporate culture, leadership, and in the competitive market. Companies also are demonstrating increasing sensitivity to the demands of shareholders, consumers, and employees and are, of course, affected by the economic and social environment. "Stakeholder capitalism," in which corporations are oriented to serve interests of involved parties, is rapidly replacing "shareholder capitalism," in which ensuring profitability for shareholders is the corporation's only purpose. For example, "benefit corporations" – which are authorized in 35 U.S. states – include positive social impact within their legally defined goals. Other examples have been reported in the philanthropic media (such as "The Rise of the Corporate Social Investor" in *Stanford Social Innovation Review*) and in the 2020 book *The Corporate Social Mind: How Companies Lead Social Change from the Inside Out.*

In 2020–2021, the COVID-19 pandemic, social justice issues, climate change, increasing poverty and income disparity, economic recession, and other disasters brought heightened pressure for business leaders to do strategic philanthropy. According to a survey by the Charities Aid Foundation of America (2020), 72 percent of corporations reported increasing their charitable contributions during the pandemic. Top areas of support included disaster relief, health, and food security. In addition, 65 percent of corporations reported allowing nonprofits to repurpose existing gifts and use the dollars for immediate needs. Corporations also responded to the events with substantial funding for social justice. According to research by Candid, they gave about $8.2 billion of the $12 billion contributed for racial equity in the United States in 2020 (Hadero 2021). Most observers agree at least some part of this new emphasis is permanent.

Additional details on corporate giving by size, type of nonprofit supported, and regional and industry variation are available from the "Publications" section of the Business Civic Leadership Center's website: www.uschamberfoundation .org/corporate-citizenship-center.

The corporate-nonprofit relationship will always be shaped by the benefits that each provides the other. The wisdom of The Fund Raising School's founder Hank Rosso (1991) remains relevant: "In accepting the gift, it is incumbent upon the organization to return a value to the donor in a form other than material" (6).

Types of Corporate Support

The most sought gift from companies is cash for special and new projects or for capital campaigns and sponsorships. However, businesses today shy away from large-ticket item requests and prefer to focus on activities that address community needs met in partnership with others, including government.

Cash contributions account for about 78 percent of total corporate giving with in-kind donations of goods making up the other 22 percent (Giving USA 2021). In-kind contributions of company products and employee time are common in certain industry groups, including tech, health, and consumer staples. In-kind giving also tends to increase significantly during natural disasters as companies respond to recovery efforts.

Workplace charitable campaigns are fundraising efforts directed at employees that are company sanctioned and supported. These campaigns are often coupled with employee volunteer programs. They have evolved greatly from being the exclusive domain of the United Way to including partnerships with single or multiple nonprofits (Giving USA Foundation 2018).

Many employers also match the donations of employees. While individual employees' personal donations are not included in Giving USA corporate giving totals, the corporate totals do include the matching monies. According to the Gates Foundation's "Double the Donation" initiative, two-thirds of Fortune 500 companies offer matching programs (doublethedonation.com). An estimated $2–$3 billion is donated through matching donations each year. However, an estimated $4–$7 billion annually set aside for this purpose goes unspent. Fundraisers can reduce this significant amount of undonated dollars simply by asking donors: "Does your employer match your charitable giving?"

Cause marketing initiatives and sponsorships are not tax deductible or strictly philanthropic, and therefore, are excluded from Giving USA figures. However, these contributions still aid nonprofits. In addition to increased revenue, sponsorship and cause marketing activities can provide new volunteers, enhanced public awareness of the nonprofit's mission, and access to potential donors and audiences.

Cause marketing is when a business donates a portion of product sales or company proceeds to a nonprofit or offers "check-out charity," a point-of-sale request to the customer at the cash register to donate to a chosen nonprofit. In return, companies receive a marketing benefit from association with the nonprofit, and often have permission to use the nonprofit's logo and branding. Check-out charity has raised $4.9 billion in the last three decades (Engage for Good 2021).

Sponsorships, in which companies pay to be associated with a project or program, are another important form of corporate support. According to IEG Sponsorship Report (2021), sponsorship revenue received by nonprofits from corporations was about equal to gift income. In addition to aligning with a corporation's philanthropic priorities, nonprofits interested in raising sponsorship revenue need to develop a menu of high-profile visibility opportunities since sponsorships are aimed at enhancing businesses' public image.

The following examples demonstrate how companies engage in multifaceted philanthropic collaborations with nonprofits.

Small Business, Big Relationship

O'Brien Toyota is an established auto dealership in Indianapolis, currently in the fourth generation of family ownership. Shepherd Community Center, a social services nonprofit located in an impoverished part of the city, annually benefits from charitable gifts from the company and the O'Brien family. The dealership includes information about Shepherd in the community involvement section of its website. The auto dealer provides discounted prices on new and used vehicles to the nonprofit's full- and part-time staff. In addition, O'Brien Toyota hired a Shepherd alum as a mechanic, helping him end his family's cycle of poverty through training and employment.

Big Corporation, Evolving Relationship

Anthem Blue Cross Blue Shield annually provides substantial charitable gifts to Gleaners Food Bank. Anthem supports Gleaners because food insecurity is the most reported unmet social need. Partnering with Gleaners allows Anthem to improve lives in the communities it serves. The company's employees volunteer to prepare food for distribution across 21 Indiana counties, and their financial donations are matched 1:1 by their employer. At the outset of the COVID-19 pandemic, Anthem made a $1.5 million gift to Gleaners to provide 7.5 million meals over a three-year period.

Models of Company Giving

Fundraisers need an understanding of the corporate context to facilitate interactions with businesses. The models (or theories) described in this section are drawn from Burlingame and Young's (1996) foundational work on corporate philanthropy utilization. They explained the motivations and considerations undergirding businesses' decisions around charitable giving and nonprofit partnerships.

Corporate Productivity Model

This model follows the basic premise that corporate giving will help the company be more profitable and return more value to shareholders. Corporate giving activities must therefore grow profits. For example, when companies give through cash gifts or product donations, direct results can include more brand visibility and sales. Or, when philanthropic contributions improve company morale, indirect results can include better employee satisfaction and productivity.

This rational aligns with the notion of "enlightened self-interest" in which the company recognizes that in doing well for others it also benefits. This suggests that the term *corporate philanthropy* is a bit of an oxymoron and that a more accurate phrase is *corporate citizenship* or *strategic philanthropy* to convey the purpose of the engagement between the company and the nonprofit.

Types of giving aligned with this model include:

- Projects that lower corporate costs, such as research grants that lower the company's internal expenditures for product development.
- Projects that help market company products, like sponsorships and cause marketing.
- Projects that enhance employee morale and thus increase productivity.
- Projects that improve the company's public image.

Fundraisers can try to articulate organizational mission and activities in ways that align with companies' needs for improved productivity. Fundraisers should communicate how gifts can contribute to the company's bottom line whether directly or indirectly.

Ethical/Altruistic Model

This notion of corporate philanthropy is based on the premise that businesses and their leaders have a responsibility to be good corporate citizens, and corporate giving and volunteering demonstrate corporate social responsibility to society. This model assumes that corporations have discretionary resources. Companies facing economic challenges are unlikely to be able to give within this model. Giving in this way requires companies to consider community priorities and how the company might partner in seeking solutions.

Types of giving consistent with this model are:

- Projects that address a known community need where the company operates or has markets.
- Projects that appeal to corporate leadership, personally or as citizens of the community.
- Projects that engage employees in community efforts to address local issues.

Fundraisers need to articulate how gifts to their organizations will benefit the community through the engagement of employees and corporate leaders.

Political Model

The political model has external and internal components. The external form is based on the idea that corporations use giving to build relationships that protect corporate power and influence governmental limits on companies. Under this model, the corporate giving program serves as a liaison to community allies.

Projects that build closer bonds between the company and carefully chosen non-profits with certain profiles are consistent with this model. Efforts that substitute for government initiative, or more accurately, minimize government intervention and portray the company as a good public citizen are typical. Environmental or arts projects are often a fit.

The internal political paradigm follows the premise that corporate giving staff members are agents within the corporate "game." The staff needs to build internal allies and prove the benefit of giving within the company. Corporate giving programs must be valuable for building of alliances with divisions, including human resources, marketing, research, public relations, and like units. Giving programs consistent with this model include employee volunteerism and educational initiatives, sponsorships, and cause marketing, as well as social service projects and short-term research endeavors.

Fundraisers need be strategic in engaging with all units of the company, not just the corporate giving unit. Projects that feature multiple interaction points are most appealing.

Stakeholder Model

The stakeholder model is based on the idea that the corporation is a complex entity that must respond to the needs and pressures of many key stakeholders, including shareholders, employees, suppliers, customers, community groups, and governmental officials. Under this framework, managing companies – small and large – is best accomplished by managing the various stakeholder interests. Thus, to be effective, corporate giving activities need to help address multiple interests.

Types of giving consistent with this model are:

- Projects including employee benefits or volunteerism.
- Projects including community education or environmental efforts.
- Projects that help consumers of company products or services.

Fundraisers can concentrate efforts on identifying stakeholder groups and developing project proposals that articulate the nonprofit mission in ways that appeal to defined groups. The nonprofit is also a community stakeholder that can be championed by the corporate giving program.

All or some of the four models described may operate in a single corporation simultaneously. Priorities also shift and change. During some periods, for example, political motivations may be more complex and particular stakeholder needs may be more pressing and visible. In other times, increased efforts to demonstrate how corporate giving affects the double bottom line (i.e., social return and financial return) may be most prevalent. Ultimately, the models are a timeless tool for creating a multi-faceted and intentional fundraising program for the business sector.

Organizing for Corporate Fundraising

Nonprofits need to consider business sector fundraising within the 14-Step Fundraising Cycle (see Chapter 12). Each step of the cycle needs to include planning on how to raise charitable donations from the private sector alongside gifts from individuals and grants from foundations.

Similar to fundraising from individuals, prospective business funders can be identified, in-person meetings with company representatives should be requested, and relationships can be cultivated. Throughout this process identifying the right person within each company, the right amount to request from that business, for the right reason, and at the right time are paramount.

The Business Sector Fundraising Case for Support

The fundraising planning cycle starts with the case for support, and a fundraising case for support designed specifically for business sector donors should address the corporate productivity, ethical/altruistic, political, and stakeholder reasons for private sector charitable giving. Recognizing the business sector's interest in utilizing philanthropy for employee recruitment, retention, and morale is important along with the realization that about two-thirds of corporate charitable support is directed toward education, health and human services, and community development. Aligning the charitable request with the corporation's core business activities also is essential.

Prospective Business Sector Donors and Donations

As the fundraising planning cycle continues, the nonprofit begins the process of describing how business sector charitable support can be aligned with the non-profit's mission. Defining how much financial support can be raised from the private sector begins by identifying potential corporate funders. The prospective donor list can be developed by consulting with: the nonprofit's board of directors; other volunteers within the nonprofit; staff colleagues; existing donors; and program participants. Prospective corporate donors also can be identified by reading local business media and observing corporate donations at other nonprofit and community events. Nonprofits also should include their vendors as potential donors.

Knowing past corporate behavior is also important to avoid "felonious philanthropy" from a company to the nonprofit. "Tainted" gifts from corporations (and individuals) should be avoided (see Chapter 2).

The business sector gift market then can be evaluated by researching companies through their corporate citizenship and sustainability reports, reviewing company websites, and talking with board members or associates with insight into the company. This information can help the nonprofit begin to understand each company's philanthropic motivations, funding priorities, and typical gift amounts.

Fundraising Vehicles and the Right Amount

The fundraising planning cycle continues with identification of fundraising vehicles. For business sector donors, this includes creating an inventory of options that companies might want to support and the public exposure that can result from donating to those specific programs, services, and activities. Options for highlighting corporate gifts can include printed and electronic materials as well as integration within direct communication with current and prospective customers. Recognition may also come through a joint advertising effort for the nonprofit or through verbal recognition at virtual or in-person functions.

A business might be interested in the bright spotlight that comes from serving as the primary sponsor of an entire event or from the naming of a program or facility. If the business donor expresses interest in recognition as an exclusive sponsor, the nonprofit should consider defining "exclusive" as within that company's product category. An expanded definition of "exclusive" to mean "the only sponsor" should derive a financial sponsorship that lands in the upper range of the nonprofit's gift range chart.

Increased visibility to federal, state, or local government is another vehicle that nonprofits can offer to corporate donors. While the entire private sector operates under various government regulations, some elements face additional public sector scrutiny. For example, banks must satisfy the federal Community Reinvestment Act while electric, water, and gas utilities are governed by state and local commissions that approve rate increases and other operating procedures. Fundraisers can offer to provide letters describing the importance of the company's charitable support to be included in community service files submitted to government regulatory agencies.

There is not a specific formula for determining the precise dollar amounts associated with various gifts or levels of public exposure for corporate donors. Nonprofits can seek guidance from board members who work in the private sector while also observing giving levels established by other local nonprofits.

Finalizing the Plan

Information then is synthesized in the next steps of the fundraising cycle as the nonprofit finalizes the list of prospective business sector donors, contact people in each business, companies' philanthropic interests, and companies' typical levels of charitable support. The nonprofit also needs to remain mindful of the timing most often associated with business sector charitable giving. Businesses budget everything, including their philanthropy. The corporate budget often follows the calendar year, and planning for next year's budget often starts in the mid-to-late summer, continues into the fall, and concludes before the end-of-year holiday season.

A fundraiser who approaches a business after the budgeting process is completed can make a favorable impression only to be informed that the company's charitable giving determinations are already made for this year and next. Fundraisers can transform this disappointing development into an opportunity by asking when the next budget planning cycle will begin and then by scheduling subsequent meetings with the company's charitable giving representative on that timeline.

Solicitation

Most corporations have an identified contact person and process, including application deadlines, located on their websites. Ongoing relationships can be developed with the people in these positions, leading to a range of philanthropic support and involvement from the company to the nonprofit. Meanwhile, small and family-owned businesses can be approached in a manner similar to cultivating individual donors. Connections between company employees and the nonprofit – ranging from board membership, to volunteering, to receiving services – also can provide an important entry point for conversations about philanthropic support.

The eventual charitable request should be tailored to the philanthropic priorities of the specific corporation. The request can include the type of giving vehicle, the dollar amount of the gift or sponsorship, and a list of options for providing the business with public visibility for supporting the nonprofit.

Stewardship

After making successful requests for charitable gifts from private sector funders, the fourteenth and final step of the fundraising cycle is stewardship. Essentials include immediate conveyance of "thank you," documentation of the contribution, and prompt follow-through in using and publicizing the gift as intended. Informing business donors of the impact of their gift and developing additional ways for companies to stay engaged help the nonprofit cultivate a longer-term relationship with corporate funders.

Conclusion

Businesses provide various forms of support for philanthropic organizations, including cash, in-kind gifts, cause marketing, and sponsorships. They can also help facilitate employee contributions of money and time and provide matching funds to build on those gifts. Corporate giving can be explained using four models detailing the various rationales, though all share a corporate concern for profit-making purposes.

Fundraisers need to demonstrate how corporate support helps the overall revenue picture of the nonprofit, serves the greater community, creates an affiliation between the company and the nonprofit, and serves company stakeholder concerns and interests. Fundraising from the business sector should be a component of nonprofits' 14-Step Fundraising Cycle, with understanding of individual companies' specific needs and interests. By developing distinctive and multi-faceted strategies for businesses, fundraisers can create lasting partnerships with fruitful outcomes for their organizations.

Discussion Questions

1. How has corporate giving evolved over time and what does the evidence suggest the future may hold for how companies give?
2. Businesses are in business to make money, not to give money away; and when they give money away, they do so to help them make money. How does this affect how fundraisers must approach businesses?
3. Review the four models of corporate giving. Think about how they may be present within the vignettes included in the "Types of Corporate Support" section.

Application Exercises

1. Write a brief fundraising case for support designed for prospective funders from the business sector that fits with your nonprofit's mission or another of your choosing.
2. With a particular nonprofit in mind, create a list of possible opportunities for visibility that can be offered to a funder from the business sector.
3. Explore the community relations webpage, corporate foundation materials, or media stories about a company's charitable activities. What kinds of contributions is the company making, and why?

REFERENCES

"Backers Prepare for Shelter Debut." 1981, November 16. *Indianapolis Star.*

"Domestic Violence Data Details Strain." 2021, January 13. *Indianapolis Star.*

"To Combat Domestic Violence, IPD Moves into Julian Center." 2000, April 4. *Indianapolis Star.*

#GivingTuesday. 2020. "After Year of Global Crisis, Millions Respond with Massive Swell of Generosity and Shared Humanity on #GivingTuesday 2020." https://hq.givingtuesday.org/after-year-of-global-crisis-millions-respond-with-massive-swell-of-generosity-and-shared-humanity-on-givingtuesday-2020/.

Abd-Allah, Umar F. 2006. *A Muslim in Victorian America: The Life of Alexander Russell Webb.* Oxford, UK: Oxford University Press.

Adloff, Frank. 2016. "Approaching Philanthropy from a Social Theory Perspective." *The Routledge Companion to Philanthropy,* Tobias Jung, Susan D. Phillips, and Jenny Harrow (eds.), pp. 56–70. London: Routledge.

Alborough, Lesley. 2017. "Lost in Translation: A Sociological Study of the Role of Fundraisers in Mediating Gift Giving in Non-profit Organisations." *International Journal of Nonprofit & Voluntary Sector Marketing,* 22(4): e1602.

Albouy, Jeanne. 2017. "Emotions and Prosocial Behaviours: A Study of the Effectiveness of Shocking Charity Campaigns." *Recherche et Applications En Marketing* (English Edition) 32(2): 4–25. https://doi.org/10.1177/2051570716689241.

Albury, Kath, Jean Burgess, Ben Light, Kane Race, and Rowan Wilken. 2017. "Data Cultures of Mobile Dating and Hook-up Apps: Emerging Issues for Critical Social Science Research." *Big Data & Society*, 4(2). https://doi.org/10.1177/2053951717720950.

Aldrich, Eva E. 2011. *Giving USA 2011 Spotlight #2: Giving by Immigrants.* Chicago: Giving USA Foundation.

Aldrich, Eva. 2016. "Fundraising as a Profession." In *Achieving Excellence in Fundraising* 4th Edition, Eugene R. Tempel, Timothy L. Seiler, and Dwight F. Burlingame (eds.), pp. 503–516. New York: John Wiley & Sons Publishers.

Alexander, Jennifer. 2000. "Adaptive Strategies of Nonprofit Human Service Organizations in an Era of Devolution and New Public Management." *Nonprofit Management and Leadership*, 10(3): 287–303.

Algoe, Sara B. 2012. "Find, Remind, and Bind: The Functions of Gratitude in Everyday Relationships." *Social and Personality Psychology Compass*, 6(6): 455–469.

Algoe, Sara B., Laura E. Kurtz, and Nicole M. Hilaire. 2016. "Putting the 'You' in 'Thank You'": Examining Other-Praising Behavior as the Active Relational Ingredient in Expressed Gratitude." *Social Psychological and Personality Science*, 7(7): 658–666.

Algoe, Sara B., Patrick C. Dwyer, Ayana Younge, and Christopher Oveis. 2020. "A New Perspective on the Social Functions of Emotions: Gratitude and the Witnessing Effect." *Journal of Personality and Social Psychology*, 119(1): 40–74.

Alliance for Strong Families and Communities and the American Public Human Services Association. 2018. "A National Imperative: Joining Forces to Strengthen Human Services." http://www.alliance1.org/web/resources/pubs/national-imperative-joining-forces-strengthen-human-services-america.aspx.

Alonso Dos Santos, Manuel, Camila Lobos, Nathalie Muñoz, Dámaris Romero, and Ricardo Sanhueza. 2017. "The Influence of Image Valence on the Attention Paid to Charity Advertising." *Journal of Nonprofit & Public Sector Marketing*, 29(3): 346–63. https://doi.org/10.1080/10495142.2017.1326355.

Alpízar, Francisco, and Peter Martinsson. 2013. "Does It Matter If You Are Observed by Others? Evidence from Donations in the Field." *The Scandinavian Journal of Economics*, 115(1): 74–83. https://doi.org/10.1111/j.1467-9442.2012.01744.x.

Alter, Joanna. n.d. "Instagram Engagement Rate Data: Average Seconds on Site." Yotpo.com. Accessed December 20, 2020: https://www.yotpo.com/blog/instagram-engagement-rate.

American Council on Gift Annuities. 2018. "2017 Survey of Charitable Gift Annuities." Smyrna, GA: American Council on Gift Annuities.

American Library Association. 2020. "Digital Literacy" Welcome to ALA's Literacy Clearinghouse. https://literacy.ala.org/digital-literacy/.

American Marketing Association (AMA). 2017. "Definitions of Marketing." https://www.ama.org/topics/marketing-definition/.

Americans for the Arts. 2018, September. "Americans Speak Out about the Arts in 2018: An In-Depth Look at Perceptions and Attitudes about the Arts in America." Americans for the Arts. https://www.americansforthearts.org/node/101584.

AmeriCorps. 2018a. "Volunteering in America." https://americorps.gov/newsroom/news/via.

AmeriCorps. 2018b. "Volunteering in U.S. Hits Record High: Worth $167 Billion." https://americorps.gov/newsroom/press-releases/2018/volunteering-us-hits-record-high-worth-167-billion.

Anderson, Albert. 1996. *Ethics for Fundraisers*. Bloomington, IN: Indiana University Press.

Andreoni, James. 1990. "Impure Altruism and Donations to Public Goods: A Theory of Warm-Glow Giving." *Economic Journal*, 100: 464–477.

Andreoni, James. 2018. "The Benefits and Costs of Donor-Advised Funds." *Tax Policy and the Economy* 32(1): 1–44.

Andreoni, James, and Ray D. Madoff. 2020. "Calculating DAF Payout and What We Learn When We Do It Correctly." NBER Working Paper w27888. Cambridge, MA: National Bureau of Economic Research.

Andreoni, James, Justin M. Rao, and Hannah Trachtman. 2017. "Avoiding the Ask: A Field Experiment on Altruism, Empathy, and Charitable Giving." *Journal of Political Economy*, 125(3): 625–653.

Anft, Michael. 2002, January 10. "Tapping Ethnic Wealth: Charities Pursue Minority Giving as Incomes Rise Among Blacks, Hispanics, and Other Groups." *The Chronicle of Philanthropy*. https://philanthropy.com/article/Tapping-Ethnic-Wealth/184929.

Angelou, Maya. 1993. *Wouldn't Take Nothing for My Journey Now*, 1st Edition. New York: Random House.

Anheier, Helmut K., and Siobhan Daly. 2004. "Philanthropic Foundations: A New Global Force?" *Global Civil Society 5*: 158–176. London: SAGE.

Ansell, Chris, and Arjen Boin. 2019. "Taming Deep Uncertainty: The Potential of Pragmatist Principles for Understanding and Improving Strategic Crisis Management." *Administration & Society*, 51(7): 1079–1112.

Aoun, Joseph E. 2017. *Robot-Proof: Higher Education in the Age of Artificial Intelligence*. Cambridge: MA: The MIT Press.

Aquino, Karl, Dan Freeman, Americus Reed II, Vivien KG Lim, and Will Felps. 2009. "Testing a Social-Cognitive Model of Moral Behavior: The Interactive Influence of Situations and Moral Identity Centrality." *Journal of Personality and Social Psychology*, 97(1): 123.

Ariely, Dan, Anat Bracha, and Stephan Meier. 2009. "Doing Good or Doing Well? Image Motivation and Monetary Incentives in Behaving Prosocially." *American Economic Review*, 99(1): 544–555.

Arnett, Jeffrey Jensen. 1997. "Young People's Conceptions of the Transition to Adulthood." *Youth & Society*, 29(1): 3–23. https://doi.org/10.1177/0044118X97029001001.

Arnett, Jeffrey Jensen. 2006. *Emerging Adulthood: The Winding Road from the Late Teens through the Twenties*. Oxford, UK: Oxford University Press.

Arum, Richard, and Josipa Roksa. 2014. *Aspiring Adults Adrift: Tentative Transitions of College Graduates*. Chicago: University of Chicago Press.

Association of Donor Relations Professionals (ADRP). "Donor Relations and Stewardship Defined." Retrieved September 15, 2021: https://www.adrp.net/assets/documents/adrpdefinitions.pdf.

Association of Fundraising Professionals (AFP). "The Donor Bill of Rights." Retrieved May 20, 2021: https://afpglobal.org/donor-bill-rights.

Association of Fundraising Professionals (AFP). 2003. "AFP Fundraising Dictionary." https://afpglobal.org/sites/default/files/attachments/2018-11/AFPFundraisingDictionary.pdf.

Association of Fundraising Professionals (AFP). 2017. "*AFP Fundraising Dictionary*." Alexandria, VA: Association of Fundraising Profession.

Association of Fundraising Professionals (AFP). 2019. "Asking Matters: Charitable Fundraising in Canada." https://afpglobal.org/asking-matters.

Association of Fundraising Professionals (AFP). 2020. "Compensation and Benefits Report." https://afpglobal.org/2020Report.

Athanassoulis, Nafsika. 2012. *Virtue Ethics.* New York: Continuum International Publishing Group.

Austin, Thad. 2017, October 24. "Giving USA Special Report – Giving to Religion." Giving USA Foundation. https://store.givingusa.org/collections/special-reports-spotlights/products/copy-of-giving-usa-special-report-giving-to-religion-digital-edition?variant=449180696585.

Axelrad, Claire. 2015, June 15. "Culture of Philanthropy: Why You Need It; Six Ways to Get It." *Guidestar* blog. https://trust.guidestar.org/2015/06/15/culture-of-philanthropy-why-you-need-it-6-ways-to-get-it/.

Badgett, M. V. Lee, and Cunningham, N. 1998. *Creating Communities: Giving and Volunteering by Gay, Lesbian, Bisexual, and Transgender People.* New York Amherst, MA: Working Group on Funding Lesbian and Gay Issues and Institute for Gay and Lesbian Strategic Studies.

Bae, Mikyeung. 2019. "Influences of Identified Victim Images on Processing Fluency." *Journal of Nonprofit & Public Sector Marketing,* 31(3): 249–273. https://doi.org/10.1080/10495142.2018.1526740.

Baghai, Pooneh, Olivia Howard, Lakshmi Prakash, and Jill Zucker. 2020, July 29. "Women as the Next Wave of Growth in US Wealth Management." McKinsey & Company. https://www.mckinsey.com/industries/financial-services/our-insights/women-as-the-next-wave-of-growth-in-us-wealth-management.

Bakar, N. B. A. 2008. "Zakat and Taxation: A Conceptual Comparison." *TAFHIM: IKIM Journal of Islam and the Contemporary World,* 2(3).

Banaji, Mahzarin R., and Anthony G. Greenwald. 2016. *Blindspot: Hidden Biases of Good People.* New York: Bantam.

Banaji, Shakuntala, and David Buckingham. 2009. "The Civic Self." *Information, Communication & Society,* 12(8): 1197–1223. https://doi.org/10.1080/13691180802687621.

Barber, Putnam, and Bill Levis. 2013. "Donor Retention Matters." Urban Institute: Center on Nonprofits and Philanthropy. https://www.urban.org/sites/default/files/publication/23231/412731-Donor-Retention-Matters.PDF.

Barnett, J., and S. Hammond. 1999. "Representing Disability in Charity Promotions." *Journal of Community & Applied Social Psychology,* 9(4): 309–314. https://doi.org/10.1002/(SICI)1099-1298(199907/08)9:4<309::AID-CASP515>3.0.CO;2-7.

Barry, Frank. 2019. "10 Surprising Church Giving Facts that You Absolutely Need to Know." Tithe.ly.https://get.tithe.ly/blog/church-giving-statistics-and-research.

Bass, Bernard M. 1985. *Leadership and Performance Beyond Expectations.* New York: Free Press.

Bass, Bernard M., and Bruce J. Avolio. 1993. "Transformational Leadership and Organizational Culture." *Public Administration Quarterly.* 112–121.

Bearman, Jessica, and Jason Franklin. 2018. *Dynamics of Hosting: Giving Circles and Collective Giving Groups.* Indianapolis: Collective Giving Research Group. https://scholarworks.iupui.edu/bitstream/handle/1805/17744/giving-circle-hosting18.pdf.

Bearman, Jessica, Julia Carboni, Angela Eikenberry, and Jason Franklin. 2017. "The Landscape of Giving Circles/Collective Giving Groups in the U.S." Collective Giving Research Group. https://scholarworks.iupui.edu/handle/1805/14527.

Behrens, Teri. 2016. "Growth in the Number of Foundations." In *11 Philanthropic Trends for 2017*, Johnson Center for Philanthropy at Grand Valley University (ed.), pp. 4–5. https://johnsoncenter.org/wp-content/uploads/2020/10/11-Trends-for-2017.pdf.

Bekkers, René. 2007. "Intergenerational Transmission of Volunteering." *Acta Sociologica*, 50(2): 99–114. https://doi.org/10.1177/0001699307077653.

Bekkers, René, and Pamala Wiepking. 2007. "Generosity and Philanthropy: A Literature Review." Science of Generosity at the University of Notre Dame. https://generosityresearch.nd.edu/assets/17632/generosity_and_philanthropy_final.pdf.

Bekkers, René, and Theo Schuyt. 2008. "And Who Is Your Neighbor? Explaining the Effect of Religion on Charitable Giving and Volunteering in the Netherlands." *Review of Religious Research*, 50(1): 74–96.

Bekkers, René, and Pamala Wiepking. 2011a. "A Literature Review of Empirical Studies of Philanthropy: Eight Mechanisms that Drive Charitable Giving." *Nonprofit and Voluntary Sector Quarterly*, 40(5): 924–973.

Bekkers, René, and Pamala Wiepking. 2011b. "Who Gives? A Literature Review of Predictors of Charitable Giving Part One: Religion, Education, Age and Socialisation." *Voluntary Sector Review*, 2(3): 337–365.

Bekkers, Rene, Sara Konrath, and David Horton Smith. 2016. "Physiological Correlates of Volunteering." *Palgrave Research Handbook of Volunteering and Nonprofit Associations*, David Horton Smith, Robert Stebbins and Jurgen Grotz (eds.). London: Palgrave MacMillan.

Bell, Jeanne, and Marla Cornelius. 2013. "Underdeveloped: A National Study of Challenges Facing Nonprofit Fundraising." Evelyn and Walter Haas, Jr. Fund. https://www.compasspoint.org/underdeveloped.

Ben-Ner, Avner, Brian P. McCall, Massoud Stephane, and Hua Wang. 2009. "Identity and In-Group/out-Group Differentiation in Work and Giving Behaviors: Experimental Evidence." *Journal of Economic Behavior & Organization*, 72(1): 153–170. https://doi.org/10.1016/j.jebo.2009.05.007.

Bengtson, Vern L., and W. Andrew Achenbaum. 1993. *The Changing Contract across Generations*. Piscataway, NJ: Transaction Publishers.

Bennis, Warren G. 2009. *On Becoming a Leader*. New York: Basic Books.

Berman, Lila C. 2015. "Donor-Advised Funds in Historical Perspective." Boston College Law Forum on Philanthropy and the Public Good 1: 5–27. https://lawdigitalcommons.bc.edu/cgi/viewcontent.cgi?article=1014&context=philanthropy-forum.

Bernholz, Lucy, Rob Reich, and Emma Saunders-Hastings. 2015, September 1. "Crowdfunding for Public Goods and Philanthropy." *Digital Civil Society* blog. https://medium.com/the-digital-civil-society-lab/crowdfunding-for-public-goods-and-philanthropy-c7c7c5976898.

Bernholz, Lucy. 2017, June 27. "Digital Literacy – Core Capacity for Today's Nonprofits." *Medium*. https://medium.com/the-digital-civil-society-lab/digital-literacy-core-capacity-for-todays-nonprofits-428fc3559ab2.

Bernholz, Lucy. 2020a, August 25. "Confronting Philanthropy's Uncomfortable Truths." *The Chronicle of Philanthropy*. https://www.philanthropy.com/article/confronting-philanthropys-uncomfortable-truths.

Bernholz, Lucy. 2020b, September 15. "Reimagining Philanthropy – Part 4 – Digital Dependence Has Obliterated the Notion of Nonprofit Independence." *The Chronicle of Philanthropy*. https://www.philanthropy.com/article/digital-dependence-has-obliterated-the-notion-of-nonprofit-independence?.

Bernholz, Lucy. 2020c, September 22. "Reimagining Philanthropy – Part 5 – What Now? The Philanthropic Future Our Democracy Needs." *The Chronicle of Philanthropy.* https://www.philanthropy.com/article/what-now-the-philanthropic-future-our-democracy-needs?

Bhati, Abhishek, and Angela M. Eikenberry. 2016. "Faces of the Needy: The Portrayal of Destitute Children in the Fundraising Campaigns of NGOs in India." *International Journal of Nonprofit & Voluntary Sector Marketing,* 21(1): 31–42. https://doi.org/10.1002/nvsm.1542.

Bingle, Benjamin S. 2017. "Community Foundation–Led Giving Days: Understanding Donor Satisfaction and Philanthropic Patterns." *The Foundation Review,* 9(4): 5.

Blustein, David L., Ryan Duffy, Joaquim A. Ferreira, Valerie Cohen-Scalid, Rachel Gali Cinamone, and Blake A. Allan. 2020. "Unemployment in the Time of COVID-19: A Research Agenda." *Journal of Vocational Behavior,* 119: 103436. doi:10.1016/j.jvb.2020.103436

Board of Governors of the Federal Reserve System (US). 2020. "Nonprofit Organizations; Total Financial Assets Held by Private Foundations, Level BOGZ1FL164090015Q" FRED, Federal Reserve Bank of St. Louis. https://fred.stlouisfed.org/series/BOGZ1FL164090015Q.

BoardSource. Leading with Intent: 2017 National Index of Nonprofit Board Practices. https://leadingwithintent.org/.

BoardSource. 2021, June. Leading with Intent: Reviewing the State of Diversity, Equity, and Inclusion on Nonprofit Boards. BoardSource. https://leadingwithintent.org/wp-content/uploads/2021/06/2021-Leading-with-Intent-DEI-Report.pdf.

Boin, Arjen. 2004. "Lessons from Crisis Research." *International Studies Review,* 6(1): 165–194.

Boin, Arjen, Sanneke Kuipers, and Werner Overdijk. 2013. "Leadership in Times of Crisis: A Framework for Assessment." *International Review of Public Administration,* 18(1): 79–91.

Bomar, Chuck. 2011. *Worlds Apart: Understanding the Mindset and Values of 18–25 Year Olds.* Grand Rapids, MI: Zondervan/Youth Specialties.

Born, Jason. Trends 2020. "Results of the Second National Benchmark Survey of Family Foundations." National Center for Family Philanthropy. https://www.ncfp.org/knowledge/trends-2020-results-of-the-second-national-benchmark-survey-of-family-foundations/.

Boswell, Stefanie S. 2012. "'I Deserve Success': Academic Entitlement Attitudes and Their Relationships with Course Self-Efficacy, Social Networking, and Demographic Variables." *Social Psychology of Education,* 15(3): 353–365. https://doi.org/10.1007/s11218-012-9184-4.

Bout, Maarten. 2018. "The Joy of Asking: An Analysis of Socioemotional Information in Fundraiser Contact Reports." MA Thesis, Lilly Family School of Philanthropy, Indiana University.

Bowman, Woods. 2006. "Should Donors Care About Overhead Costs? Do They Care?" *Nonprofit and Voluntary Sector Quarterly,* 35(2): 288–310.

Bradshaw, Pat, Vic Murray, and Jacob Wolpin 1992. "Do Nonprofit Boards Make a Difference? An Exploration of the Relationships among Board Structure, Process, and Effectiveness." *Nonprofit and Voluntary Sector Quarterly,* 21(3): 227–249.

Bragg, Rick. 1996, November 12. "She Opened the Door to Others; Her World Has Opened, Too." *New York Times.*

Breeze, Beth. 2017. *The New Fundraisers: Who Organises Charitable Giving in Contemporary Society?* Bristol, UK: Policy Press.

Breeze, Beth, and Elizabeth Dale. 2020. *Missing Out: Understanding the Female Leadership Gap in Fundraising.* London: Chartered Institute of Fundraising.

Breeze, Beth, and Jon Dean. 2012. "Pictures of Me: User Views on Their Representation in Homelessness Fundraising Appeals." *International Journal of Nonprofit & Voluntary Sector Marketing,* 17(2): 132–143. https://doi.org/10.1002/nvsm.1417.

Breeze, Beth, and Gloria Jollymore. 2017. "Understanding Solicitation: Beyond the Binary Variable of Being Asked or not Being Asked." *International Journal of Nonprofit & Voluntary Sector Marketing,* 22(4): e1607.

Breeze, Beth, and Pamala Wiepking. 2020. "Different Drivers: Exploring Employee Involvement in Corporate Philanthropy." *Journal of Business Ethics,* 165: 453–467.

Breeze, Beth, and Theresa Lloyd. 2013. "Richer Lives: Why Rich People Give." London: Directory of Social Change.

Breeze, Beth, and Wendy Scaife. 2015. "Encouraging Generosity: The Practice and Organization of Fund-raising across Nations." In *The Palgrave Handbook of Global Philanthropy,* Pamala Wiepking and Femida Handy (eds.), pp. 570–596. Hampshire, UK: Palgrave MacMillan.

Brommel, Andy. 2020, October 28. "Defining Your Case for Support." *Fundraising Communications Webinar Series.* Chicago: Campbell & Company. https://www.campbell-company.com/events/fundraising-case-for-support-2020.

Brown, Alphonce J. 2015, February. "Transparency and Accountability in Fundraising." http://philanthropicservice.com/february-2015-transparency-and-accountability-in-fundraising/.

Brown, M. Gasby, and Nuka Solomon. 2020, October 22. "Nonprofit Talk with Nuka and Gasby." *NonProfit Thursdays.* https://youtube.com/channel/UCpCYwzGcYKQoBCqE5eXX3SQ.

Brown, William A., and Chao Guo. 2010. "Exploring the Key Roles for Nonprofit Boards." *Nonprofit and Voluntary Sector Quarterly,* 39(3): 536–546.

Brudney, Jeffrey L., and Vic Murray. 1998. "Do Intentional Efforts to Improve Boards Really Work? The Views of Nonprofit CEOs." *Nonprofit Management and Leadership,* 8(4): 333–348.

Bryant, Kenzie. 2020. "MacKenzie Scott Redefines F–ck-You Money." https://www.vanityfair.com/style/2020/12/mackenzie-scott-redefines-fuck-you-money.

Bryant, W. Keith, Haekyung Jeon-Slaughter, Hyojin Kang, and Aaron Tax. 2003. "Participation in Philanthropic Activities: Donating Money and Time." *Journal of Consumer Policy,* 26(1): 43–73.

Bryson, John M. 2010. "The Future of Public and Nonprofit Strategic Planning in the United States." *Public Administration Review,* 70: S255–S267. http://www.jstor.org.proxy.ulib.uits.iu.edu/stable/40984137.

Budiman, Abby. 2020. "Key findings about U.S. Immigrants." Pew Research Center. Retrieved from: https://www.pewresearch.org/fact-tank/2020/08/20/key-findings-about-u-s-immigrants/.

Burchill, Tim. 2006. Seven Ethical "Dilemmas." In *Philanthropic Fundraising. The Hendrickson Institute for Ethical Leadership.* Winona, MN: St. Mary's University of Minnesota.

Bureau of Labor Statistics. 2019a. *Fundraisers, Occupational Outlook Handbook.* Washington DC: U.S. Department of Labor. https://www.bls.gov/ooh/business-and-financial/fundraisers.htm.

Bureau of Labor Statistics. 2019b. *Public Relations and Fundraising Managers, Occupational Outlook Handbook.* Washington DC: U.S. Department of Labor. https://www.bls.gov/ooh/management/public-relations-managers.htm.

Bürger, Tobias. 2019. "Mediatization, Marketization and Non-profits: A Comparative Case Study of Community Foundations in the UK and Germany." PhD diss., Newcastle University.

Burgoyne, Carole B., Janet Reibstein, Anne Edmunds, and Valda Dolman. 2007. "Money Management Systems in Early Marriage: Factors Influencing Change and Stability." *Journal of Economic Psychology,* 28(2): 214–228.

Burlingame, Dwight. 2004. *Philanthropy in America: A Comprehensive Historical Encyclopedia.* Santa Barbara, CA: ABC-CLIO.

Burlingame, Dwight, and Dennis R. Young. 1996. *Corporate Philanthropy at the Crossroads.* Bloomington: Indiana University Press.

Burlingame, Dwight, and Sean Dunlavy. 2016. Corporate Giving and Fundraising. In *Achieving Excellence in Fundraising,* Eugene R. Tempel, Timothy L. Seiler, and Dwight F. Burlingame (eds.), pp. 85–100. Hoboken, NJ: Wiley.

Burns, James M. 1978. *Leadership.* New York: Harper & Row.

Burns, Maree, Carole Burgoyne, and Victoria Clarke. 2008. "Financial Affairs? Money Management in Same-Sex Relationships." *Journal of Socio-Economics,* 37: 481–501.

Buse, Kathleen, Ruth S. Bernstein, and Diana Bilimoria. 2016. "The Influence of Board Diversity, Board Diversity Policies and Practices, and Board Inclusion Behaviors on Nonprofit Governance Practices." *Journal of Business Ethics,* 133(1): 179–191. https://digitalcommons.tacoma.uw.edu/cgi/viewcontent.cgi?article=1643&context=ias_pub.

Buteau, Ellie, Mark Chaffin, and Phil Buchanan. 2014. "What Donors Value: How Community Foundations Can Increase Donor Satisfaction, Referrals, and Future Giving." The Center for Effective Philanthropy. http://cep.org/wp-content/uploads/2014/04/CEP-Research_What-Community-Foundation-Donors-Value-1.pdf.

Campbell, David A., Kristina T. Lambright, and Laura R. Bronstein. 2012. "In the Eyes of the Beholders: Feedback Motivations and Practices among Nonprofit Providers and Their Funders." *Public Performance & Management Review,* 36(1): 7–30. http://www.jstor.org.proxy.ulib.uits.iu.edu/stable/23484727.

Campbell University. 2020. "Rural Case Studies: Northeast Iowa, New Mexico, Eastern Washington and New England." https://www.campbell.edu/about/research/rural-philanthropic-analysis/.

Candid. 2020. "Columbus Survey." https://cfinsights.issuelab.org/resource/2019-columbus-survey-results.html.

Candid. 2021. "Glasspockets: The Foundation Transparency Challenge." https://glasspockets.org/transparency-challenge.

Candid. 2021. "Key Facts on U.S. Nonprofits and Foundations." https://www.issuelab.org/resources/38265/38265.pdf.

Candid. n.d. "Participatory Grantmaking Special Collection." Accessed July 20, 2021: https://participatorygrantmaking.issuelab.org/

Candid. n.d. "Sustainable Development Goals." SDGFunders by Candid. Accessed September 1, 2021: https://sdgfunders.org/sdgs/.

Cao, Xiaoxia. 2016. "Framing Charitable Appeals: The Effect of Message Framing and Perceived Susceptibility to the Negative Consequences of Inaction on Donation Intention: Framing Charitable Appeals." *International Journal of Nonprofit & Voluntary Sector Marketing*, 21(1): 3–12. https://doi.org/10.1002/nvsm.1536.

Cao, Xiaoxia, and Lei Jia. 2017. "The Effects of the Facial Expression of Beneficiaries in Charity Appeals and Psychological Involvement on Donation Intentions." *Nonprofit Management and Leadership*, 27(4): 457–743. https://doi.org/10.1002/nml.21261.

Caplan, Sam. 2020, June 29. "2020: The Year That Changed Grantmaking | NpENGAGE." https://npengage.com/foundations/2020-the-year-that-changed-grantmaking/.

Carboni, Julia, and Angela Eikenberry. 2018. "Giving Circle Membership: How Collective Giving Impacts Donors." Collective Giving Research Group. https://scholarworks.iupui.edu/handle/1805/17743.

Carroll, Deborah A., and Keely Jones Stater. 2009. "Revenue Diversification in Nonprofit Organizations: Does It Lead to Financial Stability?" *Journal of Public Administration Research and Theory*, 19(4): 947–966.

Carson, Emmett D. 2001. "The Roles of Indigenous and Institutional Philanthropy in Advancing Social Justice." In *Philanthropy and the Nonprofit Sector in a Changing America*, Charles T. Clotfelter and Thomas Ehrlich (eds.), pp. 248–274. Bloomington: Indiana University Press.

Cascone, Sarah. 2020a, October 23. "After Purdue Pharma Reached a $225 Million Settlement with US Authorities, the Met Says the Name of Its Sackler Wing Is 'Under Review.'" *Artnet News*. https://news.artnet.com/art-world/sacklers-name-museum-met-1917814.

Cascone, Sarah. 2020b, July 2. "Mellon Foundation President Elizabeth Alexander Tells Us Why America's Biggest Funder of Culture Is Shifting Its Focus to Social Justice." *Artnet News*. https://news.artnet.com/art-world/mellon-foundation-social-justice-grants-1891607.

Castillo, Marco, Ragan Petrie, and Clarence Wardell. 2014. "Fundraising through Online Social Networks: A Field Experiment on Peer-to-Peer Solicitation." *Journal of Public Economics*, 114: 29–35.

CauseEffective. 2019. "Money, Power and Race: The Lived Experience of Fundraisers of Color." https://preparingthenextgeneration.org/preparing-the-next-generation/money-power-and-race.html.

CCS. 2020. "Nonprofit Fundraising Survey: Fundraising Impact of COVID-19, Edition III." https://ccsfundraising.com/insights/#publications.

CCS. 2021. "An Evolving Fundraising Climate: CCS Philanthropic Climate Survey, Edition IV." https://ccsfundraising.com/insights/#publications.

Chan, Eugene Y. 2020. "LGB+ Identification and Donations to Hurricane Irma Victims: The Role of Empathy." *International Journal of Nonprofit & Voluntary Sector Marketing*. http://doi.org/10.1002/nvsm.1691.

Chang, Chun-Tuan, and Yu-Kang Lee. 2010. "Effects of Message Framing, Vividness Congruency, and Statistical Framing on Responses to Charity Advertising" *International Journal of Advertising*, 29(2): 195–220.

Chapman, Cassandra Margot. 2019. "Toward a Triadic Understanding of Charitable Giving: How Donors, Beneficiaries, Fundraisers, and Social Contexts Influence Donation Decisions." PhD diss., School of Psychology, The University of Queensland. https://doi.org/10.14264/uql.2019.357.

Chapman, Cassandra M., Barbara M. Masser, and Winnifred R. Louis. 2019. "The Champion Effect in Peer-to-Peer Giving: Successful Campaigns Highlight Fundraisers More Than Causes." *Nonprofit and Voluntary Sector Quarterly*, 48(3): 572–592.

Charities Aid Foundation (CAF) America. 2020a. *The Voice of Charities Facing COVID-19 Worldwide*. https://www.cafamerica.org/wp-content/uploads/CV19_Report _CAF-America.pdf.

Charities Aid Foundation (CAF) America. 2020b. *The Voice of Corporate Philanthropy in Response to COVID-19 Worldwide*, vol 4. https://www.cafamerica.org/covid19report/.

Charities Aid Foundation (CAF). 2021. "CAF World Giving Index 2021." https://www. cafonline.org/about-us/publications/2021-publications/caf-world-giving-index-2021.

CharityWatch. "Our Charity Rating Process." Accessed June 30, 2021: https://www .charitywatch.org/our-charity-rating-process.

Chief Executives for Corporate Purpose (CECP). 2020. Giving in Numbers. https://cecp .co/wp-content/uploads/2020/11/GIN2020-complete-V3-11_23_20.pdf.

Chou, Eileen Y., and J. Keith Murnighan. 2013. "Life or Death Decisions: Framing the Call for Help." Yamir Moreno (ed.). *PLoS ONE*, 8(3): e57351. https://doi.org/10.1371/ journal.pone.0057351.

Cialdini, Robert B. 2001. *Influence: Science and Practice*, 4th Edition. Boston, MA: Allyn and Bacon.

Clark, Hewitt B., James T. Northrop, and Charles T. Barkshire. 1988. "The Effects of Contingent Thank-You Notes on Case Managers' Visiting Residential Clients." *Education and Treatment of Children*, 11(1): 45–51.

Clark, Lynn Schofield. 2009. "Digital Media and the Generation Gap." *Information, Communication & Society*, 12(3): 388–407. https://doi.org/10.1080/13691180902823845.

Classy. 2020. "Why America Gives 2020: How the Pandemic and Social Justice have Changed Giving." https://www.classy.org/blog/why-america-gives-covid-pandemic-social-justice-giving-trends-2020/.

Cnaan, Ram A., Kathleen H. Jones, Allison Dickin, and Michele Salomon. 2011. "Estimating Giving and Volunteering: New Ways to Measure the Phenomena." *Nonprofit and Voluntary Sector Quarterly*, 40(3): 497–525. https://doi.org/10.1177/0899764010365741.

Cohen, Steve. 2019, February 4. "The Age Gap in Environmental Politics. State of the Planet." Columbia Climate School. https://blogs.ei.columbia.edu/2019/02/04/age-gap-environmental-politics/.

Colinvaux, Roger. 2018. "Defending Place-based Philanthropy by Defining the Community Foundation." BYU L. Rev. 1.

Colinvaux, Roger. 2019. "Fixing Philanthropy: A Vision for Charitable Giving and Reform." *Tax Notes*, 162: 1007.

Colinvaux, Roger, and Ray D. Madoff. 2019, September 16. "Charitable Tax Reform for the 21st Century." *Tax Notes*, 164: 1

Collins, Chuck, Joe Fitzgerald, Helen Flannery, Omar Ocampo, Sophia Paslaski, and Kalena Thomhave. 2021. "Silver Spoon Oligarchs: How America's 50 Largest Inherited-Wealth Dynasties Accelerate Inequality." *Institute for Policy Studies*, https://ips-dc.org/report-americas-wealth-dynasties-2021/.

Community-Centric Fundraising. CCF's 10 Principles. Accessed 12 February 20210: https://communitycentricfundraising.org/ccf-principles/.

Community Foundation Atlas. 2014. https://communityfoundationatlas.org/.

Conron, Kerith J., and Shoshana K. Goldberg 2020. *LGBT People in the United States Not Protected by State Non-Discrimination Statutes*. Los Angeles: The Williams Institute.

Conway, Daniel. 2003. "Practicing Stewardship." In Hank Rosso's *Achieving Excellence in Fundraising*, Eugene R. Tempel (ed.). Hoboken, NJ: Wiley.

Council for Advancement and Support of Education. 2017. *2015 CASE Campaign Report*. Washington, DC: CASE.

Council for Advancement and Support of Education. 2021. *CASE Global Reporting Standards*, 1st Edition. Washington, DC: CASE.

Council on Foundations (COF). 2020, March 19. "A Call to Action: Philanthropy's Commitment during COVID-19." https://www.cof.org/news/call-action-philanthropys-commitment-during-covid-19.

Council on Foundations (COF). 2021. "Foundation Basics." Council on Foundations. https://www.cof.org/content/foundation-basics.

Council on Foundations (COF). n.d. "Independent Foundations." Council on Foundations. Accessed August 1, 2021: https://www.cof.org/foundation-type/independent-foundations.

Coupet, Jason, and Paul Broussard. 2021. "Do Donors Respond to Nonprofit Performance? Evidence from Housing." *Public Performance & Management Review*, 44(1): 108–135. doi:10.1080/15309576.2020.1812409.

Covey, Stephen R., and Rebecca R. Merrill. 2006. *The Speed of Trust: The One Thing that Changes Everything*. New York: Simon and Schuster.

Craver, Roger M. 2017. *Retention Fundraising: The New Art and Science of Keeping Your Donors for Life*. Medfield, MA: Emerson & Church.

Crichton, M. T., and Rhona Flin. 2004. "Identifying and Training Non-technical Skills of Nuclear Emergency Response Teams." *Annals of Nuclear Energy*, 31(12): 1317–1330.

Crittenden, William F., and Victoria L. Crittenden. 2000. "Relationships between Organizational Characteristics and Strategic Planning Processes in Nonprofit Organizations." *Journal of Managerial Issues*, 12(2): 150–168. http://www.jstor.org.proxy.ulib.uits.iu.edu/stable/40604302.

Crockett, Alasdair, and David Voas. 2006. "Generations of Decline: Religious Change in 20th-Century Britain." *Journal for the Scientific Study of Religion*, 45(4): 567–584. https://doi.org/10.1111/j.1468-5906.2006.00328.x.

Crumpton, Michael A. 2016. "Cultivating an Organizational Effort for Development." *The Bottom Line*, 29(2). https://www.emerald.com/insight/content/doi/10.1108/BL-02-2016-0010/full/html.

Cryder, Cynthia E., George Loewenstein, and Richard Scheines. 2013. "The Donor Is in the Details." *Organizational Behavior and Human Decision Processes*, 120(1): 15–23.

Cumberland, Denise M., Sharon A. Kerrick, Jason D'Mello, and Joseph M. Petrosko. 2015. "Nonprofit Board Balance and Perceived Performance." *Nonprofit Management and Leadership*, 25(4): 449–462.

Curtis, Edward IV. 2009. *Muslims in America: A Short History*. Oxford, UK: Oxford University Press.

Curtis, Edward IV, ed. 2010. *Encyclopedia of Muslim-American History*. New York: Facts on File.

Cutlip, Scott M. 1965. *Fund Raising in the United States: Its Role in American Philanthropy*. New Brunswick, NJ: Transaction Press, 1990 reprint. (Original work published in 1965.)

D5. 2016. *State of the Work*. http://www.d5coalition.org/wp-content/uploads/2016/04/D5-SOTW-2016-Final-web-pages.pdf.

Dale, Elizabeth J. 2016. "Giving Among Same-sex Couples: The Role of Identity, Motivations, and Charitable Decision-making in Philanthropic Engagement." Doctoral dissertation, Indiana University. IUPUI ScholarWorks Repository, http://hdl.handle.net/1805/10466.

Dale, Elizabeth. 2017. "Fundraising as Women's Work? Examining the Profession with a Gender Lens." *International Journal of Nonprofit & Voluntary Sector Marketing*, 22(4): e1605. https://doi.org/10.1002/nvsm.1605.

Dale, Elizabeth J. 2018. "Financial Management and Charitable Giving in Gay and Lesbian Households," *Nonprofit and Voluntary Sector Quarterly*, 47(4): 836–855.

Dale, Elizabeth, Diana Small, and Heather O'Connor. 2018. *Giving by and for Women: Understanding High-Net-Worth Donors' Support for Women and Girls*. Indianapolis: Women's Philanthropy Institute at the Indiana University Lilly Family School of Philanthropy. https://scholarworks.iupui.edu/bitstream/handle/1805/15117/giving-by-and-for-women-update180131.pdf.

Dale, Elizabeth, Debra Mesch, Una Osili, Jon Bergdoll, Andrea Pactor, Jacqueline Ackerman, and Tessa Skidmore. 2019. *All In for Women and Girls*. Indianapolis: Women's Philanthropy Institute at the Indiana University Lilly Family School of Philanthropy. https://scholarworks.iupui.edu/bitstream/handle/1805/19913/all-in-report.pdf.

Dale, Elizabeth J., Olha Krupa, Suzanne J. Walker, and Margaret F. Neitzel. 2019. *Leaving a Legacy: A New Look at Today's Planned Giving Donors*. Chicago: Giving USA Foundation.

Danso, Ransford. 2016. "Cultural Competence and Cultural Humility: A Critical Reflection on Key Cultural Diversity Concepts." *Journal of Social Work*, 18(4): 410–430.

Das, Enny, Peter Kerkhof, and Joyce Kuiper. 2008. "Improving the Effectiveness of Fundraising Messages: The Impact of Charity Goal Attainment, Message Framing, and Evidence on Persuasion." *Journal of Applied Communication Research*, 36(2): 161–175.

Davis, Gwendolyn Perry. 2011. "Foundation Fundraising." In *Achieving Excellence in Fundraising*, 3rd Edition, Eugene R. Tempel, Timothy L. Seiler, and Eva E. Aldrich (eds.), pp. 150–163. San Francisco: Jossey-Bass.

Davis, Mark H. 1983. "Measuring Individual Differences in Empathy: Evidence for a Multidimensional Approach." *Journal of Personality and Social Psychology*, 44(1): 113.

Deitrick, Laura, Tessa Tinkler, Emily Young, Colton C. Strawser, Connelly Meschen, Nanelly Manriques, and Bob Beatty. 2020. "Nonprofit Sector Response to COVID-19." *Nonprofit Sector Issues and Trends*, 4. https://digital.sandiego.edu/npi-npissues/4.

Dhingra, Naina, Jonathan Emmett, Andrew Samo, and Bill Schaninger. 2020, October. "Igniting Individual Purpose in Times of Crisis." *McKinsey Quarterly*, 4: 1–11.

Dickert, Stephan, Namika Sagara, and Paul Slovic. 2011. "Affective Motivations to Help Others: A Two-Stage Model of Donation Decisions." *Journal of Behavioral Decision Making*, 24(4): 361–376. https://doi.org/10.1002/bdm.697.

Dimock, Michael. 2019, January 17. "Defining Generations: Where Millennials End and Generation Z Begins." *Pew Research Center* blog. https://www.pewresearch.org/fact-tank/2019/01/17/where-millennials-end-and-generation-z-begins/.

Dobash, R. Emerson, and Russell P. Dobash. 2000. "Politics and Policies of Responding to Violence." In *Home Truths about Domestic Violence: Feminist Influences on Policy and Practice*, Jalna Hanmer and Catherine Itzin (eds.), pp. 187–205. New York: Routledge.

Domestic Violence Network. The State of Domestic Violence Report. Retrieved May 10, 2021: https://dvnconnect.org/wp-content/uploads/2020/12/State-of-DV-18-19-Final.pdf.

Donor Search. n.d. "3 Determiners of Donor Giving Capacity." *DonorSearch*. Accessed December 31, 2020: https://www.donorsearch.net/donor-giving-capacity/.

Donorbox. 2020. "Building a Culture of Philanthropy in Uncertain Times." https://donorbox.org/.

Dorsey, Cheryl, Jeff Bradach, and Peter Kim. 2020. Racial Equity and Philanthropy: Disparities in Funding for Leaders of Color Leave Impact on the Table. The Bridgespan Group. Available from : https://www.bridgespan.org/bridgespan/Images/articles/racial-equity-and-philanthropy/racial-equity-and-philanthropy.pdf.

Double the Donation. n.d. Corporate Sponsorships: The Ultimate Nonprofit Guide. Accessed August 1, 2021: https://doublethedonation.com/tips/corporate-sponsorships.

Dove, Kent E. 2000. *Conducting a Successful Capital Campaign*, 2nd Edition. San Francisco: Jossey-Bass.

Drezner, Noah D. 2009. "Why Give?: Exploring Social Exchange and Organization Identification Theories in the Promotion of Philanthropic Behaviors of African-American Millennials at Private-HBCUs." *International Journal of Educational Advancement*, 9(3): 147–165.

Drezner, Noah D., ed. 2013. *Expanding the Donor Base in Higher Education: Engaging Non-Traditional Donors*. New York: Routledge.

Drezner, Noah D. 2018. "Philanthropic Mirroring: Exploring Identity-Based Fundraising in Higher Education." *The Journal of Higher Education*, 89(3): 261–293. https://doi.org/10.1080/00221546.2017.1368818.

Drezner, Noah D., and Jason C. Garvey. 2016. "LGBTQ Alumni Philanthropy: Exploring (Un)Conscious Motivations for Giving Related to Identity and Experiences." *Nonprofit and Voluntary Sector Quarterly*, 45(1suppl): 52S–71S. https://doi.org/10.1177/0899764015597780.

Drezner, Noah D., and Oren Pizmony-Levy. 2021. "I Belong, Therefore, I Give? The Impact of Sense of Belonging on Graduate Student Alumni Engagement." *Nonprofit and Voluntary Sector Quarterly*, 50(4): 753–777.

Drollinger, Tanya. 2018. "Using Active Empathic Listening to Build Relationships with Major-Gift Donors" *Journal of Nonprofit & Public Sector Marketing*, 30(1): 37–51.

Drollinger, Tanya, Lucette B. Comer, and Patricia T. Warrington. 2006. "Development and Validation of the Active Empathetic Listening Scale." *Psychology & Marketing*, 23(2): 161–180.

Dubb, Steve. 2021. "Foundation Giving Numbers for 2020 Show 15 Percent Increase." *Nonprofit News | Nonprofit Quarterly* blog. Accessed August 18, 2021: https://nonprofit-quarterly.org/foundation-giving-numbers-for-2020-show-15-percent-increase/.

Duclos, R., and A. Barasch. 2014. "Prosocial Behavior in Intergroup Relations: How Donor Self-Construal and Recipient Group-Membership Shape Generosity." *Journal of Consumer Research*, 41(1): 93–108.

Dunn, Elizabeth, and Michael Norton. 2014. *Happy Money: The Science of Happier Spending.* New York Simon and Schuster.

Duronio, Margaret A., and Eugene R. Tempel. 1997. *Fund Raisers: Their Careers, Stories, Concerns, and Accomplishments.* San Francisco: Jossey-Bass Publishers.

Dwyer, Patrick C. 2015. "Gratitude as Persuasion: Understanding When and Why Gratitude Expressions Facilitate and Inhibit Compliance." PhD diss. University of Minnesota.

Dwyer, Patrick C., and Audra H. Vaz. 2020. "Gratitude and Fundraising: Does Putting the 'You' in 'Thank You' Promote Giving?" Paper presented at the 49th Annual Conference of the Association for Research on Nonprofit Organizations and Voluntary Action (ARNOVA). Convened virtually, November 11–13, 2020.

EAB. 2014, September 10. "Inside the Mind of a Curious Chameleon." https://eab.com/insights/infographic/advancement/inside-the-mind-of-a-curious-chameleon/.

Eckel, Catherine, David Herberish, and Jonathan Meer. 2014. "A Field Experiment on Directed Giving at a Public University." NBER Working Paper w20180. https://papers.ssrn.com/sol3/papers.cfm?abstract_id=2444567.

Edelman. 2020. *Edelman Trust Barometer* 2020. https://www.edelman.com/trust/2020-trust-barometer.

Eiseinger, Jesse, Jeff Ernsthausen, and Paul Kiel. 2021, June 8. "The Secret IRS Files: Trove of Never Before Seen Records Reveal How the Wealthiest Avoid Income Tax." *ProPublica.* https://www.propublica.org/article/the-secret-irs-files-trove-of-never-before-seen-records-reveal-how-the-wealthiest-avoid-income-tax.

Eisner, David, Robert T. Grimm Jr., Shannon Maynard, and Susannah Washburn. 2009, Winter. "The New Volunteer Workforce" *Stanford Social Innovation Review:* 32–37.

Ekman, Paul. 2003. *Emotions Revealed: Recognizing Faces and Feelings to Improve Communication and Emotional Life.* New York: Times Books.

Ekström, Mathias. 2012. "Do Watching Eyes Affect Charitable Giving? Evidence from a Field Experiment." *Experimental Economics*, 15(3): 530–546. https://doi.org/10.1007/s10683-011-9312-6.

Elder Jr., Glen H. 1994. "Time, Human Agency, and Social Change: Perspectives on the Life Course." *Social Psychology Quarterly*, 57(1): 4–15. https://doi.org/10.2307/2786971.

Elkas, Elizabeth A. 2016. "Management and Leadership in Fundraising." In *Achieving Excellence in Fundraising*, 4th Edition, E. R. Tempel, T. L. Seiler, and D .F. Burlingame (eds.), pp. 293–306. Hoboken, NJ: John Wiley & Sons, Inc.

Emanuel, Ezekiel J., Govind Persad, Ross Upshur, Beatriz Thome, Michael Parker, Aaron Glickman, Cathy Zhang, Connor Boyle, Maxwell Smith, and James P. Phillips. 2020.

"Fair Allocation of Scarce Medical Resources in the Time of Covid-19." *New England Journal of Medicine*, 382: 2049–2055. https://www.nejm.org/doi/full/10.1056/NEJMsb2005114.

Engage for Good. 2021. *Charity Checkout Champions*. https://engageforgood.com/guides/point-of-sale-fundraising/.

Esposito, Annamaria, and Angela Besana. 2018. "U.S. Community Foundations: Building a Generous Society in Challenging Times." *Journal of Nonprofit & Public Sector Marketing*, 30(2): 200–227. https://doi.org/10.1080/10495142.2018.1452817.

Evans, Megan L., Margo Lindauer, and Maureen E. Farrell. 2020, December 10. "A Pandemic within a Pandemic – Intimate Partner Violence during Covid-19." *The New England Journal of Medicine*, 383: 2302–2304. doi:10.1056/NEJMp2024046.

Evelyn and Walter Haas, Jr. Fund. 2020. "LGBT Giving Project 2011–2020." San Francisco: Author.

Exley, Christine. 2018. "Incentives for Prosocial Behavior: The Role of Reputation." *Management Science*, 64(5): 2460–2471.

Faculty of the Lilly Family School of Philanthropy. 2019, Fall. "8 Myths of U.S. Philanthropy." *Stanford Social Innovation Review*, 26–33. https://ssir.org/articles/entry/eight_myths_of_us_philanthropy.

Faculty of the Lilly Family School of Philanthropy. 2020, Fall. "Inclusive Philanthropy." *Stanford Social Innovation Review*, 38–43. https://ssir.org/articles/entry/inclusive_philanthropy#.

Faletehan, Aun, Elco van Burg, Neil Aaron Thompson, and Johan Wempe. 2020. "Called to Volunteer and Stay Longer: The Significance of Work Calling for Volunteering Motivation and Retention." *Voluntary Sector Review*. doi:10.1332/2040805 20X15929332587023.

Fashant, Crystal Saric, and Rebecca J. Evan. 2020. "Motivations for Volunteerism: Implications for Engagement and Recruitment." *Journal of Organizational Psychology*, 20(2).

Faust, William. 2021, February. Personal communication with Aja Pirtle.

Fender, Stacy A. 2011. "Philanthropy in the Queer Community: A Review and Analysis of Available Research and Literature on Philanthropy within the Queer Community from 1969 to 2009." MA thesis, Saint Mary's University of Minnesota.

Fetzer Institute. 2020, September. "Study of Spirituality in the United States." https://spiritualitystudy.fetzer.org/.

Fidelity Charitable. 2021. "2021 Giving Report." https://www.fidelitycharitable.org/insights/2021-giving-report.html.

Financial Accounting Foundation. 2016, August. "Financial Accounting Series: Accounting Standards Update," No. 2016–14. https://www.fasb.org/jsp/FASB/Document_C/DocumentPage?cid=1176168381847.

Fine, Allison, and Beth Kanter. 2020. "Unlocking Generosity with Artificial Intelligence: The Future of Giving." Accessed December 20, 2020: https://ai4giving.org.

Fisher, Marilyn. 2000. *Ethical Decision Making in Fundraising*. Hoboken, NJ: John Wiley & Sons.

Fishman, James J., Stephen Schwarz, and Lloyd Hitoshi Mayer. 2015. *Nonprofit Organizations: Cases and Materials*, 5th Edition. St. Paul, MN: Foundation Press.

Flandez, Raymund. 2013, May 19. "As Wedding Bells Ring, Charities Seek Support from Newly Visible Same-Sex Couples." *The Chronicle of Philanthropy.* https://www.philanthropy.com/article/as-wedding-bells-ring-charities-seek-support-from-newly-visible-same-sex-couples/.

Florsheim, Lane. 2020, August 13. "Elizabeth Alexander's Fierce Vision of Social Justice." *The Wall Street Journal Magazine.* https://www.wsj.com/articles/elizabeth-alexanders-fierce-vision-of-social-justice-11597343784.

Fomby, Paula, and Andrew J. Cherlin. 2007. "Family Instability and Child Well-Being." *American Sociological Review,* 72(2): 181–204. https://doi.org/10.1177/000312240707200203.

Forbes, Tim. 2020, February 4. "4 Ways Donation Transparency Increases Fundraising Success." *Soapbox Engage.* https://www.soapboxengage.com/blog/1843-4-ways-donation-transparency-increases-fundraising-success.

Frailey, Kerstin. 2017, January 6. "What Does the Nonprofit Sector Really Look Like?" *Guidestar.* https://trust.guidestar.org/what-does-the-nonprofit-sector-really-look-like.

Franey, Jackie W., and Russell N. James, III. 2013, October 15–17. "Trending Forward: Emerging Demographics Driving Planned Giving." National Conference on Philanthropic Planning, Minneapolis, MN.

Franks, Mary Ann. 2020. "The End of Philanthropy" In *Civic Life: What is the Long Game for Philanthropy?* D. W. M. Barker and M. Gilmore (eds.). Kettering Foundation.

Frantzreb, Arthur C. 1991. "Seeking the Big Gift." In *Achieving Excellence in Fundraising,* 1st Edition, H.A. Rosso and Associates (eds.). San Francisco. Jossey-Bass.

Frantzreb, Arthur C. 1997. *Not on This Board You Don't: Making Your Trustees More Effective.* Chicago: Bonus Books.

Fredricks, Laura. 2017. *The Ask.* Hoboken, NJ: John Wiley & Sons.

FreeWill. "Freewill Planned Giving Report 2019." https://lp.freewill.com/hubfs/FreeWill%20Planned%20Giving%20Report%202019.pdf.

French Jr., John R. P., and Bertram Raven. 1959. "The Bases of Social Power." In *Studies in Social Power,* D. Cartwright (ed.), pp. 151–157. Ann Arbor: University of Michigan.

Friedman, Milton. 1970, September. "The Social Responsibility of Business is to Increase its Profits." *The New York Times Magazine:* 122–126.

Frosch, Rachel Morello, Manuel Pastor, Jim Sadd, and Seth Shonkoff. 2009. *The Climate Gap: Inequalities in How Climate Change Hurts Americans and How to Close the Gap.* Los Angeles: University of Southern California.

Frumkin, Peter. 2006. *Strategic Giving.* Chicago: The University of Chicago Press.

Fulton, Brad. 2020. "Religious Organizations: Crosscutting the Nonprofit Sector." In *The Nonprofit Sector: A Research Handbook,* Walter W. Powell and Patricia Bromley (eds.), Stanford, CA: Stanford University Press.

Fundraising Effectiveness Project (FEP). 2019. "2018 Fundraising Effectiveness Survey Report." Washington, DC: Association of Fundraising Professionals and AFP Foundation for Philanthropy, Center on Nonprofits and Philanthropy at the Urban Institute. https://afpglobal.org/reports.

Fundraising Effectiveness Project (FEP). 2020a. "Fundraising Fitness Test (FFT)." Washington, DC: Association of Fundraising Professionals and AFP Foundation for Philanthropy, Center on Nonprofits and Philanthropy at the Urban Institute. https://afpglobal.org/feptools.

Fundraising Effectiveness Project (FEP). 2020b. "Fundraising Net Analyzer (FNA)." Washington, DC: Association of Fundraising Professionals and AFP Foundation for Philanthropy, Center on Nonprofits and Philanthropy at the Urban Institute. https://afpglobal.org/feptools.

Fundraising Effectiveness Project (FEP). 2021. "2021 Quarter 1 Report. 2021." Washington, DC: Association of Fundraising Professionals and AFP Foundation for Philanthropy, Center on Nonprofits and Philanthropy at the Urban Institute. https://afpglobal.org/FundraisingEffectivenessProject.

Furnham, Adrian, and Michael Argyle. 2014. *The New Psychology of Money*. Milton Park, UK: Routledge.

Fyffe, Saunji D. 2016, October 7. "The New Philanthropy Movement Raises New Questions." The Urban Institute. https://independentsector.org.

Galewitz, Phil. 2019, January 28. "Hospitals Check to See If Patients Are Donor-Worthy – Not Their Organs, But Pockets." *Kaiser Health News*. https://khn.org/news/hospitals-screen-patients-for-wealth-in-search-for-potential-financial-donors/.

Gallo, Marcia M. 2001. "Lesbian Giving – and Getting: Tending Radical Roots in an Era of Venture Philanthropy." *Journal of Lesbian Studies*, 5: 63–70.

Galloway, Jane. 2019. "Managing Volunteers and In-house Fundraising Groups." In *Community Fundraising*, Samantha Rider (ed.). London: Directory of Social Change.

Galloway, Scott. 2020, December 24. "Interview with Jeffrey Sonnenfeld." *THE PROF G SHOW*. https://podcasts.apple.com/us/podcast/lead-with-resilience/id1498802610?i=1000503396375.

Gamboa, Glenn, and Haleluya Hadero. 2021, September 3. "Grassroots Efforts Play Key Role in Hurricane Ida Relief." *The Chronicle of Philanthropy*. https://www.philanthropy.com/article/grassroots-efforts-play-key-role-in-hurricane-ida-relief.

Garvey, Jason C., and Noah D. Drezner. 2013. "Advancement Staff and Alumni Advocates: Cultivating LGBTQ Alumni by Promoting Individual and Community Uplift." *Journal of Diversity in Higher Education*, 6(3): 199.

Garvey, Jason C., and Noah D. Drezner. 2013. "Alumni Giving in the LGBTQ Communities: Queering Philanthropy." In *Expanding the Donor Base in Higher Education: Engaging Non-traditional Donors*, N. Drezner (ed.), pp. 74–86. New York: Routledge.

Gautier, Arthur, and Anne-Claire Pache. 2015. "Research on Corporate Philanthropy: A Review and Assessment." *Journal of Business Ethics*, 126(3): 343–369.

GenerosityForLife. n.d. "Generosity Reports." Indiana University Lilly Family School of Philanthropy. Retrieved August 1, 2021: https://generosityforlife.org/generosity-data/data-tools/generosity-reports/.

GhaneaBassiri, Kambiz. 2012. *A History of Islam in America*. Cambridge, UK: Cambridge University Press.

Gibson, Cynthia M. 2016a. "Beyond Fundraising: What Does It Mean to Build a Culture of Philanthropy?" Evelyn and Walter Haas, Jr. Fund. https://www.haasjr.org/sites/default/files/resources/Haas_CultureofPhilanthropy_F1_0.pdf.-philanthropy/.

Gilstrap, Curt A., Cristina M. Gilstrap, Kendra Nigel Holderby, and Katrina Maria Valera. 2016. "Sensegiving, Leadership, and Nonprofit Crises: How Nonprofit Leaders Make and Give Sense to Organizational Crisis." *Voluntas: International Journal of Voluntary and Nonprofit Organizations*, 27(6): 2787–2806. http://www.jstor.org.proxy.ulib.uits.iu.edu/stable/26160691.

Giridharadas, Anand. 2018. *Winners Take All: The Elite Charade of Changing the World.* New York: Alfred A. Knopf.

Give.org. 2020. *Donor Trust Report 2020: The Pandemic and a Three-Year Retrospective.* Arlington, VA: BBB Wise Giving Alliance. https://give.org/docs/default-source/donor-trust-library/2020-donor-trust-report.pdf.

Giving USA. 2018. *Giving USA Special Report: The Evolution of Workplace Giving.* Chicago: Giving USA Foundation.

Giving USA. 2020. *Giving USA: The Annual Report on Philanthropy for the Year 2019.* Chicago, IL: Giving USA Foundation.

Giving USA. 2021. *Giving USA: The Annual Report on Philanthropy for the Year 2020.* Chicago: Giving USA Foundation. https://givingusa.org/.

Giving USA Foundation. 2018. *Giving USA Special Report: The Data on Donor-Advised Funds: New Insights You Need to Know.* Chicago: Giving USA Foundation. https://givingusa.org/just-released-special-report-the-data-on-donor-advised-funds-new-insights-you-need-to-know/.

GLAAD. 2017. Accelerating Acceptance 2017: *A Harris Poll Survey of Americans' Acceptance of LGBTQ People.* New York: Author.

Glanville, Jennifer L., David Sikkink, and Edwin I. Hernández. 2008. "Religious Involvement and Educational Outcomes: The Role of Social Capital and Extracurricular Participation." *The Sociological Quarterly,* 49(1): 105–137.

Gneezy, U., E. A. Keenan, and A. Gneezy. 2014. "Behavioral Economics. Avoiding Overhead Aversion in Charity." *Science,* 346(6209): 632–635. doi:10.1126/science.1253932.

Goering, Elizabeth, Ulla M. Connor, Ed Nagelhout, and Richard Steinberg. 2011. "Persuasion in Fundraising Letters: An Interdisciplinary Study." *Nonprofit and Voluntary Sector Quarterly,* 40(2): 228–246.

Goffman, Erving. 1959. *The Presentation of Self in Every Day Life.* New York: Anchor Books.

Goldscheider, Frances K. 2012. "The Accordion Family: Boomserang Kids, Anxious Parents, and the Private Toll of Global Competition by Katherine Newman." *American Journal of Sociology,* 118(3): 821–822. https://doi.org/10.1086/667780.

Goldseker, Sharna, and Michael Moody. 2017. *Generation Impact: How Next Gen Donors Are Revolutionizing Giving.* Hoboken, NJ: Wiley.

Gopinath, Gita. 2020, April 14. "The Great Lockdown: Worst Economic Downturn since the Great Depression." *IMFBlog.* https://blogs.imf.org/2020/04/14/the-great-lockdown-worst-economic-downturn-since-the-great-depression/.

Gordon, Linda. 2002. *Heroes of Their Own Lives: The Politics and History of Family Violence.* Urbana: University of Illinois Press.

Gouldner, Alvin W. 1960. "The Norm of Reciprocity: A Preliminary Statement." *American Sociological Review:* 161–178.

Gourville, John T. 1998. "Pennies-a-day: The Effect of Temporal Reframing on Transaction Evaluation." *Journal of Consumer Research,* 24(4): 395–408.

Grace, Kay Sprinkel. 2020. "Competition or Collaboration: Where is Philanthropy Headed?" http://www.kaygrace.org/about.html.

Grant, Adam M., and Francesca Gino. 2010. "A Little Thanks Goes a Long Way: Explaining Why Gratitude Expressions Motivate Prosocial Behavior." *Journal of Personality and Social Psychology,* 98(6): 946–955.

Grant, Angelique S. C., and Ronald J. Shiller. 2020. *Diversity, Equity, and Inclusion in Advancement.* Washington, DC: Council for Advancement and Support of Education.

Grant, Kaky. 2020, September 9. "Philanthropy Will Never Be the Same after 2020: I Argue it Is Changing for the Better." Lilly Family School of Philanthropy. *Fresh Perspectives from the World of Philanthropy* blog. https://blog.philanthropy.iupui.edu/tag/kaky-grant/.

Greer, Lisa, and Larissa Kostoff. 2020. *Philanthropy Revolution: How to Inspire Donors, Build Relationships, and Make a Difference.* New York: Harper Collins.

Grimm, Jr., Robert T., and Nathan Dietz. 2018. "Where Are America's Volunteers? A Look at America's Widespread Decline in Volunteering in Cities and States." Maryland: Do Good Institute, University of Maryland. https://dogood.umd.edu/research-impact/publications/where-are-americas-volunteers.

Gross, Jennifer. 2013, September. "5 Digital Strategies to Drive Holiday Donations." https://www.thinkwithgoogle.com/marketing-strategies/video/driving-donations-digitally/.

Guo, Chao. 2007. "When Government becomes the Principal Philanthropist: The Effects of Public Funding on Patterns of Nonprofit Governance." *Public Administration Review,* 67(3): 458–473.

Gyamfi, Bright, and Kwasi Konadu. 2021, September 8. "Black Lives Matter: How Far Has the Movement Come?" *The Conversation.* http://theconversation.com/black-lives-matter-how-far-has-the-movement-come-165492.

Hadero, Haleluya. 2021, March 17. "Companies Committed Two-Thirds of Total Giving Earmarked for Racial Equity," *The Chronicle of Philanthropy.* https://www.philanthropy.com/article/corporations-become-unlikely-financiers-of-racial-equity.

Haid, Phillip. 2015, December 4. "The Ice Bucket Challenge Part 2: What Can We Learn from Why It Didn't Work." *Fast Company Magazine.* https://www.fastcompany.com/3054221/the-ice-bucket-challenge-part-2-what-can-we-learn-from-why-it-didnt-work.

Haines, William. 2006. "Consequentialism." *Internet Encyclopedia of Philosophy.* https://iep.utm.edu/conseque/.

Hall, Matthew. 2014. "Evaluation Logics in the Third Sector." *Voluntas: International Journal of Voluntary and Nonprofit Organizations,* 25(2): 307–336. http://www.jstor.org.proxy.ulib.uits.iu.edu/stable/43654317.

Hammack, David C. 2018. "Introduction." In *American Philanthropic Foundations: Regional Difference and Change,* pp. 1–30. Bloomington, IN: Indiana University Press.

Hanke, Steven. 2017, August 16. "What Do the Great Depression and the Great Recession Have in Common?" *Forbes.* https://www.forbes.com/sites/stevehanke/2017/08/16/what-do-the-great-depression-and-the-great-recession-have-in-common/.

Hansen, Ruth K. 2018. "The Role of Stigma in Writing Charitable Appeals." Doctoral Dissertation. Indiana University.

Hargittai, Eszter. 2010. "Digital Na(t)Ives? Variation in Internet Skills and Uses among Members of the 'Net Generation'." *Sociological Inquiry,* 80(1): 92–113. https://doi.org/10.1111/j.1475-682X.2009.00317.x.

Harrington, Joan, and Anita Varma. 2020. *Controversial Donors: A Guide to Ethical Gift Acceptance.* Markkula Center for Applied Ethics, Santa Clara University, Santa Clara, CA. https://www.scu.edu/media/ethics-center/social-sector-ethics/Controversial-Donors-Guide.pdf.

Hart-Brinson, Peter. 2014. "Discourse of Generations: The Influence of Cohort, Period and Ideology in Americans' Talk about Same-Sex Marriage." *American Journal of Cultural Sociology*, 2(2): 221–252. https://doi.org/10.1057/ajcs.2014.3.

Haslam, S. Alexander., Stephen Reicher, and Michael Platow. 2011. *The New Psychology of Leadership: Identity, Influence, and Power*. New York: Psychology Press.

Havens, John J., Mary A. O'Herlihy, and Paul G. Schervish. 2006. "Charitable Giving: How Much, by Whom, to What, and How?" In *The Nonprofit Sector: A Research Handbook*. New Haven, CT: Yale University Press.

Haynes, Emily. 2021a, January 12. "Fundraising Campaigns Move Forward Despite Pandemic Disruption." *The Chronicle of Philanthropy*. https://www.philanthropy.com/article/fundraising-campaigns-move-forward-despite-pandemic-disruption.

Haynes, Emily. 2021b, June 22. "Study Points to Continued Growth in Giving in 2021." *The Chronicle of Philanthropy*. https://www.philanthropy.com/article/study-points-to-continued-growth-in-giving-in-2021.

Heath, Chip, and Dan Heath. 2008. *Made to Stick: Why Some Ideas Survive and Others Die*. New York: Random House.

Heimovics, Richard D., Robert D. Herman, and Carole L. Jurkiewicz Coughlin. 1993. "Executive Leadership and Resource Dependence in Nonprofit Organizations: A Frame Analysis." *Public Administration Review*: 419–427.

Heist, H. Daniel, and Danielle Vance-McMullen. 2019. "Understanding Donor-Advised Funds: How Grants Flow During Recessions." *Nonprofit and Voluntary Sector Quarterly*, 48(5): 1066–1093.

Herman, Robert D., David O. Renz, and Richard D. Heimovics. 1996. "Board Practices and Board Effectiveness in Local Nonprofit Organizations." *Nonprofit Management and Leadership*, 7(4): 373–385.

Hershatter, Andrea, and Molly Epstein. 2010. "Millennials and the World of Work: An Organization and Management Perspective." *Journal of Business and Psychology*, 25(2): 211–223. https://doi.org/10.1007/s10869-010-9160-y.

Herzog, Patricia Snell, and Heather Price. 2016. *American Generosity: Who Gives and Why*. Oxford, UK: Oxford University Press.

Herzog, Patricia Snell, Casey T. Harris, Shauna A. Mormoto, Shane W. Barker, Jill G. Wheeler, A. Justin Barnum, and Terrance L. Boyd. 2020. *The Science of College: Navigating the First Year and Beyond*. Oxford, UK: Oxford University Press.

Hilsner-Wiles, Suzanne. 2020, March 18. "4 Ways to Engage Major Donors during the Covid-19 Crisis." *The Chronicle of Philanthropy*. https://www.philanthropy.com/article/4-ways-to-engage-major-donors-during-the-covid-19-crisis/.

Hodge, Matthew M., and Ronald F. Piccolo. 2005. "Funding Source, Board Involvement Techniques, and Financial Vulnerability in Nonprofit Organizations: A Test of Resource Dependence." *Nonprofit Management and Leadership*, 16(2): 171–190.

Horizons Foundation. 2008. *Building a New Tradition of LGBT Philanthropy*. San Francisco, CA: Author.

Hudnut-Beumler, James. 2007. *In Pursuit of the Almighty's Dollar: A History of Money and American Protestantism*. Chapel Hill, NC: University of North Carolina.

Hudson, D., J. Vanheerde-Hudson, N. Dasandi, and N. Gaines. 2016, September. "Emotional Pathways to Engagement with Global Poverty: An Experimental Analysis." 2015 Annual Meeting of the American Political Science Association, pp. 1–29.

Hui, Bryant P.H., Jacky C. K. Ng, Erica Berzaghi, Lauren A. Cunningham-Amos, and Aleksandr Kogan. 2020. "Rewards of Kindness? A Meta-analysis of the Link between Prosociality and Well-being." *Psychological Bulletin*, 146(12): 1084–1116.

Hung, Iris W., and Robert S. Wyer. 2009. "Differences in Perspective and the Influence of Charitable Appeals: When Imagining Oneself as the Victim Is Not Beneficial." *Journal of Marketing Research*, 46(3): 421–34. https://doi.org/10.1509/jmkr.46.3.421.

Hysenbelli, Dorina, Enrico Rubaltelli, and Rino Rumiati. 2013. "Others' Opinions Count, But Not All of Them: Anchoring to Ingroup Versus Outgroup Members' Behavior in Charitable Giving." *Judgment & Decision Making*, 8(6).

IEG Sponsorship Report. 2021. "What Sponsors Want & Where Dollars Will Go in 2018" www.sponsorship.com.

Ilchman, Warren Frederick., Stanley Nider Katz, and Edward L Queen II, eds. 1998. *Philanthropy in the World's Traditions*. Bloomington, IN: Indiana University Press.

Inclusive America Project. 2020, May. "Powering Pluralism: Analyzing the Current Philanthropic Landscape." Aspen Institute, Lake Institute on Faith & Giving, and Public Religion Research Institute (PRRI). https://aspeninstitute.org/programs/justice-and-society-program/powering-pluralism-analyzing-the-current-philanthropic-landscape/.

Independent Sector. 2002. *Obedience to the Unenforceable: Ethics and the Nation's Voluntary and Philanthropic Community*. Washington, DC: Independent Sector. http://efc.issuelab.org/resources/16107/16107.pdf.

Independent Sector. 2020. *Trust in Civil Society: Understanding the Factors Driving Trust in Nonprofits and Philanthropy*. Washington, DC, Independent Sector. https://independent-sector.org/wp-content/uploads/2020/06/Trust-in-Civil-Society-62420.pdf.

Indiana University. 2020. "Affinity Giving Circles." https://supportdiversity.iu.edu/giving-circles/index.html.

Indiana University Lilly Family School of Philanthropy. 2016. *The 2016 U.S. Trust Study of High Net Worth Philanthropy*. Indianapolis, IN: U.S. Trust and Indiana University Lilly Family School of Philanthropy. https://scholarworks.iupui.edu/handle/1805/11234.

Indiana University Lilly Family School of Philanthropy. 2017. *Data Set: Philanthropy Panel Study*. Unpublished. Indianapolis, IN: The Trustees of Indiana University.

Indiana University Lilly Family School of Philanthropy. 2018a. *The 2018 U.S. Trust Study of High Net Worth Philanthropy*. Indianapolis, IN: U.S. Trust and Indiana University Lilly Family School of Philanthropy. https://scholarworks.iupui.edu/bitstream/handle/1805/17666/high-net-worth2018-summary.pdf.

Indiana University Lilly Family School of Philanthropy. 2018b. *The Impact of Diversity: Understanding How Nonprofit Board Diversity Affects Philanthropy, Leadership, and Board Engagement*. Indianapolis, IN. The Trustees of Indiana University, https://scholarworks.iupui.edu/handle/1805/15239.

Indiana University Lilly Family School of Philanthropy. 2019. *U.S. Household Disaster Giving in 2017 and 2018*. Center for Disaster Philanthropy, IU Lilly Family School of Philanthropy, and Candid. https://scholarworks.iupui.edu/handle/1805/19403.

Indiana University Lilly Family School of Philanthropy. 2020a, October. *Global Philanthropy Tracker*, 1st Edition. https://scholarworks.iupui.edu/handle/1805/24144.

Indiana University Lilly Family School of Philanthropy. 2020b, July. *Higher Education and Diaspora Philanthropy in Sub-Saharan Africa*. https://scholarworks.iupui.edu/handle/1805/23421.

Indiana University Lilly Family School of Philanthropy. 2021a. *Data Set. Bank of America Study of Philanthropy: Charitable Giving by Affluent Households.* Unpublished. Indianapolis, IN. The Trustees of Indiana University.

Indiana University Lilly Family School of Philanthropy 2021b. *Everyday Donors of Color: Divers Philanthropy during Times of Change.* https://scholarworks.iupui.edu/bitstream/handle/1805/26496/donors-color-report.pdf.

Indiana University Lilly Family School of Philanthropy. 2021c. *Infographic: The Giving Environment: Understanding Pre-Pandemic Trends in Charitable Giving.* IU Lilly Family School of Philanthropy. http://hdl.handle.net/1805/26291.

Indiana University Lilly Family School of Philanthropy. 2021d. *The 2021 Bank of America Study of Philanthropy Charitable Giving by Affluent Households: Affluent Americans Expand Generosity during the Pandemic.* Indianapolis, IN. The Trustees of Indiana University.

Indiana University Lilly Family School of Philanthropy 2021e. *Charitable Crowdfunding: Who Give, to What, and Why?* Indianapolis, IN. The Trustees of Indiana University, https://scholarworks.iupui.edu/handle/1805/25515.

Indiana University Lilly Family School of Philanthropy. 2022. *Global Philanthropy Environment Index*, 2nd Edition. https://globalindices.iupui.edu/environment/index.html.

Indiana University The Fund Raising School. 2018. *Managing the Capital Campaign.* Indianapolis, IN: Indiana University Lilly Family School of Philanthropy, The Trustees of Indiana University.

Indiana University The Fund Raising School. 2021. *Principles and Techniques of Fundraising Study Guide.* Indianapolis, IN: Indiana University Lilly Family School of Philanthropy, The Trustees of Indiana University.

Institute for Social Policy and Understanding. 2021. Board Resource Development and Tracking Form. Washington, DC, and Dearborn, MI.

Internal Revenue Service (IRS). n.d. "Life Cycle of a Private Foundation." Accessed September 22, 2021: https://www.irs.gov/charities-non-profits/private-foundations/life-cycle-of-a-private-foundation.

Jackson, Kenneth W., Alandra L. Washington, and Russell H. Jackson. 2012. "Strategies for Impacting Change in Communities of Color." *The Foundation Review*, 4(1): 6. Retrieved from: http://scholarworks.gvsu.edu/cgi/viewcontent.cgi?article=1038&context=tfr.

James III, Russell N. 2009. "Health, Wealth, and Charitable Estate Planning: A Longitudinal Examination of Testamentary Charitable Giving Plans." *Nonprofit and Voluntary Sector Quarterly*, 38(6): 1026–1043.

James III, Russell N., and Michael W. O'Boyle. 2014. "Charitable Estate Planning as Visualized Autobiography: An fMRI Study of Its Neural Correlates." *Nonprofit and Voluntary Sector Quarterly*, 43(2): 355–373.

James III, Russell N., and Christopher Baker. 2015. "The Timing of Final Charitable Bequest Decisions." *International Journal of Nonprofit & Voluntary Sector Marketing*, 20(3): 277–283.

James III, Russell N. 2015a. "The New Statistics of Estate Planning: Lifetime and Post-mortem Wills, Trusts, and Charitable Planning." *Estate Planning & Community Property Law Journal*, 8: 1–39.

James III, Russell N. 2015b. "The Family Tribute in Charitable Bequest Giving: An Experimental Test of the Effect of Reminders on Giving Intentions." *Nonprofit Management and Leadership*, 26: 73–89.

James III, Russell N., and Claire Routley. 2016. "We the Living: The Effects of Living and Deceased Donor Stories on Charitable Bequest Giving Intentions." *International Journal of Nonprofit & Voluntary Sector Marketing*, 21(2): 109–117.

James III, Russell N. 2016a. "An Economic Model of Mortality Salience in Personal Financial Decision Making: Applications to Annuities, Life Insurance, Charitable Gifts, Estate Planning, Conspicuous Consumption, and Healthcare." *Journal of Financial Therapy*, 7(2): 5.

James III, Russell N. 2016b. "Phrasing the Charitable Bequest Inquiry." *Voluntas: International Journal of Voluntary and Nonprofit Organizations*, 27(2): 998–1011.

James III, Russell N. 2016c. "Testing the Effectiveness of Fundraiser Job Titles in Charitable Bequest and Complex Gift Planning." *Nonprofit Management and Leadership*, 27(2): 165–179.

James III, Russell. 2017. "Natural Philanthropy: A New Evolutionary Framework Explaining Diverse Experimental Results and Informing Fundraising Practice." *Palgrave Communications*, 3(1). https://doi.org/10.1057/palcomms.2017.50.

James III, Russell N. (2018a). "Cash Is not King for Fund-raising: Gifts of Noncash Assets Predict Current and Future Contributions Growth." *Nonprofit Management and Leadership*, 29(2): 159–179.

James III, Russell N. 2018b. "Describing Complex Charitable Giving Instruments: Experimental Tests of Technical Finance Terms and Tax Benefits." *Nonprofit Management and Leadership*, 28(4): 437–452.

James III, Russell N. 2018c. "Creating Understanding and Interest in Charitable Financial and Estate Planning: An Experimental Test of Introductory Phrases." *Journal of Personal Finance*, 17(2): 9–21.

James III, Russell N. 2019a. "Encouraging Repeated Memorial Donations to a Scholarship Fund: An Experimental Test of Permanence Goals and Anniversary Acknowledgements." *Philanthropy & Education*, 2(2): 1–28.

James III, Russell N. 2019b. "American Charitable Bequest Transfers across the Centuries: Empirical Findings and Implications for Policy and Practice." *Estate Planning & Community Property Law Journal*, 12: 235.

James III, Russell N. 2020. "The Emerging Potential of Longitudinal Empirical Research in Estate Planning: Examples from Charitable Bequests." *UC Davis Law Review*, 53: 2397–2431.

Jankowiak, Tim. 2019. "Immanuel Kant." *Internet Encyclopedia of Philosophy*. https://iep.utm.edu/kantview/.

Jeavons, Thomas H. 2016. "Ethical Nonprofit Management: Core Values and Key Practices." In *The Jossey-Bass Handbook of Nonprofit Leadership and Management*, David O. Renz (ed.), pp. 188–216. Hoboken, NJ: John Wiley & Sons, Inc.

Johnson Center. 2020. "11 Trends in Philanthropy for 2020." https://johnsoncenter.org/blog/11-trends-in-philanthropy-for-2020/.

Johnson, Craig E. 2018a. *Meeting the Ethical Challenges of Leadership: Casting Light or Shadow*, 6th Edition. Thousand Oaks, CA: SAGE.

Johnson, Paula. 2018b. "The Global Philanthropy Report: Perspectives on the Global Foundation Sector." https://cpl.hks.harvard.edu/global-philanthropy-report-perspectives-global-financial-sector.

Jones, Jeffrey M. 2020. "Percentage of Americans Donating to Charity at New Low." Gallup .com. May 14, 2020. https://news.gallup.com/poll/310880/percentage-americans-donating-charity-new-low.aspx.

Jones, Jeffrey M. 2021. "U.S. Church Membership Falls Below Majority for First Time," Gallup, March 29, 2021. https://news.gallup.com/poll/341963/church-membership-falls-below-majority-first-time.aspx.

Jones, Jennifer A. 2018. "An Unseen Lens: The Relationship between Philanthropists' Developmental Meaning Making and Philanthropic Activity." *Nonprofit Management and Leadership*, 28(4): 491–509.

Josephson, Michael. 2002. *Making Ethical Decisions*. Los Angeles, CA: Josephson Institute of Ethics.

Joslyn, Heather. 2019, August 6. "51% of Fundraisers Plan to Leave Their Jobs by 2021, Says New Survey." *The Chronicle of Philanthropy*. https://www.philanthropy.com/article/51-of-fundraisers-plan-to-leave-their-jobs-by-2021-says-new-survey/.

Josselson, Ruthellen. 1987. *Finding Herself: Pathways to Identity Development in Women*. San Francisco: Jossey-Bass.

Joulfaian, David. 2005, June. "Basic Facts on Charitable Giving." U.S. Dep't of Treasury, Office of Tax Analysis Paper 95, p. 27. https://www.treasury.gov/resourcecenter/tax-policy/tax-analysis/Documents/WP-95.pdf.

Joyaux, Simone. 2015, March 27. "Building a Culture of Philanthropy in your Organization." *Nonprofit Quarterly*. https://nonprofitquarterly.org/culture-of-philanthropy-define-philanthropy/.

Julian Center Private Collection, Indianapolis, IN.

Kaplan, Ann E. 2020. "Voluntary Support of Education: Key Findings from Data Collected for the 2018–19 Academic Fiscal Year for US Higher Education Institutions." Council for Advancement and Support of Education. https://www.case.org/resources/voluntary-support-education-key-findings-2018-19.

Kaufman, Barbara. 2003. "Stories That Sell, Stories That Tell." *The Journal of Business Strategy*, 24(3): 11–15. https://doi.org/10.1108/02756660310508155.

Kelly, Kathleen S. 1998. *Effective Fund-Raising Management*. Mahwah, NJ: Lawrence Erlbaum Associates, Inc.

Kennedy, Patrick. 2020. "Intercultural Competence for Nonprofit Fundraising." CCS Fundraising. https://ccsfundraising.com/intercultural-competence-for-nonprofit-fundraising/.

Kerrissey, Michaela J., and Amy C. Edmondson. April 2020. "What Good Leadership Looks Like During this Pandemic." *Harvard Business Review Digital Articles*. https://hbr.org/2020/04/what-good-leadership-looks-like-during-this-pandemic.

Kessler, Judd B., and Katherine L. Milkman. 2018. "Identity in Charitable Giving." *Management Science*, 64(2): 845–859.

Khanna, Tarum. 2014. "Contextual Intelligence." *Harvard Business Review*, 92(9): 58–68.

Kidder, Rushworth M. 1995. *How Good People Make Tough Choices*. New York: William Morrow.

Kim, Anne. 2017, October 4. "The Push for College-Endowment Reform." *The Atlantic*. https://www.theatlantic.com/education/archive/2017/10/the-bipartisan-push-for-college-endowment-reform/541140/.

Kim, John S., Yanna J. Weisberg, Jeffry A. Simpson, M. Minda Oriña, Allison K. Farrell, and William F. Johnson. 2015. "Ruining It for Both of Us: The Disruptive Role of Low-Trust Partners on Conflict Resolution in Romantic Relationships." *Social Cognition*, 33(5): 520–542.

Kim, Mirae, and Dyana P. Mason. 2020. "Are You Ready: Financial Management, Operating Reserves, and the Immediate Impact of COVID-19 on Nonprofits." *Nonprofit and Voluntary Sector Quarterly*, 49(6): 1191–1209.

Kim, Sung-Ju, and Xiaonan Kou. 2014. "Not All Empathy Is Equal: How Dispositional Empathy Affects Charitable Giving." *Journal of Nonprofit & Public Sector Marketing*, 26(4): 312–34. https://doi.org/10.1080/10495142.2014.965066.

King, David P. 2020, September. "Lake Institute COVID-19 Congregational Study." Lake Institute on Faith & Giving. https://philanthropy.iupui.edu/institutes/lake-institute/covid-study.html.

King, David P., Brad Fulton, Chris Munn, and Jamie Goodwin. 2019. "National Study of Congregations' Economic Practices Executive Report." Lake Institute on Faith & Giving, Lilly Family School of Philanthropy. Indianapolis, IN: The Trustees of Indiana University. www.nscep.org.

Klein, Kim. 2016, August 3. "Is Social Justice Fundraising an Oxymoron?" Open Democracy.net. https://www.opendemocracy.net/en/transformation/is-social-justice-fundraising-oxymoron/.

Klinge, Naomi, and Meg James. 2020, June 3. "Warner Music, Disney Pledge Support to Social Justice," *LA Times*. https://www.latimes.com/entertainment-arts/business/story/2020-06-03/production-companies-pledge-support-to-social-justice-groups.

Knapp, Mark L., Donald G. Ellis, and Barbara A. Williams. 1980. "Perceptions of Communication Behavior Associated with Relationship Terms." *Communications Monographs*, 47(4): 262–278.

Knight Foundation. n.d. Giving Day Playbook. Accessed September 24, 2021: https://knightfoundation.org/reports/giving-day-playbook/.

Koczanski, Peter, and Harvey S. Rosen. 2019. "Are Millennials Really Particularly Selfish? Preliminary Evidence from a Cross-Sectional Sample in the Philanthropy Panel Study." *American Behavioral Scientist*, 63(14): 1965–1982. https://doi.org/10.1177/0002764219850871.

Koenig, Bonnie L. 2004. *Going Global for the Greater Good: Succeeding as a Nonprofit in the International Community*. San Francisco: Jossey-Bass.

Kogut, Tehila, and Ilana Ritov. 2007. "'One of Us': Outstanding Willingness to Help Save a Single Identified Compatriot." *Organizational Behavior and Human Decision Processes*, 104(2): 150–157. https://doi.org/10.1016/j.obhdp.2007.04.006.

Kohli, Martin. 1988. "Ageing as a Challenge for Sociological Theory." *Ageing & Society*, 8(04): 367–394. https://doi.org/10.1017/S0144686X00007169.

Konrath, Sara. 2014. "The Power of Philanthropy and Volunteering." In *Wellbeing: A Complete Reference Guide: Volume VI: Interventions and Policies to Enhance Wellbeing*, Felicia Huppert and Cary L. Cooper (eds.), pp. 387–426. West Sussex, UK: John Wiley & Sons.

Konrath, Sara. 2017. "What's the Matter with Empathy?" *Greater Good Magazine.* https://greatergood.berkeley.edu/article/item/whats_the_matter_with_empathy.

Konrath, Sara, and Femida Handy. 2017a. "The Development and Validation of the Motives to Donate Scale." *Nonprofit & Voluntary Sector Quarterly.* 0899764017744894.

Konrath, Sara, and Femida Handy. 2017b. "5 Reasons Why People Give Their Money Away – plus 1 Why They Don't." *The Conversation.* http://theconversation.com/5-reasons-why-people-give-their-money-away-plus-1-why-they-dont-87801.

Konstam, Varda. 2015. "Running on Empty, Running on Full." In *Emerging and Young Adulthood: Advancing Responsible Adolescent Development*, pp. 183–202. New York: Springer International Publishing.

Kopczuk, Wojciech. 2007. "Bequest and Tax Planning: Evidence from Estate Tax Returns." *The Quarterly Journal of Economics*, 122(4): 1801–1854.

Kosloff, Spee, Gabrial Anderson, Alexandra Nottbohm, and Brandon Hoshiko. 2019. "Proximal and Distal Terror Management Defenses: A Systematic Review and Analysis." In *Handbook of Terror Management Theory*, pp. 31–63. Cambridge, MA: Academic Press.

Kramer, Larry. 2021, January 4. "Foundation Payout Policy in Economic Crises." *Stanford Social Innovation Review.* https://ssir.org/articles/entry/foundation_payout_policy_in_economic_crises.

Kridler, Douglas, Vikki Spruill, Dan Cardinali, and Adam Meyerson. 2017. "Letter to Orrin G. Hatch and Ron Wyden on Donor-Advised Funds." *Law School Publications*: 945. http://lawdigitalcommons.bc.edu/law_school_publications/945.

Kruglanski, Arie. 2020, March 20. "3 ways the Coronavirus Pandemic Is Changing Who We Are." *The Conversation.* https://theconversation.com/3-ways-the-coronavirus-pandemic-is-changing-who-we-are-133876.

Kübler-Ross, Elisabeth. 1997. *On Death and Dying: What the Dying Have to Teach Doctors, Nurses, Clergy, and Their Families*, 1st Touchstone Edition. New York: Simon & Schuster/Touchstone Book.

Kumar, Amit, and Nicholas Epley. 2018. "Undervaluing Gratitude: Expressers Misunderstand the Consequences of Showing Appreciation." *Psychological Science*, 29(9): 1423–1435.

Kumar, Nirmalya, and Jan-Benedict EM Steenkamp. 2013. "Diaspora Marketing." *Harvard Business Review*, 91(10): 127.

Lareau, Annette. 2015. "Cultural Knowledge and Social Inequality." *American Sociological Review*, 80(1): 1–27. https://doi.org/10.1177/0003122414565814.

Leaver, Tama, Tim Highfield, and Crystal Abidin. 2020. *Instagram: Visual Social Media Cultures.* Hoboken, NJ: John Wiley & Sons Publishers.

Lecy, Jesse D., Hans Peter Schmitz, and Haley Swedlund. 2012. "Non-Governmental and Not-for-Profit Organizational Effectiveness: A Modern Synthesis." *Voluntas: International Journal of Voluntary and Nonprofit Organizations*, 23(2): 434–457.

Lee, Young-Joo. 2019. "Scarce as Hen's Teeth: Women CEOs in Large Nonprofit Organizations." *Nonprofit Management & Leadership*, 29(4): 601–610.

Lehman, Jennifer, and Russell James III. 2018. "The Charitable Bequest Gap among African-Americans: Exploring Charitable, Religious, and Family Estate Planning Attitudes." *Journal of Personal Finance*, 17(1): 43–56.

LePere-Schloop, Megan, and Erynn Beaton. 2021. "AFP-OSU Workplace Climate Survey Preliminary Report 1." Association of Fundraising Professionals and The Ohio

State University. https://afpglobal.org/sites/default/files/attachments/blog/AFP-Workplace-Climate-Survey.pdf.

Levy, Barbara A. 2013. "Choosing a Leadership Role: A Vision for Action." In *Nonprofit Fundraising Strategy: A Guide to Ethical Decision-Making and Regulation for Nonprofit Organizations,* Janice Gow Pettey (ed.), pp. 185–212. Hoboken, NJ: John Wiley & Sons, Inc.

Li, Yannan. 2018. "A Multi-Stakeholder Perspective on Social Media Use by Nonprofit Organizations: Towards a Culture of Dialogue." PhD diss., Indiana University.

Lichter, Daniel T. 2013. "Integration or Fragmentation? Racial Diversity and the American Future." *Demography,* 50(2): 359–391. https://doi.org/10.1007/s13524-013-0197-1.

Liebling, Adam. 2020. "Disrupting Grantmaking: Matchmaking, Algorithms, Proposal-less Programs, and the Future of Philanthropy." *Peak Grantmaking,* https://www.peakgrantmaking.org/.

Liefbroer, Aart C., and Cees H. Elzinga. 2012. "Intergenerational Transmission of Behavioural Patterns: How Similar Are Parents' and Children's Demographic Trajectories?" *Advances in Life Course Research,* 17(1): 1–10. https://doi.org/10.1016/j.alcr.2012.01.002.

Light, Paul C. 2008. *How Americans View Charities: A Report on Charitable Confidence.* Washington, DC: Brookings.

Lindahl, Wesley E. 2010. *Principles of Fundraising: Theory and Practice.* Sudbury, MA: Jones and Bartlett Publishers.

Lindsay, Drew, Peter Olson-Phillips, and Eden Stiffman. 2016, October 27. "Fidelity Charitable Pushes United Way Out of Top Place in Ranking of the 400 U.S. Charities That Raise the Most." *The Chronicle of Philanthropy.* https://www.philanthropy.com/article/Fidelity-Charitable-Knocks/238167.

List, John A., and Michael K. Price. 2009. "The Role of Social Connections in Charitable Fundraising: Evidence from a Natural Field Experiment." *Individual Decision-Making, Bayesian Estimation and Market Design: A Festschrift in Honor of David Grether,* 69(2): 160–169. https://doi.org/10.1016/j.jebo.2007.08.011.

Livingston, Geoff. 2012. *How Giving Contests Can Strengthen Nonprofits and Communities.* CASE Foundation and Razoo Foundation. https://casefoundation.org/resource/giving-contests-can-strengthen-nonprofits-communities/.

Lloyd, Theresa. 2012. "Motivational Factors in International Philanthropy." In *International Charitable Giving,* Clive Cutbill, Alison Paines, and Murray Hallam (eds.). Oxford, UK: Oxford University Press.

Lu Knutsen, Wenjue, and Kathy Lenore Brock. 2014. "Introductory Essay: From a Closed System to an Open System: A Parallel Critical Review of the Intellectual Trajectories of Publicness and Nonprofitness." *Voluntas: International Journal of Voluntary and Nonprofit Organizations,* 25(5): 1113–1131.

Lu Knutsen, Wenjue, and Ralph S. Brower. 2010. "Managing Expressive and Instrumental Accountabilities in Nonprofit and Voluntary Organizations: A Qualitative Investigation." *Nonprofit and Voluntary Sector Quarterly,* 39(4): 588–610.

Lyons, Sean, and Lisa Kuron. 2014. "Generational Differences in the Workplace: A Review of the Evidence and Directions for Future Research." *Journal of Organizational Behavior,* 35(S1): S139–S157. https://doi.org/10.1002/job.1913.

Ma, Ji, and Sara Konrath. 2018. "A Century of Nonprofit Studies: Scaling the Knowledge of the Field." *Voluntas: International Journal of Voluntary and Nonprofit Organizations*, 29(6): 1139–1158.

Mack, Catherine E., Kathleen S. Kelly, and Christopher Wilson. 2016. "Finding an Academic Home for Fundraising: A Multidisciplinary Study of Scholars' Perspectives." *International Journal of Nonprofit & Voluntary Sector Marketing*, 21(3): 180–194.

MacQuillan, Ian. 2016. *Rights Stuff: Fundraising's Ethics Gap and a New Theory of Fundraising Ethics*, vol. 1.1. Plymouth UK: Centre for Sustainable Philanthropy, Plymouth University. https://www.rogare.net/normative-fundraising-ethics.

MacQuillin, Ian. 2017. *Less Than My Job's Worth: Is Fundraising a Profession? And Does It Matter If It Isn't?* Plymouth, UK: Plymouth University, Rogare. https://www.rogare.net/fundraising-profession.

Madoff, Ray D., and Roger Colinvaux. 2017. "Letter to Orrin G. Hatch and Ron Wyden on Donor-Advised Funds." *Law School Publications*: 944. http://lawdigitalcommons.bc.edu/law_school_publications/944.

Mahmood, Faiqa. 2019. "American Muslim Philanthropy: A Data-Driven Comparative Profile." Institute for Social Policy and Understanding. https:/ispu.org/american-muslim-philanthropy-a-data-driven-comparative-profile/.

Makaroun, Lena K., Rebecca T. Brown, L. Grisell Diaz-Ramirez, Cyrus Ahalt, W. John Boscardin, Sean Lang-Brown, and Sei Lee. 2017. "Wealth-associated Disparities in Death and Disability in the United States and England." *JAMA Internal Medicine*, 177(2): 1745–1753.

Mallory, Christy, Luis A. Vasquez, and Celia Meredith. 2020, July. *Legal Protections for LGBT People after Bostock v. Clayton County.* Los Angeles, CA: Williams Institute, UCLA School of Law. https://williamsinstitute.law.ucla.edu/wp-content/uploads/Bostock-State-Laws-Jul-2020.pdf.

Manning, Wendy D., Monica A. Longmore, and Peggy C. Giordano. 2007. "The Changing Institution of Marriage: Adolescents' Expectations to Cohabit and to Marry." *Journal of Marriage and Family*, 69(3): 559–575. https://doi.org/10.1111/j.1741-3737.2007.00392.x.

Martin, Del. 1976. *Battered Wives*. San Francisco: Glide Publications.

Martin, Richard, and John Randal. 2008. "How Is Donation Behaviour Affected by the Donations of Others?" *Journal of Economic Behavior & Organization*, 67(1): 228–38. https://doi.org/10.1016/j.jebo.2007.08.001.

Marts and Lundy. 2017, March. "$10M+ Gifts to Higher Education." Special Report. http://www.martsandlundy.com.

Mason, Dyana P. 2016. "Recognition and Cross-Cultural Communications as Motivators for Charitable Giving: A Field Experiment." *Nonprofit and Voluntary Sector Quarterly*, 45(1): 192–204. https://doi.org/10.1177/0899764015576408.

Mauss, Marcel. 1990. *The Gift: The Form and Reason for Exchange in Archaic Societies*, trans. W. D. Halls, Routledge. (Original work published 1950.)

Maxwell, Joseph A. 2013. *Qualitative Research Design: An Interactive Approach*, 3rd Edition. Thousand Oaks, CA: SAGE Publications, Inc.

Maxwell, Margaret M. 2011. "Selecting and Working with Fundraising Consultants." In *Achieving Excellence in Fundraising*, 3rd Edition, Eugene R. Tempel, Timothy L. Seiler, and Eva A. Aldrich (eds.), pp. 375–382. San Francisco: Jossey-Bass.

McAllister, Charn P., B. Parker Ellen III, and Gerald R. Ferris. 2018. "Social Influence Opportunity Recognition, Evaluation, and Capitalization: Increased Theoretical Specification through Political Skill's Dimensional Dynamics." *Journal of Management,* 44(5): 1926–1952.

McCrea, Jennifer, Jeffrey C. Walker, and Karl Weber. 2013. *The Generosity Network: New Transformational Tools for Successful Fund-Raising.* New York: Deepak Chopra Books.

McKeever, Brice S. 2015. "The Nonprofit Sector in Brief 2015." The Urban Institute. https://www.urban.org/research/publication/nonprofit-sector-brief-2015-public-charities-giving-and-volunteering.

McKeever, Brice S. 2018. "The Nonprofit Sector in Brief 2018: Public Charities, Giving, and Volunteering 2018." https://nccs.urban.org/publication/nonprofit-sector-brief-2018.

McKitrick, Melanie A., J. Shawn Landres, Mark Ottoni-Wilhelm, and Amir D. Hayat. 2013. "Connected to Give: Faith Communities." Los Angeles: Jumpstart. https://jumpstartlabs.org/offering/research-reports/connected-to-give/.

McLanahan, Sara, and Larry Bumpass. 1988. "Intergenerational Consequences of Family Disruption." *American Journal of Sociology,* 94(1): 130–152.

Mead, George Herbert. 1934. *Mind, Self, and Society.* Chicago: University of Chicago.

Meer, Jonathan. 2011. "Brother, Can You Spare a Dime? Peer Pressure in Charitable Solicitation." *Journal of Public Economics,* 95(7–8): 926–941.

Meisenbach, Rebecca J., Jessica M. Rick, and Jaclyn K. Brandhorst. 2019. "Managing Occupational Identity Threats and Job Turnover: How Former and Current Fundraisers Manage Moments of Stigmatized Identities." *Nonprofit Management and Leadership,* 29, 383– 399. https://doi.org/10.1002/nml.21332.

Mesch, Debra. 2010. *Women Give 2010: New Research about Women and Giving.* Indianapolis: Indiana University Lilly Family School of Philanthropy.

Mesch, Debra. 2012 *Women Give 2012: New Research about Women and Giving.* Indianapolis: Indiana University Lilly Family School of Philanthropy.

Mesch, Debra, Mark Ottoni-Wilhelm, and Una Osili. 2016. *Women Give 2016: Giving in Young Adulthood: Gender Differences and Changing Patterns across the Generations.* Indianapolis: Women's Philanthropy Institute at the Indiana University Lilly Family School of Philanthropy. https://scholarworks.iupui.edu/handle/1805/11446.

Mesch, Debra, Una Osili, Andrea Pactor, and Jacqueline Ackerman. 2015. *Do Women Give More? Funding from Three Unique Data Sets on Charitable Giving.* Indianapolis: Women's Philanthropy Institute at the Indiana University Lilly Family School of Philanthropy.

Mesch, Debra, Una Osili, Andrea Pactor, Jacqueline Ackerman, and Jon Bergdoll. 2015. *Where Do Men and Women Give? Gender Differences in the Motivations and Purposes for Charitable Giving.* Indianapolis: Women's Philanthropy Institute at the Indiana University Lilly Family School of Philanthropy, https://scholarworks.iupui.edu/handle/1805/6985.

Mesch, Debra, Una Osili, Andrea Pactor, Jacqueline Ackerman, Elizabeth Dale, and Jon Bergdoll. 2015. *How and Why Women Give: Current and Future Directions for Research on Women's Philanthropy.* Indianapolis: Women's Philanthropy Institute at the Indiana University Lilly Family School of Philanthropy.

Mesch, Debra, Una Osili, Cagla Okten, Xiao Han, Andrea Pactor, and Jacqueline Ackerman. 2017. *Women Give 2017. Charitable Giving and Life Satisfaction: Does Gender*

Matter. Indianapolis: Women's Philanthropy Institute at the Indiana University Lilly Family School of Philanthropy. https://scholarworks.iupui.edu/bitstream/ handle/1805/14283/womengive17.pdf.

Mesch, Debra, Una Osili, Jacqueline Ackerman, Jon Bergdoll, Kim Williams-Pulfer, Andrea Pactor, and Amy Thayer. 2019. *Women Give 2019. Gender and Giving Across Communities of Color.* Indianapolis: Women's Philanthropy Institute at the Indiana University Lilly Family School of Philanthropy. https://scholarworks.iupui.edu/bitstream/handle /1805/18629/women-give2019-1.pdf.

Mesch, Debra, Una Osili, Jacqueline Ackerman, Jon Bergdoll, Tessa Skidmore, and Andrea Pactor. 2020. *Women Give 2020. New Forms of Giving in a Digital Age: Powered by Technology, Creating Community.* Indianapolis: Women's Philanthropy Institute at the Indiana University Lilly Family School of Philanthropy. https://scholarworks.iupui.edu/ bitstream/handle/1805/22578/women-give2020.pdf.

Mesch, Debra, Una Osili, Jacqueline Ackerman, Jon Bergdoll, Tessa Skidmore, and Jeannie Sager. 2021. *Women Give 2021. How Households Make Giving Decisions.* Indianapolis: Women's Philanthropy Institute at the Indiana University Lilly Family School of Philanthropy. https://scholarworks.iupui.edu/bitstream/handle/1805/25383/women-give2021.pdf.

Mesch, Debra, Una Osili, Tessa Skidmore, Jon Bergdoll, Jacqueline Ackerman, and Jeannie Sager. 2020. *COVID-19, Generosity, and Gender: How Giving Changed during the Early Months of the Pandemic.* Indianapolis: Women's Philanthropy Institute at the Indiana University Lilly Family School of Philanthropy. https://scholarworks.iupui.edu/ bitstream/handle/1805/23750/covid-report1.pdf.

Mesch, Debra, Una Osili, Tessa Skidmore, Jon Bergdoll, Jacqueline Ackerman, and Jeannie Sager. 2021. *COVID-19, Generosity, and Gender: How Giving Changed during the Early Months of the Pandemic.* Lilly Family School of Philanthropy, Women's Philanthropy Institute. Available from https://scholarworks.iupui.edu/handle/1805/23750.

Meyer, Erin. 2014a. *The Culture Map: Breaking Through the Invisible Boundaries of Global Business,* 1st Edition. New York: Public Affairs.

Meyer, Erin. 2014b. "Navigating the Cultural Minefield." *Harvard Business Review,* 92(5): 119–123.

Milken Institute. 2020. "Philanthropist's Field Guide: Considering Your Philanthropy Holistically." https://milkeninstitute.org/article/considering-your-philanthropy-holistically.

Miller-Millesen, Judith L. 2003. "Understanding the Behavior of Nonprofit Boards of Directors: A Theory-based Approach." *Nonprofit and Voluntary Sector Quarterly,* 32(4): 521–547. https://doi.org/10.1177/0899764003257463.

Mills, F. 2016. *The State of Change: An Analysis of Women and People of Color in the Philanthropic Sector,* p. 36. Council on Foundations.

Mirabella, Roseanne M. 2007. "University-based Educational Programs in Nonprofit Management and Philanthropic Studies: A 10-year Review and Projections of Future Trends." *Nonprofit and Voluntary Sector Quarterly,* 36(4suppl): 11S–27S. https://doi .org/10.1177/0899764007305051.

Monaco, Michele, and Malissa Martin. 2007. "The Millennial Student: A New Generation of Learners." *Athletic Training Education Journal,* 2 (2): 42–46. https://doi .org/10.4085/1947-380X-2.2.42.

Moniz, Amanda. 2020, November 23. "The Storied History of Giving in America." *Smithsonian Magazine*. https://www.smithsonianmag.com.

Moody, Michael, Allison Lugo Knapp, and Marlene Corrado. 2011. "What Is a Family Foundation?" *The Foundation Review*, 3(4): 5.

Morewedge, Carey K., Leif Holtzman, and Nicholas Epley. 2007. "Unfixed Resources: Perceived Costs, Consumption, and the Accessible Account Effect." *Journal of Consumer Research*, 34(4): 459–467.

Morningstar. 2019. "The True Faces of Sustainable Investing Busting Myths around ESG." https://www.morningstar.com.

Morrison, Aaron. 2021, February 23. "AP Exclusive: Black Lives Matter Opens Up about Its Finances." *AP News*. https://apnews.com/article/black-lives-matter-90-million-finances-8a80cad199f54c0c4b9e74283d27366f.

Morselli, Davide, and Stefano Passini. 2015. "Measuring Prosocial Attitudes for Future Generations: The Social Generativity Scale." *Journal of Adult Development*, 22(3): 173–182. https://doi.org/10.1007/s10804-015-9210-9.

Moulton, John Fletcher. 1924, July. "Law and Manners." *The Atlantic Monthly*. http://www2.econ.iastate.edu/classes/econ362/hallam/NewspaperArticles/LawandManners.pdf.

Mundey, Peter, David P. King, and Brad R. Fulton. 2019. "The Economic Practices of US Congregations: A Review of Current Research and Future Opportunities." *Social Compass*, 66(3): 400–417.

Musick, Mark A., and John Wilson. 2008. *Volunteers: A Social Profile*. Bloomington, IN: Indiana University Press.

Nagaraj, A. J. 2013. "Gifted and Talented: What Makes a Top Fundraiser in the Age of Venture Philanthropy?" Washington, DC: Education Advisory Board. https://eab.com/research/advancement/study/gifted-and-talented-2/.

Nanus, Burt, and Stephen M. Dobbs. 1999. *Leaders Who Make a Difference: Essential Strategies for Meeting the Nonprofit Challenge*. San Francisco: Jossey-Bass.

Nathan, Sarah K., and Eugene R. Tempel. 2017. "Fundraisers in the 21st Century." IUPUI ScholarWorks. https://scholarworks.iupui.edu/handle/1805/13845.

Nathan, Sarah K., Heather A. O'Connor, Genevieve G. Shaker, and Pat D. Janin. 2021, March 17. "Supporting Small Shop Fundraisers through Peer Mentoring." *The Chronicle of Philanthropy*. https://www-philanthropy-com.proxy.ulib.uits.iu.edu/article/fundraisers-at-small-nonprofits-need-more-support-peer-mentoring-may-be-the-answer.

Nathanson, Stephen. 2014. "Act and Rule Utilitarianism." *Internet Encyclopedia of Philosophy*. https://iep.utm.edu/util-a-r/.

National Association of Charitable Gift Planners. 2017. "Guidelines for Reporting and Counting Charitable Gifts, 2nd Edition." https://charitablegiftplanners.org/standards/guidelines-reporting-and-counting-charitable-gifts.

National Association of Charitable Gift Planners. 2020. "Impact of COVID-19 on Gift Planning." https://charitablegiftplanners.org/sites/default/files/Impact-of-COVID-19-on-Gift-Planning-2020_final.pdf.

National Center for Charitable Statistics (NCCS) Project Team. 2020, June. "The Nonprofit Sector in Brief 2019." The Urban Institute, National Center for Charitable Statistics. https://nccs-urban-org.proxy.ulib.uits.iu.edu/publication/nonprofit-sector-brief-2019.

National Community Reinvestment Coalition (NCRC). 2019, September 4. "Tests Show Inferior Treatment of Minority Business Owners at Banks, and Data Shows a Steep Decline in Government-Backed Lending to Black Entrepreneurs." Press Releases, Research. https://ncrc.org/tests-show-inferior-treatment-of-minority-business-owners-at-banks-and-data-shows-a-steep-decline-in-government-backed-lending--to-black-entrepreneurs/.

National Conference on Citizenship. 2015, December 8. "New Report: 1 in 4 Americans Volunteer; 3 in 5 Help Neighbors," National Conference on Citizenship. https://ncoc.org/news/114jb730/.

National Council for Nonprofits. 2021. "Corporate Partnerships: A Guide for Nonprofits." https://www.councilofnonprofits.org/tools-resources.

National Philanthropic Trust (NPT). 2021. "2020 Donor-Advised Fund Report." https://www.nptrust.org/reports/daf-report/.tics/.

National Philanthropic Trust (NPT). 2021a. "2020 DAF Report." https://www.nptrust.org/reports/daf-report/.

National Philanthropic Trust (NPT). 2021b. "Donor-Advised Fund COVID Grantmaking Survey." https://www.nptrust.org/reports/daf-covid-survey/.

National Philanthropic Trust (NPT). 2021c. "Charitable Giving Statistics." NPTrust. https://www.nptrust.org/philanthropic-resources/charitable-giving-statis.

Neggaz, Meira. 2020. "ISPU Board of Directors Wins Leadership Award." Institute for Social Policy and Understanding. https://www.ispu.org/ispu-board-of-directors-wins-leadership-award/.

Neumayr, Michaela, and Astrid Pennerstorfer. 2020. "The Relation between Income and Donations as a Proportion of Income Revisited: Literature Review and Empirical Application." *Nonprofit and Voluntary Sector Quarterly*. https://journals.sagepub.com/doi/10.1177/0899764020977667.

Neumeier, Marty. 2007. *Zag: The Number-one Strategy of High-performance Brands: A Whiteboard Overview*. Berkeley, CA: AIGA.

Newcomb, Theodore M. 1953. "An Approach to the Study of Communicative Acts." *Psychological Review*, 60(6): 393.

Nichols, Laura, and Ángel Islas. 2015, May. "Pushing and Pulling Emerging Adults through College Generational Status and the Influence of Parents and Others in the First Year." *Journal of Adolescent Research*. 0743558415586255. https://doi.org/10.1177/0743558415586255.

NNEDV. 2020. "Domestic and Sexual Violence Fact Sheet 2020." https://nnedv.org/resources-library/domestic-violence-sexual-assault-factsheet/.

Nonprofit HR. 2019 "Talent Retention Practices." https://www.nonprofithr.com/wp-content/uploads/2019/06/Nonprofit-HR-Talent-Retention-Survey-Findings-2019-.pdf.

Nonprofit Quarterly. 2019, January 19. "Multiyear and Unrestricted: The Grants of Nonprofit Dreams Come to Life." *Nonprofit Quarterly*. https://nonprofitquarterly.org/multiyear-and-unrestricted-the-grants-of-nonprofit-dreams-come-to-life/.

Nonprofit Research Collaborative. 2015. "Nonprofit Fundraising Study." https://www.npresearch.org/comprehensive-reports.

Nonprofit Research Collaborative. 2019. "A Look at Expectations for Charitable Giving in 2020." https://www.npresearch.org/comprehensive-reports.

Nonprofit Tech for Good. 2020, September. "Global Trends in Giving Report." https://www.nptechforgood.com/research/.

Nouwen, Henri J. M., and John S. Mogabgab. 2011. *A Spirituality of Fundraising.* Henri Nouwen Society.

NPS. 2018. "2018 Online Giving Statistics, Trends & Data: The Ultimate List of Giving Stats." *Nonprofits Source* blog. https://nonprofitssource.com/online-giving-statistics/.

O'Brien, Carol L. 2005. "Thinking beyond the Dollar Goal: A Campaign as Organizational Transformation." *New Directions for Philanthropic Fundraising*, 47: 29–42.

O'Neill, Michael. 1994. "Fundraising as an Ethical Act." *New Directions for Philanthropic Fundraising*, 6: 3–13.

OECD. 2018. "Private Philanthropy for Development," *The Development Dimension.* Paris. https://doi.org/10.1787/9789264085190-en.

OECD. 2020. "Taxation and Philanthropy." *OECD Tax Policy Studies*, 27. Paris. https://doi.org/10.1787/df434a77-en.

Olson, Joann S. 2014. "Opportunities, Obstacles, and Options: First-Generation College Graduates and Social Cognitive Career Theory." *Journal of Career Development*, 41(3): 199–217. https://doi.org/10.1177/0894845313486352.

Orensten, Naomi, and Ellie Buteau. 2020. "Foundations Respond to Crisis: Toward Greater Flexibility and Responsiveness?" Cambridge, MA: Center for Effective Philanthropy. http://cep.org/wp-content/uploads/2020/12/CEP_Foundations-Respond-to-Crisis_Toward-Greater-Flexibility-and-Responsiveness_2020-1.pdf.

Osgood, Wayne D., Gretchen Ruth, Jacquelynne S. Eccles, Janis E. Jacobs, and Bonnie L. Barber. 2005. "Six Paths to Adulthood: Fast Starters, Parents without Careers, Educated Partners, Educated Singles, Working Singles, and Slow Starters." In *On the Frontier of Adulthood: Theory, Research, and Public Policy*, Richard A. Settersten, Frank F. Furstenberg, and Rubén G. Rumbaut, (eds.), pp. 320–355. Chicago: University of Chicago Press.

Osili, Una. 2020. "The Future of Nonprofit Economics, Bellwethers of Funding." *The Nonprofit Times.* https://www.thenonprofittimes.com/npt_articles/the-future-of-nonprofit-economics-bellwethers-of-funding/#.

Osili, Una, and Dan Du. 2005. "Immigrant Assimilation and Charitable Giving." https://scholarworks.iupui.edu/handle/1805/5856.

Osili, Una, Debra Mesch, Linh Preston, Cagla Okten, Jonathan Bergdoll, Jacqueline Ackerman, and Andrea Pactor. 2017. "Gender Differences in #GivingTuesday Participation." Indianapolis, IN: Women's Philanthropy Institute at the Indiana University Lilly Family School of Philanthropy. https://scholarworks.iupui.edu/handle/1805/14782.

Osili, Una, Debra Mesch, Jacqueline Ackerman, Andrea Pactor, Xia Han, and Heather O'Connor. 2018a. "How Women & Men Give around Retirement." Indianapolis, IN: Women's Philanthropy Institute at the Indiana University Lilly Family School of Philanthropy. https://scholarworks.iupui.edu/handle/1805/16758.

Osili, Una, Debra Mesch, Jacqueline Ackerman, Jon Bergdoll, Linh Preston, and Andrea Pactor. 2018b. "How Women and Men Approach Impact Investing." Indianapolis, IN: Women's Philanthropy Institute at the Indiana University Lilly Family School of Philanthropy. https://scholarworks.iupui.edu/handle/1805/16229.

Osili, Una, Sasha Zarins, Jonathan Bergdoll, Xionan Kou, Ted Grossnickle, Dan Schipp, Tim Ardillo et al. 2018. "The Impact of Diversity: Understanding How Nonprofit

Board Diversity Affects Philanthropy, Leadership, and Board Engagement." Indiana University Lilly Family School of Philanthropy, Johnson Grossnickle, and Associates and BoardSource. https://scholarworks.iupui.edu/handle/1805/15239.

Osili, Una, Jonathan Bergdoll, Andrea Pactor, Jacqueline Ackerman, and Peter Houston. 2021b. "Charitable Crowdfunding: Who Gives, to What, and Why?" Lilly Family School of Philanthropy. https://scholarworks.iupui.edu/handle/1805/25515.

Osili, Una, Sasha Zarins, Jon Bergdoll, Melissa Buller, and Anna Pruitt. 2020. "Nonprofits and Donor-Advised Funds: Perceptions and Potential Impacts." https://scholarworks .iupui.edu/handle/1805/24001.

Osili, Una, Sasha Zarins, Xiao Han, Xiaonan Kou, and Shivant, Shrestha. 2021a. "The Giving Environment: Understanding Pre-Pandemic Trends in Charitable Giving." Lilly Family School of Philanthropy. https://scholarworks.iupui.edu/handle/1805/26290.

Oyakawa, Michelle. 2015. "'Turning Private Pain into Public Action': The Cultivation of Identity Narratives by a Faith-based Community Organization." *Qualitative Sociology*, 38(4): 395–415.

Palotta, Dan. 2013. "The Way We Think about Charities Is Dead Wrong." TED. https:// www.youtube.com/watch?v=bfAzi6D5FpM.

Panagopoulos, Costas. 2011. "Thank You for Voting: Gratitude Expressions and Voter Mobilization." *The Journal of Politics*, 73(3): 707–717.

Parks, Dan. 2021, June 8. "Most Nonprofits Emerging from Pandemic Wounded but Still Operating." *The Chronicle of Philanthropy*. https://www.philanthropy.com/article/ most-nonprofits-emerging-from-pandemic-wounded-but-still-operating.

Payton, Robert L. 1988. *Philanthropy: Voluntary Action for the Public Good*. New York: American Council on Education/Macmillan Pub. Co.

Payton, Robert L., and Michael P. Moody. 2008. *Understanding Philanthropy: Its Meaning and Mission*. Bloomington, IN: Indiana University Press.

Pence, Ellen. 1987. *In Our Best Interest: A Process for Personal and Social Change*. Duluth, MN: Minnesota Program Development.

Pence, Ellen, and Coral McDonnell. 2000. "Developing Policies and Protocols in Duluth, Minnesota." In *Home Truths about Domestic Violence: Feminist Influences on Policy and Practice*, Jalna Hanmer and Catherine Itzin (eds.), pp. 41–64. New York: Routledge.

Peterson, Brooks. 2018. *Cultural Intelligence: A Guide to Working with People from Other Cultures*, 2nd Edition, Boston: Nicholas Brealey.

Petit, Stephanie. 2010, March. "A Basic Guide to Corporate Philanthropy." CGPN. https:// www.adlercolvin.com/wp-content/uploads/2017/12/A-Basic-Guide-to-Corporate-Philanthropy-00283643xA3536.pdf.

Petriglieri, Gianpiero. 2020, April. "The Psychology behind Effective Crisis Leadership." *Harvard Business Review Digital Articles*. https://hbr.org/2020/04/ the-psychology-behind-effective-crisis-leadership.

Pew Research Center. 2013, October. "A Portrait of Jewish Americans: Findings from a Pew Research Center Survey of U.S. Jews." https://www.pewresearch.org/wp-content/ uploads/sites/7/2013/10/jewish-american-full-report-for-web.pdf.

Pew Research Center. 2015, May 12. "America's Changing Religious Landscape." https://www.pewforum.org/2015/05/12/americas-changing-religious-landscape/.

Pew Research Center. 2019, June 12. "Social Media Fact Sheet." Author. https://www
.pewresearch.org/internet/fact-sheet/social-media/#who-uses-each-social-media-platform.

Pew Research Center. 2020, September 9. "Religion in America: U.S. Religious Data,
Demographics and Statistics." https://www.pewforum.org/religious-landscape-study/.

Pfeffer, Jeffrey, and R. Gerald Salancik. 1978. *The External Control of Organizations: A Resource
Dependence Perspective.* New York: Harper & Row.

Pfeffer, Jeffrey. 2019, November. "Teaching Power in Ways that Influence Students' Career
Success: Some Fundamental Ideas." Working Papers (Faculty) Stanford Graduate
School of Business, pp. 1–43.

Phethean, Christopher, Thanassis Tiropanis, and Lisa Harris. 2013. "Rethinking
Measurements of Social Media Use by Charities: A Mixed Methods Approach."
Proceedings of the 5th Annual ACM Web Science Conference, pp. 296–305.

Philanthropy Roundtable. 2021. "Who Gives Most to Charity?" *The Almanac.* https://www
.philanthropyroundtable.org/almanac/statistics/who-gives.

Philanthropy Together. 2020. "About." https://philanthropytogether.org/about/.

Pleck, Elizabeth. 2004. *Domestic Tyranny: The Making of American Social Policy against Family
Violence from Colonial Times to the Present.* Urbana, IL: University of Illinois Press.

Pogrebin, Robin, and Matthew Goldstein. 2021, March 26. "Leon Black to Step Down
as MoMA Chairman." *New York Times.* https://www.nytimes.com/2021/03/26/arts/
design/leon-black-moma-chairman.html.

Powell, Walter W., and Patricia Bromley. 2020. *The Nonprofit Sector: A Research Handbook,* 3rd
Edition. Stanford, CA: Stanford University Press.

Powers, Katie. 2019, September 3. "Shattering Gendered Marketing." *American Marketing
Association.* https://www.ama.org/marketing-news/shattering-gendered-marketing/.

Pribbenow, Paul. 1994, Winter. "Fundraising as Public Service: Renewing the Moral
Meaning of the Profession." *New Directions for Philanthropic Fundraising,* 6. Boston, MA:
Jossey-Bass Publishers.

Pribbenow, Paul. 2013. "Fundraisers and the Good Life." In *Nonprofit Fundraising Strategy:
A Guide to Ethical Decision-Making and Regulation for Nonprofit Organizations,* Janice Gow
Pettey (eds.), pp. 1–15. Hoboken, NJ: John Wiley & Sons, Inc.

Prine, Katie, and Elisabeth Lesem. 2016. "Prospective Donor and Donor Research and
Database Management." In *Achieving Excellence in Fundraising,* Eugene R. Tempel,
Timothy L. Seiler, and Dwight F. Burlingame (eds.), pp. 71–83. Hoboken, NJ: John
Wiley & Sons.

Public Religion Research Institute. 2020, December. "The Coronavirus Pandemic's Impact
on Religious Life." https://www.prri.org/research/the-coronavirus-pandemics-
impact-on-religious-life/.

Putnam-Walkerly, Kris. 2020. *Delusional Altruism: Why Funders Often Fail to Achieve Change
and What They Can Do to Transform Giving.* Hoboken, NJ: John Wiley & Sons.

Qgiv. 2021. "Donor Stewardship: Creating Lifelong Donors in 6 Steps." https://www.qgiv
.com/blog/donor-stewardship-guide.

Qu, Heng, and Jamie Levine Daniel. 2020. "Is 'Overhead' A Tainted Word? A Survey
Experiment Exploring Framing Effects of Nonprofit Overhead on Donor Decision."
Nonprofit and Voluntary Sector Quarterly. Thousand Oaks, CA: SAGE Publications.
0899764020959475.

Ragsdale, J. D. 1995. "Quality Communication in Achieving Fundraising Excellence." *New Directions for Philanthropic Fundraising*, 10: 17–31.

Rainer, Thom S., and Jess W. Rainer. 2010. *The Millennials: Connecting to America's Largest Generation*. Nashville, TN: B&H Books.

Raymo, Jim, and Judy Raymo. 2014. *Millennials and Mission: A Generation Faces a Global Challenge*. Biloxi, MS: William Carey Library.

Reese, Hope. 2020, October 13. "Laurie Santos Says Self-Care Doesn't Have to be Selfish." *New York Times*. https://www.nytimes.com/2020/10/07/health/laurie-santos-covid-happiness.html.

Reich, Rob. 2018. *Just Giving: Why Philanthropy Is Failing Democracy and How It Can Do Better*. Princeton, NJ: Princeton University Press.

Reinstein, D., and Riener, G. 2012. "Decomposing Desert and Tangibility Effects in a Charitable Giving Experiment." *Experimental Economics*, 15(1): 229–240.

Rempel, John K., John G. Holmes, and Mark P. Zanna. 1985. "Trust in Close Relationships." *Journal of Personality and Social Psychology*, 49(1): 95–112.

Rendon, Jim. 2019, June 4. "New Report Details the Barriers that Leaders of Color Face in the Nonprofit World." *The Chronicle of Philanthropy*. https://www-philanthropy-com .proxy.ulib.uits.iu.edu/article/new-report-details-the-barriers-that-leaders-of-color-face-at-nonprofits/.

Rendon, Jim. 2021, January 12. "Why Women Don't Get Ahead at Nonprofits." *The Chronicle of Philanthropy*. https://www-philanthropy-com.proxy.ulib.uits.iu.edu/article/ why-women-dont-get-ahead.

Rhode, Deborah, and Amanda Packel. 2009, Summer. "Ethics and Nonprofits." *Stanford Social Innovation Review*. https://ssir.org/articles/entry/ethics_and_nonprofits#.

Riess, Helen. 2018. *The Empathy Effect: Seven Neuroscience-Based Keys for Transforming the Way We Live, Love, Work, and Connect Across Differences*. [S.l.] Grand Haven, MI: Brilliance Publishing.

Rijn, Jordan van, Bradford Barham, and Reka Sundaram-Stukel. 2017, June. "An Experimental Approach to Comparing Similarity- and Guilt-Based Charitable Appeals." *Journal of Behavioral and Experimental Economics*, 68: 25–40. https://doi.org/10.1016/j .socec.2017.02.004.

Rind, Bruce, and Prashant Bordia. 1995. "Effect of a Server's 'Thank You' and Personalization on Restaurant Tipping." *Journal of Applied Social Psychology*, 25(9): 745–751.

Robbins, Stephen P., and Tim Judge. 2016. *Essentials of Organizational Behavior*, 13th Edition. Upper Saddle River, NJ: Pearson/Prentice Hall.

Roksa, Josipa, and Daniel Potter. 2011. "Parenting and Academic Achievement Intergenerational Transmission of Educational Advantage." *Sociology of Education*, 84(4): 299–321. https://doi.org/10.1177/0038040711417013.

Rooney, Patrick M. 2018. "The Growth in Total Household Giving Is Camouflaging a Decline in Giving by Small and Medium Donors: What Can We Do about It?" *Nonprofit Quarterly*. https://nonprofitquarterly.org/total-household-growth-decline-small-medium-donors/.

Rooney, Patrick. 2019. "Where Have All the Donors Gone? The Continued Decline of the Small Donor and the Growth of Megadonors." *Nonprofit Quarterly*. https:// nonprofitquarterly.org/where-have-all-the-donors-gone-the-continued-decline-of-the-small-donor-and-the-growth-of-megadonors/.

Rooney, Patrick, and Jon Bergdoll. 2020, March 23. "What Happens to Charitable Giving When the Economy Falters?" *The Conversation.* https://theconversation.com/what-happens-to-charitable-giving-when-the-economy-falters-133903.

Rooney, Patrick M., Xiaoyun Wang, and Mark Ottoni-Wilhelm. 2018. "Generational Succession in American Giving: Donors Down, Dollars Per Donor Holding Steady but Signs That It Is Starting to Slip." *Nonprofit and Voluntary Sector Quarterly,* 47(5): 918–38. https://doi.org/10.1177/0899764018770281.

Rose, Sharon R. 1998. "A Study of Lesbian Philanthropy: Charitable Giving Patterns." Master's thesis, University of San Francisco.

Rosen, Michael J. 2005. "Doing Well by Doing Right: A Fundraiser's Guide to Ethical Decision-Making." *International Journal of Nonprofit & Voluntary Sector Marketing,* 10(3), 175–181. https://onlinelibrary.wiley.com/doi/abs/10.1002/nvsm.11.

Rosen, Michael J. 2019, October 1. "Ethics, Fundraising, and Leadership: Avoid the Seven Deadly Sins of Fundraising." *Advancing Philanthropy Magazine,* Association of Fundraising Professionals. https://afpglobal.org/news/ethics-fundraising-and-leadership-avoid-seven-deadly-sins-fundraising.

Rosenfeld, Michael J., and Reuben J. Thomas. 2012. "Searching for a Mate: The Rise of the Internet as a Social Intermediary." *American Sociological Review,* 77(4): 523–547.

Rosso, Henry A. 1991. *Achieving Excellence in Fund Raising: A Comprehensive Guide to Principles, Strategies, and Methods,* 1st Edition. San Francisco: Jossey-Bass Publishers.

Rosso, Henry. 2010. "The Annual Fund." In *Achieving Excellence in Fundraising,* 3rd Edition, Eugene R Tempel, Timothy L Seiler, and Eva E Aldrich (eds.), pp. 51–63. Hoboken, NJ: John Wiley & Sons.

Rothenberg, Bess. 2002, March. "The Success of the Battered Woman Syndrome: An Analysis of How Cultural Arguments Succeed." *Sociological Forum,* 17(1): 81–103.

Rothenberg, Bess. 2003, October. "'We Don't Have Time for Social Change': Cultural Compromise and the Battered Woman Syndrome." *Gender and Society,* 17(5): 771–787.

Routley, Claire, and Adrian Sargeant. 2015. "Leaving a Bequest: Living on through Charitable Gifts." *Nonprofit and Voluntary Sector Quarterly,* 44(5): 869–885.

Safronova, Valeriya. 2021, January 30. "How Women Are Changing the Philanthropy Game." *New York Times.* https://www.nytimes.com/2021/01/30/style/mackenzie-scott-prisclila-chan-zuckerberg-melinda-gates-philanthropy.html.

Salamon, Lester M., ed. 2014. *New Frontiers of Philanthropy: A Guide to the New Tools and Actors Reshaping Global Philanthropy and Social Investing.* Oxford, UK: Oxford University Press.

Samek, Anya, and Chuck Longfield. 2019, April 13. "Do Thank-You Calls Increase Charitable Giving? Expert Forecasts and Field Experimental Evidence." SSRN. http://dx.doi.org/10.2139/ssrn.3371327.

Sander-Staudt, Maureen. 2011. "Care Ethics." *Internet Encyclopedia of Philosophy.* https://iep.utm.edu/care-eth/.

Sargeant, Adrian. 2001. "Using Donor Lifetime Value to Inform Fundraising Strategy." *Nonprofit Management & Leadership,* 12(1): 25–38.

Sargeant, Adrian, and Stephen Lee. 2001. "Improving Public Trust in the Voluntary Sector: An Empirical Analysis." *International Journal of Nonprofit & Voluntary Sector Marketing,* 7(1), 68–83. https://onlinelibrary.wiley.com/doi/abs/10.1002/nvsm.168.

Sawhill, Isabel V. 2014. *Generation Unbound: Drifting into Sex and Parenthood without Marriage.* Washington, DC: Brookings Institution Press.

Saxton, Gregory D., and Lili Wang. 2013, April. "The Social Network Effect: The Determinants of Giving Through Social Media." *Nonprofit and Voluntary Sector Quarterly.* 0899764013485159. https://doi.org/10.1177/0899764013485159.

Saxton, J., Harrison, T., and Guild, M. 2015. "The New Alchemy: How Volunteering Turns Donations of Time and Talent into Human Gold." https://nfpsynergy.net/free-report/new-alchemy.

Scaife, Wendy, Katie McDonald, and Sue Smyllie. 2011. "A Transformational Role: Donor and Charity Perspectives on Major Giving in Australia." The Australian Centre for Philanthropy and Nonprofit Studies, Queensland University of Technology, Brisbane, Australia. https://library.workplacegivingaustralia.org.au/a-transformational-role-donor-and-charity-perspectives-on-major-giving-in-australia/.

Schaeffer, Katherine. 2019. "The Most Common Age among Whites in U.S. Is 58 – More than Double that of Racial and Ethnic Minorities." Pew Research Center. https://www.pewresearch.org/fact-tank/2019/07/30/most-common-age-among-us-racial-ethnic-groups/.

Scharf, Kimberley, and Sarah Smith. 2016. "Relational Altruism and Giving in Social Groups." *Journal of Public Economics,* 141: 1–10.

Scherer, Shelley C. 2017. "Organizational Identity and Philanthropic Institutions: Patterns of Strategy, Structure, and Grantmaking Practices." *Nonprofit Management and Leadership,* 28(1): 105–123.

Schervish, Paul G. 2005. "Major Donors, Major Motives: The People and Purposes behind Major Gifts." *New Directions for Philanthropic Fundraising,* 47: 59–87.

Schervish, Paul G. 2008. "Why the Wealthy Give." *The Routledge Companion to Nonprofit Marketing,* Adrian Sargeant and Walter W. Wymer (eds.), p. 177. London: Routledge.

Schervish, Paul G., and John J. Havens. 1997. "Social Participation and Charitable Giving: A Multivariate Analysis," *Voluntas: International Journal of Voluntary and Nonprofit Organizations,* 8(3): 235–260.

Schervish, Paul G., and John J. Havens. 2002. "The Boston Area Diary Study and the Moral Citizenship of Care." *Voluntas: International Journal of Voluntary and Nonprofit Organizations,* 13(1): 47–71.

Schneider, Barbara L., and David Stevenson. 2000. *The Ambitious Generation: America's Teenagers, Motivated But Directionless.* New Haven, CT: Yale University Press.

Schullery, Nancy M. 2013. "Workplace Engagement and Generational Differences in Values." *Business Communication Quarterly,* 76(2): 252–65. https://doi.org/10.1177/1080569913476543.

Schuyt, T., Hoolwerf, L. K., and D. Verkaik. 2017, February. "Better Together? A Study on Philanthropy and Official Development Assistance," AFD Research Papers Series, No. 2017-57. https://www.afd.fr/en/ressources/better-together-study-philanthropy-and-official-development-assistance.

Schwadel, Philip, and Michael Stout. 2012. "Age, Period and Cohort Effects on Social Capital." *Social Forces,* 91(1): 233–252. https://doi.org/10.1093/sf/sos062.

Schwandt, Thomas A. 2007. *The SAGE Dictionary of Qualitative Inquiry,* 3rd Edition. Thousand Oaks, CA: SAGE Publications.

Schwartz, Robert A. 1968. "Corporate Philanthropic Contributions." *The Journal of Finance,* 23(3): 479–497.

Scott, Mackenzie. 2019. "Giving Pledge Letter MacKenzie Scott." The Giving Pledge. https://givingpledge.org/Pledger.aspx?id=393.

Scott, Richard, and Gerald F. Davis. 2006. *Organizations and Organizing: Rational, Natural and Open Systems Perspectives*. Routledge.

Seiler, Timothy L. 2001. *Developing Your Case for Support*. San Francisco: Jossey-Bass Publishers.

Seiler, Timothy L. 2016a. "Developing and Articulating a Case for Support." In *Achieving Excellence in Fundraising*, 4th Edition, Eugene Tempel, Timothy L. Seiler, and Dwight F. Burlingame (eds.), pp. 37–48. Hoboken, New Jersey: John Wiley & Sons.

Seiler, Timothy L. 2016b. "The Total Development Plan Built on the Annual Giving Program." In *Achieving Excellence in Fundraising*, 4th Edition, Eugene Tempel, Timothy L. Seiler, and Dwight F. Burlingame (eds.), pp. 215–223. Hoboken, New Jersey: John Wiley & Sons.

Seiler, Timothy. 2020, November. "Why and How to Fundraise During or After a Pandemic." Class Video Lecture, Philanthropy in Time of Crisis, IUPUI Lilly Family School of Philanthropy.

Seton Hall University. 2020. "Nonprofit Management Education, Current Offerings in University-Based Programs." http://academic.shu.edu/npo/.

Settersten, Richard A., Frank F. Furstenberg, and Rubén G. Rumbaut. 2008. *On the Frontier of Adulthood: Theory, Research, and Public Policy*. Chicago: University of Chicago Press.

Shaker, Genevieve G., and Deanna Nelson. 2021. "A Grounded Theory Study of Fundraiser and Major Donor Philanthropic Relationships in U. S. Higher Education." *Nonprofit and Voluntary Sector Quarterly*.

Shaker, Genevieve G., and Pamala Wiepking. 2021, July 26. "What Is Unrestricted Funding? Two Philanthropy Experts Explain." *The Conversation*. https://theconversation.com/what-is-unrestricted-funding-two-philanthropy-experts-explain-164589.

Shaker, Genevieve G., Patrick M. Rooney, Jonathon Bergdoll, Sarah K. Nathan, and Eugene R. Tempel. 2020. "Professional Identity and the Determinants of Fundraisers' Charitable Behavior." *Nonprofit and Voluntary Sector Quarterly*, 49(4): 677–703.

Shaker, Genevieve G., Patrick M. Rooney, Jonathon Bergdoll, Sarah K. Nathan, and Eugene R. Tempel. Under review. "Turnover Intention and Job Tenure of US Fundraisers."

Shaker, Genevieve G., and Sarah K. Nathan. 2017. "Understanding Higher Education Fundraisers in the United States." *International Journal of Nonprofit & Voluntary Sector Marketing*, 22(4): e1604.

Shanahan, Michael J., Erik Porfeli, Jeylan T. Mortimer, and Lance D. Erickson. 2005. "Subjective Age Identity and the Transition to Adulthood: Demographic Markers and Personal Attributes." In *On the Frontier of Adulthood: Theory, Research, and Public Policy*, Richard A. Settersten, Frank F. Furstenberg, and Rubén G. Rumbaut (eds.), pp. 224–255. Chicago: University of Chicago Press.

Shang, Jen, Americus Reed II, and Rachel Croson. 2008. "Identity Congruency Effects on Donations." *Journal of Marketing Research*, 45(3): 351–361.

Shang, Jen, and Rachel Croson. 2009. "A Field Experiment in Charitable Contribution: The Impact of Social Information on the Voluntary Provision of Public Goods." *The Economic Journal*, 119(540): 1422–1439. https://doi.org/10.1111/j.1468-0297.2009.02267.x.

Shearman, Sachiyo M., and Jina H. Yoo. 2007. "'Even a Penny Will Help!': Legitimization of Paltry Donation and Social Proof in Soliciting Donation to a Charitable Organization." *Communication Research Reports*, 24(4): 271–282.

Shen, Lijiang, and Elisabeth Bigsby. 2013. "The Effects of Message Features: Content, Structure, and Style." In *The SAGE Handbook of Persuasion: Developments in Theory and Practice*, J. P. Dillard and L. Shen (eds.). Thousand Oaks, CA: SAGE.

Shoenberger, Elisa. 2020, February 11. "What Does It Mean to Decolonize a Museum," Museumnext.com. https://www.museumnext.com/article/what-does-it-mean-to-decolonize-a-museum/.

Sica, Alan. 2012. "Polite Culture: Nice-Nellyism Suffuses Sociology." *Contemporary Sociology: A Journal of Reviews*, 41(3): 275–278. https://doi.org/10.1177/0094306112443510.

Silicon Valley Community Foundation. 2020. "2019 Annual Report." https://www.siliconvalleycf.org/annual-report-2019/by-the-numbers/.

Silva, Jennifer M. 2013. *Coming Up Short: Working-Class Adulthood in an Age of Uncertainty.* New York: Oxford University Press.

Simpson, Jeffry A. 2007. "Psychological Foundations of Trust." *Current Directions in Psychological Science*, 16(5): 264–268.

Sinek, Simon. 2011. *Start with Why: How Great Leaders Inspire Everyone to Take Action.* New York: Portfolio/Penguin.

Singer, Peter. 2015. *The Most Good You Can Do: How Effective Altruism Is Changing Ideas about Living Ethically.* New Haven: Yale University Press.

Small, Deborah A., and Nicole M. Verrochi. 2009. "The Face of Need: Facial Emotion Expression on Charity Advertisements." *Journal of Marketing Research*, 46(6): 777–787. https://doi.org/10.1509/jmkr.46.6.777_JMR6F.

Smith, Christian, and Hilary Davidson. 2014. *The Paradox of Generosity: Giving We Receive, Grasping We Lose.* New York: Oxford University Press.

Smith, Christian, Michael O. Emerson with Patricia Snell. 2008. *Passing the Plate: Why American Christians Don't Give Away More Money.* New York: Oxford University Press.

Smith, Hayden W. 1997. "If Not Corporate Philanthropy, Then What?" *New York Law School Law Review*, 41: 757–770.

Smith, Tom. 2005. "Generation Gaps in Attitudes and Values from the 1970s to the 1990s." In *On the Frontier of Adulthood: Theory, Research, and Public Policy*, Richard A. Settersten Jr., Frank F. Furstenberg, and Rubén G. Rumbaut (eds.), pp. 177–224. Chicago: University of Chicago Press.

Socialinsider. 2019, November 14. "Social Media Content Study: The Perfect Post in 2020." *Socialinsider.* https://www.socialinsider.io/blog/social-media-content-research.

Soskis, Benjamin. 2020. A History of Associational Life and the Nonprofit Sector in the United States. In *The Nonprofit Sector: A Research Handbook*, 3rd Edition. Walter W. Powell and Patricia Bromley (eds.). Stanford, CA: Stanford University Press.

Spade, Dean. 2020. *Mutual Aid: Building Solidarity during This Crisis (and the Next).* New York: Verso.

Spellberg, Denise. 2014. *Thomas Jefferson's Quran.* New York: Penguin Random House.

Spiegel, Diane. 2013. *The Gen Y Handbook: Applying Relationship Leadership to Engage Millennials.* New York: SelectBooks.

St. Amour, Madeline. 2020, February 12. "Endowments at 2-Year Colleges." *Inside Higher Education*. https://www.insidehighered.com/news/2020/02/12/community-colleges-increasingly-are-game-endowments.

Stanczykiewicz, Bill. 2020a, November. "Crisis Leadership–Responsive Fundraising." Powerpoint Presentation, Philanthropy in Time of Crisis, IUPUI Lilly Family School of Philanthropy.

Stanczykiewicz, Bill. 2020b, March 23. "Don't Stop Fundraising" [Audio podcast]. The Fund Raising School. https://soundcloud.com/thefundraisingschool/dont-stop-fundraising/s-X5kdVSbL9wH.

Stanczykiewicz, William A. 2020c. "Nonprofit Boards and Fundraising – Do Expectations Make a Difference? A Mixed Methods Study." PhD diss., Creighton University. http://dspace.creighton.edu:8080/xmlui/handle/10504/127357.

Stanford Law School Policy Lab on Donor-Advised Funds. 2020, Fall. "Are Donor-Advised Funds Good for Nonprofits?" *Stanford Social Innovation Review*. https://ssir.org/articles/entry/are_donor_advised_funds_good_for_nonprofits.

Stanger, Jeff. 2016. "Digital Fundraising." In *Achieving Excellence in Fundraising*, 4th Edition, Eugene R. Tempel, Timothy L. Seiler, and Dwight F. Burlingame (eds.), pp. 401–416. Hoboken, NJ: John Wiley & Sons Publishers.

Steensland, Brian, and Xiaoyun Wang. Forthcoming. "Philanthropy as Spiritual Practice: Contemporary Patterns and Prospects." In *Religion and Philanthropy in the United States: Contemporary Patterns and Prospects*, David King and Philip Goff (eds.). Bloomington, IN: Indiana University Press.

Stefanski, Ron. n.d. "How Declining Attention Spans Impact Your Social Media." *Muck Rack blog*. Accessed December 20, 2020: https://muckrack.com/blog/2020/07/14/how-declining-attention-spans-impact-your-social-media.

Stein, Joel. 2013, May 20. "Millennials: The Me Me Me Generation." *Time Magazine*. https://time.com/247/millennials-the-me-me-me-generation/.

Steinberg, Richard, and Mark Ottoni-Wilhelm. 2003. "Tracking Giving Across Generations." In *New Directions for Philanthropic Fundraising*, 82nd ed., 71–42. Wiley Periodicals. https://scholarworks.iupui.edu/handle/1805/6387.

Stiffman, Eden. 2019, November 5. "Flexibility Pays Off for Community Fund." *The Chronicle of Philanthropy*. https://www.philanthropy.com/article/flexibility-pays-off-for-community-fund/.

Stiffman, Eden. 2020, April 10. "How Cultivating Small Donors Led to a $10 Million Gift." *The Chronicle of Philanthropy*. https://www.philanthropy.com/article/how-cultivating-small-donors-led-to-a-10-million-gift/.

Stiffman, Eden. 2021a, March 15. "Buoyed by Small Donors, Giving Grew 10.6% in 2020, Study Finds." *The Chronicle of Philanthropy*. https://www.philanthropy.com/article/buoyed-by-small-donors-giving-grew-10-6-in-2020-study-finds.

Stiffman, Eden. 2021b, September 8. "What Drives Direct Giving and Why It Matters to Nonprofits." *The Chronicle of Philanthropy*. https://www.philanthropy.com/article/what-drives-direct-giving-and-why-it-matters-to-nonprofits.

Stiffman, Eden. 2021c, September 8. "What Drives Direct Giving and Why It Matters to Nonprofits." *The Chronicle of Philanthropy*. https://www.philanthropy.com/article/what-drives-direct-giving-and-why-it-matters-to-nonprofits?.

Stiffman, Eden, and Emily Haynes. 2019, November 5. "Anxiety in Times of Plenty." *The Chronicle of Philanthropy*. https://www.philanthropy.com/article/giving-to-the-100-top-charities-is-up-11/.

Stout, Margaret. 2019. "Pursuing Community Change through Radically Democratic Practice." In *Reframing Nonprofit Organizations: Democracy, Inclusion, and Social Change*, Angela M. Eikenberry, Roseanne M. Mirabella, and Billie Sandberg (eds.). Irvine, CA: Melvin & Leigh, Publishers.

Strickhouser, Sara M., and James D. Wright. 2015. "Agency Resistance to Outcome Measurement: Sources, Concerns, and Solutions." *Journal of Applied Social Science*, 9(2): 115–124. https://www-jstor-org.proxy.ulib.uits.iu.edu/stable/26370919.

Sulek, Marty. 2010. "On the Modern Meaning of Philanthropy." *Nonprofit and Voluntary Sector Quarterly*, 39(2): 193–212.

Swartz, Teresa Toguchi. 2009. "Intergenerational Family Relations in Adulthood: Patterns, Variations, and Implications in the Contemporary United States." *Annual Review of Sociology*, 35(1): 191–212. https://doi.org/10.1146/annurev.soc.34.040507.134615.

Tajfel, Henri, and John C. Turner. 1976. "An Integrative Theory of Intergroup Conflict." In *The Social Psychology of Intergroup Relations*, W.G. Austin and Stephen Worchel (eds.), pp. 33–47. Monterey, CA: Brooks/Cole.

Tankersley-Bankhead, B. 2020, December 2, and 2021, July 18. Email and phone conversation with Jane Chu.

Taub, Amanda. 2020, April 6. "A New Covid-19 Crisis: Domestic Abuse Rises Worldwide." *New York Times*. https://www.nytimes.com/2020/04/06/world/coronavirus-domestic-violence.html.

Taylor, Paul, and Pew Research Center. 2014. *The Next America: Boomers, Millennials, and the Looming Generational Showdown*. New York: PublicAffairs.

Teitel, Martin. 2012. *The Ultimate Insider's Guide to Winning Foundation Grants*. Medfield, MA: Emerson & Church.

Tempel, Eugene R. 1991. "Assessing Organizational Strengths and Vulnerabilities." In *Achieving Excellence in Fundraising: A Comprehensive Guide to Principles, Strategies and Methods*, 1st Edition, Hank A. Rosso (ed.), pp. 19–27.

Tempel, Eugene R. 2003. "Contemporary Dynamics of Philanthropy" In *Achieving Excellence in Fundraising*, 2nd Edition, Eugene R. Tempel (ed.), pp. 3–13. San Francisco: Jossey-Bass Publishers.

Tempel, Eugene R. 2016. "Ethics and Accountability." In *Achieving Excellence in Fundraising*, 4th Edition, Eugene R. Tempel, Timothy L. Seiler, and Dwight F. Burlingame (eds.). Hoboken, NJ: Wiley.

Tempel, Eugene R., and Timothy L. Seiler. 2016a. "Engaging the Board in Fundraising." In *Achieving Excellence in Fundraising*, 4th Edition, Eugene R. Tempel, Timothy L. Seiler, and Dwight F. Burlingame (eds.), pp. 439–450. Hoboken, NJ: John Wiley & Sons, Inc.

Tempel, Eugene R., and Timothy L. Seiler. 2016b. "Stewardship and Accountability." In *Achieving Excellence in Fundraising*, 4th Edition, Eugene R. Tempel, Timothy L. Seiler, and Dwight F. Burlingame (eds.). Hoboken, NJ: Wiley.

Thayer, Amy. "Giving to Health." 2020. In *Giving USA 2020: The Annual Report on Philanthropy for the Year 2019*, Anna Pruitt (ed.), pp. 237–258. Giving USA Foundation. https://givingusa.org/.

Thayer, Amy N., and Derrick Feldmann. 2016. "Generational Differences in Giving." In *Achieving Excellence in Fundraising*, 4th Edition, Eugene R. Tempel, Timothy L. Seiler, and Dwight F. Burlingame, (eds.). Hoboken, NJ: John Wiley.

The Economist. 2013, October 12. "Crossing the Divide: Why Culture Should be Cool." Book review of *Fish Can't See Water: How National Cultures Can Make or Break Your Corporate Strategy*. https://www.economist.com/business-books-quarterly/2013/10/10/crossing-the-divide.

The Economist. 2020, June 27. "Economists Grapple with Their Race Problem." https://www.economist.com/finance-and-economics/2020/06/25/economists-grapple-with-their-race-problem.

The Giving Pledge. 2010. "About the Giving Pledge." https://givingpledge.org/About.aspx.

The Radicati Group, Inc. n.d. "Email Statistics Report, 2019-2023 Executive Summary." Accessed December 20, 2020: http://www.radicati.com/wp/wp-content/uploads/2018/12/Email-Statistics-Report-2019-2023-Executive-Summary.pdf.

The Women's Legal Defense and Education Fund. n.d. "History of the Violence against Women Act." https://www.legalmomentum.org/history-vawa.

Theis, Michael. 2019, November 14. "Trust Gap Persists for Charities and it Hurts Giving, Study Says." *The Chronicle of Philanthropy*. https://www.philanthropy.com/article/trust-gap-persists-for-charities-and-it-hurts-giving-study-says.

Theis, Michael. 2020, April 9. "Giving from Donor-Advised Funds Surge as Pandemic Spreads." *The Chronicle of Philanthropy*. https://www.philanthropy.com/article/giving-from-donor-advised-funds-surge-as-pandemic-spreads/.

Theis, Michael. 2021, February 16. "Overall Giving Ticked Up Slightly in 2020, but Online Giving Exploded, Report Says." *The Chronicle of Philanthropy*. https://www-philanthropy-com/.

Thomala, Lai Lin. 2021, January 6. "Number of Monthly Active Users of Sina Weibo Q4 2017-Q3 2020." *Statista.com*. https://www.statista.com/statistics/795303/china-mau-of-sina-weibo.

Tierney, Kathleen J. 1982, February. "The Battered Women Movement and the Creation of the Wife Beating Problem." *Social Problems*, 29(3): 207–220.

Toce, Joseph, Byrle Abbin, William Pace, and Mark Vorsatz. 2020. *Andersen Tax LLC: Tax Economics of Charitable Giving*. Toronto: Thomson Reuters.

Toepler, S. 1999. "Operating in a Grantmaking World: Reassessing the Role of Operating Foundations." In *Private Funds, Public Purpose: Philanthropic Foundations in International Perspective*, Anheier, H. K. and Toepler, S. (eds), pp. 163–181. New York: Kluwer Academic/Plenum Publishers (Nonprofit and civil society studies).

Tremblay-Boire, Joannie. 2020. "Corporate Foundation in the United States." In *Handbook on Corporate Foundations*, Lonneke Roza, Steffen Bethmann, Lucas Meijs, and Georg Von Schnurbein (eds.). Berlin: Springer.

Turner, John C., and P. J. Oakes. 1986. "The Significance of the Social Identity Concept for Social Psychology with Reference to Individualism, Interactionism and Social Influence." *British Journal of Social Psychology*, 25(3): 237–252.

U.S. Bureau of Labor Statistics. 2020a. "Highlight of Women's Earnings in 2019." *BLS Report 1089*. https://www.bls.gov/opub/reports/womens-earnings/2019/home.htm.

U.S. Bureau of Labor Statistics. 2020b. "Making Volunteer Work Visible: Supplementary Measures of Work in Labor Force Statistics." https://www.bls.gov/opub/mlr/2020/article/making-volunteer-work-visible-supplementary-measures-of-work-in-labor-force-statistics.htm.

U.S. Census Bureau. 2017. "Real Median Household Income by Race and Hispanic Origin: 1967 to 2017." https://www.census.gov/content/dam/Census/library/visualizations/2018/demo/p60-263/figure1.pdf?utm_source=rss&utm_medium=rss.

U.S. Census Bureau. 2019a. "Quick Facts." https://www.census.gov/quickfacts/fact/dashboard/US/PST045219.

U.S. Census Bureau. 2019b. "U.S. People, Age and Sex, 2019." *Quick Facts.* https://www.census.gov/quickfacts/fact/table/US/SEX255219.

U.S. Census Bureau. 2020a. "Demographic Turning Points for the United States: Population Projections for 2020 to 2060." https://www.census.gov/content/dam/Census/library/publications/2020/demo/p25-1144.pdf.

U.S. Census Bureau. 2020b. "U.S. Census Bureau Releases New Educational Attainment Data." https://www.census.gov/newsroom/press-releases/2020/educational-attainment.html.

U.S. Census Bureau. 2021a. "Measuring Racial and Ethnic Diversity for the 2020 Census." https://www.census.gov/newsroom/blogs/random-samplings/2021/08/measuring-racial-ethnic-diversity-2020-census.html.

U.S. Census Bureau. 2021b. "Racial and Ethnic Diversity in the U.S.: 2010 Census and 2020 Census." https://www.census.gov/library/visualizations/interactive/racial-and-ethnic-diversity-in-the-united-states-2010-and-2020-census.html.

U.S. Census Bureau. 2021c. "Income and Poverty in the United States, 2020." https://www.census.gov/data/tables/2021/demo/income-poverty/p60-273.html.

U.S. Trust. 2013. "Insights on Wealth and Worth: Women and Wealth." Bank of America Corporation. https://www.ustrust.com/publish/content/application/pdf/GWMOL/ARS7ME57.pdf.

Uecker, Jeremy E., and Christopher G. Ellison. 2012. "Parental Divorce, Parental Religious Characteristics, and Religious Outcomes in Adulthood." *Journal for the Scientific Study of Religion*, 51(4): 777–794. https://doi.org/10.1111/j.1468-5906.2012.01679.x.

Uitdewilligen, Sjir, and Mary J. Waller. 2018. "Information Sharing and Decision-making in Multidisciplinary Crisis Management Teams." *Journal of Organizational Behavior*, 39(6): 731–748.

UNESCO. 2020. *Global Education Monitoring Report – Gender Report: A New Generation: 25 Years of Efforts for Gender Equality in Education.* Paris: UNESCO.

United Nations. 2018. "The Thread that Binds: Volunteerism and Community Resilience." https://www.unv.org/sites/default/files/UNV_SWVR_2018_English_WEB.pdf.

Unruh, Gregory C., and Angel Cabrera. 2013. "Join the Global Elite." *Harvard Business Review*, 91(5): 135–139.

Urban Institute. 2019. "The Nonprofit Sector in Brief 2018." National Center for Charitable Statistics. https://nccs.urban.org/publication/nonprofit-sector-brief-2018.

Urban Institute. 2020. "The Nonprofit Sector in Brief 2019." National Center for Charitable Statistics. https://nccs.urban.org/publication/nonprofit-sector-brief-2019.

Vaid, Urvashi, and Ashindi Maxton. 2017. "The Apparitional Donor: Understanding and Engaging High Net Worth Donors of Color." https://www.donorsofcolor.org/wp-content/uploads/2019/01/FinalAppDonreport4.17.pdf.

Van Eck, Clara Amy. 2017. "Changing the Message: Battered Women's Advocates and Their Fight against Domestic Violence at the Local, State, and Federal Level, 1970s–1990s." Master's thesis, Old Dominion University.

Van Knippenberg, Daan, Nathalie Lossie, and Henk Wilke. 1994. "In-group Prototypicality and Persuasion: Determinants of Heuristic and Systematic Message Processing." *British Journal of Social Psychology*, 33(3): 289–300.

Vance-McMullen, Danielle. 2018, November. "Does Giving Tuesday Lift or Shift Year-end Charitable Giving?" Paper presented at the meeting of the Association for Research on Nonprofits and Voluntary Action (ARNOVA), Austin, TX.

Vaughan, Shannon K. 2010. "The Importance of Performance Assessment in Local Government Decisions to Fund Health and Human Services Nonprofit Organizations." *Journal of Health and Human Services Administration*, 32(4): 486–512. http://www.jstor.org.proxy.ulib.uits.iu.edu/stable/41548442.

Villanueva, Edgar. 2018. *Decolonizing Wealth: Indigenous Wisdom to Heal Divides and Restore Balance.* Oakland, CA: Berrett-Koehler Publishers, Inc.

VolunteerMatch. 2021. "2020 in Review: The Impact of COVID-19 on Volunteering & the Social Sector." https://info.volunteermatch.org/2020-in-review-the-impact-of-covid-19-on-volunteering-the-social-sector.

Vu, Le. 2017a, May 15. "How Donor-centrism Perpetuates Inequity, and Why We Must Move toward Community-Centric Fundraising." Nonprofitaf.com. https://nonprofitaf.com/2017/05/how-donor-centrism-perpetuates-inequity-and-why-we-must-move-toward-community-centric-fundraising/.

Vu, Le. 2017b, May 22. "9 Principles of Community-Centric Fundraising." Nonprofitaf.com. https://nonprofitaf.com/2017/05/9-principles-of-community-centric-fundraising/.

W. K. Kellogg Foundation. 2012. "Cultures of Giving: Energizing and Expanding Philanthropy by and for Communities of Color." http://www.d5coalition.org/wpcontent/uploads/2013/07/CultureofGiving.pdf.

W. K. Kellogg Foundation. 2019. "A New Cohort of Catalyzing Community Giving Grantees in U.S., Mexico and Haiti." https://www.wkkf.org/news-and-media/article/2019/11/a-new-cohort-of-catalyzing-community-giving-grantees-in-us-mexico-and-haiti.

Waasdorp, Erica. 2021, April 26. "New Monthly Donor Stats from M+R Benchmarks." Nonprofit Pro. https://www.nonprofitpro.com/post/new-monthly-donor-stats-from-mr-benchmarks/.

Wade, Michelle. 2019. "Special Event Fundraising," Learning to Give. https://www.learningtogive.org/resources/special-event-fundraising.

Wade-Benzoni, Kimberly A., Leigh Plunkett Tost, Morela Hernandez, and Richard P. Larrick. 2012. "It's Only a Matter of Time: Death, Legacies, and Intergenerational Decisions." *Psychological Science*, 23(7): 704–709.

Wagner, Lilya. 2004. *Leading Up: Transformational Leadership for Fundraisers.* Hoboken, NJ: John Wiley.

Wagner, Lilya. 2016. *Diversity and Philanthropy: Expanding the Circle of Giving: Expanding the Circle of Giving.* Santa Barbara, CA: ABC-CLIO.

Waheer, Manar, and Avideh Moussavian. 2020, April 2. "COVID-19 Doesn't Discriminate – Neither Should Congress' Response." ACLU. https://www.aclu.org/news/immigrants-rights/covid-19-doesnt-discriminate-neither-should-congress-response/.

Walker, Darren. 2019. *From Generosity to Justice: A New Gospel of Wealth*. New York: The Ford Foundation/Disruption Books.

Walker, Julia Ingraham. 2006. *Major Gifts*. Hoboken, NJ: John Wiley & Sons.

Wang, Wendy, Kim Parker, and Paul Taylor. 2013. "Breadwinner Moms." Washington DC: Pew Research Center. http://www.pewsocialtrends.org/2013/05/29/breadwinner-moms/.

Warner, Greg. 2020, December 18. "Why QUALIFYING Donors Might Be the Silver Lining You've Been Looking For." Imarketsmart. https://imarketsmart.com/why-qualifying-donors-might-be-the-silver-bullet-youve-been-looking-for/.

Washington, Booker T. 1900. *Up from Slavery: An Autobiography*. Garden City, NY: Doubleday & Company, Inc. https://docsouth.unc.edu/fpn/washington/washing.html.

Waters, Richard D. 2009. "The Importance of Understanding Donor Preference and Relationship Cultivation Strategies." *Journal of Nonprofit & Public Sector Marketing*, 21(4): 327–346.

Weinger, Adam. 2016 May 24. "Crowdfunding & Corporate Philanthropy: Fundraising's Next Dynamic Duo?" *Crowdfund Insider*. https://www.crowdfundinsider.com/2016/05/85168-crowdfunding-corporate-philanthropy-fundraisings-next-dynamic-duo/.

Weiss, Harald E. 2012. "The Intergenerational Transmission of Social Capital: A Developmental Approach to Adolescent Social Capital Formation." *Sociological Inquiry*, 82(2): 212–235. https://doi.org/10.1111/j.1475-682X.2012.00414.x.

Westhoff, Elise. 2020, Fall. "President's Note: What Lies Ahead." *Philanthropy Magazine*. https://www.philanthropyroundtable.org/philanthropy-magazine/article/president's-note-what-lies-ahead.

Whitchurch, Jesse, and Alberta Comer. 2016, August. "Creating a Culture of Philanthropy." *The Bottom Line*, 29: 114–122. https://doi.org/10.1108/BL-02-2016-0012.

Wiemann, John M. 1977. "Explication and Test of a Model of Communicative Competence." *Human Communication Research*, 3(3): 195–213.

Wiepking, Pamala. 2021. "The Global Study of Philanthropic Behavior." *Voluntas: International Journal of Voluntary and Nonprofit Organizations*, 32(2): 194–203.

Wiepking, Pamala, and Beth Breeze. 2012. "Feeling Poor, Acting Stingy: The Effect of Money Perceptions on Charitable Giving." *International Journal of Nonprofit & Voluntary Sector Marketing*, 17(1): 13–24.

Wiepking, Pamala, and Femida Handy. 2015. The Palgrave Handbook of Global Philanthropy. Houndmills, Basingstoke, Hampshire: Palgrave Macmillan.

Wiepking, Pamala, and René Bekkers. 2012. "Who Gives? A Literature Review of Predictors of Charitable Giving II – Gender, Family Composition and Income." *Voluntary Sector Review*, 3(2): 217–245.

Wiepking, Pamala, and René Bekkers. 2015. "Giving in the Netherlands: A Strong Welfare State with a Vibrant Nonprofit Sector." In *The Palgrave Handbook of Global Philanthropy*, by Pamala Wiepking and Fermida Handy (eds.), pp. 211–229. London: Palgrave Macmillan.

Wiepking, Pamala, and Rob Beltman. 2016, September 15. "Motieven Voor Geefgedrag [Motives for Giving Behavior]." Presented at the Invited workshop at Fondsenwervingswebinars Live Event, Huis van de Gezondheid, Amersfoort, Netherlands. https://scholarworks.iupui.edu/handle/1805/25642.

Willems, Jurgen, Silke Boenigk, and Marc Jegers. 2014. "Seven Trade-offs in Measuring Nonprofit Performance and Effectiveness." *Voluntas: International Journal of Voluntary and Nonprofit Organizations*, 25(6): 1648–1670. http://www.jstor.org.proxy.ulib.uits .iu.edu/stable/43654684.

Williams-Pulfer, Kim and Una Osili. 2020, October 5. "Racial Justice Giving is Booming, 4 Trends." *The Conversation.* https://theconversation.com/racial-justice-giving-is-booming-4-trends-145526.

Wilson, K.J. 1977. *When Violence Begins at Home.* Alameda, CA: Hunter House Publishers.

WINGS. 2018, March "What Makes a Strong Ecosystem of Support to Philanthropy?" https://wings.issuelab.org/resource/what-makes-a-strong-ecosystem-of-support-to-philanthropy.html.

Winkelman, Michael. 2005. *Cultural Awareness, Sensitivity and Competence.* Peosta, IA: Eddie Bowers Publishers.

Wishart, Roewen, and Russell N. James III. In press. "The Final Outcome of Charitable Bequest Gift Intentions: Findings and Implications for Legacy Fundraising." *International Journal of Nonprofit & Voluntary Sector Marketing*: e1703.

Wolf, Dennie Palmer. 2020. "Lullaby: Being Together, Being Well." New York: Carnegie Hall. https://www.carnegiehall.org/Education/Programs/Lullaby-Project.

Women Moving Millions. n.d. "About. Our Story." Accessed January 30, 2021: https:// womenmovingmillions.org/about/our-story/.

Women's Philanthropy Institute (WPI). 2020. "COVID-19, Generosity, and Gender: How Giving Changed during the Early Months of a Global Pandemic." https://philanthropy .iupui.edu/institutes/womens-philanthropy-institute/research/covid.html.

Women's Philanthropy Institute (WPI). 2020. "The Women and Girls Index 2020: Measuring Giving to Women and Girls." https://philanthropy.iupui.edu/institutes/womens-philanthropy-institute/research/wgi20.html.

Wong, Nate, and Andrea McGrath. 2020, November 20. "Building a Trust-based Philanthropy to Shift Power Back to Communities." *Stanford Social Innovation Review.* https://ssir.org/articles/entry/building_a_trust_based_philanthropy_to_shift_power_ back_to_communities#.

Worth, Michael J. 2016. *Fundraising Principles and Practice.* Thousand Oaks, CA: SAGE.

Worth, Michael J., and James W. Asp. 1994. "The Development Officer in Higher Education: Toward an Understanding of the Role. ASHE-ERIC Higher Education Report No. 4." ERIC Clearinghouse on Higher Education, One Dupont Circle, Suite 630, Washington, DC 20036-1183.

Wright, Alyssa. 2020, September 23. "Here's How Giving Circles Prepared International Donors to Respond Quickly and Effectively to COVID-19." *Forbes.* https://www.forbes .com/sites/alyssawright/2020/09/23/heres-how-giving-circles-prepared-international-donors-to-respond-quickly-and-effectively-to-covid-19/.

Wuthnow, Robert. 2010. *After the Baby Boomers: How Twenty- and Thirty-Somethings Are Shaping the Future of American Religion.* Princeton, NJ: Princeton University Press.

Yeoman, John C. 2014. "The Economics of Using a Charitable Remainder Trust to Fund a Retirement Portfolio." *The Journal of Wealth Management,* 17(1): 40–50.

Yörük, Bariş K. 2012. "Do Charitable Solicitations Matter? A Comparative Analysis of Fundraising Methods." *Fiscal Studies,* 33(4): 467–487.

Young, Ashlee, Jaime Love, Nancy Csuti, and Christopher J. King. 2017. "Looking in the Mirror: Equity in Practice for Philanthropy." *The Foundation Review*, 9(4): 11.

Youniss, James, Susan Bales, Verona Christmas-Best, Marcelo Diversi, Milbrey McLaughlin, and Rainer Silbereisen. 2002. "Youth Civic Engagement in the Twenty-First Century." *Journal of Research on Adolescence*, 12(1): 121–148. https://doi.org/10.1111/1532-7795.00027.

YW Boston. 2020, April 13. "Our Shared Sector: Why Nonprofits Should Center Diversity, Equity, and Inclusion during the COVID-19 Pandemic." Massachusetts Nonprofit Network. http://massnonprofitnet.org/blog/shared-sector-nonprofits-center-diversity-equity-inclusion-covid-19-pandemic/.

Zakrzewski, Anna, Kedra Newsom, Michael Kahlich, Maximilian Klein, Andrea Real Mattar, and Stephan Knobel. 2020, April 9. "Managing the Next Decade of Women's Wealth." Boston Consulting Group. https://www.bcg.com/publications/2020/managing-next-decade-women-wealth.

Zarins, Sasha, and Una Osili. 2018, July 3. "Fewer Americans Are Giving Money to Charity but Total Donations Are at Record Levels Anyway." *The Conversation*. http://theconversation.com/fewer-americans-are-giving-money-to-charity-but-total-donations-are-at-record-levels-anyway-98291.

Zhai, Jiexia Elisa, Christopher G. Ellison, Charles E. Stokes, and Norval D. Glenn. 2008. "'Spiritual, but Not Religious': The Impact of Parental Divorce on the Religious and Spiritual Identities of Young Adults in the United States." *Review of Religious Research*, 49(4): 379–394.

Zimmerman, Eilene. 2020, June 18. "What Makes Some People More Resilient than Others." *The New York Times*. https://www.nytimes.com/2020/06/18/health/resilience-relationships-trauma.html.

INDEX